Germany

A New Social and Economic History

General Editors: Sheilagh Ogilvie and Bob Scribner

Germany

A New Social and Economic History

Volume 3
Since 1800

Edited by
Sheilagh Ogilvie
Reader in Economic History,
University of Cambridge

and

Richard Overy
Professor of Modern History, King's College,
University of London

A member of the Hodder Headline Group
LONDON

Distributed in the United States of America by
Oxford University Press Inc., New York

First published in Great Britain in 2003 by
Hodder Arnold, a member of the Hodder Headline Group,
338 Euston Road, London NW1 3BH

http://www.arnoldpublishers.com

Distributed in the United States of America by
Oxford University Press Inc.
198 Madison Avenue, New York, NY10016

The advice and information in this book are believed to be true and
accurate at the date of going to press, but neither the authors nor the publisher
can accept any legal responsibility or liability for any errors or omissions.

British Library Cataloguing in Publication Data
A catalogue record for this book is available from the British Library

Library of Congress Cataloging-in-Publication Data
A catalog record for this book is available from the Library of Congress

ISBN 0 340 65215 2 (hb)
ISBN 0 340 65214 4 (pb)

1 2 3 4 5 6 7 8 9 10

Typeset in 10 on 12pt Sabon by Phoenix Photosetting, Chatham, Kent
Printed and bound in Malta

What do you think about this book? Or any other Arnold title?
Please send your comments to feedback.arnold@hodder.co.uk

This book is dedicated to the memory of our friend and colleague

Bob Scribner
1941–98

who began this project but did not live to see it completed.

Contents

List of tables

List of figures

List of maps

Contents of Volumes I and II

General preface

There has long been no adequate or modern social and economic history of Germany, despite a proud tradition of German-language scholarship in the field since the nineteenth century, especially on the traditional themes of economic history (trade, capitalism, industrial production, agriculture). In part this has been the result of the scope and complexity of the German-speaking world, whose diverse developments over the centuries have made it no less difficult to produce overviews of its political history. To complicate the problem, however, there have been striking new advances in several fields of history over the past generation: historical demography and family structure; the history of disease, diet, and nutrition; material culture and daily life; the climate and ecology as historical factors. There have been new approaches to the history of social structure, work, forms of production, and the relationships between town and country, while awareness of the importance of gender has radically altered our historical perspectives. There has also been considerable interpretative reorientation. The *Annales* paradigm, with its emphasis on long-term structures and the material basis of culture and society, brought about a revolution in French historiography, but its general approach was only slowly received in German scholarship, the more so since its implicit demand for an *histoire totale* radically called into question the more compartmentalized approach of traditional social and economic history. All these developments explain why the project of a general social and economic history of Germany has become a formidable task beyond the capabilities of any one scholar.

There has been, however, a growing volume of new work in many specialist fields, which makes possible a collective attempt at a synthesis suitable for use by teachers, students, and general readers. Some recent scholarship has taken the form of traditional economic history, building on and incorporating the world of the great pioneers, while a great deal of it has also been inspired by the *Annales* school. In some areas older approaches have been cross-fertilized with the new, as in the case of agricultural history, which has profited from recent work on climatology and ecology. Newer fields of research such as demography have changed some of our commonplace generalizations, or opened up new material to historical scrutiny, as in the case of daily life. The range of expertise and coverage required to make the best use of this scholarship demands a team of authors, each of whom is a specialist scholar, summarizing, and generalizing from, the most recent research in a number of major topics. The themes of each chapter have been chosen for attention because they either encompass structures fundamental to the development of economy and society, such as population, agriculture, consumption, trade, or industry; or else they present a significant development within a given period (urbanization, welfare, science and technology). It is the aim of the work as a whole to keep in view the long-term development of economy and society in Germany, while directing attention to characteristic features of a given century or phase of socioeconomic development.

Preface to Volume III

This final volume in the series covers the modern period, from 1800 to the present day. The history of these two centuries can be approached as a single unified era for many themes, but for others falls naturally into sub-periods – a first phase of modernization and take-off up to 1914, a longer period of economic exceptionalism produced by war, defeat, and dictatorship (1914 to 1950), and then a period of remarkable recovery (1950 to the present) in which Germany regained the trajectory of the pre-1914 years.

By treating this extended period as a unity, it is possible to gain an overview of long-term structural developments in demography, agriculture, manufacturing, finance, consumption, and so on, while examining the interaction of these changes with the characteristic social and political formations of Germany in the nineteenth and twentieth centuries. The picture that emerges is one of rapid transformation, but within a framework of recognizable long-term continuities in German economies and societies.

German political unification became a reality for the first time in 1871, and was renewed in a different form in 1989. But the chapters of this book show many continuities with the territorial fragmentation which characterized German-speaking central Europe throughout the medieval and early modern periods. Local identities retained enormous social and cultural importance. Economy and society were affected by competition and conflict between different layers of government, particularly between the central *Reich* government and that of the strong *Länder* and Germany's corporate communities. And regional patterns of economic, social and demographic development in many ways continued to transcend political boundaries.

Industrialization, financial modernization, and the application of new technologies to ever-widening sectors of the economy represented striking new departures during the nineteenth and twentieth centuries, as the relatively 'backward' German economies 'caught up' with north-west Europe and the United States. But, as the contributions to this volume demonstrate, the 'revolutionized' industrial, commercial, and financial sectors shared many characteristics with their pre-industrial counterparts. State policies and state interventions continued to play a significant role in the trajectory of German economic performance, both on the regional and the national level. The visions and preconceptions of a stratum of powerful *Beamten* (civil servants) steered the economy in particular directions. And corporative occupational identities among industrial, commercial, and professional elites remained influential, perhaps most strongly reflected in the enduring concept of the German *Mittelstand*.

Agriculture, too, developed rapidly in Germany during this period, as a combination of institutional reform and new technologies transformed both agriculture itself and the social matrix in which it was embedded. But, as the chapters in this book point out, German rural life also showed long-term continuities. A stratum of noble landlords (especially in Prussia) long retained political power, economic strength, and social influence. Relationships between lord and peasant remained central in many German regions into the twentieth century. And rural images and symbols continue to exercise a powerful resonance in modern Germany to this day.

Urbanization, welfare provision, and social stratification also took great leaps forward in Germany during the nineteenth and twentieth centuries, with the transformation of a still largely rural society into one dominated by *Großstädte* and urban agglomerations, the gradual replacement of conditional community-level poor relief by increasingly universal state benefits, and the shift from a social structure dominated by 'class' to one more shaped by a plurality of 'experience'. Yet, as the discussion in this volume reveals, here there were also important continuities. Cities, welfare provision, and social structure were all channelled and constrained by conflicts between centre and localities, the enduring importance of occupational and urban community corporatism, and social exclusion experienced by substantial groups such as women and immigrants. In some German territories, urban and occupational elites long continued to regulate the marriage, settlement, and economic choices of less well-off inhabitants – an example being the notorious *politische Ehekonsens* (political permission to marry), which survived in some areas into the twentieth century.

Demographic behaviour, gender relations, and living standards also underwent striking changes in this period. Germany's unusually high mortality rates were gradually brought under control by a combination of economic development and public health measures. Fertility declined, too, with the falling demand for child workers, the growth in non-familial welfare provision, and the growing numbers of women in the labour force. Migration flows changed direction, as Germany transformed itself from a relatively stagnant economic area which exported millions of its own inhabitants into a vibrant economy which offered new opportunities to millions of immigrants from other countries. The position of women gradually improved, with female suffrage, changes in labour law, and growing welfare provision for single parents and children. Yet here, too, important continuities emerge. As the chapters of this volume show, demographic choices, women's position, and living standards remained vulnerable to rapid and sometimes catastrophic alternations of political regime, the influence of entrenched institutional structures, and long-term realities of social inclusion and exclusion.

The contributions to this final volume in the series therefore illustrate both change and continuity, shared patterns and regional specificities. On the one hand, they show how Germany participated in the rapid transformations shared by most western societies and economies in the nineteenth and twentieth centuries. At the same time, they also demonstrate vividly how German societies and economies retained the many distinctive features which had, since the medieval period, characterized this fascinating and heterogeneous central region of Europe.

Acknowledgements

This three-volume social and economic history of Germany from 1450 to the present day would not have come into being without the inspiration of our friend and colleague Bob Scribner, whose tragic and premature death in 1998 prevented his seeing this project completed. This book is dedicated to his memory.

The editors are very grateful to Jeremy Edwards, Tim Guinnane, and Paul Ryan, who were so kind as to provide detailed comments on several of the chapters of this volume.

Finally, the editors would like to thank the readers of Volumes I and II across the world who wrote to ask what had happened to Volume III. It is readers such as these who help to keep books alive.

1

The regional dimension: economic geography, economic development, and national integration in the nineteenth and twentieth centuries

FRANK B. TIPTON
University of Sydney

1.1 What is Germany? Nation and region

The sudden reunification of the former German Democratic Republic with the Federal Republic of Germany re-opened debates over the German identity that had lain dormant so long as the two Germanys were held apart and each could use the other as a convenient negative 'other' to bolster its own identity.[1] In addition, Europeans confront the related problems of the integration of this reunified Germany into Europe, of what policies a 'normal' Germany might pursue.[2] The 'German problem' has re-emerged, and the question of 'What is Germany?' remains on the agenda.

Chancellor Helmut Kohl argued during the negotiations leading to reunification that the division of Germany was both 'immoral' and 'unhistorical', and he also asserted that the integration of reunited Germany into Europe via the Maastricht treaty was not merely a question of economic harmonization, but a question of 'war and peace'. Kohl stood in a long line of German political leaders in insisting that Germany is a single entity, and he also continued a long tradition in linking the political and diplomatic issue of German unity with economic policy and regional economic development. However, there is in fact nothing unhistorical about the division of Germany. Disunity has been the norm in German history. Furthermore, the economic problems of regional integration and regional imbalance are also nothing new, and neither, unfortunately, are the social and political problems arising from uneven regional development and failure to achieve harmonious national integration.

In what follows I would like to look at the German national question from a regional standpoint. The German problem has in fact been a regional problem for a long time. Indeed the very use of the word 'German' at once defines the problem and points to the centrality of the regional question in German and central European history. For what, again, *is* Germany? And where is it? The territories typically considered 'German' possess no natural boundaries setting them off from their neighbours, so which of the many possible geographical regions should 'Germany' contain? Nor has there been any tradition of political unity. In 1667, constitutional theorist Samuel von Pufendorf described the Holy Roman Empire of the German Nation as a 'somewhat irregular body similar to a monster'. It contained nearly 2000 separate entities in 1789. They included parts of the Habsburg empire – but not all. They also included parts of the domains of the King of Prussia – but not all. Political and diplomatic history since then has been primarily concerned with which of these territories would become part of 'Germany'. It is therefore neither to geography nor to history that we should look for a simple definition of 'Germany' and 'German'.[3]

Furthermore, German economic development has been regional economic development. Variations in climate, the unequal distribution of natural resources, and the limitations of transportation technologies dictated widely disparate patterns in the early decades of the nineteenth century. The thrust of industrial change, new transportation systems, and urban centralization combined to ensure that regional structures in Germany would become ever less similar from the middle of the nineteenth century until well into the twentieth century. Germany might have been 'unified' and a newly articulated 'national' economy might be perceived, but the benefits of development were very unevenly distributed, and the consequences of that uneven distribution weighed heavily on German politics. In more recent decades, the move from industrial toward service economies has led to a broad convergence of regional economic structures, but the problem of unequal distribution of the benefits of development has remained.

As in politics and diplomacy, so too in economic development, the link between the histories of German localities and regions on the one hand, and the history of the German nation as a whole on the other, is conceptually difficult and politically contentious. From the national perspective, descriptions and explanations of economic development at the level of national aggregates by definition obscure local variations. Therefore, some call for local studies that will reveal the variety and complexity of the regional building blocks which make up the national aggregates. Yet from the local perspective, studies of economic change restricted to particular districts are by definition isolated and potentially unrepresentative.

Consequently, we also hear calls for comparative studies and for some connection between local and national perspectives.[4]

The heart of the problem lies in our understanding of the causal connections linking economic change at the local and national levels. These causal relationships connecting national aggregates and local variations are in fact unclear. From a purely statistical standpoint, we can say that national fluctuations are the weighted averages of local fluctuations, and that national fluctuations must begin in some local area. We can see, for instance, that each of the long swings evident in German economic growth during the nineteenth century was connected with a particular German region entering into the process of modern economic growth, or with an upswing or downswing in specific regional economies.[5]

Furthermore, we can say that national structural changes must begin in some locality or group of localities. Gerd Hardach, for instance, specifies not only the time, but also the place, of the beginning of Germany's industrial revolution: 'In the late summer of the year 1784 Johann Gottfried Brügelmann opened his mechanized spinning plant in Ratingen, and thereby introduced the industrial revolution in Germany.'[6] Similarly, Toni Pierenkemper insists that an understanding of the dynamics of economic change in Upper Silesia requires a close look at the localities where the most progressive iron firms were located, especially districts within the *Kreis* of Beuthen.[7] Considerations such as these seem to give a kind of priority to local fluctuations and local development in 'causing' national change. Change must begin somewhere, and therefore we can say that understanding aggregate figures requires us to pay attention to these progressive localities.

1.2 From the eighteenth to the nineteenth century

Until the middle decades of the nineteenth century, a perspective that highlights individual firms in specific districts retains some plausibility. A series of wars between the Habsburg and Hohenzollern rulers from 1740 to 1763 created a dualism that dominated central European history for a century. Following the end of the Seven Years War in 1763, this rivalry and the consequent insecurity became an important motive for 'reform' in the two major powers in German-speaking central Europe, and in many of the minor ones. These efforts added an economic dimension to the existing political divisions. Central governments attempted, though not always with complete success, to stimulate industrial development through sponsorship of new technologies. In doing so they added impetus to the efforts of individual entrepreneurs, urban communities, and proto-industrial peasant-artisan families. Government subsidies tended to go to firms with military importance, import-substitution potential, or the capacity to export luxury items. Private individuals and proto-industrial families tended to produce less expensive goods for export markets.[8]

A gap also opened between the grain-exporting districts in the north-east, roughly east of the Elbe, and the 'individualized country' (*individualisiertes Land*) celebrated by social geographer Wilhelm Heinrich Riehl to the west and south.[9] The German east was dominated economically by large estates, and socially by the owners of those estates, the Junker aristocracy. Towns were sparse and town government lay largely in the hands of representatives of the Prussian central government. From Saxony westward and southward small agricultural holdings predominated. Towns spread in a relatively dense network. Trade in foodstuffs tended to be local or regional. Exports were largely industrial products, artisan handicrafts produced by farm families or workers in the towns.[10]

We can also detect the beginnings of modern economic development, a few machine-made goods produced in factories following Brügelman's example. Aristocrats and central government bureaucrats reluctantly shared social power with the oligarchic elites who controlled the towns.[11] In both east and west, local patriotism provided the basis for broader identities, a sense of cultural distinctiveness of the sort Anthony Smith has identified as the *ethnie*, the basis of national communities.[12] As seen below, these larger regional identifications in turn fed into the debate over the shape of the 'German' nation.

The French Revolution and the Napoleonic wars brought the idea of a nation in the modern sense, an idea that 'German' writers such as Herder, Fichte, Arndt, and Jahn (a very specifically *Prussian* patriot) did much to develop and popularize.[13] A 'nation' (in the definition that continues to set the standard toward which the peoples of central and eastern Europe seem to aspire) came to be regarded as a unified, contiguous territory, inhabited by people speaking a common language, all of whom participate in the public life of the national community.[14] However, to the chagrin of German patriots, the Vienna settlement of 1815 resulted not in the creation of a single unified Germany but in the establishment of a German Confederation containing 39 separate states. Furthermore, the most significant of these states themselves contained territories whose inhabitants did not wish to belong to their putative new communities. In the south, the enlarged centralized states of Baden, Württemberg, and Bavaria faced considerable hostility from members of the smaller communities they had annexed. As for Prussia, the newly acquired territories in the Rhineland contained many individuals and communities whose desire to belong to the Prussian community was exiguous at best.[15]

As this point, although they had not grown large, districts with several truly industrial firms not only differed in their essential structure from those with only handicraft manufactures, but also probably competed with them in other regional markets. Similarly, towns whose merchants looked to interregional trade not only differed from but also competed with towns whose merchants remained local in outlook. The leaders of the progressive districts were few, but they wanted to expand. Therefore the conservative and reactionary tone of the Restoration governments generally added to the overall sense of frustration arising out of the attempts of the central bureaucracies of these states to impose their will in their new possessions. In addition, feelings of inferiority and occasional threats such as the French war scare of 1840 – the stimulus for 'Die Wacht am Rhein' and 'Deutschland, Deutschland über Alles' – helped to focus hostility towards the existing regimes around a programme of 'national' unity.

1.3 Regions and the beginnings of modern economic development

A portion of the rising tide of nationalist sentiment therefore must be attributed to local or regional opposition to central states, states that were themselves in turn envisaged as regions in a larger German national state. In Prussia, Rhinelanders and liberals such as David Hansemann sought to change state policy to suit their interests, and this meant placing Prussia at the centre of a new German government. In Württemberg, Friedrich List called for a new national government to provide the legal and physical framework for economic development in order to overcome the parochialism of the smaller states. At the same time, modern economic development began to spread outward to involve larger numbers of firms and wider geographical areas. Local patriotism, regional identities, and national aspirations therefore became bound up with the problematic linkages between local, regional, and national economic development sketched out above.

The role of consciousness is a non-economic variable with potentially important economic consequences at the regional level. The sense of belonging, of connectedness, the sense that one's region is distinct and different from others and from the 'national' community, was not only an important political fact in Germany's national history, but also an important factor in the economic sphere. The creation of regional identities is a historical process in many respects parallel to the creation of national identities. Following Benedict Anderson's analysis, we can identify the resulting identifications as the basis of an 'imagined community' within which many individuals who never meet can nonetheless feel a common bond, and who may well behave as if they belonged to a genuine primordial *ethnie* in Smith's sense.[16] Local cultures may merge into and be reformulated as regional cultures.

One of the links between regional and national change is that the political, legal, and economic structures established by the central government constitute the framework within which change occurs at the local level. So long as there was no German state, this power remained in the hands of the 39 members of the German Confederation. These states all exercised careful control over the granting of permission to open industrial establishments during the nineteenth century. The cautious and sometimes hostile attitude of the Prussian bureaucracy contrasted strikingly with the more open and flexible approach of the Saxon government, and that contrast certainly must be considered in any explanation of the relatively buoyant development of the Saxon industrial sector compared to the Rheinland during the first half of the century.[17] Furthermore, it is clear that random or arbitrary political events, for example the Prussian government's decision to remove railway securities from the category of trustee-approved investments in the 1840s, could have serious regional repercussions, in this case the sudden downturn in railway construction in the Rheinland and other areas of extensive railway promotion, which contributed to the depression of the 1840s.[18]

Still, national occurrences – in the sense of national aggregate economic measures – do not *cause* local fluctuations, and they do not *cause* local structural change. Change must begin with the decisions of individual persons. At the same time, however, national development is not *caused* by changes in local economic aggregates. National structural changes are too large to result from local changes, if we are speaking of truly small localities, or ultimately of individual persons. As contemporary developing nations know only too well, the opening of one factory in one town does not guarantee that an industrial revolution will follow. Hardach in fact recognizes this in the German case when he concludes that 'the industrial revolution as social transformation, as movement from agricultural society to capitalistic industrial society, was only finished in Germany around 1895' – that is, a full century after it 'began'.[19] So too with local districts, however progressive. In the Silesian case, rather than the single *Kreis* of Beuthen studied by Pierenkemper, a unit the size of a *Regierungsbezirk* such as Oppeln is a reasonable choice from the standpoint of analysing the impact of regional development on the national economy.[20]

At this period, the new industrial centres were as yet small, but as they expanded, their influence spread. Larger numbers of people were caught up in the change, and economic change transformed their personal and collective identities as well. From an economic/geographic perspective, we can say the regions of Germany were beginning to be more intensively involved in the process of modern economic development. From a social/psychological perspective, we can say that regions themselves were coming into being as the economy developed. In the case of the Ruhr, Wilhelm Brepohl argued in a path-breaking study that industrialization *created* a new 'people of the Ruhr' with a culture distinctively their own.[21]

The emergence of new leading sectors contributed an additional un-precedented dynamic. Previously, industrial development had centred on textiles and other consumer goods, but now it came to mean pre-eminently 'producer goods', that is, coal and iron, steam engines and machinery, and above all the construction of railways.[22] This involved not only a regional focus, but also a crucial shift of the regional focus away from the areas which had led eighteenth-century development, particularly Bohemia, Silesia, and Saxony, and towards the West. Through the middle of the nineteenth century, iron smelting required substantially greater weights of coal than iron ore, and therefore the iron industry and the industries that depended on iron tended to locate where suitable coal lay adjacent to transportation routes. The Ruhr Valley, with its hillside access to the coal deposits and its connection to the Rhine, began to emerge as a node of development.[23] The increasing importance of the Ruhr and other Rhenish-Westphalian industrial districts added weight to the Prussian economy through the 1830s and 1840s.

The establishment of the *Zollverein* tariff union in 1834 was (and is) held by many to have speeded Prussian economic development and to have accelerated development in other German states as well.[24] Shipping did increase along the Rhine in the late 1830s, but not (for instance) overland between Bavaria and Saxony, and in general the sparse data do not suggest any general, discontinuous change in the long-term rate of growth.[25] Furthermore, it is important to note that the *Zollverein* was rightly perceived by contemporaries as being pushed forward by important elements within the Prussian government at least as much as a means of strengthening Prussia's diplomatic position and undermining Austrian power in the German Confederation as for its possible 'national' economic benefits.[26] Until 1848, the Prussian government actively opposed the prime movers of modern economic development, notably railways, large-scale mining and industrial undertakings, new banking facilities, and the extension of limited liability corporations.[27] This led to political opposition against the government, especially in the Rhineland, the most rapidly developing Prussian province. A new regional identity crystallized along the fault lines where local economic interests intersected with state policy. 'Rhenish liberals' opposed their Prussian masters on a broad range of issues relating to the economic development of their province, and this opposition reinforced calls for a 'national' government that would be more sympathetic to their interests.[28]

The revolutions of 1848 represented, from this perspective, a rather paradoxical outburst of 'national' sentiment derived in large part from regional identifications.[29] Of course the programme of national unification in 1848 failed. However, in the aftermath of 1848 came a rearrangement of political and economic forces that had the effect of reinforcing the emerging regional focus of economic development in Germany. The industrial and commercial interest groups formerly in opposition now supported the Prussian government. The government in turn supported industrial development, especially the rapid expansion of the railway system, investment in the new larger mining enterprises required to exploit the deeper coal seams north of the Ruhr Valley, and a burst of development in the iron and steel industries.[30] On the other hand, liberal leaders, confident in their leadership of solid majorities in the Prussian Landtag, continued to oppose the political dominance of the Junker aristocracy in the bureaucracy and the resulting conservatism of Prussian government policy. There also remained the unfinished agenda of 'national' unification, though what this would mean, particularly with regard to Austria, was no clearer than before.[31]

Bismarck used the advantages conferred by the expansion of the railway system and rapid industrial growth, and the unfulfilled desire for national unity, to prosecute his short and successful wars against Denmark, Austria, and France. His simultaneous manipulation of intersecting but very disparate diplomatic, political, and economic interests in pursuit of his goals continues to excite admiration more than a century later.[32] Following the reunification of Germany in 1990, Helmut Kohl likened himself to Bismarck, listening for God's footsteps and seizing the hem of the divine cloak. The difference, however, is that when Bismarck said this of himself he was being disingenuous, for he himself had created the crises that he exploited. His cynical manipulation of the resulting opportunities outraged his contemporaries, including Wilhelm I, army leaders, Prussian aristocrats, government bureaucrats, and middle-class liberals.[33]

That the highly artificial creation that resulted in 1871 did in fact become a focus for individual patriotism is one of the stronger pieces of evidence for the psychological power of the 'imagined communities' which national states form. Many of Bismarck's erstwhile opponents underwent a conversion experience and forgot their previous criticisms of him and his methods, for instance historian Heinrich von Treitschke, a Saxon and a scornful critic of Bismarck who became the arch-apologist of the Bismarckian Reich.[34] Bismarck's ruthless policies were re-christened as 'compromises'. His artificial creation was asserted to be a natural organic unity and imbued with a 'moral sanctity'.[35] The selective memory imposed by the new national ideology left a blank in the historical record. Manifestly untrue assertions about 'Germany' became the mental framework of German leaders. Germans were held to be bound together by their common 'blood'. Within the new borders, suppressed regional differences were identified as merely quaint affirmations of this underlying unity, despite Paul Pfizer's observation in 1832 that different regions of Germany regarded each other with a 'jealousy that verges on national hatred'.[36] The ground was laid for a collective paranoia, a fear that the healthy German national body could be threatened from without, by the pressure of foreign bodies, and from within, by diseases spread by domestic enemies. This was the nationalism that helped push Germany towards the First and Second World Wars.

1.4 Region and nation in Bismarckian Germany

In considering the Bismarckian version of 'unification', we must note that Bismarck not only failed to solve the inherited problems of regional integration, but actually created new ones as well. For instance, even if we accept the argument that a common language is the defining factor of nationhood,[37] we see that the new 'German' state included a large number of Polish-speaking people in the eastern provinces of Prussia, that the defeat and dismemberment of Denmark had added Danish-speakers in the north, and that the annexation of Alsace and Lorraine added French-speakers in the west. With regard to German-speakers, the situation was equally ambiguous. On the one hand, the German-speaking people of Austria and Bohemia, who had been considered by many to belong within 'Germany', were not included. On the other hand, however, large groups of German-speakers in northern, central, and southern German states, who did not want to belong to the new 'German' state, were included. It is true that the 'foreign' minorities had no hope of freeing themselves.[38] It is also true that German-speakers absorbed into Prussia in 1867 and into the Bismarckian empire in 1871 came to accept quite quickly that they were 'German'.[39] As Celia Applegate argues, even in districts with strong local identities, 'regional and national loyalties could be compatible and mutually reinforcing'.[40] Nevertheless the divisions remained, and they were deepened rather than ameliorated by the pattern of economic change.

Within the new state, economic development proceeded more from the complex of links being forged among regions, than either from a uniform change in 'national' conditions or from 'regional' development. Phrased in theoretical terms, even when aggregated, changes in local economic structures do not constitute national economic change, because the creation of an interrelated set of functional exchanges is precisely what we mean by 'national' development. In other words, the national whole is more than the sum of its local parts. Thus, until the economies of emerging industrial districts have been linked to each other and to other specialized centres of supply and distribution, there can be no 'national' economy.

For Germany, this process can be traced by following the emerging pattern of the transportation network. In the 1850s, water routes ran from inland districts outward toward the sea, and railway lines had only begun to extend from the urban centres. There were virtually no connections running from east to west. 'German' regions were connected primarily to outside markets and sources of supply, not to each other. In this early period of development, growth in German regions depended on links with the international economy, on a pattern similar to that outlined for the European economy as a whole by Sydney Pollard.[41] From the 1880s onward, however, dynamics internal to the German economy seem to play a greater role, notably in the relationships of the eastern regions with Berlin and the Ruhr.[42] By 1914, the pattern of inland water routes shows clear regional nodes in the south-western, north-western, central, and eastern areas, and the major regions that were not connected by major east–west waterways had become linked by interregional railway lines. These interregional routes in turn connected the highly developed radial rail systems that had emerged in each regional economy, reinforcing the pattern of the inland waterways. The existence of a national economy is palpably obvious.[43]

In analysing the impact of the creation of new transportation facilities, we may begin with Immanuel Wallerstein's insight that it is the export of bulk products that plays the most important role for the social structure of the producing region: 'It was only with the expansion of production within the framework of a modern world economy that long distance trade could convert itself in part into bulk trade, which would, in turn, feed the process of expanded production.' According to Wallerstein, it is not the exchange of 'preciosities' but the trade in large volumes of bulk goods that results in the creation of new economic structures and the corresponding social groupings. The opportunity to sell bulk goods to consumers in core regions leads elites in peripheral regions to reorganize production, introduce new technologies, and mobilize large numbers of workers in new ways. [44]

Until the middle of the nineteenth century the development of water transportation was therefore the most important factor in determining the possibilities of regional economic development, for until the advent of the railway it was by far the cheapest form of conveying these bulk items. If the cost of construction of a canal or a usable channel in an existing river could be met, then huge savings in human and animal power could be realized.[45] Using Wallerstein's terminology, water transport routes played a crucial role in linking the peripheral and semi-peripheral areas of central and eastern Europe with the western European core regions. The penetration of the German interior by inland water routes opened opportunities in foreign markets to industrial producers in western, south-western, and central German states, and to agricultural producers in the German east. So too did the development of water transport on the Moldau and lower Danube for producers in the Habsburg lands.[46] In the core districts of Germany, early development of waterways for bulk transport reinforced the developing role of these regions in the world economy. Perhaps most importantly, the canals provided access to energy in the form of coal to the firms at the forefront of the industrial revolution. Development of the canal system gave manufacturers access to raw materials from domestic and foreign sources, and to domestic and foreign markets for sale of the products. Canals themselves often became locational factors, as industrial entrepreneurs found it convenient to site their new factories along the route. Germany shared these patterns with the other economies of western Europe. [47]

The railway added to and deepened these processes. Railways went where canals could not, and in particular they made possible the east–west connections that reoriented the trade of the regions of Germany towards each other. Seen from the perspective of the core regions, this represented an extension of the capitalist world economy into new areas of untapped labour and raw materials. At the same time, railways imposed huge demands for industrial materials, machinery, construction, and labour. From dependence on Britain for imports of machinery and technical expertise, several German regions, especially Saxony, Berlin, the Ruhr, and the Rhine-Main district, moved to become centres of production in their own right. The resulting expansionary force of their industrial sectors not only fed their own continued growth but also reinforced the process of the emergence of the national economy.[48]

Germany's rise to the status of core nation reflected the development of the national economy, one aspect of which was the emergence of the new articulated transportation network. Economic geographers have argued that this process can be conceived of as the emergence of a hierarchical structure of central places, as in Lajos Timar's emphasis on the development of urban systems:

> From the end of the XVIIIth century on – for the first time in England, then with a certain delay in other centre countries, and semi-peripheral countries as well – the nationally characteristic hierarchical system of the urban network, especially in its social respect, increasingly separates from the regional frameworks . . . a continuous system of cities is under formation.[49]

Timar's approach reflects a fairly widespread suspicion among geographers and economic historians that regional analysis poses problems of definition and conceptualization, in addition to the difficulties of causal analysis discussed above, and Timar in fact concludes that historians should dispense with the concept of 'region' entirely.[50] Some aspects of the changing occupational distributions of German cities do seem to point towards the emergence of a functionally differentiated hierarchy of urban places. However, not all cities fit into functionally defined niches, and not all those that do can be arranged by size.[51] Nor did regions arrange themselves in smoothly graded spatial hierarchies. Within the new Bismarckian empire, economic growth slowed from 1873 to 1896 compared to the 20 years preceding the empire's foundation.[52] In addition, one concomitant of development over the whole period of the Bismarckian empire's existence was an increasingly severe regional imbalance. It is significant that contemporaries perceived the resulting problems in regional terms, because their perceptual framework provided the basis for both economic and political action.

The strains of slow growth during the 'Great Depression' (1873–96) bore particularly heavily on agricultural regions and districts dominated by small-scale manufacturing. As shown in Table 1.1, this was reflected in a substantial increase in regional specialization in the three major economic

Table 1.1 Specialization in regions of Germany, 1882, 1895, and 1907

	1882	1895	1907
East			
East Prussia	34.7	40.8	46.1
West Prussia	28.5	33.9	38.6
Posen	37.7	43.9	51.4
Pomerania	19.4	26.3	32.6
Upper Silesia	14.0	11.3	14.4
Lower Silesia	2.1	4.2	7.7
District of Frankfurt	20.7	22.5	26.3
North and central			
District of Potsdam	7.2	14.7	25.9
Berlin	97.3	83.9	69.8
Mecklenburg	13.7	20.3	28.4
Schleswig-Holstein	12.0	14.7	16.3
Hannover	11.6	13.2	15.8
Hamburg, Bremen, Lübeck	86.2	75.0	62.0
Kingdom of Saxony	52.3	49.5	44.6
District of Magdeburg	7.0	2.5	1.6
District of Merseburg	11.5	9.8	11.4
West			
Northern Westphalia	14.6	10.3	9.8
Ruhr	51.3	51.8	50.7
District of Aachen	23.5	16.9	16.8
District of Cologne	21.0	27.0	30.4
Trier and Koblenz	15.7	18.2	18.1
Hessen-Nassau	3.6	5.9	3.4
South			
Bavaria	25.8	26.3	31.6
Württemberg	14.1	17.9	18.6
Baden	16.9	14.7	10.4
Hesse	19.6	18.4	18.6
Rheinpfalz	18.5	10.1	11.2
Lorraine	5.6	14.5	10.0
Alsace	4.1	1.1	4.8
Average specialization	23.6	25.2	27.1

Source: Frank B. Tipton, *Regional Variations in the Economic Development of Germany during the Nineteenth Century* (Middletown, 1976), based on occupational census data.
Method: see text.

sectors of agriculture, industry and services. Table 1.1 uses a measure of specialization derived as follows. First, in order to measure divergence from the national average, each region's total employment was multiplied by the national average share of employment in each of the three major sectors. These hypothetical figures, representing regional employment in each sector if the region did not deviate from the average, were then subtracted from actual regional employment in each sector. Finally, the absolute sum of the differences for all three sectors was expressed as a percentage of total employment in the region, yielding the measure of 'average specialization' reported in Table 1.1 – a weighted index, the ratio of all regional deviations to total national employment.

Although a region could in principle achieve a specialization approaching 200 per cent if its entire labour force was employed in a very small sector, in fact (since none of the three sectors became very small during this period), any specialization over 25 per cent can be regarded as high. A surprising number of German regions show high levels of specialization as early as 1882, and a majority show increasing specialization between 1882 and 1907. Some moved with the average, of course, and those that were already highly industrialized, such as Saxony, the Ruhr, and the urban regions showed declines as they were overtaken by the average. In addition, the index of average specialization for Germany in this period is surprisingly high by international standards, and the fact that it increases is also unusual in international perspective. The reason for this is that Germany had very large regions whose industrial sectors did not grow rapidly. The most significant (because of their political importance) were the eastern provinces of Prussia.[53]

Increasing divergence among regions within the Bismarckian empire reflected the fact that 'agricultural' regions became relatively more 'agricultural' over time. This development in turn was tied to a very heavy flow of internal migration, which is summarized in Table 1.2. The largest net out-migration was suffered by the eastern provinces of Prussia, the home of the Prussian aristocracy, while Berlin and the western industrial districts stand out as the chief beneficiaries of in-migration. Migrants responded primarily to the 'pull' of expanding job opportunities.[54] In industrial centres and in towns, demand for transportation and new construction created additional multiplier effects on the economy, resulting in what Fritz Voigt later termed 'self-feeding' growth.[55] The catchment area for migrants into German industrial and urban centres began to expand beyond Germany: by 1914 tens of thousands of Poles and Italians were working in the mines and factories of the Ruhr district.[56]

The obverse was decline in less favoured regions, and the widely lamented 'flight from the land' (*Landflucht*). Despite the widespread discussion of this problem, however, German government policy failed to address regional issues in any meaningful way. Anachronistic programmes of agricultural settlement created only 18,076 new peasant farms in East and West Prussia between 1886 and 1919.[57] Politics continued to play an important role. Railway freight rates discriminated in favour of agricultural products and against industrial goods produced in the east. Proposals for industrial development in the east which were developed by the provincial administration of West Prussia received virtually no political support.[58]

The eastern provinces of Germany, which were so badly disadvantaged by the process of economic development, however, became the sole reliable

Table 1.2 Internal migration in Germany, 1880–1910 (thousands)

From 1880 to 1890

To: From:	East	B'burg	North	Central	West	South	*Total*
East	x	281	106	122	103	12	624
B'burg	23	x	15	21	6	2	67
North	8	11	x	18	28	7	72
Central	14	49	42	x	25	15	145
West	6	12	24	17	x	39	98
South	3	10	9	26	54	x	102
Total	54	363	196	204	216	75	*1108*

From 1890 to 1900

To: From:	East	B'burg	North	Central	West	South	*Total*
East	x	249	83	90	249	14	685
B'burg	34	x	15	24	17	6	96
North	18	20	x	20	59	9	126
Central	26	58	49	x	62	22	217
West	17	19	25	12	x	47	120
South	5	16	9	24	85	x	139
Total	100	362	181	170	472	98	*1383*

From 1900 to 1910

To: From:	East	B'burg	North	Central	West	South	*Total*
East	x	233	90	11	181	16	531
B'burg	26	x	23	17	21	9	96
North	9	19	x	12	47	9	96
Central	27	72	45	x	57	28	229
West	19	24	28	20	x	39	130
South	4	14	13	17	49	x	97
Total	85	362	199	77	355	101	*1179*

Source: Computed from data on place of birth and place of residence in Walther G. Hoffmann, *Das Wachstum der deutschen Wirtschaft seit der Mitte des 19. Jahrhunderts* (Berlin, 1965), pp. 178–80.
Note: B'burg consists of the province of Brandenburg and Berlin.

electoral support of the old conservative regime. Though, as noted above, neither national minorities nor regional affiliations posed a threat to the state, nevertheless regional voting patterns in elections to the Reichstag became increasingly polarized, and this reflected the divergent interests of regional economies.[59] In this sense, Bismarck's attempt at national integration appears to have failed. In particular, the declining east became the only area in which the Conservative Party could secure majorities in elections to the Imperial Reichstag and, equally importantly, to the Prussian

Landtag.[60] This narrowing in sources of support for the government was the obverse of the rise of industry in more favoured regions and, even more ominously for the Conservatives, the rise of the Social Democratic Party. The panic this engendered in Imperial Germany's ruling circles led to increasingly desperate attempts to find some basis on which the 'nation' could be united behind the government. In the 1890s, attention turned from a 'politics of unity' (*Sammlungspolitik*), to a 'cartel of the productive classes' (*Kartel der schaffenden Stände*), and then to an increasingly risky search for a dramatic foreign policy success. In this way, regional economic development was connected to the growth of nationalism and the outbreak of the First World War.[61]

1.5 From the First to the Second World War

Regionally, the First World War was a disaster for 'Germany'. Alsace and Lorraine were restored to France, and West Prussia, Posen, and most of Silesia to a resurrected Poland. These changes could be seen as a simplification of the 'national' map of central Europe, on balance. However, the industries of Alsace, Lorraine, and Upper Silesia all suffered from being separated from previous sources of raw materials and from their most important markets in Germany. Danzig, designated a 'free city' and intended to provide Poland with an ocean port, was cut off from much of the hinterland created by the previous development of the transportation system.

Austria, despite the expressed wishes of a majority of the representatives in its constituent assembly, was not permitted to join 'Germany', and the German-speaking portion of Bohemia became part of the new Czechoslovakia. Vienna, formerly the administrative centre of the entire Habsburg empire, and a node of transportation, industry, and services comparable to Berlin, now became an outsized city of over 2 million in a country of only 8 million people. Bohemia, whose industries had attracted raw materials and shipped finished goods throughout the Empire, languished as tariff barriers cut off those previous trade relations.[62]

In the new Weimar Republic, economic development continued apace. Industry continued to expand, although 'rationalization' and concentration into cartels had the effect of further narrowing the regional focus of expansion. Growth became concentrated in the largest cities and in industrial zones where neighbouring towns grew together. Greater Berlin, the archetype of the 'metropolitan region' (*Stadtregion*), increased from 3.7 million inhabitants in 1910 to 4.0 million in 1925 and over 4.3 million in 1939, and Hamburg from 1.0 to 1.2 and 1.7 million. The new term 'agglomeration area' (*Ballungsraum*) referred to districts such as the Ruhr, the Saar, and the Rhine-Main area. In the Ruhr district, Dortmund,

Duisburg, Düsseldorf and Essen together contained over 2.1 million persons in 1933. Towards the end of the nineteenth century, German industrial development had begun to lose its previous 'island character', and now the 'islands' began to grow together.[63]

Small-scale manufacturing enterprises, and districts where they predominated, suffered. The 'individualized country' of central and southern Germany largely stagnated. Ironically, however, it was precisely during this difficult period that southern Germany was taken as the empirical framework for an immensely influential theory of urban growth, the 'central place theory' of Walter Christaller. Impressed by the regularity of the spatial distribution of southern German towns, Christaller hypothesized that as they grew, urban places would arrange themselves in regular hierarchies on a hexagonal grid, the hexagon being the shape that would minimize transportation costs from periphery to centre. City sizes and the relations among them, said Christaller, reflected scale economies in the provision of goods and services, with the largest cities acting as distribution centres for all places below them in the hierarchy. In fact, as already noted, this theory does not fit or explain the pattern of urban growth in Imperial Germany. Furthermore, the pattern of urban centres in interwar southern Germany reflected not modern industrial development, but inherited structures dating from the seventeenth century and before. Nevertheless, Christaller's central place theory is taken seriously in regional analysis to this day.[64]

During this period, German agriculture suffered even more than small industry. The decline of the remaining eastern regions, and of agricultural districts generally, continued through the 1920s and 1930s. East Prussia suffered a net loss of population, and any district above average in agricultural employment in 1907 typically had lower than average growth over the following 30 years.[65] The imperial government's programme of 'aid to the east' (*Osthilfe*) was no more effective than its programme of agricultural settlement.[66] The trajectory of German regional economic development contributed, along with the world depression, to the rise of Nazism, for when the German economy collapsed in the late 1920s, voters in agricultural districts and in the small towns of the 'individualized country' overwhelmingly gave their support to Hitler.[67]

The Second World War was another, greater disaster for 'Germany'. Not only was 'Germany' further reduced in size by territorial losses to Poland in the east, but the remnant was divided into 'West' Germany and 'East' Germany, although of course 'East Germany' was 'Central Germany' (*Mitteldeutschland*) in terms of the Bismarckian empire. Austria, defined by the victorious Allies as an 'occupied nation' rather than as part of 'Germany', again remained separate. A massive flow of population accompanied the creation of the two Germanys. Between 1945 and 1948, some 10 to 12 million persons flooded into West Germany from East Germany, Poland, Czechoslovakia, Hungary and the Soviet Union.

1.6 West and East Germany

Despite wartime destruction, West Germany possessed a strong resource base and in the division somewhat fortuitously received a particularly favourable mix of industries. West Germany also enjoyed substantial subsidies from the United States, first from the United Nations Relief and Rehabilitation Agency (UNRRA) and later through the provisions of the Marshall Plan. However, the postwar flow of refugees created a new set of regional imbalances. They concentrated in Schleswig and north-eastern Bavaria, regions with little by way of employment prospects. The government granted the refugees citizenship, rights to social services, and entitlements to pensions based on their previous status, but made no attempt to create employment in the regions where the refugees were located. Instead, in effect people were forced to move to jobs. This pragmatic combination of the provision of minimal social welfare measures to a potentially dangerous population with reliance on the private sector to create employment was enshrined in government rhetoric as the 'social market economy' (*soziale Marktwirtschaft*).[68]

East Germany, by contrast, possessed a much less favourable mixture of resources and industries, and recovery was correspondingly slower. East Germany also suffered under Soviet domination. Although 'the Soviets did not occupy Germany with specific long-range goals in mind', they needed to rebuild their own economy and insisted that East Germany conform to this aim.[69] The East Germans paid heavy war reparations, supported a large Soviet army of occupation, and were also required to maintain a large army of their own. The imposition of Soviet-style political, social, and economic institutions caused sharp declines in output. Work norms were modelled on Soviet prototypes, and the labour unions that claimed to represent the workers' interests in fact functioned as disciplinary agencies. Resentment boiled over in 1953, and was brutally repressed. Discontent continued, and 1.5 million persons moved from East Germany to West Germany between 1949 and 1961, when the East German government erected the 'Anti-Fascist Protective Wall' to block off the exit through Berlin.[70]

During the 1950s and 1960s, both West and East Germany grew rapidly. West Germany, whose economy expanded at a rate of over 5 per cent per year, benefited from the broad range of factors which contributed to the long upswing enjoyed by the entire developed world during those decades, particularly the backlog of technology which had lain fallow since the Depression, and the very rapid growth in world trade.[71] The West German 'economic miracle' rested on a very high investment ratio. West German capital formation rose to over 25 per cent of total product during the 1950s and touched 28 per cent during the 1960s.[72] Much of the investment went into the production of consumer durables, especially automobiles. A revolution in consumer spending patterns saw the share of food and drink in total consumption decline from 46 per cent in 1950 to 29 per cent in 1967.[73] Automobiles and other durables also could be exported to the

expanding markets of the new European Economic Community and overseas. Ludwig Erhard typified the western European statesmen who happily
took credit for the economic expansion during the long boom. But in effect
West Germany's 'social market economy' was never put to the test.[74]

In East Germany, the central planners emphasized the expansion of heavy
industry. Reported growth was even more rapid than in West Germany, but
benefits to consumers were limited. Official figures showed output rising
over 7 per cent each year, as capital formation accelerated from 17 per cent
of total product during the 1950s to 24 per cent during the 1960s and over
30 per cent during the 1970s.[75] The East German planners adopted the
Soviet approach of allocating resources according to the physical requirements of a given level of production. Under this physical balances approach,
because there were no prices assigned by the market to capital, raw
materials, or intermediate products, there was no way to determine the
'best' choice except through political decision. The system produced impressive results in the Soviet Union's first five-year plans in the 1930s and in
some of the eastern European countries in the 1950s and 1960s, but it
worked most effectively in the 'early' stages of economic development and
with long runs of standard products. In later stages of industrial development, and when a broad range of consumer products was required, satisfactory results were much more difficult to attain. Into the late 1960s,
however, East Germany could rely on the markets of the Soviet Union and
other eastern European regimes to absorb most of its output, and also found
markets in the European Economic Community through the opening
provided by West Germany's 'one Germany' policy.[76]

For the regional analyst, one of the interesting things about West and East
Germany is a nearly complete disappearance of the regional disparities in
sectoral structure that marked Germany before the Second World War. This
resulted from the decline in the share of agriculture and the increase in the
share of services in all major regions of the two Germanys. Coupled with
these developments was a slowing and even reversal of the growth of the
labour force and a concentration of the population into large urban centres.
These developments are shown in Tables 1.3 and 1.4. By 1987, West and
East Germany had become very similar in their overall structure.

There remained some differences: East Germany remained slightly more
agricultural and its service sector had not grown to quite the extent of that
of West Germany. Labour productivity and average incomes were far higher
in West Germany, and the gap was increasing. However, both Germanys
were industrial economies and urban societies. If we treat the two countries
as one and measure the divergence in their structures as we did above for the
regions of Imperial Germany, we obtain the figures shown in Table 1.5. We
see that in contrast to the period before 1914, average specialization for
both countries taken together never rose above 10 per cent from 1960 to
1987. East Germany diverged from the average in the final decade of its
separate existence, but the degree of divergence was significantly less than

Table 1.3 Population size and distribution by size of community in West and East Germany, 1950–87

	Total (000)	<2000 (%)	2–10,000 (%)	10–100,000 (%)	>100,000 (%)
West Germany					
1950	49,989	29.0	23.0	21.0	27.0
1960	55,433	23.0	22.0	24.0	31.0
1970	60,651	19.0	21.0	28.0	32.0
1980	61,359	n.a.	n.a.	n.a.	n.a.
1987	61,170	6.1	20.1	41.1	32.7
East Germany					
1950	18,388	29.0	23.0	27.0	21.0
1960	17,188	28.0	22.0	29.0	21.0
1970	17,068	26.0	20.0	32.0	22.0
1980	16,740	23.7	19.3	31.1	25.9
1987	16,661	23.2	18.0	31.7	27.1

Source: Hoffmann, *Wachstum*, p. 178; West Germany, Statistisches Bundesamt, *Statistisches Jahrbuch 1988 für die Bundesrepublik Deutschland* (Stuttgart, 1988), p. 60; East Germany, Staatliche Zentralverwaltung für Statistik, *Statistisches Jahrbuch der deutschen demokratischen Republik 1988* (Berlin, 1988), p. 8.

Table 1.4 Labour force size and distribution in West and East Germany, 1950–87

	Total (000)	Agriculture (%)	Industry (%)	Services (%)
West Germany				
1950	20,459	24.3	42.1	33.6
1959	25,189	15.1	47.4	37.5
1971	26,817	8.0	48.4	43.6
1980	26,328	5.5	44.1	50.4
1987	25,971	5.1	40.5	54.4
East Germany				
1960	7,686	17.0	42.1	40.9
1970	7,769	12.8	43.7	43.5
1980	8,225	10.7	45.1	44.2
1987	8,571	10.8	47.4	41.8

Source: Hoffmann, *Wachstum*, pp. 204–6; West Germany, *Statistisches Jahrbuch 1988*, pp. 100–1; East Germany, *Statistisches Jahrbuch 1988*, pp. 112, 117.

the pre-1914 national average. East Germany as a whole also diverged less from the postwar average than most of its component districts had diverged from the average before 1914. Most importantly, perhaps, there were no large 'backward' agricultural regions, and there were no regions identified exclusively with single political parties as there had been before 1914 or between the wars.

Table 1.5 Specialization of West and East Germany, 1959–87

	West Germany	East Germany	Average
1959/60	2.4	8.2	3.8
1970/1	2.2	12.7	4.6
1980	2.9	9.5	4.5
1987	6.2	19.0	9.4

Source: Computed from data in West Germany, *Statistisches Jahrbuch 1988*, pp. 100–1; East Germany, *Statistisches Jahrbuch 1988*, pp. 112, 117.
Method: See Table 1.1 and text.

Furthermore, regions within East and West Germany were much more similar to one another than had been the regions of Imperial Germany, and during the 1960s and 1970s they became even more similar. This reflected the nature of growth industries in Europe as a whole. As already mentioned, the leading sectors of the nineteenth century, the classic heavy industries of the first and second industrial revolutions, were concentrated in coal-producing districts. By contrast, the new, advanced machinery industry, electronics, and especially the modern service sector are naturally more regionally dispersed. For these industries, energy, raw materials, and transportation are much less important in determining the location of production. Even for the older heavy industries, the advent of electricity and motor vehicles loosened the bonds of raw material endowment and the rigid patterns created by water and rail transport.

In addition, there was a significant change in regional patterns of female employment. Until the 1960s, female employment patterns showed much wider regional disparities than did male employment patterns. Most women were not employed in waged work outside the home or family business; those that were employed outside the household were concentrated in a few occupations, especially textiles, clothing, and domestic service. Textiles in particular were highly concentrated in Saxony, the Rhineland, and Alsace, and domestic service concentrated in urban centres. Domestic service declined in the 1920s and virtually disappeared in the 1950s, and textiles declined as well; but from the 1960s on, increasing numbers of women were employed in a wider variety of industries. The slight decline in the total labour force in the 1970s and 1980s masks a large decline in full-time employment and a large increase in part-time employment. The largest increase was in women working in part-time jobs, as shift workers in the expanding new industrial branches, in secretarial and sales positions, and in the regionally dispersed services branches.[77]

Internationally, West and East Germany both functioned as privileged 'core' regions.[78] They drew supplies of key raw materials and food from other regions, and exported their finished products. Significantly, *all* of the regions of West Germany were among the richest in western Europe. For West Germany the 'other' regions that made this possible were the other countries of western Europe, the United States, and the Third World. In addition, West Germany could escape the threatening shortage of labour which arose in the 1960s by importing millions of 'guest workers' from Italy, Yugoslavia, and Turkey.[79]

For East Germany, the crucial source of energy and primary products, and the most important market, was the Soviet Union, although other eastern European countries also played important roles. As already mentioned, compared to West Germany, average disposable income in East Germany was low; but compared to the Soviet Union or other eastern European countries, it was high. The countries of the Council for Mutual Economic Assistance (CMEA) provided guaranteed markets for long runs of standard products, ideally suited to the conditions of planned production under the physical balances approach.[80] Labour, however, was not permitted to move among CMEA countries; the East German response to labour scarcity was an intensive mobilization of female workers, which in the 1980s reached 92 per cent of women of working age, the highest female participation rate ever recorded in the world.

Their role as core regions benefited both West and East Germany. West Germany's continual large positive balance of payments made the country the most influential voice in international financial affairs after the United States. East Germany's trade balance was more difficult to measure, because the authorities published figures only in 'valuta' marks whose relation to domestic prices is unknown.[81] However, the combination of heavy investment ratios and rising consumer spending suggests a large positive trade balance, parallel to that of West Germany. In addition, their privileged position in the network of international specialization added further buoyancy to both the West and East German economies during upswings and insulated them from the worst effects of downswings.

In the 1970s and 1980s both West and East Germany grew more slowly than during the great boom. Growth in West Germany averaged less than 2 per cent per year from 1971 to 1986, and total output actually declined in 1975, 1981, and 1982. East German figures looked better, but reported increases in output slowed to 4.6 per cent per year.[82] Manufacturers in both Germanys faced higher prices for raw materials and energy, especially oil, and the relatively easy gains from exploiting the backlog of technical innovations and from shifting workers from agriculture to industry had been exhausted. The growth rate of West German exports dropped to 4.8 per cent per year and East Germany's official figures showed a decline in the growth of foreign trade to 2.4 per cent per year.[83] These figures reflected both slower growth in foreign markets and increased competition, especially from Japan. Nevertheless, West Germany suffered much less than other western European countries or the United States, and East Germany suffered much less than other eastern European nations or the Soviet Union.

By this period, the initial postwar boom in consumer durables had passed, and the declining birth rate meant fewer new families were being formed. Virtually all West German households possessed refrigerators, televisions, and at least one automobile. The number of automobiles rose 5.5 per cent per year during the 1970s, less than a third of the rate during the postwar upswing. Across the border, limited though they were, consumer goods did begin to appear in the homes of East Germans, who enjoyed the highest standard of living in eastern Europe.[84] A majority of East German households boasted a range of household appliances: by 1987, half of East German households possessed a private automobile, up from 3 per cent in 1960 and 16 per cent in 1970.

However, the automobile represented not only East Germany's success story, but also some of the country's underlying problems. Output remained small at 200,000 per year,[85] too low to gain the economies of scale that could make the industry internationally competitive. The quality of the low-cost Trabant in particular was poor and its technology outdated. While West German automakers won sales across Europe and overseas, East German automobiles were unsaleable in those markets. At the same time, the markets in East Germany itself and in eastern Europe were limited by small populations, low incomes, and trade restrictions. The same factors affected other consumer goods, and most of the machinery industry as well.

East Germany's leaders, following Soviet examples, introduced more decentralized modes of planning in the 1960s, but these experiments were soon abandoned.[86] In the 1970s, the government introduced more substantial rewards for improvements in productivity. Higher pay, if it were to mean anything, would require larger amounts of consumer goods. This in turn implied that the rates of investment in heavy industry would have to decline. At the beginning of the 1980s, government planners attempted to improve their control over the economy by creating new and larger 'combines' (*Kombinate*), in theory both vertically and horizontally integrated, pulling together suppliers and producers across an entire industry. Each was in effect a national monopoly production and distribution unit. The director general of each *Kombinat* was supposed to work in tandem with the relevant minister. In theory, the director general, in addition to his overall responsibilities, would directly manage the largest single enterprise in the industry. This was to give him hands-on access to production costs and prices, and direct contact with other managers in the industry.

Observers believed the system to be functioning reasonably well until about 1985. The difficulties of providing both increased volumes of consumer goods and adequate levels of investment began to strain available resources. The problem remained low productivity. All eastern European regimes had difficulty providing incentives for enterprises to introduce new technologies. The regime did not reward East German managers for innovation, and the centralized planning structure did not encourage the search for genuinely new techniques.[87] In attempting to address this problem, the government designated certain industries and 'key technologies' for encouragement, and channelled funds in their direction. However, the targets were not well chosen, and the system of prices did not provide accurate evaluation of the programme. More resources were provided to the favoured industries than they could use effectively, while at the same time other industries were starved of the resources they needed to remain viable. Nevertheless the distortion and decay that resulted still remained largely hidden until the collapse in 1989.[88]

One possible explanation of the 'crisis' of the 1980s is that previously recorded rates of growth were exaggerated. The measurement of economic performance is always politically sensitive, and during the Cold War era this was even more true, for the figures were deployed as propaganda weapons in the struggle between the socialist and capitalist systems. The East German government's estimate of 'net material product' included elements of double counting and made insufficient provision for changes in the price level, which had the effect of making growth appear more rapid than it was.

Western estimates of East German growth lay substantially below the official figures, but they did place per capita income in East Germany at about three-quarters that of West Germany and two-thirds that of the United States. However, the first measures of per capita income in the 'new federal states' after 1989 showed income levels less than half of those estimated only a year before. In the absence of complete recalculations, Angus Maddison concludes the most plausible approach is to compare East Germany with Czechoslovakia, a country broadly similar in structure. 'If East German per capita growth performance in 1950–89 had in fact been like that of Czechoslovakia, its 1989 level would have been less than two-thirds of what it was imagined to be'. But, this would still mean that income levels dropped by over 25 per cent between 1989 and 1990.[89]

Meanwhile, in West Germany the broad convergence of regional structures concealed disparities, and in the era of slow growth those disparities became more painfully obvious. The most rapidly developing 'agglomeration areas' in the 1970s and 1980s were the Rhine-Main, Rhine-Neckar, Karlsruhe, Stuttgart, Nuremberg, and Munich districts. These 'southern' regions, stagnant between the wars, now enjoyed the advantages of a late start in industrialization. Their factories were newer and more modern from the outset. They specialized in innovative products at the beginnings of their product cycles, leading to more rapid growth. These new products tended to be highly research-intensive, and (as discussed in Chapter 10) research itself was an expanding industry that reinforced the locational advantages of the newer manufacturing industries. The general importance of administrative and service functions in manufacturing increased, and new *types* of service industries increased in importance. Improvements in infrastructure and other deliberate government policies made the German south more attractive. Finally, individuals, families, and firms showed a general preference to be located in the south.[90]

1.7 Regional integration in a reunited Germany

In the late 1980s, slow economic growth in East Germany fatally undermined the socialist regime. Observers had noted the wide technological gap that had opened up between West and East. In addition, the United States' embargo on sales of 'strategic' technology to socialist countries cut East Germany off from a broad range of technological breakthroughs, most obviously in the areas of electronics and computers. A series of foreign exchange crises added to these systemic problems. The Soviet Union substantially increased prices of raw materials, but eastern European markets for East German goods declined. In the Soviet Union, the confusion resulting from attempts at reform disorganized trade relations. Deficits in East German trade with West Germany and with other western countries increased.[91] The opening of the border through Hungary resulted in a haemorrhaging of young adults from the labour force. Finally, when the Soviet Union refused to continue to support the East German regime, it collapsed.

Helmut Kohl seized the hem of God's cloak, and the two Germanys became one – or rather, the three became two, for Austria once again was excluded. In the short run, 'reunification' on West Germany's terms proved disastrous for East Germany. Subjected to the full force of western competition, East German industry collapsed. The Trabant automobile became the despised symbol of the defunct system. Six months after the introduction of economic and monetary union, industrial output in East Germany had declined by 50 per cent and employment by 30 per cent.[92] The official statistics, grim as they are, may be overly optimistic. Estimates suggested that over half of the labour force in major urban centres such as Dresden and Leipzig was unemployed by mid-1991. State and local governments in the East ran huge deficits as they attempted to cope with the crisis, and they responded by making savage cuts in all areas of public-sector employment. In order to hold down the costs of unification, the federal government fixed salaries of all government employees in the East at a level 40 per cent below that of their colleagues in the West, as well as drastically reducing their pension entitlements. This had the effect, for instance, of placing a 50-year-old nursing sister in the East on the same level as a 26-year-old in the West, *less* 40 per cent.[93]

Women in particular found themselves confronting a federal government ideologically opposed to gender equality, and the imposition of the West's highly gender-segmented labour market. In contrast to East Germany, West German women were concentrated in part-time and low-paying areas, underrepresented in technical occupations, and severely underrepresented in management positions.[94] West German laws and social policies defined women primarily as wives, in theory dependent on their husbands and employed if at all for only temporary periods.[95] Hanna-Beate Schopp-Schilling, head of the women's affairs section of the Ministry of Women and Youth, insisted in 1991 that it would be 'politically naïve' to expect that the rights that East German women had enjoyed 'within the context of an undemocratically governed society and a centrally planned economy . . . should be adopted by the West German government and a West German society as a whole, which for the last 15 years did not find a political consensus to legislate these very rights for its women'.[96]

The impact on individual East Germans was mitigated by large net transfers from West to East, financed by a 7.5 per cent 'Solidarity Surcharge' levied on taxpayers and the indirect subsidy of service on government debt. By 1995, total transfers had reached DM886 billion, some 10 per cent of all government expenditure, far larger than any spending undertaken to alleviate the impact of recessions during the period of rapid growth in the postwar period. East Germany was already the most advanced eastern European economy and, thanks to the transfers, East Germans enjoyed on average a higher standard of living following reunification than before. They also gained in terms of civil liberties, political expression, and freedom of movement.

However, the federal government, in attempting both to alleviate individual suffering and to follow a free market agenda, perpetuated and possibly exacerbated regional imbalances, both between East and West and within the East. Centralized state enterprises were first broken into small units and then rapidly privatized; many were simply liquidated. The districts in which these enterprises were concentrated suffered most. Despite a decline of possibly 40 per cent in the labour force and heavy migration westward, in the mid-1990s unemployment remained around 1 million in the East, or some 13 per cent. Productivity had been very low compared to that of the West, but the dismantling of the state enterprises led to a 'severely weakened sectoral structure'. Demand remained, but the new federal states saw their previous production capacity decline by over half in 1990 and 1991. In the longer term too, dismantling state enterprises often resulted in the elimination of centralized research and development units, and a corresponding decline in employment in high technology areas.[97]

Women bore the brunt of these changes (as discussed in detail in Chapter 11). Many lost long-standing jobs and dropped out of the recorded labour force, with severe effects on their families. Those who remained suffered an unemployment rate over 20 per cent, compared to 11 per cent for men; if women were employed, they earned wages substantially lower than those paid to male workers. They lost their previous rights to first-trimester abortions, generous maternity leave, guaranteed return to employment, subsidized day care (also particularly important for university students), kindergarten, after-school care, and other benefits, all intended to make it possible for women to hold full-time jobs. Because women had made up nearly half of the East German labour force, those districts that had been doing best in terms of employment and income before reunification were the worst affected by the gender-specific consequences of the wholesale imposition of West German norms.

Divisions among regions in the West had also widened between the 1970s and the 1990s. The plight of East Germany was reproduced in districts of the West, particularly the 'old' industrial regions of the North. For example, employment in the steel industry of Nordrhein-Westfalen, which was concentrated in the Ruhr industrial district, dropped 50 per cent between 1975 and 1990. Not only had the large mines and smelters closed; medium-sized and small manufacturing firms had suffered as well.[98] In the port cities, shipbuilding and related industries showed similar declines. Expanding industries tended to be in the German South, but they also tended to employ numbers of part-time workers, many of them women.[99] Rather than moving to the expanding districts, therefore, men thrown out of work as traditional 'heavy' manufacturing jobs contracted often remained as regional pockets of unemployment, acting more as a drag than a stimulus to regional economies.

How are nation and region likely to interact in Germany in the future? On the one hand, the contemporary debates about German identity ignore regional identities, with the exception of former East Germans, whose problem is to adapt to the West German system.[100] Looking back in time, historians across a wide ideological spectrum assume the Bismarckian empire to have been founded because of an inevitable and ineluctable force of German nationalism. This view accepts the assumption made by nationalist historians following unification, that there was a single 'Germany' attempting to emerge, and that this identity was inevitable because its essence was pre-existing and unchanging. Hagen Schulze sees the period from 1815 to 1871 as one in which 'the people-nation [*Volksnation*] raises the claim to realize and develop itself within its own state; in the national state [*Nationalstaat*] it is free to govern itself, and it is free from all foreign domination'. For Thomas Nipperdey, 'the most important and fundamental point is that the German national movement, the bearer and embodiment of German nationalism, triumphed in 1871, achieved its goal: German unity, the German national state'. And for Hans-Ulrich Wehler, 'if one accepts the fundamental assumption, that nationalism was among the great, virtually irresistible motive forces of the nineteenth century, then in a comparative perspective one must accept the historical authorization of the wish to found a German national state as well'.[101]

On the other hand, the regional problems of a reunited 'Germany' may very well be subsumed under the divisions within the broader European community. It is now a cliché that 'nations' are declining in importance in the global economy, and research on 'regional' identities and their role in extended transnational contexts has proliferated. Peter Nitschke has pointed to the difficulties of abstract definitions of regional identities, and to the similarities between the creation of such identities and the processes of formation of national states.[102]

Three examples with interesting historical relevance are Baden-Württemberg, widely regarded as a leading 'southern' region, Nordrhein-Westfalen, an 'old' industrial region, and Saxony, another 'old' industrial region but in the former East Germany. In 1993 a multi-page advertisement in a major American business magazine extolled the virtues of 'Baden-Württemberg: Germany's High-Tech State' and announced that

> the economic structure of the state is characterized by very efficient and flexible medium-sized companies . . . The beautiful landscape of Baden-Württemberg, including the Black Forest and Lake Constance, numerous health resorts, and a wide range of sports facilities make the region a good place to live as well as work. Cities such as Heidelberg, Baden-Baden, Tübingen and Freiburg are synonymous with culture and tradition.[103]

In 1994 a scholarly volume entitled '700 Years of Political Co-determination in Saxony' included detailed analyses of the relations among Saxon constitutional structures, voting habits and political behaviour over the centuries. The contributors repeatedly alluded to the tension between 'tradition' and 'modernity', but also to an ongoing democratic heritage as themes in Saxon history.[104] In 1997, the first volume of a new series 'Foundations for Europe' was 'Nordrhein-Westfalen in Europe: Problems and Opportunities of the Locality', which both celebrated the state's fiftieth anniversary and addressed the role it could expect to play in 'the Europe of regions'.[105]

For the historian, the hopeful advertisement for prospective investors, the scholarly investigation of constitutional and political history, and the policy-oriented analysis of contemporary economic and political problems are all examples of the emergence of collective consciousness, and also examples of the creation of historical myths. Baden-Württemberg and Nordrhein-Westfalen are not 'historical lands' and have no legitimate claim to be regarded as coherent cultural entities. Baden and Württemberg, themselves states created artificially during the Napoleonic wars, were arbitrarily fused following the Second World War; the limits of Nordrhein-Westfalen imposed by the Allied occupation authorities in 1946 cut across the previous (and equally arbitrary) Prussian provincial boundaries. 'Saxon' history has emerged from the ban on the history of historical lands imposed by the East German government, but the conceptual limits are the borders of the present state, based on the boundaries imposed following the defeat by Prussia in 1866.

That is, despite sophisticated discussions of the meanings of regional identifications and of the relation between regional and national developments, 'regional' identity is assumed to extend over and include all of the residents of the current German federal states, but it is still sensed as problematical. 'Who are we? Where did we come from? Where are we going? And what does it mean anyhow, if we use the syllable *we* in connection with a federal state?'[106] Objectively, such unity is indeed highly problematical, and it is an equally problematical assumption historically. However, the cooperation of government agencies and private economic interests, reinforced by the educational system, may very well result in the emergence of the sense of belonging to a single community upon which a regional consciousness rests, and this consciousness in turn could have profound economic implications. If this were to be the case, and if these examples were to become typical, the 'German' problem might dissolve at last.

1.8 Notes

1 Helmut Schmitz, '"Eigenart" vs "Das Eigene": German Intellectuals in Search of a Concept of Nationhood and National Identity after Unification', *Debatte*, 6 (1998), pp. 129–47.

2 Emil Nagengast, '*Europapolitik* and National Interest: Are the Germans Normal Yet?', *Debatte*, 7 (1999), pp. 9–23.

3 Jörn Sieglerschmidt, 'Social and Economic Landscapes', in Sheilagh Ogilvie, ed., *Germany: A New Social and Economic History*, Vol. II: *1630–1800* (London, 1996), pp. 1–38.

4 Peter Steinbach, 'Territorial- oder Regionalgeschichte. Wege der modernen Landesgeschichte', *Geschichte und Gesellschaft*, 11 (1985), pp. 528–40; J. D. Marshall, 'Why Study Regions? (1)', *Journal of Regional and Local Studies*, 5 (1985), pp. 15–27.

5 Frank B. Tipton, 'National Growth Cycles and Regional Economic Structures in Nineteenth Century Germany', in Wilhelm H. Schröder and Reinhard Spree, eds, *Historische Konjunkturforschung* (Stuttgart, 1980), pp. 29–46.

6 Gerd Hardach, 'Aspekte der Industriellen Revolution', *Geschichte und Gesellschaft*, 17 (1991), pp. 102–13, here p. 102.

7 Toni Pierenkemper, 'Die privaten Hochofenwerke des oberschlesischen Industriereviers in der frühen Industrialisierung 1833–1856', *Geschichte und Gesellschaft*, 19 (1993), pp. 427–52, here p. 432, note 10.

8 See, for instance, Gustav Otruba, 'Zur Entstehung der Industrie in Österreich und zu derer Entwicklung bis Kaiser Josef II', *Österreich in Geschichte und Literatur*, 11 (1967), on Austria; W. O. Henderson, *Studies in the Economic Policy of Frederick the Great* (London, 1963), on Prussia; Wolfram Fischer, 'Ansätze zur Industrialisierung in Baden, 1770–1870', *Vierteljahrschrift für Sozial- und Wirtschaftsgeschichte*, 47 (1960), pp. 185–231, on Baden; Rudolf Forberger, *Die Manufaktur in Sachsen vom Ende des 16. bis zum Anfang des 19. Jahrhunderts* (East Berlin, 1958), on Saxony.

9 Mack Walker, *German Home Towns* (Ithaca, 1971), pp. 1–2.

10 See Sheilagh Ogilvie, 'The Beginnings of Industrialization', in Sheilagh Ogilvie, ed., *Germany: A New Social and Economic History*, Vol. II: *1630–1800* (London, 1996), pp. 263–308.

11 Walker, *German Home Towns*.

12   Anthony Smith, *The Ethnic Origins of Nations* (Oxford, 1987).
13   Friedrich Meinecke, *Weltbürgertum und Nationalstaat*, ed. Hans Herzfeld (orig. edn publ. 1907; Darmstadt, 1969); Hans Kohn, *The Mind of Germany: The Education of a Nation* (New York, 1960).
14   J. H. Hobsbawm, *Nationalism Since 1780: Programme, Myth, Reality* (Cambridge, 1990).
15   Helmut Berding, 'Staatliche Identität, nationale Integration und politischer Regionalismus', in Helmut Berding, ed., *Aufklären durch Geschichte: Ausgewählte Aufsätze* (Göttingen, 1990). Specifically on Prussia see Reinhart Koselleck, *Preussen zwischen Reform und Revolution* (Stuttgart, 1967), pp. 398–447.
16   Benedict Anderson, *Imagined Communities: Reflections on the Origin and Spread of Nationalism* (revised edn London, 1991); Smith, *Ethnic Origins*.
17   On Prussia, see Frank B. Tipton, 'Government Policy and Economic Development in Germany and Japan: A Sceptical Reevaluation', in Steven Tolliday, ed., *Government and Business* (London, 1991), pp. 66–77; on Saxony, see Hubert Kiesewetter, *Industrialisierung und Landwirtschaft: Sachsens Stellung im regionalen Industrialisierungsprozeß Deutschlands im 19. Jahrhundert* (Cologne, 1988).
18   See H. Leiskow, *Spekulation und öffentliche Meinung in der ersten Hälfte des 19. Jahrhunderts* (Jena, 1930), pp. 12–14; Reinhard Spree and Jürgen Bergmann, 'Die konjunkturelle Entwicklung der deutschen Wirtschaft 1840–1864', in Hans-Ulrich Wehler, ed., *Sozialgeschichte Heute* (Göttingen, 1974), pp. 289–325.
19   Hardach, 'Aspekte', p. 104.
20   Pierenkemper, 'Die privaten Hochofenwerke'.
21   Wilhelm Brepohl, *Industrievolk im Wandel von der agraren zur industriellen Daseinsform dargestellt am Ruhrgebiet* (Tübingen, 1957); Karl Rohe, *Vom Revier zum Ruhrgebiet. Wahlen, Parteien, Politische Kultur* (Essen, 1986), shows that the new regional culture was itself contested, notably between the expanding working class and the employers.
22   Wilhelm Treue, 'Die Technik in Wirtschaft und Gesellschaft 1800–1970', in Hermann Aubin and Wolfgang Zorn, eds, *Handbuch der deutschen Wirtschafts- und Sozialgeschichte* (Stuttgart, 1976), pp. 51–121.
23   Norman J. G. Pounds, *The Ruhr: A Study in Historical and Economic Geography* (Bloomington, 1952).
24   See Theodore S. Hamerow, *The Social Foundations of German Unification, 1858–71*, 2 vols (Princeton, 1969–72), Vol. II, pp. 120–1; Hans-Werner Hahn, *Wirtschaftliche Integration im 19. Jahrhundert: Die hessische Staaten und der deutsche Zollverein* (Göttingen, 1982).
25   Frank B. Tipton, 'The Economic Dimension in German History', in Gordon Martel, ed., *Modern Germany Reconsidered* (London, 1991), pp. 211–36.
26   See Leonard Krieger, *The German Idea of Freedom* (Chicago, 1957), p. 228.
27   Richard H. Tilly, *Financial Institutions and Industrialization in the Rhineland* (Madison, WI, 1966); Richard H. Tilly, *Vom Zollverein zum Industriestaat. Die wirtschaftlich-soziale Entwicklung Deutschlands 1834 bis 1914* (Munich, 1990).
28   Karl-Georg Faber, *Die Rheinlande zwischen Restauration und Revolution* (Wiesbaden, 1966); Koselleck, *Preußen zwischen Reform und Revolution*.
29   See Heinrich Best, *Interessenpolitik und nationale Integration 1848/49: handelspolitische Konflikte im früindustriellen Deutschland* (Göttingen, 1980).
30   Richard H. Tilly, 'The Political Economy of Public Finance and the Industrialization of Prussia, 1815–1866', *Journal of Economic History*, 26 (1966), pp. 484–97; Pounds, *The Ruhr*.

31 Eugene M. Anderson, *The Social and Political Conflict in Prussia, 1858–1864* (New York, 1968).

32 Thomas Nipperdey, *Deutsche Geschichte 1866–1918*, 2 vols (Munich, 1993), Vol. II, pp. 11–84.

33 See, for instance, Helmut Böhme, *Deutschlands Weg zur Grossmacht* (Cologne, 1966), on the Austro-Prussian war, and Otto Pflanze, *Bismarck and the Development of Germany: The Period of Unification, 1815–1871* (Princeton, 1963), on the Franco-Prussian war.

34 Karl-Georg Faber, 'Realpolitik als Ideologie: Die Bedeutung des Jahres 1866 für das politische Denken in Deutschland', *Historische Zeitschrift*, 203 (1966), pp. 1–45.

35 Heinrich von Treitschke, *Politik*, 2 vols (Leipzig, 1899), Vol. I, p. 56.

36 Paul A. Pfizer, *Briefwechsel Zweier Deutschen*, 2nd edn (Stuttgart, 1832), p. 343.

37 Hobsbawm, *Nationalism*, shows why we should not.

38 Hans-Ulrich Wehler, *Deutsche Gesellschaftsgeschichte, Dritter Band: Von der 'Deutschen Doppelrevolution' bis zum Beginn des Ersten Weltkrieges 1849–1914* (Munich, 1995), pp. 961–5, 1067–71, outlines the policy of 'Germanization' of national minorities.

39 Dan S. White, 'Regionalism and Particularism', in Roger Chickering, ed., *Imperial Germany: A Historiographical Companion* (Westport, 1996), pp. 131–55.

40 Celia Applegate, *A Nation of Provincials: The German Idea of Heimat* (Berkeley and Los Angeles, 1990), p. 14.

41 Sydney Pollard, 'Industrialization and the European Economy', *Economic History Review*, 26 (1973), pp. 636–48; Sydney Pollard, *Peaceful Conquest: The Industrialization of Europe, 1760–1970* (Oxford, 1982).

42 Frank B. Tipton, *Regional Variations in the Economic Development of Germany during the Nineteenth Century* (Middletown, 1976), Chs 6–7.

43 Andreas Kunz, 'Binnenshiffahrt', in U. Wengenroth, ed., *Technik und Wirtschaft* (Düsseldorf, 1993), pp. 382–98; Frank B. Tipton, 'The Regional Dimension in the Historical Analysis of Transport Flows', in Andreas Kunz and John Armstrong, eds, *Inland Navigation in 19th Century Europe* (Mainz and Manchester, 1994), pp. 167–80.

44 Immanuel Wallerstein, *The Modern World System*, Vol. I: *Capitalist Agriculture and the Origins of the European World Economy in the Sixteenth Century* (New York, 1974).

45 H. J. Habakkuk and Phyllis Deane, 'The Take-Off in Britain', in W. W. Rostow, ed., *The Economics of Take-Off into Sustained Growth* (London, 1963), pp. 63–82, here p. 72.

46 Milan Hlavacka, *Economic and Technical Aspects of the Elbe and Moldau Navigation in the Period of the Industrial Revolution* (Prague, 1990).

47 Kunz and Armstrong, eds, *Inland Navigation in 19th Century Europe*; G. L. Turnbull, 'Canals, Coal and Regional Growth during the Industrial Revolution', *Economic History Review*, 40 (1987), pp. 537–60, here p. 547; P. Kooij, 'Peripheral Cities and their Regions in the Dutch Urban System until 1900', *Journal of Economic History*, 48 (1988), pp. 357–71; Richard Szostak, *The Role of Transportation in the Industrial Revolution: A Comparison of England and France* (Montreal, 1991).

48 Rainer Fremdling, *Eisenbahnen und deutscher Wirtschaftswachstum 1840–1879* (Dortmund, 1975); Rainer Fremdling, 'Railroads and German Economic Growth: A Leading Sector Analysis with a Comparison to the United States and Great Britain', *Journal of Economic History*, 37 (1977), pp. 583–604.

49   Lajos Timar, 'Regional Economic and Social History or Historical Geography?' *Journal of European Economic History*, 21 (1992), pp. 391–406, here p. 400.

50   Timar, 'Regional Economic and Social History', p. 406. See John Urry, 'Some Notes on Regionalism and the Analysis of Space', *International Journal of Urban and Regional Research*, 7 (1983), pp. 122–7, here p. 123; J. D. Marshall, 'Why Study Regions? Some Historical Considerations', *The Journal of Regional and Local Studies*, 6 (1986), pp. 1–12; Horst Mazerath, 'Lokalgeschichte, Historische Urbanisierungsforschung?', *Geschichte und Gesellschaft*, 15 (1989), pp. 62–88.

51   Hans Dieter Laux, 'Demographische Folgen des Verstädterungsprozesses: zur Bevölkerungsstruktur und natürlichen Bevölkerungsentwicklung deutscher Städtetypen 1871–1914', in H. J. Teuteberg, ed., *Urbanisierung im 19. und 20. Jahrhundert. Historische und geographische Aspekte* (Cologne, 1983), pp. 65–93.

52   Tipton, 'Economic Dimension'.

53   Tipton, *Regional Variations*, covers the period 1861 to 1907, and groups federal states and administrative districts of the Bismarckian empire into moderately large units. See Rüdiger Hohls and Hartmut Kaelble, *Die regionale Erwerbsstruktur im Deutschen Reich und in der Bundesrepublik 1895–1970* (St Katharinen, 1989) for figures for individual *Regierungsbezirke* contained in post-1945 West Germany from 1895 through 1970.

54   Johan Söderberg, 'Regional Economic Disparity and Dynamics, 1840–1914: A Comparison between France, Great Britain, Prussia, and Sweden', *Journal of European Economic History*, 14 (1985), pp. 273–96, argues that the 'push' of low wages was less important. The net figures conceal much greater gross flows. See Steve Hochstedt, *Mobility and Modernity. Migration in Germany 1820–1989* (Ann Arbor, MI, 1999).

55   Fritz Voigt, *Die gestaltende Kraft der Verkehrsmittel in wirtschaftlichen Wachstumsprozessen* (Bielefeld, 1959).

56   Hans-Ulrich Wehler, 'Die Polen im Ruhrgebiet bis 1918', in Hans-Ulrich Wehler, ed., *Moderne deutsche Sozialgeschichte* (Cologne, 1970), pp. 437–55; Adolf Wennemann, *Arbeit im Norden: Italiener im Rheinland und Westfalen des späten 19. und frühen 20. Jahrhunderts* (Osnabrück, 1997).

57   Peter Quante, *Die Flucht aus der Landwirtschaft* (Berlin, 1933), pp. 196–7; see Kenneth D. Barkin, *The Controversy Over German Industrialization, 1890–1902* (Chicago, 1970).

58   Tipton *Regional Variations*, Ch. 6.

59   See, for instance, Applegate, *A Nation of Provincials*; James C. Hunt, *The People's Party in Württemberg and Southern Germany, 1890–1914* (Stuttgart, 1975); Dan S. White, *The Splintered Party: National Liberalism in Hessen and the Reich, 1867–1918* (Cambridge, MA, 1976); David Blackbourn, *Class, Religion and Local Politics in Wilhelmine Germany: The Centre Party in Württemberg before 1914* (New Haven, 1980); James N. Retallack, 'Politische Kultur, Wahlkultur, Regionalgeschichte: Methodologische Überlegungen am Beispiel Sachsens und des Reiches', in Simone Lässig *et al.*, eds, *Modernisierung und Region im wilhelminischen Deutschland: Wahlen, Wahlrecht und politische Kultur* (Bielefeld, 1995), pp. 15–38.

60   See James N. Retallack, *Notables of the Right: The Conservative Party and Political Mobilization in Germany, 1876–1918* (Boston, 1988).

61   Nipperdey, *Deutsche Geschichte, 1866–1918*, Vol. II, pp. 699–757; Wehler, *Deutsche Gesellschaftsgeschichte*, pp. 1000–4; Dirk Stegmann, *Bismarcks Erben* (Cologne, 1970); Volker R. Berghahn, *Germany and the Approach of*

War in 1914 (London, 1973). Ironically, the panic was misplaced, for 'workers did not automatically vote for the SPD'. See Brett Fairbairn, 'Political Mobilization', in Roger Chickering, ed., *Imperial Germany: A Historiographical Companion* (Westport, 1996), pp. 303–42, here p. 316.

62 Derek H. Aldcroft *From Versailles to Wall Street* (Harmondsworth, 1977); Derek H. Aldcroft and Steven Morewood, *Economic Change in Eastern Europe since 1918* (Aldershot and Brookfield, 1995).

63 Hohls and Kaelble, *Die regionale Erwerbsstruktur*, pp. 81–3.

64 Walther Christaller, *Central Places in Southern Germany* (first publ. 1933; Englewood Cliffs, 1966). See Harry W. Richardson, *Regional Economics* (New York, 1969), pp. 156–85.

65 Estimated from data in Hohls and Kaelble, *Die regionale Erwerbsstruktur*; see Dieter Gessner, 'The Dilemma of German Agriculture during the Weimar Republic', in Richard Bessel and E. J. Feuchtwanger, eds, *Social Change and Political Development in Weimar Germany* (London, 1981), pp. 134–54; Robert G. Moeller, *German Peasants and Agrarian Politics, 1914–1924: The Rhineland and Westphalia* (Chapel Hill, 1986).

66 Bruno Buchta, *Die Junker und die Weimarer Republik: Character und Bedeutung der Osthilfe in den Jahren 1928–1933* (East Berlin, 1959); Gessner, 'Dilemma'.

67 See, for instance, Thomas Childers, ed., *The Formation of the Nazi Constituency, 1919–1933* (London, 1986); Jürgen Falter and Richard Zintl, 'The Economic Crisis of the 1930s and the Nazi Vote', *Journal of Interdisciplinary History*, 19 (1988), pp. 55–85; Peter Manstein, *Die Mitglieder und Wähler der NSDAP 1919–1933*, 2nd edn (Bern, 1989); Jürgen Falter, *Hitlers Wähler* (Munich, 1991).

68 Henry C. Wallich, *Mainsprings of the German Revival* (New Haven, 1955); Martin Schnitzer, *East and West Germany: A Comparative Economic Analysis* (New York, 1972); Alan S. Milward, *The Reconstruction of Western Europe, 1945–1951* (Berkeley, 1982); Herbert Giersch, Karl-Heinz Paqué, and Holger Schmieding, *The Fading Miracle: Four Decades of Market Economy in Germany* (Cambridge, 1994), pp. 26–35.

69 Norman Naimark, *The Russians in Germany: A History of the Soviet Zone of Occupation, 1945–1949* (Cambridge, 1995), p. 465.

70 Albrecht O. Ritschl, 'An Exercise in Futility: East German Economic Growth and Decline, 1945–89', in Nicholas Crafts and Gianni Toniolo, eds, *Economic Growth in Europe since 1945* (Cambridge, 1996), pp. 489–540, here pp. 511–13.

71 Herman Van der Wee, *Prosperity and Upheaval: The World Economy, 1945–1980* (Harmondsworth, 1986); Frank B. Tipton and Robert Aldrich, *An Economic and Social History of Europe from 1939 to the Present* (London, 1987); Nicholas Crafts and Gianni Toniolo, 'Postwar Growth: An Overview', in Nicholas Crafts and Gianni Toniolo, eds, *Economic Growth in Europe since 1945* (Cambridge, 1996), pp. 1–37.

72 Computed from figures in Walther G. Hoffmann, *Das Wachstum der deutschen Wirtschaft seit der Mitte des 19. Jahrhunderts* (Berlin, 1965), pp. 825–6, and B. R. Mitchell, *International Historical Statistics: Europe 1750–1988* (New York, 1992).

73 Hoffmann *Wachstum*, pp. 698–9; Volker R. Berghahn, *Modern Germany: State, Economy and Politics in the Twentieth Century*, 2nd edn (Cambridge, 1987), p. 292; Wendy Carlin, 'West German Growth and Institutions, 1945–90', in Nicholas Crafts and Gianni Toniolo, eds, *Economic Growth in Europe since 1945* (Cambridge, 1996), pp. 455–97, here pp. 468–73.

74 See for instance Milward, *Reconstruction*, p. 425; Giersch, Paqué, and Schmieding, *Fading Miracle*, pp. 139–55.

75 East Germany, Staatliche Zentralverwaltung für Statistik, *Statistisches Jahrbuch der deutschen demokratischen Republik 1988* (Berlin, 1988). These figures in fact understate the ratio because of the very low prices that the planning authorities assigned to capital goods.

76 Hans-Dieter Jacobsen, 'The Foreign Trade and Payments of the DDR', in Ian Jeffries and Manfred Melzer, eds, *The East German Economy* (London, 1987), pp. 235–60.

77 Hohls and Kaelble, *Die regionale Erwerbsstruktur*, pp. 81–3.

78 Peter J. Hugel, 'Structural Changes in the Core Regions of the World-Economy, 1830–1945', *Journal of Historical Geography*, 14 (1988), pp. 111–27.

79 Giersch, Paqué, and Schmieding, *Fading Miracle*, pp. 126–39.

80 Jacobsen, 'Foreign Trade'.

81 Jacobsen, 'Foreign Trade'.

82 Tipton and Aldrich, *Economic and Social History*, Chs 4 and 8; Organization for Economic Cooperation and Development, *OECD Economic Surveys – Germany* (Paris, 1975, 1983, 1988); Tipton, 'Economic Dimension'.

83 West Germany, Statistisches Bundesamt, *Statistisches Jahrbuch 1988 für die Bundesrepublik Deutschland* (Stuttgart, 1988), p. 88; East Germany, *Statistisches Jahrbuch 1988*, p. 239.

84 East Germany, *Statistisches Jahrbuch 1988*.

85 United Nations, *Statistical Yearbook 1981* (New York, 1981); East Germany, *Statistisches Jahrbuch 1988*, p. 291; Vienna Institute for Comparative Economic Studies, *Comecon Data 1985* (London, 1986), p. 236.

86 Jeffrey Kopstein, *The Politics of Economic Decline in East Germany 1945–1989* (Chapel Hill, 1997), Ch. 2.

87 Raymond Bentley, *Technological Change in the German Democratic Republic* (Boulder, 1984).

88 Phillip J. Bryson and Manfred Melzer, *The End of the East German Economy: From Honecker to Reunification* (New York, 1991).

89 Angus Maddison, *Monitoring the World Economy* (Paris, 1995), pp. 131–3.

90 Wolf Gaebe, 'Disparities in Development between Agglomeration Areas in the Federal Republic of Germany', *Zeitschrift für Wirtschaftsgeographie*, 32 (1988), pp. 179–91.

91 Ritschl, 'An Exercise in Futility', pp. 517–28.

92 Leslie Lipschitz and Donogh MacDonald, *German Unification: Economic Issues* (Washington, DC, 1990); Organization for Economic Cooperation and Development, *OECD Economic Surveys – Germany* (Paris, 1991); Giersch, Paqué, and Schmieding, *Fading Miracle*, pp. 263–5; Ritschl, 'An Exercise in Futility', pp. 528–32.

93 *Die Zeit* (2 Aug. 1991), p. 5.

94 Gunnar Winkler, ed., *Frauenreport '90* (Berlin, 1990).

95 Ilone Ostner, 'Ideas, Institutions, Traditions – West German Women's Experience 1945–1990', *German Politics and Society*, 24/25 (1991/2), pp. 87–99.

96 Dorothy J. Rosenberg, 'The New Home Economics: Women in the United Germany', *Debatte*, 1 (1993), pp. 111–34.

97 Jeremy Leaman, 'Germany's Economic Unification, Five Years On', *Debatte*, 3 (1995), pp. 121–33; see Robert Halsall, 'The Treuhand: A Look Back in Anger', *Debatte*, 3 (1995), pp. 85–102. Giersch, Paqué, and Schmieding, *Fading Miracle*, pp. 262–72, and Ritschl, 'An Exercise in Futility', pp. 528–32, are far more positive in their evaluations of federal government policy.

98   Dietmar Petzina, 'Die Formierung einer europäischen Region: Probleme und Prozesse in NRW seit den fünfziger Jahren', in Wilfried Loth and Peter Nitschke, eds, *Nordrhein-Westfalen in Europa: Probleme und Chancen des Standorts* (Opladen, 1997), pp. 39–50.

99   Rosenberg, 'The New Home Economics'.

100   Schmitz, 'German Intellectuals', p. 130.

101   Hagen Schulze, *Staat und Nation in der europäischen Geschichte* (Munich, 1994), p. 209, and similar phrasing on pp. 94, 107, 268, 271, 338, 341; Thomas Nipperdey, *Deutsche Geschichte 1866–1918, Zweiter Band: Machtstaat vor der Demokratie* (Munich, 1993), p. 251; Hans-Ulrich Wehler, *Deutsche Gesellschaftsgeschichte*, Vol. III (Munich, 1995), pp. 331–2. See Frank B. Tipton, 'A New German Identity? Or the Ghost of German Idealism?' in Peter Monteath and Frederic S. Zuckerman, eds, *Modern Europe: Histories and Identities* (Adelaide, 1998), pp. 61–72.

102   Peter Nitschke, 'Was heisst regionale Identität im heutigen Europa?', in Gerhard Brunn, ed., *Region und Regionsbildung in Europa* (Baden-Baden, 1996), pp. 285–99.

103   *Fortune* (27 Dec. 1993).

104   See for instance Simone Lässig, 'Parlamentarismus zwischen Tradition und Moderne. Der Sächsische Landtag zwischen 1833 und 1918', in Karlheinz Blaschke, ed., *700 Jahre politische Mitbestimmung in Sachsen* (Dresden, 1994).

105   Elmar Brok, 'Die Zukunft des Nationalstaates – Das Europa der Regionen', in Wilfried Loth and Peter Nitschke, eds, *Nordrhein-Westfalen in Europa: Probleme und Chancen des Standorts* (Opladen, 1997), pp. 113–20.

106   Loth and Nitschke, 'Einleitung', in *Nordrhein-Westfalen*, p. 9.

|2|

Population and the economy in Germany, 1800–1990

TIMOTHY W. GUINNANE
Yale University

Germany's turbulent history in the past two centuries has left its mark on her population. The industrialization of the nineteenth century promoted rapid population growth, and the spatial concentration of that industrialization provoked enormous internal migration. Germany's relatively late economic development left the country impoverished relative to North America and some other societies for most of the nineteenth century, promoting extensive emigration. Like most of western Europe Germany experienced a sharp reduction in fertility and mortality rates during the late nineteenth and early twentieth centuries, but these transitions were more abrupt in Germany than elsewhere. Twentieth–century turmoil marked Germany's population through deaths and other demographic consequences of war and through the huge flows of refugees that followed both world wars.

This chapter traces the main developments in German population for the past two centuries, stressing connections to economic issues. I focus on population and its connection to economic and social change. This choice reflects my own background and not any judgement about the importance of culture in population developments. I cannot do justice to the profoundly regional nature of much German experience, so I will discuss only the most important regional variations. Finally, I focus on population history rather than the intellectual history or historiography of population.[1]

The reader might wonder about three basic questions. First, is quantitative demographic information from, say, the early nineteenth century at all reliable? Second, can one meaningfully speak of a 'German' population over a period that saw political unification and several changes in German territory? And third, are there not severe or even insurmountable problems posed by the fact that for much of the period discussed here, the relevant data were collected by several different statistical agencies, one each for the several states of the *Bund*, later *Reich*, and then by two different Germanys?

These are all reasonable concerns. A simple answer to the first question is that quantitative information from the nineteenth century is not necessarily less reliable than even that collected by present-day statistical agencies. On the second question, for most of this chapter 'Germany' will refer to the borders of the 1871 Reich. Loss or gain of territory affects population *size* but not demographic *rates* (such as the number of births per adult woman in a given year) unless demographic behaviour in the territory lost or gained differed materially from the rest of Germany, or the territorial changes provoked refugee flows. I discuss territorial changes where important. On the third question, the several statistical offices responsible for collecting the data discussed here usually used similar methods. A more worrisome problem concerns the geographical basis of sources. From the early nineteenth century we have basic counts of population for most territories that later comprised Germany. After the first Reich population census in 1871 we have unusually detailed, high-quality national census data. But for some questions, especially in the nineteenth century, only community-level studies provide the requisite level of detail.

The chapter is organized as follows. Section 2.1 outlines the growth of population, and discusses some basic demographic and economic issues. Section 2.2 concerns marriage, fertility, and mortality, and Section 2.3 discusses migration. Section 2.4 is a more in-depth discussion of a central demographic development of the last two centuries in Germany: the decline of fertility. Section 2.5 considers the period 1914–45 as a whole, including the demographic consequences of the two world wars and population developments during the interwar period. Section 2.6 traces the development of population patterns in the two Germanys from the Second World War until unification in 1990.

2.1 Population growth and economic development

Table 2.1 presents the total populations of Germany, France, and England and Wales for selected years in the period 1820–1990. Germany's population in the early nineteenth century was smaller than France's but nearly twice as large as England's. By 1900, slow population growth in France had left its population only slightly larger than England's and much smaller than Germany's. At the end of the twentieth century, Germany has the largest population of any European country save Russia.

Population growth reflects the balance of two forces: natural increase (or births minus deaths) and net migration (the number of immigrants minus the number of emigrants). Figure 2.1 shows the elements of natural increase in Germany, plotting the crude birth rate (CBR) and crude death rate (CDR) from 1817 to 1990. For most of the nineteenth century Germany experienced a large surplus of births over deaths. Rates of natural increase then fell in the early twentieth century and continued to fall sharply until recently. By 1972 death rates *exceeded* birth rates. As shown in Figure 2.1 and discussed in Section 2.3, however, Germany sent enormous numbers of emigrants overseas and to eastern Europe during the nineteenth century. Then, at the end of the nineteenth century, Germany became a significant recipient of immigrants in its own right. Thus the balance of forces determining the population growth rates implicit in Table 2.1 reflects dramatic changes in the elements of natural increase and in net migration.

Table 2.1 Population of Germany, France, and England and Wales, 1820–1990 (millions)

Year	Germany	France	England and Wales
1820	25.4	30.5	12.0
1850	33.7	35.8	17.9
1900	56.0	38.4	32.5
1950	69.0	42.8	43.7
1990	79.4	56.7	49.0

Note: Populations for Germany and France pertain to current borders and thus reflect territorial changes in addition to population changes *per se*. Years of national censuses vary across countries.
Sources: For 1820–50, national censuses as reported in B. R. Mitchell, ed., *European Historical Statistics, 1750–1975*, 2nd edn (New York, 1980), Series B1. For 1990, national sources reported in Bureau of the Census United States, *Statistical Abstract of the United States*, 114th edn (Washington, DC, 1994), Table 1351.

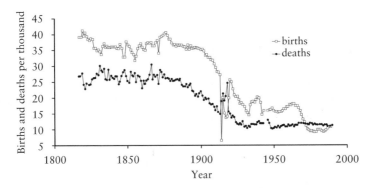

Fig. 2.1 Crude rates of birth and death, Germany, 1817–1990

Note: Post-Second World War figures for West Germany only.
Source: Michel Hubert, *L'Allemagne en mutation: Histoire de la population allemande depuis 1815* (Paris, 1995), Appendix Tables 4 and 18.

The remarkable economic development that has made Germany one of the world's leading economies began in the nineteenth century (as discussed in detail in Chapters 3–6). At the outbreak of peace in 1815 some German regions were relatively prosperous, but taken as a whole the future Reich was poor and backward relative to England, the world's first industrial country, or to other continental countries such as France. By one estimate, over 60 per cent of Germany's active population worked in agriculture in 1800, nearly double the figure for England.[2] This figure began to decline rapidly in the 1840s, and by 1900 only about one-third of the German workforce laboured in agriculture. These labour-force statistics reflect the rise and demise of household-based industrial production, and the industrialization and concomitant growth of the transportation, mining, financial, and commercial sectors of the economy. Overall GNP increased five-fold between 1850 and 1913. GNP per capita increased by two and a half times over the same period. Economic growth in the first half of the twentieth century was marred by war, inflation, and depression, but even then the German economy continued to develop in new and impressive ways (as discussed in Chapter 8). After the Second World War, West Germany entered a new period of tremendous economic growth, with an average annual growth rate of GNP of 2.7 per cent in the 1950s and over 3 per cent for the years 1960–89.[3]

There is as yet no general consensus on the causes of this economic growth. Certainly any complete accounting must include Germany's excellent endowment of key natural resources, an educational system that was able to adapt and later develop path-breaking technological innovations and to train workers in the applied skills necessary to produce new products and services (as discussed in Chapter 10), and institutional change, such as the formation of a Prussian, then a German customs union in the early nineteenth century.[4]

More important to our concerns is the effect of this economic development on population. There are several distinct lines of causation that we will simply trace here and explore in detail in the rest of the chapter. First, economic growth encourages household-formation and fertility by providing employment and higher wages to people who might otherwise defer marriage or avoid it altogether. Second, economic performance affects migration: a weak economy encourages people to leave a region or country altogether, while localized economic growth encourages migration to a particular place or city. Third, economic development may alter the nature of family life and the logic of child-rearing in ways that encourage couples to have fewer children and to provide each child with more resources. Fourth, a wealthier population may invest in the medical education and public-health infrastructure necessary to reduce mortality. Finally, economic growth and development usually implies diversification of outputs, leaving a population less dependent upon agriculture and thus less vulnerable to crop failures and other shocks to income. Population and its structure can also affect economic performance, although this is less our emphasis than the effect of the economy on population dynamics.

2.2 Marriage, fertility, and mortality, 1800–1914

Germany falls squarely within what John Hajnal described as the 'western European marriage pattern'. In this household system young people did not marry until they were able to support themselves and any offspring. Sometimes this stylized social rule was actually written into law, as in parts of Germany, as discussed below, but the norm was generally respected even where there was not such legal force. Requiring financial independence meant that young people had to wait to marry. As a result women were ordinarily in their early to mid-twenties at first marriage, and men were even older. Many adults never married at all because they never acquired financial independence or did so only late in life. This system is usually contrasted with most of Asia, where most women married and did so several years earlier than was common in western Europe.[5]

This household-formation system has two economic and demographic consequences. First, if only married women have children (which is not always true, as shown below), restrictions on marriage amounted to a form of contraception. Second, this system implies that fertility is influenced by economic conditions. Young people growing up in periods of strong economic activity will marry earlier, and more of them will marry, increasing fertility. Poor economic conditions on the other hand will reduce fertility by discouraging marriage. Many historians have argued that this relationship between population and economic activity held sway in much if not all of western Europe until the onset of industrialization.[6] But the relationship seems to break down for most western European countries during the nineteenth century.

The western European marriage pattern implies that we need to measure two aspects of marriage patterns: the age at which people marry and the proportions who never do so. Age at marriage can be established for village populations for the entire nineteenth century. John Knodel reports an age at marriage for German men of around 28 in the early nineteenth century, and an age at marriage for German women of about 26. These figures are well within the ranges reported by most other parts of Germany and western Europe.[7] For German men and women, age at marriage rose in the mid-nineteenth century only to decline again at the end of the century – at least in the combined population for all the villages Knodel studied; individual villages suggest different trends or no trend at all. When national data become available in the early twentieth century they show an average age at first marriage of 27 for men and 25 for women, an age that rises slightly in the 1920s and declines for each sex through the 1970s.[8]

Village studies cannot be used to establish the proportion who never married, unfortunately, because they are based on parish registers of marriages, births, and deaths, and so are silent about those who do not marry (and whom demographers call 'celibate'). Some studies report marital status at death, but this is only a good estimate of celibacy rates if either there is no out-migration from the area or if out-migration rates are equal for those who do and do not marry. Early censuses do not report enough detail to establish what fraction of adults had never married. The Reich censuses show that in 1871 about 9 per cent of men and 12 per cent of women aged 50–54 had never married, a figure that declined steadily into the twentieth century.[9] In 1880, levels of permanent celibacy for both men and women in Germany were, if anything, somewhat low by European standards. Within Germany, urban-dwellers were less likely to have ever married, and there was considerable variation in celibacy levels within Germany.[10]

Remarriage was another important feature of marriage patterns in the nineteenth century. In Knodel's villages 25 per cent of all marriages in the period 1800–49 involved a widow, a widower, or both. In 1850–99 this figure was 15 per cent. The decline reflects both an increase in longevity, so that marriage lasted longer before the death of one spouse, and the declining likelihood that a widow or widower would remarry. Men were more likely to remarry than were women, even when we compare people of similar ages at the time of widowhood. These trends in remarriage mirror similar trends in other western European countries.[11]

A final feature of German marriage patterns has attracted considerable attention from historians because it is unusual. In many regions of Germany and Austria, local communities had the right to refuse couples permission to marry. The historiography unfortunately cannot say how many of the couples who sought and were refused permission to marry simply lived together without marrying, but the effect of these policies on illegitimacy is a central reason for interest in this episode. The marriage restrictions (*politische Ehekonsens*, political permission to marry) were a part of the traditional system of control over rights of settlement and occupation, earlier exercised in cities by corporate bodies such as guilds and in rural areas by landlords and village communities. Prussia adopted freedom of marriage in 1794, and with the exceptions of the Kingdom of Hannover and Mecklenburg the *politische Ehekonsens* did not figure in our period for the north German states. Other German states adopted increasingly tough regulations during the early nineteenth century. By the early 1830s local governments had the right to reject requests both for legal settlement (*Heimatrecht*) and applications for marriage. The states of the North German Federation had adopted Prussian marriage law (which is to say, freedom of marriage) in 1868, and with the exception of Bavaria the entire German Empire had freedom of marriage from its foundation in 1871. Bavaria did not abandon a form of the *politische Ehekonsens* until 1916.[12]

To know how these controls affected demographic behaviour we would need to know: how many people applied for permission to marry and were refused; how many never applied for permission, assuming they would be denied; and how people who could not marry in their locality reacted to the fact. The available data on the number of couples refused permission to marry do not yield a clear picture of how effective the controls really were. Nor do we know how many people assumed their applications would be denied and so never bothered to apply. In Württemberg, marriage restrictions encouraged emigration among those whose application had been denied and among those who assumed it would be denied.[13] We can, however, ask two focused questions. Did the *politische Ehekonsens* reduce the proportion of people who married, and did it lead to increases in illegitimacy rates? North German areas with less restrictive legislation had higher proportions married than was the case in south Germany, although other influences confound the comparison. Between 1867 and 1871, a period which corresponds either to the end of restrictions or falls just after relaxation of restrictions, celibacy rates fell more in the formerly restrictive states.[14] Illegitimacy rates in the mid-nineteenth century were higher in the German states that had tough marriage restrictions, but this correlation cannot tell us whether the illegitimacy rates reflect the laws or some other feature of those states.[15] In her extraordinarily thoughtful study of the *politische Ehekonsens* in the Austrian provinces of Tirol and Vorarlberg, Mantl notes that the restriction of marriage is not by itself enough to explain high rates of illegitimacy.[16]

The marriage restrictions cannot have caused German illegitimacy on their own because births to unmarried women were a feature of demographic patterns in most European countries in the nineteenth and early twentieth centuries. Germany included two of the several European zones where illegitimacy was especially common. One was in Bavaria, the other in Saxony.[17] The index of extramarital fertility I_h, which is analogous to the index I_g for marital fertility (defined in note 21), takes values between 70 and 80 for Germany as a whole in the late nineteenth century, and falls to around 30 in the early twentieth. The overall German figures are more than twice the levels obtaining in France or in England and Wales in the same period. The national German data mask considerable regional variation. In both Bavaria and Saxony, I_h lies above 100 even at the turn of the twentieth century.[18] In Bavaria at least 20 per cent of all births were to unmarried mothers during the period 1826–69. In Prussia for the same period extramarital births were never more than 9 per cent of all births. This is true only for Prussia as a whole; in Berlin some 14–19 per cent of all births were extramarital between 1816 and 1870.[19] Scholars have long noted Germany's elevated levels of illegitimacy, and have proposed several explanations. One recent debate (not yet resolved) turns on whether nineteenth-century Germany experienced a type of 'sexual revolution'.[20]

2.2.1 Marital fertility

Changes in marital fertility behaviour were the primary feature of the demographic transition (the decline in fertility and mortality to the low rates that characterize Germany and other European countries today) discussed in Section 2.4. Prior to the decline of fertility that took place in Germany in the late nineteenth century, marital fertility levels varied considerably across the country, which was true of most of Europe, and were generally at levels that were unremarkable. Once again for the early nineteenth century we must rely on village studies. Many studies rely on an index of marital fertility (I_g) that for Germany was well within ranges found elsewhere.[21] In the early nineteenth century Knodel's Bavarian villages had fertility indices of 900, which was relatively high, but other villages had indices in the 600s and the average for all Knodel's villages was 770. Other works use published data for much larger German regions. Early published data for several German regions suggest great variation, with I_g ranging in 1861 between 852 in Württemberg and 610 in Lübeck.[22] The figure for Germany as a whole in 1867 is 760, which is somewhat higher than England and Wales at that date (674) and much higher than in France (481).[23] These differences reflect variations in the timing and pace of the fertility decline. The decline of fertility in Germany started in some areas before national data first became available in the late 1860s. Overall fertility as measured by I_f was somewhat higher in Germany than elsewhere, reflecting relatively high rates of extramarital fertility. We discuss the decline of fertility (primarily marital fertility) in more detail in Section 2.4.

2.2.2 Mortality

Figure 2.1 shows the high mortality rates obtaining in Germany in the early nineteenth century, and their substantial decline in the late nineteenth and early twentieth centuries. The decline of mortality, like the decline of fertility discussed at length in the next section, marks one of the great social changes of the past 150 years. Table 2.2 summarizes information for Germany on the expectation of life and age-specific mortality available first from village studies and later from death-registration systems. The table shows two regularities common to Germany and other western European countries. First, infant and child mortality rates before the mortality decline were very high. Much of the change in mortality over the period in question reflects

Table 2.2 Life-table measures of mortality for Germany, 1800–1994

Geographical unit and approximate period	Expectation of life at birth M	Expectation of life at birth F	Expectation of life at age 15 M	Expectation of life at age 15 F	Infant mortality rate M	Infant mortality rate F	Child mortality rate M	Child mortality rate F
Knodel's villages, 1800–49	38.7						311	
Knodel's villages, 1850–c.1900	39.4						337	
Prussia, 1816–60	26.5	28.7	38.0	38.8				
Prussia, 1831–40					183			
Germany, 1871–80	35.6	38.5	42.4	44.2	253	217	185	184
Germany, 1910–11	44.8	48.3	46.7	49.0	202	170	97	97
Germany, 1932–34	59.9	62.8	52.6	54.4	85	68		
West Germany, 1978–80	69.6	76.4	56.1	62.8	15	12		
East Germany, 1979	68.7	74.8	55.2	61.0				
Germany, 1992/4	72.8	79.3	58.5	64.0	6.5	5.1	15	12

Sources: John Knodel, *Demographic Behavior in the Past: A Study of Fourteen German Village Populations in the Eighteenth and Nineteenth Centuries* (Cambridge, 1988), Tables 3.1 and Table 3.3; Peter Marschalck, *Bevölkerungsgeschichte Deutschlands im 19. und 20. Jahrhundert* (Frankfurt, 1984), Tables 3.12–3.17; Wolfram Fischer, Jochen Krengel, and Jutta Wietog, eds, *Sozialgeschichtliches Arbeitsbuch Band I: Materialien zur Statistik des Deutschen Bundes 1815–1870* (Munich, 1983), Table 9a; Statistisches Bundesamt, *Statistisches Jahrbuch für die Bundesrepublik Deutschland* (Stuttgart, 1996), Table 3.31.

Definitions: The expectation of life is the average number of person-years to be lived by people who are of that age. The infant mortality rate is the life-table function $_1q_0$ or the chance that a new-born will die before reaching age 1. The child mortality rate is the life-table function $_4q_1$ or the chance that a child who has reached her first birthday will die before reaching her fifth birthday. Infant and child mortality rates are multiplied by 1000, so the table figures are the number of deaths per thousand people.

Notes: Infant and child mortality rates are for illegitimate and legitimate births combined. For Knodel's estimates of child mortality the periods are 1800–24 and 1850–74. I have used his 'Model West' estimate of life expectancy at birth. The figure for infant mortality rates in Prussia in 1831/40 is much lower than the comparable figures for Bavaria (296) or Saxony (266).

reductions in child and later infant mortality. High rates of mortality for infants and children create low life expectancies that are not strictly relevant to the experiences of those who survive childhood. Second, the life tables show significant differences between male and female mortality. By the end of the nineteenth century, women throughout most of Europe lived longer than men.[24]

Mortality conditions and the mortality decline in Germany differed in important respects from those elsewhere in Europe. The expectation of life at birth in Germany in 1910–11 was 49 for males and females combined, less than in other western European countries such as England.[25] One reason for Germany's low life expectancy compared to that of England was an infant mortality rate (usually measured as the number of babies per thousand births who die before reaching age one) much higher than in England or even France. In 1839 Germany's infant mortality rate was 285 compared to 151 for England and Wales, and 160 for France. Even in 1900, Germany's infant mortality rate was 229 (and those for England and France had not changed much). Only after sustained declines in the early twentieth century, reflecting changes to be discussed in detail below, did Germany's infant mortality rate converge in 1920 to the French level (131 for Germany, 123 for France, and 92 for England and Wales). Germany's mortality decline was late and abrupt compared to those of other western European countries. From the 1870s to the 1930s the overall crude death fell nearly without interruption, from over 25 per thousand people to just over 10. In the 1890s the crude death rate in Germany was approximately equal to that for France; by the mid-1920s the German death rate was much lower than in France.[26]

Mortality exhibited great variations across different sub-populations within Germany. Cities were, until the late nineteenth century, relatively unhealthy places to live, and Germany was no exception to this regularity. (Some of the apparent increase in mortality implied by moving from Knodel's villages to the national data in Table 2.2 most likely reflects the higher mortality of the urban areas included in the national data.) In 1877 life expectancy at birth for a male was five years less in a Prussian city than in a rural area, and the penalty was over three years for a female. The urban penalty in Germany declined considerably during the late nineteenth century, however, and by the early twentieth century German cities were healthier places than rural areas.

There were strong, significant relations between mortality and social class, with poorer people having higher death rates. Social-class differences in mortality suggest unequal access to the resources that encourage health and longevity. Studies of England also find important social class differences in mortality at the end of the nineteenth century.[27] These findings on social class are related to another important source of differences in mortality: legitimacy status. Virtually every statistical report or study of mortality in the nineteenth century shows that illegitimate children, who we know were quite numerous, faced mortality risks much higher than those faced by legitimate children. In Prussia as a whole, to take one example, infant mortality rates for illegitimate children were at least 50 per cent higher than for legitimate children throughout the period 1876 to 1904, and in rural areas could be twice as high.[28] The greater mortality risks for illegitimate children may reflect parental attitudes. But the more important problem was that illegitimate children were less likely to be breastfed, as their mothers were usually poor and had to work in occupations that precluded breast-feeding for any appreciable period.

Most of the early mortality transition reflected the control and then near-elimination of some infectious diseases. Diarrhoeal disease was especially important in Germany, but declined from 13 per cent to 1.5 per cent of all deaths between the 1890s and 1933. Progress against tuberculosis was slower but still steady; in the early 1890s this crippling disease accounted for 10.6 per cent of all deaths, a figure which fell to 6.7 per cent by 1933.[29]

The continuation of these trends in the twentieth century implies that nowadays life is not only longer, but also ordinarily ends in quite different ways than was the case in the nineteenth century.[30]

What caused the reductions in mortality? This question remains an active area for research and there is no real consensus for Germany or any other country. McKeown's famous argument states that the reduction in mortality during the eighteenth and nineteenth centuries was caused by improved nutrition, which in turn reflected both increased incomes and the integration of national and international food markets that reduced food costs. He argued that medicine *per se* could not have played an important role because much of the mortality decline preceded widespread use of effective medical therapies. He also argued that public-health improvements were unimportant because the major killers that declined first were not much affected by public health conditions. McKeown's argument has unfortunately become caught up in larger debates that cast economics versus something else as the prime mover in historical social change.[31]

No serious scholar has challenged McKeown's observation that the early stages of the mortality decline preceded the widespread use of effective medical therapies. For the most important killers there simply *were* no effective therapies. But this does not preclude an important role for physicians and others as advocates of hygienic and other measures that prevented disease. At the turn of the twentieth century Germany witnessed considerable propaganda for changes in lifestyle that would improve health, and for breastfeeding in particular. Doctors played an important role in this 'enforced socialization', strengthened by the role given them by the Sickness Insurance Act (1883) and by successful efforts to eliminate other practitioners from the medical market.[32] There is also clear evidence that rising incomes played a role in eliminating mortality crises before the mid-nineteenth century, and that the chronic malnutrition that characterized large parts of the European population before the twentieth century had important, negative physiological implications.[33]

But there is also little doubt that deliberate policy interventions played an important role in mortality decline. The German Empire enacted a law in 1879 that required the establishment of mechanisms to ensure the safety of food, although the actual creation of this system took many years.[34] The safety of the milk supply was especially important where cow's milk was used for infant feeding, but sterilized milk was not widely available in German cities even in the early twentieth century. Contemporaries appreciated that the summer-time spikes in infant mortality rates reflected in part the contamination of cow's milk. Another important innovation was pure water. By 1900 every German city of more than 25,000 inhabitants and about half of smaller cities had a central water system. Despite the early starts given these efforts in Germany (Berlin had a municipal water company as early as 1852, and Hamburg a central water supply in 1842), the creation of an effective system took decades.[35] The water system did not reach all dwellings immediately, and sewerage systems came even later. Thus we have to be careful with claims for the importance or non-importance of infrastructure in the mortality decline that depend on the 'date' such systems were established. Nonetheless, the public health improvements clearly played an important role in mortality decline. About 43 per cent of the decline in infant mortality from 1888–90 to 1910–12 in German cities can be attributed to water and sanitation systems.[36]

Rising incomes and changes in economic organization can have effects more subtle than those contemplated by either McKeown or his critics. This can be seen in the diffusion of municipal waterworks in the Rhineland in the period 1873–83. The decision to adopt a new water system depended not on recent outbreaks of disease, but on changes in incomes and industrial demand for water as well as inter-urban differences in the costs of such systems. In other words, the pattern of adoption of this crucial public-health intervention reflects incomes and prices.[37] At the bio-medical level, too, nutrition and infection are closely interrelated. Some diseases interfere with the body's use of nutrients. Thus eradication of some infectious diseases (especially diarrhoeal ones) improves nutrition, even without changes in food intake. In the other direction, malnutrition weakens the body's defences against infection. Many more people were exposed to tuberculosis than ever developed the disease, and one of the deciding factors in acquiring the disease was an individual's nutritional status.

The decline of infant mortality deserves special note for its connection to the issues discussed here and in the section on fertility decline below. Infants are especially susceptible to diarrhoeal infections. The public-health investments discussed above played a particular role in the reduction in infant mortality. A second factor is breastfeeding. Contemporaries noted that areas of Germany where infant mortality was relatively high, such as in Bavaria, were also areas where women ordinarily breastfed their babies for a very brief period. Breastfeeding both strengthens an infant's immune system and obviates the need for water and other fluids that may contain infectious agents. (Note that the purity of water and milk, and thus the application of public health measures, is especially important for infants who were not breastfed.)[38]

2.3 Migration and urbanization, 1800–1914

Migration has been a central feature of German history since the population movements that first brought the German people into central Europe. We will find it convenient to divide German migration in the past two centuries into four categories. The first were overseas migrants, those who left Germany for North America and other extra-European destinations. The second were migrants to eastern Europe, primarily Russia and the Habsburg lands. The third were immigrants *into* Germany. Finally, Germans moved around within Germany, and this internal migration was in large part responsible for the rapid growth of cities in the nineteenth century.

Germans, like any people, moved for a variety of reasons, including a desire to escape religious or political persecution. But the vast majority migrated to better the material aspects of their lives. The nineteenth century, as we saw earlier, witnessed tremendous economic growth in Germany. But some developments encouraged emigration from many regions. The first was the collapse of cottage industry under the weight of industrialization in Britain and later in Germany. Many rural households had scraped by with a combination of earnings from cottage industry and from agriculture, and with the decline of the former the latter was not enough. Several periods of widespread harvest failure – most notably in the early years following the peace of 1815, and then in the 'Hungry Forties' – spelt ruin for large numbers of agriculturalists. Two longer-term trends in agriculture also pushed Germans off the land. In much of south-west Germany the practice of subdividing land among heirs had produced the ever-smaller farms called 'dwarf' holdings. Many who farmed these plots combined agriculture with some other activity, but the living was precarious and it is these regions that provided many of the early nineteenth-century emigrants. In other regions, the peasant emancipation (*Bauernbefreiung*) programmes converted farmers to owners of their lands, but the conditions of sale meant that many smallholders ended up with no land at all. These emancipation programmes provoked flight from the land when the dispossessed were unable or unwilling to find employment as wage labourers in agriculture. But they could also produce an increase in the demand for agricultural labour if the new arrangements led to more intensive exploitation of the land.[39]

Mass migration from Germany overseas began after the Napoleonic wars ceased, aided in part by harvest failures in Germany's poor south-western regions and those governments' perception that allowing emigration would help improve conditions for the people who remained.[40] By the end of the nineteenth century some 5 million people had left Germany, most but not all for the United States. Figure 2.2 summarizes overseas emigration rates for the period prior to the First World War. The huge emigration of the early 1850s includes, no doubt, some political refugees in the aftermath of the 1848–49 revolutions, but most emigrants were simply reacting to the poor economic conditions in Germany that had helped spark the revolutions. Much the same is true of the 1880s, which was a period of bad harvests and falling agricultural prices associated with the importation of food from eastern Europe and the Americas. The surge in emigration during the 1860s, on the other hand, owes something to the Austro-Prussian war and the settlement that followed, and probably more to the end of civil war in the United States in 1865.[41] Other studies have demonstrated that annual fluctuations in emigration were closely tied to changes in wages and unemployment rates, at home and abroad.[42]

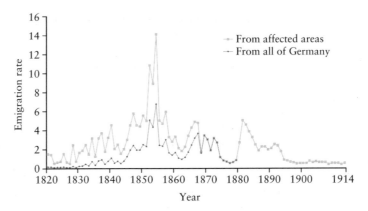

Fig. 2.2 Emigration from Germany, rate per thousand, 1820–1914.

Note: Data are for overseas emigration only. Following the approach used by some German scholars, the figure plots two different rates. Prior to about 1870, there were very few emigrants from eastern Germany, so the upper curve shows the emigration rate based only on the population of the affected (western) areas. After 1870, the two curves are identical.
Source: Peter Marschalck, *Deutsche Überseewanderung im 19.Jahrhundert* (Stuttgart, 1973), Table 4, for emigrants; and Walther G. Hoffman, *Das Wachstum der Deutschen Wirtschaft seit der Mitte des 19 Jahrhunderts* (Berlin, 1965), Table 1, pp. 172–4, for population.

Germany's emigration rates were high but not the highest in Europe even in the mid-nineteenth century.[43] Yet Germany was larger than most other countries of significant emigration such as Ireland or the Nordic countries, meaning that the total outflow from Germany was usually the largest in Europe. Where did all these migrants go? The United States drew the lion's share for the period 1847–1914, although the fraction varied over time, from a high of 93 per cent in the early 1880s to a low of 78 per cent in the last few years prior to the First World War. Other important destinations were Canada, Brazil, Argentina, and Australia.[44]

The popularity of the United States reflects several forces. For most of the nineteenth century the US drew a large majority of *most* European emigrants, a fact that reflects its size and rapid economic growth. Migration flows also have built into them a strong element of path-dependence. A migrant leaving Germany was more likely to go to a country that already had a significant number of German emigrants for several related reasons. A German emigrant may actually have been joining a specific person or family abroad. Language may also have been a draw. German emigrants were necessarily non-native speakers of the language in the major immigration countries, and going to a country that already had many Germans made it easier to acquire a job and social contacts while learning English. Finally, German emigrants could and did provide considerable information about the life and economic opportunities available in the countries to which they had gone, making it easier for a German emigrant to go to the country that already had many Germans. Path-dependence in migration means that the migration flows of one period are strongly influenced by earlier flows, and in the case of German emigration implies that the eighteenth-century migrations to the United States, however small, helped shape later overseas emigration from Germany.[45]

2.3.1 Smaller migration flows

Two further migration flows warrant mention but were relatively unimportant by the onset of the nineteenth century. One is emigration from Germany to the East. During the eighteenth century thousands of people had left the territory that would later be the German Reich and had settled in lands controlled by the Russian and Austro-Hungarian Empires. This migration continued during the nineteenth century but tapered off and was overshadowed quantitatively by overseas emigration and by movements within Germany. The beginning of these movements is difficult to date and even more difficult to distinguish from the significant movement of Germans between German states in the seventeenth and eighteenth centuries. At the beginning of the twentieth century there were large German-speaking communities in several parts of the Austro-Hungarian Empire, and in the Russian census of 1897 about 1.8 million people (1.4 per cent of the Russian population) said German was their mother tongue.[46]

2.3.2 Immigrants to Germany

Germany had been an important destination for immigrants in earlier periods. Immigrants helped make up population losses following disasters such as the Thirty Years War; the Prussian throne had invited immigrants to assist in schemes of internal colonization; and there were famous examples of importing people with skills or capital, such as the Huguenots invited to settle in Prussia. By the early nineteenth century immigration to Germany was modest. But by the last decades of the nineteenth century a new immigration flow had begun, this one mostly from the countries to the east of Germany. This new migration flow reflected Germany's rapid economic growth. At first most of these immigrants came temporarily, working in agriculture during periods of peak labour demand and returning home in the winter. Later these migrants became more permanent, working year-round in agriculture or taking industrial jobs.

The size of this immigrant flow can only be approximated. By one estimate, net immigration to Germany from elsewhere in Europe became significant in the late 1880s and in the period 1895–1905 amounted to some 40,000 people per year.[47] Another approach is to examine the number of foreign-born people

in Germany as enumerated by the census. This figure doubtless understates
the role of immigration, as it misses many thousands of people who came and
left between censuses, but it still shows a six-fold increase in foreign-born
people between 1871 and 1910.[48] At the latter date the 1.3 million foreign-
born amounted to nearly 2 per cent of the Reich's total population. Foreign
workers were more important to some regions than those total figures would
suggest. Large cities such as Berlin and Hamburg, as well as industrial regions
such as the Rhineland and Westphalia, had unusually large numbers of
foreign-born workers. In addition, some rural regions such as Mecklenburg
that had experienced heavy emigration and low rates of natural increase relied
on immigrants to make up the deficit. Germany's immigrants came from all
over Europe. But the largest groups were several nationalities of the Austro-
Hungarian Empire, who together comprised more than half of all the foreign-
born in 1910. German statistics unfortunately do not permit this sort of
precise disaggregation, but many migrants from Austria-Hungary and Russia
were Poles, and were joined in German cities by Polish-speakers from
Prussia's eastern provinces.[49]

Were these immigrants to Germany using it as a first step along the way
to some overseas destination (so-called 'stage migration'), or were migrants
to Germany in some sense 'replacing' the Germans who continued to go
overseas? The available sources do not lend themselves to a precise answer
to this question. Most migrants to large urban centres did not come directly
from the countryside, but had moved through a series of ever-larger urban
centres. This finding applies to Germans as well as immigrants. The
formation of Polish and other ethnic enclaves within Germany shows that
many immigrants stayed for long periods in Germany, even having families
and eventually assimilating into German life. What we do not know is how
many earned the wages for a transatlantic passage in Germany, or how
many left eastern Europe intending to do so but either remained in Germany
or returned to their native country when this strategy failed.[50]

2.3.3 *Internal migration and urbanization*

The industrialization process required huge increases in the labour force in
particular regions or cities. These localized demands for labour set off large-
scale internal migrations, migrations that also propelled the growth of
German cities. In 1907, nearly half the German population lived somewhere
other than the place of their birth.[51] Many of these migrations were of
relatively short distance – about 85 per cent of Germans remained in the
province in which they had been born – but even relatively short moves
could be of great economic and social significance. Some migrants to large
cities came from smaller urban centres, while for others internal migration
corresponded to a movement from agriculture to industry. Migrants from

within Germany flocked to industrial zones such as Silesia, Berlin, and Rhineland-Westphalia. With the growth of industry in south Germany later in the nineteenth century, those regions, too, became important destinations for internal migrants. Prussia's eastern provinces were an especially important source of internal migrants and accounted in 1907 for one-third of the migrants living in the Rhineland and Westphalia.[52]

Table 2.3 summarizes the growth of urban places in Germany in the nineteenth century (a process whose many implications for German society are discussed in greater detail in Chapter 6). At the start of the nineteenth

Table 2.3 Overview of German urbanization in the nineteenth century

Development of urbanization, 1816–1980

Year	Percentage of population living in urban places:			Number of
	less than 2000 people (rural)	2000 to 100,000 people	100,000 or more people	urban places with more than 100,000
1816	73.9	24.1	2.0	1
1834	73.9	24.2	1.9	1
1852	73.2	23.6	3.2	2
1871	63.9	31.1	4.8	8
1890	53.0	34.9	12.1	26
1910	40.0	38.7	21.3	48
1939	30.1	38.3	31.6	59
1961	20.7	45.1	34.2	53
1980	6.0	60.0	34.0	67
1994	8.3	59.9	31.8	84

Sizes of selected German cities before the First World War (in thousands of people)

City	About 1816	About 1850	1870	1910
Berlin	198	412	826	2071
Hamburg	128	175	290	931
Munich	54	107	169	596
Leipzig	35	63	107	679
Dresden	65	97	177	548
Cologne	50	97	129	517
Breslau	75	111	208	512
Frankfurt a.M.	42	65	91	415
Düsseldorf	23	27	69	359

Sources: Upper panel: Peter Marschalck, *Bevölkerungsgeschichte Deutschlands im 19. und 20. Jahrhundert* (Frankfurt, 1984), Table 5.5; and Statistisches Bundesamt, *Statistisches Jahrbuch für die Bundesrepublik Deutschland* (Stuttgart, 1996), Table 3.7.
Lower panel: Jürgen Reulecke, *Geschichte der Urbanisierung in Deutschland* (Frankfurt, 1985), Table 3.
Notes: In the upper panel, figures for 1816–52 are for Prussia only; figures for 1871–1939 are for the Reich; and figures for 1961–94 are for the Bundesrepublik. The 1939 figure is for the variant that includes the Saarland. City sizes in the lower panel are in thousands, and pertain to current area. The apparent decline in urbanization from 1980 to 1994 reflects the incorporation of the less urban eastern states.

century, urbanization in Germany had not proceeded far, compared to many other parts of western Europe.[53] By 1900, Germans were among the most urban people in western Europe. Statistics compiled for the 1930s showed that few countries in the world had a smaller proportion of their populations in rural areas, and Germany was second only to Great Britain in the fraction of her population who lived in cities of 100,000 or more.[54] The upper panel of Table 2.3 shows the great shift from a predominantly rural to a heavily urban society in the century prior to the First World War. Most notable is the growth of large cities, those of 100,000 or more persons. Germany had one such city as late as 1834, but 48 in 1910. These cities are distinctive to German urbanization; other urban countries, such as England, tended to have a larger fraction of their urban population concentrated in one very large city. The list of individual cities suggests the diffuse economic basis of this growth. Many cities grew ten-fold from 1816 to 1914, implying an average annual growth rate of about 2.5 per cent. More striking in its own way is the geographical concentration of urbanization. Of those 48 large cities in 1910, only 13 were in eastern or central Germany. The rest were in the western and southern regions of Germany, the regions that had experienced the most spectacular economic development during the nineteenth century.

In principle, a city's size can increase through net in-migration, through natural increase, or because the city incorporates surrounding settlements. In Laux's sample of 85 large Prussian cities, in-migration accounted for nearly half of growth from 1875 to 1905, with natural increase providing another 40 per cent. The contribution of immigrants was reflected in the age-structure of urban residents. In Prussia in 1875 the age group 16–30 comprised 30 per cent of the population in cities but only 23.6 per cent in rural areas.

2.4 The fertility transition

The rubric 'fertility transition' refers to the sharp decline in fertility rates that occurred in most western European countries during the late nineteenth and early twentieth centuries. A glance back at Figure 2.1 shows that crude birth rates began to fall in Germany in the 1870s. The decline continued, with some interruptions, until the present. More precise indicators show how marked this change was for the lives of individual men and especially women.[55] The village data mentioned earlier imply that a woman who married in her early twenties in the early nineteenth century would have eight children. The average German wife alive in the late 1880s gave birth to more than five children. Her counterpart in 1910 would have only 3.5 children, and by the 1920s this figure was down to about two children.[56] More recently fertility in Germany has fallen below the level necessary for population replacement.

The fertility transition is an active area of research and scholars debate both its characteristics and its causes. But there is little disagreement on several basic features. First, Germany's fertility transition was abrupt. Figure 2.1 shows that crude birth rates fell by half in the space of 50 years, from about 1875 to 1925, and much of that decline was concentrated in the first decade of the twentieth century.[57] No other western European country experienced such an abrupt decline in fertility. Second, the major change was in marital fertility. Overall fertility fell by 53 per cent over this period. If fertility within marriage alone had declined – that is, if marriage patterns and illegitimacy had remained constant – then overall fertility would have fallen by nearly 50 per cent, so the marital fertility decline alone accounts for most of the observed drop. Third, fertility generally declined earlier in cities than in rural areas, but this comparison is complicated by the fact that the fertility was high and its decline late in several areas with high concentrations of heavy industry, such as the Ruhr.[58] Finally, most Catholic areas had relatively late fertility transitions.

Most contemporary observers and most historians today attribute this decline in fertility to couples' efforts to have smaller families. Before discussing motivations for lower fertility we must establish which contraceptive methods couples actually used.[59] Historical demographers sometimes distinguish between 'traditional' methods of birth control and the more 'modern' methods in widespread use today. Traditional methods include sexual abstinence, male withdrawal (*coitus interruptus*), various douches, and sexual practices other than vaginal intercourse. *Coitus interruptus* seems to have been the most widely practised of these traditional birth-control methods.[60] To some readers these traditional methods for limiting family size seem unappealing. They are not as reliable as some modern methods, reduce sexual pleasure, or rely on unpleasant or even dangerous external agents. But many couples used these methods, even after alternatives were available. Over a couple's reproductive life even these methods can produce large reductions in fertility. Consistent use of withdrawal can, even taking into account its high failure rate, reduce the number of children a woman would bear by at least two-thirds.[61]

But the advent and widespread availability of more effective methods was doubtless part of the reason for the fall in German fertility. Following the vulcanization of rubber, inexpensive rubber condoms were mass-produced in Germany as elsewhere in Europe. The rubber condoms available from the 1870s were perhaps unsatisfactory, but by the early twentieth century high-quality, inexpensive condoms were available from many outlets in Germany, including drug stores, barber shops, pedlars, and through the mail. The diaphragm was a second innovation of the late nineteenth century. However, it was more expensive to use than condoms. The device itself was costly and required a medical visit to fit the device to the woman who would use it.

The dissemination of modern contraceptives in Germany took place against a complex political and social struggle. At first the Prussian and other

German governments tried to suppress both contraceptive information and the sale of the devices themselves. By the late nineteenth century, however, the health insurance funds, which managed the sickness insurance component of the social insurance system established by Bismarck (discussed in greater detail in Chapter 7), played a leading role in publicizing contraceptive methods, especially to the working classes. Most political parties in the late nineteenth and early twentieth centuries took a position on the birth-control issue. Some within Germany's feminist movement viewed the prevention of pregnancy as a basic human right, but other feminists opposed contraception. The issue of birth control occupied the attention of eugenicists concerned that the 'wrong' people would continue to have large families.[62] The question of fertility decline was also tied to concerns about Germany's ability to raise an army.

Legal prohibitions on abortion have a long history in Germany, as elsewhere. Advances in medical practice made abortions more practical in the nineteenth century than they had been earlier, and most historical discussion has focused on prohibitions during the late nineteenth and twentieth centuries. Abortion was forbidden in the Prussian legal code of 1851, the code which later formed the basis for the Reich penal code that took effect in 1872. Under this law, abortion was illegal in most circumstances and both the individual seeking the abortion and the provider were subject to imprisonment. Just how effectively the law was enforced is unknown. The Weimar Republic greatly relaxed these restrictions in 1926, only to have them reintroduced by the Nazi regime in 1933. The struggle over both contraception and abortion shows that many women wanted access to these methods for controlling their fertility. However, discussion of contraceptive techniques or abortion should not obscure the central question in the fertility transition, which is why women and men wanted to have smaller families.

2.4.1 *Causes of the fertility transition*

Interest in the history of fertility led to a large-scale project at Princeton University, commonly called the European Fertility Project. This project used district-level data to assign dates to the onset of the fertility transition in most of the countries of western Europe. The start of the fertility transition was defined as the date at which the index I_g (marital fertility) first declined by 10 per cent. By this criterion the fertility transition in most European countries began within a narrow time span. The Princeton project dates the fertility transition in Belgium at 1881; Germany, 1888; England and Wales, 1892; and the Netherlands, 1897.[63] The Princeton project's Summary volume interprets this narrow range of dates as support for the view that the fertility transition reflects a change in attitudes toward using contraception and limiting family size. Since countries with different levels of economic and social development experienced their transition at nearly the same time, the argument goes, such economic and social factors cannot have played a strong role in causing the adoption of birth control. The interpretation advanced by the Princeton authors is influential. But many scholars, including myself, have grave reservations about the methods and sources used in those studies.[64]

The Princeton project's argument that economic and social change had little to do with fertility decline has also not stood up well to new German evidence. Several studies have found, in contrast to the Princeton view, that economic and social factors played an important role in the German fertility transition. Knodel's district-level data combined with more refined statistical techniques show that industrialization was an important force in the German fertility transition and that its role increased over time. Analysis of detailed data for 407 Prussia *Kreise* in the period 1875–1910 yields even more striking findings. These administrative units are much smaller and less internally heterogeneous than the districts analysed by Knodel, and the Prussian data support use of more refined indices of social and economic development. The Prussian data show that the fertility decline in Prussia was more closely related to economic and social issues than to the cultural matters stressed by the Princeton project.[65] A project currently in progress, based on Munich registration data (*Polizeimeldebögen*), has yielded preliminary results suggesting that the fertility transition in that city started earlier than was implied by Knodel and that there were significant economic and social differences in fertility behaviour. Important social-class differences in fertility are also evident in the less precise statistical data summarized by Spree. Knodel's own village studies also imply that a fertility transition was under way in at least some parts of Germany earlier than the 1888 date suggested by the Princeton study.[66] Taken together, these studies show that in Germany at least, the fertility transition reflects in large part the social and economic transformations that drove other aspects of demographic change.

As noted above, fertility decline brought with it considerable concern about the implications of reduced population growth. Germany's transition occurred alongside a considerable decline in mortality rates, and the net effect was to *increase* the net rate of reproduction up to about 1900. Thus worries about slow German population growth appeared before changes in demographic behaviour that actually caused slower growth. In the early twentieth century, however, the effect of lower fertility dominated that of lower mortality, producing a low net rate of reproduction.[67]

2.5 War and upheaval, 1914–45

Throughout the ages, war has affected the population of a given territorial state in several ways. Soldiers die in combat and in epidemics that spread more easily through concentrated populations living in unsanitary conditions. Civilians also die at unusually high rates because military requirements reduce food, fuel, medical supplies, and other resources available for civilian use, and because population movements also spread infectious disease. In addition, a reduction in the number of new marriages as well as disruption in sexual relations for those currently married reduces the number of births. The twentieth century also introduced or made more significant three additional factors. Large-scale, deliberate attacks on enemy civilian populations in the Second World War, in Germany and elsewhere, brought civilian deaths to levels unknown in the past. Territorial reassignment after war, coupled with a heightened nationalism and intolerance of national minorities, led to tremendous population movements, as people who found themselves on the 'wrong' side of the new borders either left voluntarily or were expelled forcibly. Finally, the Second World War was accompanied by the deliberate murder of millions of civilians both in Germany and in the territories it occupied.

Scholars and propagandists have tried to estimate the numbers associated with each of war's demographic effects. By their nature the demographic events in question are difficult for even the most careful scholar to count, and given the emotional and political significance of the issue not all accounts aim to be accurate.[68] The most reliable figure is simply the population of Germany before and after the world wars. The last prewar census in 1910 showed a total population of about 65 million people. The combined population of the two Germanys in 1946, on a reduced territory, was 65 million. Thus from 1914 to 1946 Germany lost 34 per cent of her territory and on that reduced territory experienced no net population growth.

We begin with combat deaths. The First World War cost the German armies some 2.4 million men either killed or missing. This figure amounts to about 3.5 per cent of the prewar German population. The Second World War cost the German forces a total of some 3.25 million killed and missing, or about 4.7 per cent of the prewar population. Another 500,000 German civilians are thought to have died as the direct result of enemy action in the Second World War, chiefly in air raids. To this number we must add an estimate of 200,000 German Jews who either emigrated or were murdered by the German government. (The figure of 200,000 German Jews is much smaller than the total number killed in the Holocaust because most Holocaust victims were citizens of other states and not of Germany. The accepted figure for the total number of Jews murdered by the Nazi government is about 6 million.)[69] The Nazi government also murdered thousands of other people, including Roma, homosexuals, and political and religious opponents of the regime.

To these we must add two other demographic consequences of wartime conditions, an increase in non-combat civilian deaths and a decline in births. Death rates increased considerably during wartime, and birth rates decreased, as Figure 2.1 shows for the First World War. Comparable data are not available for 1944 and 1945, but the numbers for 1939–43 showed a reduced birth rate and a slightly elevated death rate. To calculate the short-run effects of the war we must estimate the number of births and deaths we would have expected in a counter-factual Germany that did not experience a war, and compare these estimates to the number of births and deaths that actually did occur. Estimates of long-term impacts are even more speculative. Some of the births that did not occur in 1916 because of war were simply deferred to the years after the war; the long-term effect on the German population of this deferral is slight. Similarly, many of the people who died because of wartime conditions in 1916 would have died within several years, even in peacetime conditions, because of normal mortality risks, implying that the long-term impact of elevated wartime mortality was less than its short-term impact. These caveats aside, reasonable estimates suggest about 2.2 million excess deaths and 2.2 million fewer than expected births in the period 1914–18. The estimates for the Second World War are 5.1 million excess deaths and a shortfall in births of about 1.7 million.[70] Thus in both wars the sum of excess deaths and fewer than expected births is greater than battlefield deaths.

The settlements in 1919 and in 1945 each required the transfer of territory to another state. Germany today is only about 65 per cent as large as the Reich before the First World War. The populations living in lost territories were not necessarily all lost to Germany. Both wars witnessed enormous migrations, as civilians first tried to flee wartime conditions or advancing armies and then afterwards as huge streams of ethnic Germans fled areas where they were now distinctly unwelcome. In June of 1925 a special office for returnees counted on German soil 1.4 million people who had been elsewhere at the outbreak of war in 1914.

The movements of civilians at the end of the Second World War were far larger and involved the deaths of many ethnic Germans, either by violence or through starvation and disease in displaced persons camps. In the last year of the war millions of civilians fled advancing armies, leaving the territories that make up Germany today with a total of 9.9 million refugees. Many of these refugees were from areas that would remain in either West or East Germany, but many others had come from areas outside Germany's post-1945 borders. In 1950, West Germany alone counted 4.5 million residents who had left areas no longer in West or East Germany. The continuing flow into West Germany in the 1950s is difficult to distinguish from another flow discussed in the next section, the thousands of Germans who fled west to escape the Stalinist regime in East Germany. Another 3.4 million West German residents were ethnic Germans who had fled areas that were not part of the Reich at the outset of the Second World War: they came from Czechoslovakia, Poland, the Baltic countries, and elsewhere in eastern Europe.

Emigration from Germany had virtually ceased during the First World War, and after the war Germans were for some years forbidden to migrate to several countries that had previously been popular destinations. Canada banned German immigration until 1923, the United States until 1921, and Australia and New Zealand until 1925.[71] But emigration rebounded soon after, and for several years reached levels unknown for decades. Official statistics put the number of emigrants in the period 1919–39 at about 720,000, with the majority going to the United States, as before the war.[72]

German emigration in the 1920s and 1930s reflected not just the situation at home, but restrictions on immigration in receiving countries. Restrictions on German immigration to the United States were not especially severe, but since they affected the largest emigrant flow these restrictions did much to redirect the emigrant flow and in some cases to hamper emigration from Germany altogether. A more serious limitation on immigration into the United States came with attempts to enforce rules against the immigration of people who might require welfare assistance once in the United States. These rules were more strictly enforced starting in September of 1930, in the wake of the Great Depression.[73]

2.5.1 Fertility in the interwar years

Recovery from the effects of the First World War in Germany was a long and slow process, hampered by political instability, uncertainty over territorial settlements and reparations payments, and the refugee flows described above. Germany, in addition, suffered both hyperinflation in the early 1920s and a particularly severe version of the Great Depression of the 1920s and 1930s. A large increase in the number of marriages in the immediate postwar years (reflecting marriages delayed during the war, as well as the remarriage of people widowed by war) helped to bring the birth rate back above the death rate in 1919, where it remained until data cease in 1943. But the birth rate then fell to levels that were, in historical perspective, very low. For most of the nineteenth century the birth rate in any year was at least 30 per thousand people, and even in 1913 there were 27.5 births per thousand Germans. In the period 1919–39 the birth rate averaged 19.5 per thousand. A continued strong diminution in mortality, especially infant mortality, was not sufficient to prevent a further reduction in the net rate of reproduction. By 1925 Germany's net rate of reproduction lay below France's, a development which was taken as a signal that Germany's fertility was at crisis levels. Coupled with the enormous human toll of the war, this decline in German fertility set off another round of soul-searching and recriminations.

A brief departure from the fertility decline took place during the period 1933–39. The German economy started recovering just before Hitler seized power in 1933, and the recovery continued throughout the peacetime regime.[74] Economic recovery alone would have encouraged new marriages and new births. In addition, the Nazi regime enacted a series of measures intended to encourage 'Aryans' to marry and to have more children. Starting in 1933, newly married couples were eligible for interest-free loans of up to 1000 Reichsmarks (RM). To qualify the couple had to agree that the wife would not work in the paid labour force and both partners had to be 'racially suitable'. For each child born to the marriage, 250 RM of the loan was forgiven, and just the interest subsidy was sizeable. To put these figures in perspective, in 1933 an unskilled building worker would earn less than 40 marks for a 60-hour week.[75] By 1940 the regime had made 1.57 million of these loans and 1.31 million births had qualified couples for partial forgiveness of their loans.[76]

Other policies reduced taxes on couples with children and offered various subsidies to those with large families. Throughout Nazi Germany families with children enjoyed preferences in housing and other markets, and promotion in army and government positions became increasingly difficult for bachelors. Part of the impetus for these measures was an effort to encourage women to leave the labour market and help reduce unemployment rates for men. The long-term impact of these policies is unclear. The economic recovery alone would have led to new marriages and an increased birth rate, and many of the births that occurred in response to Nazi subsidies in the 1930s may reflect simple changes in the *timing* of births within a marriage.[77]

2.5.2 *War and the age-structure and sex-structure of the population*

Some of the economic and demographic problems of Germany's war experience involved changes in the age-structure and sex-structure of the population. Most combat casualties were young men, and a deficit of births reduced the size of the cohort born during wartime. In 1910 the ratio of women to men in the age groups 15–45 ranged from 100 women per 100 men at age 15–25 up to 102 women per 100 men at age 40–45. In 1925 there were about 130 women per 100 men aged 30–35, and the ratio was only slightly less for other cohorts affected by the war. The same effect from the Second World War was even more severe: in 1950 there were 140 women per 100 men aged 25–40 in the two Germanys combined.[78] A long tradition in demography suggests that the necessary outcome of such sex imbalances is a cohort of women in which many can never marry. But a famous paper by the French demographer Louis Henry cautions against stressing the matter too much. The generation of French women whose most likely potential husbands were devastated by the First World War experienced only slightly elevated levels of permanent celibacy.[79] A similar adjustment occurred in Germany after the First World War; the percentage of people who had never married declined for both sexes between 1910 and 1925, but the decline was 50 per cent larger for men than for women.[80]

Changes in age-structure may also matter if they significantly alter the fraction of people who are either younger or older than working age. Again, we must be careful with hard-and-fast statements about who is too young or old to work. The age at which young people begin working and older people stop working reflects incomes, compulsory-schooling laws, and laws affecting retirement age and pensions, and the structure of the labour market. Prior to the First World War, Germany had an unusually low labour-force participation rate for men aged 65 and above.[81]

Whatever their economic impact, the effects of the wars on the age-structure of the population were significant. The deficit of births during the First World War dramatically reduced the number of children. The fraction under 15 fell from 34 per cent in 1910 to 26 per cent in 1925. The effects of the Second World War were less noticeable in this respect, partly because the reduction in births during the war was smaller and because of refugee families coming to Germany after the war. The percentage of people over 65 did increase more from 1937 to 1950 than it did over the period 1910–25, but this increase reflects the ageing of the population associated with the fertility decline, and was not necessarily the outcome of the war.

During the 1920s and 1930s the demographic forces at work in Germany – reduced fertility, reduced emigration, and the migration to Germany of ethnic Germans displaced from the lost territories – combined to produce a large increase in the number of working-age people. Between 1900 and 1933 the total population of Germany increased by 15.7 per cent, but the number of those aged 15–64 increased by 31.8 per cent. Female labour-force participation rates also rose substantially, from about 30.4 per cent in 1907 to 35.6 per cent in 1925. Labour-force participation rates for males increased even more over the same period, reflecting later retirement ages, for example.[82] This change in the age-structure of the population combined with higher labour-force participation rates played a role in the persistent high unemployment of the 1920s and in Germany's brutal experience of the Great Depression.[83]

2.6 The Germanys since the Second World War

The hardening of occupation zones into two distinct German states created for all practical purposes two distinct German populations in the period 1945–89. The ideological differences between the two Germanys, along with East German policies that bore directly on demographic patterns, led demographers to study the contrasts between the two states as clear evidence of the role, if any, of state policy in demographic behaviour. However intriguing some aspects of East German demographic policy, these comparisons are over-simplified. By its nature, the East German economy was poorer and different from its western counterpart.[84] Other aspects of life under a Stalinist regime no doubt also had their effect on the people's attitudes and desires concerning marriage and fertility. In any case, the population experience of the two Germanys differed in specifics but turned on remarkably similar basic problems.

Population in West Germany grew steadily, although more slowly than in the past, while East Germany's population declined. If we set the population of each territory to 100 in 1946, then in 1990 West Germany had 136 persons and East Germany 88. East Germany's population loss reflects the expulsions and emigration noted earlier, but owes much to feeble rates of natural increase. One result of this population decline in East Germany was that its population was even more aged than West Germany's in the 1980s.[85] The underlying cause of West German demographic stagnation and East German demographic decline was low fertility. The total fertility rate in the two Germanys moved in tandem for most of this period, with the West German total fertility rate peaking in 1966 at 2.53, and the East German in 1964 at 2.51. Fertility fell sharply thereafter in both states, although it fell further in West Germany than in East. In 1989 the total fertility rate in West Germany was 1.39 and in East Germany it was 1.57. The net rate of reproduction fell below 1 in both Germanys in the 1970s and has remained there since; in 1989 West Germany had a net reproduction rate of 0.69 and East Germany, 0.73. In the first few years following unification the East German net reproduction rate fell below that of its western counterpart.[86]

Observers have tended to focus more attention on other aspects of fertility behaviour which display greater contrasts between West and East. East German women had their children earlier in life. In most years during its existence the average age at first birth in East Germany was about two years less than in West Germany, and the difference actually widened with time.[87] Another and even more striking contrast concerns illegitimacy. The percentage of births to unmarried mothers was higher in East Germany even in the early 1950s (11–13 per cent compared to 6–8 per cent). This figure increased in both Germanys in the period 1950s–89, but more in the East. In 1989 about one-third of East German births were illegitimate, compared to 10.5 per cent of West German.[88]

The East German fertility patterns doubtless reflect many factors, but attention has focused on a set of measures enacted in the 1970s that provided financial subsidies to women who bore children and permitted most women to take a full year of paid maternity leave (policies also discussed in Chapter 11). These measures were part of a wider policy that emphasized social subsidies and state support for families, but were initially a reaction to a sharp drop in fertility that accompanied the legalization of abortion. The East German maternity policy should also be seen in the context of a society with a much higher female labour-force participation rate than West Germany (in 1983, 82.5 per cent of East German women had paid employment, compared to 55 per cent of West German women).[89] The East German policy of encouraging female labour-force participation (which, by contrast, West Germany actively discouraged) meant that women in that territory faced a higher implicit cost to bearing children.

Abortion policy proved to be one of the most serious hindrances to the integration of the two Germanys. At the time of unification, a woman in East Germany could obtain a legal abortion for almost any reason in the first 12 weeks of her pregnancy. West German law was more restrictive, forcing a woman to obtain permission from a special commission. Since these commissions are local, the actual availability of abortion varied widely within West Germany. Neither side was willing to adopt the other's abortion law at the time of unification, so the states that were formerly in East Germany temporarily had their own abortion laws.[90]

2.6.1 *Migration in the two Germanys*

Both Germanys adopted, with some reluctance, a policy of importing foreign workers to make up some of the deficit in their own workforces. Starting with Italy in 1955, West Germany signed a series of bilateral agreements with Greece, Italy, Portugal, Spain, Turkey, and Yugoslavia that enabled the recruitment of guest workers (*Gastarbeiter*) from those countries. Between 1962 and 1973 these treaties brought 9.66 million people to West Germany, although the majority eventually returned home and the net inflow was only 3.68 million. Following the oil shock in 1973, the government tried hard to limit guest worker immigration and to convince those already in West Germany to return to their homes. But continued labour immigration combined with family reunification created net immigration flows in the period 1973–88 that were smaller than earlier, but still positive.[91] West Germany's *Gastarbeiter* are legally distinct from two other sources of immigrants. West Germany instituted one of the most liberal policies on political asylum in the world, resulting in the presence of many asylum seekers (*Asylanten*). In the early 1970s asylum seekers comprised less than 1 per cent of all immigrants; by 1992 more than one-third of immigrants were asylum seekers.[92] A third category consists of ethnic Germans living outside Germany, who under the Basic Law of the Federal Republic have the right to German citizenship and to settle in Germany (*Aussiedler*). The numbers of *Aussiedler* exploded in the last years prior to unification as the disintegration of the Stalinist regimes in eastern Europe allowed ethnic Germans in Russia and elsewhere to take up residence in Germany.

Immigration into West Germany was enough to offset the low fertility of West German women and accounts for most of the population growth in the Federal Republic over the period 1960–89. In 1988 foreigners in West Germany totalled 4.5 million persons, or 7.3 per cent of the total population. The only other western European countries with foreign-born populations of larger relative size were Luxembourg (25.8 per cent) and Belgium (8.6 per cent); the next country after Germany would be France, at 5 per cent. To put this in context, in 1990, 7.9 per cent of the population of the United States was born in another country.[93] Put a different way, the size of the immigrant flow in Germany, relative to the German population, has been approximately as large in the period 1950–89 as it was for the United States at the height of immigration there (1901–10). By any reasonable standard, Germany has become an immigration country.[94]

The East German government also turned to immigrants to deal with the consequences of depopulation, but did so later and on a more modest scale. In 1989 foreigners comprised only 1.2 per cent of the East German population. Most of those had arrived in the previous few years. East Germany also drew its guest workers from different sources. Fully one-third came from Vietnam, and most of the rest came from other socialist countries in Africa and eastern Europe. East Germany's immigrants were not sufficient to offset her low fertility rates and, as we have seen, the population of East Germany declined steadily.

The heavy reliance on immigrants in West Germany especially raised uncomfortable questions about the nature of the German people. Even after recent reforms it remains difficult for an immigrant or even the child of an immigrant born on German soil to obtain German citizenship. Germany is not alone in this policy, and even countries such as France that formally accept naturalization have made it more difficult in recent years. But the sheer size of Germany's resident 'foreign' population makes this a pressing issue. The current debate over German citizenship law has both deep historical roots and practical current consequences. The process of German unification in the nineteenth century meant that the 'Germans' existed prior to a German state, and Bismarck's empire excluded some Germans while including many non-Germans (such as Poles in eastern Prussia). Thus the German state has never been coterminous with the territory occupied by the German people, in contrast to Britain or, in a different way, the United States. Moreover, the commitment to social-welfare principles in Germany means that the grant of German citizenship carries with it considerable economic rights, rights not enjoyed to anything like the same degree by British or US citizens.[95]

Some aspects of Germany's social-welfare state are directly threatened by the very low birth rates that have appeared in recent decades. A population with low fertility will, in the absence of immigration, have a relatively large number of older people. In 1871 only 4.6 per cent of the population of the German empire was 65 years old or older. In 1995 this figure had risen to 15.6 per cent in the united Germany. Sober projections imply that in the year 2040, about 30 per cent of all Germans will be at least 65 years of age.[96] In this respect Germany is in a situation similar to that of most of the European Union, and indeed most of the industrialized world. The only way to reverse this trend is to raise the fertility rate. A liberal immigration policy would have only a slight effect on population ageing, since immigrants would themselves eventually grow old. The impact of population ageing on social insurance, medical care, and related programmes is now the subject of intense concern in Germany and in other countries facing this issue. Present retirement ages, benefit levels, and other policy variables are probably unsustainable in the long run, and the future of Germany's social-welfare state depends in part on how the country faces up to this issue.

2.7 Conclusion

Wars, territorial losses, and most of all a low birth rate left the reunited Germany after 1989 with a population only about 10 per cent larger than that of the Reich at the outbreak of the First World War. But this is a very different population: living on a reduced territory and under a democratic constitutional order, the united Germany of the early twenty-first century has different political and military goals than did the Kaiserreich. Germany has also undergone what are probably the last phases of a long demographic transition begun in the nineteenth century. Germany is no longer a country of significant permanent emigration, and is now a net recipient of migrants, although ambivalently and without admitting the fact. The high birth and death rates of the early and mid-nineteenth century have been replaced by birth rates that are among the lowest in the world and death rates that imply a life expectancy at birth more than twice as long as in the early nineteenth century.

The demographic implications of this transition are clear in Germany's stagnant native population and in her rapidly ageing population. Policy-makers now grapple with the problems of maintaining social welfare benefits in a society where the retired are growing in numbers faster than the active workers who support them. Cultural observers write books with titles such as *Sterben Wir Aus?* ('Are We Dying Out?'), evoking the unlikely image of a Europe without Germans. Most interestingly, Germany today is facing up to a question it has tried to ignore for the past century: whether it is to remain a state formally defined around a particular language and ethnic community, or accept non-German immigrants as fully fledged German citizens. In facing up to these issues Germany is confronting in yet another way the difficult legacy of its turbulent past. How it responds will shape the lives of the Germans of the twenty-first century.

2.8 Notes

1 For a good introduction to the intellectual history of German population see Josef Ehmer, 'Eine "deutsche" Bevölkerungsgeschichte? Gunther Ipsens historisch-soziologische Bevölkerungstheorie', in Institut für Demographie der Öster-reichischen Akademie der Wissenschaften, ed., *Demographische Informationen* (1992–3), pp. 60–70. The best full-length study of German population in our period is Michel Hubert, *L'Allemagne en mutation: Histoire de la population allemande depuis 1815* (Paris, 1995).

2 Gerhard Heilig, Thomas Büttner, and Wolfgang Lutz, 'Germany's Population: Turbulent Past, Uncertain Future'. *Population Bulletin*, 45 (1990), pp. 4–45; P. Deane and W. A. Cole, *British Economic Growth, 1688–1959* (Cambridge, 1962).

3 Michel Hau, *Histoire économique de l'allemagne XIXe–XXe siècles* (Paris, 1994), Table A5.

4 See Frank B. Tipton, 'The Regional Dimension: Economic Geography, Economic Development, and National Integration in the Nineteenth and Twentieth Centuries' in this volume. Recent analytical economic histories for this period include Hau, *Histoire économique*; Hubert Kiesewetter, *Industrielle Revolution in Deutschland 1815–1914* (Frankfurt am Main, 1989); and Richard Tilly, *Vom Zollverein zum Industriestaat: Die wirtschaftlich-soziale Entwicklung Deutschlands 1834 bis 1914* (Munich, 1990).

5 For the basic model see John Hajnal, 'Two Kinds of Pre-industrial Household Formation System', *Population and Development Review*, 8 (1982), pp. 449–94, and John Hajnal, 'European Marriage Patterns in Perspective', in D. V. Glass and D. E. C. Eversley, eds, *Population in History: Essays in Historical Demography* (London, 1965), pp. 101–48. For two different, extended critiques of Hajnal, see Timothy W. Guinnane, *The Vanishing Irish: Households, Migration and the Rural Economy in Ireland, 1850–1914* (Princeton, 1997), and Josef Ehmer, *Heiratsverhalten, Sozialstruktur, ökonomischer Wandel: England und Mitteleuropa in der Formationsperiode des Kapitalismus* (Göttingen, 1991), pp. 64–7. For a cogent summary of regional variation in marriage patterns see Ehmer, *Heiratsverhalten*.

6 For example, E. A. Wrigley and R. Schofield, *The Population History of England, 1541–1871: A Reconstruction* (Cambridge, MA, 1981).

7 John Knodel, *Demographic Behavior in the Past: A Study of Fourteen German Village Populations in the Eighteenth and Nineteenth Centuries* (Cambridge, 1988), Table 6; Ehmer, *Heiratsverhalten*, Appendix Table 2; Michael W. Flinn, *The European Demographic System, 1500–1820* (Baltimore, 1981), Table 6.3. Knodel's extraordinary study is based on the *Ortssippenbuch*, a genealogy of everyone who lived in a village. These genealogies were only compiled for rural settlements, meaning that the detail presented in Knodel's study is not available for urban areas.

8 William H. Hubbard, *Familiengeschichte: Materialien zur deutschen Familie seit dem Ende des 18. Jahrhunderts* (Munich, 1983), Table 3.7.

9 John Knodel, *The Decline of Fertility in Germany, 1871–1939* (Princeton, 1974), Table 2.14.

10 John Knodel and Mary Jo Maynes, 'Urban and Rural Marriage Patterns in Imperial Germany', *Journal of Family History*, 1 (1976), pp. 129–68, Table 1. See also Ehmer, *Heiratsverhalten*, Appendix Table 12.

11 Knodel, *Demographic Behavior*, Tables 7.4 and 7.5; James Trussell and Timothy W. Guinnane, 'Techniques of Event-History Analysis', in David Reher and Roger Schofield, eds, *Old and New Methods in Historical Demography* (Oxford, 1993), pp. 181–205.

12 Klaus-Jürgen Matz, *Pauperismus und Bevölkerung: die gesetzlichen Ehebeschränkungen in den süddeutschen Staaten während des 19. Jahrhunderts* (Stuttgart, 1980); Ehmer, *Heiratsverhalten*, Ch. 9; Sheilagh Ogilvie, 'Population Growth and State Policy in Central Europe before Industrialization', *Centre for History and Economics Working Paper, King's College, Cambridge* (Feb. 1995).

13 Wolfgang Kaschuba and Carola Lipp, *Dörfliches Überleben: zur Geschichte materieller und sozialer Reproduktion ländlicher Gesellschaft im 19. und frühen 20. Jahrhundert* (Tübingen, 1982), pp. 328–59.

14 John Knodel, 'Law, Marriage, and Illegitimacy in Nineteenth Century Germany', *Population Studies*, 20 (1967), pp. 279–94, Tables 1 and 2.

15 Knodel, 'Law', pp. 279–94, Table 5.

16 Elisabeth Mantl, *Heirat als Privileg: obrigkeitliche Heiratsbeschränkungen in Tirol und Vorarlberg 1820 bis 1920* (Vienna, 1997).

17 Michael Mitterauer, *Ledige Mütter: zur Geschichte unehelicher Geburten in Europa* (Munich, 1983).

18 Knodel, *Decline*, Appendix Table 2.1 and Map 2.6.

19 Data from Antje Kraus, ed., *Quellen zur Bevölkerungsstatistik Deutschlands 1815–1875*, Vol. I of Wolfgang Köllmann, ed., *Quellen zur Bevölkerungs-, Sozial- und Wirtschaftsstatistik Deutschlands 1815–1875* (Boppard am Rhein, 1980), Tables 8, 27, and 33. Bavaria here excludes the Pfalz, which had much lower extramarital fertility.

20 W. Robert Lee, 'Bastardy and the Socioeconomic Structure of South Germany', *Journal of Interdisciplinary History*, 7 (1977), pp. 403–25; Edward Shorter, 'Bastardy in South Germany: A Comment', *Journal of Interdisciplinary History*, 8 (1978), pp. 459–69.

21 Knodel uses a common index of marital fertility called I_g which is defined as follows:

$$ I_g = \frac{B}{\sum\limits_{a\,=\,15\text{-}19}^{45\text{-}49} m_a F_a} $$

where B is the number of legitimate births in that year, m_a is the number of married women in the age range and F_a is the marital fertility rate of Hutterite standard. I_g is one of the four 'Princeton' indices, which are related as follows:

$$ I_f = I_g * I_m + I_h * (1 - I_m) $$

I_h is an index of illegitimate fertility defined analogously to I_g. Thus overall fertility I_f is a weighted sum of legitimate and illegitimate fertility, with the weights (I_m) being an index of nuptiality.

22 Knodel, *Decline*, Table 2.2.

23 Ansley J. Coale and Roy Treadway, 'A Summary of the Changing Distribution of Overall Fertility, Marital Fertility, and the Proportion Married in the Provinces of Europe', in Ansley J. Coale and Susan Cotts Watkins, *The Decline of Fertility in Europe: The Revised Proceedings of a Conference on the Princeton European Fertility Project* (1986), pp. 31–181, Appendix A.

24 Jacques Vallin, 'Mortality in Europe from 1720 to 1914: Long-Term Trends and Changes in Patterns by Age and Sex', in R. Schofield, D. Reher, and A. Bideau, eds, *The Decline of Mortality in Europe* (Oxford, 1991), pp. 38–67.

25 Vallin, 'Mortality', Table 3.1.

26 B. R. Mitchell, ed., *European Historical Statistics, 1750–1975*, 2nd edn (New York, 1980), Series B6.

27 Spree, *Health*; cf. Preston and Haines, *Fatal Years*.

28 Data cited in Marschalck, *Bevölkerungsgeschichte*, Table 3.16.

29 Haines and Kintner, 'Mortality Transition', Table 2.
30 Epidemics and their suppression deserve special note. By the nineteenth century most western European governments had enacted measures that limited epidemic deaths at the turn of the twentieth century to numbers that were, in historical terms, a handful. The most important exception was cholera; several German cities, most notably Hamburg, experienced severe cholera outbreaks as late as the 1890s.
31 Thomas McKeown, *The Modern Rise of Population* (New York, 1976); Simon Szreter, 'The Importance of Social Intervention in Britain's Mortality Decline *c*.1850–1914: A Reinterpretation of the Role of Public Health', *Social History of Medicine*, 1 (1988), pp. 1–39, here p. 5, to take an example from the English discussion, casts this debate as one of 'human agency' (that is, public health measures) versus 'the invisible hand' (a code-word for economics). Surely economic organization is a product of human agency.
32 Spree, *Health*, pp 186–93.
33 Robert William Fogel, 'New Findings on Secular Trends in Nutrition and Mortality: Some Implications for Population Theory', in Mark R. Rosenzweig and Oded Stark, eds, *Handbook of Population and Family Economics*, Vol. 1a (New York, 1997), pp. 413–81.
34 Spree, *Health*, pp. 139–41.
35 Jörg Vögele, 'Sanitäre Reformen und der Sterblichkeitsrückgang in deutschen Städten, 1877–1913', *Vierteljahrschrift für Sozial- und Wirtschaftsgeschichte*, 80 (1993), Table 1; Spree, *Health*, pp. 139–41; Vögele, 'Urban Infant Mortality', pp. 401–25.
36 John C. Brown, 'Public Health Reform and the Decline in Urban Mortality in Germany', in G. Kearns, W. R. Lee, M. C. Nelson, and J. Rogers, eds, *Improving the Public Health: Essay in Medical History* (Liverpool, in press).
37 John C. Brown, 'Coping with Crisis: The Diffusion of Waterworks in Late Nineteenth-Century German Towns', *Journal of Economic History*, 48 (1988), pp. 307–18.
38 Hallie J. Kintner, 'The Impact of Breastfeeding Patterns on Regional Differences in Infant Mortality in Germany, 1910', *European Journal of Population*, 3 (1987), pp. 233–61; Spree, *Health*, Tables 8 and 9.
39 Walter D. Kamphoefner, *The Westfalians: From Germany to Missouri* (Princeton, 1987); Robert A. Dickler, 'Organization and Change in Productivity in Eastern Prussia', in William N. Parker and Eric L. Jones, eds, *European Peasants and their Markets: Essays in Agrarian Economic History* (Princeton, 1975), pp. 269–92.
40 The literature on German emigration is large. Klaus J. Bade, 'Die deutsche überseeische Massenauswanderung im 19. und frühen 20. Jahrhundert: Bestimmungsfaktoren und Entwicklungsbedingungen', in Klaus J. Bade, ed., *Auswanderer – Wanderarbeiter – Gastarbeiter: Bevölkerung, Arbeitsmarkt und Wanderung in Deutschland seit der Mitte des 19. Jahrhunderts*, Vol. I (Ostfildern, 1984), pp. 259–99, is a concise summary.
41 Kevin H. O'Rourke, 'The European Grain Invasion, 1870–1913', *Journal of Economic History*, 57 (1997), pp. 775–801; Peter Marschalck, *Deutsche Überseewanderung im 19. Jahrhundert* (Stuttgart, 1973), p. 42, stresses the US Civil War as retarding emigration from Germany and re-directing some of the flow to other destinations.
42 Timothy J. Hatton and Jeffrey G. Williamson, 'What Drove Mass Migrations from Europe in the Late Nineteenth Century?', *Population and Development Review*, 20 (1994), Ch. 4.
43 Hatton and Williamson, 'What Drove', Table 1.
44 Emigration statistics from Marschalck, *Deutsche Überseewanderung*, Table 11 (cf. Marschalck, *Deutsche Überseewanderung*, Table 12). Data on emigration from

Germany require caution. See Friedrich Bürgdörfer, 'Die Wanderungen über die Deutschen Reichsgrenzen im letzten Jahrhundert', *Allgemeines Statistisches Archiv*, 20 (1930), pp. 161–96, 383–419, 537–51; and Hubert, *L'Allemagne*, pp. 105–7.

45 'Path dependence' is a term coined by economists to refer to phenomena where what happens today depends in part on an event in the past. Paul A. David, 'Clio and the Economics of QWERTY', *American Economic Review*, 75 (1985), pp. 332–7, is the basic reference. Simone Wegge, 'Chain Migration and Information Networks: Evidence from Nineteenth-Century Hesse-Cassel', *Journal of Economic History*, 58 (1998), pp. 957–86, explores this so-called 'chain migration' in the context of emigration from Hesse in the mid-nineteenth century. Walter D. Kamphoefner, Wolfgang Helbich, and Ulrike Sommer, eds, *News from the Land of Freedom: German Immigrants Write Home* (Ithaca, 1991), is a collection of letters written by German emigrants to people in Germany.

46 A recent comprehensive survey of emigration to the East is contained in Klaus J. Bade, ed., *Deutsche in Ausland – Fremde in Deutschland. Migration in Geschichte und Gegenwart* (Munich, 1992). The figures from the Russian census appear in the contribution to Bade's volume by Brandes (p. 85).

47 Bürgdörfer, 'Wanderungen', p. 539.

48 Hubert, *L'Allemagne*, Table 43.

49 Hubert, *L'Allemagne*, Appendix Table 16.

50 Dieter Langewiesche, 'Wanderungsbewegungen in der Hochindustrialisierungsperiode. Regionale, interstädtische und innerstädtische Mobilität in Deutschland 1880–1914', *Vierteljahrschrift für Sozial-und Wirtschaftsgeschichte*, 64 (1977), pp. 1–40; Peter Borscheid, 'Saison- und Etappenwanderung im Münsterland 1880–1900', *Schriften des Vereins für Socialpolitik*, NF 119 (1981), pp. 9–45; James H. Jackson, Jr, *Migration and Urbanization in the Ruhr Valley, 1821–1914* (Atlantic Highlands, NJ, 1997).

51 Hubert, *L'Allemagne*, p. 231.

52 Hubert, *L'Allemagne*, Table 33.

53 Jan De Vries, *European Urbanization 1500–1800* (London, 1984), Table 3.7.

54 Statistisches Reichsamt, *Statistisches Jahrbuch für das Deutsche Reich* (Berlin, 1940), Table 4, p. 16*; Horst Matzerath, *Urbanisierung in Preussen 1815–1914* (Stuttgart, 1985), is the most comprehensive study of urbanization in this period, although restricted to Prussia. See also Adna Ferrin Weber, *The Growth of Cities in the Nineteenth Century: A Study in Statistics* (Ithaca, 1963; 1st edn 1899), and Hans-Dieter Laux, 'The Components of Population Growth in Prussian Cities, 1875–1905, and their Influence on Urban Population Structure', in Richard Lawton and Robert Lee, eds, *Urban Population Development in Western Europe from the Late Eighteenth to the Early Twentieth Century* (Liverpool, 1989), pp. 120–48.

55 Knodel, *Demographic Behavior*, Table 10.2.

56 The sources present information in a way that requires care with definitions. The Total Fertility Rate (TFR) is the number of children born by a woman who in her lifetime experiences the same age-specific fertility rates obtaining at a given time. The Cohort Fertility Rate (CFR) gives the same number for a true cohort. The figures mentioned in the text are the total *marital* fertility rate, which is defined as the TFR but for married women only.

57 Patrick Festy, *La Fécondité des pays occidentaux de 1870 à 1970* (Paris, 1979), Table 2.

58 E. A. Wrigley, *Industrial Growth and Population Change: A Regional Study of the Coalfield Areas of North-west Europe in the Later Nineteenth Century* (Cambridge, 1962).

59 James Woycke, *Birth Control in Germany 1871–1933* (New York, 1988), is a recent history of contraception.

60 Gigi Santow, '*Coitus interruptus* and the Control of Natural Fertility', *Population Studies*, 49 (1985), pp. 19–44.

61 Paul A. David and Warren S. Sanderson, 'Rudimentary Contraceptive Methods and the American Transition to Marital Fertility Control, 1855–1915', in Stanley L. Engerman and Robert E. Gallman, eds, *Long-Term Factors in American Economic Growth* (Chicago, 1986), pp. 307–90, Table 7.8.

62 Richard J. Evans, *The Feminist Movement in Germany 1894–1933* (London, 1976); Paul Weindling, *Health, Race and German Politics between National Unification and Nazism 1870–1945* (Cambridge, 1989), and Peter Jürgen Weingart and Kurt Bayertz, *Rasse, Blut and Gene: Geschichte der Eugenik und Rassenhygiene in Deutschland* (Frankfurt am Main, 1992), provide detailed accounts of the origins and influence of thinking on 'racial hygiene' during this period. Henry P. David, J. Fleischhacker, and Charlotte Höhn, 'Abortion and Eugenics in Nazi Germany', *Population and Development Review*, 14 (1988), pp. 81–112, discuss German policy on abortion.

63 Coale and Treadway, 'Summary'.

64 For example, Timothy W. Guinnane, Barbara S. Okun, and James Trussell, 'What Do We Know about the Timing of Fertility Transitions in Europe?', *Demography*, 31 (1994), pp. 1–20.

65 John C. Brown and Timothy W. Guinnane, 'The Fertility Transition in Bavaria', *Population Studies*, 56 (2002), pp. 35–49; John C. Brown and Timothy G. Guinnane, 'Methodological Problems in the European Fertility Project: A View from Some Decades Later', unpublished working paper, Department of Economics, Yale University (2002); Toni Richards, 'Fertility Decline in Germany: An Econometric Appraisal', *Population Studies*, 31 (1977), pp. 537–53; Patrick R. Galloway, Eugene A. Hammel, and Ronald D. Lee, 'Fertility Decline in Prussia, 1875–1910: A Pooled Cross-Section Time-Series Analysis', *Population Studies*, 48 (1994), pp. 35–158; Knodel, *Decline*.

66 John C. Brown, Timothy W. Guinnane, and Marion Lupprian, 'The Munich *Polizeimeldebögen* as a Source for Quantitative History', *Historical Methods*, 26 (1993), pp. 101–18; Spree, *Health*, Tables 13–17.

67 Festy, *Fécondité*, Table 18.

68 One careful, dispassionate account is Adelheid Castell, 'Die demographischen Konsequenzen des Ersten und Zweiten Weltkriegs für das Deutsche Reich, die Deutsche Demokratische Republik und die Bundesrepublik Deutschland', in Waclaw Długoborkski, ed., *Zweiter Weltkrieg und sozialer Wandel: Achsenmächte und besetzte Länder* (Göttingen, 1981), pp. 117–37.

69 Estimate for the Franco-Prussian war from Hubert, *L'Allemagne*, p. 288. German war deaths from Castell, 'Konsequenzen', p. 117 and Table 2; they include an estimate of the number of German soldiers who never returned from prisoner-of-war camps in the Soviet Union. The Holocaust figure is uncontroversial. See, for example, Hajo Holborn, *A History of Modern Germany: 1840–1945* (Princeton, 1969), p. 810.

70 Marschalck, *Bevölkerungsgeschichte*, Tables 1.6 and 1.7.

71 Hartmut Bickelmann, *Deutsche Überseewanderung in der Weimarer Zeit* (Wiesbaden, 1980), pp. 40–1.

72 Statistisches Bundesamt, *Bevölkerung und Wirtschaft 1872–1972* (Stuttgart, 1972), p. 115; Bickelmann, *Überseewanderung*, Table 15.

73 Bickelmann, *Überseewanderung*, pp. 38–43, for the quotas and other restraints.

74 Richard J. Overy, *The Nazi Economic Recovery 1932–1938*, 2nd edn (Cambridge, 1996).

75 Gerhard Bry, *Wages in Germany 1871–1945* (Princeton, 1960), Table A-4.

76 Statistisches Reichsamt, *Statistisches Jahrbuch für das Deutsche Reich* (Berlin, 1940), pp. 53–4, Tables 12–13.

77 Friedrich Bürgdörfer, *Aufbau und Bewegung der Bevölkerung: ein Führer durch die deutsche Bevölkerungsstatistik und Bevölkerungspolitik* (Leipzig, 1935), p. 188; Friedrich Bürgdörfer, *Bevölkerungsentwicklung im Dritten Reich: Tatsachen und Kritik* (Hamburg, 1937), p. 27.

78 Castell, 'Konsequenzen', Tables 1 and 4.

79 Louis Henry, 'Perturbations de la nuptialité résultant de la guerre 1914–18', *Population*, 21 (1966), pp. 273–332.

80 Dietmar Petzina, Werner Abelshauser, and Anselm Faust, *Sozialgeschichtliches Arbeitsbuch III: Materialien zur Statistik des Deutschen Reiches 1914–1945* (Munich, 1978), Table 5c.

81 Josef Ehmer, *Sozialgeschichte des Alters* (Frankfurt am Main, 1990), Table 8.

82 Dietmar Petzina, Werner Abelshauser, and Anselm Faust, *Sozialgeschichtles Arbeitsbuch III: Materialien zur Statistik des Deutschen Reiches 1914–1945* (Munich, 1978), Table 9a.

83 Age-structures computed from Marschalck, *Bevölkerungsgeschichte*, Table 4.1. For the depression in Germany, see Richard J. Overy, *The Nazi Economic Recovery 1932–1938*, 2nd edn (Cambridge, 1996), Tables II and IV.

84 See Frank B. Tipton, 'The Regional Dimension: Economic Geography, Economic Development, and National Integration in the Nineteenth and Twentieth Centuries', in this volume. Albrecht Ritschl and Mark Spoerer, 'Das Bruttosozialprodukt in Deutschland nach den amtlichen Volkseinkommens- und Sozialproduktsstatistiken 1901–1995', *Jahrbuch für Wirtschaftsgeschichte*, 20 (1997), pp. 27–54, Table A.2, suggest that in 1946, gross domestic product per capita in the West was about 1.25 times the East German level.

85 Hubert, *L'Allemagne*, Table 56.

86 Jürgen Dorbritz, 'Bericht über die demographische Lage in Deutschland', *Zeitschrift für Bevölkerungswissenschaft*, 19 (1993–4), pp. 393–473, Table 7.

87 M. Nabil El-Khorazaty, 'Family Life Cycle and Fertility in Germany before Unification: 1947–1989', *The History of the Family*, 2 (1997), pp. 309–30, Tables 1 and 2. Dorbritz, 'Bericht', pp. 393–473.

88 Dorbritz, 'Bericht', pp. 393–473, Table 7.

89 Hubert, *L'Allemagne*, p. 405.

90 Heilig, Büttner, and Lutz, 'Germany's Population', p. 20.

91 Christoph M. Schmidt and Klaus F. Zimmermann, 'Migration Pressure in Germany: Past and Future', in Klaus F. Zimmermann, ed., *Migration and Economic Development* (New York, 1992), pp. 214–16.

92 Ralf E. Ulrich, 'The Future Growth of Foreign Population in Germany', in G. Steinman and R. E. Ulrich, eds, *The Economic Consequences of Immigration to Germany* (Heidelberg, 1994), Table 2.

93 Schmidt and Zimmermann, 'Migration Pressure', Table 1; Bureau of the Census, United States, *Statistical Abstract of the United States*, 114th edn (Washington, DC, 1994), Table 54.

94 Schmidt and Zimmermann, 'Migration Pressure', Table 3; Christoph M. Schmidt, 'Immigration Countries and Migration Research: the Case of Germany', in G. Steinman and R. E. Ulrich, eds, *The Economic Consequences of Immigration to Germany* (Heidelberg, 1994), pp. 1–19, here p. 17. Foreign women in West Germany also had higher fertility rates than German women, although that difference narrowed considerably. Ulrich, 'Future Growth', Table 4.

95 For example, Jost Halfmann, 'Immigration and Citizenship in Germany: Contemporary Dilemmas', *Political Studies*, 45 (1997), pp. 260–74.

96 Evelyn Grünheid and Reiner Schulz, 'Bericht 1996 über die demographische Lage in Deutschland', *Zeitschrift für Bevölkerungswissenschaft*, 21 (1996), pp. 345–439, Tables 28 and 30.

|3|

Land, peasant and lord in German agriculture since 1800

JONATHAN OSMOND
Cardiff University

3.1 The rural picture

Though long industrialized and eminent in modern commerce, Germany today still represents itself with agricultural images. This is particularly so in prosperous Bavaria, with its white-and-blue maypoles, dirndl dresses, leather shorts and prodigious consumption of beer, meat and offal. But elsewhere too – even in the most urban and industrialized regions – public and private festivals have a bucolic character, popular furniture aspires to the rustic, *Volksmusik* is always to be found on prime-time television, and food and drink are presented as natural products of the landscape and of German traditional practices. This is not just a touristic presentation of the glories of the German countryside and forest, a *rural* idyll; it is also a specifically *agricultural* image, presented in a very positive light.

German environmental discourse is also thorough and heartfelt. For all their ups and downs over the last two decades, the Greens have established themselves as a political force emphasizing environmental protection. Organic ('bio') production and retailing are increasing, especially in the wake of recent domestic and imported food-safety scares. And the cultural resonance of the rural and the agricultural could scarcely be better exemplified than by the reception in the 1980s of Edgar Reitz's epic *Heimat* ('Homeland'), charting the fortunes of a western German village community in the twentieth century, or by the television marathon *Der Wald* ('The Forest'), which occupied an entire evening's viewing with literary, artistic, political and scientific responses to that most evocative German phenomenon and to the threat through acid rain of *Waldsterben* ('the dying of the forest').

Throughout the last two centuries, German high culture has returned again and again to the rural and the agricultural. In the visual arts there runs a line from Caspar David Friedrich's spiritual views of mountains, forests, fields and lonely shepherds, through Wilhelm Leibl's lucid portraits of peasants in church and in the village inn, to Joseph Beuys's idiosyncratic environmentalism and Anselm Kiefer's dark exploration of blasted heaths and deep Teutonic forests. If these are some of the high points, there is also a trite, more populist genre tradition which was elevated by Hitler and the National Socialists into a state-approved image of the land and its people. The German Democratic Republic had its own version of this, with joyful harvesters trundling home together to the cooperative farm. In literature, too, one can find countless examples of light-hearted whimsy, earnest propaganda, and thoughtful depictions of farmers and landscapes through-out the different parts of Germany. For Jakob and Wilhelm Grimm in the early nineteenth century, the collection and retelling of folk tales was a task with a multitude of cultural, social and political meanings. To public acclaim, Theodor Fontane recounted his travels through the landscape of Brandenburg, and explored the social status and psychology of the *Junker* class in his novels. In the twentieth century, Oskar Maria Graf and Erwin Strittmatter turned the 'peasant novel' (*Bauernroman*) into a serious social critique of – respectively – the agricultural depression of the 1930s and the collectivization of agriculture in the German Democratic Republic in the 1950s. Hans Fallada meanwhile provided the definitive account of the peasant uproar in Schleswig-Holstein in the late 1920s and early 1930s, and the windswept shoreline of that northernmost part of Germany could not have been better portrayed than by Siegfried Lenz in *Deutschstunde*.[1] In the musical world, peasant folk song – authentic or contrived – recurs repeatedly from Schubert and Schumann, through Mahler's settings of *Des Knaben Wunderhorn* to Hannes Wader's renditions of 'Plattdeutsche Lieder' and the Breughelesque 'Buuredanz' of the Cologne band de Bläck Fööss in the 1970s.[2]

The reality of German farming today, in the West long preserved by the Common Agricultural Policy of the European Union, is characterized by the new farmhouse standing alongside the abandoned old one, by the silos and offices of the agricultural cooperatives in the villages, by the large farm machinery and the wine-growers' little tractors, and by the expanses of patchwork fields unmarked by hedges. Eastern agriculture, steered for decades before 1990 by communist planning and marked by cooperative organization, specialist concentration, over-manning and environmental neglect, is now making a painful adjustment to European Union norms. There the villages still bear the mark of dilapidation, mixed in with modern buildings GDR-style and now with the features of western capitalism. The landscape, though, looks just as it did when Caspar David Friedrich painted it.

Despite the enduring rural imagery, agriculture as a contributor to the overall German economy dwindled dramatically in the twentieth century, from approximately 30 per cent of National Product in 1900 to 2 per cent in the new Federal Republic (as can be seen in Table 3.1).[3] Similarly, in both

Table 3.1 German agriculture as a percentage of National Product, 1850–1989[a]

	1850	1860	1870	1880	1890	1900	1910	1925	1930	1938
Germany										
agriculture	47	45	40	36	33	30	25	16	18	15
industry[b]	21	23	28	32	37	40	43	49	45	52
other	32	32	32	32	30	30	32	35	37	33

	1950	1960	1970	1980	1989
German Democratic Republic					
agriculture	18	12	13	12	11
industry	52	63	58	62	63
other	30	25	29	26	26
Federal Republic of Germany					
agriculture	10	6	3	2	2
industry	44	47	46	43	40
other	46	47	51	55	58

Notes:
[a] Changes in the definition of National Product and in the categorization of economic activity mean that these are indicative percentages, rather than precise ones.
[b] Includes construction to 1910.
Sources: B. R. Mitchell, *European Historical Statistics 1750–1970* (New York, 1978), p. 428; *Statistisches Jahrbuch der Deutschen Demokratischen Republik* (Berlin, 1990), p. 104; *Kursbuch Deutschland 85/86* (Munich, 1985), p. 192; The Economist Intelligence Unit, *West Germany: Country Profile 1990–91* (London, 1990), p. 16.

western and eastern Germany the agricultural population – which made up the majority of Germans for most of the nineteenth century – declined significantly in the twentieth. In 1950, shortly after the foundation of the two postwar German republics, some 23 per cent of the workforce in the Federal Republic were still engaged in agriculture, with the figure rather higher (some 28 per cent) in the GDR. By 1970 the proportion in the GDR had fallen to just under 13 per cent, a figure below which it dipped only marginally before the end of the state in 1990, but which included many strictly non-agricultural cooperative workers. In the Federal Republic the proportion had declined more dramatically – to under 8 per cent in 1970 – and was to fall further to around 2 per cent in 1989 (as can be seen in Table 3.2). Since unification in 1990 the downward proportional trend in western German agricultural employment has continued, while in the East the proportion of those engaged in agriculture has fallen dramatically to meet it. The overall workforce percentage of farming in Germany is now between 2 and 3 per cent,[4] meaning that rural and small-town regions of Germany are now populated primarily by those who live or have opted to live in the countryside, but derive their income from non-agricultural sources.[5]

Though its numbers are therefore much depleted, the agricultural and food lobby still plays its part within German politics, as it has done on a

Table 3.2 Agricultural employment as percentage of total employment in Germany, 1861–1989

	1861	1871	1880	1890	1900	1913	1925	1930	1938
Germany									
agriculture	52	49	49	43	38	35	32	31	27
industry	26	28	28	33	35	35	38	35	41
other	22	23	23	24	27	30	31	34	33

	1950	1960	1970	1980	1989
German Democratic Republic					
agriculture	28	17	13	11	11
industry	36	42	44	45	44
other	36	41	44	44	45
Federal Republic of Germany					
agriculture	23	14	8	5	2
industry	39	45	47	42	45
other	38	41	46	53	53

Note: Agriculture includes forestry and fishing; industry includes construction but excludes mining.
Sources: A. Sommariva and G. Tullio, *German Macroeconomic History, 1880–1979* (Basingstoke, 1987), p. 27; *Statistisches Jahrbuch der Deutschen Demokratischen Republik* (Berlin, 1984), p. 109; *Statistisches Jahrbuch der Deutschen Demokratischen Republik* (Berlin, 1990), p. 125; The Economist Intelligence Unit, *West Germany: Country Profile 1990–91* (London, 1990), p. 18; G. A. Wilson and O. J. Wilson, *German Agriculture in Transition* (Basingstoke, 2001), p. 34.

grander and sometimes more ominous scale over the last two centuries. Agriculture – as daily reality, as cultural artefact, as national symbol, as economic interest, and as political rhetoric – has been a potent ingredient in the definition of German-speaking central Europe from the Continental System of Napoleon to the European Currency Union.[6]

3.2 Land and people

This survey first charts the principal features of German agriculture during this period. It then focuses on two regional examples in more detail, in order to highlight certain key characteristics and developments of German agrarian society and economy. The two contrasting experiences are, first, rural society in the largely peasant Catholic environment of Bavaria in the early years of the twentieth century and, second, Protestant *Junker* estate regions of central and eastern Germany from the nineteenth century through to forcible collectivization in 1960. Neither treatment claims to be comprehensive, but the bibliographical references indicate where further material may be found on these topics and on many more besides. In view of the huge variety of German landscapes and regional economies, a certain selectivity has been necessary in order to strike a balance between generalization and local colour.[7]

The lands of central Europe which today or in the recent past were inhabited primarily by German speakers are enormously diverse in their terrain and climate. The varieties of agriculture practised upon them have consequently been regionally distinct. Admittedly, there have been instances of significant change over the last two centuries – for instance, the almost complete disappearance of the sheep flocks (as shown in Table 3.3),[8] the introduction or abandonment of particular specialist crops, the application of scientific methods to agriculture, and widespread mechanization and land consolidation in the late twentieth century. However, certain defining features have been more or less constant. Taken together with differing practices of land inheritance and property relations, they allow for some general characterization of German agriculture over the whole period.

A broad swathe of western Germany near or adjoining the river Rhine has long been defined by owner-occupier smallholdings engaged in mixed farming, with an emphasis on small-scale cereal production, dairy, livestock, vegetables and – where the land is suitable towards the south – wine and tobacco. Widespread partible inheritance (*Realteilung*) – codified during French rule in the Rhineland at the beginning of the nineteenth century but customary in many areas before that – created a multiplicity of fragmented small parcels of land, especially in the south-west. Only in the second half of the twentieth century did government-sponsored land consolidation (*Flurbereinigung*) make substantial inroads into this situation. By contrast, the lands of the north German plain east of the river Elbe – with the exception of parts of Silesia – were defined before 1939/1945 by large entailed estates (*Fideikommisse*) and by leased concerns cultivating cereal crops, primarily rye. Mecklenburg was most pronounced as a region of these *Junker* estates, but large areas of Brandenburg, Pomerania, and West and East Prussia also came into this category. During the nineteenth

Table 3.3 Livestock numbers in Germany, 1820–1940[a]

	1820	1830	1840	1850	1860	1873	1890	1900	1915	1920	1930	1940
Millions												
cattle	9.9	10.8	12.8	13.1	13.4	15.8	17.6	18.9	20.3	16.8	18.5	19.7
pigs	3.3	4.0	5.2	5.7	6.0	7.1	12.2	16.8	17.3	15.8	23.4	21.6
sheep	...	...	...	...	28.0	25.0	13.6	9.7	5.1	5.9	3.5	4.9
poultry	...	...	...	...	...	...	...	64.1	65.2	67.8	98.2	96.6

Note: [a] 1820–60 = territory of later German Empire, excluding Alsace-Lorraine; 1873–1915 = German Empire, including Alsace-Lorraine; 1920–40 = current German territory, excluding Austria and other annexed territories.
Source: B. R. Mitchell, *European Historical Statistics 1750–1970* (New York, 1978), p. 152.

century wool, potatoes and sugar beets were important commercial products, particularly where they were favoured by terrain, soil type, or both. The fertile black-earth region of the Magdeburger *Börde*, near Magdeburg on the Elbe, for instance, came to be noted for beet production and processing; the overall development of sugar beet output can be seen in Table 3.4.[9]

After a brief phase of extreme fragmentation under the Communist 'democratic' land reform (*Bodenreform*) of 1945, larger enterprises were gradually re-established in what was now East Germany from the 1950s onwards, this time as collective farms until 1990. Between the two extremes of parcellization in the West and estate-farming in the East were and are the middling farms – largely owner-occupied but also tenanted – characteristic of many regions of central and southern Germany: in Westphalia, Thuringia, Saxony, Bavaria, Schleswig-Holstein, and elsewhere. Inheritance practices have been regionally diverse, but in one form or another *Anerbenrecht* (inheritance by one heir and the portioning-off of co-heirs) and consolidating marriage patterns tended to preserve larger holdings, even if they too were frequently fragmented into numerous separate plots.

Tables 3.5 and 3.6 give an indication of landholding patterns in Bavaria, Prussia, and Germany in the late nineteenth and early twentieth century. Around 80 per cent of agricultural land in Bavaria was occupied by middling holdings of between 5 and 100 hectares, whereas in Prussia over half the land was in holdings over 20 hectares in size, and over one-quarter in holdings over 100 hectares. This was reflected to a slightly lesser degree in the figures for Germany as a whole. It will be noted that dwarf holdings made up nearly two-thirds of all holdings in Prussia, largely reflecting partible inheritance in the Prussian Rhineland, and over one-third in Bavaria, reflecting a similar situation in the Bavarian Rhine Palatinate. In both instances, however, the area of land occupied by these holdings was only between 4 and 6 per cent of the total.

Table 3.4 Arable output in Germany, 1846–1944[a]

	1846	1850	1860	1870	1880	1890	1900	1910	1920	1930	1940	1944
Million tonnes												
wheat	1.4	1.8	2.5	2.4	3.2	3.7	4.3	4.2	2.4	4.3	4.1	3.8
rye	2.9	4.5	6.6	6.2	5.9	6.9	8.6	10.5	5.0	8.4	6.5	7.5
potatoes	7.1	10.9	11.9	20.4	22.8	27.3	40.6	43.5	28.2	50.8	54.8	41.2
sugar beet	0.2	0.6	1.6	2.3	4.7	10.6	16.0	18.2	8.0	14.9	16.5	13.7

Note: [a] 1820–60 = territory of later German Empire, excluding Alsace-Lorraine; 1873–1915 = German Empire, including Alsace-Lorraine; 1920–40 current German territory, excluding Austria and other annexed territories.
Source: B. R. Mitchell, *European Historical Statistics 1750–1970* (New York, 1978), pp. 100, 113.

Table 3.5 Agricultural landholding in Bavaria, 1882–1925[a]

Size of holding	≤2 ba	%	2–5 ba	%	5–20 ba	%	20–100 ba	%	≥100 ba	%	Total
Number of holdings (thousands)											
1882	262	38	165	24	208	31	45	6.6	0.6	0.1	682
1895	237	36	165	25	217	33	44	6.7	0.6	0.1	664
1907	242	36	162	24	225	34	41	6.1	0.5	0.1	670
1925	240	36	172	26	221	33	33	4.9	0.6	0.1	666
Agricultural area (thousand hectares)											
1882	196	4.6	549	13	2071	48	1392	32	97	2.3	4305
1895	178	4.1	553	13	2149	49	1351	31	111	2.6	4342
1907	167	3.9	547	13	2210	52	1221	29	93	2.2	4239
1925	173	4.4	577	15	2125	54	973	25	103	2.6	3952

Note: [a] Territory at census date, including Rhine Palatinate.
Source: Statistisches Jahrbuch für den Freistaat Bayern (Munich, 1926), p. 85.

Table 3.6 Agricultural landholding in Prussia and the Reich, 1907–1925[a]

Size of holding	0.05–2 ba	%	2–5 ba	%	5–20 ba	%	20–100 ba	%	≥100 ba	%	Total
Number of holdings (thousands)											
1907 Prussia	1597	59	457	17	484	18	146	5.4	15	0.5	2700
Reich	2576	56	886	19	931	20	228	4.9	19	0.4	4641
1925 Prussia	1878	63	460	15	516	17	130	4.3	15	0.5	2998
Reich	3027	59	894	18	956	19	200	3.9	19	0.4	5097
Agricultural area (thousand hectares)											
1907 Prussia	871	5.1	1501	9	4770	28	5482	32	4485	26	17,109
Reich	1506	5.5	2917	11	9075	33	8091	30	5584	21	27,173
1925 Prussia	915	5.7	1502	9	4983	31	4568	28	4140	26	16,108
Reich	1588	6.2	2924	11	9158	36	6769	26	5159	20	25,598

Note: [a] Territory of 1925.
Source: Statistisches Jahrbuch für das Deutsche Reich, (Berlin, 1928), pp. 62–3.

Tables 3.7–3.9 take the story into the post-1945 period, showing the predominance of the small to middling family farm in the Federal Republic and the replacement of this by the larger cooperative enterprise in the GDR from the mid-1950s onwards. In both instances the trajectory was towards ever-greater consolidation of agricultural concerns, most marked in the GDR, as shown by the reduction in the number of cooperatives and other socialist enterprises from over 20,000 in 1960 to under 5000 in 1989.

Tables 3.3 and 3.4 display the fortunes of livestock numbers and arable output from the early nineteenth century to the Second World War. Staples such as cereals, potatoes and root crops, plus livestock (increasingly pigs),

Table 3.7 Agricultural landholding in the Federal Republic of Germany, 1949–98

	1949	*1960*	*1970*	*1980*	*1990[a]*	*1998[a]*
Number of holdings (thousands)						
1–10 ha	1262	961	639	407	296	216
10–20 ha	256	287	268	181	129	85
20–50 ha	112	122	157	178	156	118
50–100 ha	13	14	16	27	41	51
≥ 100 ha	3	3	3	4	7	15
Total	1647	1385	1083	797	630	484

Note: [a] Territory of old Federal Republic only.
Source: G. A. Wilson and O. J. Wilson, *German Agriculture in Transition* (Basingstoke, 2001), pp. 26–8.

Table 3.8 Agricultural landholding in the German Democratic Republic, 1950–89

Utilized agricultural area by type and size of holding (%)						
	1950	*1955*	*1960*	*1970*	*1980[a]*	*1989*
Private agriculture						
≤ 5 ha	14.6	14.7	...	...	...	...
5–20 ha	55.3	44.8	...	...	...	...
20–50 ha	20.2	11.9	...	...	...	...
≥ 50 ha	4.2	1.3	...	...	...	...
Total	94.3	72.7	8.1	6.4	5.5	5.4
Socialist agriculture						
mostly ≥ 50 ha, of which:						
cooperatives (LPG)	0.0	18.6	84.2	85.8	80.3	86.6
state farms (VEG) and others	5.7	8.8	7.6	7.8	14.2	7.9
Total	5.7	27.4	91.8	93.6	94.5	94.5

Note: [a] The percentage shift between LPG and VEG/others in 1980 is due largely to a change in definition.
Sources: Jahrbuch der Deutschen Demokratischen Republik (Berlin, 1956), pp. 198–9; *Statistisches Jahrbuch der Deutschen Demokratischen Republik* (Berlin, 1990), pp. 211–12.

Table 3.9 Socialist agriculture in the German Democratic Republic, 1960–89

	1960	*1970*	*1980*	*1989*
Cooperatives (LPG)				
total number	19,313	9,009	3,946	3,844
of which:				
arable	...	...	1,047	1,162
livestock	...	...	2,899	2,682
total membership	901,490	915,119	757,462	866,676
of which:				
full-time workers	857,630	734,148	530,921	612,079
(%)	95	80	70	71
of which:				
in arable	...	...	236,641	293,433
in livestock	...	...	294,280	318,646
State farms (VEG)				
total number	669	511	469	464
Other socialist concerns				
total number	298	412	647	422

Source: Statistisches Jahrbuch der Deutschen Demokratischen Republik (Berlin, 1990), pp. 212–13.

have been crucial to small and larger cultivators alike, but there has also necessarily been local specialization dependent on soil type, land contours, water supply, and other factors. South-eastern Bavaria has specialized in wheat and locally in hops, and Schleswig-Holstein in the north and Alpine Swabia in the south were and are known for their livestock and dairy production. Finally and not to be neglected are the substantial afforested stretches of Germany used for timber, hunting, and now for tourism and recreation.

Technical and scientific advances in the nineteenth and twentieth centuries led to generally rising productivity over the period. It was set back from time to time by, for instance, potato blight in the 1840s or warfare in the twentieth century, and restricted by land reform and collectivization in the Soviet Zone and the GDR. Nonetheless, changes in crop rotation, application of animal and later artificial fertilizer, non-motorized and much later motorized mechanization, irrigation programmes, and experimentation with livestock breeding all contributed, as elsewhere in Europe, to improved yields (as shown for the twentieth century in Table 3.11).[10]

Settlement patterns reflect all the other variables, from single farmsteads (*Einzelhöfe*) in non-industrialized middling-farm areas throughout central and western Germany, through large manor houses with attached estate villages in the east, to networks of well-populated worker-peasant villages in the west. In the course of the later nineteenth century and more especially in the twentieth, the population mix in German villages and rural small towns has shifted considerably away from agricultural employment toward patterns of commuting and urban incomers. Partly for this reason, rural depopulation has been kept within bounds, although it preoccupied German agrarian ideologues from time to time.[11] Another factor in the mid-twentieth century was the influx of refugees from lands in the East lost to the re-established Polish and Czechoslovak states. Not only did the Soviet Zone of Occupation (1945–49) have to accommodate large numbers of refugees in rural areas, but the south-eastern and northern border regions of what was to become the Federal Republic had to absorb incoming populations from East Prussia, Pomerania, Silesia, and the Sudetenland, and then from the Soviet Zone/GDR itself.

Population movements in the nineteenth and twentieth centuries – primarily from east to west (as discussed in Chapter 2) – have had some impact upon the local confessional mix of rural communities, but broad distinctions since the Reformation and the Thirty Years War have prevailed to this day. Southern Bavaria, large stretches of western and south-western Germany, much of Silesia and part of East Prussia were predominantly Catholic, while in most of north and central Germany variants of Protestant observance were in the ascendant. Nonetheless, confessionally mixed villages were not uncommon in parts of central and western Germany, and neighbouring Catholic and Protestant communities were a familiar experience. The Jewish community in rural areas was very small, though it was more significant in market towns. Apart from German peasants, whose local dialects were and are mutually incomprehensible at any distance, Poles, Sorbs, Danes and the population of Alsace and Lorraine (incorporated into the Reich from 1871 to 1918) were significant in their regional populations as peasants and farm labourers.

There is a plethora of antiquarian and travel writing, and also more recent scholarly literature on the customs, festivals, and costumes of the regions of Germany.[12] In general, local distinctiveness in these matters has steadily declined since the later nineteenth century. As an English visitor of German parentage, Cecily Sidgwick, noted in 1908,

> In some parts of the Black Forest every valley has its own costume, so that you know where a man lives by the clothes he wears. There is one valley where all the girls are pretty, and on festive occasions or for church they wear charming transparent black caps with wings to them. There is another valley where the men are big-boned and blackavised, with square shaven chins and spare bodies, rather like our English legal type; and they go to church in scarlet breeches, long black velvet coats, and black three-cornered hats. Their women-folk wear gay-coloured skirts and mushroom hats loaded with heavy poms-poms (sic). In Cassel there are most curious costumes to be seen still on high days and holidays; from Berlin, people go to the Spreewald to see the Wendish peasants,[13] and in Bavaria there is still

some colour and variety of costume. But everywhere you hear that these costumes are dying out.[14]

This message was indeed a recurrent one, but many practices have been remarkably resilient. The use of local costume (*Tracht*) was promoted by the National Socialists at their official peasant festivals (*Bauerntage*) in Goslar in the Harz mountains and elsewhere, though they attempted to suppress other features of peasant independence such as the shooting clubs (*Schützenzvereine*), which were then revived in the Federal Republic.[15] *Tracht*, though not necessarily locally handmade, has also undergone periods of revival. It represents not only affiliation to the *Heimat*, but also – in that it is much more expensive than 'town clothes' – social status and special occasions.[16] It is still popular in Bavaria and in the Sorbian Lausitz, but derivative versions are to be seen through most of Germany, and not only in the countryside.

3.3 Economy and politics

The fortunes of nineteenth- and twentieth-century German agriculture were defined both by secular economic trends and by particular state intervention and political lobbying. Intrusive events such as the Napoleonic invasion, revolution in 1848–49, the wars of unification in the nineteenth century, two world wars in the twentieth, the Third Reich, and communist collectivization all played their part in defining agricultural prosperity or otherwise. As important in terms of generating social and economic change were legislation affecting the relationship between *Junker* and peasant, industrialization and emigration in the nineteenth century, and even more crucially in the second half of the twentieth century, agricultural mechanization, the motor car, television, and European subsidies.

The early nineteenth century witnessed the so-called *Bauernbefreiung* (peasant emancipation) or alternatively *Bauernlegen* (expropriation of the peasants) of the reform period in Prussia and elsewhere, and the secularization of much of the lands – particularly monastic properties – of the Catholic Church in states such as Bavaria.[17] Both these processes had considerable impact upon landownership patterns, generally shifting the rural balance of power toward the larger landowners, who were in a position to exact redemption payments and labour service from the nominally liberated peasants. The apparent abolition of serfdom in Prussia, announced in 1807 and effective from 1810, led to new forms of social dependence.

There has long been historical debate about the extent to which this period was the driving force not only behind the commercialization of large-scale agriculture, but also – because of the 'freeing' of surplus population from the land – behind German urban growth and industrialization. Both eastern and western historians have seen this period as leading to the capitalization of German agriculture, but have also been careful to point out that increased market orientation on the part of peasants and larger landowners was already in train in the late eighteenth century. Experts such as Harnisch and Hagen also see social and economic stress between peasants and *Junker* and the danger of peasant unrest as being important factors driving the Prussian reformers in the early nineteenth century.[18]

The scale of the alteration in landownership was enormous. It has been estimated that in the eastern provinces of Prussia some 30,000–40,000 peasant farmsteads and some 70,000–80,000 smaller parcels of land were lost, either by incorporation into the larger properties or by being abandoned altogether.[19] The gross loss in Prussia, according to Dipper, was in the years 1816–59 in the region of 1.33 million hectares, although the net loss was considerably less, at 0.7 million hectares.[20] The market in land was intensified by the effect of the reforms, leading not only to the displacement of the peasantry, but also to a crisis of indebtedness for many noble landowners. Henning estimates that between the 1820s and the 1870s over two-thirds of *Rittergüter* (knights' estates) changed hands, and that by 1880 nearly two-thirds of *Rittergut*-owners in eastern Germany were of bourgeois origin.[21]

The social effects of these dislocations were in certain regions and at certain times quite calamitous, with widespread rural pauperism and social unrest, exacerbated by the harvest failures of the 1840s. Increasingly, internal westward migration and then emigration to North America were the result of rural population growth and economic hardship (as discussed in Chapter 2). On the other hand, once the disastrous agricultural prices of the 1820s began to recover, there were increasing market opportunities for German farmers, particularly the larger landowners. They diversified into sugar refineries, breweries and other commercial ventures, benefited in internal trade and in export opportunities from a gradual upward trend in grain and other prices, and began to increase yields by applying the technological and scientific techniques propounded by Albrecht Thaer (1752–1828), Johann Heinrich von Thünen (1783–1850), and Justus von Liebig (1803–73) (as discussed in Chapter 10). Smaller farmers also began to participate in the cooperative financial and wholesale organizations promoted by Friedrich Wilhelm Raiffeisen (1818–88), after whom the later cooperative movement came to be named.[22]

The period from the foundation of the German Empire in 1871 to the outbreak of the First World War saw intense political debate about the role of agriculture in a rapidly industrializing society, over such matters as tariff protection against European and American competition, increased rural emigration, and the organization of the agrarian interest as a political lobby. The protective tariff introduced by Bismarck in 1879 was meant to satisfy both the *Junker* interest and that of the industrial magnates. It erected a barrier against Russian and North American grain imports, but was not necessarily to the disadvantage of smaller livestock and root-crop producers.[23] Output figures for Germany as a whole show a doubling of the number of pigs between 1860 and 1890, and a 30 per cent increase in the number of cattle (see Table 3.3). Meanwhile, potato production increased by some 130 per cent and sugar beet production by 560 per cent. The growth in wheat and rye production was much more modest, as can be seen in Table 3.4.

The organizational structures of German agriculture developed apace in the late nineteenth century. Officially politically neutral Agricultural Associations were founded to promote good farming practice, through agricultural shows, experimental programmes for crops and livestock breeding, and winter schools for farmers. Alongside these 'technical' bodies came the growth of campaigning pressure groups. The push came partly from popular rural discontent from below and partly from the organizational forays of the larger landowners from the early 1890s. The *Bund der Landwirte* (Agrarian League), founded in 1893 in protest against Chancellor Caprivi's moderately anti-protectionist trade treaties, came to exert significant – and some would say pernicious – influence within German conservatism and National Liberalism.[24] In fact, as can be seen in Table 3.10, German agricultural imports declined from 1890 to 1910 as a percentage of total German imports, but there was an even more significant decline in agricultural exports as a proportion of the total. For both larger and smaller farmers in Germany these years saw mounting indebtedness,

Table 3.10 German agricultural foreign trade, 1880–1989

Imports and exports of agricultural products and food
(as percentages of total imports and total exports of goods)

	1880	1890	1900	1910	1925	1930	1938
Germany							
imports	33.0	33.7	30.6	27.8	42.3	40.7	39.6
exports	22.4	14.2	11.2	10.2	7.2	5.5	1.2
	1950	1960	1970	1979	1985	1989	
German Democratic Republic[a]							
imports	...	...	...	...	12.2	11.0	
exports	...	...	...	...	6.5	6.8	
Federal Republic of Germany[a]							
imports	44.1	26.6	19.4	13.9	13.8	12.0	
exports	2.3	2.3	3.5	5.0	5.6	5.3	

Note: [a] Agricultural products, food, drink, and tobacco.
Sources: A. Sommariva and G. Tullio, *German Macroeconomic History, 1880–1979* (Basingstoke, 1987), pp. 49–50; *Statistisches Jahrbuch der Deutschen Demokratischen Republik* (Berlin, 1990), p. 279; The Economist Intelligence Unit, *West Germany: Country Profile 1988–89* (London, 1988), p. 33; *West Germany: Country Profile 1990–91* (London, 1990), p. 32–3.

and a failure to match improvements in productivity and marketability else-where, not just in the world overseas, but also nearer to home, in the Low Countries and Scandinavia.

The turbulent phase from 1914 to 1945 was marked by a series of major crises for all sectors of the German economy, during which the fortunes of agriculture shifted rapidly. The war years and the postwar inflation placed enormous pressure upon agricultural production and costs, and revealed many weaknesses in the productive practices of both large-scale and peasant agriculture. Undoubtedly, the inevitable loss of workers and inadequate supplies of fodder, fertilizer and fuel made life very difficult for German farmers in the First World War, but a combination of misguided official policy and farmer obduracy created severe food shortages. The positive side was that inflation eventually eradicated almost all of the debt which had been accrued by both small and large concerns.[25] In political terms, German farmers responded in generally hostile fashion to the democracy of the Weimar Republic, while organizing even more than before to plead for state assistance. Meanwhile they had lost the competitive edge against nearby high-quality production in Denmark and the Netherlands, and the further opening up of global markets.

The economic stresses of the First World War also led to more insti-tutionalized agricultural decision-making. Whereas previously the largely non-governmental agrarian bodies had sponsored technical agricultural improvements such as artificial fertilizers, stock breeding and machinery, *Reich* and *Land* authorities were now established with wide responsibility for determining production, setting prices and requisitioning produce, above all the War Food Office (*Kriegsernährungsamt*) (as discussed in Chapter 8). These powers continued after the First World War in new agricultural ministries and other authorities at national and *Land* level, the Reich Ministry for Food and Agriculture being founded in 1920. What *Junker* and peasant farmers resented as the 'controlled' or 'forced' economy (*Zwangswirtschaft*) of agriculture provoked them into direct protest against governments which they accused of socialism.[26]

The next crisis, beginning before the onset of the world economic crisis in the interwar period but severely exacerbated by it, was of renewed and severe agricultural indebtedness and falling prices. These difficulties led to widespread farm foreclosures, bankruptcy or near bankruptcy of some of the larger estates despite the notorious *Osthilfe* (Eastern Aid) extended to them, a radicalization of agricultural politics, and a susceptibility to the appeal of the National Socialists. The latter's ideological stress on farmers as the source of racial purity was swiftly expressed in the foundation under Richard Walther Darré of the *Reichsnährstand* (Reich Food Estate), in the protection of farms against forced sales and fragmentation through the *Erbhofgesetz* (Hereditary Farm Law) of 1933, and in guarantees of higher prices. However, the new rules placed limitations on farmers' decision-making in the market, and the *Erzeugungsschlacht* (Battle for Production) and the Four Year Plan revived farmers' complaints about coercion. In any case, Darré's rhetoric about the peasantry was belied by an accelerated rural exodus during the 1930s, as the industrial economy recovered. Autarkic pretensions and the Second World War once more placed German agriculture under enormous pressure to increase production, alleviated only by the fact that the territories of occupied Europe were also compelled to furnish food for the German population.[27]

For both the Soviet and the western occupying powers after 1945, food production and distribution were huge tasks.[28] Most major urban centres and some rural areas such as Brandenburg had suffered extreme damage and disruption of transport, and the population was swelled by millions of people – mainly women and children – fleeing from the East. The policies introduced in the years leading up to the founding of the two separate German states in 1949 were ideological as well as pragmatic, however, and were to determine two very different paths of development for the next 40 years. In the eastern part of Germany the economic, social and political power of the *Junker* land-owning class was destroyed not only in those territories ceded to Poland and the Soviet Union but also in the Soviet Occupation Zone of Germany (as discussed in Chapter 9). The land reform of 1945 expropriated all larger holdings (those over 100 hectares in size) and carved them up amongst farmers, farm workers and refugees from the East. During the 1950s a stop-go programme of collectivization was instigated, which from the then forcible 'collectivization spring' of 1960 until German unification in 1990 defined East German agriculture as large-scale, 'industrial' and non-individualist. Neighbouring agricultural production cooperatives (*Landwirtschaftliche Produktionsgenossenschaften*, or LPG) were amalgamated, and during the 1970s an agriculturally disastrous policy of separating livestock and arable production was introduced, with severe distortions of supply and demand, and catastrophic environmental damage.

In the three western zones and the Federal Republic which derived from them, by contrast, private property was left largely unchallenged and indeed was supported economically and ideologically by state and eventually by European subsidies. From the mid-1950s, mechanization of agriculture really took hold, even more so than in the GDR, and this led to major changes in the nature and productivity of farming. Programmes of land consolidation led to greater efficiency and productivity, but also to a depletion of the agricultural population. This was encouraged, too, by improvements in rural roads and by growing opportunities for urban employment.[29] Within a supportive European agricultural policy, the quality and marketability of West German agricultural produce thrived, and comfortably outpaced GDR yields (as can be seen in Table 3.11). Despite the growing availability and attraction of foreign delicacies, supermarket demand for domestic produce remained buoyant. Rural facilities and agricultural prices were subsided with largesse, not so much now as an inoculation against fascism as by way of deliberate Cold War contra-

Table 3.11 Arable yields in Germany, 1903–90

Yields of selected crops (tonnes per hectare)

	av. 1903–12	1938[a]	1950	1970	1990[b]
Wheat					
Prussia	2.16	...	...	...	...
Bavaria	1.61	...	...	...	...
Germany	2.03	...	...	...	...
GDR	...	2.46	2.54	3.56	4.48
FRG	...	2.23	2.58	3.79	6.58
Potatoes					
Prussia	13.74	...	...	...	...
Bavaria	11.61	...	...	...	...
Germany	13.24	...	...	...	...
GDR	...	17.30	18.12	19.57	21.25
FRG	...	16.82	24.49	27.23	39.25
Sugar beet					
GDR	...	29.10	27.31	32.01	28.65
FRG	...	32.72	36.16	44.01	54.83

Notes: [a] Future territory of GDR and FRG.
[b] 1989 in GDR, 1993 in FRG (old territory).
Sources: Statistisches Jahrbuch für das Deutsche Reich (Berlin, 1914), p. 44; *Jahrbuch der Deutschen Demokratischen Republik* (Berlin, 1956), pp. 200–1; *Statistisches Jahrbuch der Deutschen Demokratischen Republik* (Berlin, 1990), pp. 228–9, 239. G. A. Wilson and O. J. Wilson, *German Agriculture in Transition* (Basingstoke, 2001), p. 182.

distinction between the fostering of private enterprise in the West and collectivization in the East. The independent farmer was now in economic and social rather than in racial terms an epitome of the (West) German state.

German unification in October 1990 exposed East German agriculture to major crisis. Previous over-manning led swiftly to severe problems of rural unemployment, challenges to the property status of the cooperative farms caused personal and social embitterment and economic uncertainty, and exposure to western competition led – initially, at least – to a dramatic downturn in demand for local produce. This has since been reversed, but at the cost of West German appropriation of much of the agricultural and food and drink business in the East. West German agriculture, meanwhile, is not immune to the challenges posed by an increasing surplus of agricultural imports over exports (as shown in Table 3.12). Additional challenges are posed by as yet unfulfilled proposals for reform of the Common Agricultural Policy and by the prospect of Poland, Hungary and others joining the European Union, and bringing a new and potentially expensive agricultural dimension to the common economy.

Table 3.12 Agricultural foreign trade of the Federal Republic of Germany, 1967–97

Billion DM, *not inflation-adjusted*	1967	1977	1988	1997[a]
Agricultural imports	16.9	38.5	52.2	74.8
of which: European Union	7.1	14.6	34.0	47.9
Agricultural exports	2.2	12.7	26.7	43.9
of which: European Union	1.2	8.6	19.3	30.5
Balance	–14.7	–25.8	–25.5	–30.9
of which: European Union	–5.9	–6.0	–14.7	–17.4

Note: [a] 1997 = enlarged Federal Republic.
Source: G. A. Wilson and O. J. Wilson, *German Agriculture in Transition* (Basingstoke, 2001), pp. 154–6.

3.4 Peasants in Bavaria

The old Bavarian folk song, *Das Bauerndorf* ('The Peasant Village'), has in one late-twentieth-century rendition 16 verses, each listing answers to the initial choral refrain: 'What do we need in the peasant village? What do we need in the village?' The first requirement, it seems, is 'A church big and fine, a pastor (or two) who means well to folk and practises what he preaches'. There follow desiderata less pious, but bursting with the realities and the pleasures of daily rural life, among them: a bell that rings clear; a school-master who can read, write and count; a harp and bagpipes; good tobacco and snuff; a watchman who calls out the hours; a smith who shoes well; a midwife who tells no tales; a brave fire brigade; a peasant who doesn't beat his wife (and a wife who doesn't nag her husband); a maid fit for work who doesn't gaze in the mirror for six hours at a time; a baker who doesn't make the bread rolls too small; a brewer who makes sure the beer isn't watery; a cock crowing on every dung heap; a big stream to drive the mill wheel; a dance floor that doesn't creak; lamps at night; enough straw and hay, cows and pigs; and, finally, the houses full of hordes of children. 'That's what we need in the village!'[30]

It is against this aspirational view of the perfect village that we now explore the interaction of work, society, gender relations, religion and politics in rural Bavaria in the years before and immediately after the First World War. The kingdom of Bavaria, independent until 1871, was – after Prussia – the second largest German state in the empire. In the early years of the twentieth century it was still a largely agricultural economy, notwithstanding the fact that the first German railway line had been built in Protestant northern Bavaria, between Nuremberg and Fürth in 1835, and that Munich, Augsburg, and Nuremberg were developing as industrial, commercial, and administrative centres.

Needless to say, the realities of village life failed in many – but perhaps not all – respects to live up to the dream in our song. For the small peasant farmer, his family and his workers, home life, work and production were highly integrated, so a description of life on the farm itself must also include rural people's contacts with the outside world. Three topics will be highlighted here: the division of labour and living conditions on the farm, with particular reference to rural women (whose situation is also discussed in Chapter 11); the relations between the productive process of the farm and the cooperatives, markets, traders and farming organizations; and the attitudes of rural communities to the outside world, particularly to the town and city.[31]

Rural Bavaria in the early twentieth century was overwhelmingly a land of independent small farms, as can be seen from Table 3.5. Some 95 per cent of the agricultural land was farmed in small to medium-sized units by owner-occupiers, and most of the remainder by tenant farmers of the larger estates. Such estates played a very limited role in the agricultural economy of Bavaria, and even their farm-buildings were said to be less imposing than in other parts of the Reich – only two or three times the size of a large peasant farm-house. Peasant farms between 5 and 50 hectares in size predominated, making up 77 per cent of the agricultural land in 1907, although in the Rhine Palatinate and Franconia there was a strong sector of small peasant farmers, and throughout the countryside, particularly in the Palatinate and in Lower Franconia, there was a large population of small-holders, who usually had another occupation besides agriculture and whose produce was principally for their own consumption.

In Bavaria in 1907 the working population in agriculture and forestry made up 46 per cent of the kingdom's total working population, which was markedly above the figure for the empire as a whole (shown in Table 3.2).[32] Four-fifths of the total agricultural population comprised farmers and their families, while one-fifth were farm-labourers. Of the labourer population, 60 per cent were farm-hands and maids who lived on the employer's farm and were employed all year round, while 40 per cent were seasonally employed wage-labourers. Women predominated in agriculture as a whole and especially in the family-labour sector, but amongst the farm workers men had a slight majority.

As one would expect, the larger the farm the greater the percentage of the work which was performed by non-family labour, but the ratio of farm hands and maids to wage-labourers varied considerably. On medium- and large-sized peasant farms, live-in farmhands and maids were most important; on both the smallholdings and the larger estates, however, wage-labour predominated. The smallholders, of course, could not afford to pay workers for the whole year – and indeed there was not enough work to warrant this – but they would employ them for the harvest, especially of vines, hops, fruit and vegetables. Extra labour might also be used on smaller farms while the wife was having to tend a large number of small children and could only undertake work in the house.

In general, the smaller the farm, the higher the degree of female involvement, both of family and of paid labour. On the smaller holdings, women were not only numerically more important, but were also entrusted with more of the responsibility. Thus many husbands would be engaged in a trade or employed in a nearby urban industry while their wives managed the farm. In addition, there were widows who ran smallholdings by themselves, and their number was, of course, increased substantially by the First World War.[33]

Small farms depended to a considerable degree on their livestock; indeed the prestige attached by southern Bavarian farmers to the number of beasts owned was said to have led to overstocking – and the tending of animals was, apart from management of the household, the most important aspect of women's work on the farm. Only in southern Swabia, where dairy production was the overriding concern of the farmer, did he take over this role from the women. In general, the farmer's wife was responsible; since she was expected to look after the household and to provide meals for family and workers, she could not stray too far from the farmhouse, but she could supervise cattle and poultry in or near the farmyard itself.

Otherwise, the division of labour was flexible. Certain tasks might be regarded as the preserve of the women, but this did not preclude women from undertaking others when necessary. Hay mowing and loading, muck spreading and threshing – a particularly unpleasant and unpopular job – were all done by women and girls. Only the carrying of heavy loads, tree-felling, grain-harvesting, and ploughing were reserved for the men, and then not without exception, especially during the war when male labour was scarce. The importance of ploughing was such that if it could not be done by the men, the farmer's wife rather than the labourers took over. In general, the wage-labourers worked in the fields and the farm-maids in the animal sheds. Milking and the maintenance of the sheds were not always popular, however, despite the prestige, and there were complaints about the dirt and the smell. Farm-maids felt that it was difficult to keep themselves presentable and attractive, with or without a mirror to hand.

Everyone worked long hours in summer, but in winter some of the time allotted for work in fact only required being prepared for work when it arose. Of the women, the farmer's wife herself worked the longest hours – between 8 and 12 hours in winter and between 13 and 16-and-a-half hours in summer; the maids worked about 11 hours in winter and 13 hours in summer; the labourers about 8-and-a-half hours in winter and 10-and-a-half hours in summer. The labourers were not responsible for the farmhouse as the wife and the maids were, but they had their own homes to keep, which added considerably to their workload.

Sunday was the day for most free time, although the farmer's wife did sometimes have to take on tasks normally left to the maids on weekdays. All the family and the workers were expected to attend church once, but if there were only one service, there might have to be a weekly alternation of those able to go. Before the First World War at least the children of the house and workers under 18 years of age were obliged to attend religious instruction.

Sunday afternoon was free, and it was apparently difficult to get the maids to return to the farm in the early evening to feed the animals. They generally went walking or visiting in the village or further afield. Bicycles were a popular purchase with the first money saved from wages.

Rosa Kempf, who collected much of this valuable information, bemoaned the lack of intellectual stimulation available to women.[34] She reported cases of country girls of lively mind who used to copy out all the written material which they could find and learn it by heart, in an attempt to satisfy their urge to learn. By the time they reached later life, frustration had put an end even to such enterprise. Men had perhaps more scope, and there were many newspapers produced for farmers. Even so, books and papers were only read regularly in winter. Wilhelm Mattes, in his study of the Peasants' Councils in Bavaria, attributed the farmers' lack of political understanding in part to this. When in the autumn interest revived in farming politics and in outside affairs as a whole, there had been no continuity of information.[35]

Wages for farm workers were in general based on an hourly rate and supplemented, especially for those living in, by payments in kind. The rates underwent a gradual improvement from the beginning of the century, but by the 1920s did not compare favourably with those in industry. The revolution of 1918–19 had established the legality of farm workers' unions, but the absence of a tradition of collective wage-bargaining and the fact that the farm workers were dispersed amongst the small farms and lived in close contact with their employers meant that there was very little collective action. In addition, many farm workers came from agricultural back-grounds and either owned a smallholding of their own or hoped to do so at a later date. It was therefore easy for the farmers' organizations to claim that all those involved with the land shared a common cause and common interests. In fact, many seasonal labourers lived a meagre existence and suffered particularly in winter. Farm-maids and farmers' daughters, on the other hand, could in some instances amass savings. They might hope, too, to marry well and have a farm of their own; female labourers were generally older women, already married.

The Bavarian farmer's wife had a certain degree of financial responsibility, if not exactly independence. She was usually joint owner of the farm and had control over the selling of certain produce – eggs, poultry, and dairy foods in particular – and the purchase of household necessities and personal goods. Rosa Kempf was especially worried that the growing importance of cooperatives, run by and for male farmers alone, would eliminate this element of responsibility and leave the woman as nothing but a housewife, receiving an allowance from her husband. There were already signs of this in Swabia, where dairy cooperatives were flourishing, and the danger was that poultry farming would go the same way.

Before the First World War and during the Great Inflation many wealthier farmers built new dwellings or extended existing property, particularly with the addition of a second storey. By the end of the decade, however, deterioration of farming premises was widespread, as farmers experienced increasing indebtedness and could find no money to effect repairs. A grim *Bauernroman* by Oskar Maria Graf tells of a young Bavarian farmer's son who, before taking over the farm from his ageing mother in the agricultural depression, burns down the house in order to be able to build a new one with the insurance money. He cannot understand why he is not allowed to inherit when he eventually emerges from jail.[36] Graf's story implies that the act was one of desperation, but earlier in the century such occurrences were already known, or at least rumoured, even to visitors from abroad, like Mrs Sidgwick:

> [The German peasant] is a hard-working man, God-fearing on the whole, stupid and stolid often, narrowly shrewd often, having his eye on the main chance. When he is stupid but not God-fearing he dresses himself and his wife in their best clothes, puts his insurance papers in his pockets, sets his thatched house on fire, and goes for a walk. Then he is surprised that he is caught and punished. Fires are frequent in German villages, and in a high wind and where the roofs are of straw destruction is complete sometimes. You often come across the blackened remains of houses . . .[37]

Food on the larger farms in southern Bavaria was generally of good quality, for both family and workers, both groups usually eating together. In Franconia there was a custom whereby labourers brought their own food to eat, but further south, meals were provided by the farmer's wife in order to save the time which the labourers would take going back to their own homes to eat. A questionnaire administered to farm workers in southern Bavaria revealed that most of those asked had meat at least once a week, and many more often than that. A menu given as 'typical', but which is perhaps exemplary, read: first breakfast, soup; second breakfast, beer or milk and bread; midday, pork, dumpling and cabbage; late afternoon, beer and bread; and supper, soup and potatoes. There were many regional variations: except in the Palatinate and in Lower Franconia little interest was shown in either growing or eating vegetables; the diet in Lower Bavaria was a fatty one; in Swabia cheese figured prominently; and in Lower Franconia cooked sausage was more popular than in the rest of Bavaria. Although milk was an important product for many Bavarian farms, it was not greatly popular as a drink, and only replaced beer when the price of the latter was put up and angry farmers and farm workers launched an informal beer strike. Regular social drinking was not widespread in the remoter regions of southern Bavaria, but was more so further north. The Rhine Palatinate and Lower Franconia were, of course, wine regions.

The market-place was an important social centre for the farmer, and to a lesser extent for his family and farm workers. There the farmer did much of his business, learnt the latest news, and had contact with other trades, economic methods and social viewpoints. There he was exposed to political parties and farmers' pressure groups; they would organize meetings on market day in order to gain a large captive audience. One of the most important elements of every market was livestock trading, as it made up half the turnover of even the larger grain estates of Lower and Upper Bavaria. Milk was the second most important product in terms of turnover, but it was generally sold direct to a local dairy or to a cooperative, or was used on the farm. Some areas suffered from poor communications, while others – further away from an industrial centre requiring milk – benefited from convenient railways. On the whole, Bavarian farmers enjoyed relatively good market conditions, for although there were few large cities, the spread of population was sufficient to allow local disposal of goods. In the Palatinate, which had previously had access to many large centres of population, the border alterations after the First World War caused severe market problems.

The growth of the cooperative movement – that is both credit and commodity cooperatives – had continued apace since the last quarter of the previous century, and was particularly highly developed in the Palatinate, where in 1927 there were 441 organizations with a total of 54,000 members. Even there, however, traders played a still important role, and the larger farms, which did not have to group together in order to accumulate marketable quantities of uniform produce, found that they could get better prices from the traders than from the cooperatives. The trade was frequently in Jewish hands, and farmers in Zweibrücken referred, for instance, to the 'flour-Jew', the 'oil-Jew', and the 'butter-Jew'.[38] Most of all, however, Jews were involved in the cattle trade. The extension of the cooperative system was accelerated by inflation after the war, as farmers attempted to minimize their losses on paper money by cutting out the traders and dealing directly with the consumer organizations. This was a hazardous development, as the inflation and the stabilization both caused havoc with the funds of the cooperatives. In Bavaria numerous organizations collapsed, including those of three of the main farmers' unions, and had to be bailed out by the Reich authorities.

Various peasant associations operated in Bavaria before 1914 and they expanded during the 1920s.[39] Some – notably the anticlerical populist Bavarian Peasants' League (*Bayerischer Bauernbund*) – were overtly political. Others – like the powerful Bavarian Christian Peasants' Union (*Bayerischer Christlicher Bauernverein*) – lent their support to a political party, originally the Centre Party and then the Bavarian People's Party (BVP), but did not stand as a party in their own right.[40] Without exception, however, all the unions attempted to educate the peasantry in economic matters, to represent farming interests to the government, and to promote a unity of purpose amongst the agricultural population. At the local level, meetings would be held in one village and the inhabitants of surrounding villages invited to attend. Large farmers' days (*Bauerntage*) would be arranged, to which the whole family would come and participate in lectures, exhibitions, competitions and general social festivity. Advice centres on taxes, book-keeping, and other economic problems would be set up, and as times grew critical, direct action in the form of demonstrations or delivery strikes would be instigated.

Local leadership was particularly important, and reports of pockets of radical activity are nearly always associated with the presence of an effective local agitator. Some peasant leaders (*Bauernführer*) achieved wider fame or notoriety – Georg Heim, Karl Gandorfer and Franz Josef Heinz, for instance – but the power of most was exercised on the local level: the control of a leader in his home town or village could often swing the balance between two rival unions in a particular locality. Gandorfer, the leader of the radical wing of the Bavarian Peasants' League, for instance, held great sway in the grain-growing region of Mallersdorf-Pfaffenberg. He was mayor of the town, owned a large farm with an imposing farmhouse next to the church, and was also in possession of the nearby brickworks. His confidence was such that in 1926 he deliberately staged a protest against the tax system by withholding all payments and allowing the authorities to come to confiscate and forcibly auction off some of his livestock. Local traders from as far away as the next market town were intimidated by his threat of a general boycott of their businesses if they took part in the auction, so the authorities were forced, through want of bidders, to escort the animals to the railway station and take them off to sell elsewhere.

Local government reports on Bavarian rural communities complained repeatedly, especially in the years immediately following the First World War, that country people showed a disgraceful lack of concern for matters outside their own immediate environment. The Versailles Treaty passed with little comment, as did Reich elections, the Ruhr crisis, the Dawes Plan, and so on. The people only seemed interested in getting back to their old way of life, and generally enjoying themselves. In 1919 the authorities complained of lavish country weddings, dancing and music, popular theatre, fairs, races, and the smoking of expensive cigars. In 1926 it was official policy to discourage over-indulgence in the pre-Lenten *Fasching* (Carnival) celebrations.

Even if one does not share the puritanical and nationalist view of such reports, it would appear that there was rural insensitivity to the very real crises within German society. Little understanding was shown for the urban housing shortage or unemployment. The answer to the latter was that the 'loafers' in the towns should come to the land where there was plenty of work to be done. In actuality, however, farmers were unprepared to offer adequate wages, and preferred to offload the extra work onto their own womenfolk. Since at the time there were only three men officially un-employed in the Straubing area, it is perhaps understandable why farmers closed their eyes to the problems of the cities.

War, revolution and inflation did indeed exacerbate the latent hostility between town and country. Before 1914 the city was already thought to be a place of drudgery, noise and poverty, but the privations of war and the association of economic controls with urban officials, particularly Prussian urban officials, increased the distrust. In 1916 war-weariness and a desire – especially amongst the women – for the bloodshed to stop were reported from Upper Franconia, and in order to impress upon farmers that they were not the only ones making sacrifices and to encourage them to deliver their produce, factory visits to nearby cities were arranged by the Ministry of the Interior.

The revolution, particularly the events of the Soviet Republic in Munich in 1919, confirmed the rural population in its suspicion of city ways. The capital was referred to as the 'dung-heap' of Bavaria, and although impatience was expressed at the slowness of the authorities in dealing with the 'crazy terrorists', there was no desire to step in to liberate the city, and recruitment to units of the right-wing paramilitary organizations, the *Freikorps* and the *Volkswehr*, was small.

The economic upheaval of the postwar years encouraged rural xenophobia. Foreign and rich German tourists attracted to the Bavarian countryside by the plummeting Mark were resented not only for their affluence and pomp, but also because avaricious rural tradesmen put up their prices for locals and rejected their custom. On the other side of the coin, farmers themselves suffered from the ravages of desperate and resentful townspeople, who stole produce and firewood, and wantonly destroyed crops and burnt down barns. There were calls for arms and local militias to protect homes and farms.

Finally, the intrusion of officialdom into the production and marketing decisions of the farm infuriated farmers and played into the hands of the agitators. Initially, the controlled economy of the war and the immediate postwar years provided the material for opposition, and subsequently the allegedly high level of taxes and the downward trend in agricultural prices became the key issues. The so-called *Beamtenhetze* ('agitation against the officials') may have reached dramatic culmination far from Bavaria proper in the storming of the Finance Office in Bernkastel on the Mosel in 1926 and in the bomb outrages in Schleswig-Holstein a few years later. However, Gandorfer and similar peasant leaders in Bavaria maintained throughout a relentless campaign against the urban civil servants. Rural society, it was felt, was going to have to defend itself against the encroachment of the town.

The transition in Bavaria from rural protest and tumult into serious political radicalization was various and complex. In general, Protestant areas of Franconia in northern Bavaria and confessionally mixed areas of the Rhine Palatinate were susceptible at an early stage to the appeal of the National Socialists, but even southern Catholic Bavaria moved gradually from widespread support of the Bavarian People's Party to an espousal or tolerance of National Socialism. It should not be assumed that Hitler's and Darré's back-to-the-land rhetoric convinced all farmers suffering during the

Depression, but many certainly appreciated the values being expounded and chose to give the new movement a chance to prove itself.[41]

3.5 Lords and workers in East Elbia

There is enormous apparent contrast between the uproarious life of Bavarian villages and the sternly controlled estates of eastern Germany. A *Simplicissimus* cartoon of 1912 – 'East Elbia' by Eduard Thöny – shows the back of a portly *Junker* in spurred boots, with a riding crop and a whippet. In the far background is the big house, with four storeys and two side wings. Addressing a small crowd of weather-beaten country-people, doffing their caps and bending slightly in deference, the master commands, 'One liberal vote has been cast. From today the schoolmaster gets no more potatoes.'[42] The cold authority of the lords and the cowed position of the farm workers and dependent peasants were also noted by Mrs Sidgwick:

> In the eastern provinces of Germany the conditions of life amongst the poor are most unhappy. Here the land belongs to large proprietors, and until modern times the people born on the land belonged to the landlords too. No man could leave the village where he was born without permission, and he had to work for his masters without pay. Even in the memory of living men the whip was quite commonly used.[43]

There is a contrary view of benevolent control which comes across in sources from *Junker* families themselves. Libussa Fritz-Krockow paints a picture of masters and servants working loyally and happily together through the harshest of times. For her wedding in Pomerania:

> Emil Klick, the steward in Rowen, one of the villages belonging to the estate, had relatives in Klucken, a fishing village on the other side of the moor, by Lake Leba. They provided us with magnificent pike. Drambusch the forester shot three deer, and we had larded venison roast, a real delicacy, to complement the roast veal. For days before the great event, Marie the cook was receiving a constant stream of visitors. The tenant farmers' wives and the estate hands brought whatever they had, especially butter. Oodles of butter; some of it went to the baker in Glowitz, for the wedding cake.[44]

This happy event was in June 1944, as the Red Army was advancing and Germany faced total collapse. Some years before, Elard von Oldenburg-Januschau, a leading figure in the *Bund der Landwirte* and the German Conservatives, set out his paternalist view of the pleasant lot of the East Elbian farm worker:

The rural labourer has always been one of the most secure human existences. According to old convention, originating from the time before the establishment of all the various forms of insurance, the rural labourer of the German east is taken care of in his old age. He is not driven away from house and home, but continues to live on the estate and receives his old-age payment in kind. The sons of the rural labourer do not need to look around for a post or a profession. They step automatically into the position of their father. In other words: they start where their father left off.[45]

It would be churlish to suggest that there were not good employers as well as bad amongst the land-owning classes, although which category Oldenburg-Januschau occupied is left open to debate. Nor would it be wise to dismiss the loyalty, deference and respect which was felt and shown by many of the lower classes to their masters and mistresses. What is clear, however, is that the regimen for small peasants and estate labourers in the German east was a harsh one, much affected by the close links between the *Junker* class and the Prussian military.[46]

A great deal has been written about the origins and the definitions of the *Junker*, with discussion about the balance between noble and bourgeois in their social make-up and that between capitalist entrepreneurship and reactionary agrarianism in their economic behaviour.[47] The fact is that all these ingredients played their part in defining a social group which, if far from homogenous and unchanging, nonetheless had a common identity which was expressed to great effect in social, economic and political terms (as discussed in Chapter 9). The myths and the stereotypes were part of this identity.[48]

In his memoirs, Oldenburg-Januschau conveys much of the myth and the reality without apparently being aware of some of the conflicts between them. Time and again he makes statements about the importance to society of *Bodenständigkeit* (rootedness in the soil): 'For a family stands and falls with the possession of land. The home (*Heimat*) on the land holds a family together, while fluttering off to the town and leaving one's own piece of land scatters it to the four winds.'[49] The motto on the family fireplace in Januschau reinforced this rejection of the urban and the importance of staying where one belonged:

> The nobility should flee the chatter of the towns,
> And not without need leave its own hearth;
> That way its growing lineage will blossom.
> That is the old custom and right of the nobility.[50]

But he emphasizes these virtues at the same time as recounting the complicated history of land sales and purchases, bourgeois marriage alliances, heavy borrowing, and international trade which was standard practice for *Junker* families. For men to be away from home in the defence of Prussia was no conflict of interest to him, but the same could scarcely be said about politicking in Berlin or the changes over the centuries in where the family seat actually was: near Bremen, then Mecklenburg, then East Prussia, then West Prussia.

The French wars of the early nineteenth century, which reduced the family's East Prussian estate to ruins, were in a sense a catalyst for the heyday of the *Junker* in the mid-nineteenth century. The Prussian edict of October 1807, which was part of a reform programme to salvage the defeated state, ostensibly liberated the peasantry from its bondage to the aristocracy. Personal serfdom and forced service were indeed abolished, but the overall effect of this and subsequent reforms was to consolidate the power of the *Junker*, while placing their economic relationship with their labourers and dependent peasants on a different footing. The 'liberated' peasants were burdened with redemption payments for the land which they now 'owned'; they were still obliged to perform labour for and supply produce to the gentry, and they were still subject *de facto* and often *de jure* to the social, political, and judicial authority of the *Junker*. The latter meanwhile, initially at the cost of high indebtedness, had been able to consolidate and expand their landed property.

The plight of labourers, small peasants, and – not to be forgotten – the large numbers of Catholic Polish seasonal workers, was severe in the early nineteenth century. In the longer term these people provided a fund of human capital available to play its part in the industrialization of Silesia, Saxony, and Prussian territories further west. In the meantime they experienced desperate rural poverty and in the 1840s starvation. This did not mean, however, that the poor of the East were prime participants in the revolutionary events of 1848–49. It was actually only in the far south-west of Germany that there was any substantial peasant uprising. Indeed, if public pronouncements are to be believed, the peasants of Prussia sided with their lords against the turmoil in Berlin:

> We peasants from West Prussia are letting you Berliners know that, unless you soon establish decency and order in your damnable hole and restore our beloved king to his rights, we peasants shall come to make sure that you rogues shan't know whether you are coming or going. You dogs have freed the treacherous Polacks and stirred them up against us, so that they are now burning and killing. ... We peasants do not want to feed you, just so that your brood can bring us to ruin. ... We'll teach you to copy the French![51]

In this instance, as later in Bavaria, the peasantry set themselves against the depravities of the townsfolk.

By about 1860 the prosperity of the *Junker* class was probably at about its height. Rising yields, expanding markets and the eradication of earlier debt all played their part. The dynamic social mix of older families and bourgeois purchasers intensified the economic and political lobbying power of the *Junker* during the empire and the Weimar Republic, when they pressed for tariff protection against foreign competition, for the retention of their political authority based on the Three-Class-Suffrage in Prussia, and for debt relief. They had powerful friends in high places, right through to the period when Field Marshal Hindenburg was Reich President (1925–34). On their own estates they did have to face farm labour unions after the First World War, labour shortages, and – as a consequence of the Versailles treaty – the loss of a major portion of their territory in West Prussia, Pomerania and part of Silesia. The *Junker*'s sense of becoming a beleaguered social group holding out in the East against Poles and Bolsheviks confirmed them as inveterate enemies of the Republic. Military loyalty then kept most of the officer corps behind Hitler, and by the time a small number turned against him in July 1944, it was too late.

It was also too late to protect the *Junker* estates against the external enemies represented by the Soviet Union and the Poles, and the internal enemy of the returning Communists. Even before the end of the Second World War, estate owners and their families were fleeing from the most easterly territories and within months of the end of the war the *Junker* estates in the new Soviet Occupation Zone had been expropriated and carved up for new owners.

This 'democratic' land reform of the autumn of 1945 is in some respects a curious interlude in the social history of Mecklenburg, Saxony, Thuringia, and the Prussian territories of Brandenburg, western Pomerania and Saxony-Anhalt. In a matter of months the agrarian property structure of these lands was altered irrevocably by the dispossession of the large estate owners and by the influx of millions of eastern refugees. In the longer term there were surprising degrees of continuity, as large-scale agriculture was re-established from 1960 onwards. But even in the short term the break was more apparent than real. This was particularly so in those territories – Thuringia stands out – where there were relatively few larger owners and instead a middling peasant class which benefited from gaining property under the land reform. In areas such as Mecklenburg and Brandenburg, previously dominated by the *Junker* estates, there was more immediate change as the small numbers of middling to large farmers similarly saw a relative increase in their social and economic power. Throughout the Soviet Zone, though, there was virulent social antagonism between the remaining population of *Altbauern* ('old' peasants) and the settlers, *Neubauern* ('new' peasants), who were allocated small plots out of estate land. Many of the latter, especially in the north of the Zone, had enormous difficulty in the late 1940s eking out an existence and at the same time providing the food deliveries required by the authorities.[52]

There was an important gender dimension to the land reform of 1945. The temporary or permanent absence of so many men at the front meant that women made up a significant majority (around 60 per cent) of the agricultural population. The *Junker* families which provided the backbone of the officer corps were reduced to old men, women and children, and it was frequently women rather than men who faced the Soviet troops or the land reform commissions outside their mansions. In some areas of the Zone one can estimate that perhaps one-third of the expropriations, sometimes involving violence, were of women. At the other end of the social scale, women were in an even larger majority amongst the penniless refugees who were allocated plots of land to work. They were subject to hostile treatment from neighbouring *Altbauern* and to sexual violence from the Red Army.[53]

There were many different aspects to the way in which the land reform worked locally. The Communists, who were not yet strongly represented in the countryside, pledged to destroy once and for all the pernicious power of the *Junker*, and the decision to demolish the houses of many of the families was as much symbolic as a means of gaining much-needed building material.[54] They presented the reform as another, more real phase of *Bauernbefreiung* and as a spontaneous outburst of popular self-liberation. In fact, the reaction of local populations was far from uniform. Many downtrodden farm labourers genuinely relished the departure of their employers and seized their new plots with enthusiasm, while others retained a sense of loyalty and also feared for their futures as small and vulnerable proprietors. Altered social hierarchies created subtle changes in attitude over the years. This complicated mixture of responses – by then in a much-changed political context – comes over in a speech given by a young woman at a meeting for farm women in Potsdam in January 1950. She was objecting to the new regulations on farm workers' wages, insofar as they would affect employers:

> I was once a farm worker myself and worked on an estate. So I know how to stand up for the rights of farm workers. Earlier the farm worker had to keep his head down and do his work. I am very grateful that in 1946 – through the sharing out of the large landed property – we were given the opportunity once more to work our own plot of land. We took over a settlement of 16 hectares, of which 42 *Morgen* was arable land. As a former estate worker, we [*sic*] go about our work as *Neubauern* with pride. Four years have passed and we can look back with joy. We have come a long way forward. We often had difficult tasks to solve. What tasks lie in front of us in the new year? We shall continue to fulfil all our obligations. But when I think about the wage agreement, a high mountain stands in front of me. Where shall we get all the money, if we want to stay honest peasants? . . . How will the peasant clothe himself? Why do we not get a clothing card?[55]

Such a blend of different attitudes was attacked at the Potsdam meeting itself and on many other occasions around this time, as the political campaign against private farming mounted. Social divisions were exploited by the party authorities to vilify the larger peasants, who were now branded as exploiters and saboteurs. There were certainly major problems with the food supply, but that was largely because of the economic disruption caused by the land reform and the creation of so many smallholdings.

The phase of gradual collectivization, which was initiated by the ruling party from 1952 but presented as a series of voluntary acts, was also a complex social and economic phenomenon.[56] The economically vulnerable *Neubauern* frequently had a genuine interest in banding together to share labour, machinery and marketing, although as the example above displays, some now conceived of themselves as independent peasants. Middling to large peasant proprietors were generally opposed to collectivized production, but in many instances during the 1950s and even into the early 1960s formed cooperatives (*Landwirtschaftliche Produktionsgenossenschaften*, or LPG) to defend their individual and social interests *against* collectivization and to enable them to continue to employ workers on the land. Within villages social distinctions were replicated in the foundation of rival cooperatives of respectively the poorer and the richer peasants. Families and generations were divided in their responses to the pressure to collectivize.[57]

The party authorities were well aware of the complexities of the rural class structure and resolved to sort it out in one fell swoop. In the early months of 1960, all remaining East German private agriculture was collectivized by force. Though the details of cooperative organization and work remained ambiguous for a few years yet, a pattern had been imposed which not only restored large-scale agriculture to the former *Junker* estates but introduced it to the peasant areas as well (as mirrored in Tables 3.8 and 3.9). The extent of the enterprises was not coterminous with the estates of old, and in any case – despite the efforts of some heirs to reclaim what their families had lost in 1945 – the land reform expropriations were excluded in the unification agreements of 1990 from possibility of restoration. The East-Elbian *Junkers*, so resilient and adaptable over the centuries, had helped to bring upon themselves their own destruction. Oldenburg-Januschau's memoirs of 1936, the year in which he died, had closed with the verse:

> I know what I believe in,
> I know what stands firm,
> When everything here in the dust
> Blows away like dust and smoke.[58]

Nine years later it had been blown away, never to be restored.

3.6 Conclusion

Through the last two centuries in Germany the land – as property, as productive resource, as environment, and as symbol – has featured and still features strongly in social and political discourse. The people on and of that land have also been seen as crucial determinants of the German state or states: whether – the *Junker* – as archaic exploiters or as principled protectors of tradition, whether – the peasants – as primitive and uneducated threats to modern society, or as embodiments of racial stock or honest virtues. Throughout, the social and regional variety has been not only recognized but celebrated. Whether in the fragmented German geography of the early nineteenth century, in the centralizing Third Reich and GDR, or in the enlarged Federal Republic of today, Germany has valued itself in public and private as a coming together of different but related peoples, of *Stämme*, with roots in the rural. As a component of the national economy and as a proportion of the population, agriculture is now only a small fragment of what it once was, but its impact on German society will endure yet awhile.

3.7 Notes

1 Jacob and Wilhelm Grimm, *Selected Tales*, translated by David Luke (Harmondsworth, 1982); Theodor Fontane, *Wanderungen durch die Mark Brandenburg* (1862–82) and *Effi Briest* (1895); Oskar Maria Graf, *Der Harte Handel* (1935); Erwin Strittmatter, *Ole Bienkopp* (1963); Hans Fallada, *Bauern, Bonzen und Bomben* (1931); Siegfried Lenz, *Deutschstunde* (1968).

2 Hannes Wader, *Plattdeutsche Lieder* (Phonogram, 1974); *De Bläck Fööss, Links eröm, Rächs eröm* (EMI, 1977).

3 See also Geoff A. Wilson and Olivia J. Wilson, *German Agriculture in Transition: Society, Policies and Environment in a Changing Europe* (Basingstoke and New York, 2001), p. 4.

4 Wilson and Wilson, *German Agriculture in Transition*, p. 34. Note that the statistical sources vary in both the absolute employment numbers and the workforce percentage given.

5 Quantitative and qualitative analysis of this transition is to be found in: Karl Eckart, Hans-Friedrich Wollkopf, *et al.*, *Landwirtschaft in Deutschland: Veränderungen der regionalen Agrarstruktur in Deutschland zwischen 1960 und 1992* (Leipzig, 1994); Daniela Münkel, ed., *Der lange Abschied vom Agrarland: Agrarpolitik, Landwirtschaft und ländliche Gesellschaft zwischen Weimar und Bonn* (Göttingen, 2000); Wilson and Wilson, *German Agriculture in Transition*.

6 For a cultural perspective, see John G. Gagliardo, *From Pariah to Patriot: The Changing Image of the German Peasant 1770–1840* (Lexington, 1969). For a demographic treatment, see John E. Knodel, *Demographic Behavior in the Past: A Study of Fourteen German Village Populations in the Eighteenth and Nineteenth Centuries* (Cambridge, 1988).

7 General surveys and essay collections include Ernst Klein, *Geschichte der deutschen Landwirtschaft im Industriezeitalter* (Wiesbaden, 1973); Friedrich-Wilhelm Henning, *Landwirtschaft und ländliche Gesellschaft in Deutschland*, Vol. II: *1750 bis 1976* (Paderborn, 1978); Richard J. Evans and W. R. Lee, eds, *The German Peasantry: Conflict and Community in Rural Society from the Eighteenth to the Twentieth Centuries* (London and Sydney, 1986); Robert G. Moeller, ed., *Peasants and Lords in Modern Germany: Recent*

Studies in Agricultural History (Boston, London, and Sydney, 1986); Ralph Gibson and Martin Blinkhorn, eds, *Landownership and Power in Modern Europe* (London and New York, 1991), Chs 4–6.

8 In contrast to tastes in Britain, France and Italy, mutton and lamb are characteristically unpopular as meat in Germany and Poland. As overseas wool production developed, German sheep stocks declined.

9 Hainer Plaul, 'The Rural Proletariat: The Everyday Life of Rural Labourers in the Magdeburg Region, 1830–80', in Evans and Lee, *German Peasantry*, pp. 102–28.

10 Cf. Henning, *Landwirtschaft und ländliche Gesellschaft*, pp. 72–93.

11 For example, H. Böker and F. W. von Bülow, *The Rural Exodus in Germany* (Geneva, 1933).

12 Mrs Alfred (Cecily) Sidgwick, *Home Life in Germany* (London, 1908); Hans W. Singer, ed., *Deutsche Bauerntrachten: farbige Meisterbilder* (Bielefeld, 1922); Kathleen Mann, *Peasant Costume in Europe*, 2 vols (London, 1937–8); Wolfgang Kleinschmidt, *Der Wandel des Festlebens bei Arbeitern und Landwirten im 20. Jahrhundert* (Meisenheim am Glan, 1977); Christel Heinrich, 'Peasant Customs and Social Structure: Rural Marriage Festivals in the Magdeburg Region in the 1920s', in Evans and Lee, *The German Peasantry*, pp. 224–34; Ingeborg Weber-Kellermann, *Landleben im 19. Jahrhundert* (Munich, 1987).

13 A reference to the Slav Sorb population of the Lausitz.

14 Sidgwick, *Home Life in Germany*, pp. 267–8.

15 Cf. Peter Exner, *Ländliche Gesellschaft und Landwirtschaft in Westfalen 1919–1969* (Paderborn, 1997), pp. 391–404.

16 Cf. Gavin Lewis, 'The Peasantry, Rural Change and Conservative Agrarianism: Lower Austria at the Turn of the Century', *Past and Present*, 81 (1978), pp. 119–43.

17 Cf. Christof Dipper, *Die Bauernbefreiung in Deutschland 1790–1850* (Stuttgart, Berlin, Cologne, and Mainz, 1980); Hermann Schmid, *Säkularization und Schicksal der Klöster in Bayern, Württemberg und Baden 1802–1815* (Überlingen, 1975); Wolfgang Jahn and Josef Kirmeier, eds, *Glanz und Ende der alten Klöster: die Aufhebung der Klöster in Bayern 1802/03* (Munich, 1989).

18 Hartmut Harnisch, 'Peasants and Markets: The Background to the Agrarian Reforms in Feudal Prussia East of the Elbe, 1760–1807', and William W. Hagen, 'The Junkers' Faithless Servants: Peasant Insubordination and the Breakdown of Serfdom in Brandenburg-Prussia, 1763–1811', in Evans and Lee, *German Peasantry*, pp. 37–70 and 71–101.

19 Henning, *Landwirtschaft und ländliche Gesellschaft*, p. 58.

20 Dipper, *Bauernbefreiung*, p. 117.

21 Henning, *Landwirtschaft und ländliche Gesellschaft*, p. 60.

22 Henning, *Landwirtschaft und ländliche Gesellschaft*, pp. 91–3.

23 Cf. James C. Hunt, 'Peasants, Grain Tariffs, and Meat Quotas: Imperial German Protectionism Reexamined', *Central European History*, 7 (1974), pp. 311–31.

24 Cf. Hans-Jürgen Puhle, 'Lords and Peasants in the Kaiserreich', in Moeller, *Peasants and Lords*, pp. 81–109.

25 Cf. Jonathan Osmond, 'Peasant Farming in South and West Germany during War and Inflation 1914 to 1924: Stability or Stagnation?', in Gerald D. Feldman, Carl-Ludwig Holtfrerich, Gerhard A. Ritter, and Peter-Christian Witt, eds, *The German Inflation Reconsidered: A Preliminary Balance* (Berlin and New York, 1982), pp. 289–307.

26 Cf. Robert G. Moeller, *German Peasants and Agrarian Politics, 1914–1924: The Rhineland and Westphalia* (Chapel Hill and London, 1986); Jonathan Osmond, *Rural Protest in the Weimar Republic: The Free Peasantry in the Rhineland and*

Bavaria (Basingstoke, 1993). Also on the late *Kaiserreich* and the Weimar Republic, see Jens Flemming, *Landwirtschaftliche Interessen und Demokratie: Ländliche Gesellschaft, Agrarverbände und Staat 1890–1925* (Bonn, 1978); Shelley Baranowski, *The Sanctity of Rural Life: Protestantism and Nazism in Weimar Prussia* (New York, 1995).

27 Cf. Dieter Gessner, *Agrarverbände in der Weimarer Republik: wirtschaftliche und soziale Voraussetzungen agrarkonservativer Politik vor 1933* (Düsseldorf, 1976); Martin Schumacher, *Land und Politik: eine Untersuchung über politische Parteien und agrarische Interessen 1914–1923* (Düsseldorf, 1979); Stephanie Merkenich, *Grüne Front gegen Weimar: Reichs-Landbund und agrarischer Lobbyismus 1918–1933* (Düsseldorf, 1998); John E. Farquharson, *The Plough and the Swastika: The NSDAP and Agriculture in Germany 1928–45* (London and Beverly Hills, 1976); Friedrich Grundmann, *Agrarpolitik im Dritten Reich: Anspruch und Wirklichkeit des Reichserbhofgesetzes* (Hamburg, 1979); Gustavo Corni, *Hitler and the Peasants: Agrarian Policy of the Third Reich, 1930–1939* (New York, Oxford, and Munich, 1990); Oded Heilbronner, *Catholicism, Political Culture, and the Countryside: A Social History of the Nazi Party in South Germany* (Ann Arbor, 1998).

28 Cf. John E. Farquharson, *The Western Allies and the Politics of Food: Agrarian Management in Postwar Germany* (Leamington Spa and Dover, 1985); Norman Naimark, *The Russians in Germany: A History of the Soviet Zone of Occupation, 1945–1949* (Cambridge, MA, 1995), pp. 150–66. Policy on the ground did not always promote food production. British forces in western Germany displayed horticultural ineptitude by instructing producers to dig up world-famous asparagus beds in order to grow cabbages. The latter did not thrive in the specially salted soil (communication from Mr L. Westwood).

29 Modernization in western Germany is treated in Günter Golde, *Catholics and Protestants: Agricultural Modernization in Two German Villages* (New York, San Francisco, and London, 1975); Exner, *Ländliche Gesellschaft und Landwirtschaft*; Antonia Maria Humm, *Auf dem Weg zum sozialistischen Dorf? Zum Wandel der dörflichen Lebenswelt in der DDR und der Bundesrepublik Deutschland 1952–1969* (Göttingen, 1999); and Münkel, *Der lange Abschied vom Agrarland*.

30 Ulrich Seibert, ed., *Der Klampfn-Toni* (Munich, 1974), pp. 24–8.

31 This treatment derives from the following sources, which are not cited here in detail: Bavarian Main State Archive, Munich: MA 100600, 100604, 102135, 102139; MInn 72611, 73733, ML 1804; State Archive, Bamberg: K3 1787, 1788; Rosa Kempf, *Arbeits- und Lebensverhältnisse der Frauen in der Landwirtschaft Bayerns* (Jena, 1918); Alois Schlögl, *Bayerische Agrargeschichte: Die Entwicklung der Land- und Forstwirtschaft seit Beginn des 19. Jahrhunderts* (Munich, 1954); Max Spindler, *Bayerische Geschichte im 19. und 20. Jahrhundert* (Munich, 1978); Peter Urbain, *Die Umsatzstruktur südbayerischer Bauernbetriebe und ihre Bedeutung für den Betriebserfolg* (Coburg, 1933). Social and gender aspects of Bavaria in this period and before are treated in Regina Schulte, 'Peasants and Farmers' Maids: Female Farm Servants in Bavaria at the End of the Nineteenth Century', in Evans and Lee, *The German Peasantry*, pp. 158–73; and Regina Schulte, *The Village in Court: Arson, Infanticide, and Poaching in the Court Records of Upper Bavaria, 1848–1910* (Cambridge, 1994).

32 *Statistisches Jahrbuch für das Königreich Bayern* (Munich, 1911), p. 30.

33 For a discussion of women in agriculture in Saxony, see Elizabeth Bright Jones, 'A New Stage of Life? Young Farm Women's Changing Expectations and Aspirations about Work in Weimar Saxony', in *German History*, 19 (2001), pp. 549–70.

34 Kempf, *Arbeits- und Lebensverhältnisse.*

35 Wilhelm Mattes, *Die Bayerischen Bauernräte: Eine soziologische und historische Untersuchung über bäuerliche Politik* (Stuttgart and Berlin, 1921).

36 Graf, *Der Harte Handel.*

37 Sidgwick, *Home Life in Germany*, p. 274.

38 Interview with Rudolf Hamm at the Deileisterhof, near Zweibrücken, 29 Aug. 1978.

39 Jonathan Osmond, 'A Second Agrarian Mobilization? Peasant Associations in South and West Germany, 1918–24', in Moeller, *Peasants and Lords*, pp. 168–97.

40 Cf. Ian Farr, 'Populism in the countryside: the Peasant Leagues in Bavaria in the 1890s', in Richard J. Evans, ed., *Society and Politics in Wilhelmine Germany* (London and New York, 1978), pp. 136–59; Hannsjörg Bergmann, *Der Bayerische Bauernbund und der Bayerische Christliche Bauernverein 1919–1928* (Munich, 1986).

41 Cf. Geoffrey Pridham, *Hitler's Rise to Power: The Nazi Movement in Bavaria, 1923–1933* (London, 1973).

42 *Simplicissimus*, Vol. 16, No. 40, p. 715.

43 Sidgwick, *Home Life in Germany*, pp. 281–2.

44 Christian von Krockow, *Hour of the Women*, based on an oral narrative by Libussa Fritz-Krockow (London, 1992), p. 6.

45 Elard von Oldenburg-Januschau, *Erinnerungen* (Leipzig, 1936), p. 45.

46 Cf. Hainer Plaul, 'The Rural Proletariat: The Everyday Life of Rural Labourers in The Magdeburg Region, 1830–80', in Evans and Lee, *The German Peasantry*, pp. 102–28.

47 Alexander Gerschenkron, *Bread and Democracy in Germany* (Berkeley and Los Angeles, 1943); Hans-Jürgen Puhle, *Agrarische Interessenpolitik und preussischer Konservatismus im wilhelminischen Reich 1893–1914*, 2nd edn (Bonn-Bad Godesberg, 1975); Hanna Schissler, *Preussische Agrargesellschaft im Wandel: wirtschaftliche, gesellschaftliche und politische Transformationsprozesse von 1763 bis 1847* (Göttingen, 1978); F. L. Carsten, *A History of the Prussian Junkers* (Aldershot, 1989); Klaus Hess, *Junker und bürgerliche Grossgrundbesitzer im Kaiserreich: landwirtschaftlicher Grossbetrieb, Grossgrundbesitz und Familienfideikommiss in Preussen (1867/71–1914)* (Stuttgart, 1990).

48 For a contrasting picture of aristocracy in western Germany, see Gregory Pedlow, *The Survival of the Hessian Nobility* (Princeton, 1988).

49 Oldenburg-Januschau, *Erinnerungen*, p. 8.

50 Oldenburg-Januschau, *Erinnerungen*, p. 5: 'Das Geschwätz der Städte soll er fliehen, / Ohne Not vom eignen Herd nicht ziehen; / So erblüht sein wachsendes Geschlecht. / Das ist Adels alte Sitt' und Recht.'

51 *Constitutionelle Club-Zeitung*, 10 May 1848, quoted in Günther Franz, ed., *Bauernschaft und Bauernstand 1500–1970* (Limburg/Lahn, 1975), document 208.

52 For more detail, see Jonathan Osmond, 'From *Junker* Estate to Cooperative Farm: East German Agrarian Society, 1945–61', in Patrick Major and Jonathan Osmond, eds, *The Workers' and Peasants' State: Communism and Society in East Germany under Ulbricht 1945–71* (Manchester, 2002), pp. 130–50.

53 For more detail, see Jonathan Osmond, 'Geschlechtsspezifische Folgen der Bodenreform in der Sowjetischen Besatzungszone: Gutsbesitzerinnen, Bäuerinnen und Landarbeiterinnen nach 1945', in Arnd Bauerkämper, ed., *'Junkerland in Bauernhand'? Durchführung, Auswirkungen und Stellenwert der Bodenreform in der Sowjetischen Besatzungszone* (Stuttgart, 1996), pp. 153–68.

54 For instance, Saxon Main State Archive, Dresden: Ministerium des Innern (1945–1952) pp. 3739ff.

55 Federal Archive Berlin: SAPMO DY 30/IV 2/17/73, f. 45–6, cited in Osmond, 'Geschlechtsspezifische Folgen', pp. 161–2.

56 Hans Immler, *Agrarpolitik in der DDR* (Cologne, 1971); Humm, *Auf dem Weg zum sozialistischen Dorf?*; Arnd Bauerkämper, *Ländliche Gesellschaft in der kommunistischen Diktatur: Zwangsmodernisierung und Tradition in Brandenburg nach 1945* (Cologne, Weimar, and Vienna, 2002).

57 These features are discussed in detail in Osmond, 'From *Junker* Estate to Cooperative Farm'.

58 Oldenburg-Januschau, *Erinnerungen*, p. 230: 'Ich weiß, woran ich glaube, / Ich weiß, was fest besteht, / Wenn alles hier im Staube / Wie Staub und Rauch verweht'.

4

Government and the economy in the nineteenth century

FRANK B. TIPTON
University of Sydney

4.1 Introduction

It is clear that . . . the State was actively engaged in promoting the industrial revolution in Prussia. (W. O. Henderson)[1]

There would appear to be little doubt that this record of violence was connected with the experience of very rapid industrialization. (Volker Berghahn)[2]

The relationship between government and the economy in nineteenth-century Germany touches on the deepest questions of the modern world: the sources of economic growth, the impact of economic development on social and political structures, and ultimately the proper relationship between economy, society, and state. Did Germany 'succeed' or 'fail'? Is Germany 'unique'? As with so much else in German history, the evidence is ambiguous and the answers contentious.

The foundation of the Bismarckian empire was the central event of their history for three generations of German historians, and this perspective deeply affected the specialized field of economic history as well. Economic historians believed that the process of political unification, and particularly the new institutions of the empire, had stimulated exceptionally rapid industrialization.[3] In 1975 W. O. Henderson wrote that the empire 'fostered future economic progress in Germany . . . Many of the factors that had for so long hampered the expansion of industrial progress had now disappeared.'[4] During the 1970s and 1980s economic historians employing neoclassical models tended to downplay the direct economic role of the state.[5] However, the importance of the state tradition has led other historians to return their attention to government policy and 'institutional change'.[6]

General histories have continued to focus on the central role of the state, and to connect economic development with unification. Thomas Nipperdey concludes that 'in 1870 Germany still stood clearly behind England', but that by 1913 'a follower country had become a pioneer country'.[7] Hans-Ulrich Wehler lists 'an astonishing rise in the German share of world industrial production' among the 'successes of growth in the first German "economic miracle"'.[8] David Blackbourn says that nationalist historians exaggerated the role of the state, but he nevertheless argues that the Prussian government's investment in infrastructure was 'crucial'. In response to it, 'investors' confidence grew', and as a result, 'Prussia's economic and social dynamism built up a powerful head of steam behind demands for a German nation'. Following unification, 'the raft of new legislation . . . threatened to overwhelm the parliament . . . In 1871 the Empire could still have been mistaken for a reworked version of the old German confederation, minus Austria. That was no longer true by the 1880s.'[9]

Germany remains one of the most commonly cited examples of 'state-led' economic development.[10] The role of the bureaucracy has been seen as central; indeed, Germany is also one of the most commonly cited examples of 'bureaucratized polities'.[11] German observers have held that the creation of a new national community resulted in social and economic reforms imposed on society by the state, the process of unification and nation-building causing or at least facilitating the process of modernization. The bureaucracy in general, and specific government officials individually, have viewed themselves, and have been viewed by historians and social scientists as an active, progressive force, while German society has been viewed as passive and traditionalistic.[12]

Politically, however, the relation between state and society in nineteenth-century Germany appears a failure. Moreover, political failure paradoxically appears to have been rooted in the same soil as economic success. Comparing Germany with Japan, David Landes concluded that, 'In both countries, the bill for this alliance of intoxicating economic expansion and irresponsible power eventually came due, and the price proved far greater than anyone had dreamed.'[13] A generation later, Volker Berghahn argued that Germany's exceptional 'record of violence' had been 'connected with the experience of very rapid industrialization'. The central importance of the state, the creation of a new national polity, and rapid economic growth appear to have contributed to militarism, authoritarianism, and the rise of Nazism. According to this view, Germany refused to accept the political implications of the social changes brought about by economic development. Observers have held that the limits imposed on political modernization, and their disastrous consequences, reflect the idiosyncratic outcome of German history and traditions. Germany stands accused of deviating from a more normal and proper course of political development. Thus 'Germany for a century and a half has been plagued by the wrong kind of nationalism'.[14]

Intriguingly, the same bureaucracy that often receives credit for economic success is now often blamed for political failure. The idea that Germany had inherited beneficent statist traditions from the eighteenth century, and the idea that the Prussian bureaucracy in particular embodied a self-sacrificing service ethos, resulted in large part from the need of nationalist historians in the late nineteenth century to discover a usable past, to create an 'imagined community' to legitimize their new nation-state.[15] Since the Second World War, by contrast, bureaucracy has become a 'problem' in Germany. Popular accounts portray the bureaucracy as an irresponsible 'state within the state'. Social scientists have cast a critical eye on bureaucratic involvement in contemporary political decision-making, and many have called for 'reform' and 'de-bureaucratization'. Sociologists see bureaucrats as an isolated group, cut off from society (a view discussed in greater detail in Chapter 9). Political scientists point to the inefficiencies resulting from rigid inherited structures. And, looking backward, historians note the role of the bureaucracy in facilitating the rise of militarism and Nazism.[16]

This chapter focuses on two problem areas: the development of central bureaucracies, and the role of those bureaucracies in the process of modern economic growth. To do so poses serious problems. In order to judge the extent to which German government policy affected the direction and rate of economic development, we need to know how much the German economy grew. In fact, however, economists and economic historians have great difficulty measuring economic growth. Complete and consistent data are not always available, and economists disagree over how to handle even the best data. The choice of the base year dramatically affects the resulting estimate of growth, for instance, because changes in the relative prices of goods mean that a base year at the beginning of a period yields a different growth rate than a base year at the end. And, as seen below in the dispute over long cycles, the interpretation of the final estimates is also disputed.

Students of the German economy still rely on the work of Walther G. Hoffmann published in 1965, which estimates the national product of Germany in constant 1913 marks. His complex series of assumptions and underlying estimates have been criticized repeatedly.[17] Moreover, because his estimates begin only in 1850 we must rely on scattered figures as indicators of development during the first half of the century. Furthermore, Hoffmann estimated total output within the boundaries of Germany in 1913. Hence his estimates do not reveal either the patterns of development of the independent German states before 1871, or the differences among regions within states before and after unification.[18]

The absence, incompleteness, and ambiguity of the statistical record does not mean that we cannot judge the effects of government policy, but it does mean we must employ the methods of the historian as well as those of the economist. The record is in fact mixed. On the one hand, German government officials did attempt to foster and guide economic development. On the other, the initial introduction of modern industrial and transportation technologies did not result from government initiative. Furthermore, subsequent government policy toward the economy reveals a very selective and partial attitude of elite bureaucrats to any change outside their direct control. Later the German national state claimed power over broad areas, but in fact found its options severely limited by the balance of economic, social, and political forces.

However, beyond praise, blame, or a balanced judgement that truth must lie somewhere between, the story of German economic policy reveals a deeper pattern, one related more to the distribution of power than the creation of economic benefits. The relationship between the changing bureaucratic structures and the developing German economy established a remarkably durable form of interaction between the state and society, a pattern that bears partial responsibility for the tragedies of the twentieth century. And, although Germany is uniquely important for its role in twentieth-century history, the German experience both reflects and illuminates other similar patterns in the national histories of both Europe and Asia.[19]

4.2 State capacity and the role of the state in the economy

The Master said, 'The common people can be made to follow a path but not to understand it'. (Confucius, *The Analects*, VIII.9)

Little else is requisite to carry a state to the highest degree of opulence from the lowest barbarism, but peace, easy taxes, and tolerable administration of justice; all the rest being brought about by the natural course of things. (Adam Smith, *The Wealth of Nations*, 1776)

What is the role of the state in economic development? The rapid growth of the successful Asian economies over the past three decades has triggered extensive discussion, and we may draw on that debate for insight into the German story. In today's Asia no one would deny that the state plays a large role in the economy.[20] However, the extent, content, and quality of government intervention have been the objects of intense controversy. Some have interpreted this rapid growth from a neoclassical economic perspective, as the predictable outcome of market-oriented policies, the minimalist programme of 'peace, easy taxes, and tolerable administration of justice' which Adam Smith argued would allow 'the natural course of things' to lead to 'opulence'.[21] Others have interpreted this same growth from a statist perspective that emphasizes the central role of governments in guiding development, the 'path' which Confucius argued the 'common people' could be made to 'follow' but not to 'understand'.[22]

We can view the possible range of public actions and evaluate their consequences along a number of different axes. Neoclassical economists worry about the danger from 'rent-seeking coalitions', groups that attempt to use political influence to gain excessively high returns ('rents' in the jargon of economics). This obviously diverts scarce resources away from more productive uses, and market reformers fear that state-led development and state intervention will create and perpetuate conditions for rent-seeking activities, with losses that surpass any gains from state actions. But even most neoclassical economists agree that governments do have a role to play in the absence of established markets or in cases of market failure, and that such action is crucial in the structural process of transformation of a society to a more developmental model in which growth can become self-sustaining.[23]

Another point of debate has been 'state capacity', meaning not only the abilities and commitment of government officials, but also durable and effective institutional structures. Nineteenth-century Germany, like Asian economies today, was a 'latecomer' or a 'follower' country, attempting to industrialize in a world in which there were already other industrial nations. In latecomer countries the role of the state may be to substitute for the factors that served as preconditions of economic growth in the more fortunate earlier industrializers. In latecomers the state may provide the 'post-conditions' of growth, in Alexander Gerschenkron's famous formulation. Whereas in Britain private individuals accumulated the necessary capital, identified potential markets, and introduced new technologies, in follower countries these functions may be fulfilled by the state.[24] In the context of competitive international economic development, the state's task may be to 'tame' domestic and international market forces, and 'harness' them for national interests.[25] There will almost certainly be opposition to such policies, and therefore state capacity is precisely the ability 'to implement official goals, especially over the actual or potential opposition of powerful social groups or in the face of recalcitrant socio-economic circumstances'. In other words, the bureaucratic officials of a strong state must be both highly competent and autonomous.[26]

How did the bureaucracies within successful developmental states acquire their autonomy? And, why did they use their autonomy to pursue economic development rather than rent-seeking activities? Initially, it seems, meritocratic recruitment procedures play an important role. Rigorous standards of selection generate competence, and they also create a sense of unity and identity among government officials. Keeping the size of the bureaucracy small maintains its identity as an elite, and small numbers also make control and accountability easier. It is often argued that elite bureaucrats should be relatively independent of the executive. Indeed, the relationship has been described as a 'division of labour' between the tasks of ruling and reigning. In the successful states, it is argued, politicians provide space for bureaucrats by warding off interest groups that might deflect the state from its developmental priorities.[27]

These considerations relate to the initial introduction and diffusion of modern technologies. In this phase, a 'strong state' or a 'developmental state' may organize and guide resource allocation. In a later period, however, when entrepreneurial groups have emerged and the economy has begun to generate the surplus required for continued growth, the state's role may change. Rather than choosing among and introducing foreign technologies, the state must now seek to ensure a continuing 'transformative capacity', the willingness and ability to continue to seek out and develop new techniques and new products in order to maintain domestic growth and remain competitive in world markets. In successful states a complex relationship emerges in which a range of policy instruments reflects a 'shared project' between public officials and private interests. The result has been labelled 'embedded autonomy' or 'governed interdependence'. The state may offer disciplined support to private interests: it may absorb risk through subsidies and guarantees; it may sponsor privatesector governance through creation of quasi-representational institutions, and it may form specific public–private alliances to exploit opportunities for innovation.[28]

4.3 From the eighteenth to the nineteenth century: statist traditions, market reformers, and rent-seeking coalitions

A well-conducted government must be a system as well connected as if it were a system of philosophy. (Frederick the Great, *Political Testament*, 1773)

Administration became increasingly fragmentary and disorderly. A man of Frederick's intelligence and drive could sometimes make it work, but he was much less in control than conventional treatments of his regime would have us believe. (James Sheehan)[29]

The model of the developmental state certainly appears to cast an illuminating light on the tradition that German government officials inherited from Frederick the Great. Many argue that a strong state can target, support, and supervise firms and industries. To perform these functions, however, government officials must mediate between interest groups competing for scarce resources, and therefore officials must have space in which to manoeuvre and play off interests against each other. Vested interests of course support the existing equilibrium, which limits the state's access to resources, and therefore it is also argued that the state requires a high degree of centralization and high levels of internal cohesion to achieve its goals efficiently.[30] These considerations seem particularly apposite in the case of the German states, with their inherited 'corporatist' or 'state corporatist' political and institutional structures, and the repeated struggles between the centralizing desires of the monarch and the quasi-autonomous position of the nobility, the church, and urban communities.[31]

In the case of Prussia, Frederick was at war for most of the first 23 years of his reign from 1740 to 1763. His ultimate success in conquering and retaining Silesia confirmed Prussia's status as a great power as well as the role and prestige of the military in Prussian life. Frederick attempted to replace the old collegial councils he had inherited with specialized ministries, each of which would have a clearly defined area of authority and its own chain of command from the centre to the provincial and local levels. The first of these were dedicated to the army and the royal domains. Next came the *Seehandlung*, a combination central bank and overseas trading corporation. Frederick also placed the administration of Silesia under a separate department. Another ministry was established to oversee the reconstruction programme following the end of the Seven Years' War in 1763. This included extensive river reclamation projects, which opened large new areas to agricultural production, and the establishment of the *Landschaften*, rural credit banks that provided funds to large landowners. From the 1770s onward the mining and forestry ministries recruited their own lower-level personnel to serve in provincial and district offices.[32]

However, Frederick's policies were limited in both execution and intent, and scholars have disputed the balance of success and failure. Again, the debates over the Asian developmental state may help in clarifying our picture of Frederick and evaluating his lasting heritage. The developmental state poses dangers. Over time, such a state provides incentive and opportunities for rent-seeking groups to organize. An active state can provide opportunities for gain, both directly through subsidies to individuals and more indirectly to groups favoured by preferential legislation. Elite officials can become isolated, or may respond only to the interests of those with privileged access. Where the state intervenes to promote or regulate, the line between public and private may blur.[33]

Frederick did indeed isolate himself. He ruled from his office in Potsdam, with only infrequent inspection tours. He favoured the aristocracy in appointments to both military and civilian positions. His administrative changes led in some cases to overlapping jurisdictions and destructive competition among agencies. His attempt to contract out the collection of tax revenues to a private entrepreneur failed. He opposed the introduction of modern spinning and weaving machinery from England, because many of his soldiers produced textiles when not on duty, and he feared that the new technology would throw them out of work. He subsidized inefficient luxury industries in Berlin in the hope that they would earn export revenue, but he was reluctant to encourage development in his progressive western possessions.[34] As we might say today, he 'targeted' the wrong industries, or failed to 'pick winners' among candidates for support.

This was the age of 'enlightened despotism'. Frederick assumed he knew what was best for his subjects, and he interpreted any criticism or any outside initiative as a hostile threat to his authority. Most telling, perhaps, he did not encourage genuinely autonomous officials. He attempted to control everything personally. Distrust and fear bred insecurity, and despite his network of spies, he was often lied to. Even with a genius at its head, as James Sheehan emphasizes, his system did not always function efficiently, and following Frederick's death in 1786 policy drifted.

As the largest state and the most significant in the light of Germany's later history, Prussia has attracted the most interest, but Frederick was not alone. In developing our view of the general relationship among state, society, and economy, it is important to recognize that similar patterns can be seen in the history of many of the other central European states, both large and small. Numerous other would-be enlightened despots also struggled with recalcitrant corporate interests. Like Frederick, these princes, kings (and in the cases of Maria Theresa in Austria and Catherine the Great in Russia, queens) were sometimes successful and sometimes not. Among their servants were a number of officials who came to believe not only that the state should guide economic and social development, but also that they themselves rather than the ruler should be the ones responsible for formulating and executing the state's policy. Across Europe, population rose and export industries developed in response to expanding markets, but it is also important that, as in Prussia, these officials frequently failed to recognize and support development that they did not control.[35]

The French Revolution and the following series of wars threatened existing states, but also offered opportunities. The crushing defeat of the Prussian army by Napoleon at Jena brought to power in Prussia a group of younger government officials dedicated to reform led by Karl vom Stein. In 1807 and 1808 they produced a large number of edicts that touched on virtually all aspects of social and economic life. Two of the most famous were the 'emancipation' of the peasantry in the countryside, which in theory freed peasant farmers from bondage to the aristocratic landlords (as discussed in Chapter 3), and 'occupational freedom' (*Gewerbefreiheit*) in the towns, which in theory ended the powers of artisan guilds to restrict entry into manufacturing employment. New structures were introduced for central, provincial, and local government, intended to extend the range of self-administration and involve broader groups in local governance. As discussed in detail in Chapter 10, a restructuring of the educational system was begun, with the outlines of basic primary education, division into vocational training and the elite track leading to tertiary study, and the dominant role of the universities, whose outlines can still be seen today.[36]

Today's discussion of economic 'reforms' both in Asia and in Eastern Europe runs in part along similar lines. Looking at states which hope for success, market-oriented reformers recommend liberalization of production, prices, interest rates, and wages to allow them to find their 'natural' levels, deregulation of markets, dismantling of restrictive legislation, lower and simpler systems of direct and indirect taxation, and privatization of state-owned enterprises. Where government intervention is required, they continue, the state should prefer policies requiring a minimum of administrative input, having transparent costs, and minimizing opportunities for rent-seeking.[37]

Such an agenda almost inevitably damages existing interests. In the eyes of reforming officials in early nineteenth-century Prussia, occupational freedom constituted part of a broader strategy of modernization, which would extend domestic markets, and encourage specialization and efficiency, as outlined by Adam Smith.[38] However, the end to guild control over industrial employment did more than merely threaten existing master artisans with new competition. It also undermined the power of urban communities to choose their own members, because guild membership was tied to residence, marriage, and citizenship rights. Guilds in Württemberg, for instance, had been tightening entry restrictions throughout the eighteenth century. In all towns, guild members monopolized political power, and free entry into occupations threatened their position. The regulations were therefore bitterly resented and strenuously – though often covertly – resisted over the next two generations.[39]

Elite groups with access to the levers of power are in the best position to resist reforms. In Prussia the tensions between reformers and rent-seeking coalitions therefore can be seen most clearly in the agricultural sector. Frederick had opposed the eastern landlords' increasing exploitation of their peasants. He hoped to create a class of small peasant farmers, because he wanted to increase the population and provide more soldiers for his army. Influenced by English notions of aristocratic liberalism and the ideas of Adam Smith, the reformers had concluded that free workers were more efficient than unfree serfs, but also that large estates were more efficient than small farms. The 'emancipation' edict issued in October 1807 was vague, although it both protected existing peasant holdings and permitted peasants to leave the land if they wished. A further edict in 1811 stipulated that those peasants with hereditary tenure could retain their land, but those without hereditary tenure would have to surrender one-third to one-half the land they had previously farmed for themselves. The new edict also specified that all peasants owed compensation for the labour services they had previously provided to the landlords.

With Napoleon safely defeated, the old elites reasserted themselves. In 1816 the government further restricted grants of land to those peasants with holdings large enough to support a pair of oxen, and whose tenure dated from the period 1749–74. Small peasants and all those with tenure of less than two generations' duration lost their land. Between 1816 and 1850 approximately one million hectares were transferred directly from the peasants to the landlords. Those peasants who retained their land owed heavy compensation payments to the landlords. The landlords also benefited from access to credit supplied by the *Landschaften*. The

Landschaften sold bonds and lent the money to landlords. The security of mortgages on the indebted estates, plus an implicit guarantee by the government, made the bonds an attractive and secure investment, and interest rates were generally low. This additional capital allowed the landlords to enclose and drain their fields and purchase new agricultural machinery. The majority of the peasants became agricultural labourers, supplementing their wages with earnings from small plots of land allotted to them by their employers. Although agricultural productivity almost certainly improved,[40] the outcome confirmed the position of the landowning aristocracy in Prussian life.

Remembering that the reformers' motive was to increase the strength of the army helps to put the Prussian reforms in perspective. Anything that did not contribute to the military power of the state would be given a low priority or rejected. Furthermore, the amount of legislation passed is less surprising when we remember that the leaders of the reform movement were experienced officials who had been advocating these and other measures for decades. Stein, for instance, had entered the Prussian mining administration in 1780 and had served as head of the provincial administration in Westphalia from 1793 to 1802. He was well known for his criticisms of Frederick's economic policies, and he had already produced detailed proposals for administrative reform.

During this reform period, again Prussia was not unique. Reforming administrations appeared in all the German states as they struggled to maintain themselves and extend their territory while the armies marched back and forth across Europe. Sigismund von Reitzenstein in Baden and Maximilian von Montgelas in Bavaria played roles equivalent to Stein in Prussia. Programmes of peasant emancipation and occupational freedom, and divestment of state-owned or state-supported manufacturing enterprises, were adopted. An assembly of diplomats met in 1803 and approved the *Reichsdeputations-Hauptschluss* (Enactment of the Delegates of the Empire). Almost all ecclesiastical states, free cities, and independent imperial knights disappeared from the map. Their territories were absorbed by Oldenburg, Hannover, Hesse, Baden, Württemberg, Bavaria, and also by the Kingdom of Westphalia and the Duchy of Berg, which the Treaty of Vienna granted to Prussia in 1815.

The lasting economic effect of this redrawing of the map lay in the need of the surviving governments to mould their new territories into unified states. Models for doing so came from the previous experience of reforming bureaucrats, from the pattern of centralized administration in France, and from the French-style administrative structures introduced in the Kingdom of Westphalia. The new governments attempted to increase their direct control over their subjects. Self-administration by communities was replaced by central administrative direction. New administrative divisions were created, and collegial administrative organs were replaced by hierarchically organized functional ministries.[41]

4.4 The restoration: the new bureaucratic elite and the limits on economic policy

> The maintenance of the state's universal interest, and of legality, in this sphere of particular rights, and the work of bringing these rights back to the universal, require to be superintended by holders of the executive power, by (a) the executive civil servants, and (b) the higher advisory officials. (Hegel, *Philosophy of Right*, 1825, art. 289)

> The bureaucracy is the imaginary state alongside the real state; it is the spiritualism of the state. Hence everything acquires a double meaning: a real meaning and a bureaucratic one; in like fashion, there is both real knowledge and bureaucratic knowledge. (Karl Marx, *Critique of Hegel's Doctrine of the State*, 1843)

Market-oriented reformers today argue for legal changes permitting the free flow of resources; that achieved, they would prefer to remove the state from economic life. Others find a continuing case for state intervention. The Prussian reformers had tended towards market reform, but the succeeding generation of officials adopted a much more statist approach. The philosopher Hegel exercised immense influence through his position as Professor at the University of Berlin and through his *Philosophy of Right* published in 1825, a systematic handbook of administration as well as a philosophical treatise. Hegel not only considered civil servants essential to maintain the 'universal' interests of the state, but also regarded private individuals as fundamentally incapable of managing their own affairs:

> The administration of a Corporation's business by its own officials is frequently clumsy, because although they keep before their minds and are acquainted with its special interests and affairs, they have a far less complete appreciation of the connexion of those affairs with more remote conditions and the outlook of the state.[42]

In the decades following Napoleon's defeat, there was on balance a good case for the new and expanded governments of the German states to take the lead in economic development. Here, consideration of modern Asian economies can prove instructive. In the 1960s and 1970s many believed that Asian economies were threatened by 'involution', with increasing numbers of people, low levels of technology, and inadequate capital resources. Their markets, it was believed, did not function in ways that fostered development, either because of inherited values that inhibited risk-taking entrepreneurial behaviour, or because of the high levels of risk created by low income and the resulting small size of their domestic markets. Japan alone seemed to be escaping from the trap of involution, because of successful intervention by the government. Across the rest of Asia weak local governments seemed to need international assistance if anything were to be done.[43]

German states in the 1820s and 1830s faced similar problems. Growing populations required employment, and it was increasingly evident that this would have to be industrial employment. Agriculture would not absorb all the available people, and in any case rich and powerful nations were not agricultural nations. As the example of Great Britain showed, to be rich and powerful meant to be industrial. Goods produced in British factories threatened the existence of German producers, and thereby threatened the life of German states as well. But change was difficult for private entrepreneurs. The new technologies were complex, and Britain prohibited the export of machinery and the emigration of skilled workers until the 1840s. The new machines were also expensive, often beyond the means of individuals or family firms. And even if they could be obtained, installed, and made to work, there was still a high level of risk, for the limited markets of small German states might not provide sufficient sales to ensure a profit.

All these arguments were made at the time, and government officials actively debated their implications.[44] Much was in fact accomplished. In Prussia Peter Beuth headed a new Technical Institute established in 1821 in Berlin, which supported study trips to Britain (on which German officials sometimes stole plans and smuggled machinery out of the country), trained students in the new techniques, and made grants to promising industrialists.[45] Under Christian von Rother in the 1820s and 1830s, the *Seehandlung* constructed a large number of improved turnpike highways. The *Seehandlung* also invested directly in modern industrial enterprises, including mines and metallurgical plants, an advanced power-driven textile-weaving plant erected in 1842, and refineries that processed sugar beets into refined sugar.[46] These were supposed to earn profits, but in addition they were intended to produce what today would be called 'spillover' effects, that is to serve as training centres and models, and therefore they were often located in country areas. And finally, after a long diplomatic struggle pursued by Friedrich Maassen and Friedrich Motz, in 1834 Prussia succeeded in establishing the *Zollverein*, the tariff union which unified most of the German states into a single market, but which, significantly, excluded Austria.[47]

The figures against which government performance might be judged are very rough estimates. They suggest that investment rose only slightly before 1840, and that per capita income stagnated between 1825 and 1850.[48] Table 4.1 gives some selected indicators of industrial development. The linked areas of iron, coal, the railway, and steam power remained the critical leading sectors for any developing country until the last decades of the nineteenth century. In these crucial areas it is clear that, although there was some progress, the 30 years from 1820 to 1850 saw very little development in the German states. Also, as seen below, alongside the government's successes there were odd failures of policy, particularly in the areas of heavy industry and the railway.

Table 4.1 Indicators of industrial development in Germany, 1820–70

	Railway lines (km)	Iron output (000 tons)	Iron per capita (kg)	Coal output (million tons)	Coal per capita (kg)	Steam engines (total)	Steam engines (horsepower)
1820	0	96[a]	3.5[a]	1.2	46		
1830	0	122	4.2	1.7	58		
1840	469	173	5.3	3.2	98		
1850	5,856	212	6.0	5.2	147	1,416[b]	26,354[b]
1860	11,088	545	14.5	12.3	327	10,113[c]	184,649[c]
1870	19,000	1,391	34.1	26.4	647		947,000[d]

Notes:
[a] 1823.
[b] 1846, Zollverein members.
[c] 1861, Zollverein members.
[d] 1875, German Empire.
Sources: Adapted from Richard H. Tilly, 'Banken und Industrialisierung in Deutschland, 1815–1870,' in Richard H. Tilly, *Kapital, Staat und sozialer Protest in der deutschen Industrialisierung* (Göttingen, 1980), pp. 29–54, here Table 1, with additional figures calculated from data in Walther G. Hoffmann, *Das Wachstum der Deutschen Wirtschaft seit der Mitte des 19. Jahrhunderts* (Berlin, 1965).

The *Zollverein* certainly possessed the potential for creating an expanded market, but central government officials also desired to increase the power of their state. Motz had written a memo in 1817 in which he argued that Prussia should consolidate its position in North Germany as a preliminary to unifying the smaller states and excluding Austria. The motives of the smaller states were fiscal, and the generous terms offered by Prussia for entry into the *Zollverein* (Prussia bore all the costs of administration, but distributed the revenue on the basis of member states' populations, not according to the value of their trade) were clearly a bribe intended to woo them away from Austria.[49] The role of the state in economic development in education, in building model factories, and in the creation of the *Zollverein* was real enough, but it was secondary in the motives of government officials. As individual entrepreneurs began to emerge from the old communities involved in the process of growth, this led to conflict.[50]

In all German states, but particularly in Prussia, government policies toward the economy were affected by the emergence of new bureaucratic groups claiming elite status, based on universalistic norms. Hegel asserted that 'civil servants and the members of the executive constitute the greater part of the middle class, the class in which the consciousness of right and the developed intelligence of the mass of the people is found'.[51] Hegel wrote at a time when the economy was beginning to develop, and the leaders in that development were a new class of entrepreneurs who found no place in his system. In addition, the new bureaucracies came into existence at a time when demands for the creation of a new 'national' government were spreading. Conceptually separate, these processes overlapped and intersected, and individuals could easily be involved in all three at once.

The parallel movements of bureaucracy, economy, and nationalism can also be observed in Asia after 1945. The successful developmental states of Asia all created institutional structures intended to foster and guide the growth of the economy. Both market reformers and statist writers often see this as one of the lessons of growth in Japan and the 'tiger' economies, and recommend the creation of similar state structures in their would-be imitators – although for different purposes, since market reformers desire a strong state which will have the power to implement market-conforming reforms, while statist writers view the role of government agencies as to intervene and direct development. There is a danger here in either case, however. Durable and effective institutions may be deflected towards the defence of rent-seeking coalitions. Furthermore, state officials are themselves an interest group. The state's conflicting commitments, to maintain and defend property rights on the one hand, and to foster economic growth and equity on the other, may overlap and possibly conflict with the interests of powerful elites, and these may include individuals in the state apparatus.[52]

The bureaucracy has long formed an important group in German society, as discussed for the twentieth century in Chapter 9. Much of the research on the development and function of the bureaucracy in nineteenth-century Germany has focused on the influence of the Prussian tradition.[53] The thrust of this research has been to reject the notion that the professional bureaucracy and its values emerged out of the quasi-religious ethic of the Prussian state service. Bernd Wunder dismisses this view as a myth created by the patriotic 'Prussian' (*borussische*) historiography of scholars such as Gustav Schmoller and Otto Hintze around the turn of the twentieth century.[54] Furthermore, Max Weber, though critical of specific aspects of bureaucratic administration, accepted much of the mythical self-image of the Prussian-German bureaucrats in creating his immensely influential model of bureaucracy.[55]

Following Hegel's classic statement, Weber emphasized permanence of tenure and fixed salaries as the defining characteristics of bureaucracy. However, scholars across a broad range of disciplines are agreed that emergence of the bureaucracy as a social group is marked most clearly by the introduction of formal examinations.[56] In the middle of the eighteenth century German states introduced examinations testing the legal knowledge of candidates, and from the 1770s through the 1810s many states followed Prussia's example in adding a period of unpaid 'practical' work before formal appointment. In the south, candidates could support themselves with additional paid work. In Prussia, however, outside work was forbidden. The period of unpaid service was extended to five or more years, and during the 1840s the addition of a second and then a third examination further extended the period of training. In 1863 Prussia required all candidates for the higher civil service to be able to prove they could support themselves for ten years as unpaid assistants.

The development of formally examined qualifications became the basis for the claim of the bureaucracy as a whole to elite status. But in addition we need to look behind the adoption of examinations, for they served not only the interests of the bureaucrats, but those of their masters as well. Wunder says bluntly that the result of the new additional examinations was 'the exclusion of outsiders'.[57] Only those with the proper background and opinions could hope for success. Partly because of this, by the beginning of the twentieth century the class of men occupying the upper levels of the German bureaucracy had achieved an unprecedented degree of homogeneity. In their own eyes, their elite status was justified by their possession of formally certified and examined technical skills. This, they believed, placed them outside normal political processes and justified their claim to lifetime security of tenure in their positions. Weber then identified these characteristics as the 'ideal type' of *all* modern bureaucracies.

The limits these considerations of status and power placed on German economic policy can be traced in opposition to the railway, in opposition to independent entrepreneurs in heavy industry, and in the restrictive financial policies that slowed growth. The extension of the German railway system was marked by continual conflict. The numerous proposals for railways in Prussia in the 1830s and 1840s, mostly emanating from private groups in the West, emerged into a political arena in which Prussia was competing with Austria for influence in the German Confederation, in which the Prussian government was coming under increasing criticism for its inaction in the economic sphere, but in which it also had already-established economic and financial interests. Not surprisingly, the new world of industrial technologies placed severe strains on the factionalized decision-making bodies within the government.[58]

The *Zollverein* offered large potential markets, but producers required extensive transportation development before they would be able to seize the new opportunities. The highways constructed by the Prussian government were insufficient to expand the market significantly, and they often were routed inconveniently through the territory of small states, another bribe to secure the political support of those states for Prussia.[59] Railways were in retrospect the obvious solution, but the Prussian government hesitated.[60] The army was unsure at first that the railways would provide safe and efficient transport, and the initial reaction of the generals was to see railways as a competitor for scarce government funds.[61] And railways were expensive. David Hansemann's demand that 'the state build the railways' was rejected because the funds would increase the government debt. Many officials remembered the bankruptcy following Jena and therefore feared budget deficits, but the deeper reason was political. Because new government loans required the approval of an elected assembly, they would trigger promises to introduce a constitution which had been made during the wars against Napoleon and the reform period.[62]

Unwilling to construct railways itself, the government reluctantly moved towards private construction. When private railways were finally authorized in 1838, they were subjected to extremely restrictive regulations and continual administrative oversight. Officials initially opposed the telegraph, fearing its use for unauthorized political messages.[63] In 1842 the government compromised with the representatives of the provincial estates, guaranteeing 3.5 per cent interest on railway bonds and refunding the state debt at the same rate. Lines were proposed, and private construction began. Then, in 1844, the government suddenly became concerned about 'speculation' in railway shares, and prohibited further subscriptions without specific government permission. The prohibition set off a financial panic and contributed to the depression of the mid-1840s. Behind the government's decision lay a concern for eastern agriculture. Sales of the bonds issued by *Landschaften* credit banks, after rising rapidly from 1815 to 1835, had stagnated as investors turned to railways.[64]

Colleen Dunlavy has compared the early histories of railway promotion in Germany and the United States. In the 1830s and 1840s in the United States, power concentrated at the middle level of state governments, which competed vigorously to promote their economies, whereas the federal and local levels of government were relatively weak. State legislatures imposed taxes, went into debt, and spent the money to extend their transportation networks as rapidly as possible. In Prussia, by contrast, a comparatively powerful central bureaucracy stood in opposition to local interests. Although the Prussian state could define policy, those local interests could hamper its execution if they saw their interests threatened. In addition, we may add, Prussian regional interests were seen as a possible threat by the central government. Therefore, for example, the governments of Westphalia or the Rhine Province could not play the same promotional role as the governments of Pennsylvania and New York. By 1840 the United States already had 4535 kilometres of railway line open, and this rose to 14,518 in 1850 and 49,288 in 1860.[65] As can be seen in Table 4.1, the comparable figures for Germany were less than 500 kilometres in 1840, some 6000 in 1850, and still only 11,000 in 1860.

Railway development entailed expansion of the mining and metals industries, particularly in the Rhineland, but government policy consistently hindered their growth in the 1830s and 1840s. Friedrich Harkort's discovery of the possibility of smelting black-band ore containing both coal and iron went unexploited for 20 years, due to the government's insistence that only licensed coal miners work the deposits. Franz Haniel's deep mining shaft, the key to the exploitation of the coal deposits extending north from the Ruhr, was delayed ten years by bureaucratic opposition. Miners, according to government officials, were unable to manage their own affairs, a possible reflection of Hegel's patronizing statement quoted above, and also a reflection of the officials' paternal concern for society as a whole. A substantial proportion of the shareholders in Rhenish mines were women and minors, silent partners with their trust funds invested in an industry considered exceptionally safe because of extensive government control.[66]

The contrast with the United States is again instructive. Driven by the demand from the expanding railway system, subsidized by state governments, and protected by national tariffs, the US coal and iron industries accelerated past and away from Germany. Total US coal output rose from 2.2 million tons in 1840 to 7.5 million in 1850 and 18.1 million in 1860, and iron output from 291,000 tons in 1840 to 572,000 tons in 1850 and 835,000 tons in 1860.[67] Table 4.1 shows Germany at a comparable level to the United States in 1840 (or even ahead of it), but then falling far behind. German coal output was 3.2 million tons in 1840, 5.2 million in 1850, and 12.3 million in 1860. Iron output was 173,000 tons in 1840, 212,000 in 1850, and 545,000 in 1860.

Prussian commercial and industrial leaders in the 1830s and 1840s complained that there was a shortage of capital, and that it was especially difficult to obtain finance for new transportation and industrial projects. However, their difficulties did not reflect German poverty or a lack of savings. Rather, the flow of funds to would-be entrepreneurs was limited by the structure of the banking system (as discussed in detail in Chapter 5) and by government policy. Banks were typically family firms or partnerships whose banking activities had grown as a sideline to their commercial interests. In addition, for individual investors government securities and quasi-government issues such as the *Landschaften* bonds offered safe returns. Bankers reinforced this conservative prejudice. The Rothschild bank, for instance, was an alliance of five family firms in Frankfurt am Main, London, Paris, Vienna, and Milan, headed by the sons of the founder. They had grown rich by underwriting loans raised by the Prussian government early in the century, and government business remained their preference. Their resources, though large, were still limited by their personal fortunes, and they were notoriously reluctant to finance large and possibly risky industrial projects.

The Prussian government's very restrictive monetary policy further reduced the funds available. Business leaders complained that the government's refusal to increase the supply of banknotes restricted credit and hampered their activities. Government officials replied that their broader vision of the state's interest was preferable to the short-sighted views and possibly damaging impact of individual entrepreneurs. Again, the underlying issue was the distribution of political power. Banknotes were considered part of the public debt, and a substantial increase would have raised the same constitutional questions as borrowing for railway investment.[68]

Business leaders also complained that the Prussian government's suspicion of limited liability corporations hampered development. Railways and the new larger mines and blast furnaces in the Ruhr were too large for individual investors and too risky for partnerships with unlimited liability. A limited liability corporation spreads the risk of investment among large numbers of individuals, and this makes large-scale investments in new technologies easier. Many government officials, however, regarded all organizations outside their direct control as potential centres of political opposition, and therefore very few charters of incorporation were granted, only 67 between 1826 and 1850.[69] The interlocking policies affecting markets, transportation, and industrial technology from the 1820s to the 1840s reveal a confusion of motives but also an overriding concern for stability on the part of Prussian officials, some of whom would have preferred to 'slam Pandora's box shut' by slowing industrial growth.[70] Contemporaries asserted that in states where government policy was more supportive, capital seemed in less short supply and industry developed rapidly. In the Kingdom of Saxony, for instance, grants to individual industrialists exemplified a less restrictive attitude.[71]

4.5 State economic policy and the upswing of the 1850s and 1860s

Under state administration, railways are much more useful for the direct interests of the state and the public. (August von der Heydt)

Heydt ... as the ambitious head of a new ministry, interpreted his duties broadly, bending laws and encroaching upon state revenues as benefited his ministry. (James Brophy)[72]

Beginning with the 1850s, we possess Hoffmann's systematic estimates of German national product. The figures show that total output within the German borders of 1913 grew in a series of long waves, with rapid growth from 1850 to 1873, slower growth during the 'Great Depression' from 1873 to 1896, and then rapid growth again from 1896 to 1913 (as can be seen in Table 4.2). This pattern fits with the timing of the long swings in the modern world economy first identified by the Russian economist Nikolai Kondratiev in the 1920s. Both the figures themselves and their interpretation have been extensively debated. Rejected by some scholars in the 1970s on both theoretical and empirical grounds, long cycles have regained some of their popularity as an interpretative framework. Although neither as regular nor as predictable as Kondratiev surmised, they appear in a wide variety of data for the nineteenth and twentieth centuries.[73]

The long swings in total output correspond to the alternations of rapid and slow growth in the other industrialized economies. In addition, as shown in Table 4.3, the rates of growth of most of the important categories of exports showed the same pattern. After growing slowly through the 1830s and 1840s, German exports rose rapidly during the 1850s and 1860s,

Table 4.2 Employment, output, and investment in Germany, 1850–1913

	1850	1873	1895	1913
Labour force (thousands):				
Total	15,028	18,643	23,405	30,034
Agriculture	8,293	9,230	9,788	10,627
Industry	3,491	5,439	7,956	11,377
Services	3,244	3,974	5,661	8,030
Output (five-year averages, million 1913 marks):				
Total	9,555[a]	16,376[b]	27,563[c]	44,761[d]
Agriculture	4,327[a]	6,130[b]	8,708[c]	10,619[d]
Industry	2,019[a]	5,336[b]	8,535[c]	19,758[d]
Services	3,209[a]	4,910[b]	10,320[c]	14,384[d]
Percentage rate of increase:				
Total		2.73	2.39	3.08
Agriculture		1.76	1.61	1.25
Industry		4.98	2.16	5.39
Services		2.15	3.43	2.10
Output per worker (five-year averages, 1913 marks):				
Total	636	878	1,178	1,490
Agriculture	522	664	890	999
Industry	578	981	1,072	1,737
Services	989	1,235	1,823	1,791
Percentage rate of increase:				
Total		1.63	1.35	1.48
Agriculture		1.15	1.34	0.73
Industry		2.98	0.40	3.06
Services		1.12	1.79	−0.11
Capital stock (billion 1913 marks):				
Total	46.77	77.31	141.18	255.94
Agriculture	24.99	32.47	40.36	53.21
Industry	7.16	13.70	34.60	85.20
Railways	1.15	6.74	14.25	22.90
Non-agricultural housing	6.98	14.58	35.69	66.86
Government construction	6.99	9.82	16.28	27.77

Notes:
[a] 1850–5.
[b] 1871–5.
[c] 1893–7.
[d] 1909–13.
Source: Calculated from data in Hoffmann, *Wachstum.* Boundaries of 1913.

then generally more slowly during the 1870s and 1880s, and then very rapidly from the mid-1890s to 1913. If these figures can be accepted, they strongly suggest that the rate of development in each period depended substantially on Germany's participation in the movements of the world economy.[74] This clearly reduces the possible role of government policy. On the other hand, German development possessed a number of distinct features, and some of these were closely related to the actions of government officials.

Table 4.3 Yearly percentage rates of growth of exports, 1836–1913

	1837–51	*1851–73*	*1873–95*	*1895–1912*
Total	2.47	5.55	2.94	5.47
Food and raw materials				
Grains	2.61	2.45	–2.87	8.93
Coal	4.96	9.22	3.29	6.70
Semi-manufactures	3.60	8.01	5.08	7.48
Yarn	2.40	8.64	0.36	3.57
Iron	1.10	14.70	7.30	8.02
Manufactured goods	2.90	5.12	3.40	5.76
Textiles	3.05	2.73	4.43	2.53
Metalware, machinery	4.17	6.86	7.44	10.1
Chemicals	2.08	7.01	6.57	8.03

Source: Calculated from data in Hoffmann, *Wachstum*, pp. 530–2, 533–4. Three-year averages taken around the indicated year. Boundaries of 1913. Figures before 1880 are estimates based on incomplete data; see the discussion on pp. 535–6.

Once more, a comparison with twentieth-century Asian economies proves instructive. In contrast to the pessimism of the 1960s and 1970s, from the 1980s onward Asian economies grew rapidly. In a number of the most successful of these economies, 'pilot' agencies emerged as the primary institutions in the implementation of industry policy: the Ministry of International Trade and Industry (MITI) in Japan, the Economic Planning Board (EPB) in South Korea, the Council for Economic Planning and Development (CEPAD) in Taiwan, and the Economic Development Board (EPB) in Singapore. They share certain positive features, including their elite status within the bureaucracy, their acknowledged technical expertise, a clear focus, and insulation from political and interest-group pressures.[75] They also resemble one another in that they have all been highly controversial. Observers have disagreed over their success. They have aroused strenuous opposition both from private interests outside the government, who resent their interference, and from other agencies within the government, who resent their power and their expansionist tendencies.[76]

This Asian experience has parallels with nineteenth-century Germany. In contrast to the hesitant development of the 1830s and 1840s, the 1850s and 1860s saw rapid growth in a number of the German states.[77] In Prussia in particular, institutional changes made the government more responsive to the needs of emerging industries. In Prussia in 1848 the revolutionary government had established a separate Ministry of Trade, Commerce, and Public Works. Although the revolution went down in defeat, the new ministry remained, and so did the Minister, August von der Heydt. Heydt had been a merchant banker in the Rhineland and a liberal opponent of the government in the 1840s. Appointed to the ministry in December 1848, he survived in office until 1862, when he served briefly as head of the cabinet during the constitutional crisis, and then returned in 1866 to organize the financing of the war with Austria. His influence and the impact of his ministry can be seen across a broad range of state policies.

Heydt could pursue his preferred policies because of the balance of political forces within Prussia and the diplomatic struggle looming within the German Confederation. Constitutional government remained after the revolutions in most states, including Prussia. Encouraged by his conservative courtiers, Friedrich Wilhelm IV would have preferred to withdraw the new constitution, but his successive minister-presidents Friedrich von Brandenburg, Josef Maria von Radowitz, and Otto von Manteuffel all insisted that it be retained. They believed the defeat of the revolutions meant that a new struggle with Austria would begin. Repression would create internal opposition and weaken Prussia in this more important conflict. The constitution, they argued, despite granting the legislative assembly the right to approve the budget, need not interfere with bureaucratic administration. Retaining it would win internal support and therefore strengthen Prussia.[78]

In the *Landtag*, the Prussian government and its former liberal opponents of 1848 gradually moved toward an accommodation, concretely embodied in a reorganization and redirection of government finances. Industrial and commercial interests had complained both that the government was insufficiently active in support of modern industry, and that they paid a disproportionate share of taxes. Now, as can be seen in Table 4.4, taxes rose substantially, but the proportion paid by the industrial provinces declined. The share of tax revenue distributed by Heydt's ministry increased, and government spending was redirected, largely towards railway construction. After a decline through the 1830s and 1840s, the Prussian government debt nearly doubled from 1848 to 1865, and over half of the increase was spent on railways.[79] It is important that military spending rose substantially as well. This pleased the army, whose officers came overwhelmingly from the aristocratic *Junker* class. More importantly, army leaders became convinced of the strategic importance of railways as well as new improved firearms, and this implied recognition of the link between industrial development and military power.[80] For their part, liberals also were not opposed to a rising army budget, as long as the army was used to further the cause of German unity.[81] It was their suspicion that the government intended to use the army against them as in 1848, and their outrage when the government attempted to bypass the *Landtag* to implement its proposed army reforms, that led to the constitutional crisis of 1862.

Under Heydt, government policy toward industrial investment also changed significantly. Compared to the 67 limited liability corporations authorized between 1826 and 1850, 119 received approval from 1851 to 1857, and a further 82 from 1858 to 1867.[82] Most of the new corporations were in the expanding coal and iron complex in Rhineland-Westphalia.[83] Just as important, the old mining laws were reformed, taxes lowered, state supervision ended, and the privileges of the miners' guilds eliminated. By

Table 4.4 Central government spending in Prussia, 1815–66

	1821	1829	1838	1847	1849	1853	1856	1866
Spending, current prices (million thaler)	82	83	86	93	94	103	127	158
Spending, 1913 prices (million thaler)	78	65	69	79	62	102	133	147
Spending per capita, 1913 prices (thaler)	7.0	5.1	4.7	4.9	3.8	6.0	7.7	7.5
Distribution of spending (%):								
Military	27	26	31	28	29		27	29
Debt	13	14	13	8	8		11	11
Commercial[a]	16	16	16	19	27		30	31
Administrative	44	44	40	44	36		32	29
Government debt (million thaler):								
Funded, total	207		164		138		228	269
(of which, for railways)							83	105
Paper money and note issue	11		18		32		31	79
Distribution of revenue (%):								
Non-tax	34	35	34	34	35		44	51
Tax	65	65	66	66	65		56	49
Distribution of land tax (%):								
Agrarian provinces[b]	25		25					39
Industrial provinces[c]	75		75					61

Notes:
[a] Mines, forest, crown lands, railroads, postal services, and expenditures by the Ministries of Commerce and Industry to 1848 and by the Ministry of Commerce, Industry and Public Works thereafter.
[b] Pomerania, Posen, Brandenburg, Prussia.
[c] Rhineland, Westphalia, Saxony, Silesia.
Source: Adapted from Richard H. Tilly, 'The Political Economy of Public Finance and the Industrialization of Prussia, 1815–66', *Journal of Economic History*, 26 (1966), pp. 484–97.

1861 the emerging mining corporations were free to invest when and where they wanted, while wages were set by market forces and the workers' power to resist change had effectively been eliminated.[84] Trade treaties with France in 1862 and with Belgium, Britain, and Italy in 1865 opened markets for exporters, but during the upswing following the 1857 commercial crisis the new lower import duties did not damage domestic producers.

Capital for these new undertakings was more readily available than in the previous generation. In the 1850s and 1860s the supply of money (metal coins, banknotes, and bank deposits) increased much more rapidly than previously.[85] Furthermore, the less restrictive attitude towards corporate governance gradually extended to the banking sector, as discussed in Chapter 5. Looking to the French Crédit Mobilier as a model, several business groups proposed banks organized as limited liability corporations; with capital bases larger than the fortunes of any individual or family, they could actively seek out investment opportunities in expanding areas of the economy. These 'universal' banks faced the hesitancy of government officials who feared instability and speculation, the opposition of existing private bankers who feared new competition, and hostility from Heydt, himself a former private banker and now a minister who wanted to control this important area of policy. The earliest of the new banks exploited legal loopholes, as in the case of the Diskonto-Gesellschaft (1851), or established their headquarters outside Prussian jurisdiction, as in the case of Darmstädter Bank (1853). In the boom year 1856 the Diskonto-Gesellschaft was reorganized, however, and was joined by further new banks in Hamburg, Leipzig, Breslau, and in the South. Another wave of bank foundations followed the establishment of the North German Confederation in 1867, culminating in the formation of several large new corporations including the Deutsche Bank (1870) and the Dresdener Bank (1872).[86]

The figures show that the 1850s and 1860s were very good decades for the economies of the German states. There was still no 'national' economy, but on average the German economies were growing rapidly. Industrial investment had come to dominate the business cycle. Output per worker rose, and there were especially large increases in output per worker in the industrial sector. Today we expect yearly increases in productivity to result from a stream of new technologies, but in the 1850s and 1860s this kind of change was new and revolutionary. Contemporaries marvelled at the new machines displayed at shows modelled on the 1851 Crystal Palace exhibition in London. An exhibition in Karlsruhe drew 100,000 visitors in 1861, equivalent to 10 per cent of Baden's adult population.[87]

Rapid growth depended on the ready availability of credit, because the new technologies required large increases in industrial capital. The amount of capital per worker in the industrial sector rose substantially, but total productivity rose even more rapidly. Some of the 'additional' improvement in the economy's efficiency resulted from the rapid development of transportation, both the extension of the canal system and the expansion of the railway network. New canals were built, and older canals were expanded to accommodate larger vessels. Traditionally, barges had been dragged along the canals by horses, and by men and women when horses were too expensive. Now, steam power was introduced, sometimes using steam engines on the bank to draw barges along using cables attached to the vessels or to moving chains on the bottom of the canal, and sometimes to power the new larger canal boats themselves.[88]

But it was the railways that captured the imagination of the century. 'A new chapter in world history begins,' wrote poet Heinrich Heine after observing the opening of a railway line in 1843. 'With each new iron steed that travels the rails, a piece of feudalism falls into the abyss of an irrecoverable past,' declared the historian Johannes Scherr in 1858.[89] The railways themselves were an unparalleled investment undertaking, and fluctuations in railway investment dominated the industrial business cycle from the 1840s to the 1880s. Tens of thousands of labourers were mobilized for the construction of the new lines. Even more important than the increase in total length, however, was the gradual creation of connections among the producing and consuming regions in the German states. The whole was greater than the sum of the parts, and out of the many decisions to build particular lines emerged a single economy whose interdependent units were linked by the flows of goods and people along the canals and over the railway lines.[90]

The new transportation network created 'backward linkages' by providing markets for a broad range of industries. Construction required stone, cement, and timber. Steamboats, barges, rails, locomotives, and rolling stock required iron, steel, and machinery. These in turn required coal.[91] There were crucial 'forward linkages' as well. The decreasing cost of transportation reduced the prices manufacturers and farmers charged their customers. Production therefore expanded and concentrated in those districts where costs were lowest; producers in high-cost areas were forced to move, or fail. Railways and canals increased the speed and reliability of the delivery of raw materials and finished products, which meant that firms did not have to maintain such large stocks on hand. This permitted a substantial reduction in the amount of capital required for inventories. In turn, the capital released could be made available for other investments.

Keeping in mind the changing structure of the bureaucracy may provide a vantage point from which to view these changes in economic policy. If we look again at the opposition to railways within the Prussian government, we see that it came not from the emerging class of officials certified by examination, but from the older generation. Both Rother (head of the *Seehandlung*) and Karl von Nagler (Postmaster General) opposed railway construction. They feared that because of their great expense railways would be certain to lose money. In addition, railways would compete with the government's turnpikes and with the profitable freight business of the government's postal coaches, with disastrous consequences for the government's finances. Beuth, serving as finance minister, also feared the expense, and argued that the level of industrialization in Prussia did not justify investment in railways.[92]

Heydt pressed at every opportunity for extension of the government's railway system. He aimed for an integrated network of state railways. When his funding needs exceeded the legal limits of his budget or borrowing authorization, he concealed income, attempted to raise new loans, or simply violated the guidelines. On one occasion he attempted to raise money from private bankers through a complex and clearly illegal sale and repurchase of government-owned railway shares. He used his extensive powers of supervision over private railways ruthlessly, and he was accused of forcing railways into unprofitable operations such as night trains, in order to bankrupt them so they could be more easily acquired by the government. By 1858 the Prussian state railways totalled 1265 kilometres, compared to 2960 kilometres of private lines.

Heydt is a transitional and possibly unique figure, however. He was not a career bureaucrat, and his actions as minister aroused hostility both inside and outside government. Not only Beuth but also his successors as finance minister Karl von Bodelschwingh and Robert von Patow opposed Heydt's plans. Private investors were outraged at his exploitation of the legal provisions that allowed the state to impose taxes on railways that could be used to purchase their shares, in effect forcing the railway companies to pay for their own nationalization. They were further incensed over his insistence on night trains. They opposed his attempts to purge the postal and the railway departments to eliminate former revolutionary leaders or any employee suspected of 'democratic' sentiments.[93] Heydt however insisted that because of their importance railways must be run by 'reliable persons'. He also insisted that the main function of the railways was to maintain the 'authority of the state'. 'Short-sighted' private economic considerations were unimportant, and even the government's income played a subordinate role in his vision.[94]

The rapid growth of the 1850s and 1860s clearly owed much to the policies of the Ministry of Trade, Commerce, and Public Works, and to Heydt's leadership. However, his independence depended on the desire of his superiors, minister-presidents Brandenburg, Radowitz, and Manteuffel, for a minimal accommodation with the liberal majority in the *Landtag*. They wanted a healthy economy, but they did not intend to create a pilot agency to target new technologies, and they certainly did not intend that such an agency would pursue its policies independently. By the late 1850s Heydt's dogged pursuit of his and his ministry's goals had created a powerful coalition of enemies in and out of government. There were accusations of inefficiency and incompetence in his ministry, and his brief turn as head of the government in 1862 ended in a crushing electoral defeat.[95] His successor shared Heydt's lack of concern for legislative restraints on expenditure. Unlike Heydt, however, Otto von Bismarck was more than willing to exploit the fact that economic and military power had become inextricably intertwined. The Prussian army, equipped with the latest in modern arms, made efficient use of the railway system in the wars against Denmark, Austria, and France that created the Bismarckian empire.

4.6 The Bismarckian state: developmental, transformative, or predatory?

. . . conflicts become a question of power. Whoever holds the power then proceeds according to his own will, for the life of the state cannot remain still even for a second. (Otto von Bismarck, 1862)[96]

I keep in mind that, historically, authoritarian regimes have tended to outlive their usefulness. (Ferdinand Marcos, *Revolution from the Centre: How the Philippines is Using Martial Law to Build a New Society*, 1978)

The new German national government failed its first economic test. The creation of the empire was followed not by prosperity, but by a speculative boom, a catastrophic collapse in October 1873, and a depression that bore the name 'Great Depression' until the even greater disasters of the 1930s. Bismarck imposed an indemnity of 5 billion gold francs on the defeated French.[97] Both federal and state governments used the money to retire their war loans and other bond issues, for construction projects, and for generous gifts to the successful generals and politicians, notably Bismarck himself. Virtually the entire amount therefore passed almost immediately into circulation. In addition, the government introduced a new gold-backed currency, the mark, but without retiring the old silver-based currencies, and continued to mint additional silver coins.[98] This money entered an economy already in the final phase of a cyclical upswing and was therefore highly inflationary. From 1869 to 1873 banknotes and metallic currency in circulation increased by 51 per cent, and the index of investment goods prices rose by 55 per cent.[99]

Rising prices, the easy availability of capital, and the new, more lenient law of incorporation led to a large number of 'foundations', nearly 1000 companies in Prussia alone from mid-1870 to mid-1873. This is why the early 1870s in Germany are called the 'Gründerzeit', the foundation era. Many of those who had owned the government bonds that had been retired with the indemnity now turned to other forms of investment. The registered capital of incorporated enterprises increased from 473 million to 1.1 billion marks from 1869 to 1873, and the Berlin stock market rose by 50 per cent. The speculative atmosphere provided opportunities for the unscrupulous. Railway promoters in particular offered discounted shares in their companies to pay their suppliers and prayed that a continued rise in the stock market would carry their inflated capitalizations and satisfy their creditors. This was the technique employed by Bethel Henry Strousberg, the 'railway king'. Strousberg, already in difficulties since 1871, became only one among many when the collapse came. He went bankrupt, spent time in a Moscow prison for debt, and died in Berlin in 1884, the public personification of the boom and the crash.[100]

Adolf Hansemann, head of the Diskonto-Gesellschaft, and Gerson Bleichröder, Bismarck's personal banker, acted for the German government in transferring the French indemnity to Berlin. During 1872 they exploited their connections to secure large loans from the government that they used to gain control of railways, banks, insurance companies, and also breweries, traditionally the 'cash cows' used to fund takeovers. Their combinations and acquisitions may have been in the grey area where public and private interests intersect, but others had crossed the line. In February 1873 the Liberal deputy Eduard Lasker delivered a three-hour speech in the Prussian *Landtag*, during which he denounced the activities of railway promoters such as Strousberg who he claimed had paid certain high officials to exercise their influence with the Prussian Ministry of Commerce. The investigations of the ensuing royal commission resulted in the resignations of Hermann Wagener, one of Bismarck's senior advisers, and Heinrich von Itzenplitz, who had replaced Heydt as commerce minister.[101]

As seen in Table 4.2, the rate of growth of the German economy slowed for over two decades. Total output dropped in 1876 and 1877, and again in 1879 and 1880. Net investment stagnated at depressed levels through the late 1870s, rose in the late 1880s, but slumped again in 1891. The construction industry declined between 1875 and 1883, and did not regain its 1875 peak until 1892. Agricultural output grew slowly compared to the preceding upswing, and declined in several years.[102]

Bismarck cannot bear the entire blame. Although the inflationary bubble and the 1873 crisis were exacerbated by the mismanagement of the indemnity and by corrupt dealings on the part of insiders with government connections, a range of underlying factors contributed to the subsequent long downswing. A difficult transition was in progress. The German economy was becoming an *industrial* economy. By 1895, industry employed 34 per cent of the German labour force, and the share of agriculture had dropped to less than half the total. There were changes within industry as well. Although industrial investment rose both absolutely and as a proportion of national income, investment in railways slowed, reflecting the maturing of this key leading sector. The rate of increase in output per industrial worker dropped. This suggests that the easier gains of the preceding period, achieved through expanding markets and connections among previously isolated regions, had now been largely exploited.

The long cycle turned up again in the 1890s, and Germany enjoyed very rapid growth from 1895 to 1913. The upward thrust of the aggregate figures reflected the boom in industry and a parallel boom in urban construction, interrupted only slightly in 1901. High levels of industrial investment and a steady stream of new technologies led to substantial increases in productivity.[103] The industries of the 'second industrial revolution', advanced machine tools, applied chemistry, and especially electricity, emerged as the new leading sectors.[104] The production of chemicals increased 6.6 per cent per year, the output of the metals and machinery industries 8.3 per cent each, and electrical power output nearly 18 per cent per year.[105] The share of the population living in cities of over 100,000 persons rose from 12 per cent in 1890 to 21 per cent in 1910 (as discussed in Chapter 6). Employment in the construction industry increased from 1 million to 1.7 million from 1895 to 1911.[106] Margrit Grabas sees the combination of 'extensive' and 'intensive' growth represented by the linkage of urbanization and electrification as the prime motive force of the entire upswing.[107]

Germany's growth and position in 1913 can be compared to those of other established and emerging industrial economies (as can be seen in Table 4.5). The figures show Germany still well behind Britain in 1913, about equal with Japan in terms of the rate of growth of total output, and about equal with France in terms of the growth of output per person. They also show that all these European economies had been left behind by the growth of the United States. Among this select group of fortunate countries, Germany's performance was good, but not outstanding. Measures of change such as the decline in agricultural employment and urbanization also show that Germany's development was not particularly rapid compared to other European countries.[108] Despite two generations of rapid change, and despite Germany's undoubted position among the leaders in the new technologies, productivity in German industry was still only about two-thirds of British levels in 1913.[109]

These comparative figures also remind us that the pattern of German development partly reflected outside influences. Other countries experienced the downswing as well as the following upswing. Angus Maddison's estimates show that the international economy slowed in the 1870s and 1880s, but then expanded more rapidly following the mid-1890s. As can be seen in Table 4.3, exports also grew more slowly during the Great Depression of the early 1870s than over the previous two decades. They boomed during the following upswing, but Germany also became more

Table 4.5 International comparisons of German growth, 1870–1913

	1870	*1913*
Gross domestic product (millions of 1990 dollars):		
Germany	44,101	145,068
Britain	95,651	214,464
France	71,419	143,125
United States	98,418	517,990
Japan	25,505	68,933
Share of world product (%):		
Germany	2.4	5.7
Britain	5.2	8.4
France	3.9	5.6
United States	5.3	20.3
Japan	1.4	2.7
Gross domestic product per capita (1990 dollars):		
Germany	1,913	3,833
Britain	3,263	5,032
France	1,858	3,452
United States	2,457	5,307
Japan	741	1,334

Source: Angus Maddison, *Monitoring the World Economy 1820–1992* (Paris, 1995).

dependent on the world economy. The value of German exports rose from 9.5 per cent of gross domestic product in 1870 to 15.6 per cent in 1913.[110] Industrial exports boomed, but as had been the case since the 1860s, German farmers suffered from the competition of producers in eastern Europe, Canada, the United States, Latin America, and Australia. Because those farmers included the politically influential Prussian *Junker* aristocracy, the problems of agriculture became a public issue. Despite pride in Germany's accomplishments, the figures in the 1895 census set off an intense debate over the extent and meaning of Germany's transition from an 'agricultural' to an 'industrial' state (as discussed in Chapter 3).[111]

What sort of a state was the Bismarckian empire, and what role did it play in economic growth? The Bismarckian 'intervention state' continues to be portrayed as both powerful and purposive, 'a combination of individualistic and tariff- and social-political interventionist principles' according to Nipperdey.[112] Even among historians less favourable to Bismarck, such as Wehler, the state is seen as modernizing, reformist, and effective: 'State aid and damage repair, state sponsorship and direction of the so-called "free" economy, had proved themselves unavoidable.'[113]

The analysis of states and economic growth in Asia suggests that at some point successful states must alter their form. In the case of Germany, we may say that if the 1850s and 1860s represented a period of developmental state activity, then the new empire should have aimed to develop structures of embedded autonomy or governed interdependence. In the 1820s and 1830s one might have argued in favour of a 'strong' German state, prepared to force unwilling individuals and groups into new modes of behaviour. This had changed by the 1840s and, as seen above, the relationship between German commercial and industrial leaders following the 1848 revolution was marked both by accommodation and by conflict. By the later decades of the century the role of the state should have evolved towards attempting to ensure a continuing transformative capacity. Germany was no longer a consumer of technologies produced elsewhere, but had itself become a centre of technological invention. A market-oriented reformer would have suggested that the state remove itself from the economic realm, aside from the guarantee of 'peace, easy taxes, and tolerable administration of justice' which Adam Smith recommended. A statist writer would see a continuing role for the state, but a more cooperative one, a shared project between public officials and private interests.

The management of an advanced economy moving to new higher levels of productivity is a complex task and requires high levels of technical competence. As we have seen, statist writers emphasize the role of elite institutions, but also the need for these institutions to be insulated from outside pressure, while still connected to important social groups in order to persuade them to sacrifice their immediate interests to further the goals of the state. In such an 'embedded' state, politicians should reign but not attempt to rule. Rather, they should protect bureaucrats from interest-group pressures, thereby creating the space they need to guide development and manage the economy. Japan is the classic contemporary example.[114]

The range of measures introduced by the new German government certainly makes an impressive list, which can easily be extended. Henderson cites the new currency, the Imperial Railway Office, and the *Reichsbank*.[115] William Carr mentions the uniform coinage, adherence to the gold standard, the *Reichsbank*, the 'standardized and modernized' legal system, and the 1879 imperial court of appeal.[116] Blackbourn itemizes the Audit Office (1871), the Statistical Office (1872), the Railway Office (1873), the National Debt Administration (1874), the Health Department and the Post Office (1876), and the Patent Office, Justice Department and Supreme Court (1877).[117] In addition, the empire inherited and extended a wide range of official and semi-official institutions that linked public officials and private interests on a consultative basis. Regional Chambers of Commerce and Agricultural Associations had existed since the first half of the century. The national German Agricultural Council was established in 1872.[118] The Prussian State Railway Council established in 1883 advised on freight rate structures.[119]

However, the German state's capacity for direct intervention in the economy was limited. Although the Imperial government enjoyed a high degree of autonomy in areas where it was free of constitutional limits, those areas were few. The Empire was a federal state, often hamstrung by the conflict between Prussia and the other member states. Bismarck's plan for a national railway administration failed. Laws for a national railway system proposed in 1874 and 1875 were rejected, as was a plan for the sale of the Prussian state railways to the Empire. Bismarck withdrew the proposals, and Alfred von Maybach, the head of a new Prussian Ministry of Public Works that included the Prussian state railways, gained effective control over the Imperial Railway Office and the railway lines in Alsace-Lorraine. Beginning in 1879, Maybach began to purchase private lines, and by 1890 the government owned nearly all the railway lines in Prussia. In contrast to the 1850s and 1860s, during the depression of the 1870s private investors were quite happy to sell to the government. Bismarck's plans were defeated not in the popularly elected *Reichstag*, where the majority National Liberals now supported a national railway system, but in the *Reichsrat*, in which the federal states dominated. The Saxon and Bavarian governments took over private railway lines within their borders to prevent their falling into the hands of the Prussians, and the systems remained separate until 1917.[120]

The Imperial government could neither tax nor spend as it wished, because the states perceived increases in the government's budget as increases in Prussian power. Only the member states had the right to levy direct taxes. Legislation limited the amount of tariff revenue which the Imperial government could retain, and the balance went to the member states. Any resulting deficit then required contributions negotiated with the states. Fiscal policy therefore faced severe constraints, which worsened as demands on the budget increased.

In the years before the First World War, the budget deteriorated into a permanent crisis. Table 4.6 shows the dependence of the government on consumption taxes, tariffs, and income from state property such as the railways, telegraph, post, and banking services. Table 4.6 also reveals the rise in military spending, and the large gap between income and expenditures. The share of the military in net expenditures rose from 65 per cent in 1900–5 to 80 per cent in 1910–13. The government overspent its net income by 40 per cent in 1900–5 and by 20 per cent in 1910–13, when the net deficit averaged over 400 million marks per year. The outstanding debt of the imperial government rose from a negligible 16 million marks in 1876 to 4.84 billion marks in 1910.[121] Taxes and tariffs bore most heavily on those with low incomes, and the Socialist Party was most successful in those elections where taxes, tariffs, and military spending were the key issues.[122] The shortage of funds also divided the conservative parties, and tariffs, trade treaties, major construction projects such as the *Mittellandkanal* intended to connect the Rhine and Elbe, increases in the size of the army, and the expansion of the new navy, all became bitterly contested confrontations.

Monetary policy provides another means of controlling and guiding the economy, but here too the Imperial government's powers were restricted

Table 4.6 Imperial government income and expenditure, 1872–1913 (millions of marks)

	1872–75	1880–85	1890–95	1900–05	1910–13
Net income:	345	491	930	1281	2045
Total indirect taxes	224	335	623	819	1311
(of which, tariff revenue)	110	191	360	488	701
(of which, excise taxes)	114	144	263	331	610
Total direct taxes	–	–	–	–	44
Net state property income	43	101	128	275	598
Loans	–	38	193	165	40
Contributions from states	78	17	(–20)	21	50
Total expenditure:	1095[a]	776	1553	2294	3244
State property expenses				502	792
Net expenditure:				1792	2452
Military expenditure	418	461	883	1155	1965
Civilian expenditure	41[b]	312[b]	670[b]	637	487
(of which, administration)				513	338
(of which, social welfare)				124	149

Notes:
[a] Includes indemnity payments from France.
[b] Includes state property expenses.
Source: Adapted from John M. Hobson, *The Wealth of States: A Comparative Sociology of International Economic and Political Change* (Cambridge, 1997), Tables 2.5, 2.8, and 2.10.

and the effects of the actions it did take questionable. In part this reflected international conditions. The new German mark was a gold-backed currency, and under the 'rules of the game', countries adhering to the gold standard could only increase their money supply as their reserves rose. But policy played a role as well. Historians and theorists have identified a number of ways in which policy could affect the supply of credit, even under the classic gold standard.[123] In the German case, the *Reichsbank*'s statute limited its currency issue to three times its reserves, but its reserves were rising, and it had considerable freedom within its legal guidelines. Bismarck himself, who as Chancellor possessed final authority over the *Reichsbank*, intervened only twice.[124] In 1880 he called for an increase in the discount rate. In 1887 he insisted that the *Reichsbank* forbid the acceptance of Russian government bonds as security for loans. This ill-conceived bit of bullying proved a serious foreign policy error, for it drove Russia out of the Berlin money market and 'into the arms of the French', in the words of Russian foreign minister Nikolai Giers.[125]

During the Great Depression of the 1870s and 1880s, German industrial entrepreneurs once again complained that credit was scarce. The money supply rose much less rapidly than in the 1850s and 1860s, and the amount of banknotes and coins in circulation actually declined.[126] Von Dechend, *Reichsbank* president from 1876 until 1890, was highly restrictive: 'One can only create respect for one's currency if one is not embarrassed to go right up with the discount rate, so people see that one knows how to protect one's metal'.[127] Under Koch, *Reichsbank* president from 1890 to 1908, the supply of money increased more rapidly. During the upswing, the total of currency plus bank deposits rose at a rate comparable to that of the 1850s and 1860s.[128] In addition, the *Reichsbank* could extend additional credit through its discount policy. In particular, it discounted the bills of the major private banks freely. In doing so, *Reichsbank* officials claimed that they were merely responding passively to the demands of the economy, despite the clear favouritism shown to large banks and industrial firms.

Supported by the *Reichsbank*, the 'great banks' loomed over the German business landscape (as discussed in detail in Chapter 5). They believed themselves to have played a central role in the burst of investment during the upswing. 'In Germany our banks are largely responsible for the development of the empire . . . To them, more than any other agency, may be credited the splendid results thus far realized,' remarked a senior official of the Dresdener in 1908.[129] Many observers since have agreed. They argue that the government's discount policy enabled the large banks to hold more risky portfolios than would otherwise have been possible. Therefore they could both 'lend to the hilt' and support new ventures directly with their own capital.[130] The size of the great banks and their multiple functions allowed them to tailor credit and services to the stage of development of each of their customer firms, leading to gains in efficiency, and the model has been recommended as an improvement on the United States financial system.[131]

However, the government's discount policy has been criticized. A comparative view of universal banking in Italy suggests that the system does not work as well as claimed.[132] In addition, the system may have misallocated credit. The large joint-stock banks provided only a fraction of total bank credit.[133] These banks favoured with privileged access to government credit in turn had their own preferred clients, the large firms in heavy industry. They provided very little credit to consumer goods industries, and virtually none to small and medium-sized firms. The resulting segmentation and distortion of the capital market may have reduced the overall rate of growth.[134] Banks also favoured the creation of cartels. Whereas in the United States any agreement 'in restraint of trade' could be prosecuted under the Sherman Antitrust Act of 1890, in Germany a court decision in 1897 held cartel arrangements to be legally enforceable contracts.[135] The Cartel Inquiry of 1905 listed 385 cartels, including 92 in heavy industry, but the total was generally believed to be much higher. Their goal was to protect existing investment, not to innovate, and like all monopolies, when demand dropped they reduced output and increased their prices, which worsened the effect of depressions.

A final area in which the government might have exercised an influence over the economy was tariff and commercial policy. The introduction of tariffs on agricultural and heavy industrial products in 1879 has been called the 'great turning point', and even the 'second foundation of the empire'.[136] However, although there were industrial interests who wanted tariffs to protect their domestic markets in the depressed 1870s, agricultural groups at first opposed tariffs because they feared retaliation from Germany's trading partners, and the German Agricultural Council continued to oppose tariffs until 1885. The decision for tariffs reflected Bismarck's desire for a secure *Reichstag* majority, and above all the government's need for revenue. The influence of Prussia on national policy meant the influence of the landowning aristocracy, in economic policy as in other areas. In contrast to Great Britain, in particular, the Bismarckian state could not impose direct taxes on property owners, and therefore despite the initial opposition of agricultural interests, tariffs were the only available option.[137]

In turn, once tariffs were in place, any attempt to lower or eliminate them met with furious opposition from the groups that benefited. Agitation against new Chancellor Leo von Caprivi's more liberal trade policies led to the formation of the *Bund der Landwirte* in 1893, and the trade treaty with Russia passed the *Reichstag* in 1894 by a vote of only 200 to 146, with the Socialist Party voting for the government and the Conservative Party opposing it. Ten years later only the accident of the Russo-Japanese war allowed Bernhard von Bülow to extort a new treaty from Russia which maintained German tariffs at high enough levels to satisfy protectionist interests and avoid the necessity for significant direct taxes on income and property.[138]

The Empire never exercised a guiding role in the economy, either at the macro-level or at the micro-level. The *Reichsbank* appears to have been 'captured' by the private banks it should have controlled, and fiscal policy was paralysed by the influence of powerful rent-seeking coalitions. The government failed to create an elite institution with the capabilities required to provide a focused direction to economic policy. Following Heydt's departure, the independence and power of the Prussian Ministry of Trade, Commerce, and Public Works had declined. His successor Itzenplitz did not share Heydt's commitment to a state rail system. He in effect surrendered policy to his subordinates, especially Rudolf von Delbrück, a free-trader who favoured private railways, partly because he had invested in them himself. Bismarck referred to Itzenplitz as a 'signature machine' because of his willingness to authorize new private railways, and accused him of lacking the 'necessary energy' to run a large and complex ministry.[139]

But Bismarck had no desire to foster autonomous ministries or independent ministers. He relied on Delbrück's support during the constitutional conflict and the wars of unification.[140] Delbrück then served as Vice-Chancellor and head of the new Reich Chancellor's Office, with a broad brief extending over economic, financial, social, and legal policy. However, from 1873 on, Bismarck progressively reduced the scope of the office because he feared Delbrück's power.[141] In 1876 Delbrück fell, a victim of Bismarck's turn toward protective tariffs. His replacement, Karl Hofmann, 'proved himself an pliant official, who executed Bismarck's will'.[142]

Furthermore, the bureaucracy as a whole became progressively less autonomous and possibly less adequate to the tasks it faced. The Empire relied on Prussian institutions. This meant it also relied on the Prussian bureaucracy. As detailed above, the sequence of examinations allowed Prussian government officials to claim elite status and to claim further that their status reflected their technical competence. However the process also guaranteed that only those with wealth or the right connections would survive. The proportion of higher bureaucrats who were the sons of higher- or middle-level bureaucrats increased from 37 per cent in the years 1876–1900, to 44 per cent in the years 1901–18, and the proportion who were the sons of wealthy industrialists rose from 12 to 21 per cent. And, if the examination system did not produce the desired results, then the supposedly universalistic norms were violated. Wilhelm II intervened to grant exemptions to aristocrats who had failed the examinations, a disposition of patronage 'which occasionally bordered on corruption'. As a result the proportion of landowners' sons declined only slightly from 29 to 22 per cent.[143]

Under Bismarck the demands for conformity by officials became overtly political. Catholic officials suffered during the *Kulturkampf* in the 1870s, and following the decision to introduce protective tariffs Bismarck regarded any official favouring free trade in the same light as one who had failed his examination.[144] There was no 'purge' in the sense of large numbers of dismissals, but the pressure increased and the range of permissible opinion narrowed.[145] Interior minister Robert von Puttkamer issued a regulation requiring officials to vote for government-approved candidates, and Bismarck defended him, insisting that 'activity of officials in the interest of the regime is a requirement of the monarchical state'.[146] In 1883 Puttkamer demanded 'absolute, unthinking subordination of officials to the will of the all-powerful minister' who had been placed over them by the king. Behaviour was continually monitored, and any unsuitable conduct could lead to disciplinary proceedings. In 1899, an official was dismissed for renting a house to a woman thought to be a Socialist 'agitator'.[147]

As a group, the bureaucrats sincerely believed themselves to be apolitical experts, but they were neither. Narrow-minded and conformist, they were increasingly detached from Germany's emerging industrial society:

> Used to legalistic and formal ways of thinking, unexposed to the risks of life, and alien to the needs and mores of common people, this group tended to become a caste – separate but unequal, as it were, a privileged class of its own, part of the governing classes, to be sure, deserving, perhaps even indispensable, but largely unpopular.[148]

There were some 'modernizers' among the bureaucrats, concentrated in Imperial offices and in Prussian ministries requiring technical skills such as finance and public works. They favoured export industries, some measures to pacify the working classes, lower tariffs, and less regressive taxes. However, they did not form a single party as had the 1807 reformers. Their potential influence was reduced by opposition from a grouping of intransigent traditionalist conservatives, typically former rural district officials and likely to be located in the Prussian agriculture and interior ministries. And even the modernizers opposed any change in the Empire's authoritarian institutions.[149]

Observers of Asian economies have contrasted developmental with 'predatory' states. In these states incumbents use their position to create rents for their supporters, and if those groups become dependent on 'rents' (in the economist's sense of the word), even if their original influence was based on entrepreneurial activity, they may become a hindrance to further development. Such patronage politics becomes more of a problem as the range of state activities increases.[150] The range of predatory behaviour runs from links between government and business in Japan and Korea, to the more direct involvement of leaders' family members and friends in the 'crony capitalism' of Indonesia, Thailand, and Malaysia, to cases of 'kleptocracy' such as the Marcos regime in the Philippines.[151]

Bismarck was personally corrupt. He evaded income tax by under-reporting his income by about a third. He forced the University of Berlin to appoint his personal physician to a professorship, to avoid the necessity of paying him. He manipulated government subsidies and tariffs specifically to ensure the profitability of his own estates, which produced primarily timber. He regularly used insider information in buying and selling shares, and in 1890 he speculated on his own dismissal by selling his German shares before the news was released, expecting that the German market would decline.[152] As noted above, other German officials in positions of influence also enriched themselves. Wilhelm von Kardorff, the Silesian iron magnate and leader of the protectionist Central Association of German Industrialists, claimed that he had won Bismarck over to a tariff on iron by telling him that the iron industry was the largest consumer of timber.[153] True or not, the story demonstrates rent-seeking activity and the privileged access of elite groups in an authoritarian system.

Some historians have viewed the entire Imperial system as corrupt and predatory. The wasteful competition among rent-seeking groups continued under Bismarck's successors. Eckart Kehr believed that narrow interest-group pressures lay behind both domestic and foreign policies, and drove Germany into the First World War.[154] Wehler, though not accepting all of Kehr's arguments, argues that Germany's 'special path' of development resulted in the extension of state intervention in the economy and the creation of 'corporatist' representation of influential groups. Bismarck had severe difficulties controlling these pressures even with the continued support of Wilhelm I. Under the erratic leadership of Wilhelm II, consultation became an opportunity for rent-seeking coalitions to press their demands on officials. The resulting 'polyarchy' was 'permanently unstable'.[155]

Bismarckian Germany had broken through to self-sustained industrial growth and continued growing during this period, but the 'first German economic miracle' was not quite so much of a miracle as some have held. It is often argued that the Bismarckian state played a major role in this economic success, and as seen above there are certainly examples of its actions that benefited the economy. In judging success and failure, we need to remember that even the most successful developmental states and the most celebrated pilot agencies remain contentious, their accomplishments disputed and their motives frequently suspect. Nevertheless, close analysis shows a wide variety of ways in which the Bismarckian state actually failed the economy. At the highest levels, policy suffered from the continual conflict among individuals and groups, and elite bureaucrats failed to make good the deficit. In the absence of clear policy direction, one must conclude that the German economy experienced the success it did in this period despite, rather than because of, the actions of the state.

4.7 Conclusion

Every action, whether progressive or conservative, should be taken in response to the occasion, and if it develops unfavourably should be abandoned. This may entail shame, but it is to be endured; justice may be with us, but we are not to choose that course. (Okubo Toshimichi, 1873)[156]

Okubo, one of the most important leaders of the Meiji Restoration, is known as 'the Bismarck of Japan'. The analogy is not exact. One of the reasons is that Japan was already unified. Another is the remarkable unanimity and consistency of purpose of the Meiji leaders. The group of men who came to power in 1868 wanted a 'rich country' and a 'strong army' to defend Japan and Asia against the West. They consciously chose to increase their country's 'productive power' by introducing modern manufacturing industry. They believed this was unlikely to result from the initiative of private individuals, that rather, as Okubo said, it required 'the patronage and encouragement of the government and its officials'. An Industry Section was created within the newly established Home Ministry, to take the Japanese economy 'with a single leap' into the modern world.[157] The younger officials throughout the government's new centralized ministries pursued a curriculum and underwent examinations modelled on the Prussian system, which as seen above had only recently reached its final form.[158] Many of the features of the Meiji system have remained in place, and Japan has become the archetype of the developmental state against which we have been comparing the German experience.

As we have also noted, the developmental state's effectiveness has been questioned on both empirical and theoretical grounds. As in Germany, so too in Japan modern development arose out of complex structures of local communities that already produced a wide range of agricultural and industrial goods for well-established markets. However, the state did play a role, and we can say that if such a state were to guide economic development successfully, it would have to look something like an idealized version of the Japanese system, with a clear consensus at the top, specialized agencies to develop and execute policy, and trained, highly motivated officials to staff the agencies.

In eighteenth-century central Europe, a determined and energetic ruler could impose policy, but only with difficulty. Functionally specialized bureaucracies did not yet exist, and rulers had to contend with corporatist representation of a range of established interests, including the collegiate boards that supposedly executed the ruler's orders. The diverse patterns of development, including specialized agricultural and industrial production for export, proceeded without much reference to the actions of governments. As noted above, Frederick the Great's concern for Prussia's power focused narrowly on his army. He missed the importance of broader markets for mass-produced goods and the new technologies being developed to supply those markets.

The generation of market reformers, especially Stein and his colleagues in Prussia, wished to change the form of the state and to transform the economy, but the goal of the state's rulers remained to maintain and increase the state's power. In the aftermath of the wars the *Junker* landlord class and the overlapping elite of bureaucratic officials can both be seen as rent-seeking coalitions, and the struggles, for instance over the approval of railway lines, as disputes over the distribution of power as much as over the direction of economic development. The divisions, hesitancy, and reluctance of officials to encourage development during the Restoration period led to the slow growth, social imbalance, and political dissatisfaction that reached their peak in 1848.

During the upswing of the 1850s and 1860s Heydt and his ministry can be seen as a pilot agency guiding the early phases of rapid industrialization. However, Heydt's freedom of action arose not from the shared intention of government leaders but from the government's willingness to make limited concessions to the representative assembly on the one hand, and from his exercise of arbitrary power over private entrepreneurs on the other. Again the underlying motive was state power, which Heydt's superiors believed must be increased in order to prevail in the struggle against Austria. The military motive is a point of similarity with Japan, but the lack of a shared vision compared with the Meiji leaders is a substantial difference. In Prussia the mutual suspicion of elite groups led to the constitutional crisis over military spending, to Heydt's fall, and to Bismarck's rise to power.

The foundation of the Empire was followed by two decades of depression and another two decades of rapid expansion. Germany became a world power, but the role of the new state was ambiguous and frequently negative. Although the development of the world economy imposed limits on any possible policy, nevertheless Germany suffered from a lack of effective leadership and a cohesive vision. There was no new Frederick and no Meiji Restoration. Bismarck was not the Okubo of Germany, for he could never endure the shame of abandoning a course once he had chosen it. He had severe difficulties imposing his policies, and his successors failed to cope with conflicting interest-group pressures. By default, Germany was led by the upper bureaucracy, a homogeneous, closed caste convinced of its superiority and supremely confident of its abilities, yet inflexible and limited by its training and conditioning.

Rather than being corrupt, perhaps, the system was inefficient. Bluntly, Germany did not possess a system well suited to the challenges of the twentieth century. In the economic sphere, when war came, the fiscal weakness of the state undermined its war-making capacity from the outset.[159] As the war proceeded, the Empire's institutions proved increasingly inadequate to deal with the strains.[160] And, following the collapse, the resulting contradictions helped to undermine the Weimar Republic.

4.8 Notes

1 W. O. Henderson, *The Rise of German Industrial Power, 1834–1914* (London, 1975), p. 78.
2 Volker Berghahn, *Modern Germany: State, Economy and Politics in the Twentieth Century*, 2nd edn (Cambridge, 1987), p. 267.

3 Frank B. Tipton, 'The National Consensus in German Economic History', *Central European History,* 7 (1974), pp. 195–224.
4 Henderson, *The Rise of German Industrial Power*, pp. 159–60.
5 W. Robert Lee, ed., *German Industry and German Industrialization: Essays in German Economic and Business History in the Nineteenth and Twentieth Centuries* (London, 1991).
6 Richard H. Tilly, *Vom Zollverein zum Industriestaat. Die wirtschaftlich-soziale Entwicklung Deutschlands 1834 bis 1914* (Munich, 1990); Richard H. Tilly, 'German Industrialization', in Mikuláš Teich and Roy Porter, eds, *The Industrial Revolution in National Context: Europe and the USA* (Cambridge and New York, 1996), pp. 95–125.
7 Thomas Nipperdey, *Deutsche Geschichte 1866–1918*, 2 vols (Munich, 1993), Vol. I, p. 278.
8 Hans-Ulrich Wehler, *Deutsche Gesellschaftsgeschichte*, Vol. III: *Von der 'Deutschen Doppelrevolution' biz zum Beginn des Ersten Weltkrieges, 1849–1914* (Munich, 1995), p. 610.
9 David Blackbourn, *The Fontana History of Germany, 1780–1918: The Long Nineteenth Century* (London, 1997), pp. 184, 190, 266.
10 See Linda Weiss, *The Myth of the Powerless State: Governing the Economy in a Global Era* (Cambridge, 1998), Ch. 5.
11 For example, Michio Muramatsu and Frieder Naschold, eds, *State and Administration in Japan and Germany: A Comparative Perspective on Continuity and Change* (Berlin and New York, 1997).
12 For a general critique, see Frank B. Tipton, 'Government Policy and Economic Development in Germany and Japan: A Sceptical Reevaluation', in Steven Tolliday, ed., *Government and Business* (London, 1991), pp. 66–77.
13 David S. Landes, 'Japan and Europe: Contrasts in Industrialization', in William W. Lockwood, ed., *The State and Economic Enterprise in Japan* (Princeton, 1965), pp. 93–182, here p. 182.
14 Louis L. Snyder, *German Nationalism: The Tragedy of a People* (Harrisburg, 1952), p. 308. See also Ralf Dahrendorf, *Society and Democracy in Germany* (New York, 1967) and, more recently, Harold James, *A German Identity: 1770 to the Present Day* (London, 1994), and Liah Greenfeld, *Nationalism: Five Roads to Modernity* (Cambridge, MA, 1992).
15 Benedict Anderson, *Imagined Communities: Reflections on the Origin and Spread of Nationalism*, revised edn (London, 1991); Hans Rosenberg, *Bureaucracy, Aristocracy and Autocracy: The Prussian Experience 1660–1815* (Boston, 1958). See also the discussion below.
16 For instance, Bernt Engelmann, *Die Beamten: Unser Staat im Staate*, 2nd edn (Göttingen, 1994); Werner Bruns, *Zeitbombe Bürokratie: das Ende des bürokratischen Jahrhunderts* (Berlin and Frankfurt am Main, 1994).
17 Walther G. Hoffmann, *Das Wachstum der Deutschen Wirtschaft seit der Mitte des 19. Jahrhunderts* (Berlin, 1965); see Tipton, 'The National Consensus'; Carl-Ludwig Holtfrerich, 'The Growth of Net Domestic Product in Germany, 1850–1913', in Rainer Fremdling and Richard O'Brien, eds, *Productivity in the Economies of Europe* (Stuttgart, 1983), pp. 124–30; Rainer Fremdling, 'German National Accounts for the 19th and Early 20th Century: A Critical Assessment', *Vierteljahrschrift für Sozial- und Wirtschaftsgeschichte,* 75 (1988), pp. 339–55; Mark Spoerer, 'Weimar's Investment and Growth Record in Intertemporal and International Perspective', *European Review of Economic History,* 1 (1997), pp. 271–97.
18 Frank B. Tipton, *Regional Variations in the Economic Development of Germany during the Nineteenth Century* (Middletown, 1976); Rüdiger Hohls

and Hartmut Kaelble, *Die regionale Erwerbsstruktur im deutschen Reich und in der Bundesrepublik, 1895–1970* (St Katharinen, 1989).

19 See Frank B. Tipton, *The Rise of Asia: Politics, Economics and Society in Contemporary Asia* (London, 1998), Chs 12–13; Frank B. Tipton, 'Japanese Nationalism in Comparative Perspective', in Sandra Wilson, ed., *Nation and Nationalism in Japan* (London, 2002), pp. 146–62. Frank B. Tipton, 'Nationalism and Economic Development in Nineteenth Century Europe', in Adam Czarnota, Halyna Koscharsky, and Aleksandar Pavkovic, eds, *Nationalism and Postcommunism* (Aldershot, 1995), pp. 19–37, considers Germany in a comparative European context.

20 M. Shahid Alam, *Governments and Markets in Economic Development Strategies: Lessons from Korea, Taiwan, and Japan* (New York, 1989); Robert Wade, *Governing the Market: Economic Theory and the Role of Government in East Asian Industrialization* (Princeton, 1990); Linda Weiss and John M. Hobson, *States and Economic Development: A Comparative Historical Analysis* (Cambridge, 1995).

21 For instance, World Bank, *The East Asian Miracle: Economic Growth and Public Policy* (Oxford and New York, 1993).

22 For instance, Chalmers Johnson, *MITI and the Japanese Miracle: The Growth of Industrial Policy, 1925–1975* (Stanford, 1982); Chalmers Johnson, 'Political Institutions and Economic Performance: The Government–Business Relation in Japan, South Korea, and Taiwan', in Frederic Deyo, ed., *The Political Economy of the New Asian Industrialism* (Ithaca and London, 1987), pp. 136–64; Alice H. Amsden, *Asia's Next Giant: South Korea and Late Industrialization* (Oxford, 1989).

23 Michael Mann, 'The Autonomous Power of the State: Its Origins, Mechanism, and Results', in Michael Mann, *States, War and History* (Oxford, 1988); Peter B. Evans, 'The State as Problem and Solution: Predation, Embedded Autonomy and Structural Change', in Stephan Haggard and Robert Kaufmann, eds, *The Politics of Economic Adjustment* (Princeton, 1992), pp. 139–81.

24 Alexander Gerschenkron, 'Economic Backwardness in Historical Perspective', in Alexander Gerschenkron, *Economic Backwardness in Historical Perspective: A Book of Essays* (Cambridge, MA, 1962), pp. 5–30.

25 Ziya Önis, 'The Logic of the Developmental State', *Comparative Politics*, 24 (1991), pp. 109–26.

26 Theda Skocpol, 'Bringing the State Back In: Strategies of Analysis in Current Research', in Peter B. Evans, Dieter Reuschemeyer, and Theda Skocpol, eds, *Bringing the State Back In* (New York, 1985), pp. 3–37, here p. 9.

27 Önis, 'The Logic of the Developmental State', pp. 114–15; Evans, 'The State as Problem and Solution'; Peter B. Evans, *Embedded Autonomy: States and Industrial Transformation* (Princeton, 1995).

28 Evans, 'The State as Problem and Solution'; Weiss, *The Myth of the Powerless State*, Ch. 3.

29 James J. Sheehan, *German History 1770–1866* (Oxford, 1994), p. 70.

30 Mann, 'The Autonomous Power of the State'; Richard F. Doner, 'Limits of State Strength: Toward an Institutionalist View of Economic Development', *World Politics*, 44 (1992), pp. 398–431.

31 E. Hellmuth and J. Brewer, eds, *Rethinking Leviathan: The Eighteenth-Century State in Britain and Germany* (Oxford, 1999).

32 W. O. Henderson, *Studies in the Economic Policy of Frederick the Great* (London, 1963); Hubert Johnson, *Frederick the Great and His Officials* (New Haven and London, 1975).

33 Stephan Haggard, *Pathways from the Periphery: The Politics of Growth in the Newly Industrializing Countries* (Ithaca, 1990).

34 Herbert Kisch, *Die Hausindustrielle Textilgewerbe am Niederrhein vor der industriellen Revolution* (Göttingen, 1981); Rosenberg, *Bureaucracy, Aristocracy and Autocracy*.

35 See Sheilagh Ogilvie, 'The Beginnings of Industrialization', in Sheilagh Ogilivie, ed., *Germany: A New Social and Economic History*, Vol. II: *1630–1800* (London, 1996), pp. 263–308; Sheilagh Ogilvie, *State Corporatism and Proto-Industry: The Württemberg Black Forest 1590–1797* (Cambridge, 1997); Sheilagh Ogilvie, 'The European Economy in the Eighteenth Century', in T. W. C. Blanning, ed., *The Short Oxford History of Europe*, Vol. XII: *The Eighteenth Century: Europe 1688–1815* (Oxford, 2000), pp. 91–130.

36 Barbara Vogel, 'Die preussischen Reformen als Gegenstand und Problem der Forschung', in Barbara Vogel, ed., *Preussische Reformen 1807–1820* (Königstein, 1980), pp. 1–27.

37 Anne O. Krueger, 'Government Failures in Development', *Journal of Economic Perspectives*, 4 (1990), pp. 20–1.

38 Barbara Vogel, 'Die 'allgemeine Gewerbefreiheit' als bürokratische Modernisierungsstrategie in Preussen', in Dirk Stegmann, ed., *Industrielle Gesellschaft und politisches System* (Bonn, 1978), pp. 59–78; Eric D. Brose, *The Politics of Technological Change: Out of the Shadow of Antiquity, 1809–1848* (Princeton, 1993), p. 34.

39 Ogilvie, *State Corporatism*; Mack Walker, *German Home Towns: Community, State, and General Estate 1648–1871* (Ithaca, 1971).

40 Tilly, 'German Industrialization'.

41 Tipton, *Regional Variations*.

42 G. W. F. Hegel, *Hegel's Philosophy of Right*, transl. T. M. Knox (Oxford, 1976), art. 289.

43 Clifford Geertz, *Agricultural Involution: The Process of Ecological Change in Indonesia* (Berkeley, 1963); Gunnar Myrdal, *Asian Drama: An Inquiry into the Poverty of Nations*, 3 vols (New York, 1968).

44 Hermann Beck, 'The Social Policies of Prussian Officials: The Bureaucracy in a New Light', *Journal of Modern History*, 64 (1992), pp. 263–98; Brose, *Politics of Technological Change*.

45 W. O. Henderson, *The State and the Industrial Revolution in Prussia* (Liverpool, 1968), emphasizes successes; Ilya Mieck, *Preussische Gewerbe-politik in Berlin 1806–44: Staatshilfe und private Initiative zwischen Merkantilismus und Liberalismus* (Berlin, 1965), contains information on some of the failures as well.

46 Herbert Prüns, *Staat und Agrarwirtschaft 1800–1865* (Hamburg and Berlin, 1979); Wolfgang Radtke, *Die preussische Seehandlung zwischen Staat und Wirtschaft in der Frühphase der Industrialisierung* (Berlin, 1981).

47 W. O. Henderson, *The Zollverein*, 2nd edn (London, 1959).

48 Richard H. Tilly, 'Capital Formation in Germany in the Nineteenth Century', in Peter Mathias and M. M. Postan, eds, *Cambridge Economic History of Europe*, Vol. VII (Cambridge, 1978); Friedrich-Wilhelm Henning, *Die Industrialisierung in Deutschland 1800 bis 1914* (Paderborn, 1973), p. 25.

49 Leonard Krieger, *The German Idea of Freedom*, 2nd edn (Chicago, 1972), pp. 227–9; Henderson, *The Zollverein*; Hans-Werner Hahn, *Wirtschaftliche Integration im 19. Jahrhundert: die hessischen Staaten und der Deutsche Zollverein* (Göttingen, 1982); Rolf Dumke, 'Der Deutsche Zollverein als Modell ökonomischer Integration', in Helmut Berding, ed., *Wirtschaftliche und politische Integration in Europa im 19. Jahrhundert* (Göttingen, 1984), pp. 72–101.

50 Jeffrey Diefendorf, *Businessmen and Politics in the Rhineland, 1789–1834* (Princeton, 1980).

51 Hegel, *Philosophy of Right*, art. 297.
52 Evans, 'The State as Problem and Solution'; Evans, *Embedded Autonomy*.
53 G. A. Ritter, *Regierung, Bürokratie und Parlament in Preussen und Deutschland von 1848 bis zur Gegenwart* (Düsseldorf, 1983); Hansjoachim Henning, *Die deutsche Beamtenschaft im 19. Jahrhundert: Zwischen Stand und Beruf* (Stuttgart, 1984); Tibor Süle, *Preussische Bürokratietradition: zur Entwicklung von Verwaltung und Beamtenschaft in Deutschland, 1871–1918* (Göttingen, 1988); Jane Caplan, *Government Without Administration: State and Civil Service in Weimar and Nazi Germany* (Oxford and New York, 1988).
54 Bernd Wunder, *Geschichte der Bürokratie in Deutschland* (Frankfurt am Main, 1986).
55 Wolfgang J. Mommsen, *The Age of Bureaucracy: Perspectives on the Political Sociology of Max Weber* (Oxford and New York, 1974); Jürgen Kocka, 'Otto Hintze, Max Weber und das Problem der Bürokratie', *Historische Zeitschrift*, 233 (1981), pp. 65–105.
56 Bernd Wunder, 'Das Prüfungsprinzip und die Entstehung der Beamtenschaft in Deutschland', *Jahrbuch für Wirtschaftsgeschichte*, (1993), pp. 11–26.
57 Wunder, *Geschichte der Bürokratie*, p. 40; John R. Gillis, *The Prussian Bureaucracy in Crisis, 1840–1860: Origins of an Administrative Elite* (Stanford, 1971).
58 Brose, *Politics of Technological Change*.
59 Paul Thimme, *Strassenbau und Strassenpolitik in Deutschland zur Zeit der Gründung des Zollvereins* (Stuttgart, 1931).
60 See Walter Steitz, *Die Entstehung der Köln-Mindener Eisenbahngesellschaft* (Cologne, 1974).
61 Dennis E. Showalter, *Railroads and Rifles: Soldiers, Technology, and the Unification of Germany* (Hamden, Connecticut, 1975); Brose, *Politics of Technological Change*, Ch. 5.
62 David Hansemann, *Die Eisenbahnen und deren Aktionäre in ihrem Verhältnis zum Staat* (Leipzig and Halle, 1837); Diefendorf, *Businessmen*, p. 252; Brose, *Politics of Technological Change*, Ch. 7; James M. Brophy, *Capitalism, Politics, and Railroads in Prussia, 1830–1870* (Columbus, 1998), p. 33.
63 Wolfgang Löser, 'Die Rolle des preussischen Staates bei der Ausrüstung der Eisenbahnen mit elektrischen Telegraphen in der Mitte des 19. Jahrhunderts', *Jahrbuch für Wirtschaftsgeschichte*, (1963), pp. 194–208; Brophy, *Capitalism*, pp. 33–6.
64 Alfred von der Leyen, 'Die Verhandlungen der Vereinigten Ständischen Ausschüssen über die Eisenbahnfrage im Jahre 1842', *Archiv für Eisenbahnwesen*, 4 (1881), pp. 1–21; H. Leiskow, *Spekulation und öffentliche Meinung in der ersten Hälfte des neunzehnten Jahrhunderts* (Jena, 1930), pp. 8–9, 12–14; Dietrich Eichholtz, *Junker und Bourgeoisie for 1848 in der preussischen Eisenbahngeschichte* (Berlin, 1962); Brophy, *Capitalism*, pp. 36–49.
65 Colleen A. Dunlavy, *Politics and Industrialization: Early Railroads in the United States and Prussia* (Princeton, 1994); B. R. Mitchell, *International Historical Statistics: The Americas 1750–1988* (New York, 1993), p. 528.
66 Hans Spethmann, *Franz Haniel* (Duisburg-Ruhrort, 1956), pp. 159ff.; Wolfram Fischer, 'Die Stellung der preussische Bergrechtsreform von 1851–1865 in der Wirtschafts- und Sozialverfassung des 19. Jahrhunderts', in Wolfram Fischer, *Wirtschaft und Gesellschaft im Zeitalter der Industrialisierung* (Göttingen, 1971), pp. 151–2.
67 Mitchell, *International Historical Statistics: The Americas*, pp. 306, 353.
68 Knut Borchardt, 'Zur Frage des Kapitalmangels in der ersten Hälfte des 19. Jahrhunderts in Deutschland', *Jahrbücher für Nationalökonomie und Statistik*,

173 (1961), pp. 401–21; Richard Tilly, *Financial Institutions and Industrialization in the Rhineland* (Madison, 1966); Jürgen Kocka, 'Entrepreneurs and Managers in German Industrialization', in Mathias and Postan, *The Cambridge Economic History of Europe*, Vol. VII, pp. 492–589, here p. 536.

69 Horst Thieme, 'Statistische Materialien zur Konzessionierung von Aktiengesellschaften in Preussen bis 1867', *Jahrbuch für Wirtschaftsgeschichte*, (1960), pp. 285–300.

70 Brose, *Politics of Technological Change*, p. 246.

71 Tipton, *Regional Variations*; Hubert Kiesewetter, *Industrialisierung und Landwirtschaft: Sachsens Stellung im regionalen Industrialisierungsprozeß Deutschlands im 19. Jahrhundert* (Cologne, 1988).

72 Brophy, *Capitalism*, pp. 56–7.

73 Nikolai D. Kondratiev, 'Long Cycles of Economic Conjuncture', in *The Works of Nikolai D. Kondratiev* (London, 1998), I, 25–63. See Christopher Freeman, ed., *Long Wave Theory* (Cheltenham and Brookfield, Vermont, 1996); Solomos Solomou, *Economic Cycles: Long Cycles and Business Cycles Since 1870* (Manchester, 1998).

74 Frank B. Tipton, 'The Economic Dimension in German History', in Gordon Martel, ed., *Modern Germany Reconsidered* (London, 1991); Andrew Tylecote, *The Long Wave in the World Economy* (London, 1992); Angus Maddison, *Monitoring the World Economy 1820–1992* (Paris, 1995).

75 Weiss, *The Myth of the Powerless State*; Edgar H. Schein, *Strategic Pragmatism: The Culture of Singapore's Economic Development Board* (Cambridge, MA, 1996).

76 Scott Callon, *Divided Sun: MITI and the Breakdown of Japanese High Tech Industrial Policy* (Stanford, 1995). See Tipton, *The Rise of Asia*, Chs 12–13.

77 Kiesewetter, *Industrialisierung*; Wolfram Fischer, 'Ansätze zur Industrialisierung in Baden, 1770–1870', *Vierteljahrschrift für Sozial- und Wirtschaftsgeschichte*, 47 (1960), pp. 185–231.

78 Sheehan, *German History 1770–1866*.

79 Tilly, 'The Political Economy of Public Finance'.

80 Showalter, *Railroads and Rifles*.

81 Andreas Biefang, *Politisches Bürgertum in Deutschland 1857–1868: Nationale Organisationen und Eliten* (Düsseldorf, 1994).

82 Thieme, 'Statistische Materialien', p. 286; Alexander Bergengrün, *Staatsminister August Freiherr von der Heydt* (Berlin, 1908), pp. 218–20.

83 Tipton, *Regional Variations*.

84 Fischer, 'Die Stellung der pruessische Bergrechtsreform'; Wilhelm Brepohl, *Industrievolk im Wandel von den agraren zum Industriellen Daseinsform dargestellet am Ruhrgebiet* (Tübingen, 1957).

85 B. R. Mitchell, *International Historical Statistics: Europe 1750–1988* (New York, 1992), Tables G1, G2, G3; Hoffmann, *Wachstum*, pp. 814–15.

86 Richard H. Tilly, 'Banken und Industrialisierung in Deutschland, 1850–1870: ein Überblick', in Richard H. Tilly, *Kapital, Staat und sozialer Protest in der deutschen Industrialisierung* (Göttingen, 1980), pp. 29–54; Wehler, *Deutsche Gesellschaftsgeschichte*, Vol. III, pp. 85–91; Brophy, *Capitalism*, Ch. 5.

87 Blackbourn, *The Long Nineteenth Century*, p. 273.

88 Andreas Kunz, 'The Economic Performance of Inland Navigation in Germany, 1835–1935', in Andreas Kunz and John Armstrong, eds, *Inland Navigation in Nineteenth Century Europe* (Mainz and Manchester, 1994), pp. 47–78; Lars U. Scholl, *Als die Hexen Schiffe Schleppten. Die Geschichte der Ketten- und Schleppschiffahrt auf dem Rhein* (Hamburg, 1985).

89 Brophy, *Capitalism*, p. 22; Blackbourn, *The Long Nineteenth Century*, p. 280.

90 Frank B. Tipton, 'The Regional Dimension in the Historical Analysis of Transport Flows', in Kunz and Armstrong, *Inland Navigation in Nineteenth-Century Europe*, pp. 167–80.

91 Rainer Fremdling, *Eisenbahnen und deutscher Wirtschaftswachstum 1840–1879* (Dortmund, 1975); Rainer Fremdling, 'Railroads and German Economic Growth: A Leading Sector Analysis with a Comparison to the United States and Great Britain', *Journal of Economic History*, 37 (1977), pp. 583–604.

92 Brophy, *Capitalism*, p. 31.

93 Brophy, *Capitalism*, Chs 3, 4, 6.

94 Bergengrün, *Staatsminister August Freiherr von der Heydt*, pp. 144–6; Brophy, *Capitalism*, pp. 54–7.

95 Brophy, *Capitalism*, pp. 141, 152.

96 Otto Pflanze, *Bismarck and the Development of Germany*, 3 vols (Princeton, 1990), Vol. I, p. 194.

97 Fritz Stern, *Gold and Iron: Bismarck, Bleichröder and the Building of the German Empire* (New York, 1977), pp. 150–5, 320–7.

98 Nipperdey, *Deutsche Geschichte 1866–1918*, Vol. I, pp. 281, 283.

99 Hoffmann, *Wachstum*, pp. 599, 814.

100 Henderson, *The Rise of German Industrial Power*, pp. 168–70; see Wehler, *Deutsche Gesellschaftsgeschichte*, Vol. III, p. 1314 for bibliography.

101 Gordon R. Mork, 'The Prussian Railway Scandal of 1873: Economics and Politics in the German Empire', *European Studies Review*, 1 (1971), pp. 35–48.

102 Hoffmann, *Wachstum*, pp. 257, 390–5, 454–5.

103 Frank B. Tipton, 'Technology and Industrial Growth', in Roger Chickering, ed., *Imperial Germany: A Historiographical Companion* (Westport, 1996), pp. 62–95.

104 David S. Landes, *The Unbound Prometheus: Technological Change and Industrial Development in Western Europe from 1750 to the Present* (Cambridge, 1969), pp. 339–48.

105 Hoffmann, *Wachstum*, pp. 257–8, 388, 390–5, 454–5.

106 Hoffmann, *Wachstum*, pp. 197–8, 393.

107 Margrit Grabas, *Konjunktur und Wachstum in Deutschland von 1895 bis 1914* (Berlin, 1993), pp. 230–71.

108 Hartmut Kaelble, 'Der Mythos von der rapiden Industrialisierung in Deutschland', *Geschichte und Gesellschaft*, 9 (1983) (1), pp. 108–18.

109 Rainer Fremdling, 'Productivity Comparison between Great Britain and Germany, 1855–1913', *Scandinavian Economic History Review*, 39 (1991), pp. 28–42.

110 Hoffmann, *Wachstum*, pp. 530–2; Maddison, *Monitoring the World Economy*, p. 38.

111 Kenneth D. Barkin, *The Controversy Over German Industrialization, 1890–1902* (Chicago, 1970).

112 Nipperdey, *Deutsche Geschichte 1866–1918*, Vol. I, p. 281.

113 Wehler, *Deutsche Gesellschaftsgeschichte*, Vol. III, p. 662.

114 Johnson, *MITI and the Japanese Miracle*. See Weiss, *The Myth of the Powerless State*, Ch. 3.

115 Henderson, *The Rise of German Industrial Power*, pp. 159–60.

116 William Carr, *A History of Germany, 1815–1990*, 4th edn (London and New York, 1991), p. 123.

117 Blackbourn, *The Long Nineteenth Century*, p. 266. See also Nipperdey, *Deutsche Geschichte 1866–1918*, Vol. II, pp. 112–14.

118 Rita Aldenhoff, 'Agriculture', in Chickering, *Imperial Germany*, pp. 33–61, here pp. 39–40.

119 Prussia, Ministerium der öffentlichen Arbeiten, *Der Preussische Landeseisen-bahnrat in den ersten 25 Jahren seiner Tätigkeit, 1883–1908* (Berlin, 1908).

120 Frank B. Tipton, Martin Braach-Maksvytis, and Susan Newell, 'Bureaucracy and the Railway in Japan and Germany', in Olle Krantz and Lena Andersson-Skog, eds, *Perspectives on Institutional Change in the Communication and Transport Industries in the 19th and 20th Centuries* (Canton, 1998), pp. 5–32.

121 Peter-Christian Witt, *Die Finanzpolitik des Deutschen Reiches von 1903 bis 1913* (Lübeck and Hamburg, 1970); John M. Hobson, *The Wealth of States: A Comparative Sociology of International Economic and Political Change* (Cambridge, 1997), pp. 62–70.

122 Brett Fairbairn, 'Political Mobilization', in Chickering, *Imperial Germany*, p. 324.

123 See Michael D. Bordo and Finn E. Kydland, 'The Gold Standard as a Rule: An Essay in Exploration', *Explorations in Economic History*, 32 (1995) (4), pp. 423–64.

124 Carl-Ludwig Holtfrerich, 'Relations between Monetary Authorities and Governmental Institutions: The Case of Germany from the 19th Century to the Present', in Gianni Toniolo, ed., *Central Banks' Independence in Historical Perspective* (Berlin, 1988), pp. 105–59, here p. 112.

125 Wehler, *Deutsche Gesellschaftsgeschichte*, Vol. III, pp. 975–7; Nipperdey, *Deutsche Geschichte 1866–1918*, Vol. II, pp. 464–5.

126 Mitchell, *International Historical Statistics: Europe*, Tables G1, G2, G3; Hoffmann, *Wachstum*, pp. 814–15.

127 Karl R. Bopp, 'Die Tätigkeit der *Reichsbank* von 1876 bis 1914', *Weltwirtschaftliches Archiv*, 72 (1954), pp. 179–224.

128 B. R. Mitchell, *International Historical Statistics: Europe 1750–1988* (New York, 1992), Tables G1, G2, G3; Hoffmann, Wachstum, pp. 814–15.

129 J. H. Clapham, *The Economic Development of France and Germany* (Cambridge, 1936), p. 390.

130 Richard H. Tilly, 'German Banking, 1850–1914: Development Assistance for the Strong', *Journal of European Economic History*, 15 (1986), pp. 113–52; Richard H. Tilly, 'German Industrialization and Gerschenkronian Backwardness', *Revista di storia economica*, 6 (1989), pp. 139–64; Richard H. Tilly, 'An Overview of the Role of the Large German Banks up to 1914', in Y. Cassis, ed., *Finance and Financiers in European History, 1880–1960* (Cambridge, 1991), pp. 94–112.

131 Charles W. Calomiris, 'The Costs of Rejecting Universal Banking: American Finance in the German Mirror, 1870–1914', in Naomi R. Lamoreaux and Daniel M. G. Raff, eds, *Coordination and Information: Historical Perspectives on the Organization of Enterprise* (Chicago and London, 1995), pp. 257–321.

132 Caroline Fohlin, 'Fiduciari and Firm Liquidity Constraints: The Italian Experience with German-Style Universal Banking', *Explorations in Economic History*, 35 (1998), pp. 83–107.

133 Jeremy Edwards and Sheilagh Ogilvie, 'Universal Banks and German Industrialization: A Reappraisal', *Economic History Review*, 49 (1996), pp. 427–46.

134 Hugh Neuberger and Houston H. Stokes, 'German Banks and German Growth, 1883–1913: An Empirical View', *Journal of Economic History*, 34 (1974), pp. 710–31; see Rainer Fremdling and Richard H. Tilly, 'German Banks, German Growth, and Econometric History', *Journal of Economic History*, 36 (1976), pp. 416–24, and reply by Neuberger and Stokes, *Journal of Economic History*, 36 (1976), pp. 425–7.

135 Fritz Blaich, *Kartell- und Monopolpolitik im kaiserlichen Deutschland* (Düsseldorf, 1973).

136 Wehler, *Deutsche Gesellschaftsgeschichte*, Vol. III, pp. 637–57, 934–7; Nipperdey, *Deutsche Geschichte 1866–1918*, Vol. II, pp. 382–408.

137 Hobson, *The Wealth of States*, Ch. 2.

138 Hans-Jürgen Puhle, *Agrarische Interessenpolitik und preussischer Konservatismus im wilhelminischen Reich 1893–1914* (Hannover, 1966); Robert M. Spaulding, *Osthandel and Ostpolitik. German Foreign Trade Policies in Eastern Europe from Bismarck to Adenauer* (Oxford, 1997), Ch. 1.

139 Brophy, *Capitalism*, pp. 93, 152–4.

140 Wehler, *Deutsche Gesellschaftsgeschichte*, Vol. III, p. 287; Nipperdey, *Deutsche Geschichte 1866–1918*, Vol. II, p. 46.

141 Nipperdey, *Deutsche Geschichte 1866–1918*, Vol. II, p. 113.

142 Wehler, *Deutsche Gesellschaftsgeschichte*, Vol. III, pp. 642, 860.

143 Wunder, *Geschichte der Bürokratie*, pp. 80, 95.

144 Wehler, *Deutsche Gesellschaftsgeschichte*, Vol. III, p. 862.

145 Ritter, *Regierung, Bürokratie und Parlament*; John C. G. Röhl, 'Beamtenpolitik im Wilhelminischen Deutschland', in Michael Stürmer, ed., *Das kaiserliche Deutschland: Politik und Gesellschaft 1870–1918* (Düsseldorf, 1977), pp. 287–311; Margaret L. Anderson and Kenneth D. Barkin, 'The Myth of the Puttkamer Purge and the Reality of the Kulturkampf: Some Reflections on the Historiography of Imperial Germany', *Journal of Modern History*, 53 (1982), pp. 647–86; Nipperdey, *Deutsche Geschichte 1866–1918*, Vol. II, p. 134.

146 Wehler, *Deutsche Gesellschaftsgeschichte*, Vol. III, p. 863.

147 Wunder, *Geschichte der Bürokratie*, pp. 89–90; Wehler, *Deutsche Gesellschaftsgeschichte*, Vol. III, p. 1031.

148 Erich Angermann, 'Germany's "Peculiar Institution": The Beamtentum', in Erich Angermann and Marie-Luise Frings, eds, *Oceans Apart? Comparing Germany and the United States. Studies in Commemoration of the 150th Anniversary of the Birth of Carl Schurz* (Stuttgart, 1981), pp. 77–101.

149 Gary Bonham, *Ideology and Interests in the German State* (New York and London, 1991).

150 Peter Evans, 'Predatory, Developmental and Other Apparatuses: A Comparative Political Economy Perspective on the Third World State', *Sociological Forum*, 4 (1989), pp. 233–46; Faisal Yahya, 'The State in the Process of Economic Development: The Case of India', *Asian Studies Review*, 18 (1995), pp. 83–94.

151 See Tipton, *The Rise of Asia*, Ch. 13.

152 Fritz Stern, *Gold and Iron*; Pflanze, *Bismarck*, Vol. III, pp. 100–3, 186–7, 263–4.

153 Ernst Engelberg, *Bismarck: Das Reich in der Mitte Europas* (Munich, 1993), p. 227.

154 Eckart Kehr, *Der Primat der Innenpolitik*, 2nd edn (Berlin, 1970).

155 Wehler, *Deutsche Gesellschaftsgeschichte*, pp. 448–86, 662–80, 1000–37. See also Nipperdey, *Deutsche Geschichte 1866–1918*, Vol. II, pp. 699–75.

156 Ryusaku Tsunoda *et al.*, *Sources of Japanese Tradition* (New York and London, 1964), Vol. II, p. 151.

157 Masakazu Iwata, *Okubo Toshimichi: The Bismarck of Japan* (Berkeley, 1964), pp. 236–8; Tessa Morris-Suzuki, *The Technological Transformation of Japan: From the Seventeenth to the Twenty-First Century* (Cambridge, 1994).

158 Robert M. Spaulding, *Imperial Japan's Higher Civil Service Examinations* (Princeton, 1967).

159 Hobson, *The Wealth of States*, pp. 70, 256–65.

160 Roger Chickering, *Imperial Germany and the Great War, 1914–1918* (Cambridge, 1998).

$\Big|5\Big|$

Finance and industry

VOLKER WELLHÖNER AND HARALD WIXFORTH
University of Bremen and University of Bielefeld

5.1 Introduction

This chapter examines the relationship between banks and industry in the development of the German economy since the nineteenth century. Our approach to this question adopts the central hypothesis advanced by the well-known economist of the German Historical School, Josef Schumpeter, that industrial production is decisive in fostering economic change. We also follow Schumpeter in regarding the bank–industry relationship as a key component of the development process – that is, that the financial sector plays a much greater role than that of a 'veil'.[1]

In addressing the relationship between banks and industry, we place financial institutions at centre stage. This means that this survey will not discuss all facets of German financial history in the nineteenth and twentieth centuries. For instance, it cannot consider such important aspects as the role of the central bank(s) of issue and the stock market. Indeed, even our central theme cannot be dealt with exhaustively. Instead, we will focus on two important problems that have long stimulated controversy among economists and economic historians: the contribution of banks to industrial financing in Germany, and the much debated question of the 'power' of the German banks. We regard this emphasis as justified on the grounds that Germany during this period was characterized by a bank-oriented rather than a market-oriented financial system.

Chronologically, we will cover the period from 1816 to 1989. Both years mark decisive caesurae in German history. The Congress of Vienna saw a far-reaching reorganization of the European continent, which also affected the German territories. This was also the date at which the process of internal state formation began in most German states.[2] The events of 1989 were also an important caesura, since they caused a further fundamental change in the state structure of Germany. Within this period of nearly two centuries, we distinguish several phases in the development of the German bank–industry relationship. Section 5.2 discusses the early phase of German financial and industrial development, from 1816 to 1870. Section 5.3 discusses the later phase of financial development and high industrialization from 1870 to 1918, including the anomalous sub-period of the First World War. Section 5.4 examines the changing relationship between banks and industry in the Weimar Republic and under National Socialism. Finally, Section 5.5 investigates the development of German banking after the Second World War. Section 5.6 draws together what historical research on German bank–industry relations can tell us about problems of concern to present-day German society.

5.2 Banks and industry from 1816 to 1870

5.2.1 *The differentiation of the German banking system*

After the Napoleonic wars and the political reorganization of Europe at the Congress of Vienna, it became evident that the economies of most German states were strikingly backward, especially compared to the pioneer economy of industrialization, Great Britain.[3] This backwardness (discussed in detail in Chapter 4) manifested itself in a comparatively modest level of capital formation in comparison with Great Britain or France. Moreover, a high degree of scepticism within the investing population hindered the realization of many industrial projects.[4] German industrial backwardness was reflected not least in the technologies still used by the German textile industry. Whereas in Great Britain mechanization and centralization into factories had been progressing rapidly since the 1780s, in the German states the traditional domestic system whereby textiles were produced in rural households in by-employment with agriculture predominated until the mid-nineteenth century.[5] A similar state of comparative backwardness prevailed in German machine building and – from the 1830s – railway construction.[6]

Historians of earlier generations regarded German economic retardation as having been caused partly by political fragmentation, but primarily by a risk-averse banking system and inadequate capital formation. Recent research, however, suggests a more differentiated view. For one thing, there was no general shortage of capital in the German states. Difficulties in industrial financing were caused primarily by the problem of how to bundle together widely scattered sources of wealth and make them available for industrial purposes.[7] Second, given the pressures exerted by British competition on the domestic market, for example in the textile industry, it is questionable whether potential German entrepreneurs expected there to be big enough opportunities for selling industrial products to provide a lasting stimulus to the demand for investment funds. Third, as discussed in Chapter 4, most German private bankers continued to favour their traditional business of making loans to the state over industrial financing which they regarded as much riskier. Admittedly, there were important exceptions to this rule. Thus, for instance, Cologne banking houses became involved in railway financing very early on.[8] Despite this exception, German banking as a whole was not very entrepreneurial until well into the 1840s.

In general, the ability of traditional structures to survive very stubbornly remained a striking characteristic of the German economy until the crisis year of 1848. At that point, socioeconomic problems that had been mounting for a long time in German societies escalated – above all, the collapse of the traditional domestic system of rural textile production.[9] Initially, the crisis of 1848 brought into being new institutions, new legislation, and new forms of regulation in many spheres of German life. Even though in 1849 the attempts to establish parliamentary government largely collapsed, many of the new institutions and regulations survived, especially in the economic sphere. After 1848, Germany began to experience a number of stimuli that gave its industrialization a strong push forward. The railway network was extended, new technologies adopted, and attempts were made to unify the German economic area, and the most important industrial countries in Europe experienced a pronounced upturn. As discussed in Chapter 4, all these factors stimulated a powerful industrial upswing, which manifested itself particularly in railway building and heavy industry.[10]

During this expansionary phase, industrial enterprises increasingly took new institutional forms. The joint-stock company became more important among foundations of new firms and the expansion of existing ones in sectors such as railway building and heavy industry.[11] But in banking, the institutional innovation of the joint-stock company remained an exception, because of considerable political resistance. The first large bank of this type which dispensed with the right of note issue and devoted itself mainly to industrial financing was the Schaaffhausen'sche Bankverein, founded in Cologne in 1848.[12]

Against the backdrop of political and economic stabilization after 1848, it soon became clear that many of the newly founded industrial enterprises had a considerable need for capital to finance their investment process. This demand for capital by industry encouraged the establishment of additional large joint-stock banks. But the Prussian government initially refused to grant licences for new joint-stock companies. As a consequence, the Rhenish industrialist Gustav Mevissen and the Cologne private banker Abraham Oppenheim decided to set up an additional, well-capitalized, and industrially oriented lending institution outside Prussia, in Darmstadt. The model for this was the Crédit Mobilier belonging to the Perrèire brothers in France, whose activities in the German financial world had met with great acclaim. The ties of kinship between Oppenheim and the co-founders of this institution (the Paris banking house B. L. Fould et Fould-Oppenheim) meant that French bankers also took part in this project. On 2 April 1853 the Bank für Handel und Industrie (later usually referred to as the Darmstädter Bank) was granted a state licence.[13] Throughout the 1850s the Prussian government held fast to its refusal to grant licences to additional joint-stock banks, so the initiators of new banking projects in Prussian territories hit upon the expedient of establishing banks in the legal form of a 'Kommandit-gesellschaft auf Aktien' (partnership partly limited by shares), which did not have to get a state licence to do business. The most important institutions of this type for industrial financing over the following decade were the Direktion der Discontogesellschaft (originally founded in 1851 and reorganized in 1856), and the Berliner Handelsgesellschaft (established in 1856). By 1856, besides these institutions another eight additional joint-stock banks had been formed in Germany.[14]

The crisis of 1857 confronted all the newly established German banks with the first test of their viability. During this period, almost all German banks suffered more or less substantial losses. But since they mainly conducted business using their own capital, they were able to survive this critical period.[15] In the years following this crisis, German joint-stock banks tended to hold back from industrial investments. However, this restraint turned out to be a sort of calm before the storm. After victory in the war against France at the beginning of the 1870s, Germany was overtaken by a mania for founding new firms and a fever of speculative ventures. This was further intensified by the *Aktiengesetz* (Joint-Stock Company Law) of 11 June 1870, which abolished the requirement to get a state licence before operating a joint-stock company. The mania for setting up new firms mani-fested itself particularly in a spate of foundations of joint-stock companies. Whereas in the 20 years from 1851 to the middle of 1870, only 295 joint-stock enterprises came into being in Germany, 857 were formed in the following five years (up to 1874).[16] The number of joint-stock banks also grew spectacularly. Whereas at the beginning of 1870, there were still only 31 German joint-stock banks with a combined capital of 375.6 million marks, in 1872 there were 139 such banks with a combined capital of 1122 million marks.[17]

But many of these newly founded banks survived for only a very short time. In the course of the *Gründerkrach* ('foundation crash') of 1873, 73 banks, with a combined capital of 432 million marks, went bankrupt.[18] Most of them had focused less on constructively financing industry than on seeking speculative profits in company foundations and public issues. From 1870 to 1873, speculation often seemed to be more important than financing industry. The numerous bankruptcies of these 'speculative banks' during the foundation crash harmed the reputation of German joint-stock banks. Among the large banks already founded during the 1850s, the Berliner Handelsgesellschaft, the Discontogesellschaft, and the Bank für

Handel und Industrie were able to survive the crisis by pursuing more careful policies. Of the newly founded banks, it was chiefly Deutsche Bank (founded in 1870) and Dresdner Bank (founded 1872) which were to become important in later years. The concentration process which set in among the joint-stock banks after the crisis of 1873 led to a strengthening of those institutions that would later be called the Berlin *Großbanken* (Great Banks), which from this time on increasingly took over the leadership in German banking.[19]

Despite the visible and generally successful history of the joint-stock banks, which has long attracted the attention of contemporary observers and economic historians, the significance of the other German financial institutions such as savings banks and credit cooperatives must not be ignored. The private banks still played a very prominent role in this period. At least until the 1870s, they were important as founders of joint-stock banks. In addition to the Bank für Handel und Industrie which has already been mentioned, a whole array of other joint-stock banks owed their foundation mainly to the initiative of private bankers.[20] The private bankers regarded the activities of joint-stock banks not as competition but as an extension of their business, although this did not prevent them from taking part in industrial financing on their own account. Likewise, private bankers participated in issuing both industrial paper and shares in the construction of transportation infrastructure.[21] In supplying credit, asset management, trustee work, and property advice, the private bankers were able to sustain their position vis-à-vis the joint-stock banks. Tilly estimates that during the 1860s and 1870s the joint-stock banks had at their disposal total assets amounting to only about 10 per cent of those held by the private bankers. It therefore seems justified to conclude that until the 1870s the economic importance of the private bankers in Germany still surpassed that of the joint-stock banks.[22]

5.2.2 *Banks and industrial financing*

However, the fact that so many new joint-stock companies were founded and so many existing firms were transformed into joint-stock companies opened up the opportunity for joint-stock banks to act as founders of enterprises, or to provide firms with the necessary capital by taking over shares in them. The shares taken over by the banks were, as a rule, offered on the stock market to the public. However, in a few cases it proved impossible to sell them by this route, and they remained in the portfolios of the banks, leading to a longer-term bank participation in those enterprises.[23] Of course, such participations did not always arise out of a failed approach to the stock market, but could also form part of banks' calculations from the beginning. In this context, banks were motivated both by the aim of paternally fostering newly established firms and by purely speculative considerations. During the crisis of 1857, for instance, some of these banks, as well as a number of private bankers, retained their participations in the enterprises they had founded, thereby helping their industrial clientele to survive the difficult times. Generally, the long-term involvement of a bank in an industrial enterprise was institutionally supported by the bank's sending some of its directors to sit on the supervisory board of the client.[24] As time passed, this step was increasingly imitated, intensifying the relationships between banks and industry in Germany.[25]

By acting both as financiers and as founders of enterprises, German joint-stock banks, as well as prominent private bankers, took investment funds that were lying fallow, centralized them, and pumped them into industrial investment. In this way, these banks developed into relay stations in the circulation of money capital, and by doing so enduringly influenced the direction of industrial growth.[26] Savings banks and credit cooperatives did not become involved in these activities.

In which sectors did the German banks mainly become involved? The literature unanimously identifies heavy industry and especially railway building as the leading sectors in German industrialization.[27] Between 1850 and 1870, 2404.76 million marks were invested in joint-stock companies in Prussia, of which 1722.44 million were allocated to railway building alone, and a further 275.41 million to mining, smelting, and salt-making.[28] In particular, Cologne private banks such as Sal. Oppenheim jr. & Cie. and I. H. Stein both guaranteed extensive loans for the young railway companies, and participated in these enterprises via ownership of shares.[29] There are many further examples of the involvement of German banks in heavy industrial firms. Thus with the Schaaffhausen'sche Bankverein in charge, the Kölner Bergwerksverein (Cologne Mining Company) was founded in 1849 and the Hörder Bergwerks- und Hüttenverein (Hörder Mining and Smelting Company) was founded in 1852. The Alsdorf-Höngener Kohleverein (Alsdorf-Höngener Coal Company) and the Köln-Müsener Bergwerks AG (Köln-Müsener Mining Joint-Stock Company), as well as several other smaller enterprises, were also established on the initiative of the Schaaffhausen'sche Bankverein. The Discontogesellschaft, too, immediately turned to heavy industry after its reorganization in 1856, pursuant to its new statutes. Its expansion into heavy industry began in 1857 when it obtained the Henrichshütte (Henrichs Smelting-Works) in Hattingen. Parallel to this, the Discontogesellschaft devoted itself intensively to financing railway building. The same was true of the Bank für Handel und Industrie in Darmstadt, which also participated in founding machine-building companies and iron-foundries in the Ruhr region and in southern Germany. Needless to say, this kind of relationship only arose in the regions of Germany in which industrialization was already beginning. In rural areas, savings banks and credit cooperatives remained the most important financial institutions.

The first stages of German industrialization saw the formation of the basic lineaments of that specific pattern of relationships between banks and industry which was in the following decades to become a characteristic feature of economic development in the German Kaiserreich, as well as across central Europe more widely. The banks' long-term involvement in providing loans, their sending of representatives onto the supervisory boards of industrial firms, and their ownership of shares (non-trivial, at least in some cases), unquestionably gave them opportunities to influence industrial enterprises. For the most part, this situation arose when an industrial firm encountered initial difficulties and was faced with heavy competition. Especially in crisis periods such as 1856, many industrial enterprises were only able to overcome their financial bottlenecks with help from the banks. Indeed, the banks often did this more or less willingly, out of anxiety that they might lose their immobilized capital.

However, irrespective of what exactly should be understood by 'bank dominance' (a question that has yet to be clarified), and without prejudging the later period, it must be recognized that for the period before 1870 one cannot speak of a general and entrenched dominance of banks over industry in Germany. For one thing, at this period the banks themselves were only in an early phase of development and were still struggling to formulate a successful business strategy. For another, apart from capital-intensive joint-stock companies in railway building and in heavy industry, the investment needs of most industrial firms were small enough to be covered mostly by internal financing, so that there was no reason for any dominance of banks over industry. Before the 1870s, therefore, the banks were not in a position to occupy the 'commanding heights' of the German economy, the charge often levelled at them by later critics. Indeed, it should be noted that the critics of the power of the banks themselves entered the field only later, and in analysing the role and power of the banks in modern capitalist societies were thinking of the situation around 1900, which as a rule they explicitly contrasted with earlier stages of development.[30]

5.3 Banks and industry in the German Kaiserreich

5.3.1 *Consolidation and concentration in German banking, 1870–1918*

Between the foundation of the Kaiserreich and the First World War, Germany became one of the world's leading industrial states.[31] During this process, the secondary sector – industry – became the most important part of the German economy. Around 1900, for the first time the number of Germans employed in industry exceeded that in agriculture. In 1914, of the total of 31.2 million employed persons in Germany, 34 per cent were employed in the primary sector, 38 per cent in the secondary, and 28 per cent in the tertiary.[32] The total productivity of industry rose by about 90 per cent between 1873 and 1913, although the rise was much higher in metals (with 270 per cent) and textiles (with 115 per cent). Between 1871 and 1910, 6534 joint-stock companies were formed, in which a total of 9.9 thousand million marks were invested. Of these, 90 per cent were industrial enterprises, the remainder mostly banks. Of course, the industrialization process was also linked to a striking demographic and social transformation of Germany, as shown particularly by population growth (discussed in Chapter 2) and urbanization (discussed in Chapter 6).[33]

However, the changes sketched out here did not take place continuously. Rather, as discussed in Chapter 4, the long-term trend was marked by large cyclical fluctuations, and these especially influenced the banking sector. As already mentioned, during the 'foundation crash' of 1873 a large proportion of the banks founded during the preceding boom had to declare bankruptcy. Their liquidation was mainly carried out by banks that had survived the crisis as a result of more careful business policies and now greatly increased their volume of business.[34] For example, Deutsche Unionbank, founded in 1870, liquidated four lending institutions between 1871 and 1874 before it was itself taken over by Deutsche Bank in 1876. Deutsche Bank took over seven additional institutions between 1873 and 1880, while Dresdner Bank took over four.[35] According to Riesser's calculations, in 1872 there were 126 joint-stock banks, each with at least one million marks in share capital. By 1885 the centralization process had reduced their numbers to 71.[36] In the same period, the focus of German stock-market business increasingly shifted from Frankfurt am Main to Berlin. The larger joint-stock banks that initially had their main location elsewhere now established branches in Berlin, and over time these gained importance to such an extent that the central branches of these banks were moved exclusively to the capital of the Kaiserreich. This led both expert and popular opinion to become accustomed to refer to the larger institutions domiciled in Berlin as the 'Berlin Great Banks'.

Parallel to this centralization, the banking sector also expanded, largely due to the growing industrial demand for business loans. For banks to be in a position to respond properly to the growing demands of their industrial clientele for loans and public issues of shares, they were forced to expand their capital and their volume of business. During this process, many joint-stock banks ultimately turned into Great Banks and universal banks.[37]

The Great Banks sought to expand their business in two different ways. First, they entered into associations of interest with provincial banks (through exchanges of shares or founding joint subsidiaries) and took over smaller provincial institutions using funds obtained through raising capital. Second, they expanded their business indirectly, decentralizing their activities by establishing sub-branches, partnerships, agencies and branch-offices.[38] From the mid-1890s on, the Berlin Great Banks concentrated their expansionary efforts on the regional economic centres. Deutsche Bank pointed the way in 1897 when, through an exchange of shares, it secured a participation in the Schlesischen Bankverein in Breslau and the Bergisch-Märkisch Bank.[39] The extent of this expansion is illustrated by the following numbers: in 1895 the German Great Banks – i.e. Darmstädter Bank für Handel und Industrie, Berliner Handelsgesellschaft, Deutsche Bank, Discontogesellschaft, Dresdner Bank, and Schaaffhausen'sche Bankverein – had at their disposal a total of 16 branches (comprising main branches and sub-branches), 14 deposit branches and exchange offices, 11 partnerships, and one participation in another joint-stock bank. In 1911, the German Great Banks had 104 branches, 276 deposit branches and exchange offices, seven partnerships, and 63 longer-term participations in other joint-stock banks.[40] This balance sheet was completed by associations of interest with provincial banks, which themselves at this time possessed 285 sub-branches, 126 deposit branches, 21 partnerships, and 377 agencies. By 1911, the provincial banks had taken over 116 private banking houses and 45 smaller joint-stock banks.[41]

As these figures show, under the leadership of the Berlin Great Banks, a closely inter-related network of lending institutions arose in the German Kaiserreich. The outstanding position of the Berlin Great Banks in the German banking sector can be seen from the relative size of their share capital. In 1895, this amounted to 272 million marks, and by 1910 it had risen by 363 per cent to 935 million marks. The share capital of all banks with at least 1 million marks of founding capital increased by 385 per cent in this period, from 723 million marks in 1895 to 2784 million marks in 1910, while the number of banks rose from 97 to 165. Thus, although the number of institutions of this size grew by about 70 per cent, the Berlin Great Banks were nearly able to maintain their proportion of the total share capital of this size category.[42]

The Great Banks based their growth mainly on a new business policy. In the period of speculation, the joint-stock banks had financed their transactions mainly using their own capital. Now, however, they increasingly resorted to capital belonging to others, primarily depositors. The forerunner of this development was once again Deutsche Bank, which as early as 1870 began to set up deposit branches. In 1871, this bank had 8 million marks worth of deposits on its balance sheet, which by 1916 had risen to 558 million marks. The other Great Banks saw similar growth.[43] The transformation in the capital structure of the joint-stock banks reflected the general change in their business policy: as deposit business increased in significance, they lost their character as banks chiefly oriented towards establishing new enterprises and underwriting public issues of shares. The growing significance of deposits on the debit side found its counterpart on the credit side in regular lending business, especially in the form of short-term current account business, exchange discounting business, and acceptance business. That is, during the Kaiserreich the German joint-stock banks transformed themselves into institutions which combined continuous regular banking business with stock exchange business and public issues. As far as their size and range of tasks were concerned, a whole array of German joint-stock banks had developed into the well-capitalized 'universal banks' whose function as the engine of German economic growth would henceforth attract increasing scholarly attention.[44]

The universal banks grew primarily at the expense of the private bankers. Looking solely at Berlin as the banking and stock exchange centre, the number of private banking houses decreased from 538 in 1892 to only 359 in 1914. The decisive cause of this change was that many private banking houses were under-capitalized, and this prevented them from being able to satisfy the lending requirements of large industry. In addition, however, a number of changes in stock market legislation weakened the position of private bankers, especially in making public issues of shares. In 1871/2, 90 Berlin private bankers took on 394 public issues of shares, but by 1899 this business had declined greatly, with just 34 private bankers concluding only 92 public issues.[45] Many private banks were taken over by universal banks. The numbers available on this wave of takeovers vary greatly, but they suggest that about 200 institutions were affected by it.[46] A typical example of this process was the spectacular takeover of the renowned banking house M. A. Rothschild & Söhne in Frankfurt am Main by Discontogesellschaft in 1901.[47] Despite this, many private bankers continued to occupy a niche in the German banking system. Especially in providing loans to small industry and handicrafts on the regional and local level, private bankers played an important role (although one subsidiary to that played by savings banks and credit cooperatives); this was because their personal contacts with their clientele enabled them to offer greater flexibility in issuing loans than the universal bankers. Several Berlin private bankers were able to secure their competitive position by specializing in stock exchange business for foreign accounts, in arbitrage business, in buying and selling shares of smaller enterprises which were not listed (or whose shares were not regularly traded) on the stock exchange, and in advising customers on investments. Overall, however, the private bankers should be regarded as the losers during this period of consolidation and concentration in German banking. Even though they had been the initiators in founding many joint-stock banks during the speculative period, now their existence was threatened – and not infrequently eliminated – by the institutions they had brought into being.[48]

5.3.2 Banks and industrial financing in the epoch of consolidation and concentration

A characteristic feature of economic development in the German Kaiserreich was the intensification of lending relationships between banks and industry, during which a relatively stable pattern of sectoral and regional specialization developed among the universal banks. At the same time, blocks began to form, with each Great Bank seeking to create its own industrial sphere of interest. Each bank pursued the goal of becoming the exclusive provider of all lending business for the firms numbered among its clientele, although it was not always successful. This state of affairs is illustrated by several of the leading sectors of German industrialization: heavy industry, the electrical industry, and the chemical industry.

In heavy industry, as in other branches of German industry, a massive concentration set in after the foundation crisis of 1873. In some cases, it came about through mergers between firms in the same stage of production, but the most important mergers were vertical combinations between plants operating at different stages of production. Thus steelworks, blast furnaces, coal mines, and raw-materials suppliers were frequently brought together under the roof of a single industrial concern. This concentration wave culminated in the 1890s in the organization of cartels, which were initially founded as 'children of emergency', and as time passed were organized even more strictly. Outstanding examples of this development are the Rheinisch-Westfälische Kohlensyndikat (Rhenish-Westfalian Coal Syndicate), the Rheinisch-Westfälische Roheisensyndicat (Rhenish-Westfalian Pig-Iron Syndicate), and the Stahlwerksverband (Steelworks Association).[49]

In all these moves toward increasing concentration, the initiative emanated from the industry itself,[50] although it was generally 'greeted by the German banking world in the most joyful manner, and furthered by the banking world wherever possible'.[51] However, where individual firms were forced to join a cartel against their will, the decisive pressure generally came from their industrial competitors, which not infrequently harnessed the banks to further this end. By contrast, when the banks took the initiative in putting pressure on client firms to join a cartel, they generally found that such firms refused to comply. An especially spectacular case of this type arose in 1904 when Phoenix AG für Bergbau und Hüttenbetrieb (Phoenix Company for Mining and Smelting) resisted pressure by Deutsche Bank and Schaaffhausen'sche Bankverein to join the Stahlwerskverband (Steelworks Association), and was only induced to change its mind through the intervention of the industrialist August Thyssen.[52]

During the process of concentration in German heavy industry, the banks mainly acted as financiers and mediators of capital – that is, they made available to their industrial clientele the funds required for mergers by providing large loans or by placing public issues of shares. Only when firms got into serious difficulties did banks enter into longer-term participations in them. One example is Discontogesellschaft's involvement in Dortmunder Union AG für Bergbau und Stahlindustrie (Dortmunder Union Company for Mining and the Steel Industry), which caused the bank huge losses over a long period. Another is Deutsche Bank's participation in the Mannesmannröhren-Werken

(Mannesmann Pipe Works), which required injections of finance from this Berlin Great Bank to rescue it from bankruptcy.[53]

On the whole, however, heavy industrial enterprises were able to avoid coming under the tutelage of banks. In particular, large concerns such as Krupp, Thyssen, Gute Hoffnungshütte ('Good Hope Iron and Steel Works'), and Phoenix were able to exploit competition among banks to their own advantage. In many ways, banks put a lot of effort into maintaining intensive business relationships with such firms, rather than firms being brought under the thumb of the banks. The role of banks in heavy industry during the Kaiserreich has been rightly characterized as follows: 'the banks curried favour with industry, not the other way around'.[54] These examples show that the business strategies of German industrial firms prevented banks from achieving their goal of becoming the single provider of lending business to firms.

A very similar pattern can be observed in the electrical industry during the Kaiserreich. This branch of industry experienced a first, stormy boom phase during the 1880s and 1890s, during which many of its young firms relied on bank support. Large sections of the German population were very sceptical about the establishment of electrical plants, so electricity firms needed large sums of capital and the capacity to 'hold their breath' in order to survive financial droughts. Often banks had to spring to their rescue by providing capital. This was the background in 1883 for the foundation of Deutsche Edisongesellschaft (the German Edison Company), later to change its name to AEG, the first joint-stock company in the electrical industry. Berliner Handelsgesellschaft acted as 'house-bank' for this firm, and for decades fostered an intensive business relationship with AEG. Deutsche Bank, by contrast, stood at the side of AEG's most important competitor, Siemens & Halske.[55] In a number of cases, it was impossible for a single bank to cover the large capital requirements of an expanding electricity firm. As a consequence, special consortia of banks or banking groups were formed to lend to such firms. By 1900, seven large electricity concerns had emerged, in each case backed by a group of banks or a 'financial trust'. The increasing concentration of the electricity industry and the banking sector thus mutually determined and strengthened each other. By the beginning of the twentieth century, however, German electricity concerns were increasingly able to free themselves from the influence of banks by annexing their own financial trusts. Especially in the case of the two leaders in this branch of industry, Siemens & Halske and AEG, bank activity was increasingly limited to helping obtain capital and providing legal advice.[56]

Another important new sector of the German economy was the chemical industry, but here the banks played a comparatively small role. Their outstanding position on the world market endowed many German chemical enterprises with high profit margins which made them independent of economic fluctuations and substantially increased their ability to finance investments from internal funds. Consequently, banks played only a subsidiary role in the chemical industry, mainly in placing public issues of shares. Overall, this was a creditor sector, whose firms often maintained large balances with banks, and seldom had to take out loans.[57]

The basis for the relationships between banks and industry in the Kaiserreich was current account lending, i.e. pre-financing the production process through bank loans. Compared to this, the business of share issues was very much of secondary significance. During this period, as previously, it was bank loans to industry that linked the two sides, although as time passed industry was able to reduce the earlier dominance of the banks. At any rate, this is the situation suggested by existing empirical studies. The inter-relationship between banks and industry found its institutional expression in the delegation of bank directors to occupy seats on the supervisory boards of industrial firms. Particularly after the issuing of the *Aktienrechts-novelle* (Revision of the Stock Market Law) in 1884, a firm's supervisory board played a central role in deciding its business policy, since it was now responsible for monitoring strictly the firm's management. This meant that banks had at their disposal an instrument enabling them to intervene directly in the business policies of their industrial clientele, although it must be emphasized that they were not always able to make use of this instrument successfully in practice. In turn, considerations of competition meant that banks sought to obtain representatives from industry on their own supervisory boards, in the hope of forming connections with these enterprises as customers over the longer term. This system of 'interlocking directorates' became a characteristic feature of fully developed industrial capitalism in the German Kaiserreich.[58]

5.3.3 *The debate about the power of the banks*

These trends in bank–industry relationships in Germany aroused, especially after about 1900, a vigorous debate about the 'power' of the German banks which has continued (with varying intensity) ever since.[59] In two ways, this debate has implications beyond the historical context of the German Kaiserreich. Geographically, its purview was extended by the fact that a universal banking system became a characteristic feature of the financial sector not only in Germany, but also in the Habsburg Empire and several other central and eastern European countries.[60] Substantively, too, the empirical findings from German history have been used as a basis for theories about the function and position of banks in modern economies more generally. Some of these theoretical speculations, as we shall see below, have aimed to derive a general logic of development for the capitalist system as a whole.

In general terms, three schools of thought can be discerned in this debate. On the one hand, practising German bankers such as Riesser and Jeidels, not least as a result of their immediate occupational interests, defended the universal banking system as a stabilizing and efficiency-increasing element of modern market economies. In retrospect, these works are important mainly because of the wealth of material and detailed information they provide, which make them a treasure trove for historical research.

The second school of thought, by contrast, is highly critical of the universal bank system. This critical strand of argument, however, can be divided into the liberal and the Marxist critiques of bank power, which have quite contradictory policy implications. The liberal critics of the banks advanced their arguments in the context of the late nineteenth-century debate about the growing cartellization of entire branches of the economy. Liberal social scientists and economic policy-makers, especially in Austria, branded the universal banking system as a danger for a competitive economy. They regarded the large, well-capitalized universal banks, as they existed at that period in the German Kaiserreich and the Habsburg Empire, as the driving force behind cartellization. Cartels, in their view, inevitably undermined competition between enterprises, leading to market domination and misallocation of resources. These in turn they regarded as the kernels of sickness in a capitalist system which, if healthy, would be both efficient and welfare-increasing. This analysis led inescapably to a single policy recommendation: the power of the banks should be limited, in order to prevent cartellization from blocking competition, which would in turn rescue the capitalist system.[61] To create a counterweight to the powerful position of the universal banks, these liberal critics of banks demanded a system of regional lending institutions. In their view, only decentralization could ensure sufficient competition in the lending sector, and such competition was essential for an economically sensible selection process, and hence for social improvement. This line of argument is still pursued by present-day economic liberals, who demand state action against any tendencies toward monopoly in the German lending sector.[62]

The other school of bank critics consisted of Austrian Marxists, who formulated a totally different set of policy recommendations for the lending sector, based on their understanding of the Marxist theory of capital. A particularly clear and theoretically sophisticated version of this position was articulated by Rudolf Hilferding, in his 1910 book, *Das Finanzkapital* ('Financial Capital').[63] According to Hilferding, competition forced capitalists to maximize profits, and this meant they needed capital. At first, industrialists mainly borrow circulating capital, but as industrialization progresses they increasingly need fixed capital. This, according to Hilferding, was the point at which banks began to have the incentive and power to dominate industry and influence their business policies.[64] Banks can always dominate industrial firms, Hilferding held, because banks have more capital, rely less on the success of individual transactions, and hold their capital in liquid funds rather than fixed plant. As a result, Hilferding contended, banks claimed a rising share of industrial profits through interest payments, and also demanded a large share of 'founder's profits' through the premium charged in placing shares on the stock market. For Hilferding, the rising share of interest payments in industrial profits was an irreversible and inevitable feature of the capitalistic system, subjecting industrial firms increasingly to bank coercion from which they could not escape.

Hilferding's theses about the power of the banks in the capitalist system have decisively influenced socialist theorists ever since. Thus Lenin, in his study of 'Imperialism as the Highest Stage of Capitalism', took Hilferding's ideas largely on board. His analysis of 'the new role of banks in capitalism' adopted several of Hilferding's propositions while altering the emphasis.[65] After the Second World War, as the concept of 'state monopoly capitalism' ('Stamokap') gained ground among Marxist theorists, Hilferding's *Finanzkapital* experienced a renaissance. 'Stamokap' thinkers agreed with Hilferding and Lenin that the key to understanding advanced capitalism was to recognize the increasing tendency toward monopolization of the economy. They, too, argued that banking capital would inevitably merge with industrial capital to form 'financial capital'. 'Stamokap' theorists differed, however, in not expecting monopolization to exclude all forms of competition. Instead, they thought that in the final stage of capitalism, several hostile and opposing monopolistic blocks would emerge and struggle with one another.[66]

Hilferding's analysis of capitalistic development has found not only disciples but also critics, some of them bitter. Not surprisingly, opponents of Marxism reject his views on bank power as unfounded speculation.[67]

Moreover, the question still remains: What precisely is bank power? The various answers to this complicated question cannot be discussed in detail here.[68] However, in our view, any definition of 'bank power' should be based on specific details of the economic relationships between banks and industry. Any concept of power that abstracts from these specific details, or that focuses on political aspects instead, is empirically meaningless and leads into a blind alley. In our view, therefore, we can only regard banks as having 'power' over industry when they can do one or more of the following: first, control a growing share of the profits of firms in the form of interest payments; second, absorb a majority of the 'founder's profits' arising in capital transactions; third, exert massive influence over firms' business policies to the banks' own advantage.[69]

As already indicated, available empirical studies show that according to this definition, it is unjustified to speak of a general domination of banks over industry in the German Kaiserreich. Relationships between banks and industry in this period were cooperative in nature, based on a far-reaching alignment of interests. Even when conflicts arose, as occurred relatively infrequently, they were generally solved through compromises in which neither party was wholly able to subordinate the other to its interests. Occasionally, a group of industrial firms allied against the banks and successfully coerced them into behaving in a particular way.[70] Furthermore, as we shall see in the next section, there was little fundamental change in this relationship over the period that followed.

5.4 Banks and industry in the Weimar Republic and under National Socialism

5.4.1 *The development of banking during the First World War and the great inflation*

The First World War and its aftermath affected both the capital structure and the business policies of German banks in ways that can be traced back to the involvement of the lending sector in war financing. According to various authors' estimates, by the end of the war, four-fifths of the total value of all bills, half of all Lombard loans, and a quarter of all debts in the German economy were being absorbed by war finance.[71] In the second half of the war, in particular, short-term government debt made up a growing share of money owed to German banks. With government debt and hence note issues by the Reichsbank rising precipitously, from 1916 onward short-term deposits increasingly flowed into the coffers of the banks, and in order to maintain liquidity these had to be invested short-term. Since profits were high in almost all branches of industry and the central bank was printing money, there was excess liquidity in most sectors of the economy. This made bills of exchange increasingly unimportant. As a result, German banks resorted ever more frequently to treasury bills and treasury notes as forms of investment for their funds which could be liquidated at any time.

In turn, these changes in banks' lending and investment activities influenced the relationship between banks and industry. In particular, firms in industries of strategic military importance were enjoying large state orders at agreed fixed prices which meant that they could make large profits and finance their investments mainly from their own funds. Consequently, bank loans declined across large swathes of German industry, thereby visibly loosening previously close relationships between banks and industrial firms. Although not all branches of industry were equally affected by this development, on the whole bank influence on industry decreased as a result of the rapidly increasing tendency toward self-financing, the general liquidity of funds, and the war boom after 1915.[72]

In the first years of the war, the increasing concentration of the banking sector had temporarily halted. But then, in 1916, things changed. Banks, particularly the Berlin Great Banks, made use of the increasing funds and deposits to buy up (or merge with) provincial banks and private banking houses. By the end of the war, the weight of the Great Banks relative to the provincial banks and private banking houses had visibly increased. In

1914, the Berlin Great Banks had owned 46 per cent of the capital of all banks included in the statistics; by 1918, this had risen to 52.4 per cent. With deposits, the predominance of the Great Banks was even more noticeable: in 1914, they held 55.2 per cent of deposits; by 1918, it was 65.7 per cent.[73]

The same factors that determined the capital structure and business policy of banks during the First World War continued after the war ended, and even intensified: rapidly growing deposits along with high liquidity, close links between banks and state finances, and a decline in bank loans to industry linked with a loss of bank power vis-à-vis industry. In particular, the postwar years saw an even stronger increase in deposits on the one hand and short-term liabilities on the other, induced by inflation. In 1918, all lending institutions included in the statistics administered just 30 thousand million marks in deposits; by 1920, it was 84.5 thousand million. However, it must be remembered that at the end of the currency decline in 1924, deposits denominated in paper marks were converted to gold marks, and slumped heavily. In their 1924 opening balances which were denominated in gold marks, the Great Banks had deposits of only 277 million gold marks compared to 2.25 thousand million marks in 1913 – a decline to 12.3 per cent of the prewar level. Total deposits likewise declined sharply, falling from 4.84 thousand million gold marks at the end of 1913 to a mere 1.08 thousand million at the end of 1923 – only 23 per cent of the 1913 level. Taking into account mergers and takeovers, as well as the write-offs undertaken by banks, deposits in 1923 were only 20 per cent of their 1913 level.[74]

The special circumstances prevailing during the inflationary years also affected the credit side of banks' balance sheets. After the November disturbances of 1918 ended, banks had to seek out new investment opportunities for the deposits streaming ever more copiously into their coffers. The disproportionate increase in funds redeemable at short notice forced banks to seek higher liquidity in these investments. Consequently, most banks intensified their wartime practice of investing their deposits in treasury bills. By 1920, the share of treasury bills in total bank assets had risen to 48.9 per cent, before starting to fall again in 1921.[75]

Parallel to the declining importance of foreign exchange holdings, there was an increase in so-called 'nostro assets' – deposits maintained by banks with other banks or with the central bank. In 1918, they made up only 4.8 per cent of the total assets of the Great Banks; by 1921, it was 11.7 per cent. In the period of 'galloping inflation' after 1922, nostro assets comprised as much as 42.1 per cent of the total assets of the Great Banks, by a considerable margin the most important form of money investment. A substantial (although not precisely quantifiable) share of these nostro assets took the form of foreign exchange accounts held at foreign banks. These foreign assets served two purposes for the banks. First, they represented liquid investments of bank funds that were protected from devaluation. Second, from 1921 on, they were deliberately undertaken as a special way of maintaining asset values, since the deposits that flowed into such accounts were thus rescued from the devaluation of the currency.[76] The large provisions and profits which banks secured through their stock exchange and foreign exchange business also served this purpose.

These profits were generated by the stock-market rise during the inflation years, and were invested by the banks in real estate and securities. Admittedly, German banks did not display their growing holdings of securities in their balance sheets. In addition, in the final years of the inflation German banks entered large write-offs under this rubric in order to contribute to the maintenance of their assets through internal transfers to reserves. Many contemporary bank experts, however, unanimously agreed that banks were able to achieve high revenues both from their securities holdings (especially their industrial shares with high real value) and from their real estate and stock exchange business.[77] German bank directors underwent a learning process, as shown by the reorientation in bank business policies which set in particularly after 1921. They focused on exploiting the inflation (especially in their stock market and current account business) and on a deliberate policy of asset maintenance (through expanding nostro assets abroad and ownership of stocks and real estate at home). Although the profits displayed in banks' balance sheets have a low information content, they nevertheless convey the impression that most banks were benefiting from the peculiar circumstances of the postwar inflation rather than suffering from permanently poor profits.[78]

Admittedly, a comparison of balance sheets for 1913 with those for 1924 (when the gold mark started) suggests that the lending sector was one of the greatest losers from the inflation. But in fact the largest losses in bank assets had already occurred between 1914 and 1919. This, together with the reorientation of banks' business policies, suggests that German banks and their directors were successfully adapting to economic conditions during the postwar inflation. However, this is not to dispute that between 1914 and 1923 German banks did suffer losses both of their own capital and of deposits when these are converted into gold marks.[79]

Yet another finding confirms the attractiveness of banking business during the German currency decline. Between 1919 and 1923, many new banks were founded in Germany, spurred by the accelerating devaluation of the currency and the resulting increased turnover for most lending institutions, the optimism about economic trends at the beginning of the 1920s, the growing number of customers for all banks, and the high profits that banks were supposed to be able to make because of the rise in the stock market. Most of these newly established banks were small, seeking a share of the profits from the share boom, and restricting their activities to speculation. Most went bankrupt during the stabilization crisis of 1924 at the end of the currency decline, and disappeared from the picture, a situation similar to that of 1870–73.[80]

The high profits during the postwar inflation were particularly useful for the Berlin Great Banks in their efforts to continue expanding, as can be seen from the growth in their networks of sub-branches all over Germany. Besides several new foundations, many of the new sub-branches of the Great Banks arose through takeovers of smaller private banks or provincial banks together with their branch networks. Several of the Great Banks were able to become institutions of supra-regional significance solely through this expansion policy: an example is the Commerz- und Privatbank, which during the First World War and the inflation period increased its network of sub-branches by a factor of 30. Commerzbank was also involved in mergers that aroused considerable attention. In 1920 it took over the Mitteldeutsche Privatbank in Magdeburg, which brought it a new network of customers from the textile, potash, and brown coal (lignite) industries of central Germany. Unquestionably the most important merger in the German lending sector during the postwar inflation was that between the Darmstädter Bank für Handel und Industrie and the Nationalbank für Deutschland, but in this case it was a merger between two Great Banks. With this step, the Darmstädter- und Nationalbank (as the merged institution called itself) became one of those Great Banks that had most assets and sub-branches, thereby becoming a serious competitor for Deutsche Bank and Discontogesellschaft.[81]

Admittedly, the German banks were not completely able to reverse the decline in their importance relative to industry that had already become apparent during the First World War. Because of the liquidity of funds caused by the inflation, industrial enterprises were able to repay loans quickly. A number of industrialists, the so-called 'inflation kings', Hugo Stinnes, Otto Wolff, Jacob Michael, and Camillo Castiglioni, were able to build up large industrial concerns or conglomerates using large loans which they repaid in devalued marks. Hugo Stinnes' attempted takeover of the Berliner Handelsgesellschaft and Otto Wolff's similar attempt against the Discontogesellschaft show how much the power relationship between banks and industry had changed during the currency decline. Even if these are only exceptional examples, it was generally true that banks lost importance relative to industry, both in regular banking business and in public issues of shares. This was caused partly by the popular flight into material assets which meant that industrial shares could be placed with ease, and partly by the increasing establishment during the inflation period of firms' own combine banks or financing companies owned by firms. Banks increasingly became the 'companions' of their industrial clientele. This has led many to conclude that the banks lost by the inflation. However, the reorientation of their business policy sketched out above, as well as the fact that for the most part they successfully managed to maintain their assets during the postwar inflation, suggests that this view must be modified or even substantially revised.[82]

5.4.2 Banks and industrial financing
after the inflation

After the stabilization of the mark in 1924, a credit crisis set in which enabled German banks partly to re-establish their earlier position vis-à-vis industry. Given the scarcity of capital on the one hand and the considerable demand for it on the other, many smaller industrial enterprises had to take out bank loans on very unfavourable terms. This situation increased the importance of banks as the institutions allocating the available stock of capital. Nevertheless, this does not mean that the importance of the banks was increasing overall. Even after the currency decline, large industrial firms were able to defend the financial independence they had gained during the war and inflation period, as a consequence of better opportunities to raise foreign capital abroad and an ability to exploit competition among banks.[83]

Whereas large German firms had little need of external capital from banks, and set up combines during the 1920s with the help of banks but not under their direction, smaller firms (especially in the processing sector) continued to depend on bank loans and even faced increased bank influence.[84] In addition, yet another factor played a role in bank–industry relations after the inflation. After the end of the currency decline and the loss of their liquid funds, many German banks had too little capital to slake the thirst of large industry. Thus banks could not exploit the growing capital needs of large industrial firms to their own advantage. They therefore sought desperately (although vainly) to satisfy the long-term capital demand of their clients in large industry by issuing industrial bonds and debentures.

The shortage of capital in the German capital market and its weakened capital basis were responsible for the fact that the German banks could not keep pace with foreign lending institutions which were financially stronger, and which became increasingly important for German industry in this period. This is shown by the many loans taken out by German firms abroad, especially in the United States. Large foreign loans were taken out by Krupp, Thyssen, Deutsch-Luxemburgische Bergwerks- und Hütten AG (German-Luxemburg Mining and Smelting Company), and Vereinigten Stahlwerke (United Steelworks). Firms in other branches of industry did likewise.

This internationalization of banking business and of capital markets ensured that the competition among German banks, which was in any case increasing, intensified further. In the struggle to secure commissions and maintain relationships with long-standing customers, German banks often had to make far-reaching concessions in order not to lose their clientele completely. The beneficiaries of this situation were unquestionably the foreign banks, after the large combines.[85]

Against this background, it is not surprising that the merger movement and combine formation in German industry after 1924 were for the most part carried out without bank involvement. Both the foundation of

Vereinigten Stahlwerke (United Steelworks) in 1926 and the establishment of IG-Farbenindustrie in the same year took place without the influence of banks. The bank–industry relationship during this period was mainly characterized by banks' operating as mediators and advisors. When invited by members of the management team of industrial firms, bank directors acted as mediators and advisors to help their industrial clients realize their existing aims and plans. In this process, bankers often found it hard to do justice to their role as mediators. For one thing, they lacked any means of bringing about an agreement in cases of conflict, and for another the ideas and plans proposed by the banks were discarded and often not even seriously discussed. Nevertheless, in some cases industrial managers who had to take important decisions were happy to resort to bankers' expertise to achieve their aims.

After the inflation ended, German banks were fully conscious of their weakened position in the economy and their loss of importance vis-à-vis industry. At the same time, they became aware of the growth of foreign competition. Against this background, it was logical that on the eve of the world economic crisis they should seek to strengthen their competitive position through mergers and to reduce costs through synergies, thereby forming a counterweight to industry. Commerzbank led the way, when in 1929 it merged with Mitteldeutsche Kreditbank. The same year saw what was hitherto the largest merger in the German lending sector, Deutsche Bank's takeover of Discontogesellschaft. With this step, the new 'De-Di' Bank became by far the largest bank in Germany.

But the difficulties in the German banking sector could not be solved through these measures. Now as previously, German banks had serious weaknesses, particularly the making of extravagant concessions in lending conditions in order to compete for customers, a mistaken allocation of resources which one-sidedly favoured large customers. Another weakness was the ruinous competition among banks as a result of the so-called 'over-filling' of the German lending sector.[86] These developments culminated in the great trauma in the history of the German lending sector, the banking crisis of July 1931.

Although good empirical studies are still lacking, nevertheless it can be stated with certainty that the banks shared some responsibility for the 1931 banking crisis – even though it is undeniably the case that serious errors were also made by the government and the central bank. The Reichsbank's unconsidered adherence to internationally prescribed reserve guidelines intensified the 1931 crisis considerably. Nevertheless, the bank that on 13 July 1931 declared itself unable to meet payments, thereby unleashing a run on all the other banks, was the Darmstädter und Nationalbank – the very institution that between 1924 and 1929 had pursued an especially aggressive business policy in the attempt to win back lost ground vis-à-vis industry. It was this very 'Danat Bank' that had made huge loans to many large customers with insufficient security. In view of the dramatically worsening profitability of its large industrial customers faced with the world economic crisis, this business strategy had devastating effects. By freezing its loans to its large customers, the 'Danat Bank' inevitably got into payment difficulties.[87]

Bank historians have long debated two questions about this crisis. First, could the Reichsbank have rescued the 'Danat Bank' by discounting bills of exchange? Second, could the Deutsche Bank-Discontogesellschaft and Berliner Handelsgesellschaft have saved the 'Danat Bank' from collapse by taking some of its bills of exchange into their portfolios? Although conclusive empirical investigation of these questions is still lacking, it is unquestionably the case that the collapse of the 'Danat-Bank' in July 1931 started the collapse of the entire German lending sector, since very shortly afterwards both Dresdner Bank and the Rhine Province Landesbank were forced to announce their inability to meet payments. It cannot be disputed that the banking crisis of 1931 and its devastating consequences made a crucial contribution to intensifying the world economic crisis in Germany, thereby indirectly preparing the ground for the later political triumph of the Nazis.

As a consequence of the banking crisis, the German lending sector lost its independence: henceforth it was subject to the control of a so-called 'bank commissar'. The 'Danat-Bank' and Dresdner Bank were forced to merge under state auspices. In this merger, the government not only took over the share capital of the new institution (which bore the name Dresdner Bank) but also decisively determined its business policy. Commerzbank took over the Barmer Bankverein which had also collapsed during the banking crisis, but then got into difficulties itself. The government had to take over a capital participation in this bank, as well, to ensure its survival. Only Deutsche Bank-Discontogesellschaft was able to retain its autonomy. As a result of this development, by the end of the Weimar Republic a banking system had arisen in Germany which was heavily dependent on state directives and instructions. This made it easy for the Nazis to recruit the German lending sector to serve its own ends.[88]

5.4.3 The politically regulated banking system under National Socialism

The period of Nazi dictatorship from 1933 to 1945 is the darkest chapter of German history, and to this day it is largely a 'black box' as far as German banking history is concerned. For a long time, there was a shamefaced neglect by researchers of the role of the banks in the Nazi regime. Only recently have studies appeared which begin to draw back the veil of ignorance about this saddest period of German banking history.[89] Even so, many questions still remain unanswered and many aspects of the subject have not yet been dealt with. These include the 'Aryanization' of Jewish banks, the role of the banks in German war financing, the measures taken by the Nazi government to regulate banking, and the structural change within the lending sector arising from the fact that the Nazis favoured the savings banks. These themes will only be touched upon briefly here because the lack of empirical studies still prevents any detailed discussion.

After the Nazi takeover, the German lending sector, which had been weakened by the banking crisis of 1931, was immediately subjected to far-reaching state regulation. Directly after the Reichstag election of 5 March 1933, Hitler appointed Hjalmar Schacht as both President of the Reichsbank and *Generalbevollmächtiger für die Kredit- und Bankenpolitik* (Chief Representative for Lending and Banking Policy). In Schacht, Hitler, who had no expertise in lending or currency policy, chose an internationally renowned financial technocrat, with the aim of protecting the unstable German banking system from a further crisis of confidence, both domestically and abroad.

From the start, Schacht demonstrated his expert authority through successful crisis management. By swiftly convening a Commission of Inquiry as early as 1933, Schacht sought to introduce a far-reaching and long overdue modernization of the German banking system. In its report, this commission sharply criticized existing bank supervision practices, recommending direct state intervention in the business policies of the Great Banks and fundamental institutional reforms in the banking sector. Based on these recommendations, a new regulatory framework for state banking policy was laid under the auspices of Schacht and the Reichsbank. The new *Kreditwesengesetz* (Lending Law) of 1934, whose basic principles remain in force to this day, created the state Supervisory Office for Banking and endowed the German central bank with far-reaching powers of legal regulation and standard-setting. These enabled the Supervisory Office for Banking to accelerate rationalization of the lending sector through concentration of firms, and to push 'uneconomic' banks out of the market by taking away their licences. These new licensing powers were deliberately utilized by the Nazis to eliminate smaller Jewish banks, thereby serving the purposes of racist economic policies.[90]

During the first three years of Nazi domination, the Supervisory Office, the Reichsbank, and the Economic Ministry refrained from direct intervention in the business policies of the Great Banks in order to prevent political unrest. But in the case of Dresdner Bank such intervention was not even required. Through its personnel policies, which were directed by the government, this bank was already completely aligned with Nazi ideology. Because of its comparatively unattractive salaries and limited room for entrepreneurial manoeuvre, many well-qualified non-Nazi-oriented bankers withdrew their applications for management positions, thereby easing the invasion of convinced Nazis into Dresdner Bank's management.[91] The other Great Banks reacted to the racist political ideology of the regime, and its strict prescriptions, in varying ways. While a number of banks hastened to demonstrate special willingness to adapt to Nazi desires in filling high-profile management positions, and adopted opportunistic personnel policies characterized by the dismissal of Jewish members of the management, others sought to retain valuable employees as long as possible. After 1935, Nazi managers compelled banks to comply with the autarchic financing policies of the Four-Year Plan Board directed by Hermann Göring and with the economic interests of the SS. Recent research, however, shows that until 1936 Deutsche Bank, at least, opposed the desires of the Four-Year Plan Board on several matters.[92]

A well-functioning lending sector which could be exploited for the economic aspects of defence was indispensable for the expansionary aims of the Nazis. The Reichsbank deliberately directed the flow of capital, thereby enabling the public debt to rise noiselessly, via so-called MEFO-Wechsel bills. These were bills issued by the *Metallurgische Forschungsanstalt* (MEFO), an enterprise established by the heavy industrial combines to raise funds. The way this worked was that the MEFO issued its bill, then a large combine in the heavy industrial sector signed the bill a second time, after which the bill was discounted at the Reichsbank; by this means, industry was able to raise additional funds. This development initially occurred without open inflation. To implement this policy, the Reichsbank required cooperation from the business banks. Leading the German banking sector on a 'golden rein' of monetary and capital market policy, it ensured priority for the financial requirements of the state, especially defence, without appearing to inflict serious damage on the regulatory principle of autonomy of action for the banks in entrepreneurial decision-making.

Even so, banks' entrepreneurial freedom was visibly undermined by state regulation, as well as by the penetration of Nazi ideology and Nazi-oriented personnel. The Reichsbank had become the decision-making centre of the German lending sector.[93] For a long time Schacht maintained his hope of being able to control loan provision to the state and the entire German lending sector through the three offices he occupied: President of the Reichsbank, Chief Representative for the Lending Sector, and Director of the Supervisory Office for the Lending Sector.

But this hope turned out to be illusory. Increasingly, the economic requirements of rearmament took priority over the efforts of the Reichsbank and the Economic Ministry to ensure economic and financial stability in the country. One indication of this trend was the growing competition between the various institutions of the Nazi regime. In particular, the Office for the Four-Year Plan, created by Schacht's arch-rival Göring, increasingly gained influence in shaping economic policy. This office pursued an industrial policy dedicated exclusively to defence with the aim of preparing for war, without any consideration for monetary stability.

In addition, the system whereby private banking was 'directed' by the Reichsbank came under pressure because of the privileges granted to the savings banks. The savings banks had not only emerged from the banking crisis with smaller losses than the private banks, but had also profited from the regime's policies on wages, prices and foreign trade. These policies forced funds into deposits in the savings banks: from 1933 to 1938 deposits rose by 78.2 per cent, from 1939 to 1944 by 273.5 per cent. This meant that the excess purchasing power created by suppressed inflation was mainly guided into accounts at these banks. This strategy gave the Nazi regime relatively easy access to substantial funds that could be mobilized for speeding up rearmament.[94]

Under National Socialism, concentration in the lending sector reached new heights. Approximately half of all banks disappeared from active business through bankruptcy or outside takeover. This was particularly true of Jewish banks. From 1934 to 1936, the largest of these were still able to occupy a niche in the banking sector. Based on their know-how in foreign trade and stock-market business, they were able to compensate for their loss of important customers from large industry and their own weakening capital basis, and to maintain their position in the German lending sector. Now as previously, the large Jewish banks were indispensable for the German export economy because of their capital strength and their international contacts. While they lost non-Jewish customers, for the most part the Jewish portion of their clientele remained with them, favouring the rise of a relatively homogeneous Jewish economic sector. Until Schacht's dismissal as Economic Minister and President of the Reichsbank in 1936, the regulatory and racist selection of those banks allowed to stay in business had not endangered the large and renowned Jewish institutions. But with Schacht's dismissal and the disappearance of top officials at the Reichsbank who had been critical of the regime, both Economic Ministry and Reichsbank veered round toward the severe 'Aryanization' policies of Göring and Frick. Now the owners of the large Jewish banks, such as Max Warburg, were also forced out of business.[95]

Available empirical studies suggest that the behaviour of the German Great Banks with regard to 'Aryanization' was not uniform. Nevertheless, most of the large Berlin banks profited from the liquidation of their Jewish competitors, since they were able not only to take over their non-Jewish customers, thereby increasing their market share, but also to incorporate their capital. All the Great Banks became more-or-less intensively enmeshed in the 'Aryanization' of Jewish banks. Some 'Aryan' bankers did try to compensate their former competitors when they took over Jewish institutions. But most bank directors shamelessly exploited the desperation of the legitimate owners of Jewish banks. Furthermore, restrictive regulations by the Economic Ministry increasingly limited the extent to which 'Aryan' banks could pay compensation when they took over Jewish ones.

Especially radical and shameless was the behaviour of German banks in Austria after the Anschluß in 1938. Here there was a centrally coordinated policy which sought to expropriate all Jewish entrepreneurs and bankers as rapidly and completely as possible. A serious struggle developed among German banks in the Reich for the Austrian banks' large industrial share-holdings. In the competition to take over Creditanstalt, Dresdner Bank and the state-owned Reichskreditgesellschaft acted especially aggressively against Deutsche Bank. In the end Deutsche Bank was successful, in 1938 obtaining a blocking minority in the Österreichische Creditanstalt (ÖCA) and securing control of its business policy through a management contract.[96] Dresdner Bank compensated itself for this defeat by successes in the Reich Protectorate of Bohemia and Moravia. After the Sudeten Crisis of 1938, it deployed all its strength to secure the German-Czech banks' profit-able network of sub-branches.[97]

Both in the Sudeten region and in the Reich Protectorate, the activities of this bank were characterized by two strategic aims. Profit-seeking in bank-ing business merged with the obligation to support the combine-formation strategy of the *Reichswerke*. In this way, Dresdner Bank, whose manage-ment chairman Karl Rasche was particularly close to the Nazi Party, became the handmaiden of the command economy and of the Nazis' ideologically motivated economic policy. Thanks to the influence of Göring and Kehrl, Dresdner Bank was promised the Bohemian Escompte-Bank. In return, it and its new daughter-firm BEB (Böhmische Escompte-Bank) used blackmail to secure control for the Reichswerk-Konzern over key enterprises in the Czech mining and machine-building industries. Deutsche Bank obtained Böhmische Union-Bank and Deutsche Agrar- und Industriebank, two rescue cases owning blocks of shares in industrial firms strategically interesting to the combine. These transactions brought it generous tax advantages. In contrast to the situation in the 'Old Reich' and the occupied western European states, in the Protectorate no German bank showed any scruples about actively participating in 'Aryanization' or working with the Gestapo. Through their involvement in war financing as well as their collaboration with the Gestapo and other organs of the state, the German banks made themselves jointly guilty of the criminal aims and terrorist policies of the Nazi regime.[98]

Concrete research results on the overall role of the banks in the German economy during the Second World War are still not available. All that can be said here is that during the war, the German lending sector initially profited from its close inter-relationships with government organs, but was later sentenced to destruction along with the Nazi regime itself.[99]

5.5 The development of German banking after the Second World War

Even less is securely known about the recent history of German banking for the period after 1945 than for the Nazi period. Two factors are responsible for this. First, only a few detailed studies are available.[100] Second, anyone seeking to carry out such a study encounters very serious documentary problems, since access to bank and industrial archives has for a long time been explicitly restricted when it comes to the postwar period. Therefore, any statements about the contribution of banks to financing German industry after 1945 must be regarded as provisional until further notice, as must any speculations about the power of the banks in the postwar Federal Republic of Germany. Conclusions about the role of the banks in postwar Germany are still based only on statistical data; a more profound assessment of their role will only become possible through analysis of archival sources.

After 1945, far-reaching institutional changes initially appeared to be about to occur in German banking. The Allies regarded the Great Banks, along with heavy industry and the chemical industry, as some of the most important collaborators with the Nazi regime.[101] Consequently, they sought to destroy Deutsche Bank, Dresdner Bank and Commerzbank, which were supposed to be dismembered into a number of smaller institutions, each with a regional sphere of activity.[102] But in 1950/1 these plans were overturned. Out of each of the three German Great Banks, 10 or 11 smaller institutions were formed. However, this situation in turn did not last for long. As early as 1957, these three large banks were re-integrated, effectively re-establishing the *status quo ante*.[103]

Only after this period were the three successor institutions able to begin to pursue a common business policy oriented toward the future. Only after 1957, with the re-establishment of the creditworthiness of Germany, the convertibility of the *Deutschmark*, and the re-foundation of the three Great Banks, did the lines of development emerge which were to mark the German financial sector into the present day.[104]

The first phenomenon to be mentioned in this context is the process of concentration in the banking system. The number of private bankers and of small regional banks declined continually after 1957. For example, the number of private bankers fell from 245 in 1957 to 73 at the end of 1984 and 64 by the end of 1998. There were spectacular collapses of private banking houses such as that of Herstatt-Bank and the Hamburg private banking house Schröder, Münchmeyer, Hengst & Co. But the number of regional joint-stock banks (or regional banks in the form of partnerships partially limited by shares) also declined. Several of the most important mergers may be mentioned briefly: in 1970 the Berliner Handelsgesellschaft merged with the Frankfurter Bank, forming the BHF-Bank, while in 1971 the Bayerische Hypotheken- und Wechselbank entered into cooperation with the Bayerische Landesbank. Finally, in 1997 there occurred the most spectacular merger in the banking history of the Federal Republic of Germany in the postwar period when the Bayerische Hypotheken- und Wechselbank merged with the Bayerische Vereinsbank into the Bayerische Hypotheken- und Vereinsbank, and thus became the second-largest lending institution in Germany. Of similar importance was the 1995 merger of the Berliner Bank with the Landesbank Berlin and the Berliner Sparkasse to form the Bankgesellschaft Berlin.

Another characteristic of the development of the lending sector in the Federal Republic was the vigorous competition between private banks, public banks, and savings banks. Especially the latter had profited enormously in the postwar period from the 'economic miracle', rising living standards, and the resurgence in the German population's desire to save, while initially the still battered Great Banks were paying little attention to the so-called mass business among private customers. It is therefore illuminating that the Great Banks, having pulled themselves together after 1957, paid especial attention to this branch of business in order to avoid losing additional market share to the public banks and savings banks.[105]

As is well known, the first 25 years of West German economic history are regarded as the era of the 'economic miracle' (as discussed in detail in Chapter 8). During that period, the Federal Republic's extraordinarily high GDP growth rates particularly aroused the attention of contemporaries, economists and economic historians.[106] But these growth rates were only a statistical expression of far-reaching qualitative changes in the economy and society of the Federal Republic.[107] The debate about the causes of the German 'economic miracle' has not been settled. Nevertheless, findings so far do suggest that the banking system played a much less important role in influencing German economic development after 1945 than in earlier phases of German history. Unlike historians of earlier periods of German economic development, no one speculates that the banks were the engine of growth during the 'economic miracle'. This does not mean than bank finance might not have become more important for West German industry as the postwar period progressed. Particularly toward the end of the postwar boom, German firms faced changed conditions on the world market and to some extent a shortage of internal capital for investment.[108]

As a consequence of the problems in gaining access to archival material which have already been mentioned, wide-ranging qualitative statements about the relationship between banks and industry after 1945 are not possible. Available statistical material and those studies that have already been published, however, permit the following conclusions to be reached.[109] In the period between 1950 and 1989, bank loans contributed only about 12 per cent of the funds which German firms required to finance their investments. However, it is necessary to break down this period into sub-periods: during the 1960s and 1970s loan finance was more important than between 1980 and 1989. Precisely for investment in the postwar period and during the so-called 'economic miracle', more German firms required external finance than in the subsequent years. In the years of the oil crisis from 1973 to 1975, as well, which definitively ended the postwar boom, loan finance still played a role. In the 1980s its importance declined. Self-financing by firms, by contrast, expanded. Nevertheless, the fact cannot be ignored that in the period as a whole, financing through bank loans was not quantitatively important relative to total financial requirements.[110]

However, the importance of the universal banks as financiers of large industrial enterprises in the postwar period cannot be denied. This may be one reason why the debate about the power of the banks in West German society is still alive. Many politicians as well as a large swathe of German public opinion still believe that the great universal banks in particular occupy a 'strategic' position in the German economy, or even in German society.[111] The large number of supervisory board seats in German joint-stock companies occupied by bankers, their control of proxy votes, and their ownership of shares in industrial firms are still believed to be 'strategic instruments' for controlling the German economy. Public debate about the advisability of stronger restrictions on alleged bank power are fuelled by spectacular business transactions such as the hostile takeover of the Thyssen-Konzern by Krupp AG in 1997, which was believed to be a 'joint project' of the Krupp management and its house-banks.[112] Because a large number of jobs were lost as a consequence of this takeover, many politicians and large swathes of public opinion directed particular criticism at Deutsche Bank and Dresdner Bank. The same had already occurred in 1994 with the bankruptcy of the Schneider construction empire, which had been financed for a long time by Deutsche Bank. The end of the Schneider firm and the loss of hundreds of jobs evoked enormous public criticism of Deutsche Bank.

Unfortunately, there is little historical research to provide an empirical basis for the current debate about the power of the German banks. Although there are several interesting works on the question of bank power in the Federal Republic,[113] current historiography is characterized by two serious weaknesses. First, access to the required archival material is still impossible since most of the relevant holdings are closed until some future date. This means that only a modest beginning can be made at analysing the relationships between banks and industry in West Germany. Second, many authors still assess bank power over industry in terms of formal criteria such as banks' seats on industrial firms' supervisory boards. The undoubted intensification of institutional inter-relationships between banks and industry expressed in increasing numbers of bank representatives on industrial supervisory boards is unjustifiably interpreted as evidence of increasing bank influence over industry. But when bank power is assessed in terms of the more appropriate criteria formulated at the end of Section 5.3 above, this inference is by no means conclusive – as recognized in studies of the Kaiserreich and the Weimar Republic.[114] From the perspective of economic history, therefore, a conclusive assessment of bank–industry relationships in the Federal Republic of Germany is still premature. Such an assessment must await scholarly studies which do justice to the conceptual problems involved in measuring bank power, and which have carried out the requisite empirical analyses of the documentary sources.

5.6 Conclusion

In the introduction, this survey of German industry and finance over the past two centuries placed two questions at centre stage. The first concerned the German banks' contribution to long-term economic development, which is closely linked with the process of industrial investment. The second question concerned the potential power asymmetry between banks and industry, which may arise from the functional inter-relationship of the two in economic activity.

Research into German banking history has devoted special attention to particular phases of the period covered here: the early stages of industrialization, the Kaiserreich, and the 1920s. For other historical periods, especially the more recent, historical research is just beginning. Thus when it comes to the history of banking under the Nazis, at best historians can only advance plausible hypotheses. The same is true for developments after the Second World War. Any summary of bank–industry relations in Germany, therefore, is necessarily based on better information for some historical periods than for others, and on highly heterogeneous documentary sources, ranging from econometric studies to the memoirs of individual bankers and industrialists.

Nevertheless, the findings presented here unquestionably support the thesis that the German universal banking system that developed in the course of the nineteenth century influenced the long-term industrial development of the country insofar as it took strategic decisions about the allocation of financial capital. However, this influence must not be confused with a dominance of the banks over 'the rest of the economy'. For one thing, during the interwar period the universal banking system itself moved into crisis. For another, precisely in this period, but also after the end of the Second World War, banks did not play the role of financier for large segments of the Germany economy, such as small industry and the industrial 'Mittelstand' (whose importance in the German economy and society is discussed in detail in Chapter 9). Rather, this function was played by savings banks and credit cooperatives. The great universal banks, by contrast, were important much more in the financing and 'tending' of large-scale industry.

German economic fluctuations also reacted to the business policy of the large banks: in several cases – such as during the crisis of 1857 – the large German banks acted in such a way as to stabilize the entire economy. In this chapter, we have deliberately refrained from any attempt to model or quantify the influence of the banking system on industrial development in Germany over the last 200 years. For one thing, such an attempt would require methodological and theoretical reflections highly inappropriate for an introductory survey. For another, the functioning of the German economy, and with it the role of the banks in the economic process, has so enduringly changed since the nineteenth century that assumptions about the sort of influence banks exert on economic development are either too general to make concrete predictions or too specific to claim any long-term applicability.[115] In an age of 'globalization', the mechanisms linking finance with production are likely to be very different from those prevailing in the lifetime of David Ricardo, when our survey begins. It should not therefore be surprising that several separate phases can be distinguished in the relationship between banks and industry in Germany.

Let us once more briefly summarize the development of industry and finance in Germany since the early nineteenth century. Until 1848 the pioneer enterprises of German industrialization were largely compelled to do without a well-performing banking and lending system. This situation only began to change after the economic and political turbulence of 1848/9. Well-capitalized banks in the legal form of joint-stock companies began to be founded, creating institutions capable of providing the loans required by young industries. As financiers of large industrial projects and as direct investors in them, joint-stock banks played an important role in German economic development over the following decades. At the same time, through banks' ownership of industrial shares and bank seats on industrial firms' supervisory boards, there arose intensive inter-relationships between banks and industry. In this network of relationships the lending sector was not infrequently the dominant party, even though in this period the typical large German universal bank had not yet developed.

This situation was transformed during the Kaiserreich. In various branches of industry, firms were able to emancipate themselves from the banks because their business success meant they no longer required external finance. In addition, most firms were now able to do without the entrepreneurial initiative of the banks. Even now, however, banks remained indispensable for industry as providers of current account loans and in the realization of large new investments. Now that banks themselves had survived the 'childhood diseases' of their earlier years, they were better able to survive crisis periods. Banks and industry had become partners of equal rank in the economy. It is impossible to establish any unambiguous shift in power to the advantage of one or the other. The idea that German banks as a general rule held power over industry therefore lacks empirical foundation as far as the period of the Kaiserreich is concerned.

The First World War and the inflation brought the hitherto intensive relationships between banks and industry into completely new waters. Between 1914 and 1918, first armaments and later almost all sectors of industry found themselves earning high profits and able to finance investments out of their own funds. This meant that banks' industrial lending sharply decreased, and the earlier close inter-relationship between banks and their industrial clients loosened greatly. The wartime boom, high liquidity during the inflation, and the increasing tendency of firms to use internal funds for investment, reduced bank influence overall.

After the stabilization of the mark in 1924, little changed in this situation. Large German industrial firms continued to be able to maintain their financial independence, and only smaller concerns depended on the flow of capital from banks. In addition, the growing internationalization of capital markets gave rise to an increasingly severe competition among banks for customers and a growing tendency to offer loans under very favourable conditions. The German banks were too under-capitalized to maintain themselves against their foreign competitors. Even the great merger wave of 1929 was unable to alleviate this weakness, which culminated in the banking crisis of 1931.

Leaving aside the years of National Socialism during which the regulatory framework ensured that banks readily became vassals of the Nazi regime, the development of German bank–industry relations during the lifetime of the Federal Republic provides a further touchstone for the much disputed thesis about the power of banks in modern industrial societies. On this question, we are still largely lacking well-based empirical studies using material from archives and analysing business transactions. Is the German banking sector so highly concentrated that it is appropriate to characterize it as 'the power on the River Main' which dominates the commanding heights of the Germany economy, influencing important economic decisions in the banks' own interests? Do the four Great Banks – Deutsche Bank, the Bayerische Hypotheken-Vereinsbank, Dresdner Bank and Commerzbank – actually embody an influence 'towards which the rest of the economy stands in a position of dependency'?[116] From a historical point of view, any attempt to answer these questions would currently be highly speculative. But for the coming generation of researchers, these questions open up a field of study which is as interesting as it is important.

Chapter translated by Sheilagh Ogilvie

5.7 Notes

1 This view was early developed in Thorstein Veblen, *The Place of Science in Modern Civilization* (New Brunswick, 1990), pp. 279ff. For a good introduction to the fundamental differences between the various schools of economics on the theory of money, see R. Hickel, 'Die Lehre vom Gelde – neu betrachtet', in K. Diehl and P. Mombert, eds, *Vom Gelde* (Frankfurt am Main, 1979), pp. vii–lx.
2 Cf. H.-U. Wehler, *Deutsche Gesellschaftsgeschichte*, 2 vols (Munich, 1982), Vol. II, pp. 547ff.
3 On the debate concerning pioneers and latecomers in industrialization, see A. Gerschenkron, 'Economic Backwardness in Historical Perspective' in A. Gerschenkron, ed., *Economic Backwardness in Historical Perspective* (Cambridge, Mass., 1962), pp. 5–30; H. Berghoff and D. Ziegler, eds, *Pionier und Nachzügler? Vergleichende Studien zur Geschichte Großbritanniens und Deutschlands im Zeitalter der Industrialisierung. Festschrift für Sidney Pollard zum 70. Geburtstag* (Bochum, 1995); P. Deane and W. R. Cole, *The First Industrial Nation* (Cambridge, 1965); and S. Pollard, *Peaceful Conquest. The Industrialization of Europe* (Oxford, 1981).

4 Cf. K. Borchardt, 'Zur Frage des Kapitalmangels in der ersten Hälfte des 19. Jahrhunderts in Deutschland', in R. Braun *et al.*, eds, *Industrielle Revolution. Wirtschaftliche Aspekte* (Cologne, 1972), pp. 216–36; H. Winkel, 'Kapitalquellen und Kapitalverwertung am Vorabend der deutschen Industrialisierung', *Schmollers Jahrbuch*, 90 (1970), pp. 275–301.

5 On the debate about proto-industrialization, see for instance Peter Kriedte, Hans Medick, and Jürgen Schlumbohm, *Industrialization before Industrialization: Rural Industry in the Genesis of Capitalism* (Cambridge, 1981); W. Mager, 'Proto-industrialization and Proto-Industry: The Uses and Drawbacks of Two Concepts', *Continuity and Change*, 8 (1993), 181–216; S. C. Ogilvie and M. Cerman, eds, *European Proto-industrialization* (Cambridge, 1996).

6 M. Schumacher, *Auslandsreisen deutscher Unternehmer 1750–1851, unter besonderer Berücksichtigung von Rheinland und Westfalen* (Cologne, 1968); R. Fremdling, *Eisenbahnen und deutsches Wirtschaftswachstum 1840–1879. Ein Beitrag zur Entwicklungstheorie und zur Theorie der Infrastruktur* (Dortmund, 1985); D. Ziegler, *Eisenbahnen und Staat im Zeitalter der Industrialisierung. Die Eisenbahnpolitik der deutschen Staaten im Vergleich* (Stuttgart, 1996).

7 Borchardt, 'Kapitalmangel', pp. 220–5; R. Tilly, 'Germany 1815–1870', in R. Cameron *et al.*, eds, *Banking in the Early Stages of Industrialization* (New York, 1967), pp. 151–82; R. Tilly, 'Finanzielle Aspekte der preußischen Industrialisierung 1815–1870', in *Wirtschafts- und sozialgeschichtliche Probleme der frühen Industrialisierung* (Berlin, 1968), pp. 477–91; R. Tilly, 'Die Industrialisierung des Ruhrgebiets und das Problem der Kapital-mobilisierung', in R. Tilly, ed., *Kapital, Staat und sozialer Protest in der deutschen Industrialisierung* (Berlin, 1980), pp. 165–94.

8 H. Schnee, *Die Hochfinanz und der moderne Staat. Geschichte und System der Hoffaktoren an deutschen Fürstenhöfen im Zeitalter des Absolutismus* (Berlin, 1954); W. Feldenkirchen, 'Kölner Banken und die Entwicklung des Ruhrgebiets', *Zeitschrift für Unternehmensgeschichte*, 27 (1982), pp. 81–103; on the entrepreneurial perception of the market, cf. J. Kocka, *Unternehmer in der deutschen Industrialisierung* (Göttingen, 1975).

9 On the crisis of 1848, see H.-U. Wehler, *Deutsche Gesellschaftsgeschichte*, Vol. II: *Von der Reformära bis zur industriellen und politischen 'Deutschen Doppel-revolution' 1815–1845/49* (Munich, 1989), pp. 600–703; R. Hachtmann, *Berlin, 1848* (Munich, 1998).

10 On the role of railway construction in Germany, cf. the already cited works by Fremdling and Ziegler, as well as W. Steitz, *Die Geschichte der Köln-Mindener Eisenbahn* (Düsseldorf, 1974). On the development of German heavy industry in this period, see C. L. Holtfrerich, *Quantitative Geschichte des Ruhrkohlenbergbaus* (Dortmund, 1975); S. Jersch-Wenzel and J. Krengel, *Die Produktion der deutschen Hüttenindustrie 1850–1914* (Berlin, 1984), pp. 128, 409.

11 Cf., for instance, V. Wellhöner, *Großbanken und Großindustrie im Kaiserreich* (Göttingen, 1989), pp. 76ff.

12 In the course of the revolutionary events of 1848, the well-known Cologne private banking house Abraham Schaaffhausen had to discontinue payments. In order to prevent a domino effect among the industrial clientele of this insti-tution, the Prussian finance minister then in office, Hansemann, leapt at the recommendation of the Rhenish industrialist, Gustav Mevissen, to transform the collapsed private bank into a joint-stock company. On 28 August 1848, the Schaaffhausen'schen Bankverein was issued with a *Konzession* (permit to do business) by the Prussian Ministry of Trade. Cf. R. Tilly, *Financial Institutions in the Rhineland* (Madison, 1965); K. Obermann, 'Die Rolle der ersten

deutschen Aktienbanken in den Jahren 1848 bis 1856', *Jahrbuch für Wirtschaftsgeschichte*, (1960/2), pp. 47–76, here pp. 53ff; H. Böhme, 'Gründung und Anfänge des Schaaffhausen'schen Bankvereins, der Bank des Berliner Kassenvereins, der Direktion der Discontogesellschaft und der (Darmstädter) Bank für Handel und Industrie (Teil 1)', *Tradition*, 10 (1965), pp. 189–212, here pp. 193ff.

13 R. Cameron, 'Die Gründung der Darmstädter Bank', *Tradition*, 2 (1957), pp. 104–31, here pp. 112ff. On the operation of the Crédit Mobilier as a signal, see R. Cameron, *France and the Economic Development of Europe* (Princeton, 1961).

14 On the details, see J. Riesser, *Die deutschen Großbanken und ihre Konzentration* (Glashütten am Taunus, 1971), p. 647, Anlage 2; R. Tilly, 'German Banking 1850–1914. Development Assistance for the Strong', *Journal of European Economic History*, 15 (1986), pp. 113–52, here pp. 163ff.; M. Gehr, *Das Verhältnis der Banken zur Industrie in Deutschland 1850–1931* (Tübingen, 1960), p. 6.

15 See on this Gehr, *Verhältnis*, p. 15; Tilly, 'German Banking', p. 163; R. Tilly, 'Banken und Industrialisierung in Deutschland. Ein Überblick', in R. Tilly, ed., *Kapital, Staat und sozialer Protest in der deutschen Industrialisierung* (Göttingen, 1980), pp. 29–52.

16 Cf. Gehr, *Verhältnis*, p. 18.

17 Cf. Riesser, *Deutsche Großbanken*, pp. 648–50, Beilage III.

18 Cf. Gehr, *Verhältnis*, p. 22.

19 *Ibid.*, p. 26.

20 Cf. W. Zorn, 'Beiträge zur Geschichte der deutschen Banken seit 1950', *Tradition*, 1 (1956), pp. 69–74, here p. 71.

21 Cf. R. Neumann, *Der deutsche Privatbankier* (Wiesbaden, 1965), pp. 23–5.

22 Tilly, 'Germany 1815–1870', pp. 180f.

23 Gehr, *Verhältnis*, p. 10.

24 The supervisory board is a body whose members are responsible for monitoring the daily business of a company and the business strategies of its managers.

25 Gehr, *Verhältnis*, pp. 11ff.

26 *Ibid.*; as well as Obermann, 'Rolle der ersten deutschen Aktienbanken', pp. 54–56; G. Teichmann, 'Das Bankhaus Oppenheim und die industrielle Entwicklung im Aachener Revier von 1836–1855', in M. Köhler and K. Ulrich, eds, *Banken, Konjunktur und Politik. Beiträge Zur Geschichte deutscher Banken im 19. und 20. Jahrhundert* (Essen, 1995), pp. 9–23; Tilly, *Financial Institutions*, pp. 145ff.

27 See, among other studies, R. Tilly, *Vom Zollverein zum Industriestaat* (Munich, 1991), pp. 29f.; H. Kiesewetter, *Industrielle Revolution in Deutschland* (Frankfurt am Main, 1989), pp. 248–60; Wehler, *Gesellschaftsgeschichte*, Vol. 2, pp. 95–8.

28 Riesser, *Großbanken*, p. 43.

29 W. Feldenkirchen, 'Kölner Banken und die Entwicklung des Ruhrgebiets', *Zeitschrift für Unternehmensgeschichte*, 27 (1982), pp. 81–103; Ziegler, *Eisenbahnen und Staat*, pp. 110–75.

30 A survey of the debate about the power of the banks is provided by H. Wixforth and D. Ziegler, 'Bankenmacht. Universal Banking and German Industry in Historical Perspective', in Y. Cassis, G. D. Feldman and U. Olsson, eds, *The Evolution of Financial Institutions and Markets in Twentieth Century Europe* (Aldershot, 1995), pp. 249–72; H. Wixforth, 'Die Macht der Banken. Debatten, Untersuchungskonzepte, Ergebnisse', in C.-L. Holtfrerich, ed., *Arbeitskreis für Bankengeschichte, Working Papers*, 2 (1997/2) (Frankfurt am Main, 1997).

31 Cf., for instance, W. Spohn, *Weltmarktkonkurrenz und Industrialisierung Deutschlands 1870–1914* (Berlin, 1977).

32 F. W. Henning, *Die Industrialisierung in Deutschland* (Paderborn, 1973); R. Wagenführ, *Die Industriewirtschaft. Entwicklungstendenzen der deutschen und internationalen Industrieproduktion 1860–1932* (Berlin, 1933), p. 57.

33 Cf. Henning, *Industrialisierung*, p. 203; Riesser, *Großbanken*, pp. 108f. From 1870 to 1914 the population in Germany grew from 40 to 67 million. (See W. Köllmann, *Bevölkerung und Raum in Neuerer und Neuester Zeit* (Würzburg, 1965), p. 86.)

34 Gehr, *Verhältnis*, pp. 26f.

35 Riesser, *Großbanken*, pp. 515f.; P. Penzkofer, 'Entstehung und Entwicklung der privaten Geschäftsbanken Ende des 19. und im 20. Jahrhundert', in A. Grosser *et al.*, eds, *Wirtschaft, Gesellschaft, Geschichte* (Stuttgart, 1968), pp. 47–103, here pp. 63ff.; H. Wixforth, 'Bank für Sachsen oder Bank für das Reich? Zur Geschichte der Dresdner Bank 1872 bis 1914', in S. Lässig and K.-H. Pohl, eds, *Sachsen im Kaiserreich. Wirtschaft, Gesellschaft, Politik in der Reichsgründungszeit* (Cologne, 1997), pp. 309–42.

36 Riesser, *Großbanken*, p. 376, pp. 648ff.: Beilage 3; Cf. also M. Pohl, *Konzentration im deutschen Bankwesen* (Frankfurt am Main, 1982).

37 Gehr, *Verhältnis*, p. 44; Penzkofer, 'Entstehung', p. 44; Wixforth, 'Bank für Sachsen', pp. 326–8.

38 Riesser, *Großbanken*, pp. 526f.

39 Gehr, *Verhältnis*, pp. 44f.

40 These numbers are based on Riesser, *Großbanken*, p. 745: Beilage 8.

41 *Ibid.*, p. 750: Beilage 8.

42 *Ibid.*, pp. 376, 383.

43 *Ibid.*, p. 177; Gehr, *Verhältnis*, p. 32.

44 O. Jeidels, *Das Verhältnis der deutschen Großbanken zur Industrie mit besonderer Berücksichtigung der Schwerindustrie* (Leipzig, 1905), pp. 65f.; R. Tilly, 'Zur Entwicklung der deutschen Universalbanken. Wachstumsmotor oder Machtkartell?', in S. Pollard and D. Ziegler, eds, *Markt, Staat, Planung* (St Katharinen, 1992), pp. 128–56, here pp. 130ff.; Tilly, 'Development Assistance', pp. 127ff.

45 As a reaction to the 'foundation crash', the Imperial Government set up a Commission of Inquiry which was supposed to revise the stock exchange legislation. In 1896, the recommendations of this Commission were transformed into reality by the new Stock Exchange Law. The most important new regulations were the following: the minimum value of a share was fixed at 1000 marks; shares in a new enterprise could only be introduced onto the stock market one year after its foundation; providing a prospectus was obligatory; and enterprises with less than 1 million marks of share capital were excluded from being listed on the stock exchange. See on this Penzkofer, 'Entstehung und Entwicklung', pp. 66ff.; C. Wetzel, *Die Auswirkungen des Reichsbörsengesetzes von 1896 auf die Effektenbörsen im Deutschen Reich, insbesondere auf die Berliner Fondsbörse* (Münster, 1996); J. C. Meier, *Die Entstehung des Börsengesetzes von 1896* (St Katharinen, 1992).

46 Cf. Riesser, *Großbanken*, pp. 536f.; Jeidels, *Verhältnis*, pp. 56f.

47 Penzkofer, 'Entwicklung und Entstehung', p. 68. Cf. on the history of the Rothschild banking house, E. C. Conte Corti, *Der Aufstieg des Hauses Rothschild*, Vol. I: *1770–1830*, Vol. II: *1830–1871* (Leipzig, 1927/28).

48 Riesser, *Großbanken*, pp. 620f; H. Wixforth and D. Ziegler, 'The Niche in the Universal Banking System: The Role and Significance of Private Bankers within German Industry, 1900 to 1933', *Financial History Review*, 1 (1994), pp. 99–120.

49 Riesser, *Großbanken*, p. 146, pp. 572ff; Gehr, *Verhältnis*, p. 48; and Wengenroth, *Unternehmensstrategien und technischer Fortschritt. Die deutsche*

und die britische Stahlindustrie 1865–1895 (Göttingen, 1986); *Wellhöner, Großbanken und Großindustrie,* pp. 181ff.

50 Although the relationship between banks and industry in the Kaiserreich has been discussed in several studies, as a rule these are not based on the analysis of archival material. An exception is the already cited study by Wellhöner.

51 Riesser, *Großbanken,* p. 591; Cf. also Jeidels, *Verhältnis,* pp. 204ff.; Wellhöner, *Großbanken und Großindustrie,* pp. 84ff. and 242f.

52 Cf. Wellhöner, *Großbanken und Großindustrie,* pp. 84ff.

53 On the participation of Deutschen Bank in Mannesmann cf. *Ibid.,* pp. 126ff., 139ff.

54 Gehr, *Verhältnis,* p. 64. The same conclusion (with some differences) is reached by Wellhöner, *Großbanken und Großindustrie,* pp. 244f.

55 On the relationship between Deutsche Bank and Siemens-Konzern as well as that of the Berliner Handelsgesellschaft with AEG, see Wellhöner, *Großbanken und Großindustrie,* pp. 232ff.; H. Fürstenberg, *Carl Fürstenberg-Die Lebensgeschichte eines deutschen Bankiers* (Wiesbaden, 1961); Gehr, *Verhältnis,* p. 56.

56 Cf. Gehr, *Verhältnis,* pp. 61ff.; Wellhöner, *Großbanken und Großindustrie,* pp. 233ff. See also J. Kocka, *Unternehmensverwaltung und Angestelltenschaft am Beispiel Siemens 1847 bis 1914* (Stuttgart, 1969); H. Homburg, *Rationalisierung und Industriearbeit. Das Beispiel des Siemens-Konzerns Berlin 1900 bis 1939* (Berlin, 1991), pp. 27ff.

57 Cf. Riesser, *Großbanken,* p. 587; G. Plumpe, *Die IG Farbenindustrie AG. Wirtschaft, Technik und Politik 1904–1945* (Berlin, 1990).

58 Cf. Gehr, *Verhältnis,* pp. 81f.; F. Eulenburg, 'Die Aufsichtsräte der deutschen Aktiengesellschaften', *Jahrbücher für Nationalökonomie und Statistik,* 32 (1906), pp. 92–109.

59 One need only recall the lively debate among the German public about the behaviour of Deutsche Bank and Dresdner Bank during the intended takeover of Thyssen-Konzern by Krupp-Hösch AG in March 1997.

60 On the significance and development of the universal bank system in central and eastern Europe, see especially A. Teichova, 'Commercial (Universal) Banking in Central Europe – from Cisleithania to the Successor States', in M. G. Fase, G. D. Feldman, and M. Pohl, eds, *How to Write the History of a Bank* (Aldershot, 1995), pp. 125–35; D. Stiefel, 'Austrian Banks at the Centre of Power and Influence. System and Problems of Austrian Finance Capital from the 1890s to the International Economic Crisis of the 1930s', *German Yearbook on Business History 1985* (Cologne, 1986), pp. 79–90, here pp. 85f.

61 See especially F. Kleinwächter, *Kartelle* (Innsbruck, 1883); Cf. also A. Teichova, 'Rivals and Partners. Reflections on Banking and Industry in Europe, 1880–1938', in P. L. Cottrell, H. Lindgren, *et al.,* eds, *European Banking and Industry between the Wars* (Leicester, 1992), pp. 19–25; A. Mosser *et al.,* 'Das Universalbanksystem in Mitteleuropa und seine Erforschung', in A. Teichova, ed., *Banken, Währung und Politik in Mitteleuropa zwischen den Weltkriegen* (Vienna, 1997), pp. 5–22.

62 Cf. e.g. O. Graf Lambsdorff, 'Dem Machtmißbrauch vorbeugen', *Süddeutsche Zeitung* (2.6.1996), W. Eckstein, 'The Role of Banks in Corporate Concentration in West Germany', *Zeitschrift für die gesamte Staatswissenschaft* (1980), pp. 136–40.

63 R. Hilferding, *Das Finanzkapital* (Frankfurt am Main, 1968; 1st edn 1910). On Hilferding as an individual and his role in the Austrian Marxist debate about capitalist economic development, see H.-G. Haupt, 'Rudolf Hilferding', in H.-U. Wehler, ed., *Deutsche Historiker* VIII (Göttingen, 1982), pp. 56–77; H.-U. Wehler, 'Rudolf Hilferding. Theoretiker des Finanzkapitals', in P. Alter *et al.,* eds, *Geschichte und Politisches Handeln* (Stuttgart, 1985), pp. 281–95.

64 Hilferding, *Finanzkapital*, p. 96.

65 W. I. Lenin, *Der Imperialismus als höchstes Stadium des Kapitalismus* (Berlin, 1973 [1916], pp. 33f.; H. Radandt, 'Sprach Lenin von der führenden Rolle des Bankkapitals gegenüber dem Industriekapital?', *Jahrbuch für Wirtschaftsgeschichte*, (1974), Part 1, pp. 189–95.

66 K. Gossweiler, *Großbanken – Industriemonopole – Staat, 1914–1932* (Berlin, 1971), p. 34.

67 See, e.g., R. Tilly, 'Macht der Banken. Die Deutsche Wirtschaftsgeschichte und die Neue Institutionen-Ökonomie', in D. Bögenhold, ed., *Soziale Welt und Soziologische Praxis. Festschrift für Heinz Hartmann* (Göttingen, 1995), pp. 17–27.

68 See, e.g., J. Tanner, 'Die Banken und der Popanz der Macht', *Zeitschrift für Unternehmensgeschichte*, 43 (1998), pp. 19–34.

69 On this catalogue of criteria, see Wellhöner, *Großbanken und Großindustrie*, pp. 32ff.

70 Such a case occurred, for instance, in 1904, when the Duisburg mining concern 'Phoenix' was pressed by the banks to join the Stahlwerksverband (Steelworks Association), but defended itself successfully against this pressure. (Cf. Wellhöner, *Großbanken und Großindustrie*, pp. 84ff.)

71 Cf. F. Grüger, 'Die Wirkung des Krieges und der Kriegsfolgen auf das deutsche Bankwesen mit einem Rückblick auf die Vorkriegszeit', in Bankenquête, ed., *Untersuchung des Bankwesens 1933*, Part I: *Vorbereitendes Material*, Vol. I (Berlin, 1933), pp. 23–56, here p. 49; W. Prion, *Die deutschen Kreditbanken im Kriege und nachher* (Stuttgart, 1917), pp. 41, 80f.; A. Fendler, *Die Kapitalkonzentration der Berliner Großbanken 1914–1923* (Berlin, 1926), p. 18.

72 See Gehr, *Verhältnis*, p. 83; G. Hardach, 'Banking and Industry in Germany in the Interwar Period, 1919–1939', *Journal of European Economic History*, 13 (1984), pp. 203–34, here p. 206.

73 Figures according to Deutsche Bundesbank, ed., *Deutsches Geld- und Bankwesen in Zahlen* (Frankfurt am Main, 1976), p. 57.

74 Grüger, 'Wirkung des Krieges', p. 36; M. Pohl, 'Die Situation der Banken in der Inflationszeit', in O. Büsch and G. D. Feldman, eds, *Historische Prozesse des deutschen Inflation 1914–1924* (Berlin, 1978), pp. 78–97, here pp. 89ff.; 'Umschau: Die Umstellung der Berliner Großbanken', *Die Bank* (1925), pp. 55–9, here p. 57.

75 Cf. Grüger, 'Wirkung des Krieges', p. 48; C.-L. Holtfrerich, 'Die Auswirkung der Inflation auf die Struktur des deutschen Kreditgewerbes', in G. D. Feldman, ed., *Die Nachwirkungen der Inflation auf die deutsche Geschichte 1924–1933* (Munich, 1985), pp. 187–210, here pp. 206ff.; T. Balderston, 'German Banking between the Wars: The Crisis of the Credit Banks', *Business History Review*, 65 (1991), pp. 554–605, here p. 561. On the general history of the German inflation, see G. D. Feldman, *The Great Disorder. Politics, Economics and Society in the German Inflation, 1914–1924* (Oxford, 1993).

76 Cf. Holtfrerich, 'Auswirkungen', p. 203. On the increasing signficance of the financial centre of Amsterdam as a 'safe' for nostro assets of German banks, see J. Houwink ten Cate, 'Amsterdam als Finanzplatz Deutschlands 1919–1932', in G. D. Feldman *et al.*, eds, *Konsequenzen der Inflation* (Berlin, 1989), pp. 152–62.

77 On this, the bank expert Alfred Landsburg wrote: 'One indeed continually hesitated about letting fall by the wayside the enormously high profits achieved since 1921 in the realization of one's own holdings of stocks. Naturally the published figures were not wholly consistent with the reality.' (A. Landsburg, 'Die Berliner Großbanken im Jahre 1921', *Die Bank* (1921), pp. 540–56, here p. 552.)

78 Cf. Frisch, 'Die Dresdner Bank von Versailles bis Hitler', Archiv der Dresdner Bank (Frankfurt am Main, 1959) (unpublished memorandum), p. 8.

79 Pohl, 'Situation', p. 85; Hardach, 'Banking in Germany', p. 213. Cf. also the discussion by Stephen Schucker of the contribution by Manfred Pohl, in O. Büsch and G. D. Feldman, eds, *Historische Prozesse der Deutschen Inflation 1914 bis 1924* (Berlin, 1978), pp. 117f., where the positive effects of the postwar inflation for the development of banking are likewise emphasized.

80 Figures on the numbers of new foundations of lending institutions differ somewhat. Authors report, variously, 32 (1921), 55 (1922), and 99 (1923) new foundations of banks in the form of AG (joint-stock company) or KGaA (partnership partially limited by shares). Other sources refer to even higher figures, cf. Pohl, *Konzentration*, p. 305, Pohl, 'Situation', p. 87. See also P. Barret Whale, *Joint Stock Banking in Germany* (London, 1930), p. 234; W. Strauß, *Die Konzentrationsbewegung im Deutschen Bankwesen* (Berlin, 1928), p. 19; Hardach, 'Banking in Germany', p. 207. This development was not limited to Germany, but also occurred in other European states with universal banking systems; on this, see the contributions in C. Feinstein, ed., *Banking, Currency and Finance in Europe between the Wars* (Oxford, 1995).

81 Pohl, *Konzentration*, pp. 307, 328; Pohl, 'Situation', p. 85; Hardach, 'Banking in Germany', pp. 206 ff.; G. D. Feldman, 'Banks and Banking in Germany after the First World War: Strategies of Defense', in Y. Cassis, ed., *Finance and Financiers in European History* (Paris, 1992), pp. 150–9.

82 Gehr, *Verhältnis*, pp. 86, 87; H. James, 'The Causes of the German Banking Crisis of 1931', *Economic History Review*, 37 (1989), pp. 209–24, here pp. 218f.

83 Hardach, 'Banking in Germany', pp. 217f.; James, 'Banking Crisis', p. 220.

84 W. Hagemann, *Das Verhältnis der deutschen Großbanken zur Industrie* (Berlin, 1930), pp. 185ff.

85 Gehr, *Verhältnis*, p. 142; M. Wittkowski, *Großbanken und Industrie in Deutschland 1924 bis 1931* (Tampere, 1937), p. 69f.; H. Wixforth, *Banken und Schwerindustrie in der Weimarer Republik* (Cologne, 1995), pp. 514ff.; K. Lehmann, *Wandlungen der Industriefinanzierung durch Kreditanleihen in ·Deutschland* (1923/24–1938/39) (Stuttgart, 1996), pp. 53–63.

86 See on this Wixforth, *Banken und Schwerindustrie*, pp. 510f.

87 On the German banking crisis, see especially K.-E. Born, *Die deutsche Bankenkrise 1931* (Munich, 1967); R. E. Lücke, *13. Juli 1931: Das Geheimnis der deutschen Bankenkrise* (Frankfurt am Main, 1981).

88 Born, *Bankenkrise*, pp. 180–3.

89 C. Kopper, *Zwischen Marktwirtschaft und Dirigismus. Bankpolitik im Nationalsozialismus* (Bonn, 1995); C. Kopper, 'Privates Bankwesen im Nationalsozialismus. Das Hamburger Bankhaus M. M. Warburg & Co'., in W. Plumpe und C. Kleinschmidt, eds, *Unternehmen zwischen Markt und Macht* (Essen, 1992), pp. 61–73, here pp. 61–3; A. Fischer, *Hjalmar Schacht und Deutschlands 'Judenfrage'* (Cologne, 1995).

90 Kopper, *Marktwirtschaft und Dirigismus*, pp. 355. On the banking inquiry of 1933 see *Untersuchungen des Bankwesens von 1933*, Part I, Vols I and II (Berlin, 1933). Here we cannot go in detail into the individual provisions of the Lending Law.

91 Frisch, 'Die Dresdner Bank von Versailles bis Hitler', pp. 106f. In the official history of Dresdner Bank this fact is completely concealed. (H. Meyen, *120 Jahre Dresdner Bank* (Frankfurt am Main, 1992).)

92 See on this H. James, 'Die Deutsche Bank und die Diktatur 1933 bis 1945', in Lothar Gall *et al.*, eds, *Die Deutsche Bank 1870 bis 1945* (Munich, 1995), pp. 315–407.

93 Cf. especially Kopper, *Marktwirtschaft und Dirigismus*, p. 357.

94 Cf. G. Ashauer, 'Entwicklung der Sparkassenorganisation ab 1924', in Institut für bankhistorische Forschung, ed., *Deutsche Bankengeschichte*, Vol. 3 (Frankfurt am Main, 1983), pp. 279–315.

95 See on this H. Wixforth and D. Ziegler, 'The "Niche" in the Universal Banking System', *Financial History Review*, 1 (1994), pp. 99–119; H. Wixforth and D. Ziegler, 'Deutsche Privatbanken und Privatbankiers im 20. Jahrhundert', *Geschichte und Gesellschaft*, 23 (1997), pp. 205–35; C. Kopper, 'Die Arisierung jüdischer Privatbanken im Nationalsozialismus', *SoWi* (1991), pp. 111–16.

96 Cf. Kopper, *Marktwirtschaft und Dirigismus*, p. 360; James, *Die Deutsche Bank und die Diktatur*, pp. 370ff.; H. Matis und F. Weber, 'Economic "Anschluß" and German "Großmachtpolitik". The Takeover of the Austrian Kreditanstalt in 1938', in P. L. Cottrell, H. Lindgren, and A. Teichova, eds, *European Industry and Banking between the Wars* (Leicester, 1992), pp. 109–28.

97 See H. Wixforth, *Auftakt zur Ostexpansion. Die Dresdner Bank und die Umgestaltung des Bankwesens im Sudetenland 1938/39* (Dresden, 2001).

98 D. Jancik and T. Kalina, 'Banken und öffentliche Meinung in der Tschechoslowakei zwischen den beiden Weltkriegen', in A. Teichova, ed., *Banken, Währung und Politik in Mitteleuropa zwischen den Weltkriegen* (Vienna, 1997), pp. 139–57; Kopper, *Zwischen Marktwirtschaft und Dirigismus*, p. 361.

99 This assessment is consistent with the results of recent studies investigating the role of the lending sector in the Nazi economic system, based on a wide range of documentary sources. Cf. Kopper, *Marktwirtschaft und Dirigismus*, pp. 360ff.; James, 'Die Deutsche Bank und die Diktatur', pp. 405ff.

100 The most important exceptions include: M. Gerhards, *Die Industriebeziehungen der westdeutschen Banken* (Frankfurt am Main, 1982); (rather polemical) H. Pfeiffer, *Die Macht der Banken* (Frankfurt am Main, 1993); E. Czichon, *Die Bank und die Macht* (Cologne, 1995). Based on a broader range of documentary sources: C.-L. Holtfrerich, 'Die Deutsche Bank vom Zweiten Weltkrieg über die Besatzungsherrschaft zur Rekonstruktion 1945–1957', in L. Gall *et al.*, eds, *Die Deutsche Bank 1870–1995* (Munich, 1995), pp. 409–578.

101 On the entanglements of the Great Banks with National Socialism, see especially H. M. Enzensberger, ed., *OMGUS-Ermittlungen gegen die deutsche Bank 1946/47* (Nördlingen, 1985); H. M. Enzensberger, ed., *OMGUS-Ermittlungen gegen die Dresdner Bank* (Nördlingen 1987).

102 The Allied policy toward the German Great Banks is discussed in detail by T. Horstmann, *Die Alliierten und die deutschen Großbanken. Bankpolitik nach dem Zweiten Weltkrieg in Westdeutschland* (Bonn, 1991).

103 On the individual stages of this development, see Holtfrerich, 'Die Deutsche Bank', pp. 410–34.

104 M. Pohl, *Entstehung und Entwicklung des Universalbanksystems. Konzentration und Krise als wichtige Faktoren* (Frankfurt am Main, 1986), pp. 101–23; M. Dickhaus, *Die Bundesbank im westeuropäischen Wiederaufbau. Die internationale Währungspolitik der Bundesrepublik Deutschland 1948–1958* (Munich, 1996); M. Dickhaus, 'The West German Central Bank and the Construction of an International Monetary System during the 1950s', *Financial History Review*, 5 (1998), pp. 159–78.

105 Pohl, *Universalbanksystem*, pp. 140–4; H. E. Büschgen, 'Die Deutsche Bank von 1957 bis zur Gegenwart. Aufstieg zum internationalen Finanzdienstleistungskonzern', in L. Gall *et al.*, eds, *Die Deutsche Bank 1870–1995* (Munich, 1995), pp. 672–810.

106 On the development of macroeconomic aggregates in West Germany, see W. Glastetter *et al.*, *Die wirtschaftliche Entwicklung der Bundesrepublik*

Deutschland 1950 bis 1980. Befunde, Aspekte, Hintergründe (Frankfurt am Main, 1983). Detailed international comparisons are provided by A. Maddison, *The World Economy in the 20th Century* (Paris, 1989).

107 See, for instance, V. Wellhöner, *'Wirtschaftswunder'* – *Weltmarkt* – *Westdeutscher Fordismus. Der Fall Volkswagen* (Münster, 1996); B. Lutz, *Der kurze Traum immerwährender Prosperität* (Frankfurt am Main, 1989); H. Kaelble, ed., *Der Boom 1948–1973* (Opladen, 1992).

108 Cf. R. Tilly, 'Geschäftsbanken und Wirtschaft in Westdeutschland seit dem Zweiten Weltkrieg', in E. Schremmer, ed., *Geld und Währung vom 16. Jahrhundert bis zur Gegenwart* (Stuttgart, 1993), pp. 315–43, esp. p. 325. Cf. also H. Frank, 'Die Entwicklung der Marktanteile der Bankengruppen in den letzten 25 Jahren', *Die Sparkasse* 105 (1988), pp. 409–17; Deutsche Bundesbank, *Monatsberichte der Deutschen Bundesbank vom April 1989: Längerfristige Entwicklung des Bankensektors und Marktstellung der Kreditinstitutsgruppen* (1989), p. 34.

109 J. Edwards and K. Fischer, *Banks, Finance and Investment in Germany* (Cambridge, 1994).

110 See Edwards and Fischer, *Banks*, pp. 69–70.

111 See, for example, one of the prominent politicians in the CDU Party, Kurt Biedenkopf, at the Twelfth General Meeting of German Bankers (Deutscher Bankiertag) in Cologne in 1974, cited in I. Moesch and D. Simmert, *Banken – Strukturen, Macht, Reformen* (Cologne, 1976). See also 'SPD will die Machtkonzentration der Großbanken beschränken', *Frankfurter Rundschau* (27 Jan. 1995).

112 'Der Stahl-Coup oder Wo ist der Killer', *Frankfurter Rundschau* (19 Mar. 1997).

113 See, e.g., M. Gerhards, *Die Industriebeziehungen westdeutscher Banken* (Frankfurt am Main, 1982); M. Gerhards, 'Die westdeutschen Banken', *WSI-Mitteilungen*, 28 (1975), pp. 301–98; J. Esser, 'Banken und Industrie in der Bundesrepublik Deutschland', in K. Rohe *et al.*, eds, *Deutschland, Großbritannien, Europa. Politische Tradition, Partnerschaft und Rivalität* (Bochum, 1992), pp. 105–24.

114 Cf. on this especially Pfeiffer, *Die Macht der Banken*; H. Pfeiffer, *Die Macht am Main. Einfluß und Politik der deutschen Großbanken* (Frankfurt am Main, 1989); F.-U. Pappi, P. Kappelhoff, and C. Melbeck, 'Die Struktur der Unternehmensverflechtung in der Bundesrepublik', *Kölner Zeitschrift für Soziologie und Sozialpsychologie*, 39 (1987), pp. 693–717, esp. p. 715; R. Ziegler, 'Das Netz der Personen- und Kapitalverflechtungen deutscher und österreichischer Wirtschaftsunternehmen', *Kölner Zeitschrift für Soziologie und Sozialpsychologie*, 36 (1984), pp. 585–614, esp. pp. 603ff.

115 Cf. for instance H. P. Minsky, *Stabilizing an Unstable Economy* (New Haven, 1986).

116 K. Biedenkopf at the Twelfth German Bankers' Convention in Cologne in 1974.

|6|

Urbanization and social transformation, 1800–1914[1]

JOHN BREUILLY
Birmingham University

6.1 Introduction

Between 1800 and 1914, Germany made the transition from rural to urban society.[2] Urban life itself was transformed to such a degree that a town in 1800 had little in common with its namesake in 1914 apart from the name. This chapter will sketch out the course of this transformation. I distinguish three phases of urban growth. Then I consider 'typical' features for each of those phases and for the changes from one phase to the next.[3] I conclude that Germany had become an urban society by 1914.

6.2 Demography

One can identify three types of urban growth: absolute (i.e. a rise in the total urban population, henceforth *urban growth*); relative (i.e. a rise in the proportion of the urban population to the total population, henceforth *urbanization*); and average urban population (i.e. a rise in the average size of urban settlements, henceforth *city growth*). In Germany, a first phase (*c*.1800–40) was marked by urban growth, as can be seen in Figure 6.1.[4] Urban growth continued into a second phase (*c*.1840–75), accompanied by urbanization, as Figure 6.1 also shows.[5] In a third phase (*c*.1875–1914), as shown in Figure 6.2 and in Table 6.1,[6] urban growth and urbanization concentrated upon bigger urban centres and especially the big city (*Großstadt*).[7]

German population growth for some time before 1800 was rapid by contemporary standards (as discussed in Chapter 2). It was both stimulated and sustained by increases in agricultural production and productivity (as considered in Chapter 3), largely due to changes in land tenure patterns and

Table 6.1 Big-city growth in Germany, 1816/19–1910

Year	Number of cities with over 100,000 inhabitants	Average size of these cities (thousands)
1816/19	2	163
*c.*1850	4	201
1870/1	8	252
1910	48	292

Note: The table excludes Austrian cities.
Source: Derived from Jürgen Reulecke, *Geschichte der Urbanisierung in Deutschland* (Frankfurt am Main, 1985), pp. 203–4.

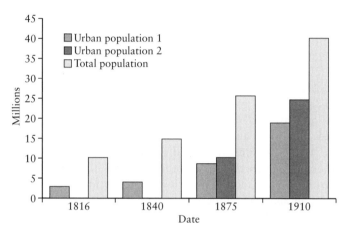

Fig. 6.1 Urban growth and urbanization in Prussia, 1816–1910
Source: Derived from data in Matzerath, *Urbanisierung in Preußen.*

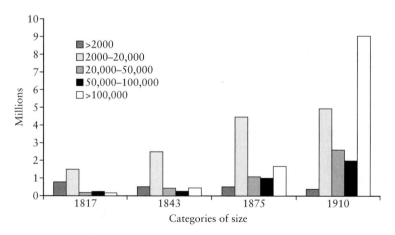

Fig. 6.2 City growth in Prussia, 1817–1910
Source: Derived from data in Matzerath, *Urbanisierung in Preußen.*

non-technological improvements which retained labour in the countryside even as the number of land-poor and landless people increased most rapidly. Much manufacturing growth was decentralized and rural, taking advantage of an increased seasonality of agricultural employment. Without the generation of new urban employment, urban growth could not outstrip general population growth. This began around mid-century which is why rural population grew as rapidly as urban population in this first phase.

Nevertheless, population growth meant urban growth. The political simplification of Germany at the beginning of the nineteenth century saw some capital cities take on additional functions. Extensive commercialization expanded market towns and trading and transport centres. Rural under-employment pushed people into towns seeking work and charity.[8] In this first phase, urban life was conditioned by the dominance of agriculture. Marriage rates were more sensitive to fluctuations in the price of food than of manufactured goods or housing.[9] Urban unemployment sharply increased following agricultural crises which depressed demand for non-food products.[10] Urban migration was cyclical and short-distance; many immigrants maintained contacts with their villages and saw urban work as temporary or seasonal.[11] Urban life was unpleasant for the poor; deaths outweighed births: urban growth depended upon immigration.[12] Where agriculture and rural industry could not support everyone, some people emigrated abroad rather than migrate to towns. Without relative expansion of urban employment, short-term growth rates of urban and rural populations moved in opposite directions, tending to cancel one another out. Population growth was most rapid in the agricultural regions of north-eastern Germany (migration levels, especially out-migration, were highest in such areas) but governmental preoccupation with over-population was greater in the more urban and densely populated territories of southern and western Germany.

From around the mid-nineteenth century parts of Germany witnessed the first phase of industrialization (as discussed in Chapters 1 and 4). This was linked to railway building which quickly attracted much capital investment, favoured economic concentration, and promoted a regional division of labour. That in turn was related to the decline of rural industry and the clearer delineation of agricultural-rural and industrial-urban areas (as discussed in Chapter 1).

The related rise of coal, iron and steel production stimulated rapid growth in areas such as the Ruhr valley. Industrialization of textile and metal-working industries based on coal-fired, steam-powered machines had similar effects. Urban growth stimulated a building boom. Although most migration was still short-distance and temporary (railway and other kinds of building work were especially suitable for such workers), and overseas emigration continued, more country-people sought work in industrializing areas and remained in those areas.[13] Small and medium-sized towns (5000 to 50,000 inhabitants) with manufacturing traditions initially grew most quickly and attracted most in-migrants. This was also the first phase of growth of the new industrial settlements, especially in coalfield areas such as the Ruhr, the Saarland and Upper Silesia. A third type of growth took place in capitals and regional centres such as Berlin, Hamburg, Cologne and Munich. There were significant social differences between these three types of concentrated population growth.

In-migrants were disproportionately in the prime working ages (17–40), male, and single, more so in industrial towns, especially the new settlements and those where industries such as mining and iron and steel making predominated. Population mobility in this second phase was much higher than net migration figures suggest. Partly this continued an older pattern of temporary migration with out-migration almost equalling in-migration, especially amongst single adults. One-third to one-half of the population moved in and out of the most rapidly expanding towns in a single year.[14] Such mobility was highest amongst lower-class immigrants although skilled workers moved for different reasons.[15]

Continued expansion of urban employment towards the end of this second phase meant that for a growing proportion of immigrants town life was coming to be regarded as a permanent state of affairs. Family migration as well as marriage rates amongst immigrants increased and with it the proportion of families within the urban population.[16] Lower-class families still moved a good deal but probably more within a town rather than from one town to another.[17] Many immigrants, at least from areas of rural industry (as opposed to peasant farming), retained traditions of early marriage and large families for a generation or two, even if these were inappropriate under urban conditions.[18] This increased urban birth rates. Death rates were depressed by the below-average proportion of old people, even if death rates for each age group remained higher than in the country-side. Consequently, more urban growth began to be generated within towns rather from in-migration, although the surplus of births over deaths continued to be higher in rural areas. Continued migration of people from countryside to town produced a relative rise in the urban population. However, in some rapidly industrializing western regions, above all the Prussian provinces of Westphalia and the Rhineland, much industrial growth was located in the countryside (mines in rural coal fields, foundries near suitable energy sources). This presents us with problems in distinguishing urban from rural settlements.[19]

After 1875 urban-industrial growth continued even during the period of the 'Great Depression' of the 1870s and 1880s. Improved long-distance transport increased food imports which released more people from agriculture. Prosperity reduced overseas emigration. After one final phase of large-scale overseas emigration in the early 1880s the pattern was one of decline. After 1900 Germany became a country of net immigration. More in-country migration was long-distance (especially from eastern Germany to western Germany and Berlin).[20] Urban birth rates began to decline from the

1870s onward, to be followed by rural birth rates some 30 years later.[21] However, rising real wages and better public healthcare reduced mortality rates, maintaining population growth. The surplus rural population continued to move into towns. It is possible, however, that by now urban centres were largely generating their own population growth and that the actual rates of migration had already begun to level out, if not decline, before the end of the century, although given the greatly increased size of the population, especially in cities, this involved many more people than earlier.[22]

The pattern of urban growth changed. Industrial employment diversified beyond railways, coal, metal, textile and building industries. New chemical- and electrical-based industries were more flexible in their choice of location, favouring proximity to the skilled labour, services and demand provided by large urban populations. Increases in disposable income generated demand for more and higher-quality consumer goods and services such as education and healthcare, all disproportionately concentrated in larger and more diversified population centres. Businesses employed more clerical workers in accounts, servicing, marketing, insurance, and so on (as discussed in Chapter 9). This caused the tertiary sector to expand more quickly than the industrial sector (perhaps encouraging more female immigration) and favoured the continued growth of the big cities. Such growth was made possible by innovations in methods of mass short-distance transportation powered by electricity and petrol. The *Großstadt* required many services which expanded old occupations and created new ones. It also evolved an increasingly complex social geography with the separation of city centres, industrial and residential areas from one another. This was linked to spatial growth through the absorption of adjoining areas. By 1914 the *Großstadt* had come to symbolize for many people a distinct way of life which threatened or promised to extend across the whole of German society.

These three cumulative stages of growth transformed the nature of the town: its legal status, politics, administration, economy, society and culture. However, this was not a simple transition from one kind of town to another but was related to the typical features of each phase and the changes between them.

6.3 Urban life around 1800

In 1800 the German town was a settlement with a privileged status which distinguished it from the surrounding countryside. Leaving aside atypical capital cities[23] and trading centres, the typical German town was small (1000–5000 inhabitants).[24] It survived through exchange with the surrounding countryside. So dependent was it on such exchange that there was frequently a ban on rural competition with 'urban' trades such as the making of shoes, clothes and furniture. This partly explains the privileged legal status of the town. Urban trades were largely controlled by guilds although such controls were in many cases being eroded. Guild rules required masters to employ limited numbers of helpers, who in turn should proceed through apprenticeship to journeyman status and, after examination, to that of a master. In theory, guilds regulated the terms under which workers were employed and obtained qualifications, took moral responsibility for them (e.g. ensuring church attendance), fixed prices and levels of output, and maintained a trade monopoly within and beyond the town.

Guild masters had automatic rights of participation in town government. This was unpaid (except for a few functionaries such as night watchmen), and was concerned with the regulation of order and managing corporate property. Keeping good order (*Polizei*) extended beyond modern policing to cover population movement, food supply, and use of leisure time.[25] The major social task was providing poor relief to indigent residents.[26] Apart from guild masters, others involved in government included property (above all, real estate) owners, lawyers, doctors, clergymen, merchants and innkeepers. Merchants dominated trading centres. Where towns were the residence of a ruler and his court (*Residenzstädte*) or a university or a large garrison, this increased the weight of state officials, academics, and military officers respectively within the urban elite. Such differences were reflected in the occupational composition of the town. Some larger, more independent towns could sustain a special elite of old wealth with hereditary rights in government: a patriciate.

Town citizenship was limited to the local propertied and occupational elites. Military officers, academics and state officials were citizens of the state, not the town. Town citizenship not only conferred political rights but was linked to exclusive rights to own real estate and practise a trade. It was passed down from father to son but could be acquired by extended residence or purchase. Town assemblies consisted either of all citizens or of representatives chosen by various categories of citizens (guild masters, real-estate owners, merchants). These usually had little formal control over the executive branch of government, whose members were often selected on hereditary or nomination principles. There was, however, no sharp distinction between legislative, executive and judicial functions, some of which rested not with the town government but with other institutions such as churches and guilds. Furthermore, close familial connections within the citizenry blurred divisions between various institutions.[27]

The rest of the town population largely divided into hereditary inhabitants (denizens)[28] and foreigners. Denizens could not be expelled. Sometimes they in turn were divided into groups with limited rights (*Schutzverwandte*, *Schutzbürger*) such as that of marriage or employment in a designated trade, and those without such rights (*Insassen*). There were Jewish settlements in some larger towns whose members had their own communal institutions but were denied access to town citizenship, acquisition of real estate, and 'honourable' trades. Richer foreigners, such as merchants, could purchase certain economic privileges such as the right to maintain a bank account or operate a warehouse. Poorer foreigners were only admitted when needed and were expelled when they could not support themselves.[29]

Population control was assisted by town walls and gates which were closed at night. The term 'foreigner' often applied not just to members of other states (whether German or non-German) but also to people born elsewhere in the state to which the town belonged. Territorial states did not have to define closely who were its members or police state boundaries because they could depend upon the local community, including towns, to do this. Similar controls operated in city-states.[30]

Townspeople generally lived and worked in the same place. The merchant might have his office in his house and his warehouse in a linked or adjoining building, backing on to a river or canal. The guild master had his workshop in his house and his assistants living with him. However, in larger towns this was often ceasing to be the case by the early nineteenth century. There were special hostels for foreign journeymen and even native journeymen often lived outside the master's house, increasingly marrying and effectively becoming permanent wage earners. In trades such as building or brewing, there was a separation between work and home, as with merchants handling large amounts of stock. Nevertheless, it was normally only a short walk from home to work. There was no local public transport and most people could not afford to keep a horse, let alone a cart or a coach. Larger towns displayed some division between richer and poorer areas but the restricted size of most towns and the lack of transport facilities imposed strict limits. More often the division would be between better housing on the street front and poorer housing off the street, clustered around courtyards. Differences in the rent for various parts of a house suggested social distinctions; cellars and attics accommodated poorer people than ground- or first-floor apartments. Buildings rarely rose beyond a second floor. Within the urban population there were sharp status divisions but members of different status groups saw a lot of one another in their every-day routines.

Towns were rarely planned, with the exception of some *Residenzstädte* where princes sought to ape the French monarchy on a small scale. Even then such planning only covered royal buildings and surrounding spaces. Where a medieval 'new town' had been established on grid lines to encourage settlement, these had long become cluttered with additional buildings, and streets had become narrow and crooked. Real-estate owners had unrestricted rights of use of their property subject to minimal rules concerning risks of fire or collapse. There was a significant amount of communal property such as fields beyond the town walls, mills and breweries. Such property was regarded as an economic asset to be used for the benefit of its communal owners, not as 'public' assets with functions distinct from those of private property.

There was little concern with 'infrastructure'. Water was obtained individually from wells or natural sources, although there might be some communal upkeep and rules (e.g. about animals using sources of water supply intended for humans). Used water was poured on to street or courtyard; at best there might be some open gutters to take it back into rivers. People and animals left their excrement on the street where it was collected more or less frequently and then either dumped into rivers or used as manure. Other waste ended up on a town rubbish heap. Heating and lighting was by open fire (wood, perhaps peat fires, tallows at best for the poor, wax candles for the rich). In crowded towns built of wood this resulted in numerous fires. Fire services were usually voluntary and amateur, fire insurance difficult or impossible. There was little or no street lighting, severely restricting movement at night.

There was little commercial provision for leisure time. Most employed people worked long hours six days a week and those without work could rarely pay for their pleasures. Churches imposed strict limits on Sunday leisure. That left evenings and holidays, the latter varying between Catholic, Lutheran, and Calvinist areas. Apart from pubs – often little more than a room in the innkeeper's house – there was no indoor provision for most people's leisure-time outside the home, which itself was small and crowded without the specialized spaces (living room, dining room, bedroom, kitchen) now regarded as the norm (as discussed in Chapter 9). There were hostels for poorer immigrants such as journeymen. Better-off residents might have access to a library or assembly room, and their larger and better appointed homes could support musical and other cultural activities. Bigger towns with people coming and going had inns, hotels and restaurants. Theatres or concert halls, other than those owned by princes and rich nobles, were mainly confined to the largest cities. Some commercial entertainment accompanied markets – exotic animals, singing, dancing, clowning, the display of wax and illuminated figures, story-telling and quackery.[31] Pilgrimages and military parades attracted crowds, along with stalls and entertainers. Much of this rather limited 'popular culture' itself became the object of urban bourgeois disapproval and even bans.[32]

Education and medical care was purchased privately by the better-off. The rich had their children tutored at home before perhaps sending their sons to a *Gymnasium* (grammar school) and subsequently a university. However, as discussed in Chapter 10, universities did not yet have much attraction for many of the urban elite (leaving aside those planning a career in state bureaucracy). A rich Hamburg merchant would prefer to place his sons in other merchant houses, preferably working for some time abroad (especially in London), learning foreign languages, commercial law and the trade.[33] For the middling sort (*Mittelstand*) there were various private schools, often with a vocational bent, which extended formal education into the teens. Many of their sons entered apprenticeships, counting houses or other training, frequently with a view to continuing in their father's trade.

Girls' education was mainly seen in relation to marriage and the raising of a family, although there was some expansion in formal schooling provision.[34] There was charitable and church schooling for poor children but many had little beyond Sunday school.[35] Charitable hospitals furnished a mixture of medical and residential care for poor people when they became sick or incapacitated by injury, disability or old age. For example, it was only in 1823 that the Hamburg government separated charitable from correctional facilities and in 1825 built one of the first general hospitals in Germany.[36] Apart from that, poor people had to rely on crude pharmacies, market quacks and folk medicine.

Except in larger towns, it was virtually impossible for collective identity or organization to develop beyond the ranks of the privileged citizenry. The major exception was journeymen who travelled from town to town and sometimes formed semi-secret occupational associations. These could organize strikes which were the object of much imperial, state, and town legislation.[37] However, in small towns the citizenry and their families made up a considerable part of the population, leading some historians to suggest that these towns were more democratic than their successors, even after the removal of privilege.[38]

Small towns were not – *pace* later conservative nostalgia – places of harmony and concord where there was a place for everyone and everyone knew their place. There were conflicts within the urban elite and between the town and outside forces. Leaving aside inevitable personal disputes, there were conflicting interests within and between town patriciates, merchants and guildsmen. Merchants disliked the guild ban on rural manufacturing; artisans objected to the narrow base of patriciate power. Such conflicts were often reflected institutionally, with the executive arm of government (*Rat, Senat*) under patriciate control, the town assembly dominated by artisans, and merchants having their own special bodies and powers. This institutional demarcation was less marked in smaller towns or in towns firmly under the control of the territorial state.

In states with powerful princes, urban autonomy was severely restricted. People could appeal to state courts; indeed, the prince might insist on choosing town judges. Civil servants, officers, and academics were citizens of the state, not the town, and could not participate in local government but equally were exempt from its authority. Policing powers, especially in larger towns and state capitals, were under state control. Nevertheless, even here towns remained legally distinct from countryside, with different modes of government, types of taxation and relationships to the state.

Urban life was not static. Apart from humdrum tensions and short-term cycles associated with good or bad harvests, population growth put pressure on towns. The sending of food, timber and other raw products from eastern Europe (including German lands) to western Europe (including other German lands) in exchange for manufactured goods, as well as the growth of rural manufacturing in textile and metal goods, stimulated the growth of strategically placed towns. Much of the expansion in population and economic activity was difficult to control within traditional corporate structures. Indeed, in areas where commercial growth and rural manufacturing were most advanced, as well as in larger towns profiting from long-distance trade, the features of the 'typical' town outlined above were rapidly disappearing by the early nineteenth century. An increasing proportion of the population, especially people at the bottom of the social scale, no longer had a corporate 'place' and were coming to be seen not as the temporary product of bad times but as a permanent fixture.[39] Some ambitious merchants and manufacturers, aided by intellectuals who looked to the very different (and to them more attractive) society taking shape in countries such as England and the Netherlands, argued for an end to the corporate order, including the privileged town.

The period 1800–15 was a time of continual warfare. Southern and western Germany, the most urbanized regions, were conquered and reorganized by Napoleon. French officials, or German officials striving to be as French as possible, imposed French ways upon German towns. On the left bank of the Rhine and in the newly established Kingdom of Westphalia legal and fiscal distinctions between town and countryside were abolished; the town became just another commune. Town walls were demolished, symbolizing the opening up of the town.[40] Guilds and other corporations were swept aside. Government was by a state-appointed mayor. A town assembly was elected by the richer inhabitants irrespective of status or occupation, and was often more exclusive than its predecessor. Replacing the old corporations, elite clubs with names like 'Casino'[41] or 'Harmonie' were founded, contributing to the formation of a new, purely wealth-based elite known by the French term *notables*. Whether these legal and political developments had a long-term significance irrespective of economic change is a matter of debate.[42]

In the rump state of Prussia after the catastrophic defeats by the French in 1806–07, urban government was legally reorganized in 1808. This retained mixed (collegial) government which was shared between a town assembly (elected on a propertied franchise rather more extensive than the French model) and the *Magistrat* whose leading official had to be confirmed in office by the state. Police powers were reserved to the state but Baron vom Stein, author of the law, hoped that towns would take more power into their own hands, saving the state money and encouraging the civic participation he felt Prussia needed if it was to free itself of French domination.

The urban population did not respond positively. In some dynamic towns one might find merchants and manufacturers, resentful of patriciate powers or guild restrictions, eagerly exploiting the new situation. More often elites found reform damaging or burdensome. In some French-controlled areas 1800–10 were prosperous years but then followed a dreadful time, culminating with the failed invasion of Russia in 1812 and its aftermath.[43] Although after 1815 there remained positive memories of French reform, by the time Napoleon fell from power his name symbolized war, conscription, billeting, requisitions, taxes, privation and suffering.

In many regions after 1815 old arrangements were restored. There were, however, important exceptions and differences. Prussia kept her 1808 law where it had originally applied, introduced another urban self-government law in 1831 for the post-1815 provinces of Westphalia, Saxony and Posen, and retained some French reforms in the Rhineland province. In 1810 Prussia had abolished guilds and these were never restored, even if there continued to be trade associations which carried out some similar functions, for example in the field of vocational training. In southern and western Germany, guilds and autonomous town powers were restored but within the context of fewer and larger territorial states which also adopted state-wide constitutions that some town citizens preferred to those of their towns. Even in the four remaining German city-states the old institutions never recovered their former authority.

Legal-administrative distinctions between town and countryside were restored. Towns had distinct and significant powers of self-government.[44] However, these varied from one German state to another. There was the 'mayoral' system of the Rhineland province with a state-appointed mayor and limited rights of budgetary scrutiny for a town assembly elected on a narrow franchise. In the rest of Prussia there was the 'collegial' system based on the laws of 1808 and 1831, where government was by a mixture of elected and appointed figures, headed by a mayor proposed by the town assembly but confirmed in office by the state. In southern and western Germany there was the 'council' system with elected councillors. However, in many cases these powers of self-government were not fully exploited until German towns took on a more dynamic role in the next phase of urban growth.

6.4 Urban growth 1800–50[45]

After the continual warfare of the 1792–1815 period there followed a period without major political upheaval until 1848. Some urban growth occurred in connection with early industrialization and the construction of textile mills and engineering works. As there were hardly any workers in such firms before 1815 these occupational groups had increased sharply by the mid-century. In absolute terms, however, there was more growth in non-industrial urban occupations which started from a larger base. The 'mass artisan' trades – masons, carpenters, cobblers, tailors, furniture makers – expanded more rapidly than the population overall, especially at the level of assistants or, where guild monopolies no longer operated, non-guilded masters. Partly this was a response to growing demand; partly it reflected pauperization and increasing competition for jobs. Some masters and merchants profited from this, employing larger numbers of workers than the traditional guild-master, both in towns (e.g. on building sites) and in the countryside (especially in textiles). In some trades, jobs were subdivided and de-skilled and more women were employed (e.g. in tailoring), often working at home. These changes were largely grafted on to a 'traditional' technology – little or no new machinery, continued combination of workplace and home – but they broke with corporate and local forms of control.[46]

Railway construction from the 1840s onwards stimulated new activity in towns connected to the rail network and promoted industrial relocation. The building of railway stations and depots, warehouses, factories and houses brought in masses of unskilled workers from over-populated rural areas, although much employment was temporary. Lifting and carrying goods was done by a combination of human and horse power and many people would stand on street corners, in docks and harbours, waiting for such work. Much more buying and selling than in modern cities took place on the street, involving both established market stall holders and itinerants. Fixed shops were also growing in importance, although small by later standards. Large retail establishments such as the department store only appeared rather later in the century and then concentrated in the larger cities. (Nowadays one could probably get more of a sense of what these places were like by visiting towns and cities in the developing world rather than in Germany.)[47]

Population growth pushed hard on food supply. At times of hardship, as during the combination of poor grain harvests and potato blight in the mid-1840s, towns were suddenly burdened with high unemployment and increased numbers of paupers, creating a sense of crisis. Where towns could keep out foreigners they did so, resisting state measures to override such powers. States saw such urban restrictions as part of the problem because they prevented people from moving to places where their labour could best be used. On 31 December 1842 the Prussian government, noted for its economic liberalism, relaxed the restrictions on poor relief which each parish (*Gemeinde*) had hitherto been able to impose on recent arrivals. Regions undergoing economic growth needed extra labour coming from greater distances and it was, in the view of the government, inefficient for these to accept and expel workers on a short-term basis. On the same day as making these changes to poor relief, the government also enacted the first clear and binding law on state membership. (The law made it clear that membership was not citizenship in the sense of political rights and obligations.) As the local boundary was relaxed the state boundary was tightened.[48] Prussia, however, remained exceptional in both its liberalization of poor relief arrangements and its refusal to adopt other illiberal measures such as marriage restrictions in the face of the growth of poverty.

Actual or threatened immigration into towns could lead to a sense of loss of control. The towns which could defend themselves (e.g. in south-west Germany where there was rural over-population but little new urban employment) saw the world beyond as a threatening place filled with people on the move trying to break into their precious urban space.[49] The towns which could not impose such controls were alarmed by poverty which, even if less than in the countryside, was more visible when it was concentrated into the crowded town. Many pamphlets were written on the 'social question', meaning the uncontrolled growth of a mass of poor people who could not be absorbed into the economy. Some advocated renewal of controls on marriage and movement; others argued that such measures were reactionary and doomed to failure and only a freer economy could adapt effectively.

The town represented both opportunity and threat. For those who benefited from growth – merchants, manufacturers, some professionals – the town became a power base and the free economy the way of the future. Such people were prominent in the liberal movement in western Prussia and parts of south-west Germany. Especially in western Prussia, new employment in textiles, metal-working, railways and related industries, a traditional absence of sharp town–country distinctions, and urban government controlled by a wealthy minority, underpinned confidence about urban growth. The economic elite did not yet envisage a future of continuous growth concentrated in towns and large-scale industry, but they did believe that their kind of people should displace the old urban order of patriciates and craft masters. This confident bourgeoisie was taking control of local government and putting its stamp on the town with new residences, railway stations, exchanges, town halls, theatres, and concert halls.[50]

For these people the town was the *Bürger-Gemeinde* (citizen/bourgeois community – the double meaning of *Bürger* is important) counterposed to the state of the prince, landed nobility, and bureaucrats. Some liberals emphasized political freedom and participation, others economic freedom and efficiency – a difference which would become increasingly apparent. Some saw the liberalized urban community as a model for wider political reform.[51]

Less confident groups living in areas where economic opportunities were not opening up and where town remained sharply distinct from countryside, or in growing towns but in stagnant or threatened occupations, saw urban growth rather differently. The growing town was dangerous. Sensationalist novels with titles like *The Mysteries of Berlin/Hamburg* (imitating Eugene Sue's popular novel *The Mysteries of Paris*) described the 'proletariat' of the bigger towns.[52] The spread of ideas advocating social upheaval, which was termed socialism or communism, caused alarm and were associated with the formation of this urban under-class. Protests, for example that of the Silesian weavers in 1844, were seen as portending revolution, which had been an *idée fixe* since 1789. In 1847 there were many food riots, including extensive disturbances in Berlin. To such anxious observers, industrialization did not provide an answer when they looked to Britain and especially to the 'shock city' of Manchester on which there was much continental writing.[53] Instead, it threatened to add to the crowded and dangerous slums of the established cities the pollution and crass social conflict of the factory-town. Urban growth, whether industrial or non-industrial, meant disorder, disease and immorality. It threatened to undermine the healthy urban community dominated by the middling sorts of people.[54]

The revolutions of 1848 appeared to confirm such fears. The triggers of revolution were urban insurrections in Paris, Milan, Vienna, and Berlin. There were demonstrations and protests in other towns. With the consequent concessions of freedom of assembly, organization and expression, and the convening of elections to parliaments, towns became the focal points for an unprecedented level of popular political activity. Even liberals assigned a higher priority to the restoration of order than to achieving constitutional government and economic freedom. Counter-revolution brought tougher state control over the towns, including a measure of urban planning, although directed at maintaining control rather than at aiding development.[55] Liberal efforts to reduce town–country distinctions and extend constitutional government to state and national level were set back.[56]

Yet appearances of urban disorder and danger were misleading. The most recently arrived and poorest urban inhabitants lacked the time, traditions, skills, expectations or connections to engage in collectively organized protest, let alone to press for social reorganization. Paradoxically, this very lack of organization and definite objectives could feed perceptions of the 'masses' as a dangerous, destructive force. Those who could organize, above all hard-pressed artisans from the 'mass trades', had limited objectives and looked to less dangerous, non-political means of realizing them as the counter-revolution gathered force. As for factory workers, these were not a particular focus of disorder, perhaps because the skilled workers were well paid and the unskilled workers were new to the life and unorganized. By the end of 1849, towns in Germany had been brought quite easily to heel.[57]

Urban life was still in thrall to the agricultural sector. The economic crisis which conditioned revolution was primarily a matter of agrarian failure, although compounded by financial and industrial depression.[58] One answer to over-population continued to be overseas emigration, now boosted by political exile which ensured that a generation of potential leaders of popular movements was lost to Germany. Yet although the mid-nineteenth-century German town was in certain respects a swollen version of its earlier nineteenth-century predecessor, there were important differences. There was a more dynamic urban middle class with reforming ideas about how to address problems of overcrowding and poverty, and there were governments like Prussia which opposed returning to restrictive, corporate ways. Railway building and early industrial development had begun to shape urban occupational structure and social geography. Town authorities recognized the need to adopt some planning powers, if only to enable purchase of properties along projected railway routes. From the 1830s onwards private gas companies, following the British lead, were supplying bigger towns with street and domestic lighting. In a few cities, as in Hamburg following a major fire in 1842, a piped water supply had been constructed (as discussed in Chapter 2), although this only became extensive after 1850.[59]

The Hamburg elite used the opportunity of the post-1842 rebuilding programme to plan a city centre designed to impress with public buildings, and straighter and wider streets, thereby pushing the poor into the suburbs beyond the city wall or closer to the harbour. There were similar projects elsewhere in Europe, sometimes with princely support, sometimes on local initiative. France set the tone with Haussmann's rebuilding of Paris, partly on security grounds, but also for reasons of hygiene and prestige. This was paralleled in Vienna, with the same displacement of the poor. Major redevelopment started in Frankfurt am Main from the late 1850s, linked to new water supplies but especially to the building of a major railway station some distance from the centre.

From mid-century on, ceremonial openings of railway stations, town halls, exchanges, theatres, concert halls, art galleries or libraries were becoming moments at which bourgeois elites boosted the image of their town and conveyed a sense of optimism. However, patterns varied greatly across Germany. There were textile towns in Westphalia where the economic elite practised a zealous evangelical Protestantism which was suspicious of secular culture and display. Where an industrial town exhibited a sharp division between a small number of large employers and a large number of wage earners there was less scope for such cultural activities, which were based on the 'middling sorts' of people.[60]

6.5 Urbanization 1850–75

Middle-class optimism appeared more realistic by the mid-1850s than in the immediate aftermath of 1848. The counter-revolution set back liberalism but spared the entrepreneurial middle class which was given unprecedented freedom to raise loans, establish companies and engage in trade. The German Customs Union (*Deutsche Zollverein*) established in 1834 was expanded with the addition of Hannover and pursued a low-tariff policy. The collapse of many small, technically antiquated firms in the 1840s cleared the path for larger and more up-to-date enterprises and a shift from rural to urban locations. The two decades *c.*1853–73 witnessed the fastest economic growth rates in Germany in modern times, only briefly set back by a financial crisis in 1857–58. Railway construction increased sharply, with concomitant economic effects. Industrialization of the Ruhr valley with its rich coal deposits took off. The western Prussian provinces, Saxony, the

Saarland, Upper Silesia, Bohemia, and big cities such as Berlin and Vienna developed as the first urban-industrial regions in Germany.[61]

Urban growth, underpinned by the expansion of new jobs in the industrial sector, outstripped general population growth and absorbed a higher proportion of excess rural population. It was not only the new sectors of railway construction, mining, iron and steel manufacture, factory textile production, and engineering which benefited. The building trade boomed. Artisans found themselves in demand in skilled jobs in the factories, meeting higher levels of demand for good-quality handicraft goods and adapting to the servicing needs of urban-industrial society. (Piped water demands plumbers; locomotives and other steam-engines need skilled maintenance and repair.) Such opportunities undermined craft resistance to industrialization and widened support for the liberal movement. Spurts in urban growth rates went in tandem with rural growth rates rather than moving inversely with them, and they varied directly with levels of prosperity. Marriage rates became more sensitive to levels of industrial employment or house rents rather than food prices. Even 'remote' rural and small-town areas altered their economic functions as they were stripped of labour and found specialist niches supplying the growing towns with various foodstuffs.[62]

Rapid and sustained growth produced distinctive problems. There was a scarcity of housing, especially for poorer people. In towns taking shape virtually from nothing, there was room to build. In some Ruhr towns large employers had the incentive and resources to supply company housing, but this never furnished all needs.[63] In well-established towns there was increased crowding and infill building or, in the larger cities where the incentive was big enough, the speculative building of high-rise blocks, the *Mietkaserne* (rent barracks) for which Berlin became notorious. As yet, people could not locate far from their place of work so such building tended to occur close to the city centre or around railway stations.

This raised issues of public health and planning, as discussed in Chapter 2.[64] Typhus and cholera epidemics stimulated a concern with polluted land and unclean water. By 1871, 17 Prussian cities had introduced communal water supplies and this increased rapidly in the next decade or so. The concern with polluted land led to the removal of cemeteries to the outskirts where gas works, water towers, and slaughter houses were also located and regulated. Street cleaning and more efficient removal of sewage to sewage fields and farms was introduced. The building of railway lines and stations required planning powers (e.g. limited powers of compulsory purchase) and the setting out of a more rational street system, especially between old town centres and railway stations. Increased population density and a heightened awareness of dangers of fire and disease meant the imposition of some standards in building and street design.

Nevertheless, by today's standards these rules and powers were limited. Planning was more about control and prevention than seeking to realize positive goals such as are associated with zoning and other modern planning measures. *Laissez-faire* values and propertied interests blocked extensive governmental intervention. So far as housing was concerned, there were hardly any rules about the interiors of buildings, and external rules concerned only such things as maximum height, number of storeys, or entries into courtyards for fire engines. Both bourgeois reformers and labour spokesmen condemned the old slums of deteriorating city-centre areas and the new slums of the speculative builders but made little headway with their alternative ideas of higher-quality provision through communal and cooperative ventures.

As for water supply, the prevalent assumption that the danger of disease lay with the pollution of ground and air meant there was as yet little attention to filtration designed to prevent the spread of water-borne bacilli. The idea of underground water-borne sewage disposal (as opposed to better collection, surface drainage and sewage fields) as yet appeared not only unnecessary but impossible in view of the costs and technical difficulties involved.

Elementary school provision lagged woefully behind the growth of a large class of children in towns.[65] There was some improvement in poor relief, especially with the spread of the influential 'Elberfeld System'. This combined more uniform regulation with an extensive use of volunteers, each responsible for maintaining personal knowledge and control of a few poor families. This rather 'illiberal' system (compared to more consistently liberal self-help schemes) did not offend middle-class sensibilities, partly because its controls provided savings, partly because something undertaken by bourgeois volunteers under the auspices of urban government did not appear to liberals as authoritarian by contrast with the older, state-dominated *Polizei*.[66]

Despite deficiencies, the new measures of control and public provision expanded the functions, powers and personnel of urban government. For many people with professional qualifications in engineering, surveying, medicine, building, finance, or law, a career in urban government appeared attractive. State governments were happy to delegate new tasks to city governments, which provided alternative political careers now that counter-revolution and Bismarck's subsequent 'unification from above' blocked constitutional progress and careers in state parliaments and ministries.

Urban elites came to regard city government as their power base. The legal measures of the 1808–48 period establishing self-government were exploited. The reactionary laws relating to local government passed in the 1850s (restoring urban–rural distinctions and restricting electoral rights) ensured that urban government became an elite monopoly. In the 1860s the sweeping away of restrictions on movement and occupational freedom ushered in an era of economic liberalism.[67] National unification accelerated these trends. Austria had its own urban development and in 1860 could credibly point to Vienna as the first German city and Bohemia as a major industrializing region. Nevertheless, city government never had the freedom and power in Austria that it achieved in Prussia. Austria's economic growth rate, although respectable, was only about half that of Prussia. In key sectors such as railway building and steel production Prussia far outstripped Austria. Prussia dominated the *Zollverein* and blocked attempts by Austria to join. None of this made Prussian-led unification inevitable but it meant that under the Second Empire these dynamic trends were vigorously promoted.[68]

Growth brought new forms of conflict. The combination of impoverished artisans, unorganized paupers and casual labourers appeared more dangerous in 1848 than actually turned out to be the case. The new generation of urban workers by 1875 was another matter. More of them had established families. With demand for skilled labour, the formation of urban-industrial working class districts and higher real wages, such workers wanted a greater share of the cake. The liberal era had seen an expansion of associations and mass literature. Under liberal auspices, workers had formed trades unions, educational associations and cooperatives. When liberals allied with Bismarck and supported restrictions on popular organization, this labour movement looked elsewhere for leadership. In predominantly Protestant towns they allied with radicals who adapted their politics to workers' interests. In Catholic areas the oppositional political Catholic movement offered communal initiatives and leadership. Bismarck's campaigns against Catholics and socialists, backed by much of the liberal middle class, only hardened and broadened this oppositional politics. It also meant that many cultural amenities for workers were provided independently of the state.[69]

These were only minority cultures within an urban population which was still very mobile and where most workers were non-unionized. Urban affairs remained dominated by a small elite. To ensure this, the electoral system was rigged in favour of this elite. After 1850 the Prussian government had adopted from the Rhenish cities a three-class franchise for the lower house of the parliament (*Landtag*) which also applied to city councils. Taxpayers were divided into three classes – an upper, middle and lower – each of which elected a third of the council. The system produced some crass results. In Essen, at some elections, the upper third of the electorate consisted of just one man, a certain Herr Krupp! Different patterns of wealth and income distribution produced wildly varying electorates from town to town. In addition to the three classes, minimum income qualifications for the vote were imposed and in some places property owners made up half the electorate. Well under half the adult male population had the vote. The first class in the franchise comprised roughly 5–6 per cent of voters, the second class 8–20 per cent of voters, and the third class the remaining 70–80 per cent. Understandably, turnouts amongst poorer voters were low. In some states a simpler system obtained; poorer people were excluded from the franchise. Only a few states, such as Baden, had a democratic system. Some states, such as Hamburg and Saxony, even altered their franchises in an anti-democratic direction when threatened by socialist advances. The result was that urban government was a bourgeois monopoly, dominated by the National Liberal Party, although town government was often represented as apolitical on the grounds that politics was the domain of the state, not the urban community.[70]

6.6 City growth and the rise of the *Großstadt*, 1875–1914

So long as the town was a privileged community, or possessed a legal identity by virtue of a special system of administration, one could use the law to distinguish town from countryside. With the abolition of guilds and the legal as well as actual realization of freedom of movement, settlement, and occupational choice, many of the legal features which defined the German town disappeared. The new constitutions of 1848–49, even when adapted in an authoritarian direction, removed the remaining elements of estate-based assemblies with special urban representation. Undemocratic franchises were based on wealth, not status. Special urban taxes were abolished or declined in significance.

There remained separate legal arrangements for urban and rural government, and in some areas these were even re-introduced in the 1850s. However, to define a town simply as a commune with urban administration raised the question of the criteria for deciding which communes should have such administration. This became a pressing problem when there was rapid population growth in a rural commune or (more rarely) population decline in an urban one. One answer was to adopt a purely quantitative approach. Before the 1860s, the law and statisticians deployed qualitative distinctions. In 1860, an international meeting of statisticians recommended a quantitative definition using a population of 2000 as the dividing point. From 1871 on, this was the operational definition used by the Imperial Statistical Office. Prussia continued to collect data on towns defined on a legal basis, which accounts for the two ways in which Figure 6.1 records urban population for 1875 and 1910.

The quantitative definition tells one nothing about population density, as it was applied to communes of widely different sizes. Recognizing that a simple definition according to whether population exceeded 2000 meant little when applied to spatially different areas, various proposals for modern and appropriate qualitative distinctions were advanced, in terms of densities, patterns of settlement and economic functions. However, these only produced multiple typologies of towns, not any agreed definition of a town as such. Furthermore, as the average size of the town increased and as the *Großstadt* became quantitatively more important as well as qualitatively distinctive, some observers, such as the social analyst and economic historian Werner Sombart, contended that the important distinction was between the big city and all other settlements.

Whether using statistical or legal definitions, after 1875 the rural population of Germany stagnated while the urban population boomed.[71] Furthermore, while urban growth had previously been concentrated in the smaller and medium-sized towns, now it was the big cities which took the lead. Partly this was a result of cities incorporating adjoining areas. There were 188 such cases between 1880 and 1910 compared to only 56 in the preceding 30 years. Of these, 133 involved 48 cities with over 100,000 inhabitants; another 46 involved smaller cities of 50,000–100,000. There were various reasons for this 'urban imperialism': acquiring land for extra housing and businesses, trying to combat the flight of the better-off to outlying regions with resultant losses in urban tax revenue, making plans for future growth. This form of big-city growth accounts for about one-fifth of the total rise in the population living in big cities (those over 100,000 population) by 1914.[72] However, the main, straightforward reason for big-city growth was that more people moved into the big cities than into other towns. Subsequently the children they had in turn added to the big-city population.

As the economy diversified and the tertiary sector grew, so the big city demonstrated many advantages. The increasing specialization and range of occupations in a mature industrial economy made it important to be able quickly to combine the right skills and resources. The big city provided this rich blend better than smaller, less complex centres.[73] In the most rapidly growing and newly established branches of the economy (chemicals, electrical products, specialized craft trades, personal services, tertiary private and public sectors), no one mineral source or transport advantage provided an overriding reason for location – but access to a dense and diverse population could well do so.

Such concentration was only feasible with further technological progress. If steam power provided the energy base for the early industrial city, electrical power and the internal combustion engine did the same for the big city. Railways were too inflexible to handle most daily mass passenger transit between work and home. Horse power created major problems of crowding and sanitation. In the 1870s, horse-drawn as well as steam-powered buses and trams proliferated in an attempt to cope with problems of city growth. We will never know how far they might have succeeded because they were quickly rendered obsolete by new technology. From the 1880s on there was rapid growth in electrically powered transport, especially the tram, and from 1900 the petrol-driven bus. These were flexible forms of transport which enabled an increased distancing of city centre, industrial areas and socially distinct residential zones from one another. There was also suburban railway growth and, from 1902, the beginning of an underground railway system in Berlin. The motorized lorry started to become important for the urban transport of goods, although use of the motor car was confined to a small elite before 1914.[74] Electric or motorized cranes not only displaced much human labour (e.g. in lifting and carting heavy goods from place to place) but made it possible to construct taller buildings in already densely crowded areas.[75]

These innovations enabled city planners to contemplate and justify urban annexation on the grounds that a more dispersed population really 'belonged to' the big city. It also allowed more firms and individuals to locate to the ever-bigger city, which began to assume a distinctive and novel geography. Nevertheless, it is arguable that such innovations enabled but did not cause big-city growth. In purely technological terms they could equally promote the opposite effect. The electric motor boosted the growth of small and decentralized enterprises. Motorized road transport permits more dispersed and flexible distributions of people and goods than do railway trains. Perhaps the concentration of electrical power supply on big cities inhibited decentralization in this period although once there were national grids that would no longer be the case. However, great increases in big-city land prices should have favoured more dispersed location. Such dispersal did take place, particularly for large-scale industrial production once the original industrial area close to the city centre had become obsolete and/or too expensive.

This trend of dispersal alongside big-city growth suggests that the two processes of industrialization and urbanization were, to some degree, becoming independent of one another. Until about 1890, urban and industrial growth in Germany were directly related and concentrated in the most rapidly growing urban areas; thereafter that relationship became less clear-cut. Already there was something post-industrial about the big city. However, trends in urban geography were more than just a function of differential land prices, as contemporaries realized when confronted with the otherwise puzzling phenomenon of slums on expensive city-centre land.

There was no single trend in the pattern of urban geography. In well-established towns which were not based on a single industry, the typical pattern was for the area extending from the old town centre to the railway station(s) to develop into a 'city centre' marked by a decline in residential population and industrial enterprises and an increase in administrative buildings, high-quality retailing, and 'cultural' buildings and spaces. Here the bourgeois elite could spend much of their work and leisure time as well as their money, even if living some distance away. Workers relocated their homes away from these centres to industrial suburbs. Many smaller enterprises tended to mix in with lower-middle-class residential districts. The rich had their exclusive residential districts, the precise location of which depended on the topography of the particular city, but which were usually well away from the industrial suburbs. Also in these suburbs could be found the establishments needed to service the big city – cemeteries, gas, electricity and water works, and slaughter houses. Throughout the different residential areas, increasingly differentiated by social class, were located a growing number of hospitals, schools and places for leisure activity.

A different pattern arose with the new industrial town. In the Ruhr, urban growth centred on the industrial enterprise rather than the other way around. Initially there was a scattering of such industrial centres. Each of them grew, getting closer to one another, until a more continuous urban agglomeration took shape. Here there was a less clearly divided social geography so long as the key production enterprise (mine, foundry) was located at the centre. Gradually, however, industrial shift and re-location (for example, when coal seams were exhausted), tertiary growth, and the residential segregation made possible by new transport technology pushed this type of city towards the pattern of the older, established type, although important differences remained. In both cases it became increasingly difficult to say where city ended and countryside began. One turn-of-the-century preoccupation came to be making that boundary clear and trying to enforce it, not, as previously, in order to demarcate economic activities from one another, but to preserve the amenities of the countryside for urban dwellers.

Big cities made urban government complex and large-scale. In Dortmund the number of urban government employees increased from 32 in 1869 to around 1600 in 1910.[76] In the period 1890–1910, per capita spending on schools in German big cities increased by a factor of six. In the two decades before the First World War, overall public expenditure in Germany rose about 2.6 per cent per annum. Breaking that down by state, Imperial and local government produces figures of 1.7 per cent, 3.2 per cent and 4.1 per cent respectively. That latter figure would be much higher if only big-city government was considered.

The state authorities no longer regarded urban government as a 'local' matter but drew up elaborate directives which established which functions were obligatory, which optional and which off-limits for city authorities. Limits were set on their taxation and credit-raising powers; city bonds could seem an attractive alternative to state loans and could have macroeconomic effects by significantly increasing levels of public debt, and influencing patterns of investment and rates of interest.[77]

Urban government was in crisis by 1900: revenues from indirect taxes intended specifically for local government were declining, leading to a heavy dependence on supplements to state income tax. Financial reform introduced by the Prussian finance minister von Miquel improved matters, but dependence on supplements was increasing again by 1914. A major problem was that the poorest cities with large working-class populations also had the greatest obligations, e.g. in elementary education.[78]

City government was professionalized. The lord mayor (*Erste Bürgermeister* in Prussia) became a career position for someone with legal training; the lord mayor of a big city usually attaining that position after having been mayor in smaller cities. An increasingly large proportion of the *Magistrat* were professional people with qualifications in medicine, building, engineering, accountancy, or law. The councillors – more and more party representatives rather than independents – could do little more than scrutinize the work of full-time professionals. Local government still depended upon an army of volunteers in matters such as poor relief, health and school boards, but these volunteers increasingly came from lower down the social scale. Until the Centre Party and the Social Democratic Party placed councils under pressure, the professionalization of urban government had few obvious political effects. National Liberals (the dominant town-hall party) and professional administrators portrayed urban government as a matter of technique and expertise without a political dimension. Nevertheless, professionalization signalled the withdrawal of the liberal middle class from close involvement in the running of the city, something accelerated by their decision to live an increasing distance from the city centre.

Expansion and professionalization took place because the tasks of urban government grew inexorably. In the 1880s the Imperial government introduced welfare reforms, including a compulsory system of sickness insurance. The funds established provided the basis for expansion of hospitals and medical provision, most marked in the bigger cities. This had to be coordinated and managed by city governments. The permanent separation of work from home, the creation of settled families in working-class districts, the confinement of waged labour to adults, and the raising of expectations all led to effective universal and compulsory elementary education. The state set down the parameters (curricula, supply and appointment of teachers) but left it to local government to furnish the buildings, teaching materials, and salaries.

City governments sought to maintain control over market-driven developments. Mass housing provided by high-density tower blocks or housing estates was built for profit but city authorities increased provision of social housing through subsidies and land grants to building societies. There were more stringent regulations about building and hygiene standards. By 1900, German big cities had introduced piped water supplies and taken over gas supplies. Electricity generation and supply was closely regulated, if not publicly owned, although often a number of city governments would combine on a regional basis. Providing trams, buses, and suburban and underground railways required powers of compulsory purchase and extensive planning. Underground sewage disposal was introduced, which was a massive investment and construction challenge, especially in densely settled and built-up areas. Some people advocated positive planning rather than just regulating private enterprise and meeting 'social' needs. From 1900 onwards there were regular meetings of German urban representatives (*Deutsche Städtetage*) and publications directed at sharing ideas about how to develop 'garden cities', 'green belts', and civic centres.

All of this altered perceptions of urban government. If urban government was seen as the property of its privileged citizenry around 1800 and as the 'community' opposed to the 'state' by mid-nineteenth century; then by 1914 it had come to be regarded as the lowest level of the state and a potentially modernizing force.

City government was also becoming explicitly politicized. Towns had always been arenas of conflict, but in the ages of the privileged citizenry or the liberal bourgeoisie this was muffled, as there were no institutions through which such conflicts could be openly channelled. This ceased with the rise of mass politics in German after 1890. The democratically elected Reichstag was no longer controlled by pro-governmental parties. By 1912, the Socialist Party had one-third of the votes and a quarter of the seats, and the Catholic Centre Party another sixth of the votes and over one-fifth of the seats. Together with left-liberal as well as ethnic parties, they could vote down government proposals.

However, this success was not repeated in state parliaments and city councils because of rigged franchises. Although these kept socialists and Catholics out of the town hall for a long time, their very use made it clear that urban government was not a matter of neutral expertise but a major resource which some controlled and were determined not to surrender to others. Arguments about education, poor relief and healthcare constantly laid bare the class nature of urban society. Indeed, political rigging made matters more divisive. By 1914, despite discriminatory franchises, the Socialist and Centre Parties were returning some candidates to councils where they gained publicity for their condemnation of those in power. At the same time, on councils, health insurance and school boards, opposition politicians were becoming involved in urban government and increasingly seeing their role in terms of practical reform rather than principled opposition. These trends would become much clearer in the Weimar Republic, when local government was democratized and treated as the lowest rung of a liberal democratic state.

6.6 Germany as an urban society

Class division was apparent in the German city by 1914. Poor working-class districts with distinctive patterns of housing and leisure produced mass support for the socialist, Catholic and ethnic parties.[79] There were separate districts for the 'middling sort'. These middling groups were expanding even more rapidly than the urban-industrial working class. In the public sector, schools, hospitals and transportation required clerks and teachers, nurses, porters, drivers, conductors, and station masters. In the private sector, the expansion of retailing, personal services, and insurance required more clerks and sales assistants. Some lower-middle-class people (artisans, shopkeepers, innkeepers) lived in workers' districts, but many, with salaries little higher than manual workers' wages (sometimes actually lower than those of skilled workers), clustered in other districts. They made different, though less clear-cut political choices, including supporting radical nationalism. In the exclusive suburbs lived the high civil servants, managers, top professionals and businessmen. The very rich built themselves country villas.[80] Urban elites still dominated the National Liberal and to some extent the Free Conservative Parties but were uncomfortable with the world of mass politics.

Yet despite these divisions some contemporaries saw the big city as a melting pot, taking people from different occupations and different regions, and imposing its own standards and its own mass culture. Almost everyone in the big city had the common experience of travelling some distance from work to home. All children went to school, even if public and private schools differed. The same parks and other public places were accessible to all. Public libraries circulated the same literature and, generally speaking, once one left aside the politically charged daily press, the same periodicals and books appealed at a popular level across classes. All German males were liable to military service, even if some served longer than others and had little chance of becoming officers. As the Socialist Party advanced electorally, it pitched its appeal less at manual workers than at all the 'little people' who suffered from high rents, rigged food prices, and unfair taxes. The Catholic Centre Party had always been populist. Increasingly liberal and right-wing parties emphasized their popular credentials, arguing that it was in the interests of *all* Germans to acquire overseas empire, or build a large navy, or maintain a large army against threatening neighbours.[81]

Anti-urbanism itself changed along with the nature of urban life. Goethe hated the big city for its chaos and visited Berlin just once. Otherwise his 'urban experience' was confined to Rome. By mid-century, the conservative sociologist Wilhelm Riehl found the city dangerous and unstable, a place where proletarians of manual and mental work challenged the traditional order based on the countryside and the small town. For people of his persuasion, the industrial city by 1880 was the antithesis of culture, with its elite consisting of vulgar materialists and its workers of sheer labour power. The city *could* be the site of civilization but more through the efforts of rulers and enlightened minorities than those of most of its modern inhabitants. Conversely, liberals and Marxists saw this urban-industrial centre as representing the future, although they differed as to what that future was.

Attitudes again changed with the spread of the German big city beyond just a few capital cities and major centres. Until now, those Germans who condemned the city echoed an ancient pastoral tradition which implied that one could always escape it. Now the big city was the place where, for good or ill, everything significant happened – establishment or *avant-garde* art, elite culture or mass culture, political and economic decision-making. This was above all the case with Berlin, by 1914 a gigantic metropolis of four million people.[82] For some critics, such as Felix Theilhaber in a book entitled *Sterile Berlin* (1913), the city diminished its inhabitants' basic biological drives and led to demographic degeneration. The city was bleeding the countryside of human resources. Agrarian protectionists deployed such arguments along with those for the need to maintain self-sufficiency in food to insist that the trend towards the 'industrial state' must be halted for the sake of national survival.[83]

Yet for other Germans the city was the magnet, the dynamic centre of all that was positive in modern life. The playwright Gerhard Hauptmann was a fierce critic of social inequality and injustice, condemned by the establishment, yet he expressed the view that 'Berlin is splendid . . . Berlin is the most wonderful city in the world. Berlin is life'.[84]

Big cities were becoming similar, although Berlin represented something unique in Germany, comparable only to London, Paris and New York. Werner Sombart saw the big city as a population centre no longer bound to any specific function. Each big city owed its existence to some original, distinctive function but to that had been added many further layers: a diverse range of goods and services, similar geographical layouts, converging building designs, common patterns of everyday life, the same apparent independence of its surroundings.

The ending of any distinct legal or privileged identity for the town in Germany and its redefinition in quantitative terms, made it difficult to decide precisely where town ended and countryside began. In the Ruhr mining area, for example, the constant extension of suburbs from the different towns threatened to make them join up with one another. Would the Ruhr end up as one gigantic city? And, if so, in what sense would it be urban as opposed to rural? Those who pressed for green belts expressed the new planning ethos which aimed to preserve the specific quality of urban as well as rural life.

The big city set the tone for German national culture. People acquired their tastes from magazines and books published in the city. What we can now see as the beginning of a mass consumer culture spread the goods associated with urban life into villages and small towns. People living in villages had family and friends in the city whom they visited or heard from. The nuclear family and the comfortable house with its front parlour was an urban middle-class ideal which became the national norm, even if impossible to realize fully for many people. However, even to have a chance of approaching that norm required the increasingly extensive practice of birth control (as discussed in Chapter 2). Just as the physical environment of the big city was clearly a made one, so people set about making their social world too.

This idea of the city and its society as *constructed* was crucial to the rise of sociology.[85] Max Weber, Ferdinand Tönnies, Georg Simmel and others tried to identify what was modern and distinctive about big-city society, as did novelists such as Heinrich Mann and Robert Musil.[86] Was it the anonymity of people from one another? Or that people related to one another only in fleeting and functional ways which encouraged a sense of fragmentation, calculation and rationalization in relationships? Was it the power of the market, the money economy, the capitalist ethic, which drove urban development in directions beyond the control of individuals or groups? Was it the massive material but artificial world which dwarfed the individual? Was it the constant flux of innovation and movement which meant that the modern was itself always changing and individuals lived in a permanent state of uncertainty and insecurity? Or, counterposed to these images of alienation, powerlessness, unceasing change, anonymity, and rationalization, were forms of solidarity actually being reproduced in the city (in workplace, neighbourhood, and family settings) which were not so unlike what existed elsewhere? Were there ways in which social transformation could humanize the big city? Had material deprivation and its related patterns of social inequality given way to mass prosperity and culture, the displacement of poverty by spiritual malaise?

These questions which contemporaries were increasingly posing by 1914 were not peculiar to Germany. What distinguishes Germany is the rapidity and completeness of its urban transformation between 1850 and 1914. Britain was a more urban society than Germany in 1914 but had already gone well down that road by 1850. The other major urban-industrial nations – France and the United States – had relatively larger rural and small-town populations than Germany. In Germany there were strong hopes and fears that the big city would impose its special nature upon the whole country. In 1800 Germany was a cluster of rural societies; by 1914 it seemed well on its way to becoming an urban nation.

Yet this appearance was deceptive. Rural and small-town life remained important; even big cities had their gardens and almost village-like districts. The First World War broke the pattern of urban and industrial growth in Germany and it was never to be resumed in the same steady way thereafter. In 1933 the National Socialists came to power, espousing an anti-city ideology which made the peasant and the small-town artisan the ideal core of the nation rather than the city-dweller, whether manual or white-collar worker.[87] Another war brought the physical destruction of many of Germany's cities. The shift away from heavy industry led to urban decline. New kinds of economic activity and communications do not obviously favour city growth. One could argue that 1914 represented the high point of German urbanization.

6.7 Notes

1 I would like to thank my colleague at Birmingham University, Dr Leonard Schwarz, who read and commented upon a draft of this chapter.

2 One can dispute the use of the term 'German society', especially before 1871. However, in an essay focused on long-term development I ignore socio-political fragmentation and Austria. Pre-1871 statistics provided apply either to the territory of the German Second Empire (except Alsace-Lorraine) or to Prussia.

3 The idea of typicality is selective but not arbitrary. It is selective because historians distinguish many types of town and many aspects of urban life as well as pointing to the unique qualities of every town. However, it is not arbitrary, as the phases identified suggest central features of towns and urban life in each phase and characteristic changes from one phase to the next.

4 In Figure 6.1, between 1816 and 1840 the urban population rises from 2.88 million to 4.07 million, but that is no faster than the total population which rises from 10.32 to 14.96 million.

5 Figure 6.1 shows the proportional growth of the urban population relative to the total population in Prussia between 1840–75. Urban population increased from 4.07 to 8.79 million, i.e. more than doubling, while total population increased from 14.96 to 25.7 million. The two different figures given for urban population in 1875 in this figure relate to two different definitions used by the Prussian government. The first and lower figure is based on a legal definition of a town whereas the second, higher figure is based upon a quantitative definition. See Section 6.4 for further consideration of this question.

6 Figure 6.2 shows how within the different categories of town, those between 2000 and 20,000 inhabitants grew especially fast between 1843 and 1875, those between 20,000 and 100,000 inhabitants quite fast between 1843 and 1910, and those over 100,000 inhabitants very fast between 1875 and 1910. Table 6.1 in turn provides more detail on the growing importance of cities with more than 100,000 inhabitants.

7 For these phases, see Horst Matzerath, *Urbanisierung in Preußen 1815–1914* (Stuttgart, 1985), pp. 9, 24–5; Wolfgang Krabbe, *Die deutsche Stadt im 19. und 20. Jahrhundert* (Göttingen, 1989), especially pp. 176ff.; Jürgen Reulecke, *Geschichte der Urbanisierung in Deutschland* (Frankfurt am Main, 1985), especially pp. 9–12. I draw heavily upon these three general studies in this chapter and forego detailed references to them when I do so. Other general studies of nineteenth-century German urban development in English include the following: G. Huck and Jürgen Reulecke, 'Urban History Research in Germany', *Urban History Yearbook*, (1981), pp. 39–54; Wolfgang Köllmann, 'The Process of Urbanization in Germany at the Height of the Industrialization Period', in *Journal of Contemporary History*, 4 (1969), pp. 59–76; Joseph Lee, 'Aspects of Urbanization and Economic Development in Germany 1815–1914', in P. Abrams and E. A. Wrigley, eds, *Towns in Society*, (Cambridge, 1978), pp. 279–93; Horst Matzerath, 'The Influence of Industrialization on Urban Growth in Prussia 1815–1914', in H. Schmal, ed., *Patterns of European Urbanization since 1500* (London, 1981), pp. 145–79; Jürgen Reulecke, 'Federal Republic of Germany', in C. Engeli and H. Matzerath, eds, *Modern Urban History in Europe, USA and Japan* (Oxford, 1989), pp. 53–71; Richard Tilly, 'Cyclical Trends and the Market Response: Long Swings in Urban Development in Germany, 1850–1914', in W. Robert Lee, ed., *German Industry and German Industrialization: Essays in German Economic and Business History in the Nineteenth and Twentieth Centuries* (London, 1991), pp. 148–84. A more general study, still of value, is A. F. Weber, *The Growth of Cities in the Nineteenth Century* (New York, 1899; repr. Ithaca, 1968).

8 For evidence which suggests that rural industry, by reducing rural unemployment, reduced migration, see Steve Hochstadt, *Mobility and Modernity: Migration in Germany 1820–1989* (Ann Arbor, MI, 1999), p. 71.

9 This is because food made the largest claim on household budgets, possibly as much as two-thirds for urban workers in mid-century Germany. See Diedrich Saalfeld, 'Lebensverhältnisse der Unterschichten Deutschlands im 19. Jarhhundert', *International Review of Social History*, 28 (1983), pp. 215–53, here pp. 236–9.

10 The time lag was important. Thus the food price increases of 1845–7, although coming down steeply in early 1848, by then were working through into higher urban unemployment rates. See Helge Berger and Mark Spoerer, 'Economic Crises and the European Revolutions of 1848', *Journal of Economic History*, 61 (2001), pp. 293–326. At the same time, during such periods of depressed economic activity (the early 1830s and the later 1850s were milder examples), migration to and from towns declined. See Hochstadt, *Mobility and Modernity*, Ch. 3.

11 Patterns of migration within states, in particular rates and types of migration, are difficult to establish, especially for the pre-1850 period. There is one very valuable source: an almost complete set of annual statistics for migration in 200 communities (*Gemeinde*) in the Prussian administrative district (*Regierungsbezirk*) of Düsseldorf in the Rhineland province. Much of the empirical data used in the work of Hochstadt and Jackson (see below) draws on this material. For an overview, see S. Hochstadt and J. Jackson, '"New" Sources for the Study of Migration in Early Nineteenth-century Germany', *Historical Social Research – Historische Sozialforschung*, 31 (1984), pp. 85–92.

The most recent major studies of these questions are Hochstadt, *Mobility and Modernity*, as well as the same author's two earlier articles, S. Hochstadt, 'Migration in Preindustrial Germany', *Central European History*, 16 (1983), pp. 195–224, and S. Hochstadt, 'Migration and Industrialization in Germany 1815–1977, *Social Science History*, 5 (1981), pp. 445–68; and James H. Jackson, *Migration and Urbanization in the Ruhr Valley 1821–1914* (Atlantic Highlands, N., 1997). These studies question earlier assumptions about an immobile 'traditional' society, the rise in geographical mobility coming only with industrialization and urbanization, and migration being mainly 'one-way' movement from 'less developed' to 'more developed' places. Hochstadt also has an extensive bibliography of secondary literature, including English-language work, and I refer the reader to this (pp. 296–327) rather than further increasing the extent of notes here.

For the legal and bureaucratic responses of German governments to cross-state migration, as well as problems of migration within some of the larger states, see Andreas Fahrmeir, *Citizens and Aliens: Foreigners and the Law in Britain and the German States 1789–1870* (New York and Oxford, 2000), especially pp. 19–43; and Dieter Gosewinkel, *Einbürgern und Ausschliessen: Die Nationalisierung der Staatsangehörigkeit vom Deutschen Bund bis zur Bundesrepublik Deutschland* (Göttingen, 2001).

12 However, Hochstadt, *Mobility and Modernity*, has persuasively argued that immigration into towns was less substantial than had previously been believed, that it became increasingly important with the rate of growth of the particular town, and that married in-migrants and the children they brought with them (plus those they had once in the town) contributed to that growth out of all proportion to their share of the total in-migration stream, because single in-migrants were much more likely to leave the town again rather than staying.

13 Hochstadt, *Mobility and Modernity*, esp. Ch. 4, shows the continued importance of temporary migration, especially amongst single adults, though his argument for a very high return of such migrants to 'smaller' communities specifically focuses on movement from cities of over 100,000 inhabitants to all smaller settlements.

14 However, we will never know how much of this movement was made up of people moving into and out of the town more than once because the sources do not enable us to identify migrants as individuals. A 50 per cent turnover could mean two distinct acts of in-migation and out-migration by one-quarter of the population.

15 For a good example of the high rate of migration and population turnover, see David Crew, *Town on the Ruhr: a Social History of Bochum 1860–1914* (New York, 1979).

16 Though see note 12 on the disproportionate contribution of married in-migrants to urban growth.

17 In part, however, this was a function of the incorporation of suburbs into the core town.

18 Heilwig Schomerus, *Die Arbeiter der Maschinenfabrik Esslingen* (Stuttgart, 1977). A short version in English of her work is 'The Family Life-Cycle: A Study of Factory Workers in nineteenth-Century Württemberg', in Richard J. Evans and W. R. Lee, eds, *The German Family: Essays on the Social History of the Family in Nineteenth- and Twentieth-Century Germany* (London, 1981), pp. 175–93.

19 I deal with definitional problems later (in Section 6.6). Here one should note that where an increase in the population of a commune from below to above 2000 inhabitants was defined as a shift from a rural to an urban settlement, 'urbanization' was simply a function of population increase. Where the rural/urban definition was legal, not quantitative, and was applied differently between regions, what counted as a 'rural' population in one place might be regarded as an 'urban' population in another.

20 For issues of internal migration and shifts from emigration to immigration, see studies in Klaus J. Bade, ed., *Population, Labour and Migration in Nineteenth- and Twentieth-Century Germany* (New York, 1987).

21 This generalization masks huge variations between towns, linked to type and dating of growth.

22 As argued by Hochstadt, *Mobility and Modernity*, Ch. 4. The distinction between rates and actual numbers is crucial. For example, the rate of in-migration into Berlin fell from 0.17 in 1871 to 0.16 in 1912 (i.e. the total number of in-migrants declined from 17 per cent to 16 per cent of the total population) but the number of in-migrants increased from 133,000 to 337,500. (Hochstadt, *Mobility and Modernity*, p. 126.)

23 There were many 'capitals', i.e. since each German state had a governmental centre. After 1815, the number was drastically reduced to 38. Nevertheless, this still gave the German urban landscape a very different quality from that of national states such as Britain and France.

24 A fine study of small towns in southern Germany is Mack Walker, *German Home Towns: Community, State and General Estate 1648–1871* (London, 1971; repr. with new introduction, 1999). There is little else in English on urban government and patterns of life in this first phase and what follows is a composite portrait drawn from German-language studies. See note 45 for general histories of Germany in English which have good sections on urban life.

25 In addition to Mack Walker, *German Home Towns*, on *Polizei* see Marc Raeff, *The Well-Ordered Police State: Social and Institutional Change through Law in the Germanies and Russia, 1600–1800* (New Haven, 1983). The subject is touched upon in the preceding volume to this by Paul Münch, 'The Growth of the Modern State', in Sheilagh Ogilvie, ed., *Germany: A New Social and Economic History*, Vol. II: *1630–1800* (London, 1996), pp. 196–232 (esp. pp. 208–10).

26 For which see Robert Jutte, 'Poor Relief and Poverty', in Sheilagh Ogilvie, ed., *Germany: A New Social and Economic History*, Vol. II: *1630–1800* (London, 1996), pp. 377–404.

27 See, for example, Richard Evans, 'Family and Class in the Hamburg Grand Bourgeoisie', in David Blackbourn and Richard Evans, eds, *The German Bourgeoisie: Essays on the Social History of the German Middle Class from the Late Eighteenth to the Early Twentieth Century* (London and New York, 1991), pp. 115–39.

28 This is the best term I can think of for those people who belonged to the town but were not citizens of it. In using it I follow others, e.g. Richard Evans in his book *Death in Hamburg: Society and Politics in the Cholera Years 1830–1910* (Oxford, 1987).

29 Fahrmeir, *Citizens and Aliens*, provides a good account of these exclusionary procedures.

30 After 1815 there were four German city-states: Bremen, Frankfurt am Main, Hamburg, and Lübeck.

31 One useful source of evidence on such leisure activity is provided by the licences that entertainers had to purchase from the town authorities to be permitted to perform at markets.

32 Much of what Ernst Schubert describes in his essay 'Daily Life, Consumption and Material Culture', in Sheilagh Ogilvie, ed., *Germany: A New Social and Economic History*, Vol. II: *1630–1800* (London, 1996), pp. 350–76 is relevant to this whole section on urban conditions around 1800.

33 Generally see Charles E. McClelland, *State, Society, and University in Germany, 1700–1914* (Cambridge, 1980). For Hamburg, see the marvellous studies by Percy Ernst Schramm, *Hamburg, Deutschland und die Welt. Leistung und Grenzen hanseatischen Bürgertums in der Zeit zwischen Napoleon I. und Bismarck. Ein Kapitel deutscher Geschichte* (Munich, 1943) and *Neun Generationen; dreihundert Jahre deutscher 'Kulturgeschichte' im Lichte der Schicksale einer Hamburger Bürgerfamilie, 1648–1948*, 2 vols (Göttingen, 1963–64).

34 See the various essays in Elke Kleinau and Claudia Opitz, eds, *Geschichte der Mädchen- und Frauenbildung*, 2 vols (Frankfurt and New York, 1996), especially in Section V of Vol. I ('Frauenbildung in der Spätaufklärung und Umbrüche um 1800') and Section I of Vol. II ('Frauenbildung und demokratische Bewegung (1830–1870)'), although many of these essays depict efforts by small minorities to resist the general neglect of formal schooling for girls. In English, see James Albisetti, *Schooling German Girls and Women: Secondary and Higher Education in the Nineteenth Century* (Princeton, NJ, 1988).

35 On popular education, see Frank-Michael Kuhlemann, *Modernisierung und Disziplinierung: Sozialgeschichte des preußischen Volksschulwesens 1794–1872* (Göttingen, 1992). English-language studies for the first half of the nineteenth century include: Anthony La Vopa, *Prussian Schoolteachers 1763–1848* (Chapel Hill, 1980); Peter Lundgreen, 'Educational Expansion and Economic Growth in Nineteenth-Century Germany', in Lawrence Stone, ed., *Schooling and Society: Studies in the History of Education* (Baltimore, 1976), pp. 20–66; Mary Jo Maynes, *Schooling for the People: Comparative Local Studies of Schooling History in France and Germany, 1750–1850* (New York, 1985); Karl Schleunes, *Schooling and Society: The Politics of Education in Prussia and Bavaria 1750–1900* (Oxford, 1989).

36 In addition to Evans, *Death in Hamburg*, see Mary Lindemann, *Patriots and Paupers: Hamburg, 1712–1830* (Oxford, 1990).

37 On artisans generally, see Friedrich Lenger, *Sozialgeschichte der deutschen Handwerker seit 1800* (Frankfurt am Main, 1988).

38 See Paul Nolte, *Gemeindebürgertum und Liberalismus in Baden, 1800–1850: Tradition, Radikalismus, Republik* (Göttingen, 1994).

39 See Jürgen Kocka, *Weder Stand noch Klasse: Unterschichten um 1800* (Bonn, 1990).

40 A comparison of a map of Frankfurt am Main in 1770 and 1822 demonstrates this dramatically. See Ralf Roth, *Stadt und Bürgertum in Frankfurt am Main* (Munich, 1996), pp. 36, 40.

41 For example, Mannheim and Aachen in 1803; Frankfurt am Main in 1805; Cologne in 1809; Dortmund in 1812. These were intended purely for sociability, and typically had a reading room, a billiard room, a card room, and dining facilities.

42 I tend to agree with those who think they did not, but the historians involved in the 'Stadt und Bürgertum' project argue that they did. See Lothar Gall, ed., *Vom alten zum neuen Bürgertum. Die mitteleuropäische Stadt im Umbruch* (Munich, 1991). This project has produced a marvellous series of books, both collections of essays comparing and contrasting different towns for specific periods and themes (such as the work cited in this note) and monographs (such as the book by Roth cited in the previous note). The series is published by R. Oldenbourg (Munich). There has also been a project on the modern bourgeoisie in Bielefeld which has given rise to a series of books published under the series title 'Bürgertum' by Vandenhoeck and Ruprecht (Göttingen). These tend to focus on problems and themes rather than specific towns as with the 'Stadt und Bürgertum' project. Again the published output has taken the form of both collections of essays and monographs. For a recent evaluation of the results of the project see Peter Lundgreen, ed., *Sozial- und Kulturgeschichte des Bürgertums* (Göttingen, 2000).

43 For the Rhineland see T. C. W. Blanning, *The French Revolution in Germany: Occupation and Resistance in the Rhineland, 1792–1802* (Oxford, 1983) and Jeffry M. Diefendorf, *Businessmen and Politics in the Rhineland, 1789–1834* (Princeton, NJ, 1980).

44 The classic study of this subject is Heinrich Heffter, *Die deutsche Selbstverwaltung im 19. Jahrhundert*, 2nd edn (Stuttgart, 1969).

45 Recent general histories of Germany in English for the nineteenth century which have good sections on urban life include David Blackbourn, *The Fontana History of Germany 1780–1918: The Long Nineteenth Century* (London, 1997); John Breuilly, ed., *Nineteenth-Century Germany: Politics, Culture and Society 1780–1918* (London, 2001); E. D. Brose, *German History 1789–1871* (London, 1997); Thomas Nipperdey, *Germany from Napoleon to Bismarck, 1800–1866* (Princeton, NJ, 1996); James Sheehan, *German History 1770–1866* (Oxford, 1989).

46 On artisans, see Lenger, *Sozialgeschichte der Handwerker*. For the development of different segments of the labour force see, in addition to Chapters 1 and 4 of the present volume, Jürgen Kocka, *Lohnarbeit und Klassenbildung: Arbeiter und Arbeiterbewegung im Deutschland 1800–1875* (Berlin, 1983). A short summary of Kocka's arguments is available in English as 'Problems of Working-Class Formation in Germany: The Early Years, 1800–1875', in Ira Katznelson and Aristide R. Zolberg, eds, *Working-Class Formation: Nineteenth-Century Patterns in Western Europe and the United States* (Princeton, NJ, 1986), pp. 279–351. For the period after 1870, see the contribution by Mary Nolan to the same book, 'Economic Growth, State Policy, and Working-Class Formation in Germany, 1870–1900', pp. 352–93.

47 A study linking the nature of street life to protest in mid-nineteenth-century Germany is Manfred Gailus, *Strasse und Brot: sozialer Protest in den deutschen Staaten unter besonderer Berücksichtigung Preussens, 1847–1849* (Göttingen, 1990).

48 The links between changing patterns of migration and definitions of state membership are considered in Fahrmeir, *Citizens and Aliens*. See also Gosewinkel, *Einbürgern und Ausschliessen*, especially Ch. 2.

49 Mack Walker, *German Home Towns*, conveys this fear very effectively. Hochstadt, *Mobility and Modernity*, makes the vital qualification, certainly for larger and growing towns, that these restrictions were aimed at immigrants seeking to settle down, not migrants moving through. Of course, controls with such intent had to keep track of the temporary migrants in order to make sure they did not succeed in staying should they try to do so.

50 For examples from the Rhineland and Westphalian provinces see Gisela Mettele, *Bürgertum in Köln 1775–1870* (Munich, 1998) and Susanne Kill, *Das Bürgertum in Münster 1770–1870* (Munich, 2001). For southern and western Germany see Frank Möller, *Bürgerliche Herrschaft in Ausgsburg 1790–1880* (Munich, 1998), Thomas Weichel, *Die Bürger von Wiesbaden* (Munich, 1997), Ralf Zerback, *München und sein Stadtbürgertum* (Munich, 1997), and Roth, *Stadt und Bürgertum in Frankfurt*. For how 'modern-minded' men, bourgeois and others, envisaged the future in the first half of the nineteenth century, see Rudolf Boch, *Grenzenloses Wachstum?: das rheinische Wirtschaftsbürgertum und seine Industrialisierungsdebatte 1814–1857* (Göttingen, 1991) and Eric Dorn Brose, *The Politics of Technological Change in Prussia: Out of the Shadow of Antiquity, 1809–1848* (Princeton, NJ, 1993).

51 See James Sheehan, *German Liberalism in the Nineteenth Century* (Chicago, 1978).

52 The novels of Charles Dickens, almost all set mainly in London, were quickly available in popular translations in German. Indeed, the 'Charles Dickens' of Germany was – Charles Dickens!

53 The study by Engels, *Die Lage der arbeitenden Klassen in England, nach eigener Anschauung und authentischen Quellen*, was published in Leipzig in 1845 and had a wide reception. An English translation of what was a study of contemporary Manchester was not published until 1887 under the title of *The Condition of the Working Class in England* and then only in the USA. The first British edition appeared in 1892, long after the death of Marx and only three years before that of Engels. This work by Engels was just one of a number of works published on the continent in the 1830–50 period which depicted Manchester as a modern hell on earth.

54 For changing and varied perceptions of the city see Andrew Lees, *Cities Perceived: Urban Society in European and American Thought, 1820–1940* (Manchester, 1985).

55 The Berlin Police President Hinckeldey in certain respects brought the old policing powers back but concentrated them into the hands of a modern police bureaucracy. Typical was his support of an expanded factory inspectorate but he added to their brief a surveillance of the political opinions of workers. For a detailed study of urban policing following the revolution, see Elaine G. Spencer, *Police and the Social Order: The Düsseldorf District, 1848–1914* (De Kalb, IL, 1992).

56 The best general study of the revolutions is Wolfram Siemann, *The German Revolutions of 1848–1849* (London, 1998).

57 A good recent collection of essays on 1848, including some on urban revolution in Germany, is Dieter Dowe, *et al.* eds, *Europe in 1848: Revolution and Reform* (New York and Oxford, 2001). A fine regional study with much on urban workers during the revolution is Jonathan Sperber, *Rhineland Radicals: The Democratic Movement and the Revolutions of 1848–49* (New Jersey, 1991).

58 For a recent consideration see Berger and Spoerer, 'Economic Crises and the European Revolutions of 1848'.

59 See Evans, *Death in Hamburg*.

60 For such polarization and lack of urban culture see Crew, *Town on the Ruhr*. By contrast, Lothar Gall conveys the sense of a very different set of social relations

and bourgeois sensibility in his study of the Bassermann family of Mannheim in *Bürgertum in Deutschland* (Berlin, 1989).

61 See Chapters 1, 4 and 5 of this volume. Apart from the general histories of nineteenth-century Germany cited earlier, see Theodor Hamerow, *The Social Foundations of German Unification 1858–1871*, Vol. I: *Ideas and Institutions* (Princeton, 1969); Vol. II: *Struggles and Accomplishments* (Princeton, 1972).

62 Hochstadt, *Mobility and Modernity*, p. 201, refers to a 're-agrarianization' of the countryside. See also Chapters 1 and 3.

63 Crew, *Town on the Ruhr*, gives examples.

64 On this subject, apart from the excellent case study by Evans, *Death in Hamburg*, more generally on urban planning see Brian Ladd, *Urban Planning and Civic Order in Germany 1860–1914* (Cambridge, MA, 1990) and Anthony Sutcliffe, *Towards the Planned City: Germany, Britain, the United States and France 1780–1914* (Oxford, 1981). On public health see the recent collection of essays edited by Jörg Vögele and Wolfgang Woelk, *Stadt, Krankheit und Tod. Geschichte der städtischen Gesundheitsverhältnisse während der epidemiologischen Transition* (Berlin, 2000). In English for the later part of the period, see Reinhard Spree, *Health and Social Class in Imperial Germany: A Social History of Mortality, Morbidity, and Inequality* (New York, 1988). See also Chapter 7.

65 See note 35, for literature on popular education in the middle part of the century.

66 On poor relief and social policy see Chapter 7.

67 A good account of liberal dominance of a big city is provided by Jan Palmowski, *Urban Liberalism in Imperial Germany: Frankfurt am Main, 1866–1914* (Oxford, 1999). More generally, see Dieter Langewiesche, *Liberalism in Germany* (London, 2000).

68 I consider these issues in more detail in *Austria, Prussia and Germany 1806–1871* (London, 2002), especially Ch. 8, 'Comparing Austria with Prussia'.

69 There is a vast literature on the German labour and socialist movement, especially for the period after 1871. The studies by Kocka, *Weder Stand noch Klasse* and *Lohnarbeit und Klassenbildung*, form the first two volumes in a series entitled *Geschichte der Arbeiter und der Arbeiterbewegung in Deutschland seit dem Ende des 18. Jahrhunderts*. The period after 1875 is considered in Vol. V by Gerhard A. Ritter and Klaus Tenfelde, *Arbeiter im deutschen Kaiserreich, 1871 bis 1914* (Bonn, 1992). There is no very up-to-date English-language survey, and the bulk of the literature focuses on organized labour and politics, for which see Gary P. Steenson, *'Not One Man! Not One Penny!': German Social Democracy, 1863–1914* (Pittsburgh, 1981) and W. L. Guttsman, *The German Social Democratic Party, 1875–1933: From Ghetto to Government* (London, 1981). For studies with more urban, social-historical concerns see Jonathan Sperber, *Popular Catholicism in Nineteenth-Century Germany* (Princeton, NJ, 1984) and Richard J. Evans, ed., *The German Working Class, 1888–1933: The Politics of Everyday Life* (London, 1982). See also Chapter 9.

70 Palmowski, *Urban Liberalism*, provides a good study of this kind of politics.

71 Births in rural areas continued to exceed deaths but migration took away the additional population.

72 By this is meant the addition made to the big-city population at the time of the extension. It does not take into account the addition made by subsequent population growth in the newly incorporated areas.

73 For a general argument about this special modern advantage of a 'rich mix' I know nothing better or more stimulating than Jane Jacobs, *Cities and the Wealth of Nations: Principles of Economic Life* (New York, 1984). However, I do not know of any study which relates her arguments to the German big city.

74 Generally see John P. McKay, *Tramways and Trolleys. The Rise of Urban Mass Transport in Europe* (Princeton, New Jersey, 1976).

75 Steel girders, concrete, and electric lighting also helped.

76 Matzerath, *Urbanisierung in Preußen*, p. 355.

77 See note 64 above for some English references. See also Karl Heinrich Pohl, 'Power in the City: Liberalism and Local Politics in Dresden and Munich', in James Retallack, ed., *Saxony in German History: Culture, Society and Politics, 1830–1933* (Ann Arbor, 2000), pp. 289–308. Although it only starts at the end of the First World War, a good sense of this kind of big-city government is conveyed in Anthony McElligott, *Contested City: Municipal Politics and the Rise of Nazism in Altona, 1917–1937* (Ann Arbor, 1998). See also his general study, *The German Urban Experience, 1900–1945: Modernity and Crisis* (London, 2001).

78 In addition to the literature on popular education cited in note 35 above, for the Second Empire see Marjorie Lamberti, *State, Society, and the Elementary School in Imperial Germany* (New York, 1989).

79 There was support for parties representing French- and Danish-speakers in Alsace-Lorraine and Schleswig respectively. Most important, however, was separate political representation for Polish-speaking citizens. Polish-speakers made up about 10 per cent of the population of Prussia, the federal state in which they were overwhelmingly concentrated. The population of Prussia was about two-thirds of the whole German population. However, Catholics and Poles tended to be disproportionately settled in rural and small-town areas compared to the population as a whole, whereas the electorate of the Socialist Party was concentrated into the bigger towns. For recent studies relating mass politics, especially elections, to social history see Jonathan Sperber, *The Kaiser's Voters: Electors and Elections in Imperial Germany* (Cambridge, 1997) and Margaret Lavinia Anderson, *Practicing Democracy: Elections and Political Culture in Imperial Germany* (Princeton, NJ, 2000).

80 For the very rich bourgeoisie see Dolores L. Augustine, *Patricians and Parvenus: Wealth and High Society in Wilhelmine Germany* (Oxford, 1994).

81 In addition to the general studies of nineteenth-century Germany cited in note 45, for the political as well as social history of the Wilhelmine period see Volker Berghahn, *Imperial Germany, 1871–1914: Economy, Society, Culture, and Politics* (Providence, 1994) and Wolfgang J. Mommsen, *Imperial Germany 1867–1918: Politics, Culture, and Society in an Authoritarian State* (London, 1995).

82 For Berlin see Gerhard Masur, *Imperial Berlin* (London, 1971).

83 For more examples of such criticisms see Lees, *Cities Perceived*, especially pp. 142–8.

84 Quoted in Alexandra Ritchie, *Faust's Metropolis: A History of Berlin* (London, 1998), p. 188.

85 This was generally the case in big-city societies, for example the rise of the 'Chicago School' of urban sociology in the United States.

86 Lees, *Cities Perceived*, considers these issues. Musil's vast novel, *Der Mann ohne Eigenschaften* (*The Man without Qualities*) is set in Vienna and is perhaps the most penetrating of all literary accounts of the big city. Arguably, Freud, working in Vienna and preoccupied with the anxieties of bourgeois patients, pioneered a theory of modern urban psychology. One can relate such arguments to numerous disciplines.

87 However, what the National Socialists preached and what they practised are two very distinct matters. A modern armaments drive and the demand for industrial labour from around 1936 undermined many of the anti-modern ideals of the movement.

7

Social policy and social welfare in Germany from the mid-nineteenth century to the present

PETER D. STACHURA
University of Stirling

The role and status of the broad field of social policy and public welfare in the modern era has for many years been the subject of intense scholarly discussion, informed by a variety of political, ideological and philosophical perspectives.[1] In Germany's case, these perspectives have been profoundly influenced by the turbulent nature of her historical development, involving, in particular, authoritarian, democratic and totalitarian phases, in which strong regional and local traditions and practices have often also played a significant part in determining the nature, extent and purpose of welfare provision. A constant and central theme of debate has been how and where to establish, within the context of industrial-capitalist society, the parameters of publicly funded state intervention vis-à-vis input from the private, voluntary sector, which embraced, most notably, confessional and liberal-Progressive organizations. In endeavouring to address and alleviate the social ills of the poorer, underprivileged classes in German society, each of these welfare groups pursued its own distinctive agenda, reflecting its particular view of how society should be constructed and what the place of the individual and his or her rights and obligations should be in that society. Consequently, this situation was often a recipe for bitter controversy and confrontation rather than cooperation and harmony among these interested groups. More recently, the debate has been considerably influenced by the Marxist-inspired concept of 'social disciplining', which argues that welfare measures directed by the state and bourgeois reformers at the poorer classes were ultimately a means of exercising social control and imposing discipline.[2]

Until the middle of the nineteenth century, poverty was widely regarded as a reflection of the moral and personal weaknesses of an individual, who thus stood condemned for violating the basic premises of Christian morality and the ethos of bourgeois respectability. Issues such as begging, vagabondage, work-shyness, unemployment, alcoholism, criminality, and delinquency were all regarded in that light. In response, poor-relief measures, which became available only after all personal and familial resources had been fully used, leaving the individual destitute, were kept to the bare minimum and were invariably administered in a demeaning, disciplinary manner. While popular acceptance of the concept of the 'deserving poor' was gaining ground, if somewhat lethargically, before 1848, the predominant attitude was still that no able-bodied person really needed or merited assistance from the public authorities.[3]

7.1 1848–1918: industrialization and its social consequences

Pre-industrial German rural society was already familiar with various social problems, including abject poverty. But new social problems, such as inadequate housing, homelessness, poor health, irregular employment, alienation, and adjustment to a new urban environment, were being created by the increasing if still comparatively modest industrial and commercial development of the period before the revolutions of 1848 (*Vormärz*). These stimulated debate within a restricted circle of observers, who became concerned that the existing means of dealing with social problems were no longer sufficient. One of the most important results was the creation in 1844 in Berlin of the middle-class, liberal-reformist organization, *Der Central-verein für das Wohl der arbeitenden Klassen* (The Central Association for the Welfare of the Working Classes), and in 1848 of the Lutheran *Innere Mission* by Johann Hinrich Wichern.[4] The former sought to provide the spiritual and material resources necessary for distressed persons to regain a place in respectable, bourgeois society, while the latter emphasized the need for a restoration of strict religious observance, family values and respect for authority and the law, as the prerequisites for the recreation of a wholly Christian society.

While these two voluntary initiatives had starkly contrasting answers to the 'social question', they helped to focus attention on poverty and the systems of poor law operating in different German states. In Prussia, for example, poor relief (*Armenpflege*) had been regulated since the end of the eighteenth century by the *Allgemeines Landrecht* (General State Law), by which the needy were given help by local bodies in their place of birth. Reforms were introduced in the early 1840s which took account of population growth and greater social and geographical mobility, trends which were accelerated, of course, by the heightened tempo of industrial-ization in mid-century (discussed in Chapter 4) and the concomitant expansion of the urban-industrial working class (discussed in Chapter 6).[5] The most important new model for the reform of the poor-relief system at that juncture was provided by the burgeoning Prussian industrial town of Elberfeld. The rationalized and decentralized 'Elberfeld system', which was targeted specifically at the deserving poor, became the blueprint throughout Germany for the organization and delivery of poor relief, charity and welfare until the advent of the Weimar Republic, and also encouraged the simultaneous expansion of the voluntary sector. How this system operated was that persons of good standing were invited by the local authority to supervise without remuneration the domestic routine, moral behaviour, and willingness to work of small groups of indigent families.

Following the unification of Germany in 1871, the first evidence appeared of the susceptibility of the welfare issue to politicization and manipulation. In the course of a difficult first decade for Chancellor Otto von Bismarck – involving, for example, economic recession, demands for constitutional reform and the *Kulturkampf* with the Catholic Church – growing numbers of industrial workers gave their support to the united Social Democratic Party (SPD). With a strong Marxist, revolutionary, and internationalist orientation, as its 'Gotha programme' of 1875 indicated, the SPD was quickly identified by Bismarck as a principal 'enemy of the Reich' (*Reichsfeind*). At the same time, the recession of the 1870s (discussed in Chapters 4 and 5) not only undermined the triumphant confidence of the *Gründerzeit*, but also further stimulated awareness of the social problems resulting from rapid industrialization. Laissez-faire attitudes, the basis of German industrial development hitherto, were now subjected to the most rigorous questioning by both government and private welfare sources.

Bismarck's response was twofold: while anti-socialist legislation was enacted with the aim of destroying the SPD, he sought to balance this tough action by introducing a series of social insurance measures covering illness (1883), industrial accident (1884), and old age and disability (1889), though not unemployment. Although this scheme of 'state socialism', with its universal coverage, compulsory participation and income-related contributions and benefits, sought to reform the poor-relief system, Bismarck's main objectives were to entice the industrial working class away from what he described as the 'international poison' of socialism and secure their loyalty to the Reich, and also to encourage the development of a healthier, more integrated workforce to meet the growing demands of German industry.[6]

Bismarck's social insurance measures were innovative in a broader European context and set the standard for others to emulate, but their impact in Germany was strictly limited in both social and political terms. The qualifying criteria for entitlement were demanding and the benefits were, in any case, very modest. Moreover, many categories of worker – in agriculture, domestic service, and small trades – were not included in the scheme. Poverty and subsequent recourse to poor relief still remained an agonizing reality for many among the German working classes. At the same time, the growth of the SPD was actually stimulated by persecution, so that when Bismarck was dismissed from office in 1890, the party had already become the largest in the country.

During the last decades of the century, as discussed in Chapter 4, the processes of industrialization and urbanization further intensified in Germany. The migration of millions of people from the countryside to the towns and cities (discussed in Chapter 6) inevitably added to the range of social ills, including unemployment, inadequate housing and sanitation, poor health and diet, limited educational opportunities, rising crime and juvenile delinquency. They demanded a fundamental reconsideration of the means to combat these problems because earlier notions of self-help and paternalism now seemed quite inappropriate. Poverty and unemployment, in particular, were increasingly understood to be the consequence of broader social and economic circumstances rather than of personal failings. Some observers called for more state intervention, extending the original Bismarckian model, while others believed that the churches and the private voluntary sector could augment their efforts. The contribution to be made by local authorities was also avidly discussed.[7] In any event, welfare provision was being viewed more and more as a way not only of alleviating social ills but also, rather more ambitiously, of redressing inequalities. It was also being emphasized that a balance had to be struck between the rights of citizenship and its responsibilities if stability and progress were to be achieved.

The debate was joined from the 1880s by a number of new social reformist organizations, of which the *Verein für Sozialpolitik* (Association for Social Policy), the *Gesellschaft für Soziale Reform* (Society for Social Reform) and the *Deutscher Verein für Armenpflege und Wohltätigkeit* (German Association for Poor Relief and Charity) were perhaps the most prominent, attracting liberal educationalists, social workers, reformers, and medical personnel. With support from organized political sources such as the Progressive Party, and later, the National Social Movement led by Friedrich Naumann, they adduced what came to be known as the liberal-Progressive *Weltanschauung* on welfare. This was an essentially bourgeois agenda aimed broadly at preserving the family and property as the foundations of society, and in particular at reform of the poor-relief system. Also to the fore was their growing conviction that the social ills of the industrial working class constituted a serious threat to the general health of the nation (*Volkskörper*) and thus to Germany's ability to meet the challenges of an increasingly competitive international arena.[8] The remedy proposed by the liberal-Progressive school, of which Wilhelm Polligkeit was the outstanding spokesman, was 'social relief' (*soziale Fürsorge*), whose aim was to reduce poverty, or eventually even to eliminate it, by addressing its inherent social causes, with priority given to tackling unemployment, bad housing, homelessness, rudimentary working conditions in factories, and criminality. In this way the poor were to be integrated into bourgeois society. From this approach the new profession of social work developed from the 1890s onward, with its own structured programmes of entry, training and qualifications.

A fresh round of welfare legislation in the 1890s by the Reich extended to a limited degree the Bismarckian provision – for example, the Workmen's Protection Act (1891), which regulated hours of work for several categories of worker and introduced measures to improve working conditions in factories. From around the turn of the century, however, public welfare provision noticeably decreased, as the German state focused on other priorities and objectives, including the expansion of its military capability and the pursuit of an ambitious foreign policy (*Weltpolitik*).

Unemployment was regarded as the most disruptive factor in working-class life, though its incidence in the generally booming period before the First World War was relatively modest: about 3 per cent on average between 1890 and 1913. The trades unions could offer a degree of support to their jobless members, the large majority of whom were skilled or semi-skilled. For its part, the SPD remained aloof from these matters, since few of its overwhelmingly skilled constituency experienced unemployment. For unskilled workers, however, unemployment meant real hardship and reliance on poor relief and charity, which, according to the Penal Code of 1871, usually involved a period in a workhouse or some sort of work camp (*Arbeitslager*). The establishment of labour exchanges (*Arbeitsnachweise*) administered by local authorities made it easier for the unemployed to find new jobs, not least by facilitating mobility, and in the first decade of the twentieth century some progress was made towards creating an unemployment insurance scheme based on the so-called 'Gent system', after the Belgian town where it originated. This involved local government supplementing the benefits paid by the trades unions to their unemployed members.[9] A universal scheme did not emerge until after the First World War.

Better health provision became another major concern of welfare agencies in response to evidence that the advance of industrial society was giving rise to diseases such as rickets and tuberculosis, and to high rates of infant mortality, which were beyond the capacity of individuals to address.[10] Social hygiene programmes sought to provide improved maternity facilities in large urban areas, and to ameliorate living and working conditions, especially of working-class children. In fact, there was increasing concern, nurtured by new perspectives relating to adolescence and young adulthood furnished by the new academic disciplines of pedagogy and social anthropology, about the overall situation of urban working-class youth, with particular focus on their conspicuous role in crime and delinquency. The traditional ethos of punishment as the remedy, embodied by the correctional system (*Fürsorgeerziehung* or *Zwangserziehung*), was now challenged by liberal ideas of educational and socialization measures, which resulted in the introduction of juvenile courts, juvenile court assistance programmes (*Jugendgerichtshilfe*), and reforms to the system of guardianship over children.

Such reforms were designed to 'rescue' working-class youths and mould them into orderly, reliable members of society. The *Kulturkritiker* of that era lent weight to this quest by emphasizing that Germany's future lay in the hands of its youth; the emergence in the early 1900s of the independent youth movement, the *Wandervogel*, was perhaps the most arresting manifestation of this view. The churches, also recognizing the importance of the young, had already established a number of organizations, including the *Christliche Verein Jünger Männer* (Christian Association for Young Men, which was Protestant) and the *Verband der katholischer Jünglings-vereinigung Deutschlands* (Federation of Catholic Youth Groups of Germany), and the SPD had followed suit with its own socialist youth association. Complementing this activity was the intervention of the Reich in the first decade of the twentieth century to protect young people from perceived dangers such as alcohol and pornographic literature. Individual German states also passed similar measures, while in 1911 legislation by the Prussian government recognized *Jugendpflege* (care for young people) as a major concern. Critics, however, regarded this intervention as having been motivated primarily by a desire to combat the spread of socialism among young workers.[11]

The increasingly well-organized and important liberal-Progressive school in the field of welfare was not, however, universally welcomed. The long-established confessional welfare organizations, in particular, were discomfited by its growing confidence, vitality and intellectual pace-setting, as well as by its support for more state intervention. While the *Innere Mission* had been the leading Protestant welfare organization since the 1840s, the Catholic contribution remained somewhat fragmented, albeit based on a reasonably firm ethical and moral understanding of 'social justice', until the creation in 1897 of the *Deutscher Caritasverband*. This was the clearest sign to date that the Catholic Church had finally acknowledged that the multifarious problems generated by a rapidly evolving urban, industrial society, for which the numerous Catholic populations in areas such as the Ruhr and Silesia provided evidence, demanded a much better organized and resourced response. The new initiative may also have been prompted by the feelings of isolation and insecurity experienced by the German Catholic Church in the aftermath of the *Kulturkampf*, giving rise to a certain intro-spectiveness, which has often been termed 'a ghetto mentality'. Although the Catholic *Caritasverband* shared important common ground with the Protestant *Innere Mission*, including a deep sense of morality and a powerful commitment to the ideas and practices of social conservatism, it succeeded in marking out in the welfare field a positive and distinctively Catholic presence.

All of these developments meant that during the last quarter of the nineteenth century the entire field of welfare had become far more complex and demanding than at any previous period, with palpable tensions among the different and, as was by then the case, competing welfare organizations. There was particular tension between the confessional and liberal-Progressive types, in view of their often very different expectations of what the provision of welfare was actually designed to achieve. To the centre of debate had also arrived the contentious issue of the nature and scope of state intervention balanced against the private, voluntary sector. Although these fundamental issues had by no means been resolved by 1914, they had been more clearly defined and were to be shaped further by the prodigious impact of the First World War.

The unanticipated length of the war and the necessary mass mobilization of the population for service in the trenches and on the 'home front' produced a series of significant and enduring changes in the fabric of German society which had implications for social policy and the provision of welfare. The large-scale employment of women and younger people in industries geared to war production alone immediately added to prewar social problems in a number of ways. Against a backdrop of governmental economizing, which included welfare cuts, the inevitable strains on and disruption of family life, the vast increase in deprivation, the spread of hunger (especially in the 'turnip winter' of 1916–17), the emergence of numerous war-disabled, widows and orphans, and working-class dis-content, especially among the young, combined to convince all parties concerned of the need for new initiatives in social welfare.[12] In addition, the government could not simply rely on propaganda to ensure the maintenance of public morale, however intense and efficaciously delivered. Propaganda had to be complemented by tangible, material help. Accordingly, and despite the unprecedented pressures on the poor-relief system, the Reich and state authorities found the means to give financial assistance to the families of servicemen (*Kriegsfamilienunterstützung*), while local governments provided supplementary welfare measures as best they could. It was hoped that the voluntary welfare groups would be able to make up any shortfalls. In addition, the National Auxiliary Service Law (*Vaterländische Hilfsdienst-gesetz*) of 1916 accorded trades unions official status as bargaining partners, in return for the right to direct labour as the government deemed appro-priate to the war effort.[13]

The overall situation was bound to intensify the debate concerning the respective roles of the state and the private sector, and the division of labour among the welfare organizations themselves. As the war dragged on and conditions on the home front deteriorated under the strain, a consensus was formed in support of the state's assumption of more responsibility for welfare provision. The enormity of the 'social question' really left no other viable alternative, though it still left open the equally difficult questions of how the public sector's contribution was to be rationalized and regulated, and also what this would mean for the future place of the private sector. Even if Germany had won the war and the Kaiserreich had continued, these matters would not easily have been resolved. The fact that they were to be addressed following Germany's defeat and collapse by a new system of government, the parliamentary democracy of the Weimar Republic, closed off certain options available only to an authoritarian regime but at the same time opened up a number of possibilities for a fresh approach.

7.2 1918–33: the rise and fall of the *Sozialstaat*

Indispensable to an understanding of the basis on which the early govern-ments of the Republic formulated their approach to social policy and welfare is an appreciation of the new political realities, above all the commanding influence in the early years of the so-called 'Weimar Coalition' parties, the SPD, the Centre Party (*Zentrum*), and the German Democratic Party (DDP). Before 1914, the SPD and the Centre (to a lesser extent) were political pariahs, in so far as they represented constituencies, the industrial working class and the Catholic population respectively, which were held in some suspicion and fear by the conservative establishment. But after 1918, they both occupied pivotal political and governmental roles in the new state, and were joined by the successors of the prewar Progressive Liberals. Moreover, all three parties were committed, albeit often for different reasons, to substantial state welfare provision. Two overarching considerations united them in the early postwar years amidst the extreme economic, social, and political instability caused by war, revolution, and the Treaty of Versailles.

First, the Republic, in response to the social problems occasioned by the war and its aftermath, was concerned to promote its reputation and acceptability in the country by pursuing a demonstrably humanitarian course in welfare for the good of the German people, in the interests of social justice, and for the regeneration of the Reich. Second, it was believed that a substantial programme of state welfare would serve an equally important political purpose, in that, following the Bismarckian pattern, it would attract the support and loyalty of the bulk of the working class, the principal recipient and beneficiary of state welfare, to the democratic order. The competition for working-class support which the SPD faced from the Independent Social Democratic Party (USPD) and the Communist Party (KPD) could only add vigour and urgency to this strategy, whose bold aim was nothing less than the construction of a veritable *Sozialstaat* (welfare state), the first in German history, in order to prevent further working-class radicalism and thus to enhance the Republic's credibility with the workers.[14]

In this endeavour, these parties also enjoyed the broad support of the voluntary sector, particularly the liberal-Progressives, who sought a more sweeping reconstruction of society that would destroy what remained of the old authoritarian state. Grouped under the umbrella organization, the *Deutscher Verein für öffentliche und private Fürsorge* (German Association for Public and Private Welfare), they were instrumental in introducing to the ongoing debate – which revolved around unemployment, the disabled, youth, widows, orphans, and pensioners – a range of related issues, such as family policy, eugenics, and the role of women and sexuality.[15] They sometimes found an ally in the newly created socialist organization, the *Arbeiterwohlfahrt*, though the confessional welfare groups, still headed by the *Caritasverband* and *Innere Mission*, were as determined as ever to preserve a spiritual-religious dimension.[16]

The first decisive steps towards the realization of this aim were the Stinnes-Legien Agreement in November 1918, heralding a new era of cooperation in industry between employers and workers, and the promulgation in 1919 of the Constitution, much of which bore the unmistakable imprint of the 'Weimar Coalition' parties. The Constitution contained many guarantees of social rights which, in turn, put in place the wider framework for later welfare legislation. For instance, Articles 7 and 9 made the Reich government responsible for poor relief, public health, maternity protection, population policy, youth welfare, and labour law, while Article 161 added a commitment to the creation of a comprehensive social insurance policy. Article 163 embodied the right of every German to work, or to be provided for in the event of involuntary unemployment. Further articles extended workers' protection and granted legal status to trades unions for the first time, allowing them to organize and negotiate wage agreements with employers through collective bargaining machinery. More improvements for the workers came through the Factory Councils Act of 1920, which created factory councils in which both sides of industry were represented. Specifically buttressing this was the establishment in 1923 of a state arbitration system under the supervision of the Reich Ministry of Labour to resolve disputes over wages and conditions.

Already before the hyperinflation crisis of 1923, and in defiance of the most unpropitious economic and political conditions, the Republic was able to lay down the embryo of what was subsequently to develop as the *Sozialstaat*. Legislation on unemployment benefits, labour exchanges, the eight-hour day, rent levels, healthcare, medical and dental provision in schools, and new housing projects paved the way, while the Juvenile Courts Law of 1923 (*Jugendgerichtsgesetz*) and the National Youth Welfare Act (*Reichsjugendwohlfahrtsgesetz, RJWG*) of 1922 were outstanding achievements. Recognizing that younger people had their own specific needs and interests, which the state had a responsibility to protect and advance, the *RJWG* provided a comprehensive range of benefits, including vocational training facilities, which began to be implemented in 1924.[17] Older workers also witnessed a narrowing of wage differentials vis-à-vis white-collar occupations, a factor in a broader redistribution of wealth in the early 1920s which resulted in rising real income levels among the working class, as discussed in Chapter 9. A significant exception to this overall positive trend was the republic's failure to restore the social insurance system and the pensions whose financial bases had been destroyed by the enormous costs and inflationary pressures of the war.[18]

All these social welfare measures showed the working class, in particular, that Germany now at long last had a state with a genuine sympathy for workers' situation, even if this still included widespread poverty, low standards of health (as discussed in Chapter 12), and serious levels of crime. It was surely no coincidence, therefore, that the workers' trades union movement played the crucial role in defeating the right-wing Kapp Putsch in 1920, or that the anti-democratic, anti-republican KPD was able in these early years to attract only a small minority of workers to its cause. Similarly, in 1923, one of the principal factors which allowed the Republic to stay afloat in the midst of intense adversity was the continued support of most of the working class. For them, the Republic was perceived to be on their side, not least because of its welfare provision on their behalf.[19]

During the relatively stable years of the mid-1920s, the *Sozialstaat* was extended further, despite the voluntary but misguided withdrawal of the SPD from participation in central government, and the continuing conflict among the various welfare groups about the content and purpose of welfare. The SPD regarded welfare as a vital stepping-stone to an ultimate socialist state, the confessional organizations sought to develop it within a Christian ethos, and the liberal-Progressives increasingly promoted secularism as a vital component of a truly democratic society.[20] In the middle stood the Reich Ministry of Labour, the agency with primary responsibility for ensuring the effective implementation of welfare legislation, in partnership with welfare or labour ministries set up by the individual German states. The Reich Ministry was led by two committed and forceful proponents of state welfare, Heinrich Brauns of the Centre Party, from 1920 until 1928, and the Social Democrat Rudolf Wissell during the period of the 'Grand Coalition' government (1928–30).[21] Also involved were a number of officially accredited organizations, including the main confessional groups, the Red Cross, and the *Arbeiterwohlfahrt*, which were grouped together in the umbrella organization, the *Deutsche Liga für freien Wohlfahrtspflege* (German League for Voluntary Welfare). There was also increasing dependence on the expanding number of professionally qualified social workers, though by the end of the 1920s many of them were becoming disillusioned by the ponderous bureaucracy and perennial in-fighting that had by then become all too common features of Weimar's welfare sphere.

Significant legislative landmarks were achieved, nonetheless, notably the National Social Welfare Law (*Reichsfürsorgepflicht-Verordnung*, RFV) in 1924, the National Basic Guidelines for the Determination, Form and Scope of Public Welfare, also in 1924, the Labour Courts Act (*Arbeitsgerichtsgesetz*) in 1926, the Working Hours Act (*Arbeitszeitgesetz*) in 1927, and the same year, arguably the crowning piece of the entire *Sozialstaat*, the Law on

Labour Exchanges and Unemployment Insurance (*Gesetz über Arbeits-vermittlung und Arbeitsversicherung, AVAVG*).[22] By abolishing means-testing, this piece of legislation enshrined the legal right of the unemployed to state benefit, subject to certain qualifying criteria. Some 17 million workers were covered, but not those in agriculture, fishing, forestry, and a few other categories. Further legislation which was designed by government to protect younger people – for instance, banning the sale of pornographic literature to juveniles and establishing a state-funded censorship office – was also passed in the mid-1920s.

In addition, in the healthier financial climate created by the introduction of a new currency (the *Rentenmark*) and adjustments to reparations payments (the Dawes Plan), welfare expenditure by the state increased by 25 per cent between 1925 and 1928, real wages went up appreciably, and a whole range of new and improved civic and social amenities was established. State education and public housing enjoyed significant investment. As discussed in Chapter 11, the cause of female emancipation, which was prosecuted by a string of women's groups, also recorded some useful improvements in relation to women's status in the labour market, maternity facilities, and opportunities in higher education and the professions. Much remained to be done for women to reach anything near equality with men, but at least a commendable start had been made. There were, of course, still many other serious social and economic problems to be resolved. Unemployment, for example, was high at certain junctures in the mid-1920s as a result of the rationalization process in industry, population growth, and the expansion of cheap female labour, and the spectre of long-term joblessness had appeared. Unsurprisingly, therefore, the unemployment insurance system was coming under considerable financial pressure some time before the onset of the Depression.

By 1929, nonetheless, the *Sozialstaat* had made impressive advances, which also considerably helped the Republic to put down firmer roots than had seemed possible only a few years earlier. The SPD, the principal driving force behind both institutions, was able to consolidate its status as the leading party as a result of the Reichstag elections in 1928, when it won some 30 per cent of the votes. The permanence of these achievements was not guaranteed, of course, and many problems and tensions remained in the welfare and broader economic and political spheres. Ominously, employers and other groups on the conservative Right, in particular, deeply resented the development of the *Sozialstaat*, because it exemplified for them the anti-capitalist and pro-working-class ethos of the Republic. They claimed that it was mainly their money, in the form of high taxes and profits, which financed welfare.[23]

The comprehensive devastation visited on Germany by the Depression changed everything, specifically by creating mass unemployment – 6 million registered, plus another 2 million or more 'invisibles' by 1932 – and its severe, diverse ramifications. The rigid deflationary policies of the government headed by Heinrich Brüning, involving drastic reductions in public expenditure, wage and salary cuts and higher taxes, and the unprecedented instability which permitted both National Socialism and Communism to flourish, had virtually destroyed the *Sozialstaat* by 1932, including, most notably, the unemployment insurance system.[24] The imposition of progressively tougher qualifying criteria for benefit entitlement, which effectively led to the restoration of means-testing, the repeated scaling down of the level of benefits to the point where they barely afforded meagre subsistence, and the eventual recourse which more and more unemployed had to make to charity, all combined to render the system a pale, discredited imitation of what it had once been. The immiseration of the industrial working class reached a new nadir, and large numbers of middle-class white-collar workers and professionals experienced the long-dreaded humiliation of being, as they saw it, 'pushed down' to the ranks of the proletariat, in terms of income, social status, and self-esteem. Unemployment, poverty, malnutrition, falling health standards, family break-ups, begging and vagabondage were widespread, and threw millions onto poor relief and charity. Employers held the upper hand over labour and wasted no time in exploiting their advantage. Those still fortunate enough to have jobs faced deteriorating wage rates for increased working hours and the ever-present threat of summary dismissal.

Just as state welfare had paid important political dividends for the Republic in the 1920s, so the disintegration of the *Sozialstaat* had disastrous implications for it in the early 1930s. Above all, the working-class support for the Republic, which had been so crucial at certain periods in the past, now either ebbed away or sank into passive disillusionment, which the emasculated SPD and trades unions were impotent to prevent. Alongside its policy of 'toleration' towards the Brüning administration, the SPD, the dominant party in many local councils, especially in Prussia, had no option but to implement the welfare cuts. Neither it nor the trades unions produced a viable policy for alleviating unemployment. The Republic collapsed in 1933 for many reasons, but among the most important was arguably the failure of the *Sozialstaat*, earlier a powerful symbol of democratic, progressive achievement, and then also of its demise.[25]

In keeping with the overall rightward political drift in the Republic during these last years, all the main welfare organizations put forward new, increasingly anti-democratic and authoritarian strategies. The very legitimacy of state welfare provision was vigorously challenged, even by the liberal-Progressive lobby, as the voluntary sector sought to regain the initiative. Right-wing political parties, paramilitary groups, employers and others on the Right all gave their support to an agenda which, in view of the political dénouement of the crisis, the advent to power of Adolf Hitler and his National Socialist Party, could only signal the termination of the conceptual and practical basis of the *Sozialstaat*, and also, indeed, of the voluntary sector, at least as constituted hitherto. A basic humanitarianism and a commitment to social justice were soon to be replaced by a ruthless agenda of political and racist expediency.

7.3 1933–45: from *Sozialstaat* to National Socialism

The flexibility of its ideology and its propaganda had allowed the Nazi Party to develop in the early 1930s as a genuine *Volkspartei* on the basis of varying degrees of support from most major sectors of the German electorate and population.[26] Besides its emphasis on nationalism, authoritarianism, anti-Marxism, racism, and anti-Semitism, the party projected the concept of a *Volksgemeinschaft*, a national community of Aryan Germans, as the. blueprint of a new and superior German society under its rule. The allegedly class-ridden, privileged, and unequal society of the Weimar era was to be replaced by a pseudo-egalitarian, meritocratic, and racist society which would be the indispensable foundation for the resurrection and long-term future of the Fatherland. For the Nazis, the *Sozialstaat* had been a product of that discredited type of society, though they were convinced that state-sponsored welfare of a different character had a vital role to play in the development of the Third Reich, not least in relation to its far-reaching efforts to exert totalitarian political and social control.

Before the *Machtergreifung*, the Nazi Party had attracted most of its support from the middle and upper classes, though by 1932 it had also succeeded in winning more and more support from the working class. Once in power, the party was especially anxious to extend its appeal in that constituency. It believed that the workers had been misled and manipulated by evil influences, above all, the left-wing parties and the trades unions, and had consequently abandoned nationalism or patriotism for internationalism, Socialism, and Marxism. This is how the Nazis explained working-class support for the November Revolution and the collapse of the Kaiserreich, and they resolved not to allow such circumstances to prevail again. The workers had to be brought back into the fold, as it were, and given the same opportunities as other classes to serve the nation. Towards that aim, the Nazis rightly concluded that a restoration of the workers' material situation was an essential first step, with welfare provision of various kinds an indispensable part of the appeal. On the other hand, many sections of the working class, reduced to despair and penury by the Depression and having largely abandoned their previous strong allegiance to parliamentary democracy and left-wing ideology, were susceptible after 1933 to the blandishments of the Nazis. Only the radical minority of workers who had supported Communism and the shrinking numbers who continued to put their trust in the SPD were initially immune. Over time, however, even many of them came to accept the new political prescription, at least passively.[27]

In short, from 1933 on, the regime, like the early Weimar Republic, brought into play, behind the provision of welfare, fundamental imperatives other than the most obvious and straightforward, the humanitarian motive. For the Hitler-centred, authoritarian regime of the Third Reich (*Führerstaat*), political and racist imperatives were undoubtedly the most important of all, for they determined the framework and the substance of social policy in general and of welfare provision in particular. In practice, this meant a 'carrot-and-stick' approach, broadly not dissimilar in this regard to that adopted by Bismarck in the 1880s. Thus, the immediate political subordination of the working class was secured by the brutal destruction in 1933 of the SPD, the KPD, and the trades unions, and by subsequent measures such as the National Labour Law of 1934, which imposed tight controls on conditions of employment and freedom of movement. The German Labour Front (DAF), into which the workers were compulsorily organized, ensured their conformity, even regimentation, while the workers, like everyone else in Germany, also became subject to the scrutiny of the police state, as embodied by the power of both the Gestapo and the SS. The racial component took shape around the notion that only Aryans were to benefit, meaning the exclusion of 'undesirables' such as Jews and Roma, and it encompassed programmes of compulsory sterilization and euthanasia for the mentally and physically disabled.

The most urgent socioeconomic task facing the regime in this respect in 1933 was to address the scourge of mass unemployment, which had fallen on the working class most of all. Before 1933, in their strident propaganda the Nazis had stressed the importance of restoring 'work and bread', although they had not developed a coherent programme of job creation. During the next three or four years, however, through a series of mainly deficit-financed initiatives, including the introduction of a massive programme of public works (the 'Reinhardt Programme'), compulsory Labour Service (*Reichsarbeitsdienst*), military conscription, rearmament, and tax and credit inducements to private industry, unemployment was reduced to the point where virtually only the physically and mentally disabled and the work-shy were without jobs. After 1936–37, there was even a shortage of, especially, skilled labour.[28] Even though wage levels were often hardly better than poor relief or charity rates, at least many workers regained the self-respect and independence which the Depression had destroyed.

The material condition of the working class was improved further by the activities of new organizations such as *Kraft durch Freude* ('Strength through Joy') and *Schönheit der Arbeit* ('Beauty of Labour'), which provided, respectively, holidays and recreational facilities, and healthier, more cheerful working conditions in factories and other places of work. The main welfare organization, the *Nationalsozialistiche Volkswohlfahrt* (National Socialist People's Welfare), oversaw a range of welfare measures for the population as a whole.[29] Medical and vocational education services for youth were soon restored to their pre-Depression levels, and a programme of slum clearance in major cities was started. The putative egalitarianism of the *Volksgemeinschaft* was supposed to be further underlined by the creation of the *Winterhilfe* (Winter Aid) and *Eintopfessen* (One-Pot-Meals) campaigns. Through all these measures, the regime maintained a steady stream of propaganda, praising the workers and emphasizing their important role as part of the national community in the new Germany.

The Nazi Party and its ancillary organizations, such as the Hitler Youth and the Stormtroopers (SA), were able to attract more and more working-class members, and not merely as a result of intimidation and coercive measures such as the Hitler Youth Law of 1936. By 1939, organized working-class resistance to the Nazis had almost completely disappeared, and a majority of workers, impressed and encouraged by Hitler's domestic and foreign 'successes', had been transformed into active or at least passive supporters. Hence, the regime claimed with considerable justification to have realized its primary objective in the welfare field.

The racist and totalitarian dynamics of National Socialism meant that after 1933 there was not to be a meaningful role in welfare for the surviving confessional and liberal-Progressive organizations. The privatization of welfare services which they had advocated in the early 1930s was never likely to be permitted by the Nazis, whose real link with the past was with those who were involved in eugenics and social anthropology, and who therefore often contributed to theories of racial superiority which the Nazis found congenial. Many of the pre-1933 voluntary groups either fell victim to the process of *Gleichschaltung* (enforced conformity) – incorporation into Nazi organizations – or were forced out of business altogether. The Catholic groups received some protection for a time under the terms of the Nazi–Vatican Concordat of 1933, but their input had been much diminished by 1939. A number of Protestant groups, which found little difficulty in adapting their own authoritarian, nationalist, and racist outlook to the new reality, were also consigned to a limited role.

By the outbreak of the Second World War, the wide-ranging nazification of German society had reduced social welfare policy to the status of a subordinate servant of the omnipotent state. Despite this, the concept of a 'national community' lacked substantive meaning by 1939, and not simply because it automatically excluded so-called 'deviant' groups, such as Jews (formally through the Nuremberg Race Laws of 1935), Roma and homosexuals. After only six years, German society was still informed to a large extent by the class divisions and attitudes inherited from the Weimar era. The social revolution envisaged by the *Volksgemeinschaft* would require a much longer period to mature fully. If a 'national community' did exist, therefore, then it was an embryonic entity, although it might have had a psychological, morale-boosting impact on an otherwise depressed population. On the other hand, perhaps the concept remained stillborn, and only possessed a semantic meaning in the world of Nazi propaganda.[30]

The upheaval occasioned by the Second World War, particularly as it broadened in scope in response to Hitler's expansionism, had no historical precedent, so that any social policy was bound to undergo major change. At the core of the Third Reich's approach was its determination to maintain as far as possible the morale of both the home and the military fronts as a vital prerequisite to final victory. This was strikingly illustrated during the earliest months of the war, when measures by the regime to increase revenue through wage restraint, higher taxes, and the closure of businesses and services deemed superfluous to the war effort met with such popular opposition that Hitler quickly ordered their partial withdrawal. Every effort was made to ensure that living standards, including social welfare provision, were kept at a high level.[31] In any case, during the period of successive victories by the Wehrmacht, from the invasion of Poland until after the attack on the Soviet Union in 1941, it was relatively easy for ordinary Germans to put up with the unavoidable petty inconveniences of wartime. Sporadic, unorganized grumbling about food and clothing rationing, and about the disruption to family and community life caused by military exigencies, did not cause undue concern.

Nonetheless, in a further effort to ensure good morale, the leader of the Institute for Labour Research (*Arbeitswissenschaftliches Institut*) of the German Labour Front, Dr Robert Ley, devised in the autumn of 1940 a very ambitious reform plan for the postwar period that included measures for better social insurance, wages and healthcare, as well as a comprehensive house-building programme. While little of the plan eventually materialized, due to opposition from some of Ley's colleagues, financial constraints, and, of course, Germany's ultimate defeat, the episode does reveal, if nothing else, the acute sensitivity of the regime to the question of morale and loyalty, particularly where it concerned the industrial working class, as already noted for the 1933–39 period. It is largely in the same light, and not necessarily for ideological reasons, therefore, that the regime's hesitation about mobilizing women workers for war production, and the postpone-ment until 1944 of measures for 'total war', should be understood. Major priority was given, though with limited success, to maintaining relatively high living standards throughout the war.[32] Consequently, and with due regard for the increasingly coercive domestic role of the SS, it cannot be said that the working class or anyone else was not generally supportive of the Reich's war effort. In 1944–45, of course, morale did begin to break down in the face of imminent catastrophe.

As the war became total and demands increased for more and more sacrifices, however, the strains on Nazi social policy and welfare increased dramatically, although in a few spheres, notably family policy, traditional structures were maintained quite effectively.[33] But the drain on manpower for war production and military service was only partially offset by the use of forced labour and compulsory drafting in countries under Nazi control. The increasingly widespread and effective Allied bombing campaign produced a housing crisis the regime was unable to solve. Food and other material shortages grew, despite the wholesale exploitation of the resources of conquered countries. The flight of millions of refugees from the East as the Red Army advanced was yet another of the developments which conspired to reduce most areas of state welfare provision by 1944/5 to a rudimentary condition. Consequently, deprivation and destitution of a type not witnessed even during the worst days of the Depression became the norm for almost all sections of the German population, with the conspicuous exception of the small farmers.

To what extent National Socialism, especially in wartime, unwittingly promoted a 'modernization' of German society is highly debatable.[34] National Socialism had always incorporated elements of the reactionary and the progressive, the revolutionary and the counter-revolutionary, the modern and the traditional, the radical and the conservative. The concept and limited implementation of the racial dynamics of the 'national community' arguably set in train a levelling-down process which was accelerated during the war through changes to the structure of the labour market, consumer choice, and mobility, so that in 1945 German society was less class-based and more egalitarian than it had been 12 years previously. Moreover, it may be said that the sheer scale and intensity of the war itself largely destroyed the traditions and ethos of the old Germany while laying the basis for a new one in 'Year Zero' (*Stunde Null*). Accordingly, as discussed in Chapter 9, society in West Germany after the war was more socially fluid, less tradition-bound and more forward-looking than at any previous time in German history.

7.4 1945–90: social policy in divided Germany

During the early postwar years, a defeated, occupied and devastated Germany hardly functioned as a normal state, and social policy and welfare amounted to little more than an attempt by the victorious Allies to provide the basic amenities of food and shelter. The chaos, which was exacerbated by the influx of some 9 million expellees and refugees from the East, reflected the unprecedented catastrophe that had befallen the country. Malnutrition, disease, cold, and black-marketeering were endemic. In the Soviet Zone of Occupation (*Sowjetische Besatzungszone, SBZ*), where a ruthless policy of confiscation, exploitation and sheer pillage was immediately set in motion, conditions were even worse. By the late 1950s, the private sector in industry, commerce and agriculture had been all but eliminated in the Soviet Zone in favour of nationalization and collectivization.

As the Cold War unfolded, a process underlined by the crisis over Berlin in 1948, the first decisive steps were taken in West Germany towards economic, social and political reconstruction. While it is true that basic infrastructure and important industries such as steel, chemicals, textiles, and machine-making had not been as badly damaged as had at first been thought, the currency reform which established the Deutschmark, the launching of the Marshall Aid programme, and the implementation of Ludwig Erhard's social market philosophy (*Sozialmarktwirtschaft*) provided the essential platform for recovery and what soon came to be known as the German 'economic miracle' (*Wirtschaftswunder*).[35] Other factors such as the revival in world trade and a concomitant demand for high-quality German exports, a highly trained and willing labour force which later had to be supplemented by millions of foreign workers (*Gastarbeiter*), the agreement of the Allies to relax economic controls, and freedom from military expenditure until the mid-1950s, combined to inaugurate a period of rising and impressive growth, full employment and prosperity in the newly created Federal Republic of Germany, lasting until the onset of world-wide recession in 1973–74.[36]

Besides advocating enterprise and competition as the key to economic success, Erhard's philosophy also recognized the state's responsibility to protect both consumers and the population at large in the interests of social justice and civic stability. This was consistent with a view throughout Europe at that time in favour of the idea of a welfare state, though what developed in West Germany in the short term was not as generous or as far-reaching as in Britain. For example, there was not a National Health Service as there was in Britain. Nonetheless, the Germans had an appalling wartime legacy to deal with, and a spectacular start was made with a necessary programme of house-building in partnership with the private sector which produced some four million new homes by the mid-1950s.[37] Tight rental controls and tenants' rights complemented this exercise. Moreover, millions of war victims of one kind or another received considerable support through the War Victims' Relief Fund (*Kriegsopferversorgung*) and the law on the 'equalization of burdens' (*Lastenausgleichgesetz*, 1952) which, through taxation measures, redistributed a certain degree of wealth from the better-off to the war-ravaged, poorer groups in German society. Over time, also, the constructive policy of cooperation between both sides of industry (*Mitbestimmung*) was sustained by full employment, rising wage levels, low prices, and more educational opportunities.

Arguably the most significant social welfare reform of the postwar era in West Germany was the introduction in 1957 of the so-called 'dynamic pension', which index-linked the level of old-age pensions to wages and salaries. Consequently, the value of pensions rose by over 50 per cent between 1957 and 1965, thus finally allowing pensioners, an expanding proportion of the population, to enjoy the fruits of the economic boom. Provision in other areas such as unemployment benefit and health insurance was also increasingly generous, and the system of public assistance (*Sozialhilfe*) was reformed in 1963 to give individuals in need the legal right to assistance from local authorities. Remarkably, by the early 1960s, West Germans enjoyed, in terms of rising wages, price stability, disposable income levels, and working hours, the highest standard of living in Europe, with the exception of Scandinavians. In a broader historical perspective, the same decade witnessed the realization through massive public expenditure of the welfare concepts of the Weimar Republic – the creation, at last, of a secure, high-quality *Sozialstaat*. This was consolidated during the chancellorship of Willy Brandt (1969–74), when further reforms enhanced the material and legal status of workers, tenants, and women.[38]

On the other hand, in what was then the German Democratic Republic, welfare provision not only was qualitatively inferior, but existed as part of a political and ideological system which was in many respects as corrupt and nefarious as that of the Third Reich. In that totalitarian, subservient Communist state, the individual's needs were of secondary importance to the imperatives of power, control and surveillance. The perennial obsession with cost-cutting was only temporarily halted in 1953 in response to the East Berlin workers' revolt, and again in 1971, with what was the most noteworthy development in provision, the adoption of a subsidy programme – dubbed 'welfare socialism' – which helped make consumer goods, albeit of generally poor quality, more widely available at low prices.[39] A few genuine advances, including the provision of crèches, sports facilities, and work for all, undeniably took place, but they all came with a political and ideological price-tag within an alien and largely unpopular system.

The oil crisis in the early 1970s, which coincided with worrying demographic trends, especially the large increase in the numbers of retired elderly people, produced a conspicuous downturn in the economies of the industrialized West. In West Germany, as in most other European countries, these events in turn gave rise to a debate about the future of state welfare and social policy, particularly as these were now far more expensive to maintain.[40] Raising taxes to meet increasing costs was generally considered to be politically unacceptable, while from the 'new Right', state welfare was shrilly denounced for being not only too expensive, but also undesirable because it allegedly promoted an economically and socially unhealthy 'dependence culture'. Free enterprise, deregulation, competition, and personal responsibility were seen as the only basis for future prosperity. In West Germany, this debate was perhaps never as vigorous as in some other countries, including Britain and the United States, for a solid consensus in favour of state welfare had been built up across all political parties and classes. It would have been political suicide for any German government to have proposed drastic changes. The only real disagreement, in fact, concerned priorities and the future rate of welfare expansion.

Although a policy of modest retrenchment was introduced by the government of Helmut Schmidt in the late 1970s and early 1980s, the welfare system was merely scaled down to a limited extent. When Helmut Kohl took over as Chancellor in 1982, even the persistent high level of unemployment (over 2 million) was not allowed to disturb unduly the evolution of the welfare system, in sharp contrast to the situation in Thatcher's Britain and Reagan's United States, where wholesale cuts were at least proclaimed to be the order of the day. Indeed, Kohl's administration to some extent improved the status of the family and rights of women through a series of legal and financial measures, thus further enhancing a quality of life that was the envy of most European countries.

As the East German economy lurched from one crisis to another during the 1980s, the Federal Republic remained sufficiently strong and well prepared to seize the opportunity, in October 1990, to realize the long-standing dream of German reunification, a goal to which Kohl had long held a deep personal commitment. The general well-being of its citizens, nurtured by a well-endowed, successful state welfare system, furnished the sharpest possible contrast with the relative poverty of its soon-to-be fellow-citizens in the eastern part of the country. An inherently buoyant western-style capitalism had triumphed incontrovertibly over a Soviet-imposed, comprehensively sterile, and discredited Communism. One of the principal challenges facing the latest version of a 'new' Germany in the final decade of the twentieth century was, therefore, to extend the former West Germany's state welfare to all its citizens. Some progress has already been made in that direction.

Over a period of about 150 years, the nature of social policy and welfare in Germany underwent as many changes as the country itself. Perhaps the most significant was the development of the role of the state as the principal provider, thus reversing its relationship with the voluntary sector of the pre-industrial and early industrial era in many parts of the country, especially in the North and South. With Bismarckian 'state socialism' as example and encouragement, the Weimar *Sozialstaat* represented in many ways the culmination of trends from the nineteenth century, but regrettably proved to be ephemeral amidst economic and political crises of unprecedented scope and severity. In the Third Reich, the state's role reached a macabre apotheosis, driven by totalitarian and racist intolerance, echoes of which resonated in the postwar Communist system of the German Democratic Republic. On the other hand, the democratic Federal Republic eventually brought to permanent and full fruition much of the welfare vision of the Weimar Republic, the basis – and at the same time a reflection – of the most stable and prosperous epoch in modern German history. From its modest beginnings in the mid-nineteenth century, social policy and welfare thus showed dramatic improvement, both quantitatively and qualitatively, to the ultimate benefit of all Germans.

7.5 Notes

1 The standard overview is C. Sachsse and F. Tennstedt, *Geschichte der Armenfürsorge in Deutschland*, 3 vols (Stuttgart, 1980/1988/1992). See also J. Frerich and M. Frey, *Handbuch der Geschichte der Sozialpolitik in Deutschland*, 3 vols (Munich, 1993).

2 For example, by C. Sachsse and F. Tennstedt, eds, *Soziale Sicherheit und soziale Disziplinierung. Beiträge zu einer historischen Theorie der Sozialpolitik* (Frankfurt am Main, 1986), and E. Reidegeld, *Staatliche Sozialpolitik in*

Deutschland. Historische Entwicklung und theoretische Analyse von den Ursprüngen bis 1918 (Opladen, 1996), pp. 243ff.; for a case study, see D. J. K. Peukert, *Grenzen der Sozialdisziplinierung. Aufstieg und Krise der deutschen Jugendfürsorge 1878 bis 1932* (Cologne, 1986). The ideas of Jürgen Habermas and Michel Foucault have been particularly influential in this debate.

3 The terms used in the discussion of welfare in Germany are diverse and frequently synonymous. The most common are *Armut* (poverty), *Armenfürsorge* and *Armenpflege* (poor relief), *Fürsorge* (social work), *Fürsorgeerziehung* and *Zwangserziehung* (correctional education), *Jugendfürsorge* (youth social work), *soziale Fürsorge* (social relief), *Sozialhilfe* (public assistance, post-1945), *Sozialpolitik* (social policy), *Sozialstaat* and *Wohlfahrtsstaat* (welfare state), *Wohlfahrt* (welfare), *Wohlfahrtspflege* (voluntary welfare work).

4 See J. Reulecke, *Soziale Frieden durch soziale Reform. Der Centralverein für das Wohl der arbeitenden Klassen in der Frühindustrialisierung* (Wuppertal, 1983).

5 See M. Doege, *Armut in Preussen und Bayern, 1770–1840* (Munich, 1991); and H. Beck, *The Origins of the Authoritarian Welfare State in Prussia. Conservatism, Bureaucracy and the Social Question, 1815–70* (Ann Arbor, 1995), pp. 39–60, 154–64.

6 W. Mommsen and W. Mock, eds, *Die Entstehung des Wohlfahrtsstaates in Grossbritannien und Deutschland, 1850–1950* (Stuttgart, 1982), pp. 71–83, 133–49; G. A. Ritter, *Social Welfare in Germany and Britain* (Leamington Spa, 1986), pp. 17–20, 28–35; and V. Hentschel, *Geschichte der deutschen Sozialpolitik (1880–1980). Soziale Sicherung und kollektives Arbeitsrecht* (Frankfurt am Main, 1983), pp. 9–28. Revisionist views characterize L. Machtan, ed., *Bismarcks Sozialstaat. Beiträge zur Geschichte der Sozialpolitik und zur sozialpolitischen Geschichtsschreibung* (Frankfurt am Main, 1994). See also G. A. Ritter, 'Sozialpolitik im Zeitalter Bismarcks', *Historische Zeitschrift*, 265 (1997), pp. 683–720.

7 The new challenges are examined by G. Steinmetz, *Regulating the Social. The Welfare State and Local Politics in Imperial Germany* (Princeton, NJ, 1993). See also W. R. Lee and E. Rosenhaft, eds, *The State and Social Change in Germany, 1880–1980* (Oxford, 1990), pp. 1–33.

8 P. Weindling, *Health, Race and German Politics between National Unification and Nazism, 1870–1945* (Cambridge, 1989), pp. 25ff., 305–57; R. J. Evans, *Death in Hamburg. Society and Politics in the Cholera Years, 1830–1910* (Oxford, 1987), pp. 508–39; M. Berg and G. Cocks, eds, *Medicine and Modernity. Public Health and Medical Care in Nineteenth- and Twentieth-Century Germany* (Cambridge, 1997), with contributions by J. Bleker on hospitals and A. Grossman on abortion.

9 H. H. Henning, 'Arbeitslosenversicherung vor 1914: das Genter System und seine Übernahme in Deutschland', in H. Kellenbenz, ed., *Wirtschaftspolitik und Arbeitsmarkt* (Munich, 1994), pp. 271–87; also A. Faust, *Arbeitsmarktpolitik im Deutschen Kaiserreich. Arbeitsvermittlung, Arbeitsbeschaffung und Arbeitslosenversicherung, 1890–1918* (Stuttgart, 1986); K. Canning, *Languages of Labour and Gender. Female Factory Work in Germany, 1850–1914* (New York, 1997); and L. A. Heilman, 'Industrial Unemployment in Germany: 1873–1913', *Archiv für Sozialgeschichte*, 27 (1987), pp. 25–49.

10 R. Spree, *Health and Social Class in Imperial Germany. A Social History of Mortality, Morbidity and Inequality* (Oxford, 1988), pp. 48–102.

11 W. Ruegg, ed., *Kulturkritik und Jugendkult* (Frankfurt am Main, 1974), pp. 23–38, 47–60, 87–114; D. S. Linton, *Who Has the Youth, Has the Future. The Campaign to Save Young Workers in Imperial Germany* (Cambridge, 1991). pp. 200ff.; E. R. Dickinson, *The Politics of German Child Welfare from the Empire to the Federal Republic* (Cambridge, MA, 1996), pp. 1–45.

12 R. Wall and J. Winter, eds, *The Upheaval of War. Family, Work and Welfare in Europe, 1914–1918* (Cambridge, 1989), pp. 417–35; J. Kocka, *Facing Total War. German Society, 1914–1918* (Leamington Spa, 1984), pp. 11–26, 115–26; U. Daniel, *Arbeiterfrauen in der Kriegsgesellschaft. Beruf, Familie und Politik im Ersten Weltkrieg* (Göttingen, 1989).

13 H.-J. Bieber, *Gewerkschaften in Krieg und Revolution. Arbeiterbewegung, Industrie, Staat und Militär in Deutschland, 1914–1920* (Hamburg, 1981), pp. 306–33. On relations between the *Verein für Sozialpolitik* and the trades unions, U. Ratz, *Zwischen Arbeitsgemeinschaft und Koalition. Bürgerliche Sozialreformer und Gewerkschaften im Ersten Weltkrieg* (Munich, 1994).

14 W. Abelshauser, ed., *Die Weimarer Republik als Wohlfahrtsstaat. Zum Verhältnis von Wirtschafts-und Sozialpolitik in der Industriegesellschaft* (Wiesbaden, 1987), pp. 33–62, 91–146; L. Preller, *Sozialpolitik in der Weimarer Republik* (Düsseldorf, 1978), pp. 296–390; G. A. Ritter, *Der Sozialstaat. Entstehung und Entwicklung im internationalen Vergleich* (Munich, 1989), pp. 112–29; Y.-S. Hong, *Welfare, Modernity, and the Weimar State, 1918–1933* (Princeton, NJ, 1998), pp. 44–75, 91–140; D. F. Crew, *Germans on Welfare. From Weimar to Hitler* (Oxford, 1998), pp. 3–15.

15 The latter theme is addressed by, for example, C. Usborne, *The Politics of the Body. Women's Reproductive Rights and Duties* (London, 1991), and A. Grossman, *Reforming Sex. The German Movement for Birth Control and Abortion Control, 1920–1950* (Oxford, 1995); 'Women and the Welfare State in the Weimar Republic', special issue of *Central European History*, 30, (1997), pp. 1–66.

16 See C. Eifert, *Frauenpolitik und Wohlfahrtspflege. Zur Geschichte der sozialdemokratischen 'Arbeiterwohlfahrt'* (Frankfurt am Main, 1993); J.-C. Kaiser, *Sozialer Protestantismus im 20. Jahrhundert. Beiträge zur Geschichte der Inneren Mission, 1914–1945* (Munich, 1989).

17 E. Jordan and J. Münder, eds, *65 Jahre Reichsjugendwohlfahrtsgesetz–ein Gesetz auf dem Weg in den Ruhestand?* (Münster, 1987), pp. 7ff., 137–51; P. D. Stachura, *The Weimar Republic and the Younger Proletariat. An Economic and Social Analysis* (London, 1989), pp. 64–93; E. Harvey, *Youth and the Welfare State in Weimar Germany* (Oxford, 1993), pp. 60–102.

18 Hentschel, *Sozialpolitik*, pp. 133ff.; W. Bogs, *Die Sozialversicherung in der Weimarer Demokratie* (Munich, 1981).

19 H. A. Winkler, *Von der Revolution zur Stabilisierung. Arbeiter und Arbeiterbewegung in der Weimarer Republik 1918 bis 1924* (Berlin, 1984), pp. 68–96; G. D. Feldman, *The Great Disorder. Politics, Economics, and Society in the German Inflation, 1914–1924* (Oxford, 1997), pp. 698–802.

20 M. Gräser, *Der blockierte Wohlfahrtsstaat. Unterschichtsjugend und Jugendfürsorge in der Weimarer Republik* (Göttingen, 1995), argues that the confessional groups thwarted the liberal-Progressives.

21 For biographical sketches of both, see P. D. Stachura, *Political Leaders in Weimar Germany. A Biographical Study* (Hemel Hempstead, 1993), pp. 18–19, 188–90.

22 K. C. Führer, *Arbeitslosigkeit und die Entstehung der Arbeitslosenversicherung in Deutschland, 1902–1927* (Berlin, 1990), pp. 342–5, 503ff.; P. Lewek, *Arbeitslosigkeit und Arbeitslosenversicherung in der Weimarer Republik, 1918–1927* (Stuttgart, 1992). On the institutional innovation of the 1927 legislation, see V. Herrmann, *Vom Arbeitsmarkt zum Arbeitseinsatz. Zur Geschichte der Reichsanstalt für Arbeitsvermittlung und Arbeitslosenversicherung, 1929 bis 1939* (Frankfurt am Main, 1993). More details in G. Gräf, *Das Arbeitsgerichtsgesetz von 1926* (Goldbach, 1993), and S. Bischoff, *Arbeitszeitrecht in der Weimarer Republik* (Berlin, 1987).

23 K. Borchardt, *Perspectives on Modern German Economic History and Policy*

(Cambridge, 1991), pp. 143–83; H. James, *The German Slump. Politics and Economics, 1924–1936* (Oxford, 1986), pp. 89–109, 209–23; J. von Kruedener, ed., *Economic Crisis and Political Collapse. The Weimar Republic, 1924–1933* (Oxford, 1988), pp. 1–19.

24 See P. D. Stachura, ed., *Unemployment and the Great Depression in Weimar Germany* (London, 1986); R. J. Evans and D. Geary, eds, *The German Unemployed. Experiences and Consequences of Mass Unemployment from the Weimar Republic to the Third Reich* (London, 1987); I. Kershaw, ed., *Weimar: Why Did German Democracy Fail?* (London, 1991). A new view can be found in W. L. Patch, *Heinrich Brüning and the Dissolution of the Weimar Republic* (Cambridge, 1998), pp. 172–219.

25 H. A. Winkler, *Der Weg in die Katastrophe. Arbeiter und Arbeiterbewegung in der Weimarer Republik 1930 bis 1933* (Berlin and Bonn, 1987), especially pp. 424–93, 626–72, 713–99, 810–68; also R. M. Huber Koller, *Gewerkschaften und Arbeitslose. Erfahrungen der Massenerwerbslosigkeit und Aspekte freigewerkschaftlicher Arbeitslosenpolitik in der Endphase der Weimarer Republik* (Centaurus, 1992); G. Schulz, *Von Brüning zu Hitler. Der Wandel des politischen Systems in Deutschland* (Berlin, 1994), pp. 863–1042.

26 Definitively assessed in J. W. Falter, T. Lindenberger, and S. Schumann, *Wahlen und Abstimmungen in der Weimarer Republik. Materialien zum Wahlverhalten 1919–1933* (Munich, 1986), and J. W. Falter, *Hitlers Wähler* (Munich, 1991), pp. 30–8, 81–135, 154–93, 285ff., 364ff. A summary is in C. Fischer, *The Rise of the Nazis* (Manchester, 1995).

27 This highly controversial theme has attracted much scholarly debate. For example, T. Mason, *Social Policy in the Third Reich. The Working Class and the 'National Community'* (Oxford, 1993); J. Caplan, ed., *Nazism, Fascism and the Working Class. Essays by Tim Mason* (Cambridge, 1995); C. Fischer, ed., *The Rise of National Socialism and the Working Classes in Weimar Germany* (Oxford, 1996); W. Zollitsch, *Arbeiter zwischen Weltwirtschaftskrise und Nationalsozialismus. Ein Beitrag zur Sozialgeschichte der Jahre 1928 bis 1936* (Göttingen, 1990); G. Morsch, *Arbeit und Brot. Studien zur Lage, Stimmung, Einstellung und Verhalten der deutschen Arbeiterschaft, 1933–1936/37* (Frankfurt am Main, 1993); E. Heuel, *Der Umworbene Stand. Die Ideologische Integration der Arbeiter im Nationalsozialismus 1933–1935* (Frankfurt am Main, 1989).

28 R. J. Overy, *War and Economy in the Third Reich* (Oxford, 1994), pp. 37–67.

29 See H. Vorlaender, *Die NSV. Darstellung und Dokumentation einer national-sozialistische Organization* (Boppard, 1988).

30 M. Burleigh and W. Wippermann, *The Racial State: Germany 1933–1945* (Cambridge, 1991), pp. 199–303; I. Kershaw: *The Nazi Dictatorship. Problems and Perspectives of Interpretation* (London, 1993), pp. 131–49. More broadly, N. Frei, *National Socialist Rule in Germany. The Führer State 1933–1945* (Oxford, 1993), and J. Dulffer, *Nazi Germany, 1933–1945. Faith and Annihilation* (London, 1996). Overshadowing everything, however, is the brilliant, magisterial new biography by I. Kershaw, *Hitler, 1889–1936*, Vol. I: *Hubris*, and *Hitler, 1936–1945*, Vol. II: *Nemesis* (London, 1998 and 2000).

31 M.-L. Recker, *Nationalsozialistische Sozialpolitik im Zweiten Weltkrieg* (Munich, 1985), *passim*; J. Noakes, ed., *Nazism, 1919–1945*, Vol. IV: *The German Home Front in World War II* (Exeter, 1998), pp. 264–301, 509–80.

32 Overy, *War and Economy*, pp. 259–414, on living standards 1939–42.

33 L. Pine, *Nazi Family Policy, 1933–1945* (Oxford, 1997), pp. 170ff.

34 Burleigh and Wippermann, *The Racial State*, pp. 7–22.

35 Details in C. S. Maier and G. Bischof, eds, *The Marshall Plan and West Germany* (New York, 1991); A. J. Nicholls, *Freedom and Responsibility. The Social*

Market Economy in Germany, 1918–1963 (Oxford, 1994); A. Kramer, *The West German Economy* (Oxford, 1991).

36 Background in D. L. Bark and D. R. Gress, *A. History of West Germany*, Vol. I: *From Shadow to Substance, 1945–1963*; Vol. II: *Democracy and its Discontents, 1963–1988* (Oxford, 1989); K. D. Bracher, T. Eschenburg, J. C. Fest and E. Jäckel, eds, *Geschichte der Bundesrepublik Deutschland*, 5 vols (Stuttgart, 1983); L. Kettenacker, *Germany since 1945* (Oxford, 1997), pp. 80–105. More specifically, A. Schildt, *Moderne Zeiten. Freizeit, Massenmedien und Zeitgeist in der Bundesrepublik der 50er Jahre* (Hamburg, 1995), and M. Wildt, *Am Beginn der Konsumgesellschaft. Mangelerfahrung, Lebenshaltung, Wohlstandshoffnung in Westdeutschland in den fünfziger Jahren* (Hamburg, 1995).

37 G. Schulz, *Wiederaufbau in Deutschland. Die Wohnungsbaupolitik in der Westzonen und der Bundesrepublik von 1945 bis 1957* (Düsseldorf, 1994), pp. 33ff., 210–52.

38 A. J. Nicholls, *The Bonn Republic. West German Democracy, 1945–1990* (London, 1997), pp. 220ff.; Jens Alber, *Der Sozialstaat in der Bundesrepublik, 1950–1983* (Frankfurt am Main, 1989), pp. 215–67.

39 H. Kaelble, J. Kocka, H. Zwahr, eds, *Sozialgeschichte der DDR* (Stuttgart, 1994), note the essay on social policy by H. G. Hockerts; D. Hoffmann, *Sozialpolitische Neuordnung in der SBZ/DDR. Der Umbau der Sozialversicherung, 1945–1956* (Munich, 1996). Something of the wider picture is given by M. Fulbrook, *Anatomy of a Dictatorship. Inside the GDR, 1949–1989* (Oxford, 1995).

40 H.-J. Brauns and D. Kramer, 'West Germany – the Breakup of Consensus and the Demographic Threat', in B. Munday, ed., *The Crisis in Welfare. An International Perspective on Social Services and Social Work* (Hemel Hempstead, 1989), pp. 124–54.

8

Economy and state in Germany in the twentieth century

RICHARD OVERY
King's College, University of London

At the beginning of the twentieth century there was a growing body of opinion among economists and politicians throughout industrial Europe that the rational management of national economies was something that could be exercised by public authorities more effectively than by unrestricted private enterprise. Among socialists such opinions were unexceptional, for they expected social ownership of the means of production to generate a more efficient economic system, but these views were not confined to the left wing of politics. In Germany one of the pioneers of 'planned economy', the businessman Walther Rathenau, lectured his peers in the early 1920s on the virtues of state regulation in opposition to the anarchy of markets, whose volatility made social crisis a natural corollary of free enterprise: 'Our politics are about the transition from the principle of private economy into that of the state'.[1] During the following decade the intellectual foundations were laid for what became known as the 'social market economy' – an economic system regulated by the state to achieve high growth, adequate welfare, and social stability. One of Germany's most senior economic thinkers, Werner Sombart, urged his compatriots in the late 1920s to accept that national economies needed national, public organization if they were to promote the public good.[2]

There is thus more than an element of irony in the fact that in twentieth-century·Germany the periods in which the role of the state was at its greatest coincided with the periods when economic performance was least impressive. During the First World War, state direction of economic resources produced massive debt, profound structural distortions, and a militant workforce. Under the Third Reich, state-sponsored economic development fuelled massive remilitarization and war, and ended with Germany divided, and its economy and urban landscape in ruins. In the German Democratic Republic, founded in 1949, the economy failed to match the exaggerated promises of the Communist leadership, and instead produced decades of low income-growth and industrial stagnation. This pattern was largely a product of circumstances. Without war, global economic crisis, and fascism, the German economy would have performed very differently, and the claims of the state would have been less onerous and distorting. Without the bitter divisions in German politics, which produced radical movements of right and left committed to some form of extensive political control over the economy, economic policy would have followed a more consensual course.

A higher level of state intervention was inevitable, given the growing complexity of the modern industrial and service economy, and the political necessity of providing higher levels of welfare and services to cope with the vagaries of the business cycle and the free market, as discussed in Chapter 7. State responsibilities expanded throughout industrialized Europe over the whole course of the century. The growth of welfare provision, regulation of agricultural marketing, state interest in stable financial markets, infra-structure investment, trade growth, etc., all involved enhanced levels of state participation. The state became a major employer in its own right. In Germany, as elsewhere, the vastly increased scale of economic activity in the twentieth century provoked the emergence of macroeconomic theory and macroeconomic policy to deal with the structure of the national economy as a whole. The claim of the German state on the national product in 1901 was 15 per cent; by 1990 that proportion had risen to 45 per cent.[3] A shift of this magnitude made the state a key player in economic development even in contexts where formal state control of the economy was neither necessary nor desired. These two elements of the relationship between state and economy in Germany are explored in what follows: the period of forced state intervention provoked by war, economic crisis and National Socialist imperialism; and the more benign long-term evolution of state regulation and responsibility.

8.1 State, war and economy

It was Adolf Hitler, in the so-called 'Four-Year Plan' memorandum which he drafted in August 1936 at his Bavarian mountain retreat in Berchtesgaden, who argued that economic life should always be subservient to the needs of politics: 'The nation does not live for the economy, for economic leaders, or for economic or financial theories; on the contrary, it is finance and the economy, economic leaders and theories, which all owe unqualified service in this struggle for the self-assertion of our nation'.[4] These sentiments bore the stamp of the widespread discourse in Germany since the First World War about the failure of the home front in the conflict, and the essential selfishness of those who ran the economic system. It was not only Hitler who assumed that the economy was there to strengthen the state and preserve the nation, rather than simply to satisfy the material aspirations of businessman or worker.

The idea of a national economy directed by the political authorities to preserve the security of the state or community grew out of Germany's catastrophic experience of defeat in 1918. Rathenau, who came to favour the rational organization of the economy by a state technocratic class, was responsible for rescuing the German war economy from disaster in 1914 by organizing a national system of raw material production and allocation.[5] He saw at first hand that neither private economic groups nor the German state were in a position in 1914 to operate, or even to understand, a macro-economic system. By 1914 the responsibilities of the German state for economic affairs were limited. Most state expenditure was undertaken by the provinces (*Länder*) and municipalities (*Gemeinden*), as discussed in Chapter 6. In 1901 two-thirds of public expenditure came from these sources, one-third from the federal government in Berlin, equivalent to only 5 per cent of the national product. Most of that expenditure went on the armed forces; national defence was the single most significant element directly financed and organized by the central state apparatus, as it was among all the major powers of Europe before 1914.[6]

The war that broke out in August 1914 confronted the German state with unprecedented demands for the mobilization and organization of the domestic economy for war. Some thought had gone into the economic implications of war between great powers in the years immediately before 1914, but there was very little serious preparation for a conflict of the scale and length of the First World War. During the four years of conflict, the relationship between the state and the economy in Germany was rapidly altered. By 1918 the state's claim on the national product had increased to an exceptional level. The ordinary budget produced a quadrupling of tax revenues between 1914 and 1918, but the extraordinary budget necessary to finance the war effort was funded by state loans, which amounted to approximately 150 billion marks in 1918, four times the size of the national product of 1913.[7] This money was used principally to secure the weapons and equipment for the armed forces from the private industrial economy, and this activity came to dominate the German economy as a whole. The financial burden was undertaken with reluctance by a state which, since its foundation in 1871, had relied on a small budget based largely on indirect taxes raised from tariffs and duties on goods. Rather than switch in 1914 to high levels of direct taxation, the government decided to fund the war by appealing to a patriotic public to subscribe to war loans. When public enthusiasm waned in 1917, the state resorted to using short-term floating debt, which it intended to pay off through financial reparations imposed on the beaten enemy.[8] German defeat left the state in 1919 with debts in excess of 150 billion marks and income from taxation of 11 billion, of which two-thirds was used to repay interest on the debt.

The state was also obliged to direct or supervise most areas of private economic activity. Again, this was done with reluctance. The assumption in 1914 was that the war would be short; only by the summer of 1915 did it become apparent that the military stalemate would require important changes on the home front if warfare were to be sustained. The most critical issue was the supply of foodstuffs and civilian goods. No serious thought had been given to rationing on a national scale, nor to the problems raised by trying to divert resources to war production in a market economy. Gradually the operations of the market were suspended. First, in August 1914, raw material production and allocation was taken over by the *Kriegsrohstoffabteilung* (War Raw Materials Department) which supervised more than 20 raw material 'corporations', each empowered to produce, allocate and distribute its own particular product. This instrument became the central element of the effort to impose some kind of macroeconomic direction. In May 1916 food supply was brought under the control of a *Kriegsernährungsamt* (War Food Office), which rationed the supply of foodstuffs and attempted to dictate agricultural prices and the structure of agricultural production. Finally in December 1916 a law on labour mobilization was passed, making all males aged 17 to 60 liable for labour conscription for work in war-essential industry. The state also assumed the right to close down enterprises, or to starve them of materials and labour. One-third of all artisan workshops closed, and the drift towards large-scale enterprise was accelerated.[9]

The purpose of the controls was to expand war production, preserve domestic morale by controlling food supply, and prevent economic egoism from subverting national needs. None of these ambitions was successfully achieved. War production proved difficult to organize on any rational basis, and it involved a great deal of waste and innumerable delays. In 1916 the armed forces, which had responsibility for war production allocated by the state, established a *Kriegsamt* (War Office), whose purpose was to provide a central apparatus for planning and procuring military equipment. Output rose during 1917 and 1918, but remained well behind plan. Food supply was difficult to organize in the face of strong resistance from farmers to what they regarded as unwarranted state interference. It proved difficult to secure adequate supplies to meet the civilian ration, and in practice the state system was circumvented by a lively black market which was impossible to police effectively. The effort to win cooperation from industry was frustrated at times by the unwillingness of industrialists to accept state control or military interference, or to deny the market by restricting profit growth. The chief difficulty was a practical one: thanks to its unique federal structure, the German state had no previous experience in running the whole national economy on its own behalf, and the private economy had no experience of operating in a context where there was, in effect, no market. The development of instruments for macroeconomic regulation or coercion was achieved through improvisation and experiment. By 1918 Germany had, despite wartime failures, a form of command economy unthinkable only four years before. Because of German resource constraints and the effects of blockade, state control was more extensive and intrusive than it proved to be among the more economically secure western Allies.

After 1919 a higher level of state economic activity remained a permanent feature in Germany, and it did so largely because of circumstances generated by the experience of the war (see Table 8.1). In the political aftermath of war the German government spent large additional sums on welfare and re-employment subsidies in addition to the costs of maintaining the state debt. The level of direct state employment rose steadily during the 1920s (in 1925 the state employed 648,000 officials and 1.18 million workers). The object was to minimize the degree of social dislocation caused by economic demobilization, and to avert social revolution. The transition from a semi-authoritarian monarchy to a democratic republic in 1919 placed the issue of welfare and social services at the centre of the political stage. The German state used economic instruments to buy political peace. In 1919 state expenditure was 55 billion marks, but income only 11 billion. By 1923 only 1 per cent of government expenditure was met by taxation.[10] The consequence of the decision to run massive deficits was a historically exceptional level of inflation and the eventual collapse of the Reichsmark which had been established in 1875/6, shortly after unification. In the summer and autumn of 1923 the mark became worthless until it was suspended as a currency in November.

The hyperinflation of 1923 was blamed at the time on the terms of the peace settlement imposed on Germany in 1919, which compelled substantial losses of territory and industrial resources and required Germany to pay annual reparations for war damage. The current historical consensus places responsibility much more firmly on the shoulders of the German government, which accepted the risks of paying for the war and postwar

Table 8.1 State expenditure in Germany in 1913 and 1925–32 (millions of Reichsmarks)

Year	State expenditure (m RM) central	local	As % of GNP central	local	total
1913	2514	3644	6.1	8.8	14.9
1925	4234	5098	11.3	13.7	25.0
1926	4836	5688	12.5	14.7	27.2
1927	5422	6205	12.8	14.6	27.4
1928	6603	6486	14.8	14.6	29.4
1929	6983	6587	15.7	14.9	30.6
1930	7799	6697	18.1	15.5	33.6
1931	7372	6567	18.8	16.8	35.6
1932	6371	6623	17.9	18.7	36.6

Source: S. Andic and J. Veverka, 'The Growth of Government Expenditure in Germany since the Unification', *Finanzarchiv*, 23 (1964), pp. 243–5.

reconstruction and welfare reforms with a weakened economy and low tax base. There were positive effects from this strategy. Re-employment was rapidly achieved, exports revived, and the German economy attracted considerable speculative investment from abroad, which helped to spread the cost of the inflation. Industry could re-equip with depreciating marks, and the productive economy expanded faster than might have been expected given the disastrous conditions of 1919. But the collapse of the currency also had serious repercussions. Since the founding of the German state, the maintenance and operation of a sound currency had been one of the chief responsibilities of the federal Reich authority and of the central bank, the Reichsbank. The failure to defend the value of the mark, though almost certainly unavoidable as a consequence of defeat in war, was widely regarded in Germany as a political failure, even as a moral lapse. The inflation wiped out the paper wealth accumulated since 1871. Bank deposits stood at 19 billion in 1913; in 1925 they totalled 608 million.[11] The inflation brought to an end Germany's first experiment in state-directed economy, and it demonstrated how poorly the German liberal economy adapted to the strains of macroeconomic management under the exceptional circumstances of war and postwar reconstruction. Although the German problem was largely a consequence of the circumstances of defeat and social upheaval, there emerged a widespread and popular view during the years of the Weimar Republic that it was the free-market capitalist system itself which was both inherently unstable and unable to protect the wider national interest, and that it should be superseded by a system more appropriate to the modern economic age.

The inflation was followed six years later by the worst slump in Germany's history, provoked by the heavy dependence on outside sources of capital (a direct result of the loss of domestic funds for investment in the inflation), low investment in agriculture and consumer sectors, and a high commitment to a narrow range of vulnerable export sectors. The slump was partly imported, partly domestic. After the experience of inflation, the state was unwilling to experiment with the economy and insisted on pursuing sound finance. In the end it was compelled to initiate policies that would prevent further economic decline, and the slump ushered in a period of increasing state regulation and direction. It also provoked a more general rejection of the liberal economic model that had served Germany well enough before 1914, in favour of a new economic order in which the domestic economy would be regulated, economic self-sufficiency (autarky) encouraged to avoid the vagaries of the world market, and new integrated trading blocs built up under German leadership, or, in extreme forms of the argument, under German imperialism. At its most radical, this economic vision embraced the idea that the economy should be brought under authoritarian political control, and regimented in ways that met the political and military requirements of the state and reduced the influence and opportunities for economic egoism.

The second period of extensive state responsibility for the economy began before Hitler became Chancellor of Germany in 1933, but it has come to be identified principally with the National Socialist regime, which between 1933 and 1939 established a new form of 'command economy'. The purposes differed from those in the war. First, the new regime wished to avoid any repetition of the failures of the liberal economy by creating a network of controls to avoid business slumps, and to maintain political stability and social peace. Second, the regime wished to organize the productive economy in ways that would allow the more rational development and exploitation of German resources. Finally, the more distant aspiration was to use what came to be called *die gelenkte Wirtschaft* (the managed economy) as an instrument for military expansion and economic imperialism in central and eastern Europe, consistent with the idea of the large autarkic area (*Grossraumwirtschaft*). Some of these ideas were National Socialist in the sense that economists in the National Socialist Party had adopted them piecemeal during the 1920s, but the idea of creating a post-liberal order and of the historical necessity for economic imperialism in Europe was widespread among the German business, political and military elites in the 1930s, who came to believe that the conventional western model of liberal capitalism was historically untenable because it only matched the self-interest of the victorious Allied powers.[12] This rejection of conventional 'western' economics was something Germany shared with those other revisionist states, Italy and Japan, which also embarked in the 1930s on experiments in state economic direction and territorial expansion. State economic policy became a function of ideology rather than economic utility.

The establishment of regulatory controls over the German economy was not the product of a single, coherent plan – indeed, National Socialists were at pains to argue that their vision of a 'people's economy' (*Volkswirtschaft*) was quite distinct from the planned economy of Stalin's Soviet Union. But the net effect of the controls was not very different in aggregate from a 'planned economy'. During 1932 and 1933, counter-cyclical 'work-creation' projects were set up; backed by state funds, they were to be labour-intensive in character, while promoting the revival of the engineering and construction industries.[13] The financial system came under close state supervision during the course of 1932 and 1933. As discussed in Chapter 5, the banks were brought under state ownership in 1932 to avoid the collapse of the whole system, and even though they were re-privatized in 1936, they lost any real freedom of manoeuvre and remained closely tied to state financial policy.[14] The capital market was also regulated by the state. New share issues required state sanction, and investment was encouraged in those areas which conformed with state military and foreign policy. Wages were controlled by state watchdogs appointed in 1934. The *Treuhänder der Arbeit* (Trustees of Labour) fixed wage rates and suspended the normal operation of the labour market. Prices were controlled during 1933–34, when upward pressure on prices was not great; when, by 1936, the economic revival produced price inflation, a new Price Commissioner was appointed, backed with dictatorial powers. State price and wage control became central to the macroeconomic direction of the economy. Finally, trade and foreign economic relations were allowed only under state licence; in September 1934 Hjalmar Schacht, President of the German Central Bank, published a so-called 'New Plan' which brought together all the ad hoc regulations established over trade and currency transactions into a single regulatory structure. The organizing principle of the productive economy remained private initiative and private ownership, but both were forced to operate in a system in which the major economic variables were dictated by state officials and agencies.

The second ambition of the National Socialist regime was to organize the productive economy along rational, corporatist lines. Each major area of economic activity was compelled to form a 'chamber' or corporation, which included all of those engaged in each branch. The whole system was run by the *Reichswirtschaftskammer* (Reich Economic Chamber). Under its broad umbrella there were 18 subordinate economic chambers (industry and trade, artisan trades, transport, energy, etc.), and six main *Reichsgruppen* (Reich groups) for industry, trade, banking, insurance, energy, and artisan trades.[15] Each of these groups spawned smaller 'economic groups' responsible for just one branch of production, a total of 47 for the main branches, and 52 for the artisan trades. This cumbersome structure produced a great deal of overlapping competence, and its functions were never well defined. The economic groups had little real executive authority, but they were the conduit for the communication and monitoring of state economic policy at every level of economic activity. German industry had a long tradition of association, as discussed in Chapter 6, and the post-1933 reforms exploited that fact by absorbing existing trade associations and cartels into the new compulsory structure. For agriculture, as discussed in Chapter 3, the system of regulation took a different form. In 1933 the *Reichsnährstand* (Reich Food Estate) was established under the National Socialist Walther Darré. This corporation embraced all those engaged on the land, but its primary function was to manage food production and marketing, and to preserve the existing structure of landholding. Price controls were initiated, and farmers were compelled to work under new organizations for collecting and selling their produce.[16]

The third ambition proved to be the most far-reaching, and was in crucial respects dependent upon the successful realization of the first two. Economic regulations helped to produce a remarkable economic revival in Germany by the mid-1930s. Although historians are critical of many of the statistical claims made on behalf of the recovery, the situation in Germany in 1931/2 presented a crisis of special magnitude which could only be overcome by state initiatives (see Table 8.2). But once the economy was stabilized and regulated, the opportunity arose to exploit that revival for the wider foreign

Table 8.2 The state and economic recovery, 1928 and 1932–38 (millions of Reichsmarks)

Year	GNP (1913 prices)	Government expenditure (current prices)	Government expenditure (1900 prices)	State investment amount (current prices)	as % of all investment
1928	57,896	23,235	13,070	6600	40
1932	42,207	17,699	12,995	2200	88
1933	45,527	18,376	13,921	2500	44
1934	50,424	21,616	15,859	4600	49
1935	56,704	21,955	15,866	6400	47
1936	63,297	23,049	16,654	8100	46
1937	70,361	26,934	18,782	8400	44
1938	77,076	37,159	25,913	10300	45

Note: GNP = Gross National Product.
Source: Andic and Veverka, 'Government Expenditure', p. 243; A. Ritschl and M. Spoerer, 'Das Bruttosozialprodukt in Deutschland nach den amtlichen Volkseinkommens-und Sozialproduktsstatistiken 1901–1995', *Jahrbuch für Wirtschaftsgeschichte*, (1997), Part II, pp. 27–54; and R. Erbe, *Die nationalsozialistische Wirtschaftspolitik 1933–9 im Lichte der modernen Theorie* (Zürich, 1958), p. 67.

political ambitions of the regime. It is important to recognize that imperial expansion and large-scale war was not a necessary outcome of the period of enhanced state intervention after 1932. There were many among the economic and military elite in Germany who favoured using the state-led economy to establish German trade and financial interests in eastern Europe from the simple fact of German economic power, without resort to physical expansion. Others, Hitler included, accepted the logic of the geopolitical arguments circulating in radical nationalist circles of the 1920s, that Germany was a natural imperial power owing to her small area and large and productive population. She needed *Lebensraum* (living space) in order to survive economically, and these additional areas could be acquired not by agreement, but only by war. The result was a neo-mercantilist outlook, in which economic well-being for one power could be achieved only by the seizure of economic resources and trading areas from others. Issues of space could only be solved, Hitler told his commanders-in-chief in November 1937, by force: 'There had never in former times been spaces without a master, and there were none today; the attacker must always come up against someone in possession'.[17]

Preparation for war and war itself dominated the economic history of the 1930s and 1940s. Just as it was possible for nineteenth-century German statesmen to assume that Prussia's economic strength had been responsible for the victorious wars of German unification, so German defeat in 1918 was attributed not to military incompetence, but to economic deficiency. In the 1930s there existed a widespread belief among politicians and soldiers alike that a strong, war-related economy was the key to German security and great-power status. The term *Wehrwirtschaft*, or 'defence economy', was used to describe this state of permanent economic mobilization for war. So central was the concept to the pattern of economic development in the 1930s that the leading German economic journal, *Der Deutsche Volkswirt* ('The German Economist'), carried a whole section devoted to issues of defence economics every week from 1935 on. The central purpose of a *Wehrwirtschaft* was to structure the economy in such a way that it could be converted quickly to war purposes, and would remain free of the threat of blockade by supplying essential materials, equipment and weapons from domestic resources. The German War Ministry established a special branch in 1934 charged with the responsibility for monitoring economic policy and development in accordance with military requirements.[18]

The economic ideas of the armed forces anticipated a second 'total war' in which the state would have to engross and deploy a high proportion of available economic resources. Hitler's regime, and Hitler in particular, embraced this concept, but enlarged it by insisting first that an adequate food basis should be supplied to avoid any prospect of a crisis of home morale in war, and second that the state should undertake an increasing share of the build-up of the physical resources necessary for large-scale war-making, in the belief that private capitalism was animated only by economic egoism. It was recognized that these political and military aims could not be realized without state direction. 'Without a plan we won't get through,' announced Hitler at the 1935 Nuremberg Party Rally.[19] During the winter of 1935/6 there was growing evidence that the rapid economic revival was faltering, partly because of competition for the limited supply of imports between rearmament and foodstuffs. At the end of the summer of 1936, Hitler himself took the remarkable step of establishing a planning apparatus armed with very great political power whose purpose was to ensure that within four years the German economy would be restructured along lines that would turn Germany into a military superpower. These primary economic aims, at least in the short term, could be met only at the expense of sharply cutting back on the growth of private consumption and exports.

It has often been argued that the Four-Year Plan, formally established by Hitler on 18 October 1936 under the direction of the air force commander-in-chief Hermann Göring, a man with no experience whatsoever of economic affairs, was a façade, masking hollow declarations of intent.[20] The reality was remarkably different. The apparatus set up from 1936 onward was the first full experiment in macroeconomic steering in Germany's history. The Four-Year Plan organization took over responsibility for foreign exchange and currency controls, price-fixing, the allocation and purchase of raw materials, the modernization of agriculture, labour train-ing, and state investment in all war-related sectors. In late 1937 the planning apparatus, based on a small group of economists in Göring's Prussian State Ministry in Berlin, was fused with the Ministry of Economics, giving it more practical opportunities for macroeconomic steering. Led by Erich Neumann and Friedrich Graml, the planning office tried to balance up the competing claims of the civilian and military economies, control the flow of trade and industrial resources, and monitor both prices and wages. The control of prices was the central instrument, designed to prevent inflation from eroding the efforts to restructure the economy towards war purposes. Under a Price Commissioner, Josef Wagner, appointed in 1936, an apparatus of 27 Price Control Offices, staffed by 224 economists and accountants, set all prices across the economy, sometimes approving rises, often not. Powers were draconian, but were seldom needed.[21]

The impact of the Four-Year Plan was extensive. It became the chief instrument for running the 'managed economy', and its influence spread into all areas of private economic activity. A high proportion of state investment was directed through the plan into the production of substitute materials – oil, textiles, rubber – and the expansion of aluminium, chemical, and iron-ore output. State investment as a whole remained a very high proportion of all investment throughout the 1932–39 period compared with the 1920s (see Table 8.3). The commitment to large-scale rearmament increased direct expenditure on the military to one-half of all state spending in 1938/9, and made necessary sharp increases in state borrowing. The indirect support for remilitarization – basic industries, transport investment, the engineering industry – ensured that the proportion of the economy devoted to war preparation was very much greater than the money spent on the armed forces themselves. By 1939 one-third of all construction workers, 28 per cent of all workers in manufacturing, and 21 per cent of those in raw material output worked on orders directly for the armed forces.[22] In three years the national product increased by almost 50 per cent in real terms, with virtually all the growth in state-sponsored areas related to war preparation. Consumer spending per capita increased only 4 per cent between 1928 and 1938 even though the net national product had grown by a third over the same period.[23]

Table 8.3 Investment in Germany, 1928–38 (billions of Reichsmarks)

Year	Public investment	Private investment	Total investment	Net investment as % of national income	State debt
1928	6.6	9.7	16.3	9.3	
1932	2.2	0.3	2.5	–*	12.3
1933	2.5	3.2	5.7	–*	13.9
1934	4.6	4.7	9.3	5.3	15.9
1935	6.4	7.2	13.6	8.8	20.1
1936	8.1	9.2	17.3	11.5	25.8
1937	8.4	10.5	18.9	13.1	31.2
1938	10.3	12.2	22.5	15.7	41.7

Note: * = net disinvestment.
Source: R. Erbe, *Die nationalsozialistische Wirtschafts politik 1933–9 im Lichte der modernen Theorie* (Zürich, 1958), pp. 54, 67, 122; B. Klein, *Germany's Economic Preparations for War* (Cambridge, MA, 1959), pp. 255–6; S. Lurie, *Private Investment in a Controlled Economy: Germany 1933–1939* (London, 1947), pp. 23, 68.

There was also a more sinister aspect to the Four-Year Plan. Göring's economic powers were absolute. The early state decrees under his signature promised severe punishments, even death, for infractions of the new economic regulations. German holders of gold and currency abroad were compelled to hand them over to the state in return for marks to be spent within Germany. Propaganda campaigns were mounted against those who squandered or hoarded resources or who exploited the black market. Göring was also given responsibility for the programme of compulsory 'aryanization' of Jewish property. From 1937 onwards a concerted campaign was mounted to expropriate Germany's Jewish population. Jewish assets were either retained by the state, sold at prices below the market value to other German owners, or (in the case of many Jewish businesses) closed down. By 1939, 110,000 Jewish businesses had been closed down or sold and the bulk of Jewish assets expropriated.[24] The Hitler regime became in economic terms a 'predatory state', seizing assets where necessary and violating the principle of private property at will. When there were no further resources to absorb within Germany, Hitler turned the regime's predatory ambitions to neighbouring states. Those occupied by German forces, beginning with Austria in 1938, found themselves the victims of an aggressive Germanization; with the coming of war in 1939 Germany looted vast resources from conquered Europe to fuel the war machine.[25] Between 1933 and 1945, German state ownership of industrial and commercial assets expanded rapidly.

During the war, the state continued to encroach further on the German economy. Some of the mistakes of the First World War were absorbed and not repeated. The levels of state expenditure during the war rose very sharply (see Table 8.4) but no serious inflation set in until after the end of the war in 1945. This situation was achieved in three ways. First, prices were rigidly controlled and rationing organized far more effectively than in the earlier conflict. Second, as discussed in Chapter 5, the banks and savings institutions (which had become little more than financial branches of the state during the 1930s) were compelled to use the rising quantity of savings to buy treasury bonds or short-term treasury bills without the state having to take the risk of relying on public subscription. Third, around one-third of German war expenses was met by contributions extorted from the occupied and satellite states.[26] Taxes were also increased, doubling tax yields, but reliance on so-called 'noiseless finance' through the banks (described in Chapter 5) avoided this time any public scrutiny of how the war was to be paid for. The ability to operate a more sophisticated macroeconomic war policy reflected substantial progress in the collecting of statistics, and the economics of national accounting.[27]

Other lessons from the First World War were not learnt. The purpose of the war economy was to produce large quantities of weapons by mobilizing the largest part of the workforce and industrial capacity for war production. By 1941 almost two-thirds of the German industrial workforce was engaged

Table 8.4 German economic performance in the Second World War, 1939–45

Year	State expenditure	Military expenditure	State revenues	State debt*	GNP** (current prices)
1938/9	39.4	17.2	17.7	27.2	119.2
1939/40	58.0	38.0	23.5	41.1	133.8
1940/1	80.0	55.9	27.2	75.8	146.0
1941/2	100.5	72.3	32.3	124.9	*152.0*
1942/3	124.0	86.2	34.7	183.6	*164.3*
1943/4	130.0	99.4	34.3	253.5	*158.2*

Notes:
All figures are in billions of Reichsmarks.
The wartime figures include revenue contributions from occupied states.
Figures in italics are best estimates.
* = figure for December each year.
** = figures for calendar year, beginning with 1939.
Source: W. Boelcke, 'Kriegsfinanzierung im internationalen Vergleich', in H. Forstmeier and
H.-E.Volkmann, eds, *Kriegswirtschaft und Rüstung 1939–1945* (Düsseldorf, 1977), pp. 55–6;
revenues from National Archives, Washington, NA T 178, roll 15, Reichsfinanzministerium,
'Statistische Übersichten zu den Reichshaushaltsrechnungen 1938 bis 1943', Nov. 1944; NNP
from Ritschl and Spoerer, 'Bruttosozialprodukt', pp. 51–2.

on military orders; in the consumer sectors some 40–60 per cent of goods
were destined for the armed forces' equipment. Civilian per capita
consumption was cut sharply, falling further between 1939 and 1941 than
in the later years of war.[28] Yet for all this, weapons output either stagnated
or grew well below the plans laid down late in 1939. The failure lay, as in
the First World War, with the absence of any central planning agency for the
war economy, any effective coordination between the three separate armed
services, and any effective policy of labour allocation. The armed forces
tried to dominate the production process and in doing so sharply reduced
the productive performance of a large sector of the industrial economy. In
two years, from 1939 to 1941, output per head in the armaments industries
dropped by 25 per cent.[29]

Unlike the experience of the First World War, when the military tightened
its grip on the economy in the second half of the conflict, in the course of the
Second World War the balance of power shifted towards civilians. In
February 1942, Hitler appointed Albert Speer as Minister for Armaments
and Munitions with the object of breaking the influence of the armed forces
and creating a mixed state-private industrial apparatus for maximizing arms
production. In three years of forced rationalization of factory practice and
the distribution of labour and materials, the output of weapons trebled.
Engineers and industrial specialists were recruited to run an organization of
Main Committees (*Hauptausschüsse*), each responsible for one major type
of weapon. The allocation of resources other than labour was undertaken
by a new Central Planning organization (*Zentrale Planung*), which like the
Four-Year Plan apparatus that it effectively superseded, operated with a
macroeconomic overview of the main variables of production. The Speer

system was a coercive one, backed by the full power of the state. By 1944, Germany was as much a command economy as the Soviet Union.[30]

The system was undermined only by the circumstances of war and the twists and turns of German politics. Persistent bombing of the German homeland disrupted the rationalization drive and placed real limitations on the expansion of production. The invasion of German-dominated Europe from three directions, east, west and south, slowly reduced the flow of resources from the conquered territories. At home, the deteriorating wartime situation led the German government to insist on costly and irrational schemes to challenge the bombing, including the development and pro-duction of expensive weapons of revenge – the 'V' weapons – and a massive programme to re-locate German industry underground. This second scheme involved half of all Germany's construction workers and disrupted attempts to extract the most from plant situated above ground.[31] Both schemes were taken over by Heinrich Himmler's SS organization, using slave labour from the network of concentration and labour camps across Germany. As the SS encroached more and more on areas of economic policy, the terror spread into the workplace. In the end Hitler decreed that the German economy should be laid entirely waste so that nothing would be left for the conquer-ing Allies. This 'scorched earth' policy was never enforced at the local level, but it was symptomatic of an extraordinary economic irrationalism that gripped the National Socialist elite in the final years of war. Whatever tech-nological and scientific progress might be attributed to modern war, there can be no doubt that war for Germany was not a net economic benefit.

The defeat of German forces and the collapse of the Third Reich brought to an end the experiments in neo-mercantilism practised since the early 1930s. It also ended the long relationship that had existed in the German lands between the state, the economy, and the power to make war, a relationship that stretched back to the Prussia of Frederick the Great. Not only was Germany again disarmed in 1945, more rigorously than in 1919, but the occupying powers, Britain, France, the United States, and the Soviet Union, were determined to eradicate what they saw as the close-knit military-industrial complex which had been sponsored by the German state for decades. The chief aim of the occupiers was to civilianize the German economy and prevent the recrudescence of state-sponsored violence and economic imperialism. In the second half of the twentieth century the relationship between state and economy for all those Germans not living in the Soviet-dominated zone in the East changed completely.

8.2 The path to the mixed economy

The development of a perverted and predatory command economy under National Socialism had been partly a product of circumstances: the aftermath of the First World War and the effects of the world slump between 1929 and 1932 both encouraged the development of a populist, radical nationalist backlash, and the emergence of a political movement committed to violent and unorthodox economics. The development of the German economy was profoundly affected throughout the century by external circumstances. So it was that the changed character of the world market after 1945 played an important part in securing the economic conditions for sustained growth of the German economy based on high export ratios and a domestic consumer boom. Between 1950 and 1969, the German economy grew at twice the annual rate achieved between 1871 and 1914, and considerably faster than other developed industrial economies.

There were also important domestic changes. Encouraged by the western Allies, who, after a brief flirtation with the idea of reducing Germany to a second-rank, predominantly agrarian economy, sponsored the revival of a benign capitalism orientated to the West, German politicians and business-men were broadly united on the need to reconstruct an economy based on stable growth, high levels of consumption and welfare, and high export ratios. Underlying this conception was an important intellectual shift. Since the 1920s, academic economists in Germany had been developing the concept of a free-market economy based on an unrestricted price mech-anism, characterized by a high level of choice, but one in which sufficient surplus could be generated for social purposes, particularly welfare pay-ments. As discussed in Chapter 7, the term used to describe this concept, usually associated with the economist Ludwig Erhard, who became economics minister in the new Federal German Republic founded in 1949, was the *Sozialmarktwirtschaft* (social market economy).[32] The ultimate object of economic policy under such a system was to promote, according to Konrad Adenauer, first chancellor of the new republic, 'the individual and his well-being'.[33]

The irony was that the achievement of this ambition relied a good deal on the economic role performed by the German state. The claims of the state on the economic product increased steadily over the second half of the century in Germany, as it did in all developed economies. In 1950 the West German state's share of GNP was 17 per cent, by 1960, 31 per cent, and by 1982, 49 per cent (see Table 8.5 for details of government expenditure). This outcome was largely a consequence of higher levels of expenditure on welfare, health, and education. Much of the money absorbed by the state was redistributed to private consumers as pensions or social-security pay-ments (the real level of state consumption remained much lower, 14 per cent in 1960, 20 per cent in 1996), but rising state claims also reflected the growing importance of the state in a wide variety of roles more closely related to economic development.

In the context of the 1950s, however, the role of the state appeared to be in retreat. During the occupation, the German economy was subject to a smothering web of restrictions and controls which stifled recovery, while the

Table 8.5 State expenditure in the Federal Republic of Germany, 1949–95 (millions of DM, current prices)

Year	Total expenditure	Per head of population (DM)	Defence	Education	Social services	State debt
1950	28,141	570	4,695	1,975	7,619	18,725
1955	51,234	991	6,078	4,196	13,715	
1960	64,555	1,180	8,450	5,559	15,455	56,716
1970	196,330	3,192	19,831	24,783	40,355	123,075
1975	527,240	8,527	32,356	53,813	248,730	253,142
1980	741,627	12,047	40,937	73,089	339,409	462,838
1985	907,128	14,867	50,849	80,977	425,957	754,693
1990	1,144,607	18,102	55,180	97,474	538,872	1,048,761
1995	1,859,062	22,771	47,708	164,606	939,487	1,974,065

Source: Statistisches Jahrbuch für die BDR (1983–2000).

rapid postwar inflation eroded savings and discouraged investment. In 1948 the currency of the western zones was stabilized and re-founded, and with the establishment of the new Federal Republic the network of Allied restrictions was rapidly dismantled. Erhard was keen to remove cartel barriers to freer trade and, in the face of strong opposition from heavy industry, a cartel law banning all trade restrictions was introduced in 1957.[34] State-owned assets, including the vast Volkswagen car plant at Wolfsburg, first set up under the Hitler regime in 1938, were privatized. The protectionist and neo-mercantilist outlook of an older generation of German managers was gradually replaced by a younger cohort of business leaders more receptive to the idea of open market competition through improvements in productivity performance and aggressive marketing. Indeed, the 'economic miracle' of the 1950s and 1960s owed a great deal to the initiatives of the private business community, who responded with growing enthusiasm to a market in which they enjoyed the sustained growth of profits for the first time since the outbreak of the First World War. Businessmen also relied on the self-restraint and economic ambitions of the workforce. After half a century of tension between labour and capital, and the harsh political discipline of the Hitler period, the organized workforce in the 1950s collaborated with government and business in holding back excessive wage claims, reducing open industrial conflict, and increasing levels of productive efficiency. Wage growth was modest but steady and continuous. In 1960 only 17,000 workers went on strike in Germany throughout the entire year; in 1965 the figure was only 6000.[35]

Nonetheless, the state had a central part to play in securing and sustaining the new economic priorities. In the words of the economist Wilhelm Eucken, a pioneer of the *Sozialmarktwirtschaft*, the state was responsible for providing the conditions for 'a viable and humane economic order', but should not actually direct the economy.[36] The state was to become an ally of the capitalist process, not its master. The most significant contribution made by the state apparatus to the German economic revival of the 1950s and 1960s was the pursuit of a stable currency. After the experience of two destructive inflations in 30 years, opinion in Germany was united on the need to maintain a stable price level and to protect the value of the mark. The population was encouraged to save rather than spend, and the trades unions were persuaded to accept low levels of wage settlements on the understanding that this was the means to secure higher levels of income and welfare in the long run. The additional savings were diverted to investment in areas likely to promote high growth, where substantial gains could be made in productivity. Throughout the Federal Republic's history, output per operator-hour grew at a faster rate than income per capita, ensuring that price levels could be kept stable and German prices on foreign markets competitive. To sugar the pill of lower income growth the government in 1951 introduced the *Mitbestimmungsgesetz* (Co-Determination Law) to allow workers to contribute half of the directors in the iron, coal, and steel industries. In 1976 the legislation was extended to cover all workers in enterprises of more than 2000 employees.

The state also helped the productive economy in other ways. Generous tax concessions and subsidies to industry to stimulate revival, totalling 28 billion marks between 1949 and 1957, boosted profits and encouraged high levels of re-investment. During the decade 1955–65 investment reached one-quarter of the national product, whereas in the 1920s it had peaked at around 16 per cent.[37] A small office in Erhard's Economics Ministry unobtrusively directed investment at key areas for growth, while more obtrusively the government promoted a major construction boom in the 1950s to repair bomb damage, build new motorways (most of the German *Autobahn* network, begun in 1934, was built after the Third Reich), and replenish and expand the housing stock. Five million houses and apartments were built between 1949 and 1959, many of them with federal or municipal subsidies.[38] The state also came to play a part in the real engine of German economic revival, foreign trade.

Throughout the period from 1914 to 1949 German economic development had been inhibited, often severely so, by isolation from the world market or poor world market conditions. Trade growth stagnated in the first half of the century following the 40 years of rising export volumes before 1914, while trade itself came to be controlled directly by the state. In the 1950s, German trade was freed from state control, and in a context of expanding world opportunities for the high-value, specialized engineering, chemical and electrical products in which Germany excelled, export levels rose sharply. The state played the part of facilitator, integrating German economic interests with the wider western world in ways that maximized trading opportunities after almost 20 years of autarkic isolation and trade restrictions. Here economic diplomacy was all-important. Germany collaborated with the GATT negotiations on reducing tariff levels, and within the framework of the Organization for European Economic Cooperation (OEEC) set up in 1948. The Federal Republic also played a major part in the process of European economic integration, which led in 1957 to the founding of the so-called Common Market, a European *Zollverein*, which helped to promote high trade growth as the Prussian customs' union had done a century before. Germany was in a strong position to supply industrial products to the other member nations, and by the 1960s two-thirds of German exports went to other European states. The German state helped to oil the wheels of the growing export boom by supplying credits, granting subventions to key export sectors, and encouraging robust marketing in areas in which German firms faced stiff competition.[39] The trade boom was sustained for most of the remainder of the century, reaching exceptional peaks in the 1980s (see Table 8.6). It was not a result simply of state help, but reflected persistently low levels of inflation and intelligent attention to quality, promotion, and after-sales. Nevertheless, the common interest of government and producer in a healthy export market put a premium on the role of the state in promoting and securing market arrangements abroad.

During the 1960s the economic boom began to falter. Foreign competition increased; full employment was secured; state spending on social priorities rose sharply; wage pressure developed from a young workforce no longer so committed to fighting the evils of inflation. Growth slowed down in the mid-1960s, and in 1967 German national product and industrial production both fell for the first time in the new Federal Republic's history. A new government replaced that of Ludwig Erhard, who had become Chancellor in 1963, a coalition of right and left in parliament committed to fighting inflation and restoring growth. The new Economics Minister, Professor Karl Schiller, an academic economist whose early work in the 1930s had been on government work-creation schemes in the National Socialist recovery, played a central

Table 8.6 Federal German trade statistics, 1950–90 (billions of DM, current prices)

Year	Exports	Imports	Balance of trade	Current account balance
1950	8.4	11.4	–3.0	–0.2
1955	25.6	24.5	1.1	2.2
1960	47.8	42.7	5.1	4.8
1965	71.7	70.4	1.3	–6.2
1970	125.3	109.6	15.7	3.2
1975	221.6	184.3	37.3	9.8
1980	350.3	341.4	8.9	–28.5
1985	537.2	463.8	73.4	48.3
1990	642.8	550.6	92.2	77.4

Source: Statistisches Jahrbuch für die BRD (1953–1992).

part in shifting state economic strategy away from Erhard's neo-liberal, free-market values, to a more Keynesian model of state economic management to counteract the business cycle, and maintain price stability and export growth. In June 1967, the Law to Promote the Stability of Economic Growth was passed, giving the state enhanced powers of macroeconomic direction. A combination of tax incentives, state investment and more effective budgetary planning restored growth. The state authorities also became brokers between capital and labour, bringing the two parties together to discuss and approve economic policy, and to accept the need for modest wage growth to counter-act inflation.

One direct consequence of the shift to a strategy of economic management was a rapid increase in the state debt, which rose from 44 billion marks in 1967 to 202 billion in 1979.[40] Unlike the growing indebtedness of the war era, however, the debts were incurred to encourage growth and social stability, and they did not lead to high levels of inflation thanks to state encouragement of industrial restructuring and high productivity growth. From 1967 onwards the Federal German economy became a genuinely 'mixed economy' in which state and private interests together promoted growth and stability, and the state made ever-increasing claims on the national product. In the 1980s a neo-liberal reaction against high state spending and responsibility, identified most closely with the American President Ronald Reagan and the British Prime Minister Margaret Thatcher, produced faint echoes in Germany. The replacement of the Social-Democrat regime in 1982 by the conservative government of Helmut Kohl was expected to bring about a reversal of the state's role in the German economy, but despite some re-privatization of state assets and stricter budgetary controls, the economy remained in essence a 'mixed' one. The state was not 'rolled back', and when the German Democratic Republic, the Communist state established in 1949 in the Soviet Zone of occupation in response to the founding of the Federal Republic, collapsed in 1989 and united with its wealthy neighbour a year later, the state had to assume even larger responsibilities for integrating the new provinces and paying the bill for the widespread unemployment and low investment provoked by union. State expenditure was a little over 1000 billion marks in 1989; by 1993 it had reached 1682 billion, or 59 per cent of the national product.[41] By this point a case might well be made that taxation and state spending did actively inhibit higher levels of aggregate economic growth, for German economic performance since the 1980s has been less clearly successful than in Britain and the United States, both of which had lagged behind Germany 20 years earlier.

The high cost of absorbing the smaller East German republic reflected the very different fortunes of the former Soviet Zone of Germany. Here, there had never been any question but that the state should play the central role in organizing and running the economy. Although the long-run aim was to increase individual well-being, just as it was in the Federal Republic, the short-term priority was to organize society and economy in ways consistent with the Stalinist/Leninist model – abolition of the private economy, collectivization of farming, emphasis on heavy industry, and central predictive planning. All of this model was exported from the Soviet Union to the German Democratic Republic. In the 1950s, a series of central economic plans were drawn up designed to show that socialist command economies were the equal of their capitalist counterparts. Heavy industry and engineering industries were expanded, representing two-thirds of industrial output in 1950, and over 70 per cent by 1970.[42] Investment ratios remained high throughout the life of the Communist state, reaching almost 30 per cent of the national product in the 1970s. Agriculture was slowly collectivized and other forms of private economic activity squeezed out by the late 1950s. All the major economic variables were regulated by the state, and trade was dominated by exchange within the Communist bloc in eastern Europe (see Table 8.7).

What this system could not supply was sustained income growth and levels of consumption likely to satisfy the workforce. Unlike the experience in the Federal Republic, output per operator-hour constantly lagged behind official prices, forcing regular confrontations with the workforce when production norms were altered or prices raised to reflect the inefficiencies of the system. In 1953 real wages were cut by one-third, provoking demonstrations in 272 cities and towns across the German Democratic Republic.[43] The regime had to balance its ambitions for high levels of aggregate economic growth with the need to placate the workforce. A combination of high state borrowing and prudent concessions on food supply and wage rates kept social protest under control, but produced an economy in which it proved very difficult to raise productivity levels when workers had little

Table 8.7 The performance of the economy of the German Democratic Republic, 1949–89 (millions of DDR marks)

Year	'Social product' nominal	real*	State expenditure	Gross investment	Industrial output*	Exports
1950	61,119	98,186	24,091	1,870	33,778	3,840
1955	106,539	166,641	38,326	5,040	64,019	9,180
1960	153,080	240,271	49,457	10,923	96,989	13,870
1965	199,106	305,153	55,759	11,215	129,566	20,620
1970	271,562	405,477	69,954	23,865	171,596	29,610
1975	361,053	532,419	114,160	27,742	231,804	47,472
1980	521,629	655,212	160,283	35,379	370,054	80,281
1985	748,613	748,613	234,392	39,562	531,976	145,060
1989	820,619	825,315	269,485	49,967	–	145,007

Note: * = prices of 1985.
Source: O. Schwarzer, *Sozialistische Zentralplanwirtschaft in der SBZ/DDR: Ergebnisse eines ordnungspolitischen Experiments (1945–1989)* (Stuttgart, 1999), pp. 255–306; F. Küchler, *Die Wirtschaft der DDR: Wirtschaftspolitik und industrielle Rahmungsbedingungen 1949 bis 1989* (Berlin, 1997), pp. 21, 27.

incentive to work harder and no threat of unemployment. This combination of price controls and low consumer output had also characterized the economy of the Third Reich in the late 1930s, where it also provoked slow productivity growth and labour hostility to changes in factory practice or work norms designed to raise output. Studies of labour policy in the German Democratic Republic have shown that the trade-off between social peace and structural inefficiency was sustained by the regime from the 1950s right through to the final collapse in 1989.[44]

In the early 1960s some attempt was made to reform the East German system following a slow-down in growth and further labour unrest. A New Economic System was introduced in 1961 which streamlined the bureaucratic apparatus of economic control, and gave greater responsibility to managers and workers to match earnings to performance. The element of crude predictive planning was modified in favour of a more economically realistic policy of price formation and resource distribution. However, the modest decentralization failed to stimulate improvements in productivity, and in the 1970s, following Ulbricht's fall in 1971, the regime returned to a more conservative model of centralized economic direction. Under the influence of the veteran economic administrator, Günter Mittag, the regime set out to raise export performance, boost the social wage (subsidies for housing, health, culture, etc.) to compensate for poor consumer goods supply, and raise output per head through constructing a system of socialist industrial corporations to match the move to merger and consolidation in the capitalist west. This attempt to reverse decentralization by instead trying to reform the command economy ended in economic disaster. The cost of subsidies rose from 8 billion marks in 1970 to 53 billion in 1988; the effort to engage more with the world economy produced slow trade growth but a vast external debt (2.2 billion in 1970, 46 billion marks in 1989); the new corporations operated with embedded inefficiencies, their cost structures and labour methods entirely inadequate to compete with western models. In 1985 every mark spent on production earned only 27 pfennigs.[45] The state economy was bankrupt by the late 1980s and the population hostile to the years of shortages, high savings that yielded nothing, and the unconvincing claims of the regime that supreme economic efforts would eventually allow Communism to overtake its capitalist rival. The collapse of the regime of Erich Honecker in 1989 owed a great deal to the self-evident inadequacy of the model of state-directed economic development.

8.3 State and economic development: some conclusions

The story of state and economy in Germany in the twentieth century is a chequered one. Rathenau's confidence that rational state management of the economy was the way of the future could never have envisaged the militarized neo-mercantilism of the Third Reich, nor the stagnant and un-enlightened statism of the Communist experiment in eastern Germany after 1945. His conception of a rational state promoting growth for the general good worked for only 30 years in the Federal Republic, from the 1970s to the end of the century, but even here there were substantial strains produced by political circumstances – the tension between social-democrat and conservative views of the state in the 1970s and 1980s, and the exceptional costs, both economic and social, of integrating the former Democratic Republic into the larger Germany created in October 1990.

The correlation between state intervention, economic well-being and social peace was an ideal, dependent for its realization on circumstances in domestic politics and international markets over which the rational economic planner could have little control. The impact of war, slump and dictatorship provoked coercive state regulation of a character and degree inherently different from the model of the economic rationalists of the early part of the century. In the most extreme case, the command economy of Hitler's Germany, the consequence was a fragmentation of the German polity united in 1871 and massive economic damage, including the destruction of much of urban Germany, the loss of all overseas assets, the expropriation and extermination of German Jews, and the expulsion of some 13 million Germans living in eastern Europe.

What effect did the mixed history of state economic responsibility have on German economic development? Without question the economy would have grown more evenly and faster over the century in the absence of external con-straints and domestic crisis. Yet it is also possible to argue that even during the periods of economic exceptionalism – 1914–23 and 1930–49 in particular – state activity could contribute positively to the long-term development of the economy. The development of macroeconomics in Germany was, for better or worse, spurred on by the necessity of organizing the state for large-scale war and coping with the aftermath of economic crisis. The architects of the postwar recovery in the Federal Republic, Ludwig Erhard and Finance Minister Fritz Schäffer, were both products of the milieu in the 1920s when issues of macroeconomic steering and business-cycle stabilization were at the centre of academic economic discourse. Germany pioneered effective collection of statistical data, and during the 1930s the Reich Economic Chamber undertook to perfect the statistical recovery of national accounts. When in September 1939 the Economics Ministry was called upon to shape wartime economic policy, Minister Walter Funk summoned a 'Committee of Professors' to advise him on taxation, consumption and price control.[46] The effective wartime financial and rationing system demonstrated the extent to which economic theory had absorbed the lessons of the recent past. Keynesianism was not by any means a British invention, and indeed when Keynes' 'General Theory' was published in 1936, German reviewers were critical of its apparent lack of rigour and exaggerated claims of originality.[47]

The state also played a continuous role in encouraging an enhanced technical threshold. This was achieved partly by long-term investment in education and training, and state support for institutions of scientific and technical research, as discussed in detail in Chapter 10. Expenditure per head on education, at constant prices, was 17.5 marks in 1913, 28 marks in 1930 and 51 marks in 1958.[48] Expenditure on research and development grew steadily over the century, but was accelerated by the demands of war and war-related technologies in chemicals, aviation, radio, and medicine. Of course, much of this research would have been undertaken, war or not; much of it benefited states other than Germany – for example, rocket technology, which was developed during the 1930s and 1940s in Germany and then transferred to the American and Soviet rocket projects after 1945. But the periods of economic crisis and exceptionalism did not reverse the important part that science and technology had historically played in German economic development in the nineteenth century.

The state also played a part in the restructuring of the German economy over the century in ways that were conducive to more rational economic development. Agriculture remained a drag on growth performance throughout the first third of the century, but under the new marketing arrangements and modernizing investment of the 1930s through to the European Economic Community's Common Agricultural Policy in the 1960s, German farmers were not free to produce what they wanted or to fix the price. The large handicraft sector was also restructured by the effects of war, inflation, and crisis. Hundreds of thousands of artisans transferred their skills to the factory during the First World War and the 1920s; during the 1939–45 war, artisan shops were closed down and millions of craft workers drafted into war work. The consequence was to increase the skill ratio of large-scale industry – true particularly of the motor industry in Württemberg and Bavaria, where much craft industry was located – and to eliminate the large number of marginal producers who had survived at the edges of the modern industrial economy down to the 1930s.

Finally, the German state has succeeded since 1945 in producing a stable financial environment to cope with the very large expenditures on social welfare characteristic of a mature industrial economy. This has involved a difficult learning curve. The currency was destroyed twice, in 1923 and 1948, and had to be reconstituted with the help of outside powers. Welfare payments could not be maintained in the 1920s without compromising the fragile economic position of the state, and, in the view of many economic critics, accelerating the drift into crisis in 1929.[49] The strategies of state financial management practised since 1949 in the Federal Republic have produced a stable environment for growth with low inflation and interest-rates, and a growth of welfare funding without compromising productivity growth and high investment ratios. This is a mix that few other developed European economies have been able to achieve in the long-term; it was not achieved in the German Democratic Republic, a fact that indicates the extent to which the beneficent effects of state policy should not be over-stated. Without a sound financial environment and comparatively low levels of long-term inflation, the private sector in the Federal Republic might well have faced higher levels of industrial conflict and tougher competition abroad, as the ailing British economy did in the 1960s and 1970s. No other contribution made by the state has been as significant in terms of Germany's sustained economic growth since the 1950s.[50]

Much, however, of what has been achieved in terms of economic development in Germany is the consequence of private initiative, as it was in the nineteenth century. The state was capable of exerting a dead hand as well as a helpful pull upwards. No history of the state in twentieth-century Germany could argue that 'modernization' of the economy has been a consequence alone of enlightened state activity. In Germany's case economic development has relied on the input of businessmen, engineers, and bankers, and of workers ambitious to improve skills and raise personal incomes. For these actors, for much of the century, the context in which they might make rational market choices has been limited by war, or by dictatorship, or by the messy economic aftermath that both produced. Germans have shown themselves to be no different from other western populations: the economy has ultimately been judged by its ability to supply rising living standards and improving standards of amenity and welfare. Where the German state has freely furthered the ambitions of businessmen and consumers, it has stimulated and invigorated economic development; where it has stifled or supervised them, economic develop-ment has been inhibited and distorted.

8.4 Notes

1 *Walther Rathenau: gesammelte Reden* (Berlin, 1924), p. 161, 'Der Höhepunkt des Kapitalismus: Vortrag in der deutschen Hochschule für Politik am 27 April 1921'.

2 G. Scheele, *The Weimar Republic: Overture to the Third Reich* (London, 1946), pp. 229–30.

3 S. Andic and J. Veverka, 'The Growth of Government Expenditure in Germany since the Unification', *Finanzarchiv*, 23 (1964), pp. 169–278, here pp. 244–5; *Statistisches Jahrbuch für die BRD 1994*, pp. 515, 682. By 1995, taxation and social expenditure represented 48.5 per cent of Gross National Product. See the discussion on the claims of the state in W. Weimer, *Deutsche Wirtschafts-geschichte: von der Währungsreform bis zum Euro* (Hamburg, 1998), pp. 454–5.

4 J. Noakes and G. Pridham, eds, *Documents on Nazism 1919–1945*, Vol. II: *State, Economy and Society 1933–1939* (Exeter, 1984), doc. 185, p. 283. For the German version, see W. Treue, 'Der Denkschrift Hitlers über die Aufgaben eines Vierjahresplans', *Vierteljahrshefte für Zeitgeschichte*, 3 (1954), pp. 184–210, here p. 206.

5 L. Burchardt, 'Walther Rathenau und die Anfänge der deutschen Rohstoff-

bewirtschaftung im Ersten Weltkrieg', *Tradition*, 15 (1970), pp. 169–96; G. Hecker, *Walther Rathenau und sein Verhältnis zu Militär und Krieg* (Boppard am Rhein, 1983), pp. 201–37.

6 Andic and Veverka, 'Government Expenditure', pp. 244–5, 262–9. On military spending see N. Ferguson, *The Pity of War* (London, 1998), pp. 105–18; and D. Stevenson, *Armaments and the Coming of War in Europe, 1904–1914* (Oxford, 1996).

7 C.-L. Holtfrerich, *The German Inflation 1914–1923* (New York, 1986), pp. 108–18.

8 There were some increases in taxation. See T. Balderston, 'War Finance and Inflation in Britain and Germany 1914–1918', *Economic History Review*, 2nd ser., 42 (1989), pp. 222–44; see, too, the recent discussion in H. Strachan, *The First World War*, Vol. I (Oxford, 2001), pp. 890–8.

9 In general, see J. Kocha, *Facing Total War: German Society 1914–1918* (Cambridge, MA, 1984); G. Hardach, *The First World War, 1914–1918* (London, 1977).

10 Holtfrerich, *Inflation*, p. 129; G. Feldman, *The Great Disorder: Politics, Economics, and Society in the German Inflation, 1914–1924* (Oxford, 1993), pp. 578–9. The figure of 1 per cent occurred right at the end of the inflation, in November 1923. In March of that year, taxes yielded 14.3 per cent of income, Treasury bills 85.3 per cent.

11 See Feldman, *Great Disorder*, pp. 845–6, on the effect of inflation on the banks. Total bank deposits declined from 33.6 billion in 1913 to 9.8 billion in 1924. On the social and political consequences, see N. Ferguson, *Paper and Iron: Hamburg Business and German Politics in the Era of Inflation 1897–1927* (Cambridge, 1995), pp. 419–45; and the essays in G. Feldman and E. Muller-Luckner, eds, *Die Nachwirkungen der Inflation auf die deutsche Geschichte, 1924–1933* (Munich, 1985), particularly P.-C. Witt, 'Die Auswirkungen der Inflation auf die Finanzpolitik des Deutschen Reiches 1924–1935', pp. 43–94, and T. Childers, 'Interest and Ideology: Anti-System Politics in the Era of Stabilization 1924–1928', pp. 1–19.

12 See for example G. Stoakes, *Hitler and the Quest for World Dominion* (Leamington Spa, 1986); W. Boelcke, *Deutschland als Welthandelsmacht 1930–1945* (Stuttgart, 1994), pp. 13–31; A. Teichert, *Autarkie und Grossraumwirtschaft in Deutschland 1930–1939* (Munich, 1984), pp. 180–219; H. Kahrs, 'Von der "Grossraumwirtschaft" zur "Neuen Ordnung": zur strategischen Orientierung der deutschen Eliten 1932–1943' in H. Kahrs et al., eds, *Modelle für ein deutsches Europa* (Berlin, 1992), pp. 9–26. For developments in economic thought, see W. Krause, *Wirtschaftstheorie unter dem Hakenzreuz* (Berlin, 1969), esp. Ch. 6. For a good example of the contemporary discourse see R. Heindel, *NS Denken und Wirtschaft* (Stuttgart, 1932): 'Liberalism is dead . . .' (p. 70); 'Freedom from the world crisis, freedom from world finance, the struggle against the capitalist West would be made possible then with the formation of a central European bloc'. (p. 89).

13 For a recent discussion, see D. Silverman, *Hitler's Economy: Nazi Work Creation Programs, 1933–1936* (Cambridge, MA, 1998), esp. Chs. iii–iv. See also B. Wulff, 'The Third Reich and the Unemployed: National Socialist Work-Creation Schemes in Hamburg 1933–4', in R. J. Evans and R. Geary, eds, *The German Unemployed* (London, 1987).

14 See C. Kopper, *Zwischen Marktwirtschaft und Dirigismus: Bankenpolitik im 'Dritten Reich', 1933–1939* (Bonn, 1995), pp. 199–208.

15 A. Barkai, *Nazi Economics: Ideology, Theory and Practice* (Oxford, 1990), pp. 116–55; see, too, R. Brady, *The Spirit and Structure of German Fascism* (London, 1937), charts II–V.

16 On agriculture under the Third Reich, see G. Corni and H. Gies, *Brot, Butter, Kanonen: die Ernährungswirtschaft in Deutschland unter der Diktatur Hitlers* (Berlin, 1997), esp. Chs. II.2, III.2, III.3.

17 Memorandum by Col. Hossbach, 10 Nov. 1937, Minutes of the Conference in the Reich Chancellery, 5 Nov. 1937 in *Documents on German Foreign Policy*, ser. D, Vol. 1, p. 30. For contemporary ideas about German economic expansion see, among many others, E. von Mickwitz, ed., *Aussenhandel unter Zwang* (Hamburg, 1938), pp. 4–5, 36–41; K. Kruger, *Deutsche Grossraumwirtschaft* (Hamburg, 1932), pp. 225–33; Wirtschafts-Hochschule Berlin, ed., *Europaische Wirtschaftsgemeinschaft* (Berlin, 1942), which contained nine chapters by leading economic experts in Germany on the complete remodelling of the European economy under German direction. On Hitler's economic thinking see R. Zitelmann, *Hitler, Selbstverständnis eines Revolutionärs* (Hamburg, 1989), pp. 195ff.

18 W. Stern, '*Wehrwirtschaft*: A German Contribution to Economics', *Economic History Review*, 2nd ser., 13 (1960/1), pp. 270–81; there is a full account of the establishment of the structure for war economics in B. A. Carroll, *Design for Total War: Arms and Economics in the Third Reich* (The Hague, 1968), pp. 78–92.

19 Bundesarchiv-Koblenz, R 7/2149, Ohlendorf papers, 'Grundsätze der Volkswirtschaftspolitik' (n.d. but October 1935), p. 9 (these papers are now deposited at the Bundesarchiv in Berlin).

20 On the plan, see R. J. Overy, 'The Four Year Plan', *German Yearbook of Business History, 2000* (Berlin, 2000), pp. 87–103. The best general account is D. Petzina, *Autarkiepolitik im Dritten Reich* (Stuttgart, 1968).

21 Bundesarchiv-Koblenz, R26 II Anh./1, H. Dichgans, 'Zur Geschichte des Reichskommissars für die Preisbildung', n.d. (1947), pp. 4–6, 9–11; R26 II Anh./2, W. Rentrop, 'Materialen zur Geschichte des Reichskommissars für die Presibildung', pp. 8–13.

22 Imperial War Museum, FD 3056/49, 'Statistical Material on the German Manpower Position during the War Period 1939–1944'.

23 Figures on the Gross National Product from A. Ritschl and M. Spoerer, 'Das Bruttosozialprodukt in Deutschland nach den ämtlichen Volkseinkommens-und Sozialproduktsstatistiken 1901–1995', *Jahrbuch für Wirtschaftsgeschichte* (1997), Part II, pp. 27–54, here p. 51. On the issue of economic restructuring and consumption, see R. J. Overy, 'The German Economy 1919–1945', in P. Panayi, ed., *Weimar and Nazi Germany: Continuities and Discontinuities* (London, 2001), pp. 33–73, here pp. 44–6, 48–9; and H. Kellenbenz, *Deutsche Wirtschaftsgeschichte*, Vol. II (Munich, 1981), pp. 453–4.

24 A. Barkai, *From Boycott to Annihilation: The Economic Struggle of German Jews, 1933–1943* (Hannover, NH, 1989), pp. 113–14, 154–5. There is a great deal of new research on 'aryanization', some of which was state-sponsored, some of it driven by business interests or party radicals. See, for example, F. Bajohr, *Arisierung im Hamburg* (Hamburg, 1997).

25 There is a very large literature on these policies. See, for example, *Nazi Gold: the London Conference 2–4 December 1997* (HMSO, London, 1998), which gives details on the expropriation of gold throughout occupied and dependent Europe, an example where race policy and predatory economics went hand-in-hand. Nor were the policies confined only to state agencies: see J. Steinberg, *The Deutsche Bank and its Gold Transactions during the Second World War* (Munich, 1999).

26 W. Boelcke, *Die Kosten von Hitlers Krieg* (Paderborn, 1985), pp. 98–102, 110–11; K.-H. Hansmeyer and R. Caesar, 'Kriegswirtschaft und Inflation 1936–1948' in Deutsche Bundesbank, ed., *Währung und Wirtschaft* (Frankfurt am Main, 1976), pp. 367–424.

27 See J. A. Tooze, *Statistics and the German State, 1900–1945* (Cambridge, 2001), Ch. vii. Tax yields rose from 17 billion RM in 1938/9 to 34 billion in 1943/4; see National Archives, Washington DC, film T178, roll 15, Reichsfinanz-ministerium, 'Statistische Ubersichtung zu den Reichshaushaltsrechnungen 1938 bis 1943', Nov. 1944.

28 This is an area of considerable debate. See R. J. Overy, *War and Economy in the Third Reich* (Oxford, 1994), pp. 274–86. See, too, R.-D. Müller *et al.*, *Das Deutsche Reich und der Zweite Weltkrieg*: Band V/I (Stuttgart, 1988), pp. 364–91. Much of the pressure on consumption exerted by high state spending existed even before the outbreak of war: see N. R. Reagin, '*Marktordnung* and Autarkic Housekeeping: Housewives and Private Consumption under the Four Year Plan, 1936–1939', *German History*, 19 (2001), pp. 162–84.

29 D. Eichholtz, *Geschichte der deutschen Kriegswirtschaft 1939–1945*, Vol. II: *1941–1943* (Berlin, 1985), p. 265.

30 On the reforms of German wartime economic administration see L. Zumpe, *Wirtschaft und Staat in Deutschland*, Vol. I: *1933–1945* (Berlin, 1980), pp. 334–44; H.-E. Kannapin, *Wirtschaft unter Zwang* (Cologne, 1966), pp. 29–79.

31 Details in Public Record Office, Kew, AIR 10/3873, British Bombing Survey Unit, 'German Experience in the Underground Transfer of War Industries' based on a German Armaments Ministry report of 11 Nov. 1944. The plan to develop 93 million square feet of underground factory space was probably the largest public works scheme ever initiated by a modern government. Only 13 million square feet of space were actually prepared.

32 A. J. Nicholls, *Freedom with Responsibility: The Social Market Economy 1918–1963* (Oxford, 1994). On Allied plans for Germany, see A. Kramer, *The West German Economy 1945–1955* (Oxford, 1989), pp. 33–67. See, too, L. Erhard, *Deutsche Wirtschaftspolitik. Der Weg der Sozialen Marktwirtschaft* (Düsseldorf, 1962).

33 K. Adenauer, *Memoirs 1945–1953* (London, 1965), p. 164.

34 V. Berghahn, *The Americanisation of West German Industry* (Leamington Spa, 1986), pp. 84–110, 156–81.

35 P. Schwerdtner, 'Trade Unions in the German Economic and Social Order', *Zeitschrift für die gesamte Staatswissenschaft*, 135 (1979), pp. 454–73, here p. 464.

36 W. Stolper and K. Roskamp, 'Planning a Free Economy: Germany 1945–1960', *Zeitschrift für die gesamte Staatswissenschaft*, 135 (1979), pp. 374–404, here p. 377. These sentiments were widespread among German academic economists after 1945, even those who had once supported greater intervention before 1939. See, for example, A. Müller-Armack, *Wirtschaftslenkung und Marktwirtschaft* (Hamburg, 1947), esp. pp. 14–37; and A. Weber, *Marktwirtschaft und Sowjetwirtschaft* (Munich, 1949), pp. 185–233.

37 W. Glastetter, G. Högemann and R. Marquardt, *Die wirtschaftliche Entwicklung in der Bundesrepublik Deutschland 1950–1989* (Frankfurt am Main, 1991), p. 89. See, too, the general discussion on sources of growth, in R. Klump, *Wirtschaftsgeschichte der Bundesrepublik Deutschland* (Wiesbaden, 1983), esp. pp. 58–72, 98–100.

38 J. Diefendorf, *In the Wake of War: the Reconstruction of German Cities after World War II* (New York, 1993), pp. 18–42. The state supplied 55 per cent of the 91 billion marks spent on house building through subsidies and direct investment between 1950 and 1959. On road building and state help for transport, see P. Spary, *Wachstums-und Wohlstandseffekte als Entscheidungskriterien bei öffentlichen Strassenbauinvestitionen* (Berlin, 1968), pp. 29–34.

39 On trade policy, see H. J. Jung, *Die Exportförderung im wirtschaftlichen Wiederaufbau der deutschen Bundesrepublik* (Cologne, 1957); W. Hankel,

'Germany's Economic Nationalism in the International Economy' in W. L. Kohl and G. Baseri, eds, *West Germany: A European and Global Power* (Lexington, MA, 1980), pp. 23–9; Stolper and Roskamp, 'Planning a Free Economy', pp. 391–4; and H. Müller, 'The Reconstruction of the International Economic Order after the Second World War and the Integration of the Federal Republic of Germany in the World Economy', *Zeitschrift für die gesamte Staatswissenschaft*, 137 (1981), pp. 344–66.

40 A. Sommariva and G. Tullio, *German Macroeconomic History 1880–1979* (London, 1987), p. 239.

41 *Statistisches Jahrbuch für die BRD 1994* (Wiesbaden, 1994), p. 515.

42 On the economy of the German Democratic Republic, see O. Schwarzer, *Sozialistische Zentralplanwirtschaft in der SBZ/DDR: Ergebnisse eines ordnungspolitischen Experiments (1945–1989)* (Stuttgart, 1999); and F. Küchler, *Die Wirtschaft der DDR. Wirtschaftspolitik und industrielle Rahmenbedingungen 1949 bis 1989* (Berlin, 1997).

43 J. Kopstein, *The Politics of Economic Decline in East Germany, 1945–1989* (Chapel Hill, NC, 1997), p. 36.

44 On the Third Reich see, in general, R. Hachtmann, *Industriearbeit im 'Dritten Reich': Untersuchungen zu den Lohn-und Arbeitsbedingungen in Deutschland 1933–1945* (Göttingen, 1989); T. Siegel, 'Wage Policy in Nazi Germany', *Politics and Society*, 14 (1985), pp. 1–51. On the experience in the German Democratic Republic, see Kopstein, *Politics of Economic Decline*, esp. Chs. 3 and 6.

45 Kopstein, *Politics of Economic Decline*, p. 99.

46 Bundesarchiv, BA R7/xvi 7, Professorenausschuss to Reichswirtschaftsministerium, 16 Dec. 1939, report on wartime finance.

47 See, for example, A. Forstmann, 'Arbeit oder Beschäftigung? Kritische Betrachtungen zu J. M. Keynes "Allgemeiner Theorie der Beschäftigung"', *Finanzarchiv*, 5 (1937), pp. 375–468.

48 Andic and Veverka, 'Growth of Government Expenditure', pp. 264–5.

49 See, for this, K. Borchardt, *Perspectives on Modern German Economic History and Policy* (Cambridge, 1991), Chs. ix, x; J. von Kruedener, ed., *Economic Crisis and Political Collapse: the Weimar Republic* (Oxford, 1990).

50 On financial policies, see W. Dreissig, 'Zur Entwicklung der öffentlichen Finanzwirtschaft seit dem Jahr 1950', in Deutsche Bundesbank, ed., *Währung und Wirtschaft*, pp. 691–742; and B. Sprenger, *Das Geld der Deutschen: Geldgeschichte Deutschlands von den Anfängen bis zur Gegenwart* (Paderborn, 1991), pp. 248–58.

9

Social structure in the twentieth century

CHRISTINA BENNINGHAUS, HEINZ-GERHARD HAUPT, AND
JÖRG REQUATE
University of Bielefeld

At the beginning of the twenty-first century, there is little agreement among sociologists about the extent to which differences between social strata still exist in German society, or about their importance relative to other kinds of social differentiation, such as those between the sexes and the generations. German society as a whole pays much less attention to social inequality nowadays than in the 1970s.[1] Risks such as environmental damage and unemployment seem to affect all social groups, and social differences are now perceived more as the expression of different lifestyles and interests than as the consequence of social origins or social position.[2] Some sociologists go so far as to maintain that the enormous improvement in overall living standards since the 1960s – the so-called 'elevator effect' – has meant that in the last 20 years what Gerhard Schulze terms the 'experience-oriented society' has replaced the 'competitive society' with its class struggles.[3] No longer is the struggle to improve or secure one's status the chief concern, but rather the attempt to shape one's life according to one's own ideas about what constitutes happiness.

While social scientists are thus questioning the survival and importance of social inequality in present-day Germany, a glance at the late nineteenth century yields a much clearer picture. At that time, contemporaries regarded different social groups as occupying mutually antagonistic positions. Thus, for instance, the political economist and historian Gustav Schmoller complained in 1873 about the 'deep chasm which transsects our social environment', and 'the struggle which nowadays divides employers and workers, the property-owning and propertyless classes'.[4] So should we regard the history of German social structure in the twentieth century as a transition from a class society to an 'experience-oriented society'? This chapter asks how social stratification in Germany changed in the course of the twentieth century, and whether and to what extent this involved a decline in the importance of social differences. Long-term developments in social structure were brought about not only by general modernization processes such as industrialization and urbanization, but also by the economic and political crises (and the wars) of the first half of the century, and by state policies, which affected social structure both in periods of dictatorship and under the modern welfare state. Additional important roles were played by organized interest-groups such as unions and associations.

Sociological concepts about society reflect existing social structures, and thus themselves constitute historical sources for studying past societies. But at the same time they also prescribe the context of meaning used in describing a society both by its own members and by outsiders; and this means they influence the theoretical frameworks used by historians in interpreting that society. For this reason, this chapter begins by surveying the most important theories of social stratification in Germany.[5] It then uses selected aggregative data to trace the long-term changes in German social structure over the twentieth century. Finally, it discusses the three large social groupings that were most important for German social structure in the twentieth century: the elites, the middle classes, and the workers.

For the 1945–90 period, wherever explicit reference is not made to the German Democratic Republic, the discussion relates to West Germany. As shown by recent studies of the social history of the German Democratic Republic, its society cannot be adequately described using classical models of stratification.[6] The social policies of the German Democratic Republic leadership, which were emphatically directed at increasing equality, led to a significant reduction in inequalities based on earning opportunities, property, and education. Old elites lost their influence, differences in income and lifestyles disappeared, and the dividing lines between the workers (who were regarded as vectors of the state) and other social groups became increasingly blurred. The result was a society that was socially homogeneous compared to other parts of Europe: in the words of Klaus Tenfelde, probably the 'most equal society that has ever existed, or probably ever will exist, in central Europe, with the possible exception of the Czechoslovak Socialist Republic'.[7] Admittedly, the social history of the German Democratic Republic does not consist solely of this process of declining social differentiation. Here, too, new elites were formed, although their position was based not so much on economic capital as on political power and the resulting access to resources. Models of stratification developed to describe capitalist societies are thus only of limited use in analysing the social history of the German Democratic Republic. Furthermore, the data essential for analysing social structure were often not collected in the German Democratic Republic for political reasons, so that direct comparisons between East and West Germany are possible only in particular fields.

9.1 Sociological models of class and stratification and their influence on historical research

The concept of class that has exercised the most important political influence is unquestionably that of Karl Marx. His well-known dichotomistic class-model – ownership versus non-ownership of the means of production – has also informed many historical studies. In the former eastern bloc, especially in the German Democratic Republic, Marxist analyses even became the basis of the official writing of history. But even in studies using a less dogmatic Marxist analysis than the politically constrained studies carried out in the German Democratic Republic, it soon emerged that Marx's dichotomistic model of class was not adequate for understanding the complexity of social stratification and the processes by which it changes, especially in the twentieth-century context.[8]

A more flexible approach, which has in the meantime become more influential among historians in the Federal Republic of Germany, is that of Max Weber.[9] Like Marx, Weber regards classes as being based on economic factors. That is, classes are groups of people possessing approximately the same opportunities in the market. For Weber, the basic distinction is between the property-owing classes and the earning classes. Unlike Marx, Weber does not assume that the propertyless earning classes necessarily have common interests and hence inevitably develop a class-consciousness that in turn leads to their pursuing common ends. This may indeed take place, but only when the causes and consequences of that class's common circumstances are clearly perceived; and other factors, such as the possibility of forming associations and the existence of a recognizable opponent, also play a role. Thus Weber divests the Marxist concept of 'class' of its historical and political teleology, thereby getting rid of the idea that 'objective interests' derive from the immediate situation in which a class finds itself. Furthermore, Weber's use of the plural – property-owing *classes* and earning *classes* – conveys a much more differentiated picture of society than the Marxist dichotomy. For Weber, the various earning and property-owning classes do not yet form social units as such; they only become so through 'commercium' and 'connubium' – that is, through social transactions and marital ties. Weberians define social classes as being distinguished by 'totalities of class situations, between which people easily move and indeed typically do move from one generation to the next'.[10] For historians concerned with social stratification in general or with particular social formations, this raises the question of the extent to which economically determined, objective class situations give rise to social groups that act together politically.

For much of the twentieth century, the class theories of Marx and Weber remained the starting-point for analyses of social stratification in Germany, particularly ones that viewed social differences as determined by economic factors. Both Marxist and non-Marxist analysts of class took pains to refine their respective models in order to provide the best possible explanation of social realities and social change.[11] As a result, particularly non-Marxist, but also ultimately Marxist, analysts accepted the existence of a more or less differentiated middle stratum, or of several middle classes. But although this meant that theoretical models became more differentiated and descriptive, they still often left out of account other important factors that were central for explaining social inequality.

These included the state and its social policies, as well as a variety of cultural factors. State social policy can be regarded as aiming to reduce social inequalities and the disadvantages arising from the large differences in individuals' market situations in such a way as to maintain social harmony. This applies particularly to those partially or wholly excluded from income-earning activity: children, elderly people, and the ill. But the German sociologist Rainer Lepsius has pointed out that state social policies not only reduce existing inequalities but also create new ones. This leads him to argue that the Weberian property-owning and earning classes must be enhanced by a concept of a 'public provision class' (*Versorgungsklasse*), which he defines as 'constituting a class insofar as differences in access to public goods and services determine people's access to goods, their external circumstances, and their inward destinies'.[12] One justified objection to Lepsius's model is that 'pure' public provision classes hardly exist, since pensions and unemployment payments (i.e. state provision) are closely linked to previous earned income. Nevertheless, in examining social inequality it is important to recognize that the regulations and payments of the welfare state have a non-trivial influence on the economic situation of large sections of the population (as discussed in Chapter 7).

Even more than social policy, cultural factors have in the last quarter of the twentieth century increasingly been regarded as important in analysing social inequality. A particularly influential figure in this context has been Pierre Bourdieu, who integrated into his analyses not only economic capital but also 'cultural capital' (education) and 'social capital' (social relationships).[13] Nevertheless, Bourdieu stayed quite close to the usual materialistic explanatory models, since he too regarded economic living conditions as greatly affecting the accumulation of the two other sorts of capital, and as influencing the emergence of class-specific patterns of thinking, perception, and values. In this view, cultural factors still exercise relatively little autonomous effect on an individual's location in the social hierarchy.

Unlike Bourdieu, who focuses on an empirically objectifiable socio-cultural analysis of class, recent German studies, such as those of Ulrich Beck and Gerhard Schulze, place much greater emphasis on the subjective perception and the subjective shaping of one's own life situation. Two things have brought about this shift toward analysing society in terms of non-material factors. For one thing, at latest since the 1950s, the concept of 'class society' has been retreating into the background in Germans' own descriptions of their society. Thus when in the 1950s Helmut Schelsky claimed that during the structural upheavals after the two world wars considerable upward and downward mobility had taken place, he was not wholly mistaken. However, to speak of postwar German society as a 'levelled-out middle-stratum society' or 'melting-pot' in which class had disappeared, as Theodor Geiger did, was only possible if one stressed *perceptions* of social inequality over its realities, which remained un-diminished.[14] The second reason for the increasing importance of non-material factors in analysing social structure is the fact that, although great social differences continue to exist, overall social well-being has noticeably increased and social differences now exist within these much higher average living-standards (the 'elevator effect'). Closely related to this is a much-discussed shift in values toward post-material attitudes, and a related emphasis on the importance of how the individual conducts his or her own life. According to Ulrich Beck and others, the generally higher level of well-being makes inequalities less visible. A lasting process of individualization has 'mixed society up', largely dissolved class society, and created new 'milieus' to which one belongs not because of 'objective' factors but rather because one chooses to do so.[15]

Thus in recent sociological thinking the concept of 'milieu' has become the most serious competitor with that of class. Among historians, the concept of 'milieu' has also seen a boom in recent years but is used rather differently. The influential work by Rainer Lepsius distinguishes four 'social and moral milieus' in twentieth-century Germany: the Catholic, the conservative, the bourgeois Protestant, and the socialist.[16] In contrast to class theories, the milieu concept views religion as having its own role in forming society, a role that runs straight across all models of class and stratification. Milieu models regard these four German 'milieus' as having undergone considerable dissolution since the 1960s, just as models of 'class' regard the old class formations as having broken down. Since this chapter is about social *stratification*, this concept of 'milieu' will not play any further role here.

9.2 Aggregate social change in twentieth-century Germany

German social structure underwent enormous transformations during the twentieth century. Long-term changes in the composition of the population and the structure of earnings had already begun in the nineteenth century, as discussed in Chapters 2, 3, and 4. In the twentieth century, German social structure was affected both by largely unplanned processes such as industrialization and urbanization, and by state action, particularly educational expansion and welfare policy. At the same time, despite all these changes, particular aspects of social inequality turned out to be very enduring. Poverty and deprivation manifested themselves in new ways, but (as discussed in Chapter 7) did not become things of the past. This section explores the changes in German social structure on the basis of various aggregative social indicators.

9.2.1 Population change

In the first third of the twentieth century, as discussed in Chapter 2, the population growth of the nineteenth century continued. The number of people living within the frontiers of the German Empire rose from 60.5 million in 1913 to 68.6 million in 1938, although the Second World War then caused it to fall to 64.2 million (45.7 million in the western zones and 18.5 million in the German Democratic Republic). However, as early as 1961 German population size surpassed its prewar level, with 73.3 million in the Federal Republic and the German Democratic Republic combined. The huge wave of refugees out of the German Democratic Republic up to 1961 caused its population to fall from 18.5 million in 1945 to 17.1 million in 1961, but in the Federal Republic population grew continuously: from 45.7 million in 1945 to 56.2 in 1961, finally reaching 66.1 million in 1995. In the mid-1990s, the reunited Germany, despite a smaller territory, had a larger population than the old German Empire, with 81.6 million inhabitants.[17]

Population growth has essentially two components: on the one hand the so-called natural factors, the birth rate and the death rate; and on the other, migration movements. Both are closely connected with changes in social structure. As discussed in Chapter 2, the most noticeable secular trend in the natural factors during the twentieth century has been the decline in the birth rate and the rise in life expectancy. This decline in the birth rate can primarily be observed among the lower strata: over the course of the twentieth century, the combination of poverty and large families of children has begun to disappear, although the process is not yet complete. Social inequalities in the face of sickness and death, by contrast, have proved to be particularly tenacious. Material well-being and satisfaction with one's own occupational and general life situation still leads to longer life expectancies than do material deprivation and dissatisfaction, as discussed in Chapter 12. Counter to the widely held view, for instance, heart attacks are not so much a 'managerial illness' as a fate experienced disproportionately by members of the lower strata.[18]

Despite the decline in the surplus of births over deaths, the total number of inhabitants in Germany nevertheless rose in the course of the twentieth century and, as discussed in Chapter 2, this was mainly because of in-migration. Between the late nineteenth century and the present day, Germany changed from a land of emigration to one of immigration.

Whereas between 1890 and 1893 nearly 1.3 million Germans emigrated to the 'New World', in the following decades emigration overseas declined perceptibly, even though it temporarily increased again during periods of economic crisis such as in the Great Inflation and the 1950s when over 2 million Germans migrated to the United States, Canada, and Australia.[19] The terror of the National Socialist state after 1933, especially the persecution of political opposition groups such as the Communists, Social Democrats, and Democrats, and the expulsion of the Jews, meant that emigration both to neighbouring European states and overseas took on a dramatic character for those involved in it, but in quantitative terms it was quite limited. Of the 400,000 Jews living in Germany under the Weimar Republic, approximately half emigrated, and thereby remained alive. Since they often occupied leading positions in the economy, legal life, scholarship, and literature, their emigration involved a huge loss for German society.

The twentieth-century redrawing of political frontiers also caused large migration movements. After the Versailles agreements in 1919, approximately 700,000 people left the areas ceded to Poland and France in order to settle in areas that remained German, while 300,000 emigrated from Germany to Poland and 150,000 Ruhr-Poles emigrated to France. This exchange led to a net population gain for Germany. After 1945, flight and expulsions from the eastern areas of the former German Empire (amounting to more than 10 million people between 1945 and 1950) greatly increased and changed the population of Germany. In the short term, the refugees escalated the economic and social problems of particular villages and towns, and absorbed a lot of attention from the authorities. But in the medium term, they provided additional labour that was beneficial for the reconstruction of the country, and contributed to changes in the confessional and political structure of East and West German society and to the destruction and transformation of traditional social 'milieus'. Throughout the following decades, political support was given to the so-called 'Aussiedlung', which enabled 'German-descended' inhabitants of eastern European states to migrate to the Federal Republic. Between 1988 and 1994 alone, almost 2 million people took advantage of this possibility.[20]

The Federal Republic also benefited from the stream of refugees leaving the Soviet Zone and the German Democratic Republic up to the building of the Wall in 1961. Before 1949, 1.3 million people had already fled to the western zones, and between then and 1961 another 2.29 million did so, while only 500,000 people migrated from the Federal Republic to the German Democratic Republic. This migration from east to west unquestionably weakened the German Democratic Republic, since the refugees included many skilled workers and a disproportionate proportion of the young intelligentsia – engineers, school teachers, university teachers, doctors, pharmacists, and lawyers. The rising demand for labour in the Federal Republic from the late 1950s onward meant that these refugees were rapidly integrated into West German society and filled noticeable gaps.[21]

Especially during the 1960s, the population of the Federal Republic was increased through the systematic recruitment of foreign labour, euphemistically called *Gastarbeiter* ('guest workers'). Around 14 million Italians, Greeks and Turks moved to the Federal Republic between 1955 and 1973; however, most did not remain, with 11 million returning to their home countries. 'Of the 4.8 million workers still to be found in the Federal Republic in 1989', according to the migration researcher Klaus Bade, 'almost 3 million belonged to, or were descended from, the "guest worker" population that had immigrated from the former "recruitment countries"'. In actuality, the inflow of 'guest workers' initially meant that the lower stratum of the population increased in size, as will be discussed later in greater detail. But for quite a few years now two clear tendencies can be seen within the immigrant population. First, this group has come to resemble that of the German-descended population in its proportion of self-employed persons, although not in its pattern of qualifications or wealth. Second, the second and third generations of immigrants show unmistakable tendencies toward upward social mobility.

Since its foundation, the Federal Republic has thus been one of the most important immigrant societies of the world.[22] With 4.9 per cent foreigners in the population in 1970 and 8.8 per cent in 1995, Germany has *de facto* developed into a multicultural society. But, as shown by the absence of a law regulating immigration, the occurrence of xenophobic excesses, and the slowness with which foreigners are becoming citizens, German society has not yet come to terms with this process, either politically or culturally.[23]

9.2.2 Changes in the structure of employment

The social and economic structure of Germany has been dramatically transformed since the 1880s. This can be seen first in the clear decline in the importance of agriculture, both as an employer and as an economic sector, as discussed in Chapter 3. Whereas in 1895, 36 per cent of all inhabitants of the German Empire still earned a living from agricultural activities, in 1978 it was 6 per cent, and in 1996 as low as 3.2 per cent. By contrast, the industrial sector continues to be an important employer. In 1895, industry provided jobs for 39 per cent of all employed Germans, and by 1970 this had risen to 49.4 per cent. In the following 25 years, however, the importance of the secondary sector declined: by 1995, only 35.9 per cent worked in this sector. By that date, a majority of employed Germans no longer worked in industrial or craft businesses, but instead in shops and offices. Whereas in 1895 around one-quarter of employed Germans worked in the service sector, by 1970 this had risen to 41.5 per cent and by 1995 to 60.9 per cent. Within the service sector, trade and transportation continued to play an important role, but have now been joined by consulting, advertising, and research.[24]

This sectoral shift has been accompanied by changes in occupational roles. Self-employed people made up nearly a quarter of all employed Germans in 1895, but the decline in agriculture together with the process of concentration in commerce, crafts, and industry caused this to fall to only 16 per cent at the foundation of the Federal Republic, and only 9.8 per cent by 1997. At the same time, self-employment became less attractive as an occupational role model. In particular, the assistance of family members on farms, small shops or small workshops, carrying out tasks important for business survival but usually poorly paid, has greatly declined. Whereas in 1907 family members of self-employed persons made up 15 per cent of all earners, and in 1961 still 10.3 per cent, by 1997 it was only 1.0 per cent. Thus employment in family business has become a very marginal phenomenon in Germany.

The twentieth century witnessed a dramatic increase in the number of salaried or white-collar employees (*Angestellten*), who made up 4.7 per cent of all German earners in 1882 and 47.4 per cent in 1997. At the same time, the internal structure of this group changed, with a huge expansion in its range of activities. Increasingly, it also included women: about one-quarter of all white-collar employees were women in 1925, rising to almost one-half by 1970. From 1900 onward, white-collar employees became important in public service administration, industrial enterprises, department stores, and offices. Civil servants (*Beamten*) also increased in number, from 4.7 per cent of all employed Germans in 1882 to 6.9 per cent in 1997, but their growth rate and overall social importance remained well behind that of the white-collar employees. Civil servants are a group which had and still has a special relationship of loyalty and trust vis-à-vis the German state, and which the state provides with symbolic and real gratification; but nowadays they are being more harshly criticized than ever before, and in the context of discussions about 'deregulation' there are proposals that *Beamtenstatus* (civil servant status) should be restricted to those working in the police, army and judiciary.[25]

Until well into the 1980s, workers and their families made up the largest group in German society. In 1882, 57.4 per cent of all German income-earners were agricultural or industrial workers, falling to 34.8 per cent by 1996. In agriculture in particular, wage-work disappeared almost completely, while in industry, jobs shifted from the traditional industries of mining, steel making, and textile production to the modern growth industries of chemicals and electronics. Throughout the twentieth century and despite these changes, the proportion of women among workers remained relatively constant, at about 30 per cent (as discussed in Chapter 11).[26]

Like other occupational groups, workers were divided by religious affiliation, regional loyalties, qualifications, and earning opportunities. Nevertheless, through mutual association in unions and political parties, they achieved an improvement in their social situation which in the 1960s manifested itself in much better real incomes, consumption opportunities, leisure, and social security. In the course of the century, the focus of their activities shifted from the traditional industries of mining, steel making, and textile production to the modern growth industries of chemicals, electricity, and electronics, especially for men, while women remained over-represented in the remaining branches of industry. In this process, as already mentioned, the proportion of women among workers remained relatively constant, at about 30 per cent.

9.2.3 *Education and social structure*

The nineteenth and twentieth centuries witnessed the rapid expansion of the German educational system, as also discussed in Chapter 10. Around 1900, the vast majority of German children left school at the age of 13 or 14 and started to work full time, learning the necessary skills either on the job or within a formal apprenticeship. Today, young people remain in full-time education for at least ten years and often receive their vocational training in schools.[27]

Since the 1920s, the German education system has been characterized by a tripartite division. After attending primary school for four years, children are placed in one of three types of school – *Hauptschule, Realschule* or *Gymnasium* – in which they typically stay for the rest of their school years. The *Hauptschule* leads only to the basic German school-leaving certificate, achieved at age 15–16. The *Realschule* leads to a certificate, achieved at age 16–17, necessary for admission to technical schools and higher vocational education. The *Gymnasium* leads to a certificate called the *Abitur*, achieved at age 19–20, which permits entrance to university. In recent decades, the *Gesamtschule*, which was originally intended to replace the old system by integrating all pupils into the same schools, has been added to this system.

The relative importance of these different schools has shifted remarkably over the last century. This can best be illustrated by examining the school experience of German 13-year-olds. In 1900, only 6 per cent of all 13-year-old boys attended the *Gymnasium*, a proportion which had risen to 15 per cent by 1931 and further expanded after the Second World War, reaching 22 per cent in 1970 and 29 per cent in 1990. The *Realschule* attracted about 5 per cent of 13-year-olds in the interwar period but gained importance after the war with 16 per cent in 1970 and 26 per cent in 1998. As the *Gesamtschule* nowadays is attended by about 10 per cent of all 13-year-olds, the importance of the *Hauptschule* has diminished considerably. While more than three-quarters of all 13-year-olds attended a *Hauptschule* in 1952, this proportion had fallen to only one-third of all boys and one-quarter of all girls of this age group by the late 1990s.[28]

Parallel to the growing importance of the *Gymnasium*, university education has become more common in Germany, as discussed in Chapter

10. The number of students increased from about 50,000 in 1900 to 120,000 in 1920 and 410,000 in 1970. Since then it has quadrupled, reaching 1,640,000 in 1995.[29] As these figures suggest, the West German educational system expanded greatly after the war. Especially between 1962 and 1975, when investment in schooling and training increased from 3 to 5.5 per cent of German GNP, and nine years' school attendance became compulsory, educational levels clearly improved. Whereas in 1960, 71 per cent of German school-leavers still finished school with the *Hauptschulabschluss* or even without any certificate and only 6 per cent of school-leavers obtained the *Abitur*, the corresponding figures for the mid-1990s were 30.5 per cent and 30 per cent.[30]

In the German Democratic Republic, the expansion of the educational system started earlier, as it was supposed to contribute to the politically desired dissolution of class society. The 'bourgeois monopoly of education' was supposed to be broken down by the abolition of divisions within the education system, by expanding further education, and by special support for children of workers and farmers. If one relies on official data, which exaggerate the proportion of 'workers' children' for ideological reasons, the level of education among citizens of the German Democratic Republic rose rapidly from the 1950s on, especially among the children of workers. Thus in 1958, for example, more than half of all college students in the German Democratic Republic were classified as 'workers' children'.[31] Over the decades that followed, however, the regime restricted educational opportunities. Out of fear of an 'over-production' of academics, access to the *Abitur* and thus to university was choked off. This gave rise to fierce competition for places, in which workers' children were at a particular disadvantage. In the 1980s and 1990s, counter to all propaganda to the contrary, such children enjoyed worse educational opportunities in East than in West Germany.[32]

Looking at the entire German population, the expansion of the educational system has led to great generational differences in educational achievement. Members of the younger generation are far more likely to have received secondary education.[33] Furthermore, an ever-growing proportion of 16- to 30-year-olds is still in education, experiencing a new life-stage which sociologists are terming 'post-adolescence'.[34]

During the 1960s, the expansion of the West German educational system was seen as an opportunity to reduce social differences. Under the slogan of 'equality of opportunity', a meritocratic ethos postulated that individuals' social status should be based on their abilities rather than their social origins or their sex. Thus educational planners and politicians focused on the educational disadvantages experienced by women, workers' children, and the poor, as well as the inadequate coverage of rural areas.

With some justification, women can be regarded as the 'winners' of the educational expansion in Germany. During the last decades, their educational disadvantages have all but disappeared. Among the graduates of the *Realschule* and the *Gymnasium*, girls are slightly over-represented.[35] Among university students, the proportion of female students rose from only 2 per cent in 1908 to 19 per cent by the beginning of the 1930s, was then noticeably depressed again under National Socialism, but reached 28 per cent by 1960. During the following decades it increased continuously, reaching 43 per cent by 1994.[36] However, among the higher academic qualifications women are still found in lower proportions than men. In 1995 women achieved only 32 per cent of all doctorates and only 13 per cent of all *Habilitationen* (the German 'second doctorate', necessary for obtaining a tenured job as a university academic).[37] Furthermore, gender differences in choice of occupation and subjects studied are still marked. Although women did benefit disproportionately from the expansion in educational opportunities, they were often unable to turn this 'cultural capital' to account on the labour market. Thus, as also discussed in Chapter 11, earning opportunities of German women remain significantly worse than those of men with equal educational qualifications.[38]

In West Germany, as in other European countries, educational expansion did not reduce educational differences between social strata. Although the proportion of workers' children able to attend a *Gymnasium* increased from 7 per cent in 1976 to 12 per cent in 1989, at the same time this proportion also increased among children of other social strata: among children of white-collar employers, for instance, from 31 per cent to 40 per cent.[39] Parents' education and income continue to influence German children's educational opportunities considerably: at the beginning of the 1990s, about three-quarters of children of civil servants with higher education attended a *Gymnasium*, compared to only 14 per cent of children of apprenticeship-trained workers, and only 7 per cent of children of unskilled workers.[40] Thus the German educational expansion enormously increased the overall educational level of the population, but did not do away with social inequalities in achieving these higher educational qualifications.

Whereas it proved possible to reduce regional differences in the supply of education, the integration of foreign young people into the German school system has remained inadequate. In 1994, only 8.8 per cent of foreign school-leavers achieved the *Abitur*, compared to 24.9 per cent of school-leavers of German origin. By contrast, 43.6 per cent of foreigners finished their schooling only with the basic school-leaving certificate from a *Hauptschule*, while this was the case for only 25.4 per cent of their fellows of German origin.[41] Since higher education suited to the labour market is an essential factor in social integration, this educational gap means that foreigners in Germany are still threatened with social marginalization.

Over the course of the twentieth century, educational qualifications have unquestionably become less socially exclusive in Germany and an increasing number of people, especially women, have benefited from educational expansion. Nevertheless, sociologists point out two paradoxes in this educational expansion. The first consists of a simultaneous upward and downward valuation of educational qualifications. School and university matriculation are more and more valued because they have increasingly become prerequisites for occupational advancement, especially in managerial positions. But at the same time academic graduation alone leads less and less automatically to high occupational positions, and this has led to its devaluation. For academics, both income advantages and job security have declined over the last 25 years. The second paradox is the fact that expanding educational opportunities have not in themselves led to greater equality of opportunity. The unambiguous winners of the educational expansion are the children of the middle service-sector strata and the old middle stratum. This has meant that they have increased their advantage over workers' children, especially the children of untrained and apprenticeship-trained workers, who seldom profited from the educational expansion.[42]

9.2.4 *Income distribution and poverty*

Despite great social changes, increased opportunities for social mobility, improvements in educational levels, and transformations in lifestyles and housing, fundamental aspects of social inequality appear to be enormously enduring. Even today, German society is marked by considerable gender differences, unequal distribution of income and wealth, and the continued existence of poverty.

German women's earning opportunities and career prospects continue to be considerably worse than those of men, as discussed in detail in Chapter 11. According to data for the mid-1990s, women's gross earnings are about 30 per cent lower than men's, and family obligations disadvantage women substantially more than men in planning their lives.[43] Compared to the beginning of the twentieth century, clear improvement in women's opportunities can be observed in many spheres – ranging from voting rights to educational opportunities – but the leading positions in German society are still reserved mainly for men.

Unequal income distribution also continues to prevail, unaffected by the overall rise in real wages. Thus the highest-earning 20 per cent of the German population earned 45 per cent of total national income in 1950, and still as much as 43 per cent in 1980 and 38 per cent in 1995; the corresponding figures for the lowest-earning 20 per cent of the population were 5 per cent in 1950, 7 per cent in 1980, and 9 per cent in 1995.[44] There are also large income differences among occupational groups. Self-employed households have the highest average incomes: according to data for 1993, they dispose of twice as much income as the average German citizen. Civil servants and white-collar employees also earn more than average, while workers, farmers, pensioners, unemployed people, and welfare recipients are forced to survive on below-average incomes.[45]

Overall, despite growing national income, the gap between rich and poor in Germany has not been closed. Admittedly, income inequality in Germany is no higher than in other western European countries, is less extreme than in England and Ireland, and is much lower than in the United States.[46]

The distribution of wealth shows even clearer differences. In 1993 average gross household wealth in the former Federal Republic (West Germany) was 65,300 DM. However, 21 per cent of German households had wealth of less than 10,000 DM, amounting to only 1.4 per cent of total gross national wealth. By contrast, 5.6 per cent of households had gross money wealth over 200,000 DM – that is, almost one-third of the total gross money wealth in Germany was concentrated in the hands of one-twentieth of the population.[47]

Finally, stubborn outcrops of poverty still survive in twentieth-century German society. By contrast with earlier centuries, twentieth-century poverty was no longer a question of physical survival, since food shortages were only experienced in times of war and postwar crisis. While the inter-war period was a time of severe economic hardship for many Germans, with little increase in real wages and extremely high rates of unemployment during the Depression, the economic boom of the postwar decades nurtured hopes that poverty would 'wither away'. However, these hopes did not turn into reality, even though the extent and the causes of poverty have certainly changed.

Quantitative statements regarding the extent of poverty are difficult, as definitions of poverty have to be adjusted to changing historical and cultural circumstances. In the postwar period, a political definition of poverty has been used which equates the poor with those people eligible for social assist-ance. While their number was low in the postwar decades, comprising only 1.2 per cent of the population in 1969, it then rose continuously, encompassing 2.8 per cent of the population in 1994 and 3.3 per cent in 1996. However, as not everybody entitled to social assistance actually claims benefits, it has been estimated that about 5 per cent of the German population in 1996 could be regarded as poor.[48]

A different picture emerges when poverty lines are defined using the economists' and sociologists' concept of 'equivalent income'. The 'equivalent income' of a household is defined as its disposable income adjusted for its specific size and composition. This is because larger households need larger incomes than smaller households to reach a given level of economic well-being: thus a four-person household with an income of DM60,000 annually has a lower level of economic well-being than a two-person household with the same income level. To calculate a household's 'equivalent income', an equivalence scale is used, which reflects assumptions about how different characteristics, such as household size and composition, relate to the amount of income different types of households need to achieve an equivalent standard of living. The equivalent income of one household can then be compared directly with the equivalent income of another household of a different size and composition, or with the average 'equivalent income' of German households as a whole.

Relative poverty can then be measured by comparing a household's equivalent income with the average equivalent income of all German households; this measure has the advantage that it controls for differences in household size and composition. In this context, 'severe poverty' has been defined as 40 per cent of average equivalent income in the economy as a whole, 'poverty' as 50 per cent of average equivalent income, and 'low income' as 60 per cent of average equivalent income. Using this categorization, 'in 1995 more than one-twentieth of the total German population lived in "severe poverty", a good tenth lived in "poverty", and about one-fifth in "the sphere of low income"'.[49]

Although poverty seldom lasts long, nevertheless large groups in German society face the risk of impoverishment at some time in their lives. Thus between 1990 and 1995, 22.9 per cent of the German population underwent phases of 'relative poverty'.[50] Compared to the past, fewer of them were elderly people or females, even though these groups were disproportionately represented compared to non-elderly males. Poverty in Germany at the end of the twentieth century was concentrated particularly in households of unemployed people, foreigners, single parents, and numerous children.[51]

Despite rising real wages across the century, a wider range of consumption possibilities, and rising average living standards, structures of inequality have survived in Germany, as reflected in gender differences, income gaps, and divergent experiences of poverty. Women's movements, labour unions, and (albeit timidly) organizations for the homeless and the poor, have protested and continue to protest about these inequalities in life chances and occupational opportunities, but have not been able to do away with prevailing inequalities.

9.3 Structural changes within large social groups

Within German society, it is possible to observe social groups that are distinguished from one another according to a wide variety of criteria: income, wealth, education, and prestige. As time has passed, the composition of these groups has changed so much that they can hardly be encompassed using a single set of analytical concepts. White-collar groups at the end of the twentieth century no longer have much in common with those of the period around 1900. One can speak of a 'bourgeoisie' (*Bürgertum*) at the end of the Kaiserreich and under the Weimar Republic, but not for the German Democratic Republic. Nevertheless, the discussion that follows adopts a crude social division into 'upper', 'middle', and 'lower' groups. This has two advantages: first, it corresponds to the historian's customary distinction between elites, middle strata, and lower strata; and second, it also corresponds with present-day German citizens' picture of their own society, as reflected in opinion polls.[52]

9.3.1 Elites

German society at the end of the nineteenth century and the beginning of the twentieth is frequently described as a sharply segregated class society. In this, it was not fundamentally different from other industrialized European societies of the time. Nevertheless various peculiarities can be discerned, especially with regard to the elites.

Compared to other western European countries, what is noticeable about German society at the beginning of the twentieth century is the special role of the nobility (as already discussed in Chapter 3), together with the strong position of the military and the bureaucracy. Unlike in England or France, where nobility and upper bourgeoisie had merged into a comparatively homogeneous elite long before, in Germany the nobility – above all the famous Prussian *Junker* – had largely succeeded in defending its corporate privileges at the top of class society, and in maintaining not only its economic but also its political power.[53] Although parts of the German nobility suffered great losses of land in the course of the nineteenth century, land ownership remained the basis of noble self-definition in Germany into the twentieth century. A stable core of noble landowners was able not only to retain its landed property, but also to extend it substantially. Admittedly, as research studies justifiably emphasize, land ownership was not synonymous with wealth. Nevertheless, in 1914 the large noble landowners still stood at the pinnacle of the scale of wealth in Germany.[54]

In sustaining this dominant social position, the decisive factor was that the German nobility, on the basis of a solid economic underpinning, had succeeded in maintaining its political power in the government, the administration, the diplomatic service, and not least the military of early twentieth-century mass society. However, the revolution of 1918 unquestionably spelt the beginning of the end of noble political power in Germany. Admittedly, most of the higher German civil servants remained in office even after the revolution. But whereas in 1914, nobles still made up 90 per cent of all regional administrators (*Landräte*) in Pomerania, and as many as 40 per cent even in the Rhine Provinces, by 1930 only 14 out of 480 Prussian regional administrators were nobles (less than 3 per cent). Over the same period, the number of noble civil servants in the upper administrative echelons declined by about one-third, although the Foreign Office remained a bastion of the nobility. Of the 161 leading noble civil servants in 1921, 62 (39 per cent) were still in office in 1933.[55]

But the abdication of the Kaiser in 1918, the resignation of the 19 surviving princes, and the dissolution of the Upper Chamber (dominated by the nobility even outside Prussia), deprived the nobility not only of its traditional offices at court and its surviving political functions, but also quite generally of its prestige and influence, and (not least) of a large proportion of those channels of influence which had enabled noble pressure groups to go on securing their interests. With the election of Hindenburg as President of the Reich, parts of the conservative noble agrarian lobby in particular saw a chance of bringing these channels back to life. And when the so-called 'cabinet of the barons' was appointed in 1932, this lobby actually temporarily regained control of the levers of political power. But by then the nobility had long relinquished any formative role in German politics. Politically fragmented and unified only in their aim of 'surmounting' the Republic, non-trivial sections of the nobility, particularly substantial groups within the corporative associations of the nobility, approached ever closer to the National Socialists or went over to them completely. But Nazi gratitude was very limited. In the longer term, the nobility continued to lose importance. Although there was a large proportion of nobles among the resisters of 20 July, this probably had a great deal to do with the fact that it was clear to many that a defeat under Hitler's leadership would lead not only to territorial losses but to a final loss of importance for the nobility. Politically, and with the expropriation of their land in the Soviet Occupation Zone also economically, the German nobility as a social group decisively and finally lost its position in 1945. In specific leading groups in West German society – for instance in the diplomatic corps – the nobility continued to be clearly over-represented, quite apart from the fact that a whole array of noble families, undamaged by all the upheavals, succeeded in maintaining and extending their economic position under the new conditions of economic prosperity after 1949.[56]

In the 1970s, it was argued that the strong position of the German nobility under the Kaiserreich showed that the German bourgeoisie lacked 'bourgeois' qualities, and should instead be regarded as a 'feudalized' bourgeoisie. In the meantime, however, this view has been considerably revised. This is particularly the case with regard to the German educated bourgeoisie which, in the judgement of Hans-Ulrich Wehler, must be seen as a 'politically powerful bourgeois formation, which shaped norms, modes of conduct, and life goals' under the Kaiserreich.[57] The educated bourgeoisie – both those pursuing civil service occupations and those pursuing what were termed the 'free' professions – succeeded in inducing the state to provide far-reaching guarantees of their security and position. In any case, civil servants could be sure of the special esteem of the state which, after all, they them-selves to a considerable extent represented. But the 'free' (or, as they are sometimes called, 'unfree') professions, such as doctors, lawyers, engineers, secondary-school teachers and others, also succeeded in gaining state support for their numerous aims, not least control over access to their occupations – a major contrast with the Anglo-Saxon professional model, which developed without state guarantees.[58]

Against this background of a comfortable, state-guaranteed position at the beginning of the twentieth century, it was the educated bourgeoisie in particular that experienced the First World War, the 1918 revolution, and the 1923 hyperinflation as dramatic turning points. In addition to its feeling of being under threat by a burgeoning working class pushing for political influence, the educated bourgeoisie experienced real losses from the hyper-inflation, which particularly affected those whose savings were held in banks rather than in the form of substantial material assets. A sense of crisis had already been spreading among the bourgeoisie since the turn of the century. The rise of the working class, growing urbanization, and the changes these brought about in the bourgeois society of notabilities (especially in towns and cities), the increasing perception of society as a 'mass society': these are only a few key phrases describing the changes which gave the bourgeoisie – probably above all the educated bourgeoisie – the feeling that it might be losing the role it claimed as motor and measure of social progress. Indeed, the beginning of the Weimar Republic appeared to provide dramatic confirmation of previously rather vague bourgeois fears of being increasingly put on the defensive by advancing modernization. The state, which had hitherto protected the interests of the educated bourgeoisie both inside and outside the civil service, now appeared to be too weak to sustain such guarantees, and no longer desirous of doing so. This led the bourgeoisie, particularly members of the 'free' occupations, to turn away from the new state in disappointment. The bourgeois occupational organizations saw one of their chief successes as being the way in which they cooperated with the state to dampen the consequences of cyclical crises by means of bureaucratic monitoring. But the Weimar state democratized and modernized the system, and despite a significant over-supply of academics succeeded in improving access by women and other underprivileged groups. In various ways, the Weimar state put pressure on the professions to reform, and the corporative professional associations regarded this as a threat to all the achievements of their policies of professionalization.

Anxieties about loss of social and economic power brought many members of the educated bourgeoisie into opposition against the Weimar state, but did not necessarily reflect the real situation of each occupational group. University lecturers, like all civil servants, had 'suffered dispropor-tionately from the inflation caused by the war', but they had also profited disproportionately from the economic upturn. At the end of the 1920s, their incomes were 40 per cent above the prewar level and 4–6 times the average worker's wage (compared to only 2–3 times the average worker's wage before the war).[59] The other bourgeois occupations, too, were able largely to consolidate their material position up to the end of the 1920s. The educated bourgeoisie could also count among its long-term successes in the first third of the twentieth century the tendency for managers of businesses increasingly to hold academic and professional qualifications. Furthermore, at least in the first half of the twentieth century, there was a clear and continuing rise in the proportion of sons of the upper educated bourgeoisie in the German economic elite. But this did not reconcile the bourgeoisie to the Weimar Republic or even lead them actively to accept the opportunities the Republic might have offered for an expansion of bourgeois liberalism. Instead, large sections of the educated bourgeoisie in general and the professions in particular threw themselves into the arms of the National Socialist system, which had explicitly stated that it wanted nothing to do with precisely this bourgeois liberalism. Admittedly, the professions could regard themselves as having 'improved' their own position in the short term at the expense of the Jews and left-wing liberals, but only insofar as they did not regret their complete loss of occupational autonomy.

The Weimar Republic and especially the National Socialist period have been characterized as years of crisis for the bourgeoisie, eventually leading to its 'dissolution'. However, this crisis had in part been caused by the bourgeoisie itself. In particular, numerous young academics at German universities had made a very substantial contribution to bringing it about. Although regarding 'bourgeoisie' and 'liberalism' as equivalent had always been problematic, in German universities powerful energies were directed at 'freeing' future elites from 'the ballast of liberalism'.[60] Thus the bourgeoisie also played a considerable role in increasing the power of 'anti-bourgeois' National Socialism. Even in 1933, outside central politics there was hardly any changeover in the elite, with two important exceptions. One was the expulsion of the very few liberal officials, for instance in the administration and justice system. The other was the expulsion of Jews from all spheres of public life, and thus of course from leading positions in it. Recent research has emphasized how deep the traces were of the 'dejudification' carried out by the Nazis, especially among managers in the banking system (as discussed in detail in Chapter 5).[61]

The extent to which 1945 saw a discontinuity in the composition and recruitment of the German elite differed greatly between the two German states founded in 1949. The American sociologist L. J. Edinger distinguished three different patterns of continuity within the West German elite after 1945. The clearest break with the prewar period occurred among the political elites and the union leaders. None of the leading Nazi functionaries returned to a political post or to any other leading position after the war. The most unbroken continuity, by contrast, Edinger discerns in the Catholic Church, and to a lesser extent in the Protestant church and the universities. The third pattern was one in which a very few people with excessively close links to the Nazi apparatus of domination were dismissed, whereas the vast majority returned to their posts after a short phase of denazification.[62] This pattern can be observed in the administration and in the officer corps, and probably also in other spheres. Recent studies have stressed the enormous continuities throughout much of the twentieth century in the German justice system and among Germany's economic elites. Political caesurae, not least 1945, had surprisingly little impact on the composition of Germany's economic leaders, who underwent the same experience as the German educated elite both inside and outside the civil service: after a short-lived wave of dismissals, the management teams of German firms returned to their original posts, with very few exceptions.[63] Radical change was experienced only by the political elite and (as already mentioned) by the nobility, which now finally ceased to be the leading group in society.

This final dismissal of the nobility as the leading stratum in society, together with the beneficial consequences of economic growth, misled scholars such as Helmut Schelsky into assuming that social differences in general had been levelled out.[64] But very soon, sociologists pointed out that the upper and upper middle strata continued to dominate West German society, a pattern that only began to change with the educational expansion of the 1960s and 1970s.[65] Over the long term, access to the elite has increasingly opened up in the case of higher managerial positions, as shown by the increasing difficulty of passing on such posts from father to son. In the 1950s it was still to some extent possible for managerial families to engage in 'dynasty building', but nowadays this has almost completely died out.[66]

It is still an open question to what extent the concept of 'bourgeoisie' (*Bürgertum*) and 'bourgeois-ness' (*Bürgerlichkeit*) can still be applied to the upper and middle social strata of the Federal Republic of Germany. Admittedly, it is generally agreed that the Federal Republic has approached nearer to the ideal of 'bourgeois society' or 'civil society' than any previous German society. But in this process, has the German bourgeoisie completely disappeared, or only changed its form? This question is frequently posed, with as yet no conclusive answer.[67]

By contrast with the broad continuities in composition and recruitment of elites in the Federal Republic, hardly any society can ever have brought about a more radical discontinuity in its leading personnel than the German Democratic Republic. Unlike in the Federal Republic, where the expertise of the old leading strata in the economy, the administration, the military and the justice system was regarded as indispensable, in the German Democratic Republic the selection of personnel for key social positions was unambiguously dominated by political considerations. One symptom of this was the rapid emergence of so-called *Volksrichter* (people's judges), who were supposed to prevent the old personnel of the justice system from returning to their inherited positions. Admittedly, in some spheres, especially the universities, an effort was made to retain 'bourgeois' lecturers, especially in the natural sciences.[68] But here, too, by the time the Berlin Wall went up in 1961 the German Democratic Republic had lost a large proportion of its experts. First politics and then the scarcities it created meant that in the German Democratic Republic, more than ever before or after in any German society, opportunities for upward mobility were opened up to children of the lower strata, especially children of workers.

This big turnover in the elite, the ostentatious break with the past, and the opportunities for upward mobility it implied, must have made a non-trivial contribution to the relative legitimacy enjoyed by the German Democratic Republic at the beginning of its existence, despite all the repression. But the initial dramatic opening of the universities to workers' children was followed by an increased social closing which set in as early as the end of the 1950s. Privileged access to education by the bourgeoisie had been removed, but was increasingly being replaced by educational privileges for the socialist intelligentsia. Whereas in 1954 about half of those starting university came from workers' families, by 1989 it was at most 7–10 per cent; in the same period, the proportion of children of university or college graduates rose from 12 to 78 per cent of the total.

The educational expansion in the two German states also increased the proportion of female students. However, in both Germanys female university graduates failed to gain access to leading positions in society. Nevertheless, this was true to a differing extent in the two German states. In the German Democratic Republic, the leading positions in politics, the economy, the justice system, and not least the universities continued to be reserved almost exclusively for men. But compared to West Germany, in East Germany there were more females in the management of firms and women were more active in the justice system. In the 1980s in West Germany women made up 18 per cent of judges and public prosecutors, compared to about 50 per cent in East Germany. It is justifiably emphasized that when the German Democratic Republic came to an end and its labour market went into crisis, this hit women much more severely than men, as discussed in Chapter 11. Although precise figures are not available for all sectors, it is at least clear that it affected women in academic occupations less than in other spheres of activity. Nevertheless, at the beginning of the 1990s, in the territory of the former German Democratic Republic 21 per cent of all engineers were female, a proportion three times as high as in the territory of the former Federal Republic.[69]

But despite some structural and personal continuities, the collapse of the German Democratic Republic in 1989 brought about deep-reaching structural changes in the composition and recruitment of elites. The positions of power, which had been monopolized by the 'new socialist intelligentsia', had to be largely vacated. In politics, in administration, in the justice system, in the military, in the broadcasting organizations, and in some sectors of the universities, there occurred a partial West German take-over of East Germany. Unlike after the collapse of the National Socialist regime, where at least in West Germany old elites returned to their positions after a short interruption, after the collapse of the German Democratic Republic a reservoir of West Germans was available to fill the vacuum in the elite created by political change.

9.3.2 *The middle strata*

Ever since Aristotle the concept of the 'middle' has stood for measure and moderation, compromise, and balance. This metaphor has always been applied to societies, and has been especially widely used in Germany. Unlike in Britain or France, in Germany this ideological view of the middle social stratum has been driven by state policy and the lobbying of occupational interest groups. After 1880, the term *Mittelstand* – a German word meaning literally 'middle estate', for which there is no English equivalent, although it is sometimes translated loosely as 'middle class' – was no longer used for the bourgeoisie but instead referred to craftsmen and shopkeepers. After the turn of the century, it was increasingly also applied to the so-called 'new *Mittelstand*' of white-collar employees (*Angestellten*) in technical, commercial and bureaucratic occupations. The state, the corporate organizations of craftsmen and shopkeepers, and the corporate associations of white-collar employees, all portrayed the *Mittelstand* as a guarantee of a harmonious society in the face of the increasing anonymity of life and the polarization of social forces. Into the present day, *Mittelstand* has remained an important category used by master craftsmen, shop proprietors, and white-collar employees to describe themselves, although its importance has varied and diminished over time. Among white-collar employees its importance declined after about 1960, but as late as 1974 the President of the *Zentralverband des deutschen Handwerks* (Central Association of German Crafts), Paul Schmitter, explicitly appealed to basic elements in *Mittelstand* ideology: the craftsman was 'still, even today, the link between capital and labour', and – as his predecessor had put it in 1969 – 'in craft workshops still, even today, the desire for cooperation and the sense of community has survived'.[70]

One of the peculiarities of German social development is that, long into the twentieth century, the middle of society operated not as a sphere of competition and unhindered mobility, but rather as a space structured by the state and by occupational corporatism. The continuity of these definitions, and their transformation over time, can be traced both in state action and in the development of corporate organizations of master crafts- men, shopkeepers, and white-collar employees.[71]

Conservative groups and governments in particular, but before 1933 also the political centre, lauded the social qualities of the *Mittelstand,* drawing a clear distinction between it and the working class in order to support the status quo, indeed often to pursue reactionary social goals. From the conservatives of the Kaiserreich to the CDU/CSU after 1949, the German right has often supported at least some of the demands made by *Mittelstand* lobbying groups. In the Kaiserreich, craft workers enjoyed more extensive protection than any other social group: H. A. Winkler has appropriately termed it 'social protectionism'. Craft organizations called *Innungen*[72] (a revival of an old German term for guilds) were able to impose compulsory membership on all masters in a locality if certain conditions were met;

chambers of handicrafts (*Handwerkskammern*) arose as institutions in public law; and training of apprentices was confirmed as a monopoly of master craftsmen. Shop proprietors and white-collar employees also profited from this state protection. In particular German states, warehouse taxes were imposed to protect shopkeepers.[73] White-collar employees enjoyed a special status in businesses, which was reflected in the fact that they were paid monthly, had holiday entitlements, and enjoyed superior working conditions; these privileges were confirmed in the 1911 *Reichs-versicherungsordnung* (Imperial Insurance Ordinance), which separated their medical and old-age provision from that of the workers.[74] In the 1950s, the German government (supported even by SPD votes) confirmed the *Grosse Befähigungsnachweis* (Great Certificate of Qualification), which permitted only those holding the title of master craftsmen to set up work-shops, a regulation passed by the Nazis to satisfy a long-standing demand of the corporate organizations of craftsmen; this law also sought to restrict opening a retail shop only to those able to display a certificate of expertise. It was only several years later that this attempt was wrecked through a veto of the *Bundesverfassungsgericht* (Federal Constitutional Court).[75] After 1949, the distinction between white-collar employees and workers was weakened in several ways: it became possible for white-collar employees to be outvoted by workers in elections, and the material and legal differences between white-collar employees and workers were reduced.

The Weimar Republic adopted a completely different attitude to the *Mittelstand*. As politics began to be determined by the alliance between large industry and the workers' movement, and hence economic perform-ance, economic rationalization, and an increase in competition became ever more important, subsidies to maintain *Mittelstand* interests became much less central. Thus it was not until 1932 that the Brüning government gave way to pressure by the shopkeepers for a prohibition against the establish-ment of dime stores.[76]

Under National Socialism, policy fluctuated between two poles. On the one hand, the Nazis sought to gain the adherence of master craftsmen and shopkeepers by granting concessions to them. On the other hand, the need to prepare for war and then to conduct warfare meant that the Nazis sought to rationalize craftwork and shopkeeping, as well as production and administration. Thus Nazi policy toward the *Mittelstand* took on a Janus face. At the beginning, the National Socialist government granted demands that the corporate organizations of craftsmen had been making since the Kaiserreich, for instance with the *Grosse Befähigungsnachweis* (Great Certificate of Qualification). But at the same time, in the process of Nazi economic coordination, the corporate associations and chambers of the craftsmen were dissolved and integrated into the *Deutsche Arbeitsfront* (German Workers' Front). During the war, matters progressed as far as a so-called *Auskämmung* ('mopping up') of the craft sector, leading to a decimation in the number of craftsmen.[77]

The policy of the German Democratic Republic also fluctuated between the imperatives of providing for economic needs and the desire to bring about structural changes in distribution and production. When providing for needs moved to centre stage, collectivization slowed down. When structural policies became more important, the number of craft workshops and retail shops declined. But unlike in West Germany, East German governments consistently sought to break down distinctions between workers and white-collar employees: their primary goal was an idealized working class, not an ideologically overcharged middle stratum.[78]

Another peculiarity of German society was that the middle stratum not only enjoyed considerable state privileges, but also organized itself into a dense network of corporative occupational organizations and *Mittelstand* associations. The long survival of guilds, which were definitively abolished in all German territories only with the foundation of the Empire in 1871, meant the survival of very strong corporative traditions in craft circles. These traditions favoured the spread of the so-called *Innungen*, corporate groups formed by master craftsmen; the term *Innung* itself was taken over from one of the many German terms for 'guild'. The 1897 *Handwerker-novelle* (Supplementary Bill on Craftsmen) actually provided that all crafts-men could be compelled to become members of an *Innung*, so long as a majority of the independent master craftsmen of that occupation in that town opted for it. Although master craftsmen in the western provinces of Prussia and in southern Germany mostly stayed away from the *Innung* movement, nevertheless by 1907 almost 500,000 craft masters were organized into *Innungen*. By 1926 as many as 70.9 per cent of all German craft masters belonged to an *Innung*, although on the part of 79 per cent of them this was not a voluntary choice. Thus nineteenth-century German craftsmen succeeded in creating a form of interest-group representation which issued certificates of mastership, journeymanship, and apprentice-ship, and which has survived in Germany into the present day.

In their corporative organization, craftsmen were more successful than shopkeepers, who generally had to maintain their position in chambers of commerce dominated by large merchants and overseas traders. Before 1933, shopkeepers possessed their own independent chambers only in Hamburg and Bremen. But both shopkeepers and craftsmen (although not a majority of them) belonged to the *Mittelstand* associations. The one that attracted most attention was unquestionably the *Reichsdeutsche Mittelstandsverband* (*Mittelstand* Association of the German Empire), founded in Magdeburg in 1913 with the explicit aim of opposing the 'gold and red internationals' – i.e. Jews and social democrats. Then, under the Weimar Republic, the *Mittelstandspartei* (*Mittelstand* Party) sought to appeal to small-scale tradesmen, but enjoyed only moderate success – indeed, after 1930 very little. In the Federal Republic after 1949 there was a specifically *Mittelstand* current within the CDU/CSU, but outside these two political parties the *Mittelstand* did not take on any independent organizational form.[79]

This *Mittelstand* orientation also dominated sections of the white-collar movement. As among craftsmen, so also among white-collar employees, there was a powerful tendency to form associations. As early as 1907, approximately every third white-collar employee belonged to an association. Admittedly, these early white-collar associations did not all resemble unions: most of them repudiated strikes and some accepted entrepreneurs as members. But the First World War and its aftermath ended this apolitical situation, increasing support for associations regarding themselves as political, such as the social democratic *Afa-Bund* (*Arbeitsgemeinschaft für Angestelltenverbände*) in the early Weimar Republic, and later the 'liberal' *Gewerkschaftsbund der Angestellten* (GdA) and the *Deutsch-Nationalen Handlungsgehilfenverband* (DHV). Between 1920 and 1930, these numbered 1.4 million members among them: i.e. before the National Socialists took over power, 35 per cent of all German white-collar employees were organized into such associations. In the Federal Republic after 1949, this high degree of mobilization was never re-attained: the proportion of white-collar employees belonging to either the independent *Deutsche Angestellten Gewerkschaft* (DAG) or the *Deutsche Gewerkschaftsbund* (DGB) decreased from 28 per cent in 1953 to 19 per cent in 1970. Thus in the Federal Republic the *Mittelstand* orientation which had become so important before 1933 because of the sharp distinction between the white-collar movement and the workers' movement, declined in importance among white-collar employees, unlike among small-scale tradesmen.[80]

For all these corporative associations that proliferated up to 1933, membership involved not only adopting a programme but also participating in a whole way of life. Such an association often formed a sub-milieu in which particular activities, values, and ways of life predominated. Collective banquets and processions, youth activities and singing, expeditions and reading evenings were all regarded as appealing to the association's members. This whole social milieu was almost completely destroyed by the events of 1933, and after 1945 was never again restored to any significant extent in either of the two Germanys.[81]

The fundamentally *Mittelstand* orientation of small-scale tradesmen and white-collar employees in Germany, and their anxieties about their status in the wake of hyperinflation and world economic crisis, also helps to explain their vulnerability to National Socialism. The Nazis used anti-capitalist rhetoric, promises of change, and nationalism to manipulate for their own ends what Theodor Geiger has termed the 'panic of the *Mittelstand*'. A great deal of the literature about German craftsmen, shopkeepers, and white-collar employees in the 1920s and 1930s focuses on why a majority of them voted for the NSDAP and many even became party members. However, this teleological explanation has been criticized by those who stress differentiation within occupational groups and variation in their reactions to National Socialism.

It is an indisputable fact that the old and new *Mittelstand* was over-represented in the NSDAP. In Bavaria in 1933, 21 per cent of NSDAP members were non-rural self-employed people, while 28 per cent were white-collar employees and civil servants. Their proportion in the party member-ship was double their weight in the population. But only 2 per cent of all master craftsmen, shop proprietors, and white-collar employees in Bavaria were politically active in the NSDAP. Nor did this picture change when the NSDAP came to power. Members of the *Mittelstand* were especially strongly represented among Nazi members, but beyond this general fact there are important differentiations to point out. The 'Nazification of the *Mittelstand*' was greater among shopkeepers than among master craftsmen, more wide-spread in the north than in the south, and stronger in Protestant than in Catholic areas. Current research tends to stress the inclusive character of the NSDAP, and to ask more thoroughly about its non-*Mittelstand* supporters. Excessive concentration on the role of the *Mittelstand* has for a long time obscured both the vulnerability of workers to National Socialist ideology and the responsibility of the bourgeois elite for the Nazis' coming to power.[82]

This high degree of corporate organization and the political support for the interests of small-scale tradesmen and white-collar employees made it possible to slow down and cushion the social consequences of structural changes in crafts, shopkeeping, and the tertiary sector. But ultimately these structural changes could not be prevented. During the twentieth century, the traditional-style middle groups in German society became ever smaller and more differentiated. One clear indicator is the decline in the proportion of self-employed persons among German earners, a decline that accelerated rapidly after the Second World War. The number of craft workshops fell from 849,000 at the foundation of the Federal Republic to 500,000 in 1977; in the German Democratic Republic, it fell from 250,000 in 1955 to only 83,000 in 1982. This decline was caused by industrial concentration in both Germanys, and in the German Democratic Republic also by policies unfavourable to craftsmen.

The decline in the number of small-scale producers also affected shop-keeping, although a bit later on. Urbanization ensured that shop numbers increased up to 1939, but in the Federal Republic they declined after the war, falling from 600,000 in 1950 to 346,000 in 1975.

But at the same time as crafts and commerce were undergoing these profound transformations, the sphere of white-collar employees was expanding. The non-manual labour force, which largely meant white-collar employees, made up only 10 per cent of all earners in the German Empire in 1910, but 21 per cent in the Federal Republic by 1950, and 46 per cent by 1980. White-collar employees found jobs especially in the service sector, the public sector, and above all in businesses in the chemical industry, machine building and the new technologies. Between 1950 and 1970, the number of white-collar employees in the Federal Republic doubled.[83]

This long-term trend reflected structural changes in the economy. In commerce and crafts, large and wealthy firms profited from these changes, at the expense of the one-person businesses that had been part of the proletarian survival strategy. Except during the world economic crisis and the Nazi period, the German economy saw an increasing number of employees per business and a rising turnover per employee. This change favoured enterprises with lots of capital and a high turnover, and led to diverging destinies for different groups of proprietors. There was as big a gap in income opportunities and business perspectives between a large clothing retailer and the owner of a corner shop as between the owner of a flourishing garage and the owner of a shoe-repair workshop. Of course, these differences had existed since the beginning of the century, but with the growing pressure to invest more capital in individual businesses the gaps between proprietors of different businesses unquestionably increased. With the improved employment situation and the expanding consumer goods industry after 1960, one-man shops and craft workshops lost the important social function that they had fulfilled in the nineteenth and the first half of the twentieth century, that of providing supplementary income for workers' families in periods of unemployment, sickness and old age.[84]

Among white-collar employees, too, there were worlds of difference between the high-earning top positions and the middle managers or office workers. There were big gaps in salary between technicians, salesmen, managers, and office workers, and this generated different ways of life and different educational options. The white collar and tie, which had traditionally symbolized a whole range of social privileges, were no longer the monopoly of white-collar employees; indeed, many white-collar technicians were active on the production end of businesses, and in department stores and offices were often being replaced by women. In particular, increased female work in offices and stores changed the position of white-collar employees. By 1980, 55.9 per cent of all earning females in Germany were working as white-collar employees or civil servants, generally in lower and poorly paid positions.

The traditional middle groups in German society increasingly unravelled under the pressures exerted by an increasing division of labour, business concentration, and growing differentiation of occupations and positions. Nowadays, the middle group in Germany is so far from representing a single entity that no political group is seeking to restore it. It has not disappeared from political rhetoric – Gerhard Schröder's SPD has just now discovered it – but what it now refers to is a composite social complex with a multitude of self-definitions. Nowadays German politics is dominated no longer by the *Mittelstand*, but rather by a vaguely defined 'middle'.[85]

9.3.3 The workers

The word 'worker' conjures up an image of heavy, physical, industrial work. It evokes thoughts of miners, metal workers, or assembly-line workers in the car industry, of male bodies streaming with sweat, of alcohol, political agitation, unions and strikes. This image emerged in the course of the nineteenth and the twentieth centuries both as a terrifying picture and as a means of self-identification, even though it corresponded only partially to the actual composition, appearance or behaviour of workers. Thus throughout the twentieth century, about 30 per cent of 'workers' were female, and hence bore no relation to the stereotypes.

While the proportion of women among workers remained remarkably constant, the distribution of workers among the different sectors of the German economy changed a great deal. Thus the proportion of workers (of either sex) employed in agriculture fell continually throughout the century, from 21 per cent in 1907, to 11 per cent in 1950, to only 2 per cent in 1977. Workers of both sexes increasingly worked in the secondary sector: in 1900 about half of all workers worked in industry and crafts, but by 1970 it was 72 per cent.[86] This concentration of workers in the secondary sector occurred at the same time as a huge expansion in the economic importance of the tertiary sector, which has employed a majority of all German earners since the 1980s. This has led to a decline in the proportion of 'workers' among wage earners: in the interwar period about three-quarters of all wage earners were workers, but by 1977 this had fallen to one-half, and by 1993 it was only 36 per cent. Nowadays most German earners are white-collar employees or civil servants. However, compared to other highly developed western societies, Germany still seems to be 'over-industrialized'.[87]

Workers can still be distinguished from white-collar employees and civil servants, despite enormous transformations in the world of work, by their lower level of education and training, their lower social prestige, and the physical nature of their work, which brings with it significantly higher risks of illness and accident. But at the same time, workers share many characteristics with lower white-collar employees, for instance their low levels of autonomy and economic security.[88] Neither at the beginning of the twentieth century nor at its end did German workers themselves form a homogeneous group. Differences in training levels, sex, and age were and still are important, although religion, important in the first half of the century for the formation of social milieus, has declined in importance. Ethnic differences, by contrast, remain central determinants of training and occupational opportunities within the stratum of workers into the present day.

9.3.3.1 BRANCHES OF INDUSTRY, GROWTH IN TECHNOLOGY, AND THE IMPORTANCE OF TRAINING

Within industry, male and female workers are concentrated in different branches. This segregation of the labour market has survived throughout the twentieth century despite changes in particular branches of industry.[89] Thus whereas jobs in mining, once a dominant branch of industry, declined rapidly after the Second World War, new earning opportunities for men arose in the chemical, metal, electronics, and fine machine-building industries. For women, the textile and clothing industries offered most employment in the first half of the century, but in the 1950s when these sectors began to be rationalized and to move away to low-wage countries, new female jobs arose in the electronics industry.[90]

Over the twentieth century, working conditions changed in different ways in the various sectors and branches of industry. Two important influences have been the increasing mechanization and rationalization of work, and the widespread changes in the size and structure of businesses. Despite fears to the contrary, new technologies have not led to a declining level of qualifications for workers. Likewise, it turned out to be a fallacy that physically heavy work, whether unskilled or semi-skilled, would disappear with technological advance, and that a general rise in qualifications would set in. Instead, workers have become much more heterogeneous than they were in 1900, with regard both to their working conditions and to their levels of qualification.[91]

Throughout the twentieth century, male workers of German origin had a generally high and rising level of qualifications. As early as the interwar period, only about a third of male workers of German origin did unskilled work. By 1970, this proportion had further declined to around 20 per cent.[92] The large group of skilled workers was trained through craft or industrial apprenticeships. The so-called 'dual system', established at the beginning of the century, obliged apprentices to attend vocational schools at the same time as undergoing training; in these schools they learnt both vocational skills and general educational subjects. This was supposed to prevent training from becoming too specialized and to prepare the apprentice for a wide variety of possible jobs in the relevant occupational field.[93]

The 'dual system' for male apprentices was also supported by employers as early as the Kaiserreich, and under the Weimar Republic it was extended to girls. But on the whole the training of female workers remained lower than that of males. From the interwar period to the 1970s, a majority of female workers were untrained. According to a survey of 1994, 84 per cent of female workers were unskilled or semi-skilled.[94]

Throughout the twentieth century, females and foreigners made up the lower stratum of the workers. Ever since the deliberate recruitment of foreigners into Germany began in the 1960s, dirty, heavy, and dangerous jobs which German workers were unwilling to do have been taken over by immigrants. At the same time, males of German origin successfully dominated the 'working elite' of master craftsmen and foremen, which was characterized by upwardly mobile aspirations and by working conditions similar to those of the middle classes in the service sector.

9.3.3.2 CHANGES IN LIVING STANDARDS

In the nineteenth century, the social strata below the bourgeoisie often suffered oppressive poverty, particularly as a consequence of under-employment. But toward the end of that century, as discussed in Chapters 7 and 12, German workers' living standards began to improve and the most extreme forms of deprivation began to disappear. Famine, which had still recurred in Germany up to the mid-nineteenth century, now disappeared under the impact of agricultural improvements. Excessive child labour, too, became a thing of the past. Real wages of workers in industry, trade and transportation almost doubled between the foundation of the German Empire in 1871 and the First World War. At the same time, the working day became shorter, and the position of workers' families was further improved by the creation of self-help organizations and the passage of social legis-lation under Bismarck.[95]

The Weimar Republic, by contrast, saw widespread economic crisis in Germany. Although the working day became shorter and the welfare state expanded, as discussed in Chapter 7, this benefited only those who could find work on the notoriously lax German labour market. In the Kaiserreich, unemployment was usually less than 3 per cent, but in the 1920s and 1930s it became a mass experience. According to the occupational census carried out in the summer of 1933, even though the worst crisis was already past, 36 per cent of workers were unemployed (compared to only 24 per cent of white-collar employees). Effective support for so many unemployed people was impossible in the framework of the unemployment insurance system created in 1927, so the world economic crisis led to immiseration for many German workers' families.[96]

During the Nazi period, not only did workers experience rising real wages, but the racist ideology also provided workers of 'Aryan' origin with new social status. During the war, the employment of forced labourers made German workers into quite a privileged group. In spite of the destruction of the working-class political movement, such economic and social improve-ments led to a neutralization and partial social integration of the working class during the Nazi period.[97]

After the Second World War, workers' living standards in West Germany improved to an explosive and unexpected extent, as discussed in Chapter 12. Between 1950 and 1970, real wages of German industrial workers tripled. This rapid rise in real wages, coupled with an expand-ing welfare state and almost full employment after 1960, meant that for many workers' families, life lost its proletarian character: material need and insecurity, which had been characteristic of workers' lives in the nineteenth and early twentieth centuries, now almost completely disappeared. Family income, which until 1950 had been spent almost 75 per cent on food, clothing, and rent, now increasingly left room for new purchases. Televisions, cameras, and refrigerators moved into workers' households, and during the 1960s many workers were able to buy cars.[98]

At the same time as living standards rose, the working week of industrial workers shortened. The paid working week had been 48 hours in the 1920s and was still that length in the immediate postwar period, but now it was gradually reduced. Paid holidays had often lasted only three days a year in the 1920s, but were now greatly extended. In the early 1970s, the five-day week had become almost universal, and by 1995 industrial workers of both sexes had an average working week of only 38 hours. But these figures convey only a limited impression of the real growth in leisure. It was only from the 1950s onward that the time not filled up with income-earning work could actually be turned into 'free time' as a result of the growth in real wages. Previously (and perhaps nowadays once more) it tended to be used instead for moonlighting in the black economy.[99]

At the same time as real income and leisure thus increased, the social security of workers and their families also improved, as discussed in Chapter 7. Whereas in the first half of the century, unemployment, illness, and old age had still inevitably led to poverty for workers' families, with the expansion of the welfare state from the 1960s onward this ceased to be the case. Unemployment insurance, paid sick leave, and index-linking of pensions meant a huge fall in social risks for German workers' families.

Thus the period after 1960 saw clearly improved material living conditions and a striking decline in livelihood risks for German workers. This justifies describing German workers as being 'de-proletarianized' during this period, even though many aspects of social inequality have shown themselves to be very enduring.

9.3.3.3 THE PROLETARIAN WAY OF LIFE

In the pre-industrial world, many adults remained unmarried throughout their whole lives, as discussed in Chapter 2. But during the nineteenth and early twentieth centuries, German society was increasingly composed of families, a development that reached its highpoint in the first decades after the First World War. This also affected workers: under the Kaiserreich, but particularly in the interwar period, it became normal for workers of both sexes to establish families.[100] However, the family life of the lower strata did not correspond to the expectations of bourgeois observers: especially in the period before the First World War, it was characterized by lack of space, material deprivation, large numbers of children, and little intimacy. Bourgeois observers regarded workers' often unhealthy dwellings, the close cohabitation of families with outside lodgers, the fact that children and adults slept together, the labour force participation of mothers and their allegedly irrational householding, and workers' consumption behaviour, as adding up to a set of fundamental causes for widespread immiseration, alcoholism, and sexual illnesses among the working class.

The property-owning bourgeoisie had already generally begun to reduce its fertility rate in the second half of the nineteenth century, as discussed in Chapter 2. After the turn of the century, survival chances for infants rose, leading other groups in German society to begin limiting births as well. Particularly noticeable is the transformation in reproductive behaviour among workers' families formed in the first third of the twentieth century. According to the 1939 census, among urban workers' families formed before 1905, 47 per cent had seven or more children, compared to only 33 per cent for families founded between 1905 and 1909, and only 24 per cent for those founded between 1910 and 1914.[101] Under the Weimar Republic, average child numbers in proletarian families continued to decline. Now young workers' wives desired to have only two children, just like their bourgeois counterparts. Only 35 per cent of marriages formed between 1922 and 1925 resulted in three or more children. Even Nazi propaganda failed to reverse this general trend toward lower fertility. Nowadays, differences across social strata in reproductive behaviour have almost completely disappeared in Germany. The number of children is low in all social strata. This results not only from a considerable decline in the number of large families, but also from a huge increase in the proportion of women remaining childless throughout their lives. While 90 per cent of women born in 1940 brought at least one child into the world, one-quarter of all women born in 1960 remain childless. Here, stratum-specific differences can be observed, in that educated women remain childless more often than female workers. In the course of the twentieth century, in short, typical family size in Germany has become ever more similar to the bourgeois ideal of the small family.[102]

The same is true for workers' housing. Under the Kaiserreich and the Weimar Republic, workers' housing was perceived as being very precarious, and consequently huge, publicly funded housing programmes were established to combat 'the housing question', as discussed in Chapter 7. This gave rise to large numbers of new dwellings (as can be seen, for instance, in Hamburg), which particularly benefited young, trained workers. But on the whole poor housing remained a characteristic of proletarian family life into the 1950s.[103] Yet one should not place too much reliance on the picture painted by the various works of social criticism published during the prewar and interwar periods, which referred particularly to the housing situation in Berlin. In the first half of the twentieth century, average dwelling space for workers' families varied enormously across German regions. Thus in interwar Hannover, for instance, workers' families usually had dwellings with a kitchen and three rooms, although no larger than 50 square metres in total size. Here it was less the size of the dwelling than the way the space was used that irritated bourgeois observers. Workers were regarded as not using available space 'rationally'; by this, bourgeois observers (and, indeed, the workers' movements themselves, beginning in the 1920s) meant that that there should be separate bedrooms for parents and children, separate bedrooms for daughters and sons, and plain, functional furniture. Instead, workers' families tended, wherever possible, to use one room as 'the good parlour', and often continued to favour large and ornate furniture.[104]

The depredations of the Second World War and the need to find shelter for refugees after 1945 intensified the German housing crisis anew in the immediate postwar period. Here, workers' families suffered most. It was only from the 1960s on that their housing situation improved, as a consequence of public housing construction and the general rise in living standards. In the decades that followed, many workers began to be able to buy housing rather than renting it. Whereas in 1950 only 6 per cent of workers' households in the Federal Republic lived within their own four walls, by the 1980s this was true for 29 per cent of unskilled and semi-skilled workers, and for 43 per cent of skilled workers.[105] Nowadays, there-fore, workers inhabit housing similar to that of other social strata, although families with low incomes or large numbers of children still have to live in smaller, poorer dwellings located in disagreeable neighbourhoods.[106]

Throughout the twentieth century, German workers' families did not depend solely on the income-earning work of the man. Workers' wives also contributed to the family income in a wide variety of ways: through economical and labour-intensive housekeeping, through by-employment, and through formal income-earning work outside the household. In the first half of the century, it was also common for work by older children to make an important contribution to the family's material situation. The ideal of the housewife-marriage, which continues to be widespread among workers into the present day, was far from possible for many German workers' families. Thus in 1925, 23 per cent of workers' wives were active in the labour force. Admittedly, this rate clearly declined after the Second World War, falling to 16 per cent by 1950, but by 1957 it had risen again to 31 per cent, and by 1969 to 46 per cent. Wives of unskilled and semi-skilled workers had higher labour force participation rates than wives of skilled workers. But it was material necessity that appears to have caused workers' wives to enter the labour force, whereas wives of higher social strata took jobs more often out of a desire for independence and self-realization, which have now become a matter of course for the younger generation of German women.[107]

The twentieth century also saw a decline in the lack of space, the work-centredness, and the forced modesty that had previously characterized family life among workers. It is incomparably more difficult to assess whether personal relationships within workers' families and the style of upbringing of workers' children also changed. For the interwar period, Heide Rosenbaum finds that different styles of upbringing coexisted in the families of German workers. Thus parent–child relations in traditionally oriented workers' families continued to be strongly hierarchical in nature. Children were expected to be obedient and tractable, and little account was taken of their individual needs. In families with social democratic beliefs, by contrast, mothers and fathers often devoted great attention to their children and these children's development. For these families, as well, however, bourgeois notions of intimate and comradely parent–child relationships continued to be an alien concept.[108]

The postwar period saw a convergence in the aims and practices of child rearing among different German social strata. The past few decades have seen an increasing predominance of child-rearing views that emphasize children's self-confidence and seek to further their individual self-determination. This view also places great stress on helping children develop a capacity to form their own judgements and a sense of responsibility. Such child-rearing aims are increasingly observed among workers, too, but there are still stratum-specific peculiarities. Thus workers appear to place more stress on obedience, good manners, orderliness, and cleanliness, and are more willing to enforce these aims using disciplinary techniques such as corporal punishment, confinement, and prohibitions. These child-rearing aims may partially mirror workers' experiences within their own working world, which is still often characterized by little independent decision-making.[109]

9.4 Conclusion

German social structure changed greatly in the course of the twentieth century. The nobility lost its socially dominant position. New elites arose. Once important occupational groups, such as independent farmers and miners, have declined greatly in significance. Income-earning work has changed its face altogether, so that the service sector is now the most important source of employment. Living standards generally rose, gradually in the first half of the century owing to the wars and the economic crises, but very rapidly in the postwar period, and this has clearly changed the lifestyles of all strata of the population. The expansion of education has likewise affected all demographic groups, and has especially revolutionized the position of women. Overall, the children and youths of today spend much more time in the school system than was the case in earlier generations. Correspondingly, the training profile of the German population has changed greatly, as a consequence of the growing need for qualified employees on the one hand and of individual attempts at upward mobility on the other. The once large group of unskilled and semi-skilled workers has shrunk, and consists nowadays overwhelmingly of foreigners.

But despite these huge transformations, German social structure has at the same time been characterized by troubling continuities. Social differences appear to be very long-lived and resistant. Neither the expansion in education of the 1960s and 1970s nor the general increase in living standards has led to a disappearance of differences among social strata. Recent sociological studies therefore emphasize the continuing existence of social differences, albeit in forms specific to modern welfare societies. According to Rainer Geißler, nowadays social differences are multi-dimensional, with differences between social strata existing in parallel with other differences between sexes and ethnic groups. In addition, the general increase in economic well-being has made social differences less visible. But differences between social strata, according to Geißler, remain important determinants of differences in opportunities.[110]

This opinion runs counter to widespread views, both among sociologists and in German society at large, which hold that there are few important differences between social strata in present-day Germany, and that the earlier competitive struggle within a hierarchically divided society has been replaced by a peaceful coexistence of groups with different lifestyles. Within this 'experience-oriented society', according to Gerhard Schulze, people no longer strive mainly to improve or maintain their status; instead, their 'basic existential problem' is 'to experience their lives'.[111] If it is appropriate to regard present-day Germany as this sort of 'experience-oriented society', then any analysis of social structure which focused on differences between strata would be almost completely obsolete.

Interestingly, recent sociological research has sought to combine these two perspectives, taking into account both sets of empirical findings: increasing individualization and 'experience-orientation' on the one hand, but also the stubborn survival of differences between social strata on the other. According to the sociologist Thomas Schnierer, experience-orientation operates as a 'vent' that makes the competitive struggle for attractive social positions more endurable. Schnierer argues that this works in two ways. First, if there is a consensus within society that social differences result not from obstacles to social mobility but from lifestyle decisions, then occupying a low social position becomes much easier to put up with: members of under-privileged social groups and those losing the competitive struggle for attractive social positions can bring 'experience-orientation' into play to obscure their own lack of opportunities. But experience-orientation not only makes lack of privilege and lack of success more endurable; it also makes it possible to 'package' the enjoyment of privilege and competitive success as a form of 'experience' or 'self-realization', in a way that fits into the social contract. If, for example, one can regard studying abroad simply as a form of self-realization, or buying shares as a form of leisure-time gambling activity, then the fact that they maintain or improve one's social status becomes an apparently unintended side-effect, for which one does not have to have a guilty conscience. Thus the fact that, in reality, Germans do appear to be becoming more 'experience-oriented' does not indicate that social inequality is being dismantled in German society. Rather, experience-orientation is a psychological reaction to the continuing existence of social inequality, a 'vent' for the frustration that would otherwise be created by the bitter competitive struggle for attractive social positions.[112]

Chapter translated by Sheilagh Ogilvie

9.5 Notes

1 Thomas Schnierer, 'Von der kompetitiven Gesellschaft zur Erlebnisgesellschaft? Der "Fahrstuhl-Effekt", die subjektive Relevanz der sozialen Ungleicheit und die Ventilfunktion des Wertewandels', *Zeitschrift für Soziologie*, 25 (1996), pp. 71–82.

2 Ulrich Beck, *Risikogesellschaft. Auf dem Weg in eine andere Moderne* (Frankfurt am Main, 1983); Ulrich Beck, 'Jenseits von Stand und Klasse? Soziale Ungleichheiten, gesellschaftliche Individualisierungsprozesse und die Entstehung neuer sozialer Formationen und Identitäten', in Reinhard Kreckel, ed., *Soziale Ungleichheiten* (Göttingen, 1983), pp. 35–74.

3 Gerhard Schulze, *Die Erlebnisgesellschaft. Kultursoziologie der Gegenwart* (Frankfurt am Main, 1992).

4 Gustav Schmoller, 'Die Eisenacher Versammlung zur Besprechung der sozialen Frage', *Jahrbücher für Nationalökonomie und Statistik*, 20 (1873), pp. 1–12, here p. 6.

5 For a good guide to theories of social inequality, see Stefan Hradil, *Soziale Ungleichheit in Deutschland*, 7th edn (Opladen, 1999), pp. 95–142. For a new survey of theories of social stratification from the end of the eighteenth to the end of the twentieth century, see Hans-Ulrich Wehler, 'Soziale Stratifikation und Stratifikationstheorien', in Hans-Ulrich Wehler, ed., *Umbruch und Kontinuität. Essays zum 20. Jahrhundert* (Munich, 2000), pp. 185–214; on German society's own self-definition in the first two-thirds of the twentieth century, see additionally Paul Nolte, *Die Ordnung der deutschen Gesellschaft. Selbstentwurf und Selbstbeschreibung im 20. Jahrhundert* (Munich, 2000).

6 Heike Solga, *Auf dem Weg in eine klassenlose Gesellschaft? Klassenlagen und Mobilität zwischen Generationen in der DDR* (Berlin, 1995).

7 Klaus Tenfelde, 'Einige Ergebnisse', in Peter Hübner and Klaus Tenfelde, eds, *Arbeiter in der SBZ-DDR* (Essen, 1999), pp. 889–95, here p. 889.

8 It is well known that Karl Marx nowhere worked out his class theory in the form of a consistent model. From the rich literature on the Marxist conception of class, see especially Ralf Dahrendorf, *Soziale Klassen und Klassenkonflikt in der industriellen Gesellschaft* (Stuttgart, 1957); for a good, brief summary with details of the main relevant points in Marx's works, see Hradil, *Soziale Ungleichheit*, pp. 99ff.

9 See esp. Max Weber, *Wirtschaft und Gesellschaft* (Tübingen, 1980), pp. 177–80 and pp. 531–40; for a quick introduction with details of further literature, see Hradil, *Soziale Ungleicheit*, pp. 105ff.

10 Weber, *Wirtschaft und Gesellschaft*.

11 For class theories linked to those of Marx, see especially Erik Olin Wright, *Classes* (London, 1985); for non-Marxist theoretical approaches to class, see Theodor Geiger, *Die soziale Schichtung des deutschen Volkes* (Stuttgart, 1932; repr. Darmstadt, 1972); Dahrendorf, *Soziale Klassen*; Robert Erikson and John Goldthrope, *The Constant Flux. A Study of Class Mobility in Industrial Societies* (Oxford, 1992).

12 M. Rainer Lepsius, 'Soziale Ungleichheit und Klassenstrukturen in der Bundesrepublik', in Hans-Ulrich Wehler, ed., *Klassen in der europäischen Sozialgeschichte* (Göttingen, 1979), pp. 166–209, here p. 179.

13 Pierre Bourdieu, *La distinction. Critique sociale du jugement* (Paris, 1979).

14 Theodor Geiger, *Klassengesellschaft im Schmelztiegel* (Cologne, 1949); Theodor Geiger, *Die soziale Schichtung des deutschen Volkes. Soziographischer Versuch auf statistischer Grundlage* (Darmstadt, 1967); Helmut Schelsky, *Wandlungen der deutschen Familie in der Gegenwart* (Stuttgart, 1949).

15 Beck, *Risikogesellschaft*; for criticisms of this, see among others, Karl Ulrich Mayer and Hans Peter Blossfeld, 'Die gesellschaftliche Konstruktion sozialer Ungleichheit im Lebenslauf', in Peter Berger and Stefan Hradil, eds, *Lebenslagen, Lebensläufe, Lebensstile* (Göttingen, 1990), pp. 297–318.

16 M. Rainer Lepsius, 'Parteiensystem und Sozialstruktur. Zum Problem der Demokratisierung der deutschen Gesellschaft', in Gerhard A. Ritter, ed., *Deutsche Parteien vor 1918* (Cologne, 1973), pp. 58–80.

17 Peter Marschalck, *Bevölkerungsgeschichte Deutschlands im 19. und 20. Jahrhundert* (Frankfurt am Main, 1984), *passim*; see also the statistics in Dietmar Petzina *et al.*, eds, *Sozialgeschichtliches Arbeitsbuch, III. Materialien zur Statistik des Deutschen Reiches 1914–1945* (Munich, 1978), pp. 27–36.

18 See Reinhard Spree, *Soziale Ungleichheit vor Krankheit und Tod. Zur Sozialgeschichte des Gesundheitsbereichs im Deutschen Kaiserreich* (Göttingen, 1981); Ingbert Weber, 'Soziale Schichtung und Gesundheit', in Rainer Geißler, ed., *Soziale Schichtung und Lebenschancen in der BRD*, 2nd edn (Stuttgart, 1994), pp. 195–219; Andreas Mielck, *Soziale Ungleichheit und Gesundheit: empirische Ergebnisse, Erklärungsansätze, Interventionsmöglichkeiten* (Bern, 2000).

19 Rainer Geißler and Thomas Meyer, 'Struktur und Entwicklung der Bevölkerung', in Rainer Geißler, ed., *Die Sozialstruktur Deutschlands*, 2nd edn (Opladen, 1996), pp. 333–57, here p. 346.

20 Geißler and Meyer, *Struktur und Entwicklung*, p. 352.

21 See Klaus J. Bade, *Homo Migrans. Wanderungen aus und nach Deutschland. Erfahrungen und Fragen* (Essen, 1994), pp. 17–52.

22 Geißler and Meyer, *Struktur und Entwicklung*, p. 346.

23 Klaus J. Bade, ed., *Das Manifest der 60. Deutschland und die Einwanderung* (Munich, 1994), p. 72.

24 See the statistics in Hradil, *Soziale Ungleichheit*, p. 85.

25 Hradil, *Soziale Ungleichheit*, pp. 85–6; Jürgen Kocka, *Die Angestellten in der deutschen Geschichte 1850–1980. Vom Privatbeamten zum angestellten Arbeiter* (Göttingen, 1981).

26 Hradil, *Soziale Ungleichheit*, pp. 87–90; Erhard Hertrich, 'Vom Wandel der Erwerbsmöglichkeiten', in Wolfgang Ruppert, ed., *Die Arbeiter. Lebensformen, Alltag und Kultur von der Frühindustrialisierung bis zum 'Wirtschaftswunder'* (Munich, 1986), pp. 93–103.

27 For a general introduction to the German school system see Peter Lundgreen, *Sozialgeschichte der deutschen Schule im Überblick*, Vol. II: *1918–1980* (Göttingen, 1981). See also Hradil, *Soziale Ungleichheit*, pp. 144–77.

28 Peter Lundgreen, 'Schule im 20. Jahrhundert. Institutionelle Differenzierung und expansive Bildungspolitik', in Dietrich Brenner and Heinz-Elmar Tenorth, eds, *Bildungsprozesse und Erziehungsverhältnisse im 20. Jahrhundert* (Weinheim, 2000), pp. 140–65, Table 1.

29 Lundgreen, 'Schule im 20. Jahrhundert', Table 2.

30 Hradil, *Soziale Ungleichheit*, p. 154

31 Gero Lenhardt and Manfred Stock, *Bildung, Bürger, Arbeitskraft. Schulentwicklung und Sozialstruktur in der BRD und der DDR* (Frankfurt am Main, 1997), p. 150.

32 Geißler, *Sozialstruktur*, pp. 254–5; Solga, *Auf dem Weg*.

33 Walter Müller and Dietmar Haun, 'Bildungsungleichheit im sozialen Wandel', *Kölner Zeitschrift für Soziologie und Sozialpsychologie*, 46 (1994), pp. 1–42, here p. 14.

34 Thomas Meyer, *Modernisierung der Privatheit. Differenzierungs- und Individualisierungsprozesse des familialen Zusammenlebens* (Opladen, 1992), pp. 133–5.

35 Hradil, *Soziale Ungleichheit*, p. 157.
36 Geißler, *Sozialstruktur*, pp. 277–8.
37 Hradil, *Soziale Ungleichheit*, pp. 159–60.
38 Geißler, *Sozialstruktur*, pp. 181–8.
39 Helmut Köhler, *Bildungsbeteiligung und Sozialstruktur in der Bundesrepublik* (Berlin, 1992), p. 57.
40 Geißler, *Sozialstruktur*, p. 262, Table 12.4.
41 Hradil, *Soziale Ungleichheit*, p. 167, Table 8.
42 Geißler, *Sozialstruktur*, p. 263.
43 Hradil, *Soziale Ungleichheit*, p. 227.
44 Hradil, *Soziale Ungleichheit*, p. 224, Table 16.
45 Richard Hauser and Irene Becker, 'Zur Entwicklung der personellen Verteilung der Einkommen in West- und Ostdeutschland 1993 bzw. 1990 bis 1994', *Sozialer Fortschritt*, 45 (1996), pp. 285–93, here p. 286.
46 Jürgen Kohl, 'Armut im internationalen Vergleich. Methoden, Probleme und empirische Ergebnisse', in Stephan Leibfried and Wolfgang Voges, eds, *Armut im modernen Wohlfahrtsstaat* (Opladen, 1992), pp. 272–99, here p. 283.
47 Edeltraut Guttmann, 'Geldvermögen und Schulden privater Haushalte Ende 1993', *Wirtschaft und Statistik* (1995), pp. 391–9, here p. 399.
48 Hradil, *Soziale Ungleichheit*, p. 244.
49 Hradil, *Soziale Ungleichheit*, p. 245.
50 Statistisches Bundesamt, ed., *Datenreport 1997. Zahlen und Fakten über die Bundesrepublic Deutschland* (Bonn, 1997), p. 521.
51 Geißler, *Sozialstruktur*, pp. 186–8.
52 Heinz-Herbert Noll, 'Wahrnehmung und Rechtfertigung sozialer Ungleichheit 1991–1996', in Heiner Meulemann, ed., *Werte und nationale Identität im vereinten Deutschland* (Opladen, 1998), pp. 61–84.
53 Hans-Ulrich Wehler, *Deutsche Gesellschaftsgeschichte*, Vol. III: *Von der 'Deutschen Doppelrevolution' bis zum Beginn des Ersten Weltkrieges 1849–1914* (Munich, 1995), pp. 805–25, 1276–9.
54 Heinz Reif, *Adel im 19. und 20. Jahrhundert* (Munich, 1999), pp. 11f.
55 See Iris von Hoyningen-Huene, *Adel in der Weimarer Republik. Die rechtlich-soziale Situation des reichsdeutschen Adles 1918–1933* (Limburg, 1992), pp. 224, 228.
56 Reif, *Adel*, pp. 54f.
57 Hans-Ulrich Wehler, 'Wie bürgerlich war das Deutsche Kaiserreich?', in Jürgen Kocka, ed., *Bürger und Bürgerlichkeit im 19. Jahrhundert* (Göttingen, 1987), pp. 243–80.
58 Konrad Jarausch, *The Unfree Professions. German Lawyers, Teachers, and Engineers 1900–50* (Oxford and New York, 1990); Konrad Jarausch, 'The Decline of Liberal Professionalism 1867–1933', in Konrad Jarausch and L. E. Jones, eds, *In Search of Liberal Germany* (Oxford, 1990), pp. 261–86.
59 Christian Jansen, *Professoren und Politik. Politisches Denken und Handeln der Heidelberger Hochschullehrer 1914–1933* (Göttingen, 1992), p. 29.
60 Hans Mommsen, 'Die Auflösung des Bürgertums seit dem späten 19. Jahrhundert', in Kocka, ed., *Bürger*, pp. 288–315; Bernd Weisbrod, 'Die Krise der bürgerlichen Gesellschaft und die Machtergreifung von 1933', in Hans-Ulrich Wehler, ed., *Scheidewege der deutschen Geschichte. Von der Reformation bis zur Wende 1517–1989* (Munich, 1995), pp. 171–82.
61 Dieter Ziegler, 'Kontinuität und Diskontinuität der deutschen Wirtschaftselite 1900 bis 1938', in Dieter Ziegler, ed., *Großbürger und Unternehmer: die deutsche Wirtschaftselite im 20. Jahrhundert* (Göttingen, 2000), pp. 31–53, esp. pp. 48ff.
62 L. J. Edinger, 'Continuity and Change in the Background of German Decision-Makers', *The Western Political Quarterly*, 14 (1961), pp. 17–36.

63 On this continuity of German elites, see Wilfried Loth and Bernd A. Rusinek, eds, *Verwandlungspolitik. NS-Eliten in der westdeutschen Nachkriegsgesellschaft* (Frankfurt am Main, 1998).

64 Schelsky, *Wandlungen*; Helmut Schelsky, 'Die Bedeutung des Schichtungsbegriffs für die Analyse der gegenwärtigen Gesellschaft', in Helmut Schelsky, ed., *Auf der Suche nach Wirklichkeit. Gesammelte Aufsätze* (Düsseldorf, 1965), pp. 331–65. For a good guide to Schelsky's theses, see H. Braun, 'Helmut Schelskys Konzept der nivellierten Mittelstandsgesellschaft und die Bundesrepublik der 50er Jahre', *Archiv für Sozialgeschichte* 29 (1989), pp. 199–223.

65 Geißler, *Sozialstruktur*, esp. pp. 90ff.

66 Michael Hartmann, 'Kontinuität oder Wandel. Die deutsche Wirtschaftselite zwischen 1970 und 1995', in Ziegler, *Großbürger*, pp. 73–92.

67 Hannes Siegrist, 'Ende der Bürgerlichkeit? Die Kategorien "Bürgertum" und "Bürgerlichkeit" in der westdeutschen Gesellschaft und Geschichtswissenschaft der Nachkriegsperiode', *Geschichte und Gesellschaft*, 20 (1994), pp. 549–83; Klaus Tenfelde, 'Stadt und Bürgertum im 20. Jahrhundert', in Klaus Tenfelde and Hans-Ulrich Wehler, eds, *Wege zur Geschichte des Bürgertums* (Göttingen, 1994), pp. 317–53.

68 Ralph Jessen, *Akademische Elite und kommunistische Diktatur. Hochschullehrerschaft in der Ulbricht-Ära* (Göttingen, 1999).

69 For the figures relating to the German Democratic Republic, see Geißler, *Sozialstruktur*, pp. 240ff., 265, 285.

70 Cited in Heinrich August Winkler, 'Stabilisierung durch Schrumpfung: Der Gewerbliche Mittelstand in der Bundesrepublik', in Werner Conze and M. Rainer Lepsius, eds, *Sozialgeschichte der Bundesrepublik Deutschland. Beiträge zum Kontinuitätsproblem* (Stuttgart, 1983), pp. 187–209, here pp. 202f.

71 See Heinz-Gerhard Haupt, 'Les classes moyennés existent-elles en Allemagne?', in S. Guillaume, ed., *Histoire et historiographie des classes moyennes dans les sociétés développées* (Talence, 1998), pp. 21–32.

72 'Innungen' were voluntary, self-governing craft bodies which obtained official status within the political framework of the Kaiserreich; an 'Innung' became compulsory when more than half the masters of an occupation in a town opted for it.

73 Heinrich August Winkler, 'From Social Protectionism to National Socialism: The German Small-Business Movement in Comparative Perspective', *Journal of Modern History*, 48 (1976), pp. 1–18; Heinrich August Winkler, *Mittelstand Demokratie und Nationalsozialismus. Die politische Entwicklung von Handwerk und Kleinhandel in der Weimarer Republik* (Cologne, 1972); Uwe Spiekermann, *Warenhaussteuer in Deutschland. Mittelstandsbewegung, Kapitalismus und Rechtsstaat im späten Kaiserreich* (Frankfurt am Main, 1994).

74 Jürgen Kocka, *Angestellte zwischen Faschismus und Demokratie. Zur politischen Sozialgeschichte der Angestellten: USA 1890–1940 im internationalen Vergleich* (Göttingen, 1977), pp. 28ff.

75 Winkler, *Stabilisierung*, pp. 199ff.

76 Winkler, *Mittelstand*.

77 See H. A. Winkler, 'Der entbehrliche Stand. Zur Mittelstandspolitik im "Dritten Reich"', *Archiv für Sozialgeschichte*, 17 (1977), pp. 1–40; Adelheid von Saldern stresses the advantages of Nazi power for the artisans, in *Mittelstand im 'Dritten Reich'. Handwerker – Einzelhändler – Bauern* (Frankfurt am Main, 1979).

78 Friedrich Lenger, *Sozialgeschichte der deutschen Handwerker seit 1800* (Frankfurt am Main, 1988).

79 Winkler, *Mittelstand*.

80 Jürgen Kocka and Michael Prinz, 'Vom "neuen Mittelstand" zum angestellten Arbeitnehmer. Kontinuität und Wandel der deutschen Angestellten seit der Weimarer Republik', in Conze and Lepsius, *Sozialgeschichte*, pp. 210–55.

81 Up to now there has been no detailed research into the destinations of the organized *Mittelstand*, nor on the survival of the way of life they represented; on this, see B. Holtwick, *Der zerstrittene Berufsstand: Handwerker und ihre Organizationen in Ostwestfalen-Lippe 1929–1953* (Paderborn, 2000).

82 For a summary of existing research, see G. Crossick and H. G. Haupt, *The Petite Bourgeoisie in Europe 1780–1914. Enterprise, Family and Independence* (London, 1995), pp. 216ff.; and Rudi Koshar, ed., *Splintered Classes: Politics and The Lower Middle Classes in Interwar Europe* (New York, 1990).

83 Kocka and Prinz, *Vom 'Neuen Mittelstand'*, p. 249.

84 Lenger, *Sozialgeschichte*, pp. 203ff.

85 Konrad Adam, *Staat machen: warum die neue Mitte keine ist und wir die alte Mitte brauchen* (Berlin, 1999).

86 Josef Mooser, *Arbeiterleben in Deutschland 1900–1970. Klassenlagen, Kultur und Politik* (Frankfurt am Main, 1984), pp. 28–30.

87 Whereas in 1993 58 per cent of all German earners worked in the tertiary sector, the corresponding figures for the USA and England were 73 and 71 per cent respectively; see Geißler, *Sozialstruktur*, p. 138.

88 Geißler, *Sozialstruktur*, p. 168.

89 For an overview of the major shifts in the labour force participation of women see Angelika Willms-Herget, *Frauenarbeit: zur Integration der Frauen in den Arbeitsmarkt* (Frankfurt am Main, 1985).

90 Mooser, *Arbeiterleben*, pp. 30–5.

91 Geißler, *Sozialstruktur*, pp. 170f.

92 Mooser, *Arbeiterleben*, pp. 59f.

93 On the dual system see Karlwilhelm Stratmann and Manfred Schlösser, *Das Duale System der Berufsbildung. Eine historische Analyse seiner Reformdebatten* (Frankfurt am Main, 1990).

94 Geißler, *Sozialstruktur*, p. 171.

95 Mooser, *Arbeiterleben*, pp. 73ff.

96 See Richard J. Evans, *The German Unemployed: Experiences and Consequences of Mass Unemployment from the Weimar Republic to the Third Reich* (London, 1987); Peter Lewek, *Arbeitslosigkeit und Arbeitslosenversicherung in der Weimarer Republik 1918–1927* (Stuttgart, 1992).

97 Ulrich Herbert, 'Arbeiterschaft im Dritten Reich', *Geschichte und Gesellschaft*, 15 (1989), pp. 320–60.

98 Mooser, *Arbeiterleben*, pp. 80–2.

99 Geißler, *Sozialstruktur*, p. 167.

100 Klaus Tenfelde, 'Arbeiterfamilie und Geschlechterbeziehungen im Deutschen Kaiserreich', *Geschichte und Gesellschaft*, 18 (1992), pp. 179–203.

101 Christina Benninghaus, *Die anderen Jugendlichen. Arbeitermädchen in der Weimarer Republik* (Frankfurt am Main, 1999), p. 67.

102 For detailed information on numbers of children, see Karl Schwarz, 'Kinderzahl der Frauen der Geburtsjahrgänge 1865–1955', *Zeitschrift für Bevölkerungswissenschaft*, 17 (1991), pp. 149–58; Karl Schwarz, 'Rückblick auf eine demographische Revolution. Überleben und Sterben, Kinderzahl, Verheiratung, Haushalte und Familien, Bildungsstand und Erwerbstätigkeit der Bevölkerung in Deutschland im 20. Jahrhundert im Spiegel der Bevölkerungsstatistik', *Zeitschrift für Bevölkerungswissenschaft: Demographie*, 24 (1999), pp. 229–81.

103 On workers' housing see Mooser, *Arbeiterleben*, pp. 141–60; Karl Christian Führer, *Mieter, Hausbesitzer, Staat und Wohnungsmarkt: Wohungsmangel und Wohnungszwangswirtschaft in Deutschland 1914–1960* (Stuttgart, 1995); and

Adelheid von Saldern, *Häuserleben. Zur Geschichte des städtischen Arbeiterwohnens vom Kaiserreich bis heute* (Bonn, 1995).

104 Heidi Rosenbaum, *Proletarische Familien. Arbeiterfamilien und Arbeiterväter im frühen 20. Jahrhundert zwischen traditioneller, sozialdemokratischer und kleinbürgerlicher Orientierung* (Frankfurt am Main, 1992).

105 Geißler, *Sozialstruktur*, p. 168.

106 Geißler, *Sozialstruktur*, p. 66.

107 Mooser, *Arbeiterleben*, pp. 85–7.

108 Rosenbaum, *Proletarische Familien.*

109 Martin Feldkircher, 'Erziehungsziele in West- und Ostdeutschland', in Michael Braun and Peter Mohler, eds, *Blickpunkt Gesellschaft 3: Einstellungen und Verhalten der Bundesbürger* (Opladen, 1994), pp. 175–208.

110 Rainer Geißler, 'Kein Abschied von Klasse and Schicht. Ideologische Gefaren der deutschen Sozialstrukturanalyse', *Kölner Zeitschrift for Soziologie and Sozialpsychologie*, 48 (1996), pp. 319–38.

111 Schulze, *Erlebnisgesellschaft.*

112 Schnierer, 'Von der kompetitiven Gesellschaft zur Erlebnisgesellschaft?'.

10

Science, technology, and society in Germany from 1800 to the present

WOLFHARD WEBER
University of Bochum

The meanings attached to the terms 'Germany', '(natural) science', and 'technology' have changed a great deal in the past 200 years.[1] For one thing, as discussed in Chapter 1, Germany looked very different in 1815, compared to how it looked in 1870, 1918, 1945 or 1990. This chapter will therefore refer to the geographical area covered by the 'kleindeutsch' ('small German') political solution reached in 1864/70, leaving aside other German-speaking areas of Europe. In the post-1945 period, the discussion will mainly focus on the Federal Republic of Germany, although developments in the German Democratic Republic will be mentioned where appropriate.

The meaning of 'science' or 'natural science' has also changed greatly over the past two centuries. Until 1800, it referred to the systematic gathering of knowledge about nature (in the sense of the Greek term *physis*). Then it began to take on the meaning of research into the inner relationships among natural phenomena. In Germany, this was at first its exclusive meaning, and even later it was still linked with a strong interest in the speculative search for truth, or what was called 'natural philosophy'. After 1810, science and technology sharply diverged: natural science and natural philosophy were directed towards developing knowledge that was removed from practical application, more concerned with discovering the truth than with serving a useful purpose.

Up until 1800, *Technologie* ('technology') had been widely taught in German universities within economic studies, as a subject whose purpose was to help princely officials provide guidance to craftsmen and industrialists. The explicit aim was to encourage exports, thereby furthering the country's finances and industry. But after 1810, 'technology' as a subject began to be banned from German universities, precisely because of its orientation toward practical usefulness. Indeed, this tension between 'truth-oriented' scientific research and 'useful' technical research was to continue to characterize German society for the following two centuries.

To what extent, then, did the natural sciences provide the basis for technical innovations in Germany? This question will concern us for the entire period. Basic scientific discoveries have undoubtedly often constituted points of departure for technical processes. But seldom did a scientific discovery lead directly to an innovation. As a rule, a scientific discovery showed a pathway toward an innovation for which there had long been a demand, and scientific methods again became necessary when technical processes had to be rationalized.

This chapter is divided into three chronological sections. The first covers the period up to about 1880, with an internal break around 1850. The second covers the period up to the 1960s, with another break around 1925. The final section covers the period between the 1960s and the present day. These periods do not overlap with dates of major political changes in Germany. Instead, they were the dates at which large parts of the German population began to deal with technology in fundamentally new ways – deal with it, rather than conceptualize it. The natural sciences develop according to quite different rhythms from other aspects of life, independently of national traditions: their development must be seen as an autonomous impulse toward understanding the world, one largely removed from social developments. Yet scientists have always lived in this world and received their stimulus from it, and this justifies a social history of the sciences.

10.1 The period to 1880

10.1.1 German society

Around 1810, the most influential forces in German civil society were the nobility, the upper bureaucracy, and a few established industrialists in domestic (i.e. pre-factory) industries. Members of these groups who were interested in reforming the encrusted structures of German society – including its educational system and its industrial technologies – enjoyed considerable freedom of action in the first two decades of the century, although the climate for reform visibly worsened after about 1820.[2] Nevertheless, the establishment of a customs union among German states in 1834 encouraged the formation of organized interest groups to represent their members' views at the periodic renegotiations of the terms of this common market.[3] The revolutions of 1848 saw the creation, in social clubs, of the forerunners of the first German political parties. After 1848, German parliaments, too, enjoyed wider powers. It was this that made possible far-reaching political and economic changes such as the shift toward free trade in the 1850s, which opened up an unimaginable variety of avenues for the application of technical processes.

An important question in recent research on the history of science and technology relates to the 'modernity' of developments in Germany during this period, compared to Britain or America.[4] But it is surely impossible to define what is 'normal' so far as modernity is concerned. Britain took a very long time to industrialize, and the European states and regions that followed it into industrialization had to adapt their social and technological endowments under commercial pressure from early industrialized countries if they did not want to fall into dependency on them. However, this literature on comparative 'modernity' probably has in mind a very specific component of Anglo-American modernity, namely the removal of industrial techniques from the direct control of the central state to become available to enterprises and other organs of civil society, and in Germany this took a very long time.

German states had already seen some attempts to reorganize society and disburden it of its feudal elements before 1800, as discussed in Chapter 4. This was particularly the case in the larger territorial states, where traditional connections to Paris and trade influences from England were felt more strongly, and in the republican city-states, especially the port cities of Hamburg and Bremen, which relied more on trade than on production. Where an enlightened officialdom had been able to influence princely administrations, cautious attempts at peasant emancipation had taken place, justice systems had been given new foundations,[5] and educational opportunities had begun to be transformed.

Two manifestations of these developments were the rapid growth of economic and scholarly journals, and the much greater opportunities to travel despite the many borders that still survived between different German territories. German rulers had already realized before the French Revolution that it was difficult to move their subjects to new courses of action through authoritarian decrees, unless they themselves personally participated in these developments. The old Empire had actually roused itself in 1804 to eliminate the ecclesiastical territories which constituted a particular obstacle to enlightenment, to subordinate them to secular princes, and in this process to secularize the school system, even if not quite so extensively as in France. The defeat of most German states by Napoleon led, especially in Austria and Prussia, but also in other German territories, to considerable efforts at reform, particularly in technical education, and these were to retain momentum well into the middle of the nineteenth century.

The forces working for this consisted of a small, liberal, mainly bourgeois bureaucracy, and it was this group which also initiated most of the early attempts to develop technology and science in Germany after 1800. One example was the introduction of *Gewerbefreiheit* (freedom of occupations, i.e. abolition of guild restrictions in the industrial sector) in Prussia in 1810 by Hardenberg. But in other German territories, even advanced Saxony, this only occurred formally in 1862. Moreover, the interest of German bureaucracies in consolidating their powers by developing technology was actually a very pre-industrial phenomenon. In eighteenth-century Germany, technical experts (such as engineers) had been found almost solely in positions where they were directly serving the political ruler, mostly in a military sense, although to some extent also in agriculture and crafts. Thus there were very considerable continuities in the relationship between German society and technology from the pre-industrial to the industrial period.

10.1.2 German science

Before 1800, established views of science had also already begun to undergo substantial changes. This applied both to the self-image of individual scientific disciplines (such as chemistry) and to the ambitions of scientific organizations (such as the Academy of Sciences or the École Polytechnique).[6] But it was around 1800 that the natural sciences arose in Germany for the first time as recognizable scholarly and university disciplines. They began to pursue a strategy of orienting themselves increasingly toward research, and to this end they moved into the universities, which had been newly re-established as elite organs of the *Bildungsbürgertum* (educated bourgeoisie). In this process, research ceased to be simply a matter of learned men being patronized by princes, and became a public concern pursued in a university context. As a result, from the very beginning these natural sciences had to pay attention to the demands made on them by society. They also had to secure society's 'permission' to pose hitherto unheard-of questions about 'nature', and to follow new paths in answering such questions. At the same time, the natural sciences had to develop appropriate instruments and measuring devices, since human senses are not as a rule capable of precise quantification of phenomena. Developing measuring instruments had far-reaching effects on German science and thus on German society, since the 'materialization' of scientific answers which they brought with them was almost always deeply shocking to existing, socially conservative mentalities, which were accustomed to thinking in terms of organic and spiritual relationships.

There were also shocks in store on the worldly level. After Germany's defeat by Napoleon, most German universities faced financial disaster. Many were dissolved outright because of lack of students. Others were re-opened in the newly merged German states, although the number of students remained small. The Friedrich-Wilhelm University, for instance, was opened in 1810 in Berlin. It gave absolute priority to 'basic' scholarly disciplines, those directed at the search for truth and research into classical antiquity, favouring them above disciplines dedicated to useful purposes.

For the first time German universities included philologists, who were to form the core of the teaching body in the *Gymnasien* (university-oriented secondary schools, discussed in Chapter 9). The reformers of the German universities in this period shifted Master's studies out of the universities into the very demanding *Gymnasien* where Greek, Latin, and philosophy were compulsory subjects. In 1834, the *Abitur* examination was established, which pupils sat in these schools under the supervision of church and state; the *Abitur* remains the examination for university entrance in Germany (as discussed in detail in Chapter 9).

During these reforms, the technical sciences were completely removed from German higher education, on the grounds that they were useful rather than being dedicated towards the quest for truth.[7] Nevertheless, some natural sciences survived in the philosophical faculties, insofar as they could claim to fall under the heading 'natural philosophy', i.e. to be involved in the speculative search for truth. Other violations of the idea that the German university was dedicated to truth rather than usefulness also soon made themselves apparent. Jurisprudence managed to maintain its university status (on the basis of its closeness to philosophy), as did medicine (on the basis of its link with the natural-philosophy concept of the 'life force').

In a variety of ways, the view that universities were supposed to serve the quest for truth was overtaken by reality. Thus medicine engaged in systematic observation of phenomena such as infections, and gradually deciphered the causes of recurring epidemics, thereby demonstrating that human health was not an inevitable state of being, but rather could be affected by useful interventions. This insight ran parallel to a recognition in other sciences, that industrial production processes could be improved by taking appropriate steps. Justus Liebig, for instance, opposed the 'natural philosophy' approach to chemistry, and showed how chemical experiments and appropriate manuring could increase soil fertility and reduce the frequency of famines.[8] Declining soil fertility and population growth had presented social reformers with insoluble theoretical and practical diffi-culties. Now a subject which had hitherto been regarded only as an auxiliary discipline for pharmacology offered a chance to escape the Malthusian trap. Thus during the great famine of 1845/6 the government of Baden established several professorships of chemistry, the beginning of a fertilizer industry which would soon begin to flourish.[9]

In every formal sense, however, German universities continued to try to exclude the 'useful' disciplines. After 1810, the technological cameralist disciplines, which until 1806 had generally attracted the largest audiences, were no longer represented in German universities. After the July Revolution of 1830, German universities pushed even more forcefully for the exclusion of the 'practicians', who were also suspected of revolutionary tendencies. Those who wished to gain appropriate training in technical fields for use in the world had to turn to institutions outside the university system.

At this period, very few such institutions yet existed. For those wishing to pursue economic occupations, the Ministry of Commerce provided support for technical training in (poly-)technic schools or *Gewerbeinstitute* (Industrial Institutes). Expert technical knowledge for state and military needs was only available in Berlin via the military academies. In France, such knowledge could be obtained at the École Polytechnique, but this institution was rejected by Berlin for fear of revolution. It did find a home in Baden in 1825 at the Karlsruhe Polytechnic School, but had little immediate influence on the transformation of Baden's antiquated industrial technology.

Only in Prussia did reform involve the decision to develop a system of commercial and industrial education which would train people for the economy rather than for the state. Admittedly, for a long time high fees and low teachers' salaries meant that the quality of the training and the number of students remained very modest. Nevertheless, after the revolutions of 1848, the professors in this system pushed for an increase in their social status and for a fully academic institutional organization. In order for this to take place, it was necessary to have a full-value *Abitur* entrance requirement, which was achieved in 1876. It was also necessary for the existing technical colleges to be transformed into schools of general education, which was achieved with the establishment of the *Oberrealschulen* in 1882.[10] Both were brought about through parliamentary initiatives.

The content of the teaching in these colleges also gradually changed. An important model was the *Eidgenössische Technische Hochschule* (Swiss Technical College) established in Zürich in 1856, based on the principles of higher mathematics. German admiration for the success of this Zürich model brought about a gradual transformation of schools for 'practicians' into colleges concentrating much more on mathematics, physics, and chemistry, and teaching these subjects at higher levels of difficulty. This reached its apogee in 1876/9 with the very late merging of the Construction Academy and the Industrial Academy in Berlin into a technical college. Only as a result of a pedagogical strategy oriented toward predictability and the material sciences did the subject-matter taught at these institutions achieve the level of a technical science.

10.1.3 Technology and commerce in Germany

In concrete terms, the technological side of Germany's industrialization effort was initially simply a race to catch up as soon as possible with England, France, and the United States. The most important impetus toward doing so was provided by the constant expansion of German markets as a result of the customs union (after 1834) and then German unification (after 1871). Even so, as discussed in Chapter 2, hundreds of thousands of Germans were forced to emigrate because of the lack of subsistence opportunities at home.

After 1813, the Prussian state financed experimental workshops and machines, with the aim of creating models for industrialization by its citizens, as discussed in Chapter 4. It only ceased to engage in such paternalistic behaviour after 1851, when the parliament forced through a liberalization of economic management in the coal-mining sector. Until then, corporative political considerations had prevented the liberalization of this branch of industry.[11]

Technological development in Germany was also aided by numerous immigrants. The transmission of new technical knowledge through personal mobility by expert individuals had been well known for centuries, as shown by the recruitment of German technical experts by England in the sixteenth century and by Russia in the eighteenth. But now the flow of migrants moved in the opposite direction, from other countries into Germany. Now, too, these migrants brought with them not so much craft skills as those needed for building machines and transportation systems. Entrepreneurs and technicians began to move to Germany, often with financial assistance. Sometimes this created sociopolitical tensions, since such immigrants naturally placed their own economic interests above the group interests of the local inhabitants or those affected by their business decisions. It was always much easier when such immigrants were engaged in building up completely new industries, as Belgians and Englishmen did in the Ruhr region, or as when French ideas gave rise to the gas motor and later to the internal combustion engine.[12] Such enterprises as these brought with them much less social unrest than the development of factories in textiles, an industry which already existed in the form of non-factory cottage production.[13]

However, this race to catch up with early-industrializing countries did not see Germany developing many fundamentally innovative products. It was thought that the way to compete was by under-cutting imports, in the way that had been customary for centuries. It was not until the American Centenary Exhibition in Philadelphia in 1876 that the dilemma faced by German industry was explicitly articulated by Franz Reuleaux, Rector of the Berlin Technical College. He argued that supplying 'cheap and nasty' products in a competition to offer ever-lower prices for already established wares was not the way for German industry to provide livelihoods for Germany's numerous inhabitants.[14] Instead, Reuleaux wanted to improve German technological performance so that German industry could create new, high-quality products. He had come to Berlin from the Swiss Technical College in Zürich and sought to make the technical subjects taught at the Berlin Technical College 'scientific' by subsuming them under 'kinetics', the study of the laws of motion. He and his colleagues did not lack insight into the details of technical processes or their links with practical applications. But their ideas were still in advance of their time, and did not yet fit into the self-image of German technical colleges. Problems such as friction called for laboratories, not for museums.

German industrialists also had to learn that industrial success was influenced not only by technological innovations but also by their financing. Before 1848, the Prussian state was highly indebted and was administered by fearful officials. As discussed in Chapter 4, this exercised a braking effect on German industry, which was strongly criticized by entrepreneurs. This was only alleviated by new and more liberal – some would say too liberal – legislation governing shareholding after 1871, as discussed in Chapter 5.[15]

The early 1870s saw a number of far-reaching changes in German society and political life which also affected science and technology. The new German Empire was formed in 1871, and although it initially suffered from having too few primary responsibilities, its political importance gradually expanded. Then, in 1873, the German economy experienced a significant downturn, affected also to some extent by economic crises in America and Austria. This resulted in a far-reaching transformation not only of German political culture, but also of science, technology, and society. Bismarck, who feared for the cohesion of the recently founded German Empire, followed the examples of America and France by offering tariff protection to the endangered branches of industry and agriculture. Then, in 1877, he authorized the establishment of a patent office under the direction of Werner von Siemens, because the emerging sciences of chemistry and electrical engineering were finding that they had to protect their own processes and inventions. He also, as discussed in Chapter 7, provided the German population with three all-encompassing social insurance systems: for sickness, industrial accidents, and old-age pensions. Finally, he authorized a number of structural changes in the education and university systems which were implemented by the Prussian parliament and had substantial effects on the other German states. The example of England had done its duty, and Germany was now following its own path.

10.2 From 1880 to the 1960s

10.2.1 German society

The long period from 1880 to 1970 saw an unusually dynamic and continuous growth of industrial production in Germany. As discussed in Chapter 6, this structural change took place not in a centralized way in the capital cities – despite the enormous growth of Berlin – but rather in a polycentric way, in which the different German regions continued to compete with one another, as well as with foreign regions. At first glance, it might seem that the First World War, the Weimar Republic, the National Socialist Reich, the Second World War, and the reconstruction of a democratic Federal Republic of Germany after 1945, display quite different structures from one another. Nevertheless, this period is actually quite homogeneous, viewed from the perspective of the development of science-based industries under the aegis of the German nation-state. The imaginations of German scientists and engineers were oriented towards great national goals, as these had been developed during the Kaiserreich. Furthermore, there was the widely held self-image of German society which believed that in order to achieve these goals both education and research must be financed by the state.

Germany's new experience of liberal, capitalist economic cycles in the 1860s and 1870s had brought 'new men' into influential positions. It had also endowed the younger generation which was affected by these developments with a substantial dose of both positivist science and scepticism about liberal economic cycles. These attitudes also involved a certain scepticism about the idea of using technical developments to solve social problems. In addition, German engineers adopted ideas about cyclical processes and the importance of thrift, quite counter to the positivistic, linear euphoria about 'progress'.[16] This dissatisfaction took on a political form in the later 1870s, with the strengthening of the socialist movement and its rejection of the Kaiserreich, which in turn evoked very intense anti-socialist and soon also anti-Semitic tendencies. As discussed in Chapter 9, the latter ideas gripped the younger generation of German students in particular, with great – indeed, ultimately fateful – consequences.

German society reacted to the long economic crisis after 1873 on a number of levels. Alongside prohibitions against the socialist party, there arose efforts at social integration through social insurance (discussed in Chapter 7) and educational changes (discussed in Chapter 9 and later in the present chapter). There also arose protective mechanisms such as cartels and associations which sought to stabilize the internal market and also the political system. This policy resulted in a greater self-confidence in Germans' own technological achievements.

The technical shaping of industrial production, however, does not rest on top-level research alone. Just as important, if not more so, is the opening – and opening-up – of scientific and technical educational careers. Arguably the most influential component of the response to the economic crisis of the 1870s, as far as German science and technology were concerned, was the opening up of new opportunities for professional advancement through the strengthening of scientific and technical education after the long depression of the 1870s. New opportunities in science and technology were supposed to ensure upward social mobility for a small group of 'officers', something desired both by industry and by a German Empire pushing toward external expansion as a great power and at the same time supporting the social structures of the Kaiserreich.

In 1879, during the liberal phase, the professors in the technical sciences achieved equality with those in the universities. Then, in 1899, the degree of 'Doctor of Engineering' began to be granted at the Technical College in Berlin and at nine other colleges. Almost immediately after 1880 the question arose of equipping the electrical (and mechanical) engineers and the chemists with experimentation rooms and laboratories. The new technical college in Berlin attracted a large number of students from the beginning. Other technical colleges, such as the one in Darmstadt, were not successful during the 1870s and only survived by acting entrepreneurially: Darmstadt, for instance, negotiated substantial help from industry in establishing the discipline of electrical engineering which helped secure its future.[17] Nevertheless, the number of students attending technical colleges grew rapidly, and only began to stagnate after the crisis of 1901/2.

After the crisis of the 1870s, Germany's emerging industrial (lower) bourgeoisie favoured a type of school that would simultaneously provide a general education (with modern languages and sciences) and lead on to admission to a technical college, the *Oberrealschule*. This type of school began to be set up from 1882 onward in Prussia, and substantially improved the theoretical knowledge of German technical experts. This created a need to train teachers in the requisite natural sciences, and that in turn increased the number of lecturers.

But the most drastic change was the restructuring of middle-ranking technical education in the final decades of the nineteenth century. In exchange for accepting the various new social insurance programmes, German industry demanded the creation of a state-financed technical education system with admission requirements below the level of the *Abitur*. In Prussia, this led in 1890 to the foundation of the *technische Mittelschulen* (technical middle schools), which then commenced to grow very rapidly. In 1893, there were already four technical middle schools with a budget of 100,000 marks; by 1908 these had expanded to 11 technical middle schools, with a budget of 10.5 million marks – and Prussia was already spending 4 million marks on its four technical colleges. After 1918, the technical middle schools were renamed *Höhere Technische Lehranstalten* (higher technical educational establishments), but from the start they had been equipped with laboratories, just like technical colleges. These institutions generated a large stratum of graduates who were responsible for redirecting toward the sphere of production the research results generated in the technical colleges. It was these developments that led an English observer of the German educational system, Dawson, to remark in 1908 that 'Science, education, application, and an equal regard for small as for large things – these, in the main, are the causes of Germany's success as a rival in the market of the world.'[18] Rivalries between these different types of technical education, as well as with other schools, were resolved by a new board, the DATSCH (*Deutscher Ausschuß für technisches Schulwesen* or German Commission on Technical Schools), which gave German technical education very uniform contours.

At the end of the nineteenth century, the first two generations of German industrialists and bankers to become wealthy began to work toward extending the university system by establishing numerous private foundations – not just in Prussia, but also in other German territories. In an effort to bring cohesion among the various competing regions of Germany, the circles surrounding the Kaiser developed the notion of a foundation, with a strong technical emphasis, for the entire Empire. The Empire had already given way to 15 years of pressure from Werner von Siemens, and in 1886 established a research institute, the *Physikalisch Technische Reichsanstalt* (Imperial Institute of Physical and Technical Studies) to provide a home for the systematic study of the emerging subjects of electrical engineering and electrophysics, as well as for the new forms of measurement and equipment which they required. This was done mostly to benefit the economy, but the Imperial state with its military requirements hoped to benefit as well. Similar institutions, for instance for the investigation of technical questions arising from railway accidents, had already been established at the beginning of the 1870s as appendages to university departments. The Imperial Institute of Physical and Technical Studies was also distinctive in that it provided a context for collaboration between theoretical groups of researchers (surrounding Hermann von Helmholtz) and more practically minded groups (surrounding the development of instruments). This Institute soon constituted an important potential source of lecturers for the technical colleges.[19]

Very gradually, traditional German academics were beginning to give up their resistance to the establishment of science research institutes outside universities. At the same time, the great associations of technical scientists – especially that of the chemists, who wanted a national institute of chemistry – continued to exert pressure. Finally, the Kaiser proclaimed his intention to create a foundation, the *Kaiser-Wilhelm-Gesellschaft zur Förderung der Wissenschaften* (Kaiser Wilhelm Society for the Promotion of Sciences, abbreviated as KWG), which was established in 1911.[20] Its task was to promote active collaboration between science and practical applications, and to provide assistance in cases where the state was unable to do so promptly or adequately. In addition, Kaiser Wilhelm Institutes were to be established in particularly important fields of research, and unified in the south of Berlin (Dahlem) into a 'Little Oxford'. In the event, the Kaiser Wilhelm Society turned out to be an exceptionally effective scientific organization. At the same time, however, it became an institution in which science and the upper Prussian bourgeoisie united to fortify their dominance in the society of the Kaiserreich. The sociologist Max Weber regarded the Kaiser Wilhelm Society as a state-capitalist enterprise.[21]

The directors of the Kaiser Wilhelm Institutes were to be appointed by the state, but their selection and especially their financing were to be ensured by the participation of private donors. However, existing institutions and the Prussian Academy of Sciences ended up exerting a very strong influence on the whole process. This meant that in the event, greatest prominence was given to the natural sciences, and hardly any to technology. By 1914, Kaiser Wilhelm Institutes had been founded for zoology, chemistry, experimental therapy, hard coal research, work physiology, the Bibliothecia Herziana in Rome, biology, physiology and brain research, physics, and German history. The closest to the ideas of the industrial sponsors was the Kaiser Wilhelm Institute for Hard Coal Research, which was the first to be founded outside Berlin, near Essen in the Ruhr region, and which by 1920 had made considerable achievements in improving coking, obtaining liquid and gaseous fuels from coal and coke, and synthesizing rubber from coking gases.[22]

After 1918, with the Kaiser no longer present as a protector of science, both the Kaiser Wilhelm Institutes (which lost all their capital during the great inflation) and German universities as a whole suffered from a great shortage of funding. This, together with the international boycott of German science, was widely regarded by Germans as unjust. These interests gave rise to a unique team effort among Germany's top research institutions, the formation in 1921 of the *Notgemeinschaft der Deutschen Wissenschaft* (Emergency Society of German Science), organized on the model of the Kaiser Wilhelm Society.[23] So, from 1921 on, the budget of the Reich itself always planned an appropriation for science and research. Nonetheless, German industrial interests provided about 30 per cent of the budget of the Kaiser Wilhelm Society and continued to maintain their own subject-specific associations which they themselves controlled and which were much better financed – three associations for chemistry and one for physics, all with a special emphasis on applied work.[24] In the Kaiser Wilhelm Society, applied research received more support than before.

These developments gave rise to the three different spheres in which scientific research in Germany is still conducted to this day. First, there was academic research, which was largely determined by academics themselves. It was carried out on the one hand in universities and technical colleges, and on the other in the non-university organizations mentioned above, the Kaiser Wilhelm Institutes (nowadays transformed into Max Planck Institutes). Not surprisingly, the large number of Nobel Prize winners generated by these Kaiser Wilhelm Institutes focused public interest on them.

Second, there was industrial research. This also occurred through state funding, after the establishment of the German Federal Atomic Ministry in 1955, followed by that of Federal Ministry for Research and Technology in 1982.

The third way in which scientific research was conducted in Germany was through state-directed research or research carried out for government departments, for example on questions relating to material science or military technology. Occasionally, such research was carried out in conjunction with universities, but more often with non-university institutions.

In Prussia up to 1945, for example, it occurred in the fields of meteorology, geodesy, astrophysics and astronomy, vaccination science, water research (hygiene), food and agriculture (sugar, fermentation, weights and measures, hydraulic engineering).

Although the academies, the universities, and to a certain degree even the Kaiser Wihelm Institutes all distanced themselves from applied research, nevertheless in a few prominent cases this distance was overcome. After 1918, in the Kaiser Wilhelm Society the only funds for new research purposes were provided either by industrial foundations with particular purposes,[25] or through money from the government of the Reich; there was no longer any inflow of general funding.[26] In 1919 the Kaiser Wilhelm Society took over research into aviation which had previously been a military matter,[27] but whose point of departure had been Ludwig Prandtl's theory of boundary layers, developed in the Göttingen Institute. By doing this, the Reich rescued this branch of research from the aviation ban imposed by the Allies, clearing the way for research into gliding and for cooperation with the Soviet Union which was also heavily promoting research into these questions.

Then, in 1928, the *Deutsche Forschungsrat für Luftfahrt* (German Research Council for Aeronautics) was founded, largely as a result of the awakening interest of the Weimar Republic and its military. The aim was to create a joint coordinating centre for state, science, and economy to provide expert opinions, research programmes, and prospective investigations of aviation technology. However, the funding for all of this remained quite limited. Only with the National Socialist regime did it begin to be much more extensively promoted, when in 1936 the *Deutsche Forschungsanstalt für Luftfahrt* (German Research Institute for Aeronautics) was founded with the decisive help of Hermann Göring. In the course of German rearmament from 1935 onward, the relevant Kaiser Wilhelm Institutes were provided with generous funding, and were also removed from the influence of the Kaiser Wilhelm Society by being subordinated to the *Reichsforschungsrat* (Reich Research Council).[28] They were, for example, supposed to push forward research into aviation motors, solve the problems of high-altitude flight, and improve aerial navigation, all questions closely linked with the militarization of aviation.[29] Their organization can even be characterized as the first large-scale research institution, when after 1942 10,000 scientists were brought together to work toward the development of warplanes and several thousands on rocket weapons,[30] even if they were not organized so strictly and on such a large scale as in the Manhattan project for the development of the atomic bomb in the United States, which is generally regarded as having provided the model for large-scale research institutions after 1945.

In 1945, these and other military-oriented large-scale research institutions and departments were dissolved in Germany. Research bans were imposed on aviation, nuclear physics, space research, and radar technology, and only began to be dismantled after 1952. Unlike before 1945, German scientists and engineers now more or less voluntarily followed the offers of the victorious powers to change their places of work.[31]

In the Soviet Occupation Zone, in the first two years after the end of the war, about 2000 individuals (scientists, technicians, and skilled workers) were taken away to the Soviet Union to work in nuclear research, aviation and rocket construction programmes. The first of them returned in 1950, the last in 1956. In order to keep these top-level specialists, and also scientists such as Max Steenbeck, Gustav Hertz, and Peter A. Thießen, in the country, the German Democratic Republic set up the *Amt für Technik* (Technology Office), specifically to make funding available for aviation research; it was dissolved in 1961 with the breaking-off of aircraft manufacturing. The first nuclear power plant, however, did start operating by 1957.

In 1955, when the German Democratic Republic received sovereignty, the German (prewar: Prussian) *Akademie der Wissenschaften* (Academy of Sciences) was completely remodelled on the Soviet model and was assigned the role of the top scholarly committee in the state, and the *Forschungs- gemeinschaft* (Research Community) emerged as the favoured inner circle.[32] But the top natural scientists who were returning from the Soviet Union wanted to have a continuation of the old, pre-1945 *Reichsforschungsrat* (Reich Research Council), with its proximity to the government and to government finance. To this end, they pushed through a Research Council called the *Beirat für naturwissenschaftlich-technische Fragen* (Sub- Committee for Questions of Natural Science and Technology) within the Ministerial Council of the German Democratic Republic, with Thießen at its head and 45 members. It is less well known that the German Democratic Republic, as well, planned large-scale research institutions after 1955 which were also to be directed by former top Nazi physicists.[33]

This arrangement was to some extent admired in West Germany, where scientists always found themselves wrestling with mixed institutions full of politicians, such as the *Wissenschaftsrat* (Science Council). Apparently in competition with the new arrangements in the German Democratic Republic, the Federal Republic of Germany, which also achieved sovereignty in 1955, also created large-scale research institutions, above all due to pressure from Werner Heisenberg. Just like in the post-1918 period, a major concern was the tapping of energy reserves, which physicists and chemists promised to do by exploiting nuclear energy.

After 1945, the western Allies, despite their painful experience with fascist Germany, were much more cautious in excluding Germany from the inter- national community of researchers than they had been after 1918. In this, a role was probably played by the hope that this would enable them to make use of Germany's remaining resources. Furthermore, after the Potsdam Conference in 1945, Germany was supposed to be turned into a federal entity in all matters, and limited from building up central state power. Each of the victorious Allied powers therefore sought to make attractive offers to the top figures in German science to suit their own needs. As mentioned above, this resulted in Ferdinand Porsche working in France, and Werner von Braun and others in the United States (e.g. in the field of aviation medicine). A number of German physicists had been interned in England in 1945/6 and interrogated about their intentions with regard to the atomic bomb.[34]

After 1945, the famous scientific associations which still existed in Germany were only hesitantly revived. The appointment of the communist Robert Havemann as President of the Kaiser-Wilhelm Society by the authorities in East Berlin was not a success: most of the scientists in the Kaiser-Wilhelm Society not only were anti-communist, but also regarded the former presidents of the Society, Max Planck and Otto Hahn, as their representatives. However, for the association to be permitted by the British to operate again, it had to get rid of its name, and from 1946 onward it was renamed the Max Planck Society. With the rise of the Cold War, it was mainly the Americans who promoted communication within the often divided associations, and furthered their reactivation. The British promoted the creation in March 1949 of the *Deutsche Forschungsrat* (German Research Council) in Göttingen. Under the direction of the physicist Adolf Windaus it was considered the centre of research in the natural sciences. It encompassed the three West German Academies and the Max Planck Society. Then in March 1951 this new *Deutsche Forschungsrat* merged with the *Notgemeinschaft* (Emergency Society) which had been established in 1921, to form the *Deutsche Forschungsgemeinschaft* (German Research Community); this latter institution operated more democratically than the former *Forschungsrat* in finding assessors for proposed projects.

In the first third of the twentieth century, many German engineers and scientists had become convinced that basic scientific research was susceptible to planning. In West Germany after the Second World War, this led to the creation of a large number of research institutes which – as in 1900 and 1925 – were supposed to enable Germany to overcome its backwardness relative to other nations. In the early years of the new Federal Republic, these consisted of the Max Planck Institute for Nuclear Research and for (Nuclear) Shipbuilding (set up in 1960, the 'Otto Hahn' being launched in 1969), the Hahn-Meitner Institute, and Deutsches Elektronen Synchroton. But the legacy of the previous domination of German science by the mandarins led to conflict about what was the correct path: the nuclear research plant in Jülich was founded by Leo Brandt (the most important motor of research policy in North Rhine-Westphalia) in competition with the nuclear research centre in Karlsruhe in Baden.[35] There were considerable tensions with the Nuclear Ministry in Bonn, which favoured the Karlsruhe institute for foreign policy reasons. In the end, the American light-water reactor in Karlsruhe got the upper hand. This was mainly because after 1953, the Americans were prepared to deliver enriched fissionable material, and also to release information about many technical processes, in order to prevent the Soviets from using it for civilian purposes and keep the British out of the market.

10.2.2 German industry and technology

The long period from 1880 to 1970 saw a very ambivalent relationship between German society and industry on the one hand, and German science and technology. There evolved an enormous German pride in outstanding scientific discoveries and extraordinary technical innovations, a pride increasingly enunciated in published form after about 1920.[36] But the way in which Germans made use of technology began to manifest a remarkable and in certain ways fateful drive toward recognizing the potential benefits of technology while at the same time neglecting its economic and worldly dangers. Such questions were generally 'solved' in Germany through national debates about cartellization and rearmament. But, as shown by the experience of the two world wars, these solutions tended to be the opposite of constructive. After 1933 in particular, German engineers – and Germans at large – did not recognize the necessity to control certain uses of technology, despite the growth of persecution within Germany, German military aggression abroad, and the unrestrained use of many scientific and technical processes and experiments regardless of any customary notions concerning the limits to human degradation.[37]

Germany saw a particularly widespread tendency for links to be formed between members of the various natural sciences and the technical fields in which their ideas could be applied: physicists in materials analysis and electrical technology; chemists in re-conceptualizing the properties of materials and in medicines; engineers in constructing the machines necessary for both research and production. This situation mirrored, in a sense, the German Reich itself, which was characterized by enormous social and regional differentiation. Indeed, Germans' scientific and technical achievements were often used as a justification for setting up this very Reich, against initial opposition to it. Many upwardly mobile individuals came to Germany from neighbouring countries, with a view to achieving personal fulfilment through scientific success. As already mentioned, Germany had not just a single centre of development, but a whole array of competing centres. One can only pose the question whether these numerous upwardly mobile people played their own special role in later German abuses of technological possibilities.

The German scientists and engineers who participated in the First World War alongside the military were above all those who regarded the remarkable expansion of the Germany economy from 1890 onward as a sign that Germany was a 'chosen' society, and who used this to underpin German claims to world domination along Darwinian lines. Very early on, it was noted that this might at the same time compensate for the unresolved conflicts arising from social tensions within German society. Large sections of German public opinion, especially in academic milieus, were not prepared to undertake a sober analysis of Germany's defeat in the Great War. As a result, in the years after 1930, they were easy prey for the radical

National Socialists, who exploited what they claimed was the unjustified humiliation of Germany after the war in order to persecute inconvenient critics as well as democrats, and to let loose a religious war against 'racially less valuable' and 'ideological' opponents. Admittedly, this all occurred with a constant invocation of the national community (*Volksgemeinschaft*), to whom great social concessions were made on paper, at the expense of the Germans who were killed or driven into exile and the European peoples who were conquered.

After 1945, the German engineers and scientists who had been persecuted by the Nazis were seldom remembered. Instead, two cultures confronted one another within German society. One emphasized the misuse of scientific and technical achievements; the other culture, a less public one, stressed the fact that Germany had lost the war despite having better and more sophisticated technology and science. The fact that one's assessment of technology always involves its responsible use only entered these people's consciousness – despite the V2 rockets and the bombing of cities – when the nuclear bomb was used. It was only decades later, when the harm caused to complete non-participants, even to the unborn, became clear, that this awareness was transferred to nuclear power plants and to other scientific experiments (e.g. in macro-biology), and was articulated in public protests.

The other major post-1945 development was the fact that in Germany especially, but also in most other European countries, after a few years of reconstruction there occurred a huge increase in the consumption of technical appliances (as discussed in Chapter 12).[38] To a considerable extent, the war had set a development in motion which would later be used for civilian purposes: information technology is a particularly vivid example of this. In Germany, this reorientation of technology to civilian uses was particularly striking.

10.2.2.1 THE SOCIOPOLITICAL MANAGEMENT OF TECHNOLOGICAL RISKS

But in 1880 this was still far in the future. During German industrialization, the initial challenge was to work out ways for society to deal with the problems which inevitably arose in constructing or applying new technical devices. Initially, Germany had simply followed decentralized, non-state models of dealing with technical accidents, which had been developed during industrialization in Britain. But from 1880 onward, the German state increasingly intervened, particularly by passing new legislation. As early as 1838, German states had already passed laws requiring compensation for railway accidents to be provided according to the principle of absolute liability.

In dealing with the problems caused by steam boiler explosions, Germany took over Britain's insurance solution, whereby the owners of steam-powered factories formed so-called *Dampfkesselüberwachungsvereine*

(Steam Boiler Supervision Associations), followed in 1873 by a *Internationaler Verband der Dampfkesselüberwachungsvereine* (International League of Steam Boiler Supervision Associations). After the end of the 'British' period, in 1884, Bismarck (as Minister of Trade and Industry) created a rival, the *Zentralverband der Preußischen Dampfkesselüberwachungsvereine* (Central League of Prussian Steam Boiler Supervision Associations) which was made responsible for carrying out regular inspections of steam engines. Despite the fact that these were actually private associations, the German state assigned more and more responsibilities to them as time passed: for automobiles, then for inflammable substances, and so on. It was not until 1936 that the lack of transparency in this monitoring system which had grown up historically was eliminated by the establishment of the *Reichsverband der Dampfkesselüberwachungsvereine* (Reich League of Steam Boiler Supervision Associations). After 1946, regional Steam Boiler Supervision Associations arose, forming a League, the *Vereinigung der Dampfkesselüberwachungsvereine*, which had similarly all-encompassing powers. In Germany it was not until the 1970s that there was any competition among these associations. Even then, as privately registered associations they remained responsible for the security of nuclear power plants, but most of all they are known for their compulsory regular technical inspections of every car and every elevator in Germany.

Risks to employees arising from improper use of technology had already been made the responsibility of firms quite early on, in 1869, based on the principle of liability for injury to workers caused by intentional and negligent acts. But it was not until 1878 that the state inspectorate of industry obtained influence over the technical organization of machines and arrangements inside industrial plants, by securing the right of regular inspections. From 1884 onward, German firms had to provide compulsory accident insurance for their workers, in order to be able to compensate them for accidents in the workplace. These efforts triggered campaigns, especially during the Weimar period, which were noticeably oriented toward American models. The question of occupational illnesses remained unsolved for a long time and was only tackled after 1925 under considerable international pressure. Enduring and modernized solutions were created only after the Social Democrats came to power in 1969 and established an entire ministry to deal with such matters.

10.2.2.2 ELECTRICITY

In the early twentieth century, the age of mass production was rapidly approaching. In this era, it would become absolutely essential to be able to implement rationalization and standardization. But German industry was very slow in undertaking these steps, which only began to be implemented in 1916 under pressure from the armaments programme. This pressure resulted in a development which was very beneficial for German industry in general, the definition of the *Deutsche Industrie Norm* (German Industry Norm), the origin of the initials 'DIN' which still appear in many industrial standard measures in Germany (and throughout the world). Even then, it was not until the 1920s that Germany began to take on board American developments such as Fordism and Taylorism for organizing the mass production of goods.

Likewise, the new branches of industry which arose in Germany in the years after 1880 were initially characterized by a remarkable uncertainty. Although Siemens had already demonstrated the possibility of electric propulsion in 1879, it did not put it into effect until it was challenged by the new financing model adopted by AEG and by a severe crisis in 1901/2 which 'cleansed' the market of competitors. Even then, it was necessary not merely to build power plants, but also to awaken and develop the demands of customers by providing appropriate electrical appliances and equipment.[39] In 1891, Oskar von Miller had demonstrated that electrical three-phase current was susceptible to being conveyed over considerable distances in a way that was economically viable at least to some extent. This set off a far-reaching construction of an electrical grid in Germany. This also began a wealth of experiments and technical developments in which experienced instrument-makers were just as important as finding solutions to controlling the new 'electricity grid' system. After 1917, this grid not only covered the towns, but also extended into agricultural areas, and constituted the first significant step in bridging the gulf between rural and urban lifestyles (the second being the spread of the automobile after 1950).[40] Even so, the German state's military concerns delayed the electrification of the German railways for another two generations.

The Ruhr steel enterprises, despite their frequent conflicts over scientific matters, eagerly adopted the new form of energy provision represented by electricity. First they enduringly improved the heat flow in their factories through the exploitation of waste heat from blast furnaces for electricity generation. Then, spurred by incentives arising from the highly cartellized structure of their industry, they began to use coal gas to drive large-scale gas machines and generators. Soon they established an electricity grid which was to become the most important in Germany, the Rheinisch-Westfälisches Elektrizitätswerk AG (RWE). In the 1920s the very high-voltage lines of this grid stretched from the Dutch border, via Cologne (where it used bituminous coal), all the way to the Alps (where it relied on dams).[41] The most important source of its dominance was RWE's generous and widely accepted offer to municipalities to participate financially in the grid. Not surprisingly, the National Socialist technocrats did not regard this private electricity supplier favourably, and forced it to build and participate in its own gigantic military electrical grid.[42]

From the 1920s on, the American technocratic movement had sought to disseminate the view that electricity – like railways previously and high-speed highways later on – represented a high-grade and complex technical system that held out the hope of reducing unemployment and creating greater social justice. The German technocratic movement, as well, sought to turn electricity distribution into a key to political order, and was thus one of the first movements to recognize the fact that technical systems could be influenced by society and hence planned. For this reason, electricity played a major role in the evolution of German cultural attitudes toward new technologies.[43]

10.2.2.3 CHEMICALS

The field of technology and industry in which Germany was unquestionably dominant in global terms was chemistry. The laboratories of the German chemical industry and the chemistry chairs in German universities developed, through their patenting strategy, an exceptionally dense network and an absolute superiority in the production of chemical products throughout the world. This branch of industry was correspondingly large and influential. Very soon, it was able to free Germany from the necessity of importing nitrogenous fertilizer by combining techniques in chemistry and in electrical engineering, thereby synthesizing nitrogen through the Haber-Bosch process. It also made possible the large-scale production of synthetic methanol, which was used especially as a basic raw material in organic chemical techniques, as a fuel additive, and in synthetic rubber production. These successes strengthened German chemical engineers' sense that almost anything was feasible.

After the First World War, German chemistry worked under a twofold stimulus: the worldwide anxiety about an energy bottleneck, and a specifically German postwar feeling of being cut off from hard coal resources in Upper Silesia and the Saar, and of possessing very limited oil deposits. This was the background which supported German chemists' development of the high-pressure process for the production of complex hydrocarbon bonds. The bituminous coal region of central Germany, which had already been exploited as a power centre for nearby industrial centres, saw the building of the Leuna-Werke in 1916; this helped to create a giant centre of chemical production in this region (which was after 1945 to become the East German chemicals centre). The connections forged between chemists, physicists, and engineers in fields such as chemical technology created the basis for the development of high-pressure chemistry, in order to use hard coal to produce oil and later also synthetics. The increasing importance of synthetic fibres after 1930 was a consequence, among other things, of the field of polymer chemistry conceptualized by Hermann Staudinger. In 1931, IG Farben succeeded in working out how such fibres could be spun, but they were intended much more for industrial use than for consumer use, since the American fibre Perlon and the British fibre Dralon represented superior competing products.

The autarkic economic policies pursued by the National Socialist regime, although (as discussed in Chapter 8) they failed to endow Germany with the desired economic autarky, nevertheless had the effect of promoting German research in this field of chemistry, particularly the high-pressure (Bergius) process used by IG Farben and the lower-temperature process developed by Franz Fischer at the Kaiser-Wilhelm Institute for Coal Research in Mülheim on the Ruhr. However, these autarkic policies had a lasting legacy, especially for East Germany. After 1945, the large-scale chemical industries which were oriented toward an autarkic conception of the German economy lay in the Soviet Occupation Zone and were firmly anchored in the minds of those in power there as productive establishments. It was probably a structural benefit for West Germany that it was deprived of these old industries, and instead oriented itself toward American petroleum-based processes.

10.2.2.4 IRON, STEEL, AND MACHINE TOOLS

Perhaps the greatest contrast with the high-technology emphasis in the German chemical industry was provided by the German iron and steel industry. Despite the fact that iron and steel were the basic metals of early industrialization, German iron and steel firms neglected to build up their own research laboratories. The big, fundamental innovations in processes came over to Germany from Britain, and the electrical process introduced at the beginning of the twentieth century came over from France. It was not until 1917 that the Kaiser-Wilhelm Institute for Iron Research was established, and not until the 1920s that German steelworks began to set up research laboratories of their own.[44] Indeed, it was only under considerable pressure from its customers – and because it became possible to produce liquid oxygen in large quantities – that the German steel industry undertook the factory research necessary to develop the oxygen process during the 1940s.

Not only did early industrialization rely on the efficient production of raw iron and steel, but it required the introduction of new, higher-quality varieties and products, such as T-girders for construction purposes. These began to arrive from the 1880s onward. Again, the machine-tool industry was at first dominated by Britain and the United States, with Germany far behind. But from 1905 onward, Georg Schlesinger in Berlin brought it to new heights of quality by extensively re-conceptualizing it in terms of precision and adaptability. This was to endow the German machine-tool industry by the 1920s with a strong export position which was to endure to the present day. Its development went hand in hand with a rationalization of the manufacturing process in the way envisaged by Taylor and Ford, which was introduced into Germany from 1925 onward. Not only Hitler, but also the founders of Volkswagen, oriented themselves towards these maxims.

The success in German machine-tool building was in turn indispensable for the large-scale motor building industry, which began to emerge in Germany around 1900.[45] The assembly industries also began to develop, as made-to-measure production was combined with electric and petrol-motor-driven machines. Initially it grew modestly, but then from the 1930s to the 1950s it expanded fast. In motor vehicle manufacturing and later aircraft production, Germany had no large social stratum with substantial purchasing power; indeed, the First World War and its consequences actually annihilated in Germany a large portion of the potential purchasing power in this sector. However, Germany had a large number of craftsmen and mechanics who were keen to experiment, and they eagerly tackled the wealth of problems that had to be solved if fast-running motors,[46] electric ignition, and vehicle suspension and superstructure were to be presented to the public. To achieve this, large-scale mechanics, fine mechanics, and electrical engineering had to develop hand in hand. Initially, the leading markets for these were in France, soon afterwards in Britain, and then in the United States.

10.2.2.5 RADIO AND TELEVISION

The technology for the wireless transmission of information was developed in a context of furious international competition, but German scientists played an important role in the process. The physicists (such as Heinrich Herz) studying the use of electromagnetic waves had simultaneously to develop the technical ideas and the necessary instruments, particularly a variety of different amplifier valves.[47] The first wireless conversation in Germany took place in 1913, but the technology only really began to be emphasized after the First World War. The war had exerted a considerable stimulus on the technical development of this communication technology, especially through the concept of the 'tethering' of large numbers of listeners to each broadcaster. Germany saw the beginning of regular radio programming in 1923. This gave rise to an early wave of consumer goods, as listeners had now to be fitted out with the necessary equipment. In this process, the National Socialists played a particularly distinctive role in the Germany of the 1930s. There were cycles of innovation which continued throughout the Second World War, not only in the continued expansion of radio, but also in the spread of the telephone in the 1960s and 1970s.

Electromechanical recording processes, together with the development of a long-playing record through the innovation of closer groove intervals, expanded the production of communication media. Stereophonics arose (in Britain) after 1932. Finally, the German firm IG Farben developed synthetic tapes with iron powder lamination for audiotape equipment. In this way, a data storage medium was invented which was much more efficient, which could easily be adapted to a wide variety of requirements (e.g. both analogue and digital), and which was to remain important to the end of the twentieth century.

Then, in the late 1950s, television arrived. As a result of the mechanical picture reduction which had already been developed for the cinema, television proved to be much faster to change over to than radio, and much more easily transmitted. The first fully electronic television transmission was brought about by the German Manfred von Ardenne in 1930. The first regular broadcasts took place in 1932 in the United States, with Britain and Germany following. After 1965, colour television benefited from continued improvements emanating from Telefunkengesellschaft, which was jointly operated by Siemens and AEG. Together with the automobile, this led to a lasting decline in the importance of public places for sociopolitical protest, compared to their staging for the media. The student protests of the mid-1960s were to be the last 'spontaneous' political demonstrations.

How can we summarize the relationship between society, science, and technology in Germany during the long period from 1880 to 1970? The activities and values of German engineers were always deeply embedded in their pride in the development of a German nation. But it would be a gross exaggeration to portray Germany's more than 80 years of successful industrial development as having resulted from its heroic wealth of original technical developments. However effective the new forms of organization adopted by large-scale scientific institutions might have been, technical artefacts had to be produced and sold in line with market requirements. Germany's strength seldom lay in making big macro-inventions (although the chemical industry might be an exception to this rule); rather, it resided in making small micro-innovations. German debates about technical innovations were always complex, complicated, and carefully weighed up, and characterized by a slowness which was often torturous. With technical innovations arising in other countries – such as railways, automobiles, and telephones – Germany nonetheless checked them carefully and tended to develop German variants. To a very striking extent, German manufacturers added to the usual heroic maxims of large scale and speed, considerations such as thrift and circulation. These four maxims – together with the slogan 'catch up on backwardness' – were the basic components of the German attitude toward technology not only over these 80 years, but over the entirety of the past two centuries, as will become even more apparent in the final section of this chapter.

10.3 From the 1960s to the present day

10.3.1 German society

The last section of this chapter discusses the past 40 years, a period whose contours are still only emerging. It can certainly be stated that in this period German society's relationship with science and technology was shaped by a much less pronounced sense of national confidence, a stronger emphasis on the individual, and a greater sensitivity to environmental issues. Nevertheless, it continued (and continues) to be characterized by great public enthusiasm for large-scale technological projects of a violent nature, such as weapons systems, the Strategic Defence Initiative, and space travel. That is, there is still considerable support in Germany for the old basic attitude of highly industrialized economies toward technology: bigger, faster, higher. In addition, the German economy continues to depend on exports, even of products which do not satisfy environmental considerations: the products of the chemical industry, of the manufacturing industry (such as cars), and of the plant manufacturing industry continue to make up the backbone of German exports.

The late 1950s saw a new political consciousness emerge in West Germany, emphasizing the importance of organizing education and science on a much broader basis, i.e. of involving in it a much larger circle of people (as discussed in Chapter 9). This parallelled the move to an economy which was much more strongly consumer-oriented than ever before (as discussed in Chapter 12). The immediate trigger for this view, in addition to the democratization of Germany after 1945, was the American Sputnik shock. In order to compete with Soviet imperialism, it was thought to be essential to strengthen western countries' scientific and mathematical training. Few noticed that the actual reform of higher education which then ensued in Germany involved precisely the opposite: it was not science and mathematics, but rather languages and political education that expanded most noticeably.

At this juncture, all the democratic parties in Germany were dominated by an enthusiasm for the United States, which arose from the view that it was mainly the United States which Germany had to thank for its own re-admission to the community of civilized nations.[48] As in many other European countries, this was to change in the mid-1960s. In Germany, this was caused not just by the Vietnam War and the United States' continued nuclear tests. It resulted equally from indigenous inter-generational conflict between young people and their parents. In Germany, this was particularly acute because the parental generation was tarred with the brush of its own failures in the pre-1945 period, which fatally weakened its debating position against the younger generation. Even the large-scale criminal trials of Nazi war criminals during the 1960s, which were supposed to show that Germany had left behind its Nazi past, did not prove particularly satisfactory, and did not counteract the enormous extent to which the older generation in Germany was regarded as having forfeited its authority. This led to a breakdown in any widespread acceptance of the system of upbringing which the parents themselves had undergone and which had traditionally imposed considerable restrictions on the young. The younger generation also began to demand and enjoy much greater attention to their own consumer preferences and their own specifically youth culture. This post-1960s German youth movement resembled the German youth movement of the beginning of the twentieth century in resisting excessive restrictions, but differed from it in not placing its hopes in a strong German nation-state.

The common ground shared by the German youth movement and by all the German opponents of the market economy and liberal capitalism which emerged from the 1960s onward was that of 'security'. This concern for 'security' – understood on a variety of levels – was no new, post-1965 phenomenon, but rather one that had been developing continuously since the 1880s, including during the Nazi era. 'Security' included, for example, the ever more perfect organization of medical insurance and a much more extensive programme for the continued payment of wages in cases of illness (as discussed in Chapter 7). It also involved the universal acceptance of the idea that economic well-being, like health, was a question of politics and could be brought into being. The social democratic and liberal government which was in power in Germany between 1969 and 1981 adopted this position, which it termed *Modell Deutschland* (the German Model). Unfortunately it remained a model, but fortunately, it was a less dangerous 'German Model' than the one blueprinted a hundred years earlier by anti-Semites and anti-socialists.

It is therefore not surprising that when in 1989 the Soviets gave up the German Democratic Republic, a majority of German young people opposed German unification, declaring themselves willing to accept the existence of several German states in Europe – precisely because unification held so many uncertainties. It was much more the decision of the departing generation (together with the United States, which wanted Germany to become a stronger partner in NATO) that led to German unification. The same rejection of risky decisions can be seen in the current widely held German attitude to genetic technology, despite the fact that it is the second-fastest growing sector of German industry after chemicals. Both patterns of behaviour underscore a traditional German attitude towards technical innovations, emphasizing caution and risk-minimization much more than euphoric enthusiasm for progress.

10.3.2 German science

Scientific work in large-scale research institutes in Germany in the last third of the twentieth century has been distinguished by four notable characteristics. First, there has been the collaboration of many scientific disciplines and teams of researchers on common projects, often around large pieces of equipment. Second, there has been the fact that research was directed towards goals which were held to be socially or politically relevant and economically useful. Third, there has been the fact that the funding derived overwhelmingly from the public sector. And fourth, there has been the dualism between the political setting of goals on the one hand and the relative autonomy of the scientists on the other.

The political conditions of the 1950s subordinated state sponsorship for the sciences in Germany to the primacy of economic and defence policies. The distribution of the scarce available resources took place according to *ad hoc* principles, which envisaged that the funding authorities would monitor projects according to the rules governing the state budget. Science underwent an organizational splintering which was mirrored in the confusion among areas of responsibility and sources of funding.

In the 1950s, the German Federal Government financed science through making general grants of funding which were not specified for particular purposes. But in the mid-1960s, 'planning euphoria' arrived in Germany from the United States. As a result, in 1969 the German *Wissenschaftsministerium* (Science Ministry) implemented a new regulatory framework, according to which large-scale research institutions were to be financed 90 per cent by the federal government and 10 per cent by the particular German state in which the institute was located. Research planning, financial planning, efficiency inspections, overall management, and detailed controls now entered the set of instruments used by state research policy.

'Planning', which had already been widely discussed since the 1920s, became the catch-phrase of the 1970s. Admittedly, many scientists active in basic research and brought up in the mandarins' tradition found it hard to adjust to this concept. Not only Julius Speer, who was President of the *Deutsche Forschungsgemeinschaft* (German Research Community) between 1964 and 1973, but also many other scientists, saw a fundamental contradiction between planning and freedom of research. Nevertheless, the intense demands science made on financial resources ultimately led to the acceptance of planning in the research arena.

This can be seen in the development of aerospace science in West Germany between the 1960s and the 1970s. In 1962 the German Federal Government had declared research into space and space travel to be fields of particular importance.[49] It demanded that energies be focused on aerospace research, and Secretary of State Wolfgang Cartellieri reproached German science for not engaging in sufficient research. The American example of NASA was now regarded as being the best model for Germany. But in 1965, German aerospace research was not yet in a position to put forward coordinated research plans. Only in that year did a fundamental rethinking begin. For this rethinking, the economic downturn of 1966 (discussed in Chapter 8) was certainly also partly responsible. In addition, talented specialists were beginning to emigrate out of Germany. In the era of the European Space Plan, a rapid solution had to be found. March 1968 saw the establishment in the Ministry for Scientific Research of an *Arbeitsgruppe Forschungsplanung* (Working Group for Research Planning) for aviation and aerospace research and the merger of all institutions involved in this field, into the *Deutsche Forschungs- und Versuchsanstalt für Luft- und Raumfahrt* (German Institution for Research and Experimentation in Aviation and Aerospace). It was only in this period that 'planning' asserted itself as the key concept governing basic research, even though scientists themselves had already been doing it for two generations.[50]

The establishment of the *Gesellschaft für Mathematik und Datenverarbeitung* (Society for Mathematics and Data-Processing) in 1968 was essentially also a matter of political planning by the federal government. It was regarded as essential that computers, which were often delivered by industry without adequate software, be equipped with appropriate programming languages. In this, the convention for the development of the machine-independent programming language ALGOL had created the nucleus of a research community. But it was not until the end of the 1960s that this gave rise to the discipline of information science. The federal government was already promoting the German Computing Centre in Darmstadt, which had been founded in 1962 by the *Deutsche Forschungsgemeinschaft* as a supra-regional computing centre and research institute for numerical mathematics. However, the Society for Mathematics and Data-Processing was not uncontroversial, chiefly because of the strategic weaknesses of its director, but also because of the fact that competing proposals were put forward.

With such a large number of large-scale research institutes in Germany, it seemed reasonable to try to coordinate their common interests, which they actually did by forming the *Arbeitsgemeinschaft der Großforschungseinrichtungen* (Working Community of Large-Scale Research Institutions) in 1970, without any interest or promotion by the ministry. But planning also included the re-organization of certain large-scale research centres, no easy undertaking given the inflexible German law regarding public service, under which as a rule no one can be dismissed after having been employed for five years. Unlike the Max Planck Society, which can simply ordain that one of its institutes close down, it required laborious negotiations to arrive at re-organizations of the large-scale research centres of Geesthacht and Jülich. By 1996, Germany had 16 large-scale centres, including three in the new, formerly East German states (for molecular medicine, environmental science, and geo-research). These centres were mostly privately organized but publicly funded, and had around 25,000 employees. They disposed of a good third of all personnel, and more than 50 per cent of all funding, in the entire sphere of non-university and state-financed research. In addition, the Max Planck Society operated 70 institutes (including eight in the new, formerly East German states), and the Fraunhofer Gesellschaft (for applied sciences) operated 36 (plus ten in the new states).

By contrast with West Germany, in East Germany research institutes were spared such adjustment to new research practices such as international cooperation. Initially, research funding in the East was greatly increased in favour of industrial research in the Academy of Sciences. In 1958, university research received 17 million marks compared to 93 million for the Academy; in 1961 the universities were still receiving only 17 million, while the Academy's funding had risen to 140 million marks.[51] The German Democratic Republic wanted to engage in all the multiplicity of research fields undertaken in West Germany in order to remain interesting for scientists who might otherwise seek to emigrate, although the building of the Berlin Wall partially solved this problem. Not only this, but it also wanted to produce special achievements in particular sectors such as chemistry, despite not having oil reserves at its disposal. This created a conflict which remained unresolved. Under Ulbricht, there was an attempt to build up the German Democratic Republic as the 'model state' for a socialist economy, which was supposed to be led via the Ministry for Science and Technology and its planning of research. But these attempts failed, at the latest with the building of the Wall. This failure forced Ulbricht to resign in May 1971. Honecker immediately shifted to the strategy of expanding consumption, and permitted Günter Mittag in particular to create huge conglomerates ('kombinate') whose sheer size operated mainly to perpetuate the unprofitable character of numerous production lines. The only exceptions were in machine tool manufacturing. It proved impossible for East Germany to catch up with the huge productivity increases experienced in West Germany (as in other liberalized economies) as a result of electronic data processing, especially after the worldwide increase in the prices of raw materials in the mid-1970s. East German employees were not appropriately trained to do this, nor did the retrospective adjustment to the state's economic plan, which occurred every year, provide information about the actual economic situation.

Probably the most important changes in German science and technology during this period took place in the education system. The American Sputnik scare gave rise to debates about the German education system in the Federal Science Council, which in 1960/2 put forward a number of recommendations for the development of the *wissenschaftliche Hochschulen* (scientific colleges). As a result, these colleges were hugely expanded, particularly between 1965 and 1975. The fastest growth in technical education was seen in the *Fachhochschulen* (specialist colleges). These colleges occupy the level just below that of the technical universities, and although they had their origins in the 1930s began to emerge much more clearly in the last quarter of the twentieth century. After an initial phase of uncertainty, in the 1980s German politicians became very enthusiastic about this particular path for technical training (as well as training in economic, social, administrative, and welfare matters), not least because it requires almost school-like attendance from students, and ensures that they sit their final examinations after only three years. Below these *Fachhochschulen* (specialist colleges) lies a stratum of non-academic *Fachoberschulen* (specialist upper schools) which, unlike the technical colleges, do not require that applicants have the *Abitur* (university entrance examination). Below these, in turn, lies the so-called 'dual training system' which is obligatory for all apprentices. It bears this name because it is organized in such a way that apprentices are trained in the practicalities of their speciality, but also spend one to two days a week in the classroom, thereby combining empirical and systematic learning.

Recent decades have seen a relative decline, however, in expenditures on science and education in Germany. While the number of students in colleges has doubled since 1975, the number of teachers has only increased very slightly. In addition, a number of new universities have been founded, but budget appropriations for university funding have stagnated. This has changed the nature of German universities as scholarly institutions. In the consciousness of their students, German universities increasingly appear to be simply a continuation of school, which can be attended without costs and without entrance examination. After 1990, the education system of the former East Germany was aligned with that of the West: the Academy of Sciences was merged into the western one with deployment of all of its 24,000 scientists, and the East German *Gymnasium* had a much more demanding final level added to it. All these unification questions delayed reform for another decade. Now Germany is facing the probability of structural reform in order to achieve harmonization across the European Union (arising from the Bologna agreement of 1999 concerning Bachelors' and Masters' Degrees). This seems likely to bring about extensive changes in the technical colleges as they have existed in Germany since the nineteenth century. In addition, a new element is entering the German system, in the shape of private-sector specialist colleges which are being set up in low-investment subjects such as economics and management, although none have been set up in technical subjects; their main aim is training for large firms. The technical colleges are nowadays adding a focus on improving their graduates' social skills, particularly their ability to represent technical developments and products in the economic and political spheres.

10.3.3 *German industry and technology*

Since the 1960s, Germany has seen one new wave of consumption after another (as discussed in Chapter 12). These consumption waves have mainly been directed at furnishing German households with the variety of goods which are now seen as necessary: washing machines, kitchen appliances, televisions. A central question is whether this mechanization of the household has shifted the balance in people's preferences between home and work life.

These new waves of technological advance have affected German consumption patterns much more than production patterns. In fact, Germany began to lose out to Japan in producing and developing these products as early as the 1960s. By means of pirate copies, higher precision, lower costs, and above all digitalization, Japanese producers achieved much greater advances than German ones, which continued to pay too much heed to maintaining the informal barriers between different status groups among the engineers. The same occurred in German ship building and car making during the 1960s and 1970s. Japanese industry overtook and then surpassed Germany, as it did the established industrialized countries. Germany failed to adapt its delivery systems quickly enough to new forms of operation and to global markets. Such adaptation was hindered by traditional thinking, vested interests in the camps of both managers and unions, and handed-down social structures, such as the sharp separation between research, production, repair, and sales departments. Likewise, the expectations held both by the United States and by Germany's partners in the European Community, that Germany should deregulate and open up its markets, have created predictable problems. Strongly cartellized sectors such as iron, steel, and coal have opened up only very slowly and in fact have been reproduced on the EU level. Even now, the German hard coal industry sells its output for 300 per cent the level of prices on the world market, with the difference being paid by the German taxpayer, yet its almost 100,000 employees and managers occupy the top band in the wage hierarchy!

Perhaps the most visible technological change in West Germany in the last third of the twentieth century was the spread of the automobile. The car has also been central to growing sociopolitical debate in Germany about limiting the use of technology. Indeed, the German fascination with cars and the pollution they create became (along with nuclear power plants) the basis of the German environmental movement. By contrast with the older generation of Germans, whose valuation of technology was shaped by their own experiences of war and economic distress, the members of the German environmental movement wanted to strengthen the role of the 'enlightened' consumer in the process by which technology was created. This led them to place much more importance on 'reason' and 'security' in the use of technology, rather than on the principles of 'trial and error' and 'risk-taking' which have always been central to technological innovation. In doing so, however, the environmental movement was ignoring the fact that (as discussed in Chapter 12) a majority of the German population regarded mass consumer objects, including cars and aeroplanes, as achievements of the social system they lived in. They regarded themselves as being entitled to enjoy these goods, and they were not willing to give them up. Indeed, such goods were an essential component of the modernization paradigm of individualization. Thus the car, for instance, has long ceased to be solely a means of transportation: instead, it has become an extension of the individual's personal domestic sphere, protecting him or her from excessively close contact with new social environments. In return for this benefit, people are willing to accept very long daily journeys – along with their ecological consequences.

The other sphere in which technology has fundamentally shaped German society in the last third of the twentieth century is electronic data processing. It had its origins in some pioneering electrotechnical machines built by Konrad Zuse from 1941 onward, and in the large, clumsy electronic machines developed for logistical purposes in the last years of the Second World War. Then, in 1947, the first transistor was built in the United States, although it was not immediately able to compete with tube technology, which was still susceptible to further development. It was not until 1958 that the breakthrough occurred, again in the United States, with the first integrated circuit, first used in the consumer sector in Japan and Europe, then in the United States. In 1964 there were still ten transistors per 0.5 cm² of chip, but by 1980 this had increased to 50,000, and by 1985 it had reached one million. Parallel to the development of the transistor was the invention of cybernetics, first devised by Norbert Wiener in 1947. This was supposed gradually to replace human beings by machines in managing and monitoring technological processes. The needs of the military (in processing information obtained through air surveillance) combined with civilian needs (particularly the desire of airlines and shipping firms to process masses of data very quickly) to stimulate huge increases in computing capacity. After 1960, the general adoption of ALGOL got rid of the tiresome problem of the large number of independently developed programming languages.

Thus computing started out as mainly a military project, but rapid miniaturization enabled computers to be put into action in space travel and armaments, and later in almost all spheres of production and consumption. So unexpectedly fast has one development followed on the heels of another, that it would not be exaggerating to describe it as the 'industrialization of information'. Even though information technology was not actually developed in Germany, it has exercised enormous influence over the German economy. The model of Silicon Valley, which in the 1970s emerged as a development centre for the application of integrated circuits in industrial processes, has since the mid-1980s constituted an organizational model for many German universities, which helped to set up and promote technology parks in their immediate surroundings. The subsequent breakdown of Silicon Valley has still not entered into the discussions of the German planning administrations.

Personal computers have also contributed to the revolutionizing effects of computers in all sectors of German economy and society since the 1980s. Although it began mainly as a device for game playing, the PC soon began fundamentally to change the whole infrastructure and periphery of the firm, and to permeate the German economy. Yet despite the fact that Germany had a substantial store of electronic know-how, no dominant German computer manufacturing has arisen. The same is true of France, suggesting that that country also suffers from a similarly encrusted hierarchical structure in its research sector.

10.4 Conclusion

The outlines of the relationship between society, science, and technology in Germany in the last third of the twentieth century are still only emerging. Nevertheless, it is clear that two important questions remain central to this complex of issues as Germany moves into the twenty-first century.

First, the development of science and technology in Germany over the past two centuries has been determined, to a very distinctive extent, by Germany's emerging self-perception as a 'nation'. The question is whether this self-perception will now be transferred to Europe, or whether German identity will survive as a distinct regional identity within Europe.

Second, up to now almost all of those within German society who have participated in education and science, and benefited directly from it, have done so at no tuition cost to themselves – i.e. they have been educated, and have pursued scientific and technical research at public expense. The question is whether this will continue to be the case, or whether Germany will see a move toward transferring at least some of the costs of education and science to those who directly benefit from them. This in turn would give a much stronger influence to industry, which has traditionally not shown a great deal of interest in subjects beyond the realm of its own business.

Chapter translated by Sheilagh Ogilvie

10.5 Notes

1 For English literature on this subject, see Charles Singer, *A History of Technology*, 8 vols (Oxford 1958/1984); and, from the perspective of economic history, David Landes, *The Unbound Prometheus* (Cambridge, 1969). Comparative surveys in German include Akos Paulinyi and Ulrich Troitszch, *Mechanisierung und Maschinisierung* (Berlin, 1991); Wolfgang König and Wolfhard Weber, *Netzwerke von Stahl und Strom* (Berlin, 1990); and Hans-Joachim Braun and Walter Kaiser, *Seit 1914. Energiewirtschaft, Automatisierung, Information* (Berlin, 1992). See also Ulrich Troitzsch and Wolfhard Weber, *Technik. Von den Anfängen bis zur Gegenwart* (Stuttgart, 1987). A summary of a large number of heterogeneous approaches can be found in Armin Hermann, ed., *Kultur und Technik*, 9 vols (Düsseldorf, 1990–95).

2 Erich Dorn Brose, *Technology and Science in the Industrializing Nations 1500–1914* (Atlantic Highlands, New Jersey, 1998), is the most recent book about long-term developments prior to 1800. Eric Dorn Brose, *The Politics of Technological Change in Prussia. Out of the Shadow of Antiquity 1809–1848* (Princeton, 1993), offers the best introduction to the problem of Germany's early technological transformation.

3 After 1834, the customs union was renewed every 12 years.

4 See Arteen Marcia Tuchmann, 'Institutions and Disciplines: Recent Works in the History of German Science', *Journal of Modern History*, 69 (1997), pp. 298–310.

5 Reinhart Koselleck, *Preussen zwischen Reform und Revolution. Allgemeines Landrecht, Verwaltung und soziale Bewegung von 1791–1848* (Stuttgart, 1967);

Hans-Ulrich Wehler, *Deutsche Gesellschaftsgeschichte*, 2 vols (Munich, 1987/1995); Thomas Nipperdey, *Deutsche Geschichte*, 2 vols (1983/1993).

6 See John Hubbel Weiss, *The Making of Technological Man. The Social Origins of French Engineering Education* (Cambridge, MA, and London, 1992); Roger Hahn, *The Anatomy of a Scientific Institution. The Paris Academy of Science 1666–1803* (Berkeley, 1971); Karl Hufbauer, *The Formation of the German Chemical Community 1720–1795* (London, 1982).

7 This did not apply to the higher mining officials and the architects, who completed their studies in specialized academies.

8 R. Stephen Turner, 'Justus Liebig versus Prussian Chemistry. Reflections on Early Institute-Building in Germany', *Historical Studies in the Physical Sciences*, 13 (1982), pp. 129–62.

9 Peter Borscheid, *Naturwissenschaft, Staat und Industrie in Baden 1848–1914* (Stuttgart, 1976).

10 Peter Lundgreen and André Grelon, eds, *Ingenieure in Deutschland 1770–1990* (Frankfurt am Main, 1994); Peter Lundgreen, 'Engineering Education in Europe and the USA 1750–1930. The Rise to Dominance of School Culture and the Engineering Professions', *Annals of Science*, 47 (1990), pp. 33–76; Wolfgang König, 'Zwischen Verwaltungsstaat und Industriegesellschaft. Die Gründung höherer technischer Bildungsanstälten in Deutschland in den ersten Jahrzenten des 19. Jahrhunderts', *Berichte zur Wissenschaftsgeschichte*, 21 (1998), pp. 15–122; Wolfgang König, 'Technical Education and Industrial Performance in Germany. Triumph of Heterogeneity', in Robert Fox and Anna Guagnini, eds, *Education, Technology and Industrial Performance in Europe 1850–1939* (Cambridge, 1993), pp. 65–87.

11 Eric Dorn Brose, *The Politics of Technological Change in Prussia, 1809–1948* (Princeton, NJ, 1993).

12 In the form of the 'Otto Motor' or petrol motor.

13 Sidney Pollard, *Peaceful Conquest. The Industrialization of Europe 1750–1970* (Oxford, 1981).

14 Franz Reuleaux, *Briefe aus Philadelphia* (Braunschweig, 1876), edited by H. J. Brian (Weinheim, 1982).

15 Richard H. Tilly, *Financial Institutions and Industrialization in the Rhineland 1815–1870* (Madison, WI, 1966).

16 See Hans-Liudger Dienel, *Herrschaft über die Natur? Naturvorstellungen deutscher Ingenieure 1871–1914* (Stuttgart, 1992). For a general view of the precursors to this era, with an excellent discussion of the German aspects, see Joachim Radkau, *Technik in Deutschland. Vom 18. Jahrhundert bis zur Gegenwart* (Frankfurt am Main, 1989).

17 Wolfgang König, *Technikwissenschaften. Die Entstehung der Elektrotechnik aus Industrie und Wissenschaft zwischen 1880 und 1914* (Chur, 1995).

18 W. H. Dawson, *The Evolution of Modern Germany* (London, 1908), pp. 95ff.

19 Davin Lee Cahan, *An Institute for an Empire. The Physikalisch-Technische Reichsanstalt 1871–1918* (Cambridge, 1989).

20 This foundation was planned to serve 'research into nature'. Thanks to continued pressure from the universities, there was no more mention of technology. Private donations for institutes dedicated to technology were sometimes not even made use of: Wolfram Fischer, ed., *Die Preußische Akademie der Wissenschaften zu Berlin 1914–1945* (Berlin, 2000). On the Kaiser-Wilhelm Society now, see Rudolf Vierhaus and Bernhard vom Brocke, eds, *Forschung im Spannungsfeld von Politik und Gesellschaft. Geschichte und Struktur der Kaiser-Wilhelm-/Max-Planck-Gesellschaft* (Stuttgart, 1990).

21 This fateful situation, in which universities (which were sceptical of technology) and natural scientists (who were favourable toward technology) worked together

with the technology-promoting Wilhelm II and the industrialists, is vividly described in its various warped ideological manifestations in Jeffrey Herf, *Reactionary Modernism. Technology, Culture and Politics in Weimar and the Third Reich* (Cambridge, 1984).

22 Manfred Rasch, *Geschichte des Kaiser-Wilhelm-Instituts für Kohlenforschung 1913–1943* (Weinheim, 1989).

23 To this organization belonged the *Akademien der Wissenschaften* (Academies of Sciences), all *wissenschaftliche Hochschulen* (scientific colleges), the Kaiser-Wilhelm-Gesellschaft, the *Deutsche Verband Technisch-wissenschaftlicher Vereine* (German League of Technical-Scientific Associations) which united all the engineering and architectural associations – as well as the venerable *Gesellschaft Deutscher Naturforscher und Ärtzte* (Society of German Naturalists and Physicians).

24 These were the *Justus-Liebig Gesellschaft zur Förderung des chemischen Unterrichts* (Justus-Liebig Association for the Promotion of Teaching in Chemistry), the *Emil-Fischer Gesellschaft zur Förderung der chemischen Forschung* (Emil-Fischer Association for the Promotion of Research in Chemistry), the *Adolf-Baeyer Gesellschaft zur Förderung der chemischen Literatur* (Adolf-Baeyer Association for the Promotion of Chemical Literature), and the *Helmholtz-Gesellschaft zur Förderung der physikalisch-technischen Forschung* (Helmholtz Association for the Promotion of Research in Physics and Technology).

25 These included chemistry, metallurgy, research into dyes and leathers, Silesian coal research, and iron research.

26 Among other fields promoted were labour physiology, biology, physics, silicates research, hydrology and water-power, microbiology, anthropology, breeding research, medical research, and cell physiology.

27 Helmuth Trischler, *Luft- und Raumfahrtforschung in Deutschland von 1900 bis 1970. Politische Geschichte einer Wissenschaft* (Frankfurt am Main, 1992).

28 For the period after 1933, see Margit Szöllösi-Janze, *Science in the Third Reich* (New York, 2001); on the controversy over whether Nazi Germany promoted basic or applied science, see Helmut Maier, *Wehrhaftmachung und Kriegs-wichtigkeit. Zur rüstungstechnischen Relevanz des Kaiser-Wilhelm-Instituts für Metallforschung in Stuttgart vor und nach 1945* (Berlin, 2002).

29 The main 'research-targets' were metal hull and jet propulsion, as shown by the examples of Papst von Ohain in 1939 and Frank Whittle in 1941.

30 On this complex, see Michael J. Neufeld, *The Rocket and the Reich. Peenemünde and the Coming of the Ballistic Era* (New York, 1997).

31 Burkhard Ciesla and Mathias Judt, eds, *Technology Transfer out of Germany after 1945* (Amsterdam, 1996).

32 Raymond G. Stokes, *Constructing Socialism. Technology and Change in East Germany 1945–1990* (Baltimore, 2000).

33 Agnes Tandler, 'Geplante Zukunft. Wissenschaftler und Wissenschaftspolitik in der DDR 1955–1971' (PhD dissertation, European University Institute, Florence, 1997).

34 Mark Walker, *Die Uranmaschine. Mythos und Wirklichkeit der deutschen Atombombe* (Munich, 1992), published in English as *German National Socialism and the Quest for Nuclear Power 1939–1945* (Cambridge, 1989).

35 The research landscape at that time is summarized in Leo Brandt, ed., *Aufgaben Deutscher Forschung* (Cologne, 1952).

36 Authors such as Hans Dominik or Anton Zischka should be mentioned in this connection.

37 Karl-Heinz Ludwig, *Ingenieure im Dritten Reich* (Düsseldorf, 1968).

38 Axel Schildt and Arnold Sywottek, eds, *Modernisierung im Wiederaufbau. Die westdeutsche Gesellschaft der 50er Jahre* (Bonn, 1993).

39 Wolfgang Koenig, 'Science-Based Industry or Industry-Based Science. Electrical Engineering in Germany before World War I'. *Technology and Culture*, 37 (1996), pp. 70–101.

40 A first 'scientific-technological' breakthrough in agriculture had been the use of artificial fertilizers around 1860.

41 On the RWE, see Dieter Schweer and Wolf Thieme, eds, *Der gläserene Riese. RWE – ein Konzern wird transparent* (Wiesbaden, 1998). On Stinnes, see Gerald D. Feldman, *Hugo Stinnes* (Munich, 1998). On the technical system, see Thomas P. Hughes, *Networks of Power. Electrification in Western Society 1880–1980* (London, 1983); Edmund N. Todd, 'Technology and Interest Group Politics: Electrification of the Ruhr, 1886–1930', (PhD dissertation, University of Pennsylvania, 1984); Edmund N. Todd, 'A Tale of Three Cities: Electrification and the Structure of Choice in the Ruhr 1886–1900', *Social Studies of Science*, 17 (1987), pp. 387–412.

42 Helmut Maier, 'Bernhard Goldenberg', in Wolfhard Weber, ed., *Ingenieure im Ruhrgebiet* (Münster, 1999), pp. 149–83.

43 Stefan Willecke, *Die Technokratiebewegung in Nordamerika und Deutschland zwischen den Weltkriegen* (Frankfurt am Main, 1994).

44 Manfred Rasch, 'Erfahrung, Forschung und Entwicklung in der (west-) deutschen Eisen- und Stahlerzeugung', *Ferrum*, 68 (1996), pp. 4–29.

45 Mikael Hård, *Machines are Frozen Spirit: The Scientification of Refrigeration and Brewing in the Nineteenth Century – A Weberian Interpretation* (Frankfurt am Main, 1993).

46 Donald E. Thomas, *Diesel. Technology and Society in Industrial Germany* (Tuscaloosa, AL, 1987). On the important role of theoretical approaches in manufacturing of diesel motors, but also on refrigeration technology up to and including gas liquefaction, see Hans Liudger Dienel, *Ingenieure zwischen Hochschule und Industrie. Kältetechnik in Deutschland und Amerika 1870–1930* (Göttingen, 1995).

47 Frank Thomas, *Telefonieren in Deutschland. Organisatorische, technische und räumliche Entwicklung eines grosstechnischen Systems* (Frankfurt, 1995).

48 See Alf Lüdtke, Inge Marssolek, and Adeleid von Saldern, eds, *Amerikanisierung. Traum und Alptraum im Deutschland des 20. Jahrhunderts* (Stuttgart, 1996).

49 Trischler, *Luft- und Raumfahrtforschung.*

50 The 'planning euphoria' can also be traced back to the technocratic visions of the technocracy movement in the 1920s, as well as to the development planning which occurred during the 1920s and 1930s in the course of the organization of transportation systems. In the post-1945 period, after the completion of the greater part of the clear-up work at the end of the 1950s, these notions surfaced once again; see Helmut Schelsky, 'Planung der Zukunft. Die rationale Utopie und die Ideologie der Nationalität', *Soziale Welt*, 17 (1966), pp. 155–72.

51 P. Friess and P. Steiner, eds, *Forschung und Technik in Deutschland nach 1945. Katalog des Deutschen Museums Bonn* (Munich, 1995).

|11|

Women and the family

LISA PINE

South Bank University, London

Using a broadly chronological framework, this chapter analyses the main developments, trends, and policies that affected women and the family in Germany throughout the nineteenth and twentieth centuries, focusing upon the most significant eras in terms of change: the nineteenth century; the First World War and the Weimar Republic; the Third Reich; and the post-1945 period. The nineteenth century saw the transition from *das ganze Haus* ('the whole house') to the nuclear family as the dominant family form. It also witnessed the first women's movements that campaigned for changes in the role of women. The impact of the First World War upon German society in general and upon the family in particular was also significant in the context of change. The Weimar Republic was a time of ambivalence of attitudes – the breaking of old taboos and a simultaneous conservative backlash – as German society modernized. The Third Reich was a period of great significance both in terms of its ideology and its policies towards women and the family, and in terms of its impact upon subsequent history. The experiences of women and the family in German society took two separate paths in the post-1945 era, as different regimes in East and West Germany made their mark. These paths reconverged in 1990 with German reunification, and the chapter ends with a brief consideration of the post-reunification era.

11.1 The nineteenth century: the changing family form

In the early modern period, the predominant German family form was that of the *Haushaltsfamilie* or *das ganze Haus* ('the whole house').[1] This 'domestic community' was composed not only of blood relations but also of individuals who worked for the household, such as servants, farmhands, apprentices, and journeymen. In pre-industrial society, productive function was of great significance in the composition of the household. Each member of the household performed a specific task. The social unit of the household had a clearly defined, strict hierarchical structure. This was necessary because the household functioned as a unit of production. The household was run jointly by the *Hausvater* (literally 'house-father' or patriarch) and the *Hausmutter* (literally 'house-mother' or mistress of the household), although each had different areas of authority. The *Hausvater* exercised legal guardianship rights over all members of the household.[2] In most cases the *Hausvater* headed the family, although on average some 15 per cent of rural households and some 20 per cent of urban households were headed by females. The *Hausvater* was responsible for the general organization of the household, wielding authority over his wife, children and employees. The *Hausmutter* was in charge of the internal economy of the household, which was her exclusive domain.[3]

The Industrial Revolution brought in its wake a dramatic change to the traditional German family model, involving a separation between workplace and residence.[4] This meant that the 'domestic community' was replaced as the dominant social unit by the *Familie* ('family'), composed of parents and their offspring. Non-relatives who had previous been members of the household now resided outside it.[5] This transition instigated a new era for the bourgeois family, which became a private domain of social interaction and reproduction. Servants were not included in this intimate sphere. In the family, privacy and sentimentality prevailed and the relationship between parents and children was strengthened. The exclusion of non-related persons from the household meant that 'the household of the family' became the dominant form.

However, as Mitterauer and Sieder have pointed out, changes in the family form from the pre-industrial period to the era after the Industrial Revolution must be assessed with care. There was no general historical trend in this era from the large to the small family, nor from a multi-generational family type to an isolated nuclear family form.[6] Contrary to popular belief, changes in the family were the result not of a reduction in family size, but of transformations in the constitution of the household, engendered by the changes in its functions. As the family lost its function as a unit of production, its perceived size declined as servants and other non-related persons were now outside it.

The separation of dwelling and workplace also brought with it a redefinition of the division of labour within the family unit, as production was removed from the household. The former close collaboration between the *Hausmutter* and *Hausvater* in administering the household – in which the former was an active partner – gave way to a completely different situation, in which male and female spheres became separate, both in location and in activity.[7] From the 1820s onwards, with the transition from the traditional household to the bourgeois family, the term *Hausmutter* was increasingly replaced by the word *Hausfrau* ('housewife').[8] Her role changed from that of domestic producer to that of domestic consumer.

Middle-class women believed that the new, bourgeois family form was superior. They looked down upon both rural wives, whom they considered to be vulgar, unfeminine and unsophisticated, and women of the aristocracy, whom they regarded as selfish, egotistical, immoral and dishonourable. The new German bourgeoisie of the late eighteenth and early nineteenth centuries dissociated itself from both, as well as from the old middle class of guilded craftsmen, innkeepers, retailers and merchants, in whose households, as in the case of farming families, women were still fully integrated into the production process. The new bourgeoisie made its own innovations and sought to differentiate itself from other classes.

The main factor that distinguished a middle-class lifestyle was the absence of work among women. The bourgeois household could live on the income of the male provider, thus leaving the *Hausfrau* free from the need to do outside work. In contrast to the leisure of the middle-class woman, the working-class woman had to work an average of 12 to 14 hours a day, as well as look after a large number of children and take care of her household.[9] Working-class women were employed in the textile industry as semi-skilled labour, but also in the food, paper and tobacco industries, and in domestic service.[10] The working-class family was very much dependent upon the mother's as well as the father's income, and children aged ten and over were also obliged to work.

In agricultural families, where subsistence depended upon what was produced on the farm, the division of labour was based on gender. The farmer and household head took care of the fields, with the assistance of his sons and farmhands. His wife had many functions. She took care of the household in terms of bed-making, tending linen and clothing, washing, sewing, and cleaning. She supervised work in the dairy barns, the kitchen and cellar, as well as the rearing of livestock. She was in charge of training her daughters and of the work of female servants.[11] In such families, with distinct labour functions, the work of the *Hausmutter* and *Hausvater* was of equal value and importance in maintaining the estate. But men and women did not have equal status within the family hierarchy. In the majority of cases, the traditional patriarchal family structure remained firmly entrenched, with the *Hausmutter* being subordinate to the *Hausvater*.[12]

The same family structure, with the man as indisputable head of the household and guardian of his wife and children, also applied to families of the upper class. But the families of the nobility had a different lifestyle altogether. In aristocratic families, children were isolated from their parents, reared and educated instead by servants, governesses, and private tutors. As in other strata of society, daughters were brought up with the aim of marriage, but relations between marital partners were often rather distant. Many aristocratic couples lived quite separate lives – with separate bedrooms, frequent absences from home on the part of the husband, and leisure trips, for example to spas, on the part of the wife, so that spouses were held together only by joint social duties. Women, free from the burden of work and of raising their children, were able to indulge in leisure pursuits and other activities, including, if they wished, extra-marital affairs, without appearing to lose their honour, as this was a tacitly accepted part of their way of life.

The early nineteenth century saw the further development of the German bourgeois family, with a distinctive style of furnishing and design (*Biedermeier*), for which the housewife and mother took responsibility.[13] Her role was to create a cohesive and stable home environment and to rear and protect her children. Women were the providers of family cohesion. The socialization of children took place within the family. The mother brought up her children with values of industriousness, ambition, self-control and thrift. Women had three roles – as wives, mothers and housekeepers. Their priorities lay in that order, too – to their husbands first, then to their children, and finally to their household. A woman's work in the household made possible and safeguarded her husband's success outside it. In this period, the bourgeois family had servants to do menial tasks and house-work, such as scrubbing, heavy cleaning, washing and ironing, and nannies to look after the children and take them out for walks. Hence, the middle-class housewife's duties were more concerned with supervising her staff and keeping up the appearance of her household in line with its social status. The family was portrayed as the haven of order and tranquillity. The image of idyllic family life prevailed as the norm, with the housewife's qualities of grace and effortlessness perceived as charming, feminine virtues. The house-hold was a centre of warmth and love.

Marriage was the only acceptable status for the daughters of the middle class. A married woman shared the social position and standing of her husband. But the marital relationship was unequal. The German Civil Code of 1900 placed a series of legal restrictions upon married women.[14] A married man could annul any contract made by his wife and prohibit her from earning her own living. In addition, the German Civil Code granted all responsibility for marital affairs to the husband, not the wife. The husband also controlled his wife's dowry, property and inheritance. As parents, it was the father, not the mother, who took the major decisions about children's education and future. Children also had to seek their father's consent before marrying. The marital relationship was very different for a man than it was for a woman. For a man, marriage was only part of his life, which was supplemented by his profession and social contacts outside the home. For a woman, the domestic sphere was her only one. Her relationship with her husband, and the bearing and rearing of her children made up her entire world. Very few opportunities existed for married women to earn their own living. Tradition held that only those women who were unmarried could seek employment.

The mid-nineteenth century witnessed the emergence in Germany of a wider urban middle class, whose core was made up of civil servants, judges, lawyers, doctors, university lecturers, and teachers. This new urban bourgeoisie distinguished itself from the other inhabitants of the large towns in terms of its professional practices, dress, housing, and cultural norms. Men of the professional middle class met in clubs and coffee houses, and became more and more oriented to the world outside the home. In contrast, their wives remained very much inside the home. Their role was to supervise their servants, to keep up the appearance of wealth and luxury, to decorate their homes lavishly and to host tea parties and dinner parties, in order to demonstrate the success of their husbands' business or profession. Hence, whilst men became increasingly involved in the public sphere, women remained within the private sphere. Women's work within the domain of the home complemented that of men outside it.[15] The notions of natural gender polarity and of separate but complementary spheres of action for women and men were the key aspects of change in gender relations that began during the last decades of the eighteenth century and characterized the nineteenth century.[16]

11.2 The nineteenth century: the emergence of the women's movement and women's role in public life

The nineteenth century also saw the gradual participation of German women in public life (for example, many women attended the Hambach Festival in 1832), and some women were involved in organizations to care for the poor, usually under the aegis of the church. Yet even such activities by women outside the household did not contradict traditional ideas about the nature and place of females. Such women were simply transferring their perceived feminine qualities, such as selflessness and compassion, to an environment outside their own homes.[17]

Louise Otto (1819–95) was the most prominent and active member of the first women's movement in Germany, which developed in 1848. In April 1849, she claimed that women should have 'the right to be responsible and self-determining citizens of the state'.[18] But even such statements were intended to be understood within certain parameters as determined by the rules of correct behaviour and accepted gender roles for women. Even the strident women of the 1848 revolution had clear notions about a woman's place and they did not seek emancipation in this sense. In general, German women limited their public activities at this time to indirect, rather than direct, political action. For example, they set up their own female gymnastics clubs. This in itself was a new development. One of their major demands in 1848 was the expansion of education for girls, beyond the traditional subjects of needlework, languages, drawing, and music.

From the 1850s onwards, middle-class German women set up Sunday schools to teach working-class girls how to knit and sew, organized home economics courses, established day nurseries at which working women could leave their young children, and set up 'people's kitchens' for working-class families.[19] The Association for the Further Education and Intellectual Exercise of Working Women, set up in Berlin in 1869, was one of many such organizations aimed at providing education and welfare services to working-class women. Middle-class women's groups became involved in these activities for a number of reasons, including a sense of distress and horror at the plight of working-class women, but also in order to try to disseminate their own values, which they considered to be correct and proper, more widely in German society. The response of working-class women was ambivalent, but this did not deter the bourgeois women, who had the opportunity to engage in spheres of socially constructive activity outside the household, from becoming involved in such community welfare projects.

From the 1880s onwards, more and more local authorities in Germany began to acknowledge the efforts of women in welfare work. Whilst some women involved in infant care and poor relief were paid by local authorities for their efforts, others undertook such work voluntarily. These areas of work, along with an expansion in housing and healthcare services, gave rise to increasing professional opportunities for women in Germany.[20] Middle-class women felt suited to this type of activity – transferring their motherly skills and attributes from their homes to the community, and giving this work the same care and attention they gave to their own families and household responsibilities. They also thought that they had a duty to do such work. They believed that social problems could be ameliorated by educational measures, so they set an example to working-class women about how to look after children and run a household. The middle-class family model – the patriarchal nuclear family – with the husband as the breadwinner and the wife as homemaker began to be widely accepted, and was gradually emulated by many working-class families. Bourgeois family structures and gender roles came to be pursued by both the urban and the rural working classes.

In the late nineteenth century, the German women's movement began to call for limited changes to the traditional pattern. It claimed that women were equal to men in value, although not in nature.[21] It did not wish to abolish the concept of a gender-based division of labour and it did not present a challenge to the notion that the primary importance of women was within the family. What it did fight for was a change in the legal status of married women, so that their husbands would no longer be in charge of their property. It also called for women to be able to play a role in cultural, societal and economic activities outside the family. Although in the late nineteenth century the German women's movement still thought that the female sex was 'destined for motherhood', it also believed that women's work for the family needed to gain higher ideological status and that women's work in raising the next generation and promoting the welfare of society and good values needed to be given credit.[22] The other main belief shared by the majority of bourgeois women's associations in Germany was that women who needed to be or who chose to be in employment should be protected by the state, for example by means of effective labour policies and maternity protection for working-class women, and greater job opportunities in the educational and welfare sectors for middle-class women.

They also campaigned for women's suffrage and asserted that women should have the right to better education and to university entrance.[23] In 1900, Baden opened its universities to women for the first time, followed by Prussia in 1908. There had been similar calls for women's entry into higher education in Britain in the second half of the nineteenth century. The University of London was the first English university to award women degrees on the same terms as men, in 1878.[24] Oxford and Cambridge allowed women to attend college, but did not grant them degrees until after the First World War and the Second World War respectively. In France, higher education for women was very restricted in this period, as only a few private schools prepared girls for university.[25] By 1913–14, there were 3649 women enrolled as students (6.3 per cent of the total number of students) at German universities. Access to higher education was a great success for the women's movement in Germany, but voting rights for women took longer to achieve.

Associations of working-class women first came into being in Berlin and other large towns in the 1880s, and by the end of that decade working-class women became increasingly involved in the activities of the SPD (Social Democratic Party).[26] Clara Zetkin, the first leader of the German working-class women's movement, made a speech at the International Workers' Congress in Paris in 1889 on the subject of 'The Emancipation of Women', in which she argued that limitations on women's employment should be abolished because it was only through work outside the family that working-class women could gain economic independence. She further held that 'full emancipation' could only be achieved through socialism and therefore urged women to join the SPD. In the 1891 Erfurt Programme, the SPD advocated universal suffrage and called for 'the abolition of all laws which place women at a disadvantage to men in public and civil law'.[27] These were very progressive demands for the time.

Like the middle-class women's movement, the working-class women's movement became increasingly involved in social and welfare projects for mothers and children. It set up committees for the protection of children, and organized outings and hikes for working-class children. There was a considerable degree of overlap between the aims and activities of the working-class and middle-class German women's movements. Both still esteemed motherhood very highly and both were involved in similar types of welfare activity. Yet they did not perceive themselves as a united force for the emancipation of women. Class still clearly separated them. There was a patent lack of cooperation between the two movements, whose leaders believed they were fighting for different aims. Working-class women were against the idea of 'common sisterhood' (in Zetkin's phrase) with women of the bourgeoisie.[28] For their part, middle-class women's organizations considered the working-class women's groups to be too radical and militant. Hence, in the period before the First World War, class kept the two German women's movements apart, despite their common overlap on the issues of the political and legal equality of women.

11.3 The First World War and the Weimar Republic: modernity and reaction

Despite the changes that had occurred in the status of women and in the family form in Germany during the course of the nineteenth century, the family continued to be seen as a symbol of stability and continuity at the beginning of the twentieth century. The First World War acted as a catalyst for social and economic change. Its modernizing impact was felt throughout German society as it brought about a significant upheaval in family life and created substantial transformations in traditional attitudes and values. It also created some important changes in women's role in society, as females became increasingly incorporated into the labour market and were given public recognition for their work. The national catastrophe gave German women the opportunity to assert themselves in efforts on behalf of their nation and made them more visible in society.

The First World War engendered a disruption of family life and many challenges to traditional practices. The call-up of some 9 million men, half of whom were married, by the end of 1915 meant that many families suddenly lost their breadwinners.[29] Conscription meant a decrease in family income, as the wartime supplements to soldiers' families were inadequate to meet their basic requirements. Conscription also created a social vacuum, in the sense that countless families now lacked the patriarchal authority upon which the functioning of family life had previously depended.[30] Working-class families suffered the most, as they were too poor to buy foodstuffs in bulk or on the black market. Even families whose men were not conscripted suffered financially, as real earnings for male industrial workers decreased by about one-third between 1914 and 1918. In many cases, women had to go out to work in order to make up the shortfall in family income. At first, it was hard for women to find employment, but the labour shortage created by conscription and the demand for the production of armaments meant that after 1916, more and more women found their way into the German workforce. Indeed, by the beginning of 1917, a massive campaign was launched to encourage women to work; thus female labour was mobilized for the war economy. High wages for unskilled and semi-skilled labour acted as a spur for many married women who had not worked previously to take up jobs in industry. This was especially the case in the engineering, metallurgical, and chemical industries, in which there was a huge increase in the number of female workers. Simultaneously, the number of women working in the textile industry declined, so that by the end of 1918, the number had halved by comparison with the prewar period.[31] In the factories, as women replaced men who had been conscripted, the distinctions between separate spheres of work for men and women no longer prevailed. The number of women working outside the home had in any case been growing in the decades prior to the outbreak of war, and the war seemed to accelerate this trend, as well as to break down traditional notions about the types of job for which women were suitable.[32]

The war also consolidated and speeded up trends in German social policy that had begun prior to 1914, in particular welfare measures for working-class women. Middle-class women also became engaged in a much wider range of voluntary and social work than ever before, and received public recognition for their efforts. Many local women's organizations, which had already been involved in such activities before the war, increased their efforts to help the needy, for example by setting up soup kitchens, organizing clothing supplies, and making jam and preserves for working women and indigent families.[33] The National Women's Service was set up in August 1914 to coordinate such efforts, as women now saw themselves as 'fighters on the home front'. This voluntary work achieved an elevated status as patriotic duty and public service.

The immediate aftermath of the war brought a host of economic and social problems to Germany, including inflation and unemployment. Inflation eroded the material foundations of middle-class family life (as discussed in Chapters 5 and 10). It meant that many families lost their savings and no longer had the financial resources to uphold the style of life to which they had been accustomed. At a more personal level too, the war engendered difficulties. These included bereavement for women whose fathers and sons had died in battle, and also the burden of caring for the many men who returned home disabled or psychologically disturbed. In addition, there was a significant trend of 'homecoming divorces'. As society readjusted to peacetime conditions, women were expected to leave their jobs to make room for demobilized men and to facilitate men's re-entry into family life.

The impact of the war and the revolution of November 1918 created important changes in German society. The old imperial order collapsed, making way for a new experiment in liberal democracy. One of the most significant developments in the new constitution of the Weimar Republic was that women achieved equal suffrage.[34] Almost 90 per cent of women utilized their new right to vote in the elections of January 1919, and 9.6 per cent of those elected to the Weimar National Assembly were women.[35] Women's equal voting rights had been achieved earlier in a number of other

European countries, such as Finland (1906) and Norway (1913), but much later in others, such as France (1944) and Italy (1945). In Britain, the Representation of the People Act of 1918 granted women over the age of 30 the right to vote, but equal suffrage was achieved only a decade later in the Equal Franchise Act of 1928.[36]

New educational initiatives on sexual hygiene and birth control (discussed in Chapter 2) were introduced by organizations such as the Association for Sexual Hygiene and Life Reform, and the National Union for Birth Control and Hygiene, set up in 1923 and 1928 respectively.[37] There was a movement towards a more rational approach to sex, with an emphasis upon sexual health and hygiene, such as contraception advice and information about venereal disease. The open and public discussion of issues such as sexuality and methods of contraception was a completely new trend.[38] In 1926, a Reichstag majority voted for a change in the abortion legislation, consolidating Paragraphs 218–20 of the Penal Code into a single paragraph, Paragraph 218, and reducing the severity of sentences for abortion.[39] Yet, simultaneously there was a call for traditional values and protection of the genetic stock of the nation. The Weimar Republic was characterized by an ambivalence towards liberalization and the dropping of old taboos. There were some significant moves towards modernization, but the impact of these generated a conservative backlash.

Modernization in Weimar society saw advances in healthcare and welfare (as discussed in Chapter 7), and a boom in the leisure industry, with many cinemas, theatres, clubs, and cafés springing up in the cities, which themselves were growing larger and larger because of the movement of people from the countryside to the towns. Urbanization and modernization were the key trends which offered the 'new woman' a liberated lifestyle. Many young women moved to the cities to work in seemingly glamorous jobs, as secretaries, shorthand typists, shop assistants, and waitresses. They grew in confidence as they earned their own money, became independent of their families, cut their hair into the fashionable bob, smoked cigarettes, and dressed in modern, casual styles. However, this image did not apply to the majority of German women: on the whole there was no real questioning of traditional male and female stereotypes during the Weimar Republic, and gender roles were still quite rigidly defined.

The proportion of women in employment during the Weimar era remained broadly constant at about one-third, rising slightly to 35.6 per cent in 1925.[40] Of these, the number employed in agriculture and domestic service dropped, the number employed in industry rose slightly, whilst the number of women in white-collar jobs and in public-sector employment doubled. The largest single category of working women, those in family businesses, remained almost constant. Yet the Weimar Republic did not witness complete economic liberalization for women. After the First World War, there was a reversal in the trend of women in 'men's jobs' in transportation and heavy industry, as men returned to oust women from such positions. The significant change instigated by the war, however, was the influx of women into administrative, welfare, and educational work. In this sense, the *soziale Mütterlichkeit* ('social motherliness') advocated by the women's movement was fulfilled, with women taking jobs that could benefit from their feminine qualities.[41] But even in these spheres of work, women generally performed lower-paid tasks, whilst men took on the more responsible and better-paid roles (as discussed in Chapter 9). And where men and women did the same job, the latter received lower rates of pay. In fact, the modernization of techniques and the concentration of ownership meant that jobs were reshuffled in such a way that left women near the bottom of the pile. Working-class women were increasingly pressed into unskilled work. The electrical, chemical, and metallurgical industries which were being transformed by the installation of new machinery and production lines employed women as unskilled and semi-skilled labour. In 1925, more than 20 per cent of the workforce in the chemical and electrical industries were women.[42] Hence, the harassed peasant's wife, the underpaid industrial worker, and the exploited sales and office girls perhaps had some reason to respond to calls for a romanticized, idealized past. Modernization had meant emancipation, but the latter did not always meet expectations. Additional burdens on women or unfulfilled hopes left many of them thinking that they would be better off in traditional roles.[43]

According to its critics, modernization also engendered sexual promiscuity, rising divorce and abortion rates, falling birth rates, and higher numbers of illegitimate children being born. Such trends were considered to be signs of the demise of the family. So, too, was the rapid trend towards smaller family sizes (discussed in Chapter 2). Crude birth rates declined faster in the 1920s than at any other time in German history.[44] The decline in the birth rate was seen by conservative forces not as a 'rationalization of sex life' but as a 'national catastrophe'. Many religious and conservative groups sprang up in the aftermath of the First World War, and campaigned against women's emancipation, against birth control and against abortion. Such groups included the League of Queen Louise and the Evangelical Women's Federation. Other groups were concerned with the sharp decline in the nation's birth rate, such as the National League of Large Families, which promoted families with four or more children as a reaction against the Weimar trend of the 'two-child' family. Hence, the position of women in the Weimar Republic was mainly determined by a constant struggle between those forces aiming at emancipation and those more traditional forces, which campaigned against the 'new woman' and her objectives. Attitudes in Weimar Germany towards women were still, in many cases, conservative and reactionary. For example, the German National People's Party (DNVP) and the Catholic Centre Party favoured traditional, polarized gender roles. The effects of the economic crisis in 1929 compounded such attitudes. Women who aspired to a 'modern' lifestyle were chastised for failing to meet their obligations to their families and to the nation.

Demographers and population policy experts were full of gloom and doom about the effects of these changes upon the future of the nation. They predicted the 'death of the nation' as a result of the widespread use of contraception and the limiting of family size to two children. They were also worried about the qualitative future of the nation, and especially concerned that it was the 'better-off' circles (i.e. the middle and upper classes) that were limiting the number of their offspring, and squandering money selfishly upon luxury goods for themselves instead of having large families, whilst the 'lower strata of society', whose offspring – often illegitimate – were not always 'valuable', were 'reproducing indiscriminately'.

Hence, there was a call for women involved in commerce and public employment to return to traditional peasant and rural lifestyles, away from the decadence and depravity of the big cities, and to work in 'acceptable' forms of occupation (for example, as domestic helps or in family businesses) if indeed they had to work at all. In 1932, Chancellor Brüning introduced a new decree, 'The Law Governing the Legal Status of Female Civil Servants and Public Officials' against 'double-earners', which meant that a married woman could be dismissed from public service if her husband already earned a wage.[45] This law was intended to remove women from the workplace and to vacate positions for men, at a time of acute job shortages. Although its introduction had very little impact upon the labour market, this law was significant as a demonstration of the prevalent ideological stance that a married woman's first place should be in the household.[46] Germany was not unique in discouraging 'double-earners'. In Britain, the informal 'marriage bar' applied to professional and white-collar women before the First World War was formalized in 1919, when married women were dismissed from a wide range of occupations, including teaching, nursing, and the civil service.[47]

In many ways, the mid-1920s were years of comparative stability for the German family, as most people sought an ordered home and a sense of peace and security. The family was a place of refuge. The Weimar era gave social support to families, in the form of housing (both by rent subsidies and by the construction of low-income housing) as well as improving health services, as discussed in Chapter 7. Household appliances, such as vacuum cleaners, electric irons, and washing machines, were new additions to middle-class homes during this period, too. With them came new norms of greater efficiency and organization of the household, and more exacting standards of hygiene and comfort. Women's time and effort on basic chores was saved by the introduction of such domestic appliances, but they did not lighten the burdens for housewives and mothers in reality. Instead, their impact was to free up time for other household or family tasks, perhaps aimed at greater comfort or living standards, or more time and energy put into the upbringing of children.

The position of the family waned once again with the effects of the economic crisis engendered by the Wall Street Crash in 1929. This time it was largely a financial burden that families faced. The economic crisis eroded the material basis of middle-class family life, as savings were lost, and of working-class family life, as mass unemployment meant that workers lost their jobs and incomes. This placed a considerable strain on the mother to search for cheap provisions, mend damaged clothes, and maintain the cohesion of the family. Young unemployed family members sometimes left home, wandering across Germany, and even beyond the borders, to relieve the strain on the family of 'unnecessary eaters'.[48]

The economic climate of the early 1930s created many social rifts, for example between the employed and the unemployed, and between the older and younger generations. Inter-generational conflict sharpened considerably as parents lost their status and prestige through unemployment and impoverishment, and many were no longer in a position to provide their children with protection and security. Such tensions were advantageous to the Nazi Party, which capitalized upon the 'crisis of the family'. Loss of savings and financial security, as well as utter desperation and the host of other problems associated with the Depression, attracted many women to vote for the Nazi Party – which promised employment and recovery of the economy – with the hope that they would be able to feed their families again. In addition, the ideological image of women promoted by the Nazis found ready acceptance among many women as well as men during the last years of the Weimar Republic, despite the fact that National Socialist ideology made no secret of being completely at odds with women's emancipation. Women formed a significant part of the Nazi vote. They cast their votes for a whole variety of reasons, not just gender-related ones. Hence, in their search for a party that would solve all of Germany's economic and social problems, and put an end to the recent political instability, the number of women voting for the Nazi Party steadily increased from 1928 onwards, so that by the elections of March 1932, the same number of women as men voted for the Nazi Party.[49]

11.4 The Third Reich: the centrality of racial policy

The National Socialists attributed the dwindling birth rate to the spiritual and ideological setbacks that had affected German society in the years preceding their own *Machtergreifung* ('seizure of power'). The senseless, extravagant enjoyment of the individual during the Weimar Republic had taken precedence over collective moral obligations. Hence, 'duty' towards the community through kinship and family, marriage and childbirth, had been lost in a flurry towards 'internationalism', 'pacifism', and 'racial mixing'. The National Socialists claimed that the Weimar governments had encouraged egocentricity and independence, with taxation laws that showed a hostility to marital and familial life. Bachelorhood and childless marriages had been completely acceptable in Weimar society. The average family had had two children, whilst large families had been seen as abnormal, and as inimical to the good of society. Large families, often living in poverty and hunger, had been the objects of scorn and pity in Weimar society. They were looked down upon by small middle-class and well-to-do families. According to the National Socialists, it was these large families, with four or more children, that were fulfilling their biological obligations to the continued existence of the nation.

From 1933 onwards, Weimar attitudes were completely reversed. Nazi leaders and eugenicists believed that the worth of a nation was shown in the preparedness of its women to become valuable mothers, and that Germany had to become a fertile land of mothers and children. Whilst men fought on the battlefield, women also had a battle to fight – to produce a new generation of Germans. Parents of large families were to be proud of their 'swarm of children'. Now there was a stigma attached to being unmarried or childless, with increasing peer pressure amongst colleagues to marry and have children. The Nazis promoted the new ideal of the *kinderreiche Familie* ('many-child family'), comprising four or more children, hereditarily healthy, politically reliable, and socially responsible.[50]

The National Socialists' objectives of an increased birth rate, racial homogeneity, and a regimented social life invaded the private domain of the family quite profoundly.[51] The Nazi regime reorganized and expanded the public health system, making it a modern tool for enforcing Nazi population and racial policy. Its policies had a considerable impact upon laws relating to racial hygiene, marriage, divorce, birth control, and abortion. In July 1933, the Law for the Prevention of Hereditarily Diseased Offspring was passed, calling for the compulsory sterilization of individuals suffering from certain 'hereditary diseases'. These included 'congenital feeble-mindedness', 'schizo-phrenia', 'manic depression', 'Huntingdon's chorea', 'hereditary blindness', 'hereditary deafness', and 'serious physical deformities'. In addition, chronic alcoholics could be compulsorily sterilized. The law was officially declared to embody the 'primacy of the state over the sphere of life, marriage and family'. Between January 1934 – when the decree came into effect – and the outbreak of war in September 1939, approximately 320,000 people (0.5 per cent of the German population) were sterilized under the terms of this law.[52] The quantitatively and strategically most important group sterilized were the 'feeble-minded'. This category made up some two-thirds of those sterilized, and almost two-thirds of these were women.[53] Many of these people were of German ethnicity, but from the poorest sectors of society, whilst others were from ethnic-minority groups or were inmates in asylums and psychiatric institutions.

Marriages between 'racially pure', 'healthy' Germans and the 'unfit' or 'racially inferior' were prohibited by means of new Nazi legislation in 1935.[54] The Law for the Protection of German Blood and Honour – one of the Nuremberg Laws – banned marriages and sexual relationships between

Jews and 'Aryans'. The Law for the Protection of the Hereditary Health of the German People or Marriage Health Law required all prospective spouses to produce a 'certificate of fitness to marry', issued by the local health authorities.[55] Such certificates were denied to those with serious infectious or 'hereditary' diseases. These measures demonstrate that, to the National Socialists, marriage was not a free community of two people, but purely an institution for procreation. The biologization and medicalization of marriage led to a significant restriction of individual liberties.

On the positive side, a marriage loan scheme was introduced in 1933 in order to promote early marriages between healthy, 'Aryan' partners. Interest-free loans of up to 1000 Reichsmarks were made to German couples in the form of vouchers for the purchase of furniture and household equipment. The granting of a loan was conditional upon the woman giving up paid employment. The two main reasons for this were to encourage women back into the home and to create job opportunities for men. The loans were to be repaid at the rate of 1 per cent per month. But the sum to be repaid was cut by one-quarter for each child born to the couple, so that, in effect, on the birth of the fourth child repayment was waived altogether. This measure was aimed at encouraging newly-weds to start having children as quickly as possible. In 1937, the revocation of the prohibition on women's paid employment as a prerequisite of the loans resulted in a sharp increase in applications. In 1939, 42 per cent of all marriages were loan-assisted. However, the loans did not have the desired effect of boosting the nation's birth rate. The long-term trend towards one- and two-child families was not altered appreciably by this measure, as the loans were inadequate to cover the costs of a larger family. Couples granted marriage loans on average had only one child.[56]

In 1938, a reform of the German marriage law was introduced, incorporating a new divorce law that facilitated divorce. 'Premature infertility' became a ground for divorce, as did either partner's 'refusal to procreate', in both cases because the primary purpose of marriage, the preservation and increase of the race, could not be fulfilled. A divorce could also be granted if the couple had lived apart for three years or more and the marriage had 'irretrievably' broken down. By 1941 21,293 men and 6648 women had filed for divorce on the grounds of the 'irretrievable breakdown' of their marriage. In the same period, 'premature infertility' accounted for 383 divorces and 'refusal to procreate' for 1771 divorces.[57] The facilitation of divorce, however, did not stem from liberal ideals or from any attempt on the part of the regime to ameliorate the position of private individuals. Instead, it was for the benefit of the German nation. The objective was to dissolve marriages that were of no value to the *Volksgemeinschaft* ('national community'). The logic behind this law was that once a divorce had been granted, the two partners involved might remarry and provide the nation with children. Contradictory though it may have seemed, the 1938 divorce law was another method by which the National Socialist regime sought to fulfil its population policy objectives.

The pronatalist imperatives of the Nazi regime could not be met given the prevailing climate in German society of relatively easy access to birth control advice and contraceptives, and with the effects of the relaxation of the abortion laws during the Weimar era. The birth control, marriage, and sexual counselling centres set up during the Weimar Republic were either closed down by the new Nazi government or absorbed into the public health offices. This suited the political aims as well as the pronatalist ambitions of the Nazi regime, since many of these centres were run by the KPD (German Communist Party). The Nazi regime was able to use the Law for the Protection of the People and State of 28 February 1933 to ban birth control organizations on the grounds that they were 'Marxist'. However, the practice of birth control in Germany could not easily be eradicated by the regime. Nazi laws and propaganda merely meant that such practices were reduced and continued underground, rather than being eliminated altogether. The real crackdown occurred in January 1941, when Himmler's Police Ordinance categorically banned the production and distribution of contraceptives, but even this did not ensure total success for the regime in this respect.

In May 1933, the National Socialist government tightened up the abortion laws once again. Paragraphs 219 and 220 were reintroduced. Paragraph 219 stated that any person who advertised, exhibited or recommended articles or procedures for abortion could be fined or imprisoned for up to two years. Paragraph 220 prescribed the same punishment for any person publicly offering his or her services, or those of a third party, to carry out an abortion. Abortion on eugenic grounds, however, was permissible, and in some cases, even mandatory. Illegal abortionists were increasingly punished by imprisonment, rather than by fines. In 1936, Himmler created the Reich Central Office for the Combating of Homosexuality and Abortion, headed by Josef Meisinger, to deal with matters of 'public morality'. Abortion and homosexuality were conceptually linked, as both implied individual choice. In 1937, the anti-abortion campaign led by the Gestapo intensified, with nine times as many abortionists facing legal charges as in the previous year. During the war, measures against abortion became increasingly stringent. It was made almost impossible to have an application for a legal abortion approved, which led to an increase in the number of illegal abortions. In 1943, a new sub-paragraph was added to Paragraph 218, which stated that the death penalty could be imposed upon any person who continuously impaired 'the vitality of the German nation' by carrying out abortions.

With the aim of regenerating the 'body of the nation', Nazi policy increased state intervention into the private sphere, on racial and biological grounds. Under National Socialism, family rights were suppressed as the regime aimed to control, define, and categorize both sexuality and the family. This was in clear contrast to the liberal conception of the family as the last place of refuge for the individual against the encroachment of state intervention.[58] Despite its allegations about the negative implications of the

Weimar period for the family and its claims to re-establish the true meaning of the family after the 'liberal capitalists' and 'Marxists' had destroyed its 'moral foundations', the Nazi regime, in reality, itself undermined the German family in an unprecedented way.[59] It did so by subjecting the family to state encroachment and mechanisms of control, by reducing its socialization function, by attempting to remove its ability to shelter emotionally and to provide for its members, and by subjecting it to the racial thinking that was so central to Nazi ideology. The implication of the National Socialist era for the German family was the ultimate destruction of the private sphere, in physical and practical terms, as well as morally and spiritually.

11.5 The post-1945 era

The Second World War had far-reaching implications and consequences for the German family, creating almost impossible circumstances for intimate and stable family life to be conducted. Men at the front suffered physical mutilation and psychological scarring, unsure if they would survive the war to resume family life. Many women who were used to their husbands making the decisions and dealing with family finances had to manage on their own. The conscription of farmers and male farm labourers created additional hardships for rural women, who had to cope with both their sources of livelihood and their families single-handed. In the cities and industrial areas, too, women bore the strains of industrial work and maintenance of their families on their own, struggling for survival under circumstances of rationing, bombings, and fear. Their daily life was dangerous, demanding them to be 'both mindless and brave'.[60] There was much solidarity amongst women, who found themselves in similarly desperate situations. Female relatives helped each other with work, shopping, and looking after children. In the absence of relatives, women turned to female colleagues, friends, and neighbours for help and support. Networks of support among women were widespread and provided much-needed mutual relief. Air raids had disrupted normal life and many families were made homeless and dispossessed. Many women and children had been evacuated from the cities to rural areas, and families separated in the process.

As a consequence of the war, water and gas supplies to many homes had been destroyed, and food and clothing were in short supply. These problems were worse in urban areas than in the countryside, but the aim everywhere was 'to get through'.[61] Women cut clothes out of old military uniforms, formed knitting needles out of bicycle spokes and made yarn out of potato sacks. Food rations were meagre and shortages were severe, especially in the winter of 1946–47. One Berlin woman recalled the situation: 'During the war we were bombed, but had assurances of getting food supplies; when the war ended, there were no more bombing raids, but there was also nothing to eat.'[62] Hence, the immediate postwar period brought about feelings of joy and relief, but also disappointment.

By the end of the war, the German economy was shattered, and some two-fifths of the population had been displaced and dispossessed. There was a tremendous housing shortage, as about one-quarter of all homes had been destroyed by the effects of the war. In the cities, over 50 per cent of housing had been destroyed. In 1946, there were some 6 million dwellings too few for the needs of the German population.[63] People whose homes had survived the war had to make rooms available to refugees or homeless families. The impact of the war upon family life had been disastrous. Almost 4 million men had died in battle and 11.7 million men were prisoners of war in 1945. This meant that millions of women had to be self-reliant. Lack of food and sleep brought emaciation and chronic exhaustion to many women, who had to work as rubble clearers or in semi-skilled and unskilled jobs, and who often gave up their food for their children. The search for food included foraging expeditions and resort to the black market. Women had to be resourceful and good at improvisation, as they were forced to prepare meals with few ingredients and sometimes without energy supplies. A study of 498 Berlin families in 1946–47 concluded that: 'The burden of day-to-day work carried out by most women has become not only more complex and difficult, but is also increasing disproportionately to the scant opportunity they have to recover their strength through eating and sleeping.'[64]

The homecoming of husbands and fathers had been long awaited by families that had been separated for between three and nine years. Women hoped that with the return of their husbands, their lives would be made easier. However, when men returned home, many women could scarcely recognize their husbands, who were emaciated or maimed, or both. The women faced perhaps their hardest task, to provide the understanding, emotional balance, rebuilding of confidence, and encouragement needed by so many totally beaten and desperate men.[65] The process of recovery and rehabilitation was a lengthy one, and its strain frequently resulted in the physical and psychological exhaustion of women. Many men were unable or unwilling to adjust to their new situation, which exacerbated the already difficult circumstances of their families. For example, they often refused to change their attitudes and expectations and, despite their powerlessness, acted like domestic tyrants. This often resulted in conflicts and arguments between spouses. Rising divorce rates, reaching a postwar high of 87,013 in 1948, demonstrated that it was not easy for married couples to reformulate their relationships after years spent apart, as too much had changed.[66]

Years of separation took their toll on family life. Both men and women were confronted with changes in the physical appearance of their partners. Feelings of reserve and alienation made it hard for many married couples to communicate with each other. In addition, it was difficult for them to recount painful experiences to each other. Other problems also contributed to the destabilization of families, such as sexual distance between spouses and difficulties in the relationships between children and their recently returned fathers.[67] Many children were unable to recognize their fathers on their return home. Younger children, in particular, had often had no knowledge of their fathers, sometimes having only seen photographs of them. Elder sons, in the absence of their fathers, had become the confidants of their mothers and ersatz fathers to their siblings. With the homecoming of their fathers, there inevitably ensued a conflict about the recognition and maintenance of this status. Many fathers were unwilling to accept it and many sons were unwilling to give it up. Older children, in general, resented their fathers for treating them still as children, when they had been forced to grow up faster as a consequence of the war. They rebelled against their fathers and felt alienated from them. This placed mothers in the difficult position of trying to maintain some degree of harmony and balance within the family.

Hence, in the immediate aftermath of the war, during a period of great upheaval and hardship, German women were confronted with considerable challenges. Although they were 'visible' in non-traditional work, such as clearing away the ·rubble left by the Allied bombings, this activity was considered to be an extension of their 'special nature' and their feminine qualities of self-sacrifice.[68] And with the growing sense of a return to the notion of working father and *Hausfrau* mother, by 1949 women's contributions had become 'invisible' again. This ideal was celebrated in the new West German state: even though many women worked, either through choice or through financial necessity, the description of their role in the public discourse made that work invisible. In this sense, very little had changed. The prevalent attitude was that both the cohesion of the social order and men's public position depended upon women's private role.[69]

The division of Germany into two separate states under very different political systems saw divided fortunes and experiences for women and the family in East and West Germany.[70] In the East, the family had to conform to the norms of socialist rule in the German Democratic Republic (GDR). Families were places to 'eat, sleep and watch television', not places to nurture the individuality and personal development of their members.[71] There was little scope for flexibility even in the private sphere – the overall aim was to fit into society as normal, constructive members. In this sense, circumstances were not that different from the National Socialist era in practical and emotional terms. By contrast, in West Germany in the 1950s everyday family life began to regain a sense of unity and concord.[72] In 1953, the German Federal Republic set up a new Ministry for Family Concerns headed by Franz-Joseph Wuermerling. Its chief aims were to overcome the housing shortage, to give financial support to families by means of tax relief and family allowances, and to promote family values.[73] This was a reflection of the status regained by the family as a source of renewal and order. By the early 1950s, the family in the German Federal Republic had regenerated, stabilized, and strengthened itself. Once again, it became a source of emotional support to its members, something it had not been permitted to be under the Nazi dictatorship. It was also considered to be an important element in the stability of the state.[74]

The socialist order in East Germany, along with proclaiming an end to inequality in society in general for political and economic reasons, also claimed to do away with sexual inequality.[75] It instigated a series of measures to enable women to combine motherhood and employment, including the establishment of a comprehensive system of child-care facilities, child benefits and allowances, and paid leave after childbirth and during children's illnesses. For example, the 'baby year' entitled women to paid leave for the first year of a child's life. In the GDR in 1989, 90 per cent of all women between the ages of 16 and 60 were part of the workforce. Employment was a normal part of women's lives in the GDR. Yet housework and care for the family were still very much considered to be women's responsibilities. Within the private sphere of the family, women were still housewives, albeit with the help of full-time child-care facilities, such as crèches and kindergartens that were located close to either their home or their place of employment. Women and men generally believed that they were treated equally in the GDR. Access to employment for women was taken as equality. But although the majority of women were employed, few attained positions of leadership or reached the top in their professions. Employment practices underpinned this inequality, with women's pay being one-third lower than that of men.[76] Such wage differentials between women and men existed irrespective of their occupations, qualifications or status.

The West, by contrast, saw a resurgence in traditional gender stereotypes in the early 1950s. The family policy pursued by the Federal Republic at this time reflected conservative attitudes. There was a call for a return to normality and security after the disarray of the Nazi era and the war.[77] A study by the sociologist Helmut Schelsky in 1955 concluded that the events of the war and the immediate postwar era had posed an 'exceptional danger to the family', but that this had ultimately revived regenerative forces which served to strengthen the family.[78] In a fragmented and disrupted society, the family had emerged as the 'last bastion, the ultimate place of safety'. The family merited restoration and preservation, but not rethinking or restructuring.[79]

Certainly this conservatism also applied to the question of women's status and role. There was a trend to restore the old familial order, in which traditional gender roles were encouraged, with the man as breadwinner and the woman as child-rearer. German women's magazines promoted the image of the housewife as appealing. Single, divorced, and widowed women were marginalized and the nuclear two- or three-child family became the accepted norm once again.[80] The percentage of married women working outside the home went down in 1950 to 25 per cent, its lowest point in the twentieth century.[81]

In 1949, Article 3 of the German Federal Republic's Basic Law (*Grundgesetz*) established equal rights for women and men.[82] In contrast to the Weimar Constitution, which granted only civil equality, in 1949 equal rights were intended to apply in all areas of life. But the 1900 Civil Code was not necessarily changed in accordance with this, until July 1958 when the Equal Rights Law came into effect, finally abolishing certain forms of male authority, such as right of decision over all questions pertaining to married life. Married women now had the right to take up paid employment. The law also established joint ownership of property as the norm, giving each partner the right of disposal over his or her individual wealth.[83] This was a very late development in comparison to Britain, where married women had achieved control of their earnings in 1878 and control of their property in 1882.[84]

The 1950s witnessed a boom in consumer goods and domestic appliances, as well as trends in consumption of more expensive foods and luxury goods (as discussed in Chapter 12).[85] Rising social aspirations led German married women into the workplace. Many of them went out to work because they wished to raise their general standard of living, rather than as a result of economic need. The 1960s saw considerable changes in West German society. By 1961, the proportion of married women at work had increased again to 32.8 per cent.[86] The women's liberation movement of the 1970s built upon this change, arguing that all people, regardless of gender, should have the opportunity for self-realization and fulfilment. It launched a campaign for the repeal of the abortion law.[87] It made other new demands, calling into question the whole principle of the gender-based division of labour both inside and outside the home.[88] As in Britain, its radical rejection of housework and of the traditional role of women in the family was what distinguished the German women's movement of the 1970s from any that had gone before.[89] In contrast to the situation in East Germany, women's motivation for employment in West Germany was linked to a critical view of traditional gender stereotypes of women as housewives and mothers. Hence, whilst the bourgeois nuclear family became the societal norm, the gender polarity and separation of male and female spheres associated with it was gradually eroded.

By 1980, 48.3 per cent of married women in West Germany were going out to work, following an expansion of job opportunities in the service sector and the civil service.[90] With the average size of the West German household decreasing to 2.3 members in 1990 and with the decline in the birth rate, women were not out of place in the 'man's world'. Household and children required less time and energy on the part of women.[91] Women fulfilled the role of housewife and mother for a short period of time, if at all, interrupting their career paths for only a few years. Many women combined family and work by seeking part-time employment. Despite the disadvantages of part-time jobs, they were much in demand by married women as they offered a greater degree of flexibility than full-time work.[92] Motherhood and employment could be complementary activities and many women opted to combine these roles, rather than having to choose between the two.

Another reason for the popularity of part-time employment was that German school hours ended at lunchtime, which made it very hard for women with children to take up full-time employment.

After the reunification of Germany in 1990, the view of employment being the norm for women from the former GDR persisted. The majority of women continued to combine their roles as mothers and workers in the lifestyle to which they had grown accustomed under socialism.[93] But East German women entered the reunified Germany with many disadvantages, including lower pay, qualifications, and occupational status, and more familial duties than either men and West German women. In the new market economy, their position was weak. The social and economic changes that took place after the reunification served to weaken their position further. Whereas during the GDR era, the two-child family had been perceived as the norm, after the reunification, the birth rate fell markedly as women decided to have children either later or not at all. In the 1990s, East German women, especially those of the younger generation, decreased their familial commitments and moved closer to the West German model of the one-child family.[94] Women from the former GDR became attracted to more individualistic and independent lifestyles. The number of marriages dropped dramatically, as women chose to live outside conventional family units. These trends towards one-child families and common-law partnerships changed women's lives quite considerably compared to the GDR period when *Muttipolitik* ('Mummy-policies') shielded women – including single mothers – from some of the difficulties involved in their dual roles as mothers and workers. Indeed, without protective measures to assist them, single mothers were the first to be pushed out of the labour force and even forced into poverty in the competitive post-unification economy.[95]

In the GDR, whilst incomes were low and luxuries uncommon, poverty was almost unknown.[96] Families could live on very small incomes because state subsidies kept rents low, basic goods were cheap, and domestic energy costs remained unchanged over a period of 40 years. Low income in the GDR did not have the same implications as it did after the reunification. Suddenly, the cost of living in the former GDR rocketed – for example, rents increased by almost 300 per cent between October and December 1991 and a further 140 per cent in the following year. These changes brought an unprecedented experience of destitution and poverty to many sectors of society whose position during the GDR era had been relatively secure; these included working women and single mothers. Unemployment also hit East German women very hard after the reunification. Women were less protected than men by special measures to cushion or defer unemployment; they were forced into early retirement more quickly than men, and they were less successful in retraining and finding new jobs.

Since reunification, the women of former East Germany have had to redefine their lives.[97] Their status as mothers is no longer protected as it was in the GDR era and although they still have the motivation to work, their prospects for employment have been reduced. They have increasingly chosen to reduce the size of their families or even to remain childless altogether.[98] Hence, motherhood plays a less significant role in the lives of women from the former East Germany than it did during the GDR era. Societal norms have changed – protection and support for mothers is not available in the same way as before, the two-child family is less common, and women are seeking more flexible patterns of employment where this is possible. Part-time work and fewer children is what more women are seeking. This is a very different situation from during the GDR, when working full-time was an accepted way of life for women, as was a larger number of children within a conventional marriage.[99]

11.5 Conclusion

In the eighteenth and nineteenth centuries, the German household was very different from how it became in the twentieth century. Functions of production and consumption were very closely bound up in 'the whole household', as were male and female spheres of activity. The *Hausvater* and *Hausmutter* were jointly responsible for the running of a household and making a living. Industrialization brought a change to this traditional pattern, by removing from the household its productive function and creating clearly separate domains for men and women. It heralded a new gender-based division of labour in which men operated outside the home and women worked inside it.

In addition, two particularly significant issues about the position of women in mid-nineteenth-century Germany should be noted. First, middle-class women and their organizations did not seek to abolish the notion of the gender-based division of labour. In 1849, Louise Otto firmly repudiated the idea that she was advocating women's emancipation. The German women's movement still followed traditional rules of femininity, but advocated women's right to self-development within the family and society, such as becoming involved in education and social welfare. Second, working-class women did not have any sense of 'sisterhood' with the women of the middle classes, whom they essentially regarded as their employers, despite the attempts of middle-class women's organizations to support and help them.

The First World War had a considerable impact upon the German family and upon the role of women in German society. Yet the impact and achievements of the women's movement diminished considerably during the course of the Weimar period. Once the right to vote had been achieved, together with a constitutional promise of equality, progress dwindled and the organized women's movement itself was crippled. In addition, despite the rhetoric of emancipation in the Weimar Republic, patriarchal ideology and attitudes remained dominant in German society. The old assumptions about women's roles had not been abandoned. Even the Federation of German Women's Associations and the Social Democratic women's movement both believed that motherhood was a woman's first duty, although it was one which had to be recognized and valued more highly. And the tensions created by the new demands on women had not been resolved. There remained no doubt in Weimar society that family duties were of prime significance and no solution emerged on how a woman might combine work and family demands.

The Third Reich also offered no progress, not least because the policies of the National Socialist era towards women and the family were so inconsistent in nature. In some instances they mirrored the Nazis' reactionary ideology, yet in others they appeared quite revolutionary. The Nazi regime ultimately achieved the destruction of the family as a social unit. It imposed a strict supervision and control of birth, marriage, and sexuality, and simultaneously emptied the household of its members.[100] Ultimately, both Nazi policy and the impact of the Second World War left the German family in total disarray.

There have been marked changes in the contemporary era. Modern German women are far less tied to their families than before and the revolutionization of birth control by the Pill in the 1960s has meant that sex for women is no longer just a reproductive function.[101] Contemporary German society is moving away from strictly traditional family relations, for example towards common-law partnerships rather than marriages, and family relationships in which individual members can attain self-fulfilment and autonomy with the support of the family unit. The family should not be perceived as a static structure. It has developed and changed over time, both in historical form and function, so that the patriarchal family structure with its emphasis upon the authority of the husband and father over the wife and children has lost its significance.[102] Social norms and expectations have altered from a framework based upon patriarchy and an authoritarian, hierarchical system within the family to greater equality, participation, individuality, freedom, and partnership within family life. In many cases, the family sphere is still important, but it is no longer the only sphere. Decreasing family sizes, a reduction in time expended on household chores because of raised standards of living and the purchase of consumer durable goods and time-saving devices, the loosening of traditional conventions, and increased opportunities for women to participate in work outside the home and to contribute to social and political life are amongst the most prominent trends in German society at the beginning of the twenty-first century.[103]

11.6 Notes

1 This term has been rejected by a number of historians, including Michael Mitterauer and Reinhard Sieder. They suggest instead the term *Hausgemein-*

schaft ('domestic community'). See M. Mitterauer and R. Sieder, *The European Family: Patriarchy to Partnership from the Middle Ages to the Present* (Oxford, 1982), p. 9.

2 I. Weber-Kellermann, 'The German Family between Private Life and Politics', in A. Prost and G. Vincent, eds, *A History of Private Life*, Vol. V: *Riddles of Identity in Modern Times* (Cambridge, MA, 1991), pp. 503–37, here p. 504.

3 On the role of the *Hausmutter*, see M. Gray, 'Prescriptions for Productive Female Domesticity in a Transitional Era: Germany's *Hausmütterliteratur*, 1780–1840', *History of European Ideas*, 8 (1987), pp. 413–26.

4 Weber-Kellermann, 'The German Family between Private Life and Politics', p. 504. On the changes to the household in this period, see H. Medick, 'The Proto-Industrial Family Economy: The Structural Function of Household and Family during the Transition from Peasant Society to Industrial Capitalism', *Social History*, 1 (1976), pp. 291–315, and E. Shorter, *The Making of The Modern Family* (New York, 1975).

5 Mitterauer and Sieder, *The European Family*, pp. 6–7.

6 *Ibid.*, p. 43.

7 U. Frevert, *Women in German History: From Bourgeois Emancipation to Sexual Liberation* (Oxford, 1993), p. 15.

8 Gray, 'Prescriptions for Productive Female Domesticity', p. 413.

9 On the experiences of working-class women, see L. Abrams, 'Martyrs or Matriarchs? Working-Class Women's Experience of Marriage in Germany before the First World War', *Women's History Review*, 1 (1992), pp. 357–76.

10 Frevert, *Women in German History*, pp. 85–93.

11 Gray, 'Prescriptions for Productive Female Domesticity', p. 422.

12 Frevert, *Women in German History*, p. 23.

13 *Ibid.*, pp. 66–7.

14 *Ibid.*, p. 322.

15 On this, see K. Hausen, 'Family and Role Division: The Polarisation of Sexual Stereotypes in the Nineteenth Century – An Aspect of the Dissociation of Work and Family Life', in R. Evans and W. Lee, eds, *The German Family: Essays on the Social History of the Family in Nineteenth- and Twentieth-Century Germany* (London, 1981), pp. 51–83, here pp. 63–4.

16 L. Abrams and E. Harvey, eds, *Gender Relations in German History: Power, Agency and Experience from the Sixteenth to the Twentieth Century* (London, 1996), pp. 19–20.

17 On the experiences of women in nineteenth-century Germany, see J. Fout, ed., *German Women in the Nineteenth Century* (New York and London, 1984), R. Joeres and M. Maynes, eds, *German Women in the Eighteenth and Nineteenth Centuries: A Social and Literary History* (Bloomington, 1986), and I. Weber-Kellermann, *Frauenleben im 19. Jahrhundert* (Munich, 1983).

18 Frevert, *Women in German History*, p. 76.

19 *Ibid.*, p. 101.

20 *Ibid.*, p. 104.

21 U. Frevert, 'Gender in German History', in M. Fulbrook, ed., *German History since 1800* (London, 1997), p. 515.

22 Frevert, *Women in German History*, p. 126.

23 On female education, see J. Albisetti, *Schooling German Girls and Women: Secondary and Higher Education in the Nineteenth Century* (Princeton, 1988).

24 J. McDermid, 'Women and Education', in J. Purvis, ed., *Women's History: Britain, 1850–1945* (London, 1995), pp. 107–30, here p. 112.

25 B. Anderson and J. Zinsser, *A History of Their Own: Women in Europe from Prehistory to the Present*, Vol. II (London, 1988), p. 188.

26 Frevert, *Women in German History*, pp. 138–9.

27 *Ibid.*, p. 141.
28 *Ibid.*, p. 147.
29 Frevert, *Women In German History*, p. 154.
30 R. Sieder, *Sozialgeschichte der Familie* (Frankfurt am Main, 1987), p. 212.
31 Frevert, *Women in German History*, p. 156.
32 On women's work in the First World War, see U. Daniel, *The War from Within: German Working-Class Women in the First World War* (Oxford, 1997), pp. 37–126.
33 Frevert, *Women in German History*, pp. 160–1.
34 On the background to the achievement of women's suffrage, see R. Evans, 'German Social Democracy and Women's Suffrage, 1891–1918', *Journal of Contemporary History*, 15 (1980), pp. 533–57.
35 Frevert, *Women in German History*, p. 169.
36 S. Bruley, *Women in Britain since 1900* (London, 1999), p. 82.
37 Frevert, *Women in German History*, p. 189.
38 On contraception, see C. Usborne, *The Politics of the Body in Weimar Germany: Women's Reproduction Rights and Duties* (London, 1992), pp. 119–33.
39 L. Pine, *Nazi Family Policy, 1933–1945* (Oxford, 1997), pp. 19–20.
40 D. Peukert, *The Weimar Republic: The Crisis of Classical Modernity* (London, 1991), p. 96.
41 *Ibid.*, p. 97.
42 Frevert, *Women in German History*, p. 184.
43 On the gap between perception and reality of emancipation in the Weimar Republic, see R. Bridenthal and C. Koonz, 'Beyond Kinder, Küche, Kirche: Weimar Women in Politics and Work', in R. Bridenthal, A. Grossmann, and M. Kaplan, eds, *When Biology Became Destiny: Women in Weimar and Nazi Germany* (New York, 1984), pp. 33–65.
44 Weber-Kellermann, 'The German Family between Private Life and Politics', p. 515.
45 Peukert, *The Weimar Republic*, p. 97.
46 Frevert, *Women in German History*, p. 198.
47 On this, see Bruley, *Women in Britain*, pp. 20–1, 61, 69.
48 Sieder, *Sozialgeschichte der Familie*, p. 225.
49 M. Burleigh and W. Wippermann, *The Racial State: Germany 1933–1945* (Cambridge, 1991), p. 243.
50 On this, see Pine, *Nazi Family Policy*, pp. 88–116.
51 *Ibid.*, pp. 8–46.
52 G. Bock, 'Racism and Sexism in Nazi Germany', in Bridenthal, Grossmann, and Kaplan, eds, *When Biology Became Destiny*, pp. 271–96, here p. 279.
53 G. Bock, 'Antinatalism, Maternity and Paternity in National Socialist Racism', in G. Bock and P. Thane, eds, *Maternity and Gender Policies: Women and the Rise of the European Welfare States, 1880s–1950s* (London and New York, 1994), pp. 233–53, here p. 236.
54 On what follows, see Pine, *Nazi Family Policy*, pp. 15–19.
55 This law, with its requirement of 'certificates of fitness to marry' had similarities to the 'politische Ehekonsens' in the nineteenth century, discussed in Chapter 2 of this volume. The 'politische Ehekonsens' continued to be the law in the North German Confederation until 1868 and in Bavaria until 1916.
56 J. Stephenson, *Women in Nazi Society* (London, 1975), p. 47.
57 G. Czarnowski, 'The Value of Marriage for the *Volksgemeinschaft*: Policies Towards Women and Marriage under National Socialism', in R. Bessel, ed., *Fascist Italy and Nazi Germany: Comparisons and Contrasts* (Cambridge, 1996), pp. 94–112, here pp. 107–8.
58 J. Donzelot, *The Policing of Families* (London, 1980), p. 5.

59 See Pine, *Nazi Family Policy*, pp. 179–83.
60 A. Tröger, 'German Women's Memories of World War II', in M. Higonnet *et al.*, eds, *Behind the Lines: Gender and the Two World Wars* (New Haven, 1987), pp. 285–99, here p. 297.
61 Sieder, *Sozialgeschichte der Familie*, p. 240.
62 Cited in S. Meyer and E. Schulze, *Wie wir das alles geschafft haben: alleinstehende Frauen berichten über ihr Leben nach 1945* (Munich, 1984), p. 92.
63 C. Kleßmann, *Die doppelte Staatsgründung: Deutsche Geschichte 1945–1955* (Göttingen, 1982), p. 39.
64 H. Thurnwald, *Gegenwartsprobleme Berliner Familien. Eine soziologische Untersuchung* (Berlin, 1948), p. 86.
65 U. von Kardorff, *Berliner Aufzeichnungen. Aus den Jahren 1942–1945* (Munich, 1962), p. 293.
66 R. Moeller, *Protecting Motherhood: Women and the Family in the Politics of Postwar West Germany* (Berkeley, 1993), pp. 29–30.
67 Sieder, *Sozialgeschichte der Familie*, pp. 237–8.
68 M. Höhn, 'Frau im Haus und Girl im Spiegel: Discourse on Women in the Interregnum Period of 1945–1949 and the Question of German Identity', *Central European History*, 26 (1993), pp. 57–90, here p. 63.
69 *Ibid.*, p. 75.
70 On this, see H. Shaffer, *Women in the Two Germanies. A Comparative Study of a Socialist and a Non-Socialist Society* (New York and London, 1981).
71 E. Kolinsky, 'Women after *Muttipolitik*', in E. Kolinsky, ed., *Between Hope and Fear: Everyday Life in Post-Unification East Germany* (Keele, 1995), pp. 177–200, here p. 181.
72 E. Kolinsky, *Women in West Germany: Life, Work, Politics* (Oxford, 1989), p. 78.
73 A. Nicholls, *The Bonn Republic: West German Democracy 1945–1990* (London, 1997), p. 105.
74 Höhn, 'Frau im Haus und Girl im Spiegel', p. 81. On this period, see also R. Moeller, 'Reconstructing the Family in Reconstruction Germany: Women and Social Policy in the Federal Republic, 1949–1955', in R. Moeller, ed., *West Germany under Construction: Politics, Society, and Culture in the Adenauer Era* (Ann Arbor, 1997), pp. 109–33.
75 Kolinsky, 'Women after *Muttipolitik*', p. 177.
76 *Ibid.*, p. 178.
77 Moeller, *Protecting Motherhood*, p. 213.
78 H. Schelsky, *Wandlungen der deutschen Familie in der Gegenwart* (Stuttgart, 1960), pp. 63 and 87.
79 Moeller, *Protecting Motherhood*, p. 213.
80 Frevert, *Women in German History*, pp. 266–7. See also, Kolinsky, *Women in West Germany*, pp. 78–9.
81 Moeller, *Protecting Motherhood*, p. 217.
82 On this, see Moeller, *Protecting Motherhood*, pp. 38–75.
83 See Frevert, *Women in German History*, pp. 278–81.
84 Anderson and Zinsser, *A History of Their Own*, p. 361.
85 *Ibid.*, p. 268. On women as consumers in West Germany, see E. Carter, 'Alice in the Consumer Wonderland: West German Case Studies in Gender and Consumer Culture', in Moeller, ed., *West Germany under Reconstruction*, pp. 347–71, and E. Carter, *How German is She? Postwar West German Reconstruction and the Consuming Woman* (Ann Arbor, 1997). See also, J. Loehlin, *From Rugs to Riches: Housework, Consumption and Modernity in Germany* (Oxford, 1999).

86 Moeller, *Protecting Motherhood*, p. 217.

87 Frevert, *Women in German History*, pp. 294–5.

88 Moeller, *Protecting Motherhood*, p. 224.

89 Frevert, *Women in German History*, pp. 288–92. On Britain, S. Rowbotham, *A Century of Women: The History of Women in Britain and the United States* (London, 1999), p. 401.

90 *Ibid.*, p. 270.

91 Kolinsky, *Women in West Germany*, p. 85.

92 Frevert, *Women in German History*, p. 272.

93 H. Nickel, 'Women and Women's Policies in East and West Germany, 1945–1990', in E. Kolinsky, ed., *Social Transformation and the Family in Post-Communist Germany* (London, 1998), pp. 23–36, here p. 31.

94 Kolinsky, 'Women after *Muttipolitik*', p. 179.

95 *Ibid.*, p. 180.

96 On what follows, see *ibid.*, pp. 188–91.

97 D. Dodds and P. Allen-Thompson, eds, *The Wall in my Backyard: East German Women in Transition* (Amherst, 1994), a collection of interviews of 18 East German women, is a useful source on the impact of the reunification.

98 Kolinsky, 'Women after *Muttipolitik*', p. 194.

99 On changes in the post-reunification era, see E. Kolinsky 'The Family Transformed: Structures, Experiences, Prospects', in Kolinsky, ed., *Social Transformation and the Family*, pp. 207–17.

100 See Pine, *Nazi Family Policy*, p. 182.

101 Frevert, *Women in German History*, p. 320.

102 Mitterauer and Sieder, *The European Family*, p. 21.

103 For a recent survey of women and the family in Germany, see E. Kolinsky, 'Women in the New Germany', in G. Smith, W. Paterson, and S. Padgett, eds, *Developments in German Politics*, 2 (London, 1996), pp. 267–85.

12

Anthropometrics, consumption, and leisure: the standard of living[1]

JÖRG BATEN
University of Tübingen

12.1 What does the 'standard of living' mean for human beings?

A nineteenth-century Bavarian day-labourer had two dreams: a wonderful meal with as much butter as he could eat and enough income to be able to marry. In 1979, while a successful architect in Dresden was bored of travelling to the Black Sea and had a desire to see southern France, his colleague in Hamburg just wanted to live without the fear of becoming unemployed. A First World War soldier from North Friesia equated standard of living with coming home without major injuries, while an Italian construction worker living in Karlsruhe in 1893 cherished the dream of buying a brick factory back home and becoming an entrepreneur with a high income. A higher standard of living is what all of these Germans wanted.

These imaginary individuals – drawn from certain stereotypes of nineteenth- and twentieth-century German history – all shared a common bundle of aspirations: a high income, a long and healthy life, good nutrition. But each individual placed special weight on different components of this bundle: the right to marry, the ability to travel, job security, life expectancy, nutrition and health, income and social status.[2] This multidimensionality of human preferences means that there is a large number of possible ways to assess people's quality of life. The relevant components and indicators can be broken down as follows.

Incomes and prices: real income (i.e. income adjusted for changes in the value of currency) reflects differences in purchasing power across time periods, geographical units, and social strata. Measured in terms of indicators such as per capita gross domestic product (GDP) or real wages, it is the most commonly used indicator of living standards.

Life expectancy: in many ways complementary to the income approach to standards of living, measuring life expectancy at birth (or at later ages) provides an indication about average health and longevity. A high income is certainly of much lower value if individuals do not have the time to spend it.

Education: the ability to read and write, and more sophisticated aspects of educational attainment, may enable people to lead more fulfilled lives. Education also often implies an ability to improve one's purchasing power in the future.

Income inequality: as people often do not value their income in absolute terms, but rather relative to what they regard as a possible income, perceived living standards are often affected by income inequality. Strong deviations between actual purchasing power and perceived poverty are quite common. To illustrate this, Amartya Sen has cited the example of the American definition of the poverty line during the 1980s, which was still 50 times higher than the average income in India at the same period.[3]

Social status: another relative measure of living standards in a society is social status. The happiness of certain social groups is decided not only by purchasing power, but also by the way in which the rest of society values their social status.

Leisure: the number of working hours per day or per lifetime is an important component of the standard of living, particularly when one considers such historical phenomena as the enormously long working days of children in nineteenth-century factories.

Other components: there is a large number of additional components of living standards, such as freedom of individual choice, political freedom, and the opportunity to buy certain products. These can be among the hardest aspects of living standards to measure and assess.

This multidimensionality of human welfare cannot be fully captured in a concise survey of two centuries of German living standards.[4] This chapter therefore adopts the strategy of identifying a primary indicator that is measurable over the entire time period, and then comparing the other components of living standards with this indicator. This primary indicator cannot be real GDP per capita, because this has not yet been estimated in a reliable way for the first third of the time period under consideration. In addition, German national income estimates for the period before 1945 are still heavily disputed (see Figure 12.1 for the most widely cited series).[5] Somewhat more reliable for the early period are real wage estimates, although these suffer from a lack of information about underemployment and other factors. Life expectancy has been estimated for a number of villages and regions, but not for Germany as a whole (as discussed in Chapter 2).[6] Information on educational attainment, leisure and income inequality is still scarce and scattered. We will discuss some of the available information below, but none of these measures of living standards is avail-

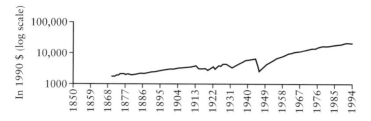

Fig. 12.1 GDP per capita in Germany, 1850–1995

Source: Maddison, *Monitoring*, pp. 194–5.

able for Germany over the entire period we are interested in. There is one measure, however, which does not suffer from these disadvantages: human stature.

Recent research has devoted a great deal of attention to studying human stature as an index of the standard of living. The rationale behind this project is that if a large enough number of individuals is studied, individual genetic determinants average out, and the average height of a population reflects the standard of living that population experienced: above all the quantity and quality of nutrition it enjoyed, but also its disease environment, and the physical exertion demanded from it because of its workload. This indicator has the important advantage that it is available for Germany over the last two centuries at a low level of regional aggregation and for social strata whose income is normally unknown: housewives, noblemen, subsistence-oriented peasants, and many others.

Height is strongly influenced by nutrition, and nutrition in turn is a good indicator of various aspects of the standard of living. The quantity and quality of nutrition is mostly determined by income, or, more precisely, by consumption. Two-thirds of consumption was spent on food in nineteenth-century German lower-class households, and this proportion was still as high as 50 per cent in Germany in the 1950s.[7] Nutrition itself influences health and longevity.[8] Under-nourishment is also held to be associated with poor development of children's intellectual and motor skills, so that in some situations height may also be correlated with educational attainment.[9]

Thus the height of a population can be thought of as a proxy index for several components of that population's living standards. Admittedly, by comparison with other indices such as the Human Development Index[10] (HDI) proposed by the United Nations, the weighting of the different factors contributing to the height variable is not fully clear, because of the complicated and time-variant biological processes that lead to the average stature of a population. But in combination with other indices of living standards, height can provide valuable insights into the development of human well-being in a society.

Particularly interesting are the time periods when biological indicators (height and mortality) and purchasing-power indicators (income and prices) diverge from one another. In an international context, the divergence between heights and real wages in both Britain and America in the 1820–40 period has attracted a great deal of interest. In this chapter, we will see that biological indicators and purchasing-power indicators diverged in Germany during the Nazi period. During this period of rising incomes in Germany, there was an anthropometric decline, and this has caused historians to revise their estimates of what was happening to living standards in Nazi Germany.[11]

In this chapter, we will therefore use human heights as a central indicator for assessing the standard of living in Germany over the past two centuries, but will also combine it with other measures of living standards where these are available. Furthermore, we will see how the evidence on Germany contributes to our wider understanding of what is actually measured by different indicators of living standards.

12.2 The early nineteenth century: the German agrarian reforms

In the early nineteenth century, Germany was unambiguously an agrarian economy, as discussed in Chapter 3. While the share of agriculture in the British economy had declined to 22 per cent by that date, the corresponding figure for Germany was still 56 per cent.[12] Not surprisingly, the most important debate about living standards in early nineteenth-century Germany focuses on an agricultural question: the influence on living standards of the agrarian reforms (often called the *Bauernbefreiung* or 'emancipation of the peasants'). These reforms profoundly changed the social relations and the economic system experienced by the majority of the German population that still worked in agriculture. The abolition of serfdom (*Leibeigenschaft*) and of feudal obligations intensified the trend towards a 'capitalist' agriculture in Germany.

As Georg Friedrich Knapp famously argued in 1887, this change in property rights and labour relations increased the productivity of the German agricultural sector, but only at the cost of widespread rural impoverishment.[13] In Prussia, those peasants who enjoyed better property rights had to make redemption payments – often one-third to one-half of a peasant's plot was transferred to the large land-owner (the *Junker*). Knapp also reported that the peasants with inferior property rights often lost their farms outright, becoming wage-labourers on the holdings of the large landowners.[14] The pauperization of the German rural lower classes, particularly around the mid-nineteenth century, is regarded by many historians as having been a result of this development.[15]

Other authors have criticized this view. Friedrich-Wilhelm Henning, for instance, argues that while the Prussian peasants lost a significant portion of their previous plots, they gained a similar magnitude of property from the division of the commons.[16] The net effect was that the *Junker* received this portion of the arable land. The poorer peasants who had depended on using the commons were the group that experienced particularly hard times after the agrarian reforms. Knut Borchardt notes that scarcity of land may not have been the greatest problem facing agriculture in East Prussia, since it proved possible to expand the total arable land area by a considerable amount between the early and mid-nineteenth century.[17] Hans-Ulrich Wehler stresses the importance of missing credit opportunities for the smaller farmers, although they were still able to survive as a social class and to improve their productivity.[18]

The second hypothesized effect, the development of a rural proletariat, has been ascribed by Robert Dickler not to the agrarian reforms, but rather to the long-run development towards capitalistic agriculture in Germany, which had already started in the eighteenth century.[19] It must be recognized that the historiographical tradition attributing a large share of the responsibility for rural proletarianization to the agrarian reforms may not be free of ideology. The powerful political role of the East-Elbian *Junkers* from the late nineteenth century through to the Nazi period created an incentive for liberal and left-wing German economists to portray them as having robbed peasants of their land. Later economic historians of the German Democratic Republic (GDR) emphasized this point so as to help legitimate the collectivization of agriculture in East Germany.

The discussion that follows will begin by considering the timing of the agrarian reforms and some theoretical issues concerning them. It will then assess empirically how the different types of agrarian reform in selected regions of Germany affected measures of living standards in these regions.

In Prussia, one of the main events of the *Bauernbefreiung* consisted of the *Preußische Reformen* of 1807 and 1811, whose aim was to clarify labour relations and the question of serfdom. In Prussia, the period of greatest change in agrarian regions was the 1820s.[20] In the south German territories of Bavaria and Württemberg, by contrast, agrarian reform occurred much later, with the most important reforms beginning only after the revolutions of 1848. Saxony initiated its agrarian reforms during the 1830s, and gained a reputation for implementing them without major disadvantages for its farmers. Matters were similar in Hannover and Baden, which started their reforms early, but completed them quite late. In these parts of Germany, financial institutions helped the farmers to pay their obligations, and only a very few farmers lost their farms.

These differences in timing were important. Because Prussia implemented most of its agrarian transformation during the 1820s and the decades that followed, the hunger crisis of the 1840s hit its land-poor and landless groups particularly hard.[21] Bavaria, Württemberg, and Baden had the additional advantage that their agrarian reforms were largely implemented after the mid-nineteenth century, a period during which no major hunger crisis occurred. In those territories, the famines of the mid-nineteenth century cannot be blamed on the agrarian reforms.

The ethical and legal issues surrounding the German agrarian reforms are almost impossible to judge without deciding certain political questions. First, was it actually necessary that the landlords be compensated for the loss of the feudal obligations (rents and labour services) which peasants owed them before the *Bauernbefreiung*? Second, if it was judged that the landlords did have to be compensated, then should the peasants pay the whole amount or should the state cover a certain share of the redemption payments, as the government of Baden did? If we follow the leading contemporary view that the feudal lords had to be compensated, a number of economic questions then arise: is it more efficient to impose a long-term obligation on farmers that has an effect similar to that of an additional tax, or to deprive farmers of part of their plots but leave them debt-free thereafter? The answers to these questions depend both on the initial productivity of farms and the initial wealth of the peasants, and on the optimal size and structure of farm for the predominant types of agricultural production.

According to Dickler, the long-run trend was in any case towards larger farms with the organizational capabilities for exporting grain. If producing grain and exporting it along the large East-Elbian rivers was the most productive option, then in principle the *Junkers* should have been able to pay relatively high wages. A reasonable income distribution might have generated a higher income for all than an alternative agrarian economy with many small-sized plots. However, the political system in Prussia prevented trades unions from struggling for higher wages for workers. Indeed, the agrarian reforms may have helped to stabilize the *Junker* stratum, and these large landowners certainly prevented political change and increased government spending on education. The implication would be that the agrarian reforms could have reduced the level of education indirectly. These indirect sociopolitical results of the agrarian reforms were arguably their greatest disadvantage.

Furthermore, it must be recognized that Dickler's view that large-scale export-oriented agriculture was more efficient applied only to the period before the 1870s. When Knapp wrote his influential study in the 1880s, the capitalist East-Elbian system was once again in crisis, owing to the fact that new transportation technologies were now permitting large-scale grain imports from the New World and eastern Europe. During this 'European grain invasion', the western and northern German agricultural regions which specialized in meat and dairy products did much better than the eastern German regions which specialized in grain.[22]

Is it possible to test the effects of the reforms empirically? While a comparison between Prussia and the other states would be appealing, the difference in the timing of the reforms between different German territories means that such comparisons have only limited reliability. Too many other factors changed between the early reforms in Prussia and the comparatively late reforms in the other German territories.

However, the evidence that we do have does not support the Knapp thesis. Saxony, with its reputation for mild agrarian reforms, certainly did not perform well on living standards during the nineteenth century. Nutritional status in Saxony was among the worst in Germany (as can also be seen from Map 12.3),[23] mortality rates were above average, and income inequality was high, as a relatively high income per capita contrasted with low wage-rates.[24]

In late-reforming Bavaria, available evidence on the development of living-standard indicators suggests stagnation. People's heights were not increasing between the 1820s and the mid-nineteenth century, and real

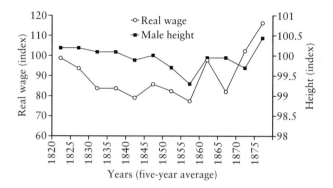

Fig. 12.2a Male heights and real wages in Bavaria (nineteenth century)

Source: Baten, *Ernährung*, p. 97.

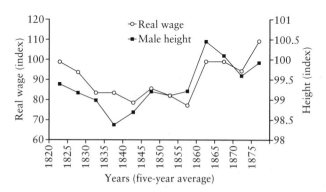

Fig. 12.2b Female heights and real wages in Bavaria (nineteenth century)

Source: Baten, *Ernährung*, p. 96.

wages were actually declining (as shown in Figures 12.2a and 12.2b). Mortality rates actually increased in the 1840s. Finally, inequality both in nutritional status and in wealth[25] significantly increased in Bavaria between the early and mid-nineteenth century (as can be seen from Figure 12.3). While farmers were more or less able to keep their height advantage between 1815–19 and 1835–39, unskilled day-labourers lost 2 centimetres in height. This evidence suggests that the adversity of the mid-nineteenth-century crisis, which Knapp attributed to the agrarian reforms, also manifested itself in Bavaria, a territory which did not really start its agrarian reforms before mid-century.

One opportunity for direct comparison is provided by the differences in agrarian reforms within Prussia, which can be categorized on a scale from 'mild' to 'harsh' according to how much land the peasants lost. In the eastern province of Prussia (which must be distinguished from the whole Kingdom of Prussia), peasants had previously mostly been 'owned' by the state, which treated them relatively mildly; consequently, the agrarian reform observed in this province can be labelled 'mild'. In the eastern provinces of Posen and Pomerania, by contrast, peasants lost a particularly high share of their previous plots or became dependent agricultural workers; thus the agrarian reforms here must be labelled 'harsh'.[26] In addition, many farmers in the western provinces of the Kingdom of Prussia – the Rhineland, Westphalia, the province of Saxony, and even Brandenburg – were rich enough to redeem

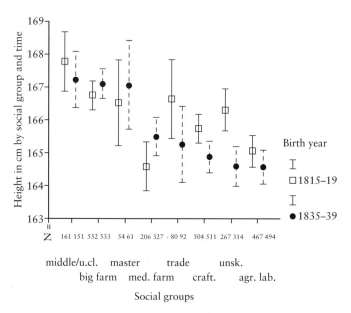

Fig. 12.3 Height inequality in Bavaria, 1815–39

Source: Baten, *Ernährung*, p. 163.

their feudal obligations with a lump-sum payment or had favourable property rights. These differences were caused by the initial agrarian setting in these provinces, rather than by government policy, but the agrarian reforms in these areas can still be categorized as 'mild', since peasants lost their land to a much lesser extent. In Silesia, by contrast, farmers were hit hard by the reforms.

If we can devise measures of living standards for these different provinces of the Kingdom of Prussia, then we can see whether the mildness or harshness of the agrarian reforms had any significant impact on standards of living. How can we measure changes in living standards across regions of Prussia? Attempts to quantify regional living standards in Prussia before 1900 always depend on proxy indicators, because the available data are scarce.

Knut Borchardt estimated regional living standards by measuring the numbers of physicians, assuming a constant elasticity of people's demand for medical services over time and across regions; these figures are shown in Table 12.1, columns 5 and 6.[27] His main finding was that regional living-standard differentials in Prussia remained constant over time, with only Silesia declining from a middle to a low position, while the Rhineland improved its position.

Gerd Hohorst constructed income estimates by assuming that the correlation between the share of agriculture in the economy and income in 1913 (and between the number of cattle per capita and income) remained constant over time; these figures are shown in Table 12.1, columns 3 and 4.[28] Because Silesia, for example, had a large industrial population, its income was estimated as being relatively high. Indeed, it might have been overestimated, given that productivity and wages were much lower in Silesia than in the western districts.[29] A greater reliability may be attributed to Hohorst's estimated changes over time: according to his calculations, Silesian industry stagnated whereas the Rhenish economy expanded rapidly.

Another way of measuring living standards across different Prussian regions is by examining changes in people's heights. We can obtain an anthropometric record for Prussia from the proportion of conscripts categorized as unfit because they did not meet the Prussian army's minimum height requirement; this information is shown in Table 12.1, columns 7 and 8. This indicator can be used to examine living standards during two stages of the agrarian reform process in Prussia. First, we have rejection rates of those conscripts measured immediately after the strongest wave of agrarian transformation in 1831. Second, we have rejection rates measured in 1854, during the mid-century period of nutritional crisis.[30]

It is important to distinguish between the more urban districts (such as Berlin, Danzig, Stettin, and Stralsund) and the more rural ones, as the effects of the agrarian reforms may have differed between urban and rural areas. Among the eastern rural districts, nutritional status in 1831 was worst in the provinces of Prussia and Posen, and better in Pomerania and

Table 12.1 Welfare indicators for Prussian provinces, 1831–65

(1)	(2)	(3)	(4)	(5)	(6)	(7)	(8)	(9)
		'Uncorrected' income		Physicians per capita		Malnutrition (rejection rate)		Pop. crises
Region	Reform type	Level, 1831	Growth, 1831–58	Rank 1825	Rank 1861	Level 1831	Change, 1831–54	No. per district 1817–65
Eastern rural districts								
Prussia	mild	88.1	1.9	9	8–9	26.3	4.8	9
Posen	harsh	98.9	-3.2	8	9	29.1	6.9	8
Pomerania	harsh	87.1	3.9	7	7	17.8	1.7	1
Brandenburg	mild	99.7	5.1	5	5	8.70	12.8	2
Eastern urban districts								
Prussia (Danzig)	mild			9	8–9	36.8	-13.7	9
Pomerania (Stettin/Strals.)	harsh			7	7	12.9	-3.4	3
Brandenburg (Berlin)	harsh			1	1	9.3	-7.3	9
Industrial and western								
Silesia	harsh	107.1	-0.9	4	6	25.2	3.4	5
Saxony	mild	105.2	2.1	2	2	10.7	7.8	2
Westphalia	mild	105.9	1.1	3	4	3.9	7.4	4
Rhineland	mild	107.9	21.3	6	3	9.6	11.4	2

Notes on columns:

(3) 'Uncorrected' income estimated by Hohorst, *Hungerkrisen*, p. 45, based on industrial share and cattle per capita (Prussian average = 100), see text. Urban districts are not separated out.

(4) Percentage growth from 1831 to 1858 (related to income in prices of 1913).

(5) Physicians per capita, the welfare indicator used by Borchardt, *Regionale*, rank in 1825: 1 = best, 9 = worst. Underlined numbers signify that regional aggregation is not fully congruent.

(7) Rejection rate for reasons of height in the Prussian military (an indicator for nutrition), level in 1831.

(8) Change in rejection rate between 1831 and 1854 (source: Baten, *Einfluß*).

(9) Number of population crisis years (for definition see text) per district (*Regierungsbezirk*), as estimated by Bass, *Hungerkrisen*.

Brandenburg. Thus both mild and harsh types of reform produced both high and low rejection rates on grounds of low height. This suggests strongly that agrarian reforms did not have any systematic influence on living standards. The same is true for increases in rejection rates between 1831 and 1854. There was less increase in the rural part of the province of Prussia than in the province of Posen, and much less increase than in the province of Brandenburg; however, the increase in rejection rates was higher in the province of Prussia than in Pomerania. Since both Posen and Pomerania followed the harsh type of *Bauernbefreiung*, again the agrarian reforms seem to have no systematic effect on living standards.

The rejection rates for these eastern provinces of the Kingdom of Prussia were enormously high, much higher than in the wealthier West. The western provinces of the kingdom were already doing better in the early period: thus, for example, Westphalia had only about 4 per cent rejected conscripts, the Rhineland only 10 per cent. Even though their rejection rates increased considerably between 1831 and 1854, their level remained lower than in the East: Westphalian rejection rates increased by 7 per cent, the Rhenish rates by 11 per cent. Interestingly, all districts with declining rejection rates contained the large urban trading centres of the East: nutritional status improved in urban Brandenburg (Berlin's rejection rate declined by 7 per cent), Prussia (Danzig's rate declined by 14 per cent), and Pomerania (Stettin's rate declined by 4 per cent, Stralsund's by 3 per cent). One could conjecture that this was because agricultural commercialization helped to improve urban food supplies. However, more research on the Prussian anthropometric record would be necessary to explore this possibility.

Another way of assessing living standards is by examining mortality rates. Hans-Heinrich Bass estimated the number of population crises between 1816 and 1859 by defining a 'crisis year' as a year in which population growth was more than 50 per cent below the long-run growth path; these figures are shown in Table 12.1, column 9.[31] It is possible that this procedure overestimates the number of crisis years in districts with rapidly growing populations (such as Berlin), since a higher total growth might imply higher variance. However, Bass's estimates are valid for comparisons among rural districts. Bass's results do not provide support for the Knapp thesis that the agrarian reforms were responsible for the crisis in living standards in Germany around the middle of the nineteenth century: in the province of Prussia with its milder agrarian reforms, the number of population crises was higher than in the districts with harsher reforms. Pomerania actually did best in this respect, even better than the western provinces of the Kingdom of Prussia, in spite of its rapid population growth.[32]

What can we conclude about the effect of the nineteenth-century German agrarian reforms on living standards? Knapp argued that the agrarian reforms caused considerable economic hardship around the middle of the nineteenth century. However, indicators of mortality and nutritional living standards do not support Knapp's argument. The agrarian reforms were milder in the western provinces of the Kingdom of Prussia, but this part of the Kingdom was already doing better from the beginning, as far as living standards were concerned. Among the eastern provinces of Prussia, it is impossible to detect any systematic effect of the agrarian reforms on living standard indicators. However, the long-run impact of the Prussian type of agrarian reform may still have been substantial, given that it probably helped to stabilize the power of the large landowners – although, as Henning pointed out, many formerly feudal Prussian estates were actually bought by the increasingly wealthy industrialists.[33]

12.3 Industrial development and German living standards in the late nineteenth century

The nineteenth century saw increasing structural change in the German economy, as it shifted from agriculture to industry. During the 1860s, this structural change accelerated: the large German industrial cities began to attract large-scale migration, and by the eve of the First World War Germany had become an industrial nation.[34] The debate on German living standards during this period of time focuses on the effects of industrial development. Similar to the 'pessimist' views about living standards during the British industrial revolution, many German historians have argued that industrialization created the so-called *Soziale Frage* ('social question'). This was the question of whether the dividends from rapid industrial development were so unequally distributed across German society that working-class living standards failed to improve for the first two or three generations.

Would we expect industrialization to have been good or bad for late nineteenth-century Germans? On the one hand we would expect there to have been higher wages and incomes in industry (the 'modern' sector) during an economic transformation. The modern sector has to pay higher wages to attract workers from the traditional sector, and as industrial production was more capital-intensive, its labour productivity was higher. On the other hand, public health might have been worse in the newly emerging, rapidly urbanizing centres of industrial activity. Given the low level of nineteenth-century medical knowledge, higher incomes might not have translated into better health (as discussed in Chapter 2). Furthermore, as Smits and van Zanden have recently warned us, the productivity gap between industry and agriculture in the twentieth century does not automatically apply to the nineteenth century or earlier: in the Netherlands, for example, agricultural productivity was higher than industrial productivity as late as 1850.[35]

To answer the question of how industrialization affected German living standards, let us begin by comparing the level of industrialization in different German regions with several indicators of living standards in these regions at one particular time. Later we will turn our attention to the development of German living standards over time.

A good proxy for measuring how industrialized a region was is by measuring how low a share of its population still worked in agriculture. According to this proxy measure, as Map 12.1 shows, the most industrialized German regions in the early nineteenth century were located in Saxony, the Rhineland, and Westphalia.[36] The core Saxon industrial region was surrounded by a larger industrial region extending between Breslau in Silesia, Hildesheim, and Potsdam. The most agricultural regions were those at the eastern frontiers of Germany, in southern Germany, and in the north-west of Germany between Münster and Mecklenburg. This regional structure did not change much in the following century, as similar maps for 1895, 1925, and 1939 would show.

How do these differences in industrialization across German regions compare with their mortality experience in the nineteenth century? As can be seen from Map 12.2, mortality appears to be negatively correlated with industrialization across Germany: the larger the share of industry in a region's economy, the lower the mortality rate.[37] It seems possible that the percentage of the population working in industry was positively correlated with per capita income, as was certainly the case in the early twentieth century.[38] It appears that the higher incomes in industry were sufficient to allow a better provision of nutrition and health-related resources. The most deadly regions were the agrarian east and south of Germany, whereas the industrial regions of Germany did relatively well, including such heavily industrialized districts as Arnsberg, Düsseldorf, and Wiesbaden. An exception to this rule was Saxony, particularly Leipzig and Zwickau, which had above-average mortality rates.

Another exception to the generally deadly effect of agriculture on living standards is provided by north-western agricultural regions such as Aurich or Schleswig, which ranked at the top in terms of life expectancy. However, this was probably because they specialized in cattle-farming which was a profitable business during this period of time (in regions close enough to urban markets), and because the inhabitants of those regions also had direct nutritional advantages: living in a cattle-farming area allowed cheaper access to protein, as milk was not easy to transport. In addition, as Robert Lee argues, it was the labour-intensity of grain production in particular that led women to neglect breastfeeding of their children.[39] Thus the difference between agricultural regions specializing in grain production and those specializing in cattle farming explains some of the remaining differences in mortality, and statistical tests support this view.[40]

Protein availability is also reflected in the height of military recruits, as can be seen from Map 12.3. Saxony, the earliest and most rigorously industrialized German state with a low protein production per capita, had very short recruits. Similar levels of malnutrition occurred in Silesia and the

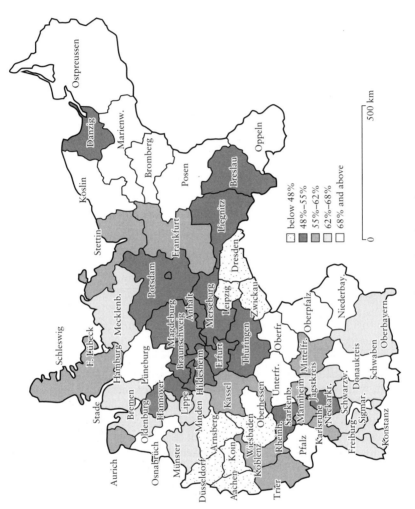

Map 12.1 Share of agricultural population in 1849

Source: Baten, *Ernährung*, p. 163.

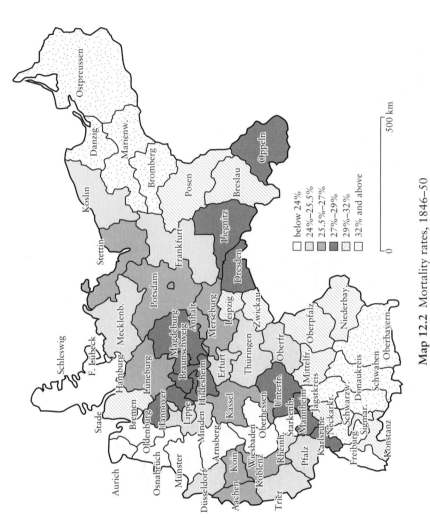

Map 12.2 Mortality rates, 1846–50

Source: Frank, *Regionale*, Data Appendix.

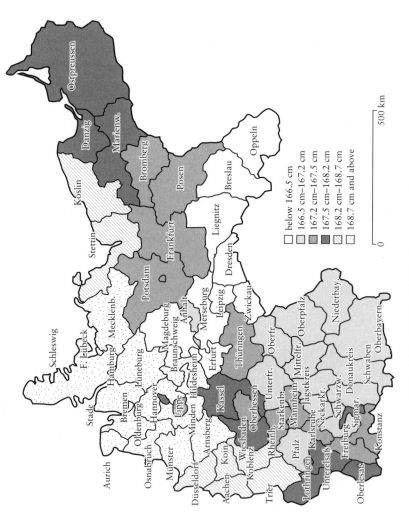

Map 12.3 Male height in German provinces, 1906

Source: Evert, E., 'Körpergröße der Militärpersonen', *Zeitschrift des Königlich Preußischen Statistischen Bureaus*, Ergänzungsheft, 28 (1908), pp. 154–7.

Prussian province of Saxony (especially in Magdeburg, Erfurt, and Merseburg). Westphalia, the famous late-developing industrial centre of iron, steel, and coal, had tall recruits. The agricultural extremes are found in the favourable nutritional experience of the German north-west, and in the malnutrition of agricultural Bavaria and the Prussian north-east.

How do these results compare with other indicators of living standards? The few available data on educational attainment confirm the East–West differences in living standards across Germany. In 1841 literacy rates were as high as 93–8 per cent in the west of the Kingdom of Prussia. But at the eastern edge of Prussia, Polish-speakers had much lower rates: in Posen literacy was only 59 per cent.[41] Again an exception, Saxony already achieved a literacy rate of 98.8 per cent in the 1840s, whereas both its nutrition and life expectancy records were clearly below average throughout the nineteenth century.[42]

Another relevant living standard component is the quality of housing. However, while some data are available on urban housing (which was miserable for workers during the 1860s and afterwards slightly improved), we have almost no quantitative information on rural housing.[43]

A somewhat different picture emerges if we consider changes over time instead of levels. Harald Frank argued that the rapid development of industry in the Ruhr region caused its mortality to increase during the 1860s and early 1870s.[44] Was this true? We can test this by defining rapidity of industrialization in terms of the growth rate in the share of industrial occupations in a region between 1849 and 1882. Those regions with a rapid increase in non-agricultural occupations (more than 10 per cent) can be distinguished from a medium group and from the slow industrializers with 5 per cent or less increase (as shown in Figure 12.4). Between 1859–65 and 1872–75, mortality rates were indeed increasing most strongly in the regions that industrialized most rapidly, whereas the slow industrializers did not experience much increase in mortality between those early periods. But in later periods, the rapidly industrializing regions did better: as early as 1879–82 the mortality rates of rapidly industrializing regions were lower than those of slowly industrializing regions, and this trend continued until 1925–28.[45] The short period of higher mortality in the rapidly industrializing regions in the 1870s can probably be attributed to diseases that spread more easily in large industrial towns, such as cholera, typhus, and tuberculosis.[46] The Franco-Prussian war of 1870/1 caused additional mortality-related stress.

This period of disproportionate mortality in rapidly industrializing regions was relatively short in Germany, especially compared with Britain. To some extent, this can be ascribed to timing. The difficult nutritional situation in late eighteenth- and early nineteenth-century Europe that supports the 'pessimist' view of the British Industrial Revolution affected the German industrial regions much less, because they were relatively small at that time. When German industrialization accelerated in the 1860s and in the final decades of the nineteenth century, food supply was generally much

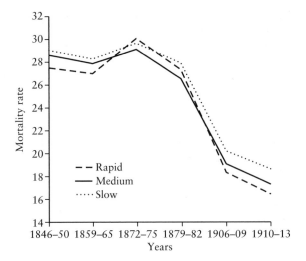

Fig. 12.4 Mortality rates in German districts, 1846–
1913, by rate of industrialization (1849–82)

Source: Frank, *Regionale*, Data Appendix.

less of a problem in Europe, as agricultural and transport technology were
more advanced.

Of course, this does not mean that rapid economic development put no
pressure on German people in the nineteenth century. The enormously long
working hours must have had terrible effects, and they also applied to
children. Table 12.2 presents some of the scarce quantitative evidence we
have on nineteenth-century working hours. Meinert estimated an incredible
80-hour working week in industry for the period around 1860. However,
Gömmel's estimate for Nuremberg of a 65-hour working week was probably
closer to the truth. During the late nineteenth century, the working week
declined, reaching 57 hours in 1910/14, creating more leisure for German
workers. This downward trend continued steadily, but at a slower rate,
during the twentieth century, except (as we shall see below) during the Nazi
period.[47] The enormous increase in leisure during the twentieth century is
certainly a major component in increased German living standards.

It can be concluded that the German industrial development of the 1850s
and 1860s led to deterioration in some components of living standards.
However, as early as the 1860s, the situation was already gradually starting
to improve. If we consider the development over time of height and life
expectancy, the decades of rapid German industrialization from the 1860s to
the end of the century can be characterized as a period of progress. Even in
rural Bavaria, the 1860s were the turning point after many decades of height
stagnation and real wage decline (Figures 12.2a and 12.2b), especially for
lower-class women. This corresponds to the fact that during the 1860s life

Table 12.2 Weekly working hours in German industry, alternative estimates, 1811–1989

Period	Gömmel	Meinert*
1811	61.1	
1821	61.1	
1835	62.1	
1845	61.9	
1850	63.5	
1860	64.8	80–85 (1830/60)
1870	66.5	78 (1860/1870)
1880	64.3	72 (1875/1880)
1890	62.5	66 (1885/1890)
1900	58.4	62 (1895/1900)
1913	55.0	57 (1910/14)
1919/23		48
1925		50.5
1929		46
1932		41.5
1935		44.5
1939		48.5
1944		48.5
1950		48
1959		45.5
1970		40
1989		38.6

Note: * 1970 and 1989 from Pohl, *Lebensarbeitszeit*, pp. 21–2.
Sources: Gömmel, *Wachstum* (refers to Nuremberg); Meinert, *Entwicklung* (cited in Hoffmann, *Wachstum*, pp. 213–14).

expectancy at age 20 increased significantly, and women in particular enjoyed for the first time their natural longevity advantage over men (as can be seen from Figure 12.5). In a similar vein, Sophia Twarog has found that male heights in Württemberg increased between the early 1850s and the 1860s, and also increased around 1890.[48] German life expectancy started to rise continuously in the last decades of the nineteenth century.

In conclusion, German industrial development – in spite of some major drawbacks arising from long working hours and urban crowding – had relatively few and transitory adverse effects on health and living standards, at least if one compares it with the situation in the agricultural regions of Germany. The correlation between the share of the population that was industrial and the level of mortality among German regions was negative around 1850 and again around 1913, probably because the industrial regions had a higher income. Yet, as we have seen, the agricultural regions themselves were far from homogeneous. Significant differences in nutrition, health, and income can be found between the north-western regions specializing in protein production, and the eastern and south-eastern regions which were growing the major share of Germany's starches.

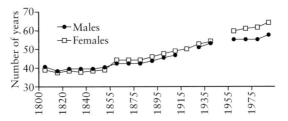

Fig. 12.5 Remaining life expectancy at age 20 in Germany (periods after the Second World War, Federal Republic of Germany)

Source: Imhof, *Lebenserwartungen*, pp. 409–10.

12.4 Times of war, times of uncertainty

12.4.1 *The First World War*

War, hunger, and pestilence have always accompanied one another. Military blockades create hunger, so they have often been used to weaken the military power of the enemy. Plagues follow famines and often reinforce the shortage of foodstuffs. In 1916/17, however, when hunger returned to Germany, it still came as a shock to the population, because the preceding three decades had seen an enormous and unprecedented degree of economic development: food shortages seemed to have been banished forever. Even supplies of the scarcest foodstuff of the nineteenth century, animal protein, had increased substantially during the period leading up to the First World War in Germany. Between the early 1890s and 1913, the per capita supply of animal protein in Germany increased by about 26 per cent, from 47 to 59 grams per person per day.[49] These absolute numbers must not be directly compared with today's nutritional recommendations. The disease environment, housing situation, and hard physical work characteristic of Germany around 1900 would have required a much higher nutrient input to achieve the net nutritional status characteristic of modern Germans. However, the improvements before the First World War were substantial, and the hope of having abolished hunger was ubiquitous throughout Germany. It was rapidly destroyed by the initiators of the First World War.

It has been argued that Germany lost the war mainly because it was short of food.[50] This argument has recently been closely re-examined by Avner Offer. Before the war, Germany imported 19 per cent of its caloric consumption and 27 per cent of its proteins. As the Allied forces succeeded in suppressing most of Germany's food imports during the war, animal protein in particular became a major problem. The same amount of inputs allocated to producing beef yields only 12–20 per cent of the calories and protein one obtains if those same inputs are allocated to producing grain.

Pork was slightly more efficient than beef, but still produced a caloric content less than 50 per cent that of grain.

For this reason, in 1914/15, a German government commission decided to commit the enormous *Schweinemord* (literally 'pig-murder'). Between August 1914 and April 1915, one-third of the German swine herd was slaughtered. This led to an increase in grain production. However, since the government commission did not have sufficient storage capacity for the additional grain, it had to leave the grain lying on the farms. Since meat prices were rising, many farmers decided to feed the grain to their remaining pigs, and about one-third of the civilian grain ration 'disappeared', as Offer put it.

The large German cities – which were growing during the war as the war industries attracted more and more workers – suffered particularly severely from serious food shortages, and the large port cities such as Hamburg and Bremen were not able to import their foodstuffs as they had previously. But in spite of these enormous problems, Offer concludes that the German population was not really starving during the First World War. Calories were still available in sufficient amounts, except in the winter of 1916/17 and the summer of 1918. It was mainly animal protein that was missing.[51]

Another way of measuring the impact of the famine and epidemics that occurred in Germany during the First World War is by examining changes in people's heights. In Stuttgart, the heights of schoolchildren were measured annually from 1911 onwards in massive numbers; this information is shown in Figure 12.6. These data derive from a relatively large industrial city, where one would expect the sensitivity of heights to changes in nutrition to be greater than in the countryside or in smaller towns. All the series observed in Stuttgart declined during the war years. This suggests serious declines in living standards, since in the twentieth century even stagnation in heights must be regarded as an indication of nutritional problems, given the more or less continuous increase in the knowledge of hygiene and the quality of medical care[52] during this century.[53] The heights of the youngest Stuttgart girls reached their lowest point in 1917, and those of 8- and 9-year-old girls were lowest in 1918. The heights of Stuttgart boys reached their lowest points in 1918 and 1919. This different chronology between boys and girls is too small to be interpreted as indicating differential treatment of sexes, but we would not want to leave the possibility unmentioned. More research on twentieth-century height data is clearly a desideratum.

Heights of growing individuals are affected most strongly in the year following the nutritional insult.[54] Therefore, the Stuttgart height records confirm the chronology provided by other sources: the winter of 1916/17 and the summer 1918 were the worst years of the century in terms of German nutritional status.[55] If we assume that the distribution of proteins between children – on which we have data – and adults was not completely different from what it was in the prewar period, our data support the view that nutritional problems must have contributed heavily to dissatisfaction within the German population during the later war years.[56]

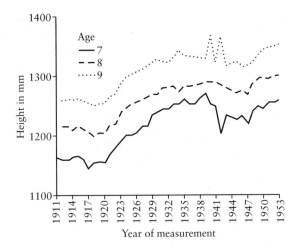

Fig. 12.6a Height of Stuttgart girls, 1911–53

Source: Tanner, J. M., *Foetus into Man: Physical Growth from Conception to Maternity*, 2nd edn (Cambridge, MA, 1990), p. 130.

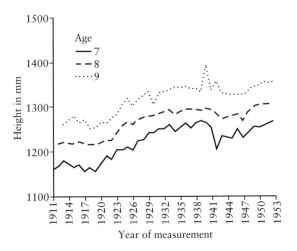

Fig. 12.6b Height of Stuttgart boys, 1911–53

Source: Tanner, *Foetus into Man*, p. 130.

12.4.2 *The Weimar years and the world economic crisis*

The Weimar years are notorious for the unstable development of the German economy, as shown in Figure 12.1. The inflation and hyperinflation posed major problems during the years up to 1923/4, despite the fact that a certain amount of success in exports was achieved during the milder inflation years of 1920/1. The late 1920s have been characterized by Borchardt as 'crisis before the crisis', indicating a very unstable development of the German economy. Then 1930–33 saw the World Economic Crisis, which was far more severe in Germany than in any other country.[57]

One of Borchardt's most hotly debated arguments is that of the 'profit squeeze'. According to Borchardt, the political situation in Germany during the Weimar years led to a major redistribution of income in favour of the workers and the government. This left little profit for entrepreneurs, which meant they had little ability or incentive to invest.[58]

Workers gained not only in terms of income, but also in terms of leisure, as can be seen in Table 12.2. At a period during which the German government perpetually claimed to be unable to pay war reparations, nevertheless there occurred considerable expenditure on infrastructure and especially dwelling houses for workers, as discussed in Chapter 7. This led to improved housing conditions – especially for the poorer sections of society – and improved hygiene, as many densely populated parts of cities were connected to sanitary systems for the first time. On the other hand, the 'profit squeeze' led during the late-1920s to a high level of structural unemployment – even before the World Economic Crisis – and this caused a decline in living standards for those people who were seeking jobs.[59]

This means that our expectations with regard to German living standards during this period are ambiguous. As the poorest sections of the population influence the record of living standards particularly strongly, one might expect to observe a stagnation due to unemployment and uncertain future prospects. On the other hand, redistribution policies might imply increasing living standards, if there was enough income to be redistributed.

What light is shed on these theoretical considerations by the data on German heights in this period? In large industrial towns such as Stuttgart and Leipzig, heights in fact increased dramatically during the Weimar period, as can be seen in Figures 12.6 and 12.7. After recovering their prewar levels around 1921, heights grew very strongly until around 1931.[60] After that, during the economic crisis, they continued to increase modestly in Stuttgart, although little, if at all, in Leipzig. Between 1919 and 1930, the increase in Leipzig heights was 6.7 centimetres. In the same period, the increase in Stuttgart heights was 8.4 centimetres for girls and 8.7 centimetres for boys. Admittedly, children's heights are more sensitive to changes in the environment than adult heights, because not only the level but also the speed of growth increases. Nevertheless, the contribution of the Weimar years to the overall twentieth-century height increase in Germany was enormous.

This amazing increase in human stature in Germany during the Weimar period is mirrored in household surveys. Reinhard Spree found that Germans' consumption of starches, especially potatoes, decreased between 1907 and 1927/8, whereas their consumption of protein-rich meat (and of

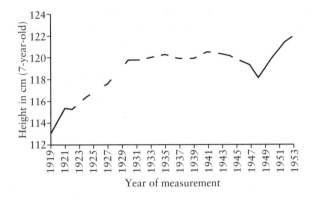

Fig. 12.7 Heights of Leipzig schoolchildren, 1919–53

Source: Hilda Marcusson, *Das Wachstum von Kindern und Jugendlichen in der Deutschen Demokratischen Republik* (Berlin, 1961), p. 13.

sugar) increased.[61] The largest part of this increase and the greatest improvement in quality probably took place during the middle Weimar years.

During the economic crisis of 1930–33, Stuttgart schoolchildren continued to become taller, while those of Leipzig did not.[62] The Stuttgart development is somewhat puzzling, because weekly real earnings decreased by 15 per cent between 1929 and 1932, and total per capita production fell by 22 per cent; these national data are shown in Figure 12.1.[63] On the other hand, an economic rule called 'Engel's law' tells us that such an economic crisis tends to reduce basic consumption much less than luxuries. Before the economic crisis of 1930–33, German workers were already consuming quite a few 'luxury' items. This meant that their first response to the crisis would have been to cut back on these luxuries long before they reduced basic consumption. When we examine aggregate consumption estimates during this period in Germany, animal protein consumption fell only slightly, by about 1 gram per day, or 1.5 per cent (as can be seen in Table 12.2). If we take into account that probably less protein was wasted or fed to animals during the crisis years, the modest height increase in Stuttgart is not implausible.

Compared with Leipzig, the disamenities of the economic crisis in Stuttgart were relatively modest, because entrepreneurs there tried to keep their staff as long as possible. The new automobile companies and other modern industries of the Neckar area required large investments in workers' human capital (mainly their skills) which would have been lost if employers let them go.[64] In the more traditionally structured industrial area around Leipzig, where people's heights more or less stagnated during the crisis, unemployment figures were much higher, suggesting a higher vulnerability of this area.[65]

Another interesting finding in this context is that the composition of animal protein consumed by Germans changed considerably in this period.

Cheaper, but more nutritious, dairy products were consumed instead of meat (as can be seen from Table 12.2, column 2). The percentage of meat proteins consumed by the average German fell by 1.5 per cent between 1929 and 1932/33.

Another interesting finding is that, according to the estimates of Hoffmann, expenditure on medical services continued to increase during the economic crisis of 1930/33.[66] Total expenditures on physicians in Germany increased dramatically during the late 1920s and continued to increase during the crisis years, from 766 million marks in 1930 (prices of 1913) to 790 million marks in 1932 and 803 million marks in 1933.[67] This figure is based solely on the number of physicians, and thus does not even capture the technological progress that probably increased productivity of medical care in this period.

Interestingly, aggregate national mortality rates were declining during the Weimar years *and* during the World Economic Crisis, reaching their lowest point in 1932, but then rising somewhat during the early years of National Socialism (as can be seen from Figure 12.8).[68] The increase in German mortality between 1932 and 1935 or 1937 was visible in nearly all age groups. According to Spree, German male life expectancy decreased between 1932 and 1938.[69]

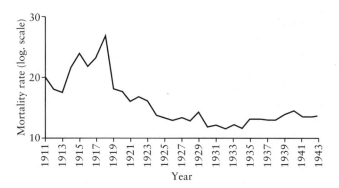

Fig. 12.8 Death rates in Germany (military losses excluded), 1911–43

Source: Mitchell, International Historical Statistics, p. 102.
Note: From 1917, Alsace-Lorraine excluded; from 1919, ceded territories; from 1922, Eup/Upper Silesia.

12.4.3 *The Nazi period*

Perhaps the most astonishing fact in the history of German living standards in the nineteenth and twentieth centuries is that – at least as measured by changes in human heights – living standards stagnated during the early Nazi period, as can be seen in Figures 12.6 and 12.7.[70] The slight decline in German heights during the Second World War, and the strong nutritional insults suggested by heights during the early postwar years, are much less surprising. Likewise, the nadir reached by German nutrition in 1946/7 is well documented from other sources. So, too, is the increase thereafter, which emerges clearly from the height records for German children.

For the early Nazi period, however, one would expect to observe height increases. After all, the German economy was undergoing a recovery from the crisis it had experienced in the early 1930s.[71] Most narrative recollections of contemporaries mention a rising standard of living for those Germans who did not belong to the groups persecuted by the Nazis. Per capita GDP was significantly increasing in Germany, according to Angus Maddison (based on Hoffmann's figures) by a hefty 35 per cent between 1932 and 1936 (as can be seen from Figure 12.1).[72] Not only was GDP per capita rising, but also, as Dietmar Petzina emphasizes, real wages saw an upward trend after 1933. In spite of the official policy of fixing wages and prices to the level of 1933, both nominal and real wages were tending to rise, starting from their very low level after the 1930/3 crisis.[73] According to Petzina's calculations, by 1938 German real wages had recovered their level of 1928/9.[74] One would also expect public health to have improved as a result of the enormous attempts of the Nazis to organize the whole population, particularly children and adolescents, into organizations such the *Hitler Jugend* which promoted efforts in the field of public health. Finally, tourist institutions (such as *Kraft durch Freude*) provided working-class consumers with unprecedented opportunities to take holidays away from home.

Why, then, do we observe a decline rather than an improvement in our central indicator of living standards, children's heights? There are a number of reasons. For one thing, although per capita GDP was greatly increasing, much of the additional production coming out of the German economy was spent on military equipment and could not be allocated to increasing personal consumption. For another, although real wage rates were recovering, Richard Overy has argued that real *earnings* in Nazi Germany failed to regain their 1920s level.[75] Furthermore, both Petzina and Overy agree that the recovery in real wages was relatively modest compared to the increase of total GDP, leading to an income redistribution in favour of the government and groups such as the self-employed and the owners of capital.[76] In addition, the modest recovery of real wages was accompanied by longer working hours. Between 1933 and 1939, the number of hours worked per week increased every year, in contrast to the Weimar period when the trend had been in the opposite direction.[77] This meant that the leisure component of the standard of living was significantly reduced.

But the most important factor explaining the stagnation of German children's heights in the Nazi period is the fact that the quality of nutrition deteriorated. As discussed in Chapter 8, the National Socialists sought to transform the German economy, which before the First World War had been strongly integrated into world markets, into an autarkic economy, in food consumption as in all other sectors. Since Germany had been a considerable importer of animal products, this policy of pursuing autarky created enormous problems in providing the German population with animal protein and fat. Contemporaries discussed this issue intensively under the technical heading *Fettlücke* (shortage of fat).[78] Up to 1936, German consumption of both fats and animal proteins increased much more slowly than GDP, because of the forcible government curbs on imports from Denmark and other protein-producing countries (as can be seen from Table 12.3). In 1937/8, consumption was somewhat higher. However, Overy presents archival material showing that German workers' households were consuming 18 per cent less meat in 1937 than in 1927, making up for it by increased starch consumption.[79]

In the run-up to the Second World War, a great deal of attention was devoted in Germany to nutritional issues. The National Socialists wanted at all costs to avoid the upheavals experienced during the First World War. The Nazis' *Lebensraum* ideology was partly based on the following line of reasoning: if it was impossible to produce enough cattle in an autarkic Germany, then Germany should occupy the land of neighbouring countries to the east. During the Second World War, the military and political authorities in Germany continued to be greatly concerned that German soldiers or their families at home might suffer from malnutrition. One strategy was to deprive the occupied countries of food. It has been estimated that in 1942/3, some 45 per cent of German grain consumption, and 42 per cent of German fat and meat consumption had either been stolen from the occupied countries or else produced within Germany by forced labourers.[80]

Other strategies adopted by the Nazi government to secure nutrition included ideas whose clumsiness can best be illustrated by an example.[81] As fat was in particularly short supply in autarkic Nazi Germany, a firm called the *Märkische Seifenfabrik* in Witten an der Ruhr had the idea of producing

Table 12.3 Protein consumption from milk, meat, and eggs (per capita and day), 1890–1936

	Protein in g	% of proteins from meat
1890	47.1	37.2
1913	58.8	35.6
1928	60.6	39.5
1929	60.7	38.5
1930	60.3	37.8
1931	60.4	38.2
1932	59.9	37.0
1933	59.5	37.0
1934	61.2	39.8
1935	59.9	39.2
1936	61.1	37.8

Source: Teuteberg, 'Der Verzehr von Nahrungsmitteln in Deutschland'.

artificial fat from hard coal. This fat was not used for industrial purposes – as one might have imagined from the raw material – but rather was actually included in the food parcels sent to soldiers, for human consumption! Unsurprisingly, it was very unpopular due to the fact that it was absolutely tasteless. To improve its taste, colour and vitamin content, the *Märkische Seifenfabrik* decided to buy a large plot of land, plant carrots, extract carotene and add it to the artificial fat. From the remaining carrot material, they produced jam. The company bought a large agricultural estate relatively cheaply near the town of Lahr in Baden, by promising that an army research institute would be founded in Lahr.[82] The idea of creating food from hard coal illustrates how difficult the nutritional situation can be in an industrial economy striving for autarky. It also illustrates the enormous trust the National Socialists had in modern technological methods for improving consumption under ideological constraints.

12.5 The two Germanys: differences in conventional and in biological standards of living

12.5.1 Does socialism make you shorter and die earlier?

With the introduction of different economic and political systems in the two parts of Germany after the Second World War, living standards also evolved in different directions. No one would doubt today that conventional living standards in the German Democratic Republic (East Germany) were much lower than in the Federal Republic (West Germany), although the shadow economy might have narrowed the statistical estimates based on the formal economy by a few percentage points.[83] Bart Van Ark recently estimated that in East Germany in 1987, value added per person employed in manufacturing was only 32 per cent of the West German level.[84] Hartmut Kaelble provided figures on the numbers of cars, telephones, books, and mailed letters per capita in both Germanys which strongly support the view that there was a very substantial difference in their living standards.[85]

At first sight, it may seem logical that lower per capita GDP should lead to lower levels of such biological measures of living standards as life expectancy and net nutritional status. However, there are several factors which might have moved East Germany up to a comparable level with West Germany when it came to such biological components of human well-being.

First, it is possible to imagine that the general level of welfare was already so high that what was missing in the poorer East Germany was only some of the above-mentioned 'decencies' of living – cars, telephones, books, postal services – whereas food, for example, may not have been in short supply.

Second, the socialist redistribution policy in the East might have provided special benefits for the least productive social groups, the ones who might have dropped out of the social security networks in the West. In East Germany, housing rents were low and foodstuffs were sold at low prices due to government subsidies. Meat consumption, in particular, was strongly subsidized by the state, as has been emphasized by Stephan Merl.[86]

Third, East Germany was characterized by a good supply of medical services in the countryside. In West Germany, by contrast, the supply of health-related goods in rural areas showed some surprising lags: it was the urban centres which consumed much of the advanced medicine.

On the other hand, the supply of some health-related products (for example, specialized drugs) was generally more uncertain in a socialist economy. This even applied to some perishable foodstuffs such as milk which were important for health outcomes, although equivalent animal protein might have been obtained by East Germans from less perishable foods such as bacon which were more resistant to the problems of central planning.

Perhaps most importantly for its population's biological standard of living, East Germany adopted 'dirtier' production methods, as its leaders sought to catch up with the higher conventional living standards and consumption levels in the West. Industrial production in the south of the German Democratic Republic was heavily based on *Braunkohle* (bituminous coal), and this created enormous health problems. Starting in 1962, the Humboldt University in East Berlin undertook specialized epidemiological research comparing morbidity rates in the heavily industrial district of Halle (which produced 15.3 per cent of East Germany's industrial output) to rates in the relatively unpolluted Neubrandenburg district (which produced only 1.1 per cent of the country's industrial output).[87] In March 1962, 0.278 per cent of Halle's inhabitants were unable to work because of bronchitis, compared to only 0.096 per cent in Neubrandenburg. The corresponding values for September 1962 were 0.096 per cent and 0.045 per cent. This difference was statistically significant and – according to the Humboldt University study – was caused by the enormous quantity of dust in the air in the industrial areas. In Halle, the number of foggy days per year increased decade by decade over the twentieth century, from only 13.5 in 1891–1900 to 64 in 1961–68. In 1970, the lung capacity of children from the chemical district of Bitterfeld was found to be much lower than that in rural Schwerin. An analysis of 1700 schoolchildren found that human growth was retarded by ten months in the chemical district of Bitterfeld compared to healthier localities in the German Democratic Republic. By 1978, this retardation had been reduced to 'only' six months.[88] These very evident health problems led to a brief period during the early 1970s when there was some public promotion of ecological ideas in East Germany. An environmental law was promulgated (the 1970 *Landeskulturgesetz*), and a Ministry for Environmental Issues was created in 1971.[89] But economic problems – among them the two oil price shocks of the early to mid-1970s – soon led the East German government to abandon these experiments.

During the latter existence of the German Democratic Republic, its socialist leaders were so desperate for western currency which would enable them to import scarce goods that they went so far as to 'sell' some of their population's biological standard of living, if we can regard environmental pollution as one aspect of human welfare. For example, they offered the Schönberg waste disposal area to waste transports from the West, because the Federal Republic had enormous problems in finding disposal areas. Officials also tolerated toxic material mixed into this waste.[90]

Measures of life expectancy and to a certain extent human stature confirm that East Germany had a lower biological standard of living than the West. Both indicators displayed a continuous upward trend after the Second World War, in East and West alike. Up to the 1970s, it is possible that life expectancy increased as fast in East as in West Germany, although one cannot be sure that the German Democratic Republic's government statistics were not falsified: the basic mortality statistics for non-infants in the German Democratic Republic after the mid-1960s are reliable, whereas other published figures are clearly problematic.[91] But during the 1970s and 1980s the figures show much slower progress in life expectancy in the East than in the West, and this is probably no statistical artefact. The 2.8 additional years for women and 2.6 years for men that West Germans were able to enjoy represented a clear advantage in biological standard of living over their East German counterparts. Certainly, during the later years of the German Democratic Republic, life expectancy was increasing much more slowly than in the Federal Republic, and during the last two decades before the Wall came down, longevity in the East was substantially lower than in the West (as can be seen from Table 12.4).

Regional analyses bear out this picture. Harald Frank analysed mortality rates on the regional level in East and West Germany. He found that – after

Table 12.4 Life expectancy in East and West Germany, 1969–95

Base years	West men	West women	Base years	East men	East women	Difference men	Difference women
1969–71	67.3	73.6	1970	68.1	73.3	–0.8	0.3
1975–77	68.6	75.2	1976	68.8	74.4	–0.2	0.8
1980–82	70.2	76.9	1981	69.0	74.8	1.2	2.1
1985–87	71.8	78.4	1986–87	69.8	75.8	2.0	2.6
1988–90	72.6	79.0	1988–89	70.0	76.2	2.6	2.8
1991–93	73.1	79.5	1991–93	69.9	77.2	3.2	2.3
1993–95	73.5	79.8	1993–95	70.7	78.2	2.8	1.6

Sources: Riphahn and Zimmermann, *Transition's Mortality*, p. 4, who report values from various issues of the *German Statistical Yearbook* and, prior to 1991, the *Statistical Yearbook* of the GDR.

controlling for age structure – mortality was much higher in any East German district than in any West German district in 1985–87.[92] Particularly high mortality rates (but also a high average age) and particularly low fertility rates were found in the three Saxon districts, whereas the opposite was true for the agricultural north.[93]

The same pattern can be seen in comparisons of average human heights between the two Germanys. East German heights were generally somewhat lower than West German ones, although different studies arrive at different estimates. Holle Greil finds that in the 1980s East Germans aged 20–24 were on average 178.1 centimetres in height, compared to 178.7 for West Germans – a fairly small difference.[94] On the other hand, Michael Hermanussen compares the heights of 18-year-olds in the 1980s, and finds that East German males were 3.7 centimetres shorter than their West German counterparts, while East German females were 2.8 centimetres shorter than West German ones. He argues that his figures (published by East German anthropologists) were considered to be representative, and that the same is true for the western figures.[95] As we cannot examine the exact methods by which these different measurements were taken, we can only conclude that East Germans were at least 0.6 centimetres shorter than West Germans in the 1980s. Even this cautious measure, however, taken together with the lower life expectancy, suggests a lower biological standard of living in the former German Democratic Republic.

12.5.2 Stature and mortality before and after unification

What was the effect of German unification in 1990 on the biological standard of living? Hermanussen found that after 1990 East German (male) military conscripts manifested a surprising increase in height. He found that the difference between male heights in East and West Germany decreased from 2.2 centimetres in 1989 to only 1.4 centimetres in 1992, only 1.1 centimetres centimetres in 1993, and only 0.6 centimetres in 1994.[96] The first step in this remarkable pattern of convergence in heights can be partly explained by the previously different age at measurement, which had been 17.9 years in East Germany, whereas in West Germany (and the later cohorts of East Germans after unification) it was 19.5 years. But the subsequent decrease in the height differential between East and West must have been caused by other factors. Migration is an unlikely explanation, because one would not expect all the tall people to remain in eastern Germany. Surprisingly, as Hermanussen points out, convergence only took place among males in the later years of adolescence: eastern German children's heights did not increase. Holle Greil has pointed out that eastern German female heights did not increase either.[97]

The divergent development in the heights of adolescent males and females in East and West Germany after unification might be explained by differences in labour market policies and child-care provision between East and West. In the former German Democratic Republic, the socialist policy of putting women to work and taking special care of children (discussed in Chapter 11) might have resulted in relatively more and better resources being allocated to these groups. In capitalist market economies, young males might have a higher income expectation, so that the allocation of resources within households could have shifted in their favour.

Further light is shed on this unresolved puzzle by the development of mortality rates in the years following German unification. Available data suggest that mortality rates deteriorated in eastern Germany during this period, although mainly for those in the middle age groups around age 40. Eberstadt, and Riphahn and Zimmermann studied the determinants of this surprising demographic development.[98] They found that certain gender-specific age groups were most at risk. In general, *female* mortality decreased in eastern Germany after unification; only women in the age group 35–45 experienced some increase in mortality between 1989 and 1991. Eastern German men in this 35–45 age group also saw an increase in mortality. In the first few years after unification, younger eastern German males also experienced increased mortality, but their death rates moved back to normal values relatively fast. By contrast, as late as 1994 eastern German males around age 40 still had mortality rates 10–20 per cent higher than before unification.

One may speculate that younger people adjusted more easily to the new situation, while men of 35–45 years are typically in a life phase in which they want to apply the knowledge they have obtained up to that point. Not being able to do so, and instead being faced with uncertainty and often unemployment, it seems likely that they experienced strong psychosocial stress. Riphahn and Zimmermann conclude that the increased mortality rates among eastern German men of this age group were mostly caused by over-consumption of alcohol, and by circulatory and cardio-vascular problems which were also related to psychosocial stress.[99]

It is interesting that women were much less sensitive to this development, even though (as discussed in Chapter 11) they were the main victims of the high unemployment which emerged in eastern Germany after unification. Only middle-aged women in eastern Germany saw some increase in their mortality rates after unification. For eastern German women as a whole, by contrast, life expectancy improved considerably, mostly because of falling mortality risks for elderly women and, to a lesser extent, for very young females. Interviews of eastern German individuals after unification suggested that men suffered more than women from the psychosocial stress of unemployment, because – in accordance with traditional gender roles – males felt more loss in social status from losing their jobs.

12.6 Conclusion

Different judgements about German living standards, and hence about different periods of German history, emerge when one compares traditional welfare indicators with biological measures of the standard of living.

The first part of this chapter considered the impact of the agricultural reforms and the rapid industrial development on nineteenth-century German regional living standards. With regard to the agrarian reforms, Knapp's famous argument that the productivity of agriculture was increased at the expense of widespread rural impoverishment can now be confronted with a variety of empirical evidence which casts considerable doubt on this view. Once one takes into account differences in the initial living standards of different German regions, and differences in the timing of the agrarian reforms in different German territories, one finds that the agrarian reforms in fact had no systematic effects on living standards. Regions in which the reforms were particularly harsh did not develop much worse (or better) living standards than regions where agrarian policies were milder. The crisis in German living standards around the middle of the nineteenth century, and the increasing inequality during this period, can be observed even in territories such as Bavaria where the agrarian reforms only began to be effective later on.

German industrialization greatly accelerated from the 1860s onward. This had some harsh but transitory effects on mortality rates during the 1860s and 1870s. Particular sections of the German population (in particular, children and inhabitants of regions such as Saxony and Silesia) certainly experienced the worst aspects of industrial development. But compared with agricultural regions, the average industrial region did better in most respects. Mortality rates tended to be lower, and nutritional status and income tended to be higher in industrial regions than in agricultural ones. Furthermore, industrialization in Germany achieved the ability to provide a decent standard of welfare quite rapidly, at least compared with Britain and Belgium. The milder German path to industrialization was partly caused by the fact that it began industrializing so much later. It may be that the adverse development of biological living standards in countries such as Britain and Belgium was caused by other characteristics of the period at which they industrialized – the late eighteenth century to the mid-nineteenth century – rather than merely by the fact that they were industrializing. Moreover, German politicians had the chance to learn from the British case with regard to urban public health and social insurance policies, to name just two examples.

In the twentieth century, the 1920s stand out as an astonishingly favourable period for German living standards. Net nutritional status measured by anthropometric methods (i.e. human stature) increased very strikingly during this period, whereas the other decades between 1910 and 1950 were more or less times of stagnation.

Another particularly interesting set of results relates to the Nazi period. First there is the stagnation of heights among urban schoolchildren during the National Socialist regime, an outcome mainly caused by the Nazis' striving for national economic autarky. Furthermore, there was a significant increase in mortality between 1932 and 1937, which suggests that biological standards of living were declining even for the non-persecuted groups in Nazi Germany.

After the Second World War, Germany saw a stable increase in nutritional status and life expectancy in both East and West. However, especially from the 1970s onward, East Germany performed much less well. Comparing the two Germanys after the Second World War – in spite of some controversial figures – it can be concluded that not only material well-being but also the biological standard of living was lower in the eastern part. Lifespans were significantly shorter in the last two decades of the German Democratic Republic, and human stature was probably somewhat lower. After reunification, East German mortality has only begun to catch up in very recent years, although for male adolescents net nutritional status may have begun to improve somewhat earlier.

In sum, this chapter has presented quantitative material to evaluate the effects on living standards of some of the most important changes in German social and economic history over the last two centuries. Many of the indicators on German living standards which are available to historians are still subject to dispute, and require much further research to improve them. However, the possibility of assessing the impact of government policies and changes in economic structure on living standards using quantitative measures provides a very important supplement to contemporaries' – necessarily subjective – judgements.

12.7 Notes

1 For important comments and suggestions, I thank Christoph Buchheim, Bernard Harris, Axel Heitmüller, John Komlos, Michael Kopsidis, Sheilagh Ogilvie, Richard Overy, Douglas Puffert, Reinhard Spree, and Andrea Wagner. Michael Haines provided important hints. Financial support from the DFG (German Science Foundation) is gratefully acknowledged.

2 On the plurality and other theoretical dimensions of the standard of living see Amartya Sen, *The Standard of Living* (Cambridge, 1994), esp. pp. 1–18; and Sebastian Coll and John Komlos, 'The Biological Standard of Living and Economic Development: Nutrition, Health and Well-Being in Historical Perspective', in Clara Eugenia Nunez, ed., *Debates and Controversies in Economic History. Proceedings of the Twelfth International Economic History Congress* (Madrid, 1998), pp. 219–82, here pp. 233–5.

3 Sen, *Standard*, p. 18.

4 Suggestions for further reading include Erich Wiegand and Wolfgang Zapf, eds, *Wandel der Lebensbedingungen in Deutschland. Wohlfahrtsentwicklung seit der*

Industrialisierung (Frankfurt, 1982); Wolfram Fischer, ed., *Lebenstandard und Wirtschaftssysteme. Studien im Auftrage des Wissenschaftsfonds der DG BANK* (Frankfurt am Main, 1995); and Hannes Siegrist, Hartmut Kaelble, and Jürgen Kocka, eds, *Europäische Konsumgeschichte. Zur Gesellschafts- und Kulturgeschichte des Konsums (18. bis 20. Jahrhundert)* (Frankfurt am Main, 1997).

  5 Ritschl and Spoerer estimated the GDP level of the prewar and interwar years to be somewhat lower than Maddison estimated on the basis of various Hoffmann estimates, but the growth rates during the 1920s and 1930s, for example, were not significantly modified. Angus Maddison, *Monitoring the World Economy* (Paris, 1995), pp. 130 and 194–5; Walter G. Hoffmann *et al.*, *Das Wachstum der deutschen Wirtschaft seit der Mitte des 19. Jahrhunderts* (Berlin, 1965); Albrecht Ritschl and Mark Spoerer, 'Das Bruttosozialprodukt in Deutschland nach den amtlichen Volkseinkommens- und Sozialproduktsstatistiken', *Jahrbuch für Wirtschaftsgeschichte*, 97 (1997), pp. 27–54.
  6 Arthur E. Imhof, ed., *Lebenserwartungen in Deutschland, Norwegen und Schweden im 19. und 20. Jahrhundert* (Berlin, 1994).
  7 Manfred Lohr, 'Langfristige Entwicklungen der Arbeitslosigkeit in Deutschland', in Wiegand and Zapf, *Wandel*, pp. 237–335.
  8 Among a vast literature, see C. E. Taylor, 'Infections, Famines, and Poverty', *Journal of Interdisciplinary History*, 14 (1983), pp. 484–502, here p. 486.
  9 S. R. Osmani, 'Nutrition and the Economics of Food: Implications of Some Recent Controversies', in J. Dreze and A. Sen, eds, *The Political Economy of Hunger*, Vol. I (Oxford and New York, 1990).
 10 The HDI gives equal weights to the income, literacy, and life expectancy variables. Declining marginal utility is assigned to income increases at a high level.
 11 Charles H. Feinstein, 'Pessimism Perpetuated: Real Wages and the Standard of Living in Britain during and after the Industrial Revolution', *Journal of Economic History*, 58 (1998), pp. 625–58.
 12 Knut Borchardt, 'Wirtschaftliches Wachstum und Wechsellagen 1800–1913', in Hermann Aubin and Wolfgang Zorn, eds, *Handbuch der Wirtschafts- und Sozialgeschichte*, Vol. II (Stuttgart, 1976), pp. 198–275, here p. 215.
 13 Georg Friedrich Knapp, *Die Bauernbefreiung und der Ursprung der Landarbeiter in den älteren Theilen Preußens* (Leipzig, 1887).
 14 Hartmut Harnisch, 'Statistische Untersuchungen zum Verlauf der kapitalistischen Agrarreformen in den preußischen Ostprovinzen (1811 bis 1865)', *Jahrbuch für Wirtschaftsgeschichte*, 74 (1974), pp. 149–83; Friedrich Lütge, 'Über die Auswirkungen der Bauernbefreiung in Deutschland', in Friedrich Lütge, ed., *Studien zur Sozial- und Wirtschaftsgeschichte. Gesammelte Abhandlungen* (Stuttgart, 1963), pp. 174–223; Knut Borchardt, 'Regionale Wachstumsdifferenzierung in Deutschland im 19. Jahrhundert unter besonderer Berücksichtigung des West-Ost-Gefälles', in Wilhelm Abel, ed., *Wirtschaft, Geschichte und Wirtschaftsgeschichte: Festschrift zum 65. Geburtstag v. Friedrich Lütge* (Stuttgart, 1966), pp. 325–39.
 15 Knapp, *Bauernbefreiung*; Harnisch, *Untersuchungen*.
 16 Friedrich-Wilhelm Henning, *Handbuch der Wirtschafts- und Sozialgeschichte Deutschlands*, Vol. 2: *Deutsche Wirtschafts- und Sozialgeschichte im 19. Jahrhundert* (Paderborn, 1996), p. 70.
 17 Borchardt, *Wachstumsdifferenzierung*; Hans-Ulrich Wehler, *Deutsche Gesellschaftsgeschichte*, Vol. I (Munich, 1987), p. 422, gives much lower estimates.
 18 Wehler, *Gesellschaftsgeschichte*, Vol. II, p. 33–53.
 19 Robert A. Dickler, 'Organization and Change in Productivity in Eastern Prussia', in William N. Parker and Eric L. Jones, eds, *European Peasants and their Markets. Essays in Agrarian Economic History* (Princeton, 1975), pp. 269–92.

20 Harnisch, *Untersuchungen*, p. 157. Even though the whole process lasted until the end of the century, if the final mortgage payments are considered.

21 It is possible that those of the landless who received their wages largely in kind did relatively well. However, this social group as a whole certainly had much higher mortality from nutrition-related diseases. Hannover also did well even though it started early, but north-western Germany had less serious problems in general, as discussed below.

22 Kevin O'Rourke, 'The European Grain Invasion, 1870–1913', *Journal of Economic History*, 57 (1997), pp. 775–801.

23 It was not much different around mid-century, as the anthropometric evidence suggests; see Ernst Engel, 'Die physische Beschaffenheit der militärpflichtigen Bevölkerung im Königreich Sachsen', *Zeitschrift des Statistischen Bureaus des Königlich Sächsischen Ministeriums des Innern*, 4 (1856), pp. 61–116.

24 The real wages given in Jörg Baten, *Ernährung und wirtschaftliche Entwicklung in Bayern, 1730–1880* (Stuttgart, 1999), p. 49, and the wages published in the periodical *Centralblatt* (1892), are much lower for Saxony than the (total) income estimates reported in Borchardt, *Regionale*, p. 117, would suggest.

25 In the Palatinate region of Bavaria, the share of wealth held by the top 10 per cent increased from 44 per cent around 1840 and 1850 to 50 per cent in 1860 and 49 per cent around 1875 (calculated from recruitment lists in the Landesarchiv Speyer).

26 Harnisch, *Untersuchungen*.

27 Borchardt, *Regionale*.

28 Gerd Hohorst, 'Wirtschaftswachstum und Bevölkerungsentwicklung in Preußen 1816 bis 1914' (PhD dissertation, University of Münster, 1978); Harald Frank, *Regionale Entwicklungsdisparitäten im deutschen Industrialisierungsprozeß 1849–1939* (Münster and Hamburg, 1994).

29 Jörg Baten, 'Der Einfluß von Einkommensverteilung und Milchproduktion auf die regionalen Unterschiede des Ernährungsstandards in Preußen um die Mitte des 19. Jahrhunderts: Ein anthropometrischer Diskussionsbeitrag', *Archiv für Sozialgeschichte*, 36 (1996), pp. 69–83.

30 We cannot directly compare this rejection rate with those of other states, due to data limitations which are explained in detail in Baten, *Einfluß*.

31 Hans-Heinrich Bass, *Hungerkrisen in Preußen während der ersten Hälfte des 19. Jahrhunderts* (St Katharinen, 1991), pp. 43–7.

32 Baten, *Ernährung*, p. 44

33 Henning, *Handbuch*, p. 74.

34 See Borchardt, *Wachstum*.

35 Jan P. Smits and Jan L. van Zanden, 'Industrialization and Income Inequality in the Netherlands 1800–1914', in Clara Eugenia Nunez, ed., *Trends in Income Inequality during Industrialization: International Economic History Association Conference, Session B12* (Madrid, 1998), pp. 91–102, here p. 96.

36 Saxony: districts Dresden, Leipzig, Zwickau. Rhineland: Düsseldorf, Cologne, Aachen, plus the more agricultural Koblenz and Trier. Westphalia: Arnsberg plus Münster and Minden.

37 While these mortality rates are not age-standardized, the research of Lee on age-specific mortality rates in general supports the raw figures: see W. Robert Lee, 'Regionale Differenzierung im Bevölkerungswachstum Deutschlands im frühen neunzehnten Jahrhundert', in Rainer Fremdling and Richard H. Tilly, eds, *Industrialisierung und Raum. Studien zur regionalen Differenzierung im Deutschland des 19. Jahrhunderts* (Stuttgart, 1979), pp. 192–228, here p. 214.

38 At least for Prussia in 1913, per capita income and the share of the labour force in non-agricultural occupations were highly correlated (correlation coefficient 0.79).

39 Lee, *Regionale Differenzierung*, p. 220; Hallie J. Kintner, 'The Determinants of Infant Mortality from 1871 to 1933' (PhD dissertation, University of Michigan, 1982), p. 220.

40 A regression of mortality rates on percentage of the labour force in industry and height (as a proxy for protein availability) explains 51 per cent of the variation in mortality rates in 1910–13. The two variables explain similar shares of the variation in mortality.

41 Hans-Ulrich Wehler, *Deutsche Gesellschaftsgeschichte*, Vol. II (Munich, 1987), p. 485.

42 Between 1841 and the early 1880s, average literacy in Germany increased by some 8 per cent, and by 1900 illiteracy had virtually disappeared; see Sophia Twarog, 'Heights and Living Standards in Germany, 1850–1939: The Case of Württemberg', in Steckel and Floud, *Health*, pp. 285–330, here p. 320. More rigorous studies on alternative indicators of educational attainment in Germany, particularly during the nineteenth century, are still a desideratum. Hoffmann observed that expenditures on education and recreation as a percentage of total private consumption increased slowly from 0.6 in 1850/4 to 1.3 in 1910/13, somewhat higher during the Weimar (2.8) and Nazi period (3.6) and particularly after the First World War (5.2). See Hoffmann, *Wachstum*, p. 139.

43 Elisabeth Gransche and Franz Rothenbacher, 'Wohnbedingungen in der zweiten Hälfte des 19. Jahrhunderts 1861–910', *Geschichte und Gesellschaft*, 14 (1988), pp. 64–95.

44 Frank, *Regionale*.

45 Those mortality figures are not adjusted for age, but the development is similar if infant mortality rates are compared.

46 Lee, *Regionale Differenzierung*, p. 219.

47 Hoffmann, *Wachstum*, pp. 213–14; Hoffmann's figures are based on Ruth Meinert, 'Die Entwicklung der Arbeitszeit in der deutschen Industrie 1820–1956' (PhD dissertation, University of Münster, 1958), whose weak evidence for the time period up to the 1860s has never been checked, except by Rainer Gömmel, *Wachstum und Konjunktur der Nürnberger Wirtschaft (1815–1914)* (Stuttgart, 1978), pp. 190–1. See also Baten, *Ernährung*, Ch. 5, for alternative regional proxies. Good overviews on the development of working hours are given in Hans Pohl, ed., *Die Entwicklung der Lebensarbeitszeit* (Stuttgart, 1992).

48 Twarog, *Heights*.

49 Estimated from Teuteberg's figures on meat, dairy products, and eggs, excluding fish because of its regionally restricted supply. Following Rainer Beck's tables, eggs were assumed to contain 130 g protein per kg, milk 33 g and meat on average 170 g. The increase was rapid until around 1900, with two shorter crises around 1893 and 1901/02, and slow but steady until 1913. See Rainer Beck, *Naturale Ökonomie* (Berlin, 1986); Hans J. Teuteberg, 'Der Verzehr von Nahrungsmitteln in Deutschland pro Kopf und Jahr seit Beginn der Industrialisierung', *Archiv für Sozialgeschichte*, 19 (1979), pp. 331–88.

50 The following discussion is based on Avner Offer, *The First World War. An Agrarian Interpretation* (Oxford, 1991), pp. 21–78.

51 On the flu epidemic during First World War, see J. Winter, *The Great War and the British People* (Basingstoke, 1986), p. 121.

52 Although one could argue that the knowledge and use of therapeutic techniques and medical care improved much more rapidly after 1945 than previously.

53 Even if the gross nutritional intake of animal proteins did not increase in every year, nutrients were used more efficiently. Only countries and regions with severe problems, such as the Soviet Union and China, did not participate in the increase. In the following discussion of heights, we will consider not only height decline but also height stagnation over a period of five, six, or more years as a signal of

nutritional problems. Internationally, the twentieth century was a period in which continuous increases in physical stature were typical. In the United Kingdom, especially in the prosperous south-east, children's heights increased continuously. On the following, see Bernard Harris, 'The Height of Schoolchildren in Britain, 1900–1950', in Komlos, *Stature*, pp. 25–38. In other areas, with higher unemployment rates, heights stagnated during crisis years, but normally for no longer than a couple of years. In areas such as Glasgow or the Welsh Rhondda, characterized by 'old' industries and high unemployment rates, there was some stagnation until the early 1920s, but afterwards a continuous increase; see Harris, *Height*, pp. 32–4. For example, the increases in height in Croydon, a town south of London, followed an almost exactly linear trend. The same is true for Swedish heights, whose upward trend was almost perfectly continuous during the twentieth century; see Lars G. Sandberg and Richard H. Steckel, 'Was Industrialization Hazardous to Your Health? Not in Sweden!', in Steckel and Floud, *Health*, pp. 127–59, here p. 150. In the United States, heights in each decade were higher then in the previous one, even during the Great Depression, except for African-American females; see Jialu Wu, 'How Severe was the Great Depression? Evidence from the Pittsburgh Region', in Komlos, *Stature*, pp. 129–52, here p. 137.

54 James Tanner, 'Introduction: Growth in Height as a Mirror of the Standard of Living', in Komlos, *Stature*, p. 3; for a detailed time series analysis, see Jörg Baten, 'Height and Real Wages: An International Overview', *Jahrbuch für Wirtschaftsgeschichte*, forthcoming.

55 Offer, *First*, p. 53. For a more detailed discussion of the demographic impact of war, see the articles in Richard Wall and J. Winter, eds, *The Upheaval of War* (Cambridge, 1988), especially pp. 9–42.

56 Whether the lack of animal protein also contributed to lower efficiency of workers in the militarily relevant industries or even the soldiers, has to remain in the field of speculation until we know more about this sort of relationship. On the relationship between nutrition, height, and efficiency see John Strauss and Duncan Thomas, 'Health, Nutrition, and Economic Development', *Journal of Economic Literature*, 36 (1988), pp. 766–817.

57 Knut Borchardt, 'Zwangslagen und Handlungsspielräume in der grossen Wirtschaftskrise der frühen dreissiger Jahre: Zur Revision des überlieferten Geschichtsbildes', *Bayerische Akademie der Wissenschaften, Jahrbuch*, 79 (1979), pp. 85–132. For a recent overview on the different opinions on the 'Borchardt Controversy', see Mark Spoerer, 'Weimar's Investment and Growth Record in Intertemporal and International Perspective', *European Review of Economic History*, 1 (1997), pp. 271–97.

58 Many arguments have been put forward against Borchardt's view: see, for example, Carl-Ludwig Holtfrerich, 'Was the Policy of Deflation in Germany Unavoidable?', in Jürgen von Kruedener, ed., *Economic Crisis and Political Collapse. The Weimar Republic 1924–33* (New York, 1990), pp. 63–80; and Richard Overy, *War and Economy in the Third Reich* (Oxford, 1994), p. 40, who argues that labour costs were low by international standards.

59 Pierenkemper, *Standard*.

60 This reflects – due to the lag structure of heights – the last year before the World Economic Crisis became really catastrophic.

61 Reinhard Spree, 'Klassen- und Schichtbildung im Medium des privaten Konsums: vom späten Kaiserreich in die Weimarer Republik', *Historical Social Research*, 22 (1997), pp. 29–80, here p. 47.

62 1931–34 in the height record.

63 Calculated from Gerhard Bry, *Wages in Germany* (Princeton, 1960), p. 362.

64 This can also be measured by Württemberg's overtaking of Baden in terms of industrial production and electricity demand; see Jörg Baten, 'Regionale

Wirtschaftsentwicklung, öffentliche Elektrizitätswirtschaft und Erster Weltkrieg in Baden und Württemberg: ein quantitativ-graphischer Vergleich', *Historical Social Research*, 16 (1991), pp. 69–112, here p. 104.

65 The unemployment rates in Leipzig compared with Stuttgart were: 27 per cent vs 15 per cent in December 1931, 29 per cent vs 15 per cent in July 1932; 29 per cent vs 17 per cent in January 1933 (number of unemployed per number in labour force); the source for this is *Statistische Beilagen zum Reichsarbeitsblatt*, various issues.

66 Hoffmann, *Wachstum*, p. 677.

67 By contrast, population grew only from 65.1 million to 66.0 million in the territory under consideration, see Hoffmann, *Wachstum*.

68 Brian R. Mitchell, *International Historical Statistics: Europe 1750–1988*, 3rd edn (New York, 1992), p. 102.

69 *Statistisches Jahrbuch für das Deutsche Reich 1934*, p. 33; *Statistisches Jahrbuch für die Bundesrepublik Deutschland*, p 40; Reinhard Spree, 'Der Rückzug des Todes. Der epidemiologische Übergang in Deutschland während des 19. und 20. Jahrhunderts', *Historical Social Research*, 23 (1998), pp. 4–43, here p. 28.

70 The following discussion relates only to the population that was regarded by the National Socialists as 'German'. It is impossible to make statements about increasing living standards in Germany without mentioning those sections of the population who suffered or were murdered under the Nazi regime: Jews, Roma, homosexuals, active left-wing politicians, and many other groups.

71 Even though not everyone accepts the decrease in unemployment between 1932 and 1935 at face value. Silverman expressed doubts about the Nazi statistics but did not estimate the degree of falsification; see Dan Silverman, 'National Socialist Economics: The Wirtschaftswunder Reconsidered', in Barry Eichengreen and Timothy Hatton, eds, *Interwar Unemployment in International Perspective* (Dordrecht, 1988), pp. 185–220.

72 Maddison, *Monitoring*, p. 130 and 194–5; Hoffman, *Wachstum*.

73 Dietmar Petzina, *Autarkiepolitik im Dritten Reich. Der nationalsozialistische Vierjahresplan* (Stuttgart, 1968), p. 167.

74 *Ibid.*

75 Overy, *War*, pp. 263–4.

76 See Dietmar Petzina, *Die deutsche Wirtschaft in der Zwischenkriegszeit* (Wiesbaden, 1977), p. 148; and recently Mark Spoerer, *Von Scheingewinnen zum Rüstungsboom. Die Eigenkapitalrentabilität der deutschen Industrieaktiengesellschaften 1925–1941* (Stuttgart, 1996).

77 Bry, *Wages*, p. 48.

78 On the *Fettlücke* see Gustavo Corni and Horst Gies, *Brot – Butter – Kanonen. Die Ernährungswirtschaft in Deutschland unter der Diktatur Hitlers* (Berlin, 1997), pp. 309–14.

79 Overy, *War*, p. 264. He also stresses the decline in quality described in the discussion that follows.

80 L. Burchardt, 'The Impact of the War Economy on the Civilian Population of Germany during the First and Second World War', in W. Deist, ed., *The German Military in the Age of Total War* (Leamington Spa, 1985), pp. 40–70, here p. 53, cited from Corni and Gies, *Brot*, p. 554.

81 On the following, see Jörg Baten, 'Die wirtschaftliche Entwicklung der Stadt Lahr im 20. Jahrhundert', in Stadt Lahr, ed., *Geschichte der Stadt Lahr im 20. Jahrhundert* (Lahr, 1993), pp. 45–66, here pp. 56–7.

82 After the war, chemical production in other fields was relatively successful, the name was changed to *Imhausen Chemie (Lahr)*, and this firm became famous in the 1980s because it was accused of building a chemical warfare factory in Qaddafy's Libya.

83 For a recent overview, see Oskar Schwarzer, *Sozialistische Zentralplanungs-wirtschaft in der SBZ/DDR: Ergebnisse eines ordnungspolitischen Experiments (1945–1989)* (Stuttgart, 1999).

84 Bart van Ark, 'Convergence and Divergence in the European Periphery: Productivity in Eastern and Southern Europe in Retrospect', in Bart van Ark and Nicholas Crafts, eds, *Quantitative Aspects of Postwar European Economic Growth* (Cambridge, 2001), pp. 271–326, here p. 284. See also Wilma Merkel and Stefanie Wahl, *Das geplünderte Deutschland. Die wirtschaftliche Entwicklung im östlichen Teil Deutschlands von 1949 bis 1989* (Bonn, 1991).

85 Hartmut Kaelble, 'Europäische Besonderheiten des Massenkonsums 1950–1990', in Siegrist, Kaelble and Kocka, *Europäische Konsumgeschichte*, pp. 169–203.

86 Stephan Merl, 'Staat und Konsum inder Zentralverwaltungswirtschaft. Rußland und die ostmitteleuropäischen Länder', in Siegrist, Kaelble and Kocka, *Europäische Konsumgeschichte*, pp. 205–41.

87 On the following, see Gerhard Würth, *Umweltschutz und Umweltzerstörung in der DDR* (Frankfurt am Main, 1985), pp. 70–2.

88 Regional control groups were also considered.

89 *Ibid.*, p. 31. As early as the 1950s, Reinhold Lingner argued for a more ecological style of agriculture, after the GDR's official enthusiasm for the Stalinist and Soviet type of large industrial production in agriculture destroyed many natural hindrances against soil erosion, such as trees and hedges; see *ibid.*, p. 23.

90 *UmweltMagazin* (July, 1989), pp. 28–31.

91 In particular, cause-of-death data and all varieties of production figures were problematic. See Regina Regina T. Riphahn and Klaus F. Zimmermann, 'The Transition's Mortality Crisis in East Germany', *UNU/WIDER – Research for Action*, 42 (1997), pp. 9–10, citing Nicholas Eberstadt, 'Demographic Shocks after Communism: Eastern Germany, 1989–93', *Population and Development Review*, 20 (1994), pp. 137–52.

92 Frank, *Regionale*, pp. 198–201. See also Chapter 2 of the present volume.

93 Calculated from the 1984 figures from *Statistisches Jahrbuch der DDR* (1986).

94 Holle Greil, 'Age- and Sex-Specifity of the Secular Trend in Height in East Germany', in Komlos and Baten, *Biological*, pp. 483–96.

95 Michael Hermanussen, 'Catch-Up in Final Height after Unification of Germany', *Acta Medica Auxologica*, 29 (1997), pp. 135–41. Astonishingly, according to these studies, children were not shorter.

96 Hermanussen, *Catch-Up*.

97 Greil, personal communication (1997).

98 Nicholas Eberstadt, 'Mortality and the Fate of Communist States', *Communist Economies and Economic Transformation*, 5 (1993), pp. 499–517, cited from Riphahn and Zimmermann, *Transition's Mortality*.

99 Riphahn and Zimmermann, *Transition's Mortality*, p. 42. Another explanation that has not been satisfactorily examined is selective migration: if more healthy people left, mortality rates among the remaining inhabitants might have increased.

Index